*Considerations
on the Principal
Events of the
French Revolution*

Madame de Staël

❀ ❀ ❀ ❀ ❀ ❀ ❀ ❀ ❀ ❀ ❀ ❀

CONSIDERATIONS
ON THE PRINCIPAL
EVENTS OF THE
French Revolution

GERMAINE DE STAËL

Newly Revised Translation of the 1818 English Edition

Edited, with an Introduction and Notes,
by Aurelian Craiutu

❀ ❀ ❀ ❀ ❀ ❀ ❀ ❀ ❀ ❀ ❀ ❀

LIBERTY FUND

Indianapolis

Introduction, note on the present edition, annotations, bibliography, index, © 2008 by Liberty Fund, Inc.

Frontispiece: Portrait of Madame de Staël by Anne-Louis Girodet de Roucy-Trioson, ca. 1800–1824. © The Gallery Collection/Corbis. Reproduced by permission.

Printed in the United States of America

C 10 9 8 7 6 5 4 3 2 1
P 10 9 8 7 6 5 4 3 2 1

Library of Congress Cataloging-in-Publication Data
Staël, Madame de (Anne-Louise-Germaine), 1766–1817.
[Considérations sur les principaux événemens de la Révolution françoise. English]
Considerations on the principal events of the French Revolution / Germaine de Staël; edited and with an introduction by Aurelian Craiutu.
p. cm. Includes bibliographical references and index.
ISBN 978-0-86597-731-0 (hc: alk. paper) ISBN 978-0-86597-732-7 (pbk.: alk. paper)
1. France—History—Revolution, 1789–1799—Causes. 2. France—History—Revolution, 1789–1799—Influence. 3. Staël, Madame de (Anne-Louise-Germaine), 1766–1817—Political and social views. I. Craiutu, Aurelian. II. Title.
DC138.S713 2008
944.04—dc22   2008029586

LIBERTY FUND, INC.
8335 Allison Pointe Trail, Suite 300
Indianapolis, Indiana 46250-1684

Contents

Introduction

Liberty! Let us repeat her name . . . for all that we love,
all that we honor is included in it.

—*Madame de Staël*

A Thinker for Our Times:
Madame de Staël, Her Life and Works

Very few individuals have left as deep a trace on their age as Anne Louise
Germaine, Baronne de Staël-Holstein (1766–1817). She was one of the
greatest intellectuals and writers of her time, and the influence of her
works crossed national borders, cultures, and disciplines. Her powerful
and sparkling personality impressed everyone she met, from Byron and
Chateaubriand to Tsar Alexander I and Napoléon. Staël's popularity was
such that in 1815, soon after Napoléon's fall from power, one of her contemporaries observed that "there are three great powers in Europe: England, Russia, and Madame de Staël."[1]

Life of Madame de Staël

Who was this powerful woman accepted into the most exclusive circles
of her time and destined to become one of the most famous French
writers? Born on April 22, 1766, Madame de Staël belonged to the distinguished Necker family, at one point among the richest families in Europe.
Germaine's mother, Suzanne Curchod, was a highly educated woman
from Lausanne who closely supervised her daughter's education, seeking

1. See Fairweather, *Madame de Staël*, 3.

to give her a truly encyclopedic knowledge of disciplines as diverse as mathematics, languages, geography, theology, and dance. Madame Necker held a famous salon attended by such celebrities as Voltaire, Diderot, Holbach, Helvétius, d'Alembert, Gibbon, Hume, and Walpole.

Madame de Staël's father, Jacques Necker (1732–1804), a Swiss Protestant, had risen to prominence as a banker in Paris. He made a name for himself in the political realm as Louis XVI's minister of finance and was a leading actor during the initial stages of the French Revolution. Necker is remembered today for taking the unprecedented step in 1781 of making public the country's budget, a novelty in an absolute monarchy where the state of finances had always been kept a secret. Necker, who thought this custom both unlawful and ineffective, realized that public opinion had become an invisible power exercising a major influence on the country and the court. Justifying his decision, Necker wrote: "Darkness and obscurity favor carelessness, [while] publicity can only become an honor and a reward."[2] The public success of Necker's *Compte rendu* was tremendous: more than three thousand copies were sold the first day of its publication.

Necker was also the author of important books in which he vigorously defended liberty, constitutionalism, and moderate government: *On the Executive Power in Large States* (1792), *On the French Revolution* (1796), and *Last Views on Politics and Finance* (1802). Necker's reflections on the French Revolution, an unduly ignored masterpiece, are a detailed account of his conduct during the turbulent events of 1788 and 1789, and especially during the month of July 1789, when his dismissal by King Louis XVI was followed by the fall of the Bastille and his subsequent recall by the monarch. In his political writings, Necker justified his preference for a tempered monarchy similar to the one existing in England, and he became one of the leading theorists of executive power in modern political thought.[3]

Madame de Staël achieved fame as a novelist, political thinker, sociologist of literature, and autobiographer. To her thorough education she added vast political experience and an intense personal life that blended

2. Necker, *Compte rendu* (Paris, 1781), 1–2.
3. For an interpretation of Necker's political ideas, see Grange, *Les idées de Necker.*

love and politics in an original way, as her rich correspondence demonstrates.[4] A romantic and restless soul, Madame de Staël attracted the friendship of the most important men of her age, from Talleyrand, Goethe, and Benjamin Constant to J.-C.-L. Simonde de Sismondi, Prosper de Barante, and August Wilhelm von Schlegel. She witnessed firsthand the most important events of the French Revolution, which she followed closely from Paris and, later, from her exile at Coppet, in Switzerland, where she lived between 1792 and 1795, anxiously watching from a distance the rise of the Jacobin democracy, the Terror, and the fall of Robespierre on 9 Thermidor.

Her health declined in 1816, and in February 1817 she became bedridden. Her mind remained as sharp as ever, though, and Staël had the opportunity to reflect one more time on her extraordinary life and achievements. In a letter to Chateaubriand she confessed: "I have always been the same: lively but sad. I love God, my father, and liberty."[5] She died on July 14, 1817, at the age of fifty-one.

Works of Madame de Staël

Staël's first major book, *Letters on the Works and Character of J.-J. Rousseau*, appeared in 1788 and established her reputation in the Parisian circles of that time. In the aftermath of the Revolution she gained a long-awaited opportunity to again pursue her literary interests and also to become involved in politics. She published *On the Influence of Passions on the Happiness of Individuals and Nations* in 1796, followed four years later by *On Literature Considered in Its Relations to Social Institutions* (1800).[6] Her famous novel *Delphine* appeared in 1802, and *Corinne* was published five years later. After 1795, Madame de Staël returned to Paris for longer sojourns, commented on the major political events of the day, and formu-

---

4. For an excellent selection from Staël's correspondence, see Solovieff, *Madame de Staël, ses amis, ses correspondants. Choix de lettres (1778–1817).*

5. Quoted in Solovieff's introduction to *Madame de Staël, ses amis, ses correspondants. Choix de lettres,* 16.

6. An American edition of this book was published under the title *The Influence of Literature upon Society* (Boston: W. Wells and T. B. Wait and Company, 1813).

lated various policy proposals meant to bring the Revolution to a successful end.

In 1797 she completed the initial part of her first major political work, *On the Current Circumstances Which Can End the Revolution,* whose full text was not published until 1979. The republican tone of this book might surprise readers familiar only with Staël's later political writings, which portray her as an enthusiastic defender of constitutional monarchy *à l'anglaise.* Inspired by the principles of the Enlightenment, she put forward a powerful critique of the excesses of the Jacobins while also taking to task the errors of the ultraroyalists who sought to reverse the course of French history. In order to "close" the Revolution, Madame de Staël favored a republican form of government based on popular sovereignty, representative government, and respect for private property, seen as the foundation of all political rights. She also expressed concern for the low public-spiritedness of the French, which she regarded as a corollary of the disquieting civic apathy fueled by the country's postrevolutionary fatigue.[7]

In 1803 Madame de Staël was forced into exile by Napoléon. Her unfinished memoir, *Ten Years of Exile,* recounts her peregrinations in Europe and documents her critical attitude toward the imperial government. *On Germany* was completed in 1810. In it she praises Prussia and never mentions Napoléon, who had waged an eight-year war against that country. The book did not appear in France because the police confiscated the volume's proofs and type blocks and the ten thousand copies already printed. *On Germany* was finally published in London in 1813. Napoléon, angry and humiliated by Staël's defiant refusal to remove some offending passages, emphatically forbade the publication of the book because it was allegedly "un-French."[8]

Shortly before her death in 1817, Madame de Staël completed her last

7. A similar concern can be found in Benjamin Constant's famous lecture, "The Liberty of the Moderns Compared to the Liberty of the Ancients," which drew inspiration from various ideas of Madame de Staël.

8. The word "un-French" was General Savary's. See his letter to Madame de Staël in Herold, *Mistress to an Age,* 491–92. For more information, see *Ten Years of Exile,* pt. II, chap. i, 101–10.

and arguably most important political work, *Considerations on the Principal Events of the French Revolution*. She managed to revise only the first two volumes and a part of the third one. A French edition of *Considerations* was published in 1818 by her son and her son-in-law, Auguste de Staël and Victor de Broglie, respectively, assisted by her friend August Wilhelm von Schlegel. A three-volume English translation of the book came out the same year in London, but the translator's name was not mentioned on the front page.

Madame de Staël and Napoléon

Madame de Staël's hatred of tyranny and passionate defense of freedom were bound to clash with the institutions of the new regime of Napoléon Bonaparte. Staël met Napoléon for the first time in 1797 and later recalled that she felt unable to breathe in his presence. She became a fierce critic of the First Consul when his absolutist and bellicose tendencies became evident. Napoléon, Madame de Staël argued, subjected his critics to countless persecutions and engaged the country in extravagant military campaigns, taking pleasure only in the violent crises produced by battles. "Emperor Napoléon's greatest grievance against me," Staël wrote in the opening chapter of *Ten Years of Exile*, "is my unfailing respect for true liberty."[9] She deplored the absence of the rule of law in France and argued that public opinion itself was powerless without the authority of the law and independent organs to express it. A famous political figure during that time, Staël was received in the most select circles in England, Germany, Sweden, Austria, and Russia. Tsar Alexander I, who gave Madame de Staël a Russian passport, enjoyed her company and conversation and welcomed her to Russia. At Coppet, she rallied a powerful opposition to Napoléon that brought together many friends of liberty who had become the Emperor's staunchest critics.

Her admiration for Prussia, expressed in *On Germany*, clearly conveyed her opposition to Napoléon. By praising the German culture and spirit, Madame de Staël offered a thinly veiled critique of the Emperor's policies.

9. *Ten Years of Exile*, 4.

A believer in the benefits of the cross-fertilization of ideas, she suggested that France needed an influx of new foreign ideas and, above all, freedom to overcome its political predicament.

In 1814 Madame de Staël welcomed the restoration of the Bourbon monarchy. She returned to Paris, where she followed with great interest the debates on the new Chamber of Deputies while also seeking to recover the two million livres that her father had loaned to the French state during the Revolution. She claimed that the Charter of 1814 contained all the political principles that had previously been advocated by Necker, but she also expressed her concerns about the long-term viability of the new constitutional text. This odd mixture of royal concession and political contract was, she argued, inferior in many respects to the unwritten English constitution based on a sound balance of powers.[10]

The Ideas of *Considerations*

The first years of the Bourbon Restoration provided an open arena for vigorous political debates among partisans of the Old Regime, supporters of constitutional monarchy and representative government, and those who wanted to continue the Revolution. The debate over the legitimacy of the principles of 1789 forced the French to come to terms with the violent episodes of the French Revolution. Not surprisingly, most of the historical writings published during the Bourbon Restoration display an unusual degree of political partisanship, as historians sought to use the lessons of the past to justify their own political agendas. Those who *wrote* history during this time often also tried to *make* history. Liberal writers such as Guizot, Constant,[11] and Madame de Staël insisted that the initial episodes of the Revolution should be seen neither as a prelude to the Terror nor as a complete break with the feudal past, but instead as the inevitable outcome of factors that had been at work for a very long time in the Old Regime. In advancing this argument they were often obliged to

10. For more details, see Herold, *Mistress to an Age*, 544–49, 562–78. On the Charter of 1814, see Aurelian Craiutu, *Liberalism Under Seige*, 70–75.

11. Constant discusses Staël's *Considerations* on pp. 840–52 of his essay "De Madame de Staël et de ses ouvrages," in Benjamin Constant, *Oeuvres*, ed. Alfred Roulin.

resort to a selective reading of the past, one that insisted either on discontinuities or on long-term social, cultural, and political patterns. But regardless of their sophisticated hermeneutical strategies, all French liberals of the time shared two common characteristics: they defended the principles of representative government and constitutional monarchy, and they admired the English model that had successfully blended liberty and order and protected the country against revolutionary turmoil. Staël memorably captured the new liberal catechism in *On the Current Circumstances* when arguing that, in France, liberty was ancient and despotism modern.[12]

Considerations aimed at contributing to this rich and intense historical debate, even if in some respects it was fundamentally a composite that added few original points beyond the sometimes exaggerated praise of Necker's political views and actions.[13] Yet, Madame de Staël's unique perspective, combining firsthand political experience and a subtle intellect with an elegant style and passionate voice, offered a convincing justification of the principles of constitutional monarchy that had inspired the authors of the Charter of 1814. It is important to remember that Madame de Staël did not intend to write a purely historical work retracing step by step the main events and phases of the French Revolution and its aftermath. As she stated in a short foreword to the original edition, her initial goal was to write a book examining the actions and ideas of her beloved father, Jacques Necker, who looms large in the pages of this book. But in the end, Madame de Staël went beyond her original goal and offered a comprehensive view of the main events and actors of the French Revolution. By strongly criticizing Napoléon's actions and legacy, she put forward a vigorous liberal agenda that championed the principles of constitutionalism and representative government. Thus, *Considerations* consolidated Madame de Staël's image as a passionate friend of liberty who feared mob rule and violence and advocated political moderation, the rule of law, and representative government.

12. *Des circonstances actuelles qui peuvent terminer la Révolution et des principes qui doivent fonder la république en France*, 273.

13. See Gauchet, "Staël," in *A Critical Dictionary of the French Revolution*, 1009.

The title of Staël's book was probably a rejoinder to Joseph de Maistre's *Considerations on France,* originally published in 1796 (a new edition came out in 1814), while some of Staël's ideas might have been a response to Burke's *Reflections on the Revolution in France* (1790). Although Burke saw the French Revolution as the result of accidental forces that brought forth the sudden collapse of the Old Regime in 1789, Madame de Staël viewed the events of 1789 as the outcome of the general development of European civilization.[14] Thus, she challenged not only the ultraroyalist opponents of the Revolution, who wanted to restore the old alliance between throne and altar, but also those who argued that the Revolution had been the mere result of accidental or transitory causes. She saw the events of 1789 as part of a greater historical development that consisted of three eras: the feudal system, despotism, and representative government. According to this interpretation, the same social and political forces that had brought about the Revolutions of 1648 and 1688 in England were also the prime cause of the revolutionary wave in France a century later: "Both belong to the third era in the progress of social order—the establishment of representative government. . . ."[15] In other words, far from being fortuitous, the fall of the Old Regime in 1789 was in fact the inevitable outcome of a long historical evolution that could not have been arrested by the efforts of a few individuals.

In this regard Staël's analysis anticipated Tocqueville's meticulously researched diagnosis of the internal crisis of the Old Regime. By focusing on the lack of public spirit and the absence of a genuine constitution prior to 1789, she demonstrated that the Revolution was an irreversible phenomenon that arose in response to the deep structural problems of the Old Regime. Although she stopped short of claiming (like Tocqueville) that the real Revolution had actually occurred prior to 1789, Madame de Staël's account gives the reader a strong sense of the inevitability of the events of that year.

All these ideas loom large in the first two parts of the book in which

14. This idea also is at the heart of François Guizot's *Histoire de la civilisation en Europe* and his *Histoire de la civilisation en France.*

15. *Considerations,* pt. I, chap. i, 24–25.

Staël reflects on the state of public opinion in France at the accession of Louis XVI and discusses Necker's plans for finance and his famous account of the kingdom's finances. Other important topics include the plans of the Third Estate in 1788 and 1789, the fall of the Bastille, and the actions of the Constituent Assembly. About the latter, Madame de Staël has many good things to say, in contrast to Burke's more negative account that highlighted the Assembly's excesses and limitations. In her view, the achievements of the Assembly ultimately outweighed its shortcomings: "We are indebted to the Constituent Assembly for the suppression of the privileged castes in France, and for civil liberty to all. . . ."[16] It was the Constituent Assembly that effaced ancient separations between classes, rendered taxes uniform, proclaimed complete freedom of worship, instituted juries, and removed artificial and ineffective restraints on industry. Above all, the decrees of the Constituent Assembly established provincial assemblies, spreading life, emulation, energy, and intelligence into the provinces. In this regard, it is worth pointing out again the similarity between Staël's interpretation of the political dynamics of the initial phase of the Revolution and Tocqueville's. Both believed that the events of the first half of 1789 displayed sincere patriotism and commitment to the public good, combining enthusiasm for ideas with sincere devotion to a noble cause that made a lasting impression on all true friends of liberty in France.[17]

Yet, Madame de Staël was far from being an unconditional admirer of the Constituent Assembly. In fact, she criticizes it for having displayed an excessive distrust of executive power that eventually triggered insuperable tensions between the King and the representatives of the nation. The Constituent Assembly wrongly considered the executive power as an enemy of liberty rather than as one of its safeguards. The Assembly proceeded to draft the constitution as a treaty between two opposed parties rather than as a compromise between the country's various social and political

16. Ibid., pt. II, chap. iv, 190.
17. "I have never met," Tocqueville wrote in *The Old Régime*, "with a revolution where one could see at the start, in so many men, a more sincere patriotism, more disinterest, more true greatness. . . . This is 1789, a time of inexperience doubtless, but of generosity, of enthusiasm, of virility, and of greatness, a time of immortal memory." (*The Old Régime and the Revolution*, vol. I, 208, 244)

interests. It "formed a constitution as a general would form a plan of attack,"[18] making a harmonious balance of powers impossible and preventing the import onto French soil of bicameralism. The unfortunate choice of a single chamber was incompatible with the existence of effective checks and balances capable of limiting the growing power of the representatives of the French nation.

Staël's *Considerations* also vindicates, albeit in a moderate tone, the principles of 1789 that sought to improve the system of national representation and the right of the Third Estate to full political representation. The boldest claim of this part of the book is that France lacked a true constitution and the rule of law during the Old Regime. The *parlements*[19] were never able to limit the royal authority, which had retained the legal right to impose a *lit de justice*.[20] Moreover, the Estates General were convened only eighteen times in almost five centuries (1302–1789) and did not meet at all between 1614 and 1789. Although the *parlements* could (and occasionally did) invoke the "fundamental laws of the state" and asserted their right to "register" the laws after they had been "verified," it was not possible to speak of the existence of a genuine constitution in the proper sense of the word. "France," Madame de Staël wrote, "has been governed by custom, often by caprice, and never by law. . . . the course of circumstances alone was decisive of what everyone called his right."[21]

Staël did not hesitate to list a long series of royal abuses, including arbitrary imprisonments, ordinances, banishments, special commissions, and *lits de justice* that infringed upon the rights of ordinary citizens and were passed against their will. In her view, the history of France was replete with many attempts on the part of the nation and the nobles to obtain rights and privileges, while the kings aimed at enlarging their prerogatives and consolidating their absolute power. "Who can deny," Madame de Staël concludes in this important chapter (part I, xi), "that a change was

18. *Considerations*, pt. II, chap. viii, 211.

19. The *parlements* were sovereign courts of law and final courts of appeal for the judicial districts of the country.

20. A special session of the *Parlement of Paris* called by the monarch to impose the registration of his royal edicts.

21. *Considerations*, pt. I, chap. xi, 104.

necessary, either to give a free course to a constitution hitherto perpetually infringed; or to introduce those guarantees which might give the laws of the state the means of being maintained and obeyed?"[22] On this view, the Revolution of 1789 appeared justified insofar as it sought to put an end to a long reign based on arbitrary power and obsolete and costly privileges.

In other chapters from parts II and III, Staël criticizes the blindness and arrogance of many political actors whose actions and ideas paved the way for the Terror of 1793–95. She also denounces the institutionalization of fear fueled by the perverse passion for equality displayed by the French. "True faith in some abstract ideas," she argues, "feeds political fanaticism"[23] and can be cured only by the sovereignty of law. Her conclusion is remarkable for both its simplicity and its accuracy: liberty alone can effectively cure political fanaticism, and the remedy for popular passion lies above all in the rule of law. The institution that alone can bring forth ordered liberty is representative government; it is the only remedy through which "the torches of the furies can be extinguished" and that can adequately promote limited power, a proper balance of powers in the state as well as the right of people to consent to taxes, and their ordered participation in legislative acts.

Part IV examines the Directory and the rise of Napoléon Bonaparte. Madame de Staël draws an unflattering (and somewhat biased) portrait of the future emperor by emphasizing not only his unbounded egotism and intoxication with power but also his lack of emotion combined with an unsettling air of vulgarity and political shrewdness. Staël pays special attention to analyzing Napoléon's rise to power in the aftermath of the Terror, believing that he was not only a talented man but also one who represented a whole pernicious system of power. She claimed that this system ought to be examined as a great political problem relevant to many generations. As she memorably puts it, no emotion of the heart could move Napoléon, who regarded his fellow citizens as mere things and means rather than equals worthy of respect. He was "neither good, nor violent, nor gentle, nor cruel. . . . Such a being had no fellow, and therefore could

22. Ibid., pt. I, chap. xi, 111.
23. Ibid., pt. III, chap. xv, 354.

neither feel nor excite sympathy. . . ."[24] Intoxicated with the "vile draught of Machiavellianism" and resembling in many respects the Italian tyrants of the fourteenth and fifteenth centuries, Napoléon managed to enslave the French nation by shrewdly using three means. He sought to satisfy men's interests at the expense of their virtues, he disregarded public opinion, and he gave the French nation war for an object instead of liberty.[25] Through these means he managed to dazzle the masses and corrupt individuals by acting upon their imagination and captivating them with a false sense of greatness.

These chapters convincingly illustrate Staël's hatred of absolute power and shed light on her staunch opposition to the Emperor, for whom she held a deep aversion.[26] Anticipating a common *topos* of Restoration liberal thought, she notes that Napoléon's absolute power had been made possible by the leveling and atomization of society, and she explains his fall from power by pointing out the influence of public opinion and the inevitable limits of that power. In the end, Madame de Staël argues, Napoléon left a nefarious legacy that strengthened the coercive force of centralization and fueled the atomization of society. The system of egoism, oppression, and corruption he founded derailed the normal political development of the country and wasted countless resources. Being a man who could act naturally only when he commanded others, Napoléon degraded the French nation, which he used to advance his own political ambitions and plans. In *Ten Years of Exile*, Madame de Staël wrote that since Napoléon's character was "at war with the rest of creation," he ought to be compared to "the Greek flame, which no force of nature could extinguish."[27]

Parts V and VI of the book contain a vigorous defense of representative government in France and offer a detailed examination of the English po-

---

24. Ibid., pt. III, chap. xxvi, 409.

25. For more details, see ibid., pt. IV, chap. iv, "Progress of Bonaparte to Absolute Power."

26. She recollected their first meeting as follows: "Yet nothing could triumph over my invincible aversion for what I perceived in him. I felt in his soul a cold sharp-edged sword, which froze the wound that it inflicted." (Ibid., pt. III, chap. xxvi, 409–10)

27. *Ten Years of Exile*, 93.

litical system, culminating in moving praise of political liberty and limited power. The political agenda of *Considerations* is illustrated by chapters xi and xii of part V, in which Madame de Staël examines the system that the Bourbons and the friends of liberty ought to have followed in 1814. Worth noting here is Madame de Staël's passionate defense of decentralization and self-government as two effective means of combating Napoléon's legacy of centralized despotism. Opposing those who believed that the French were not made for liberty, Staël points to the rising force of public opinion and warns that every effort to sail against the new democratic torrent will be futile in the long term. After reminding her readers that hypocrisy in the pursuit of liberty is more revolting than its complete denial, she adds confidently: "Let this torrent enter into channels, and all the country which it laid waste will be fertilized."[28]

Part VI contains a detailed account of the main principles undergirding representative government, liberty, and public opinion in England. Madame de Staël did not seek to be a neutral observer of the English scene; her normative approach stemmed from her belief that France must imitate the political institutions of England in order to overcome its legacy of despotism and centralization. "That which is particularly characteristic of England," she noted in a Burkean vein, "is a mixture of chivalrous spirit with an enthusiasm for liberty"[29] fostering a fortunate balance between all social classes, which makes the English nation seem, "if we may say so, one entire body of gentlemen."[30] Unlike the French nobles, the English aristocrats were united to—and identified themselves with—the nation at large and did not form a privileged caste detached from the management of local affairs. Of special interest will be the discussion of the relationship between economic prosperity, legal protection, rule of law, and political freedom, as well as the discussion of the seminal influence of religion and morals on political liberty, anticipating Tocqueville's analysis of religion as a bulwark of political freedom in America. Referring to the English government, Staël writes: "The government never interferes in what can

28. *Considerations*, pt. V, chap. xi, 606.
29. Ibid., pt. VI, chap. iv, 671.
30. Ibid., pt. VI, chap. iv, 671.

be equally well done by individuals: respect for personal liberty extends to the exercise of the faculties of every man."[31] Madame de Staël also praises the balance of power between Crown and Parliament, the countless opportunities for improving the political system without any major convulsion, and the fortunate balance between old and new political and legal forms giving liberty both the advantage of an ancient origin and the benefits of prudent innovation. She saw in publicity and freedom of the press the two pillars of representative government that create a strong bond between the governed and their representatives: "Public opinion bears the sway in England, and it is public opinion that constitutes the liberty of a country."[32]

The last chapter of the book, "Of the Love of Liberty," memorably summarizes the reasons why people need freedom and are ready to die for it. Madame de Staël's vigorous appeal to liberty can still inspire us today: "Liberty! Let us repeat her name with so much the more energy that the men who should pronounce it, at least as an apology, keep it at a distance through flattery: let us repeat it without fear of wounding any power that deserves respect; for all that we love, all that we honor is included in it. Nothing but liberty can arouse the soul to the interests of social order."[33]

The Reception of *Considerations*

Soon after its publication, *Considerations* became a classic *sui generis* in France and was regarded as a first-rate contribution to the ongoing political and historical debate on representative government and its institutions in nineteenth-century France and Europe. Staël's book was praised for having opened the modern era of French liberalism.[34] It was hailed as

31. Ibid., pt. VI, chap. iii, 653.
32. Ibid., pt. VI, chap. iv, 668.
33. Ibid., pt. VI, chap. xii, 753–54.
34. For an account of the reception of Madame de Staël's work, see Frank Bowman, "La polémique sur les Considerations sur la Révolution française," *Annales Benjamin Constant*, 8–9 (Lausanne and Paris: Institute B. Constant and Jean Tonzot), 225–41. For an analysis of the liberalism of the Coppet group (Necker, Staël, Constant, and Sismondi), see Lucien

a genuine hymn to freedom based on a perceptive understanding of the prerequisites of political freedom as well as on a detailed analysis of the social, historical, and cultural contexts within which political rights and political obligation exist. As time passed, however, the book fell into oblivion and shared the fate of French nineteenth- and twentieth-century liberals who became marginalized and ignored in their own country. Not surprisingly, *Considerations* went out of print for more than a century, from 1881 to 1983.

Considerations triggered a number of powerful critiques among Staël's contemporaries, who disagreed with some of its ideas and interpretations. One such critical response came from Stendhal, who was put off by Staël's exceedingly harsh treatment of Napoléon. Another came from the pen of Jacques-Charles Bailleul, who published an extensive, two-volume (chapter by chapter) critique of the book.[35] But it was Louis de Bonald, a leading writer himself and a prominent representative of the ultraroyalists, who put forward the most trenchant critique of Staël's book. In *Observations on the Work of Madame de Staël Entitled "Considerations on the Principal Events of the French Revolution"* (1818), Bonald argued that Madame de Staël failed to give an impartial account of the Revolution, preferring instead to reinterpret its main events in order to vindicate her father's actions and legacy. The Catholic Bonald went further and attacked Staël's political ambitions as well as her liberal principles and values and Protestant outlook. Ultraconservatives like Bonald and Maistre disagreed with Staël's emphasis on the inevitability of the Revolution as well as with her claim that France did not have a proper constitution prior to 1789. If there was anything inevitable in the Revolution, Maistre claimed, it concerned God's punishment for the excesses of the Enlightenment. Not surprisingly, some regarded the Revolution as a unique (and Satanic) event in

---

Jaume, ed., *Coppet, creuset de l'esprit libéral,* especially the essays by Lucien Jaume ("Coppet, creuset du libéralisme comme 'culture morale,'" 225–39), Luigi Lacchè ("Coppet et la percée de l'État libéral constitutionnel," 135–56), and Alain Laquièze ("Le modèle anglais et la responsabilité ministérielle," 157–76).

35. The full title of Bailleul's book is *Examen critique de l'ouvrage posthume de Mme. la Bnne. de Staël, ayant pour titre: Considérations sur les principaux événemens de la Révolution française.*

history that displayed a degree of destruction and human depravity never seen before.[36]

Madame de Staël and America

Finally, it is important to point out that Madame de Staël had a deep appreciation for the principles of American democracy and that her writings and ideas exercised a significant influence on prominent nineteenth-century American intellectuals such as George Ticknor and Henry James. Inspired by Staël's *On Germany*, they studied German culture and made decisive contributions to the development of American higher education and intellectual life.[37] Staël exchanged many letters with important figures such as Gouverneur Morris, Albert Gallatin, Thomas Jefferson, and Pierre Samuel du Pont de Nemours (who emigrated to America after Napoléon's coup d'état of 18 Fructidor).

Moreover, Madame de Staël had numerous investments (land, bonds, and stocks) in the United States, valued by some accounts at approximately one and a half million francs. In 1809–10 she even contemplated coming to America with her family in the hope of finding a new home far away from Napoléon's grasp.[38] Although focused predominantly on business issues, her correspondence with her American friends touched on important events in America such as slavery, the expansion to the West, and the Louisiana Purchase. To Jefferson she confessed in 1816: "If you

36. This thesis looms large in Maistre's *Considerations on France*, in which he argued that the Revolution contained no single element of good, being "the highest degree of corruption ever known, . . . pure impurity, a horrible assemblage of baseness and cruelty." (Maistre, *Considerations on France*, 38–39)

37. On this topic, see Pochmann, *German Culture in America*, and Hawkins, *Madame de Staël and the United States*.

38. See Madame de Staël's statement (from 1810) in *Ten Years of Exile*, 102: "I was still determined to go to England by way of America," and Savary's acknowledgment: "You are aware, Madam, that we allowed you to leave for Coppet only because you expressed the desire to go to America." (quoted in Herold, *Mistress to an Age*, 491–92) Also see the letters of May 22 and 28, 1809, written from Coppet by Sismondi, Staël's close friend, confirming Staël's intention to cross the ocean to find in the New World the freedom and security missing in France. Excerpts from the two letters can be found in Hawkins, *Madame de Staël and the United States*, 39.

succeeded in doing away with slavery in the South, there would be at least one government in the world as perfect as human reason can conceive it."[39] At the same time, Madame de Staël was worried that by fighting against England the United States vicariously helped Napoléon and his despotic regime.

It was this concern that prompted her to work toward bringing the two countries together. While in London in 1814, she was instrumental in setting up an appointment between the American secretary of the treasury, Albert Gallatin, and Russia's tsar, Alexander I. The meeting had a powerful symbolic connotation because Russia's involvement gave a strong warning to England against continuing its war with America. In September 1814, she wrote to Gallatin that the United States rather than England was the true defender of liberty: "It is you, America, that interest me now above all, aside from my pecuniary affairs. I find you to be at the present moment oppressed by the party of liberty and I see in you the cause that attached me to England a year ago."[40] Back in Paris, she received John Quincy Adams and continued her correspondence with Jefferson. "Our family," she wrote to him in 1816, "is still a little intellectual island where Franklin, Washington, and Jefferson are revered as in their own country."[41] Shortly before her death, she told George Bancroft in Paris: "You are the vanguard of the human race, you are the future of the world."[42]

These testimonies demonstrate that more than a decade before Tocqueville, Madame de Staël sincerely admired the Americans and unambiguously praised their dedication to political liberty, foreseeing the rise of the young nation to the status of superpower. "There is a people who will one day be very great," she wrote in *Considerations*. "These are the Americans. . . . What is there more honorable for mankind than this new world,

---

39. Chinard, "La correspondance de Madame de Staël avec Jefferson," 636 (quoted by Hawkins, *Madame de Staël and the United States,* 5).

40. Quoted by Hawkins, *Madame de Staël and the United States,* 54.

41. Chinard, "La correspondance de Madame de Staël avec Jefferson," 636 (also quoted by Berger in his introduction to *Politics, Literature, and National Character,* 27).

42. *Life, Letters, and Journals of George Ticknor,* vol. I, 132–33. It is worth pointing out that Madame de Staël was familiar with La Rochefoucauld-Liancourt's *Voyage dans les États-Unis d'Amérique fait en 1795, 1796, et 1797.*

which has established itself without the prejudices of the old; this new world where religion is in all its fervor without needing the support of the state to maintain it; where the law commands by the respect which it inspires, without being enforced by any military power?"[43] Her prophetic words continue to inspire us today, as new constellations of ideas and political factors challenge us to rethink the role of American democracy in the twenty-first century.

Aurelian Craiutu
Indiana University, Bloomington

43. Staël, *Considerations*, pt. VI, chap. vii, 707.

Note on the Present Edition

In recent years the English-speaking academic world has witnessed a renewed interest in the writings of Alexis de Tocqueville and Benjamin Constant. New English translations of Tocqueville's and Constant's political works have been published by prestigious presses, and special issues on their writings have appeared in important academic journals. Unfortunately, the same cannot be said of Madame de Staël, the other principal figure of nineteenth-century French political thought. None of her major political works are available in English at the present moment, and she remains an unknown figure among political theorists, vaguely linked to Constant, with whom she had a close intellectual and personal relationship.[1]

The lack of recognition given to Madame de Staël's political writings in the Anglo-American world is both disappointing and surprising given her stature as one of the greatest writers and political thinkers of the nineteenth century. Readers interested in the debates on the events and legacy of the French Revolution can only regret the absence of an English translation of Staël's *On the Current Circumstances Which Can End the Revolution*. Similarly, they have been deprived of access to the old English edition of her *Considerations on the Principal Events of the French Revolution* because it has been out of print for almost two centuries (the book appeared in 1818). Perhaps even more surprising is the neglect of Staël's

---

1. In 2000 Transaction Publishers republished a selection from Madame de Staël's writings on politics, literature, and national character. Translated and edited by Morroe Berger (the original edition appeared in 1964), this anthology includes a seventeen-page fragment from Staël's *Considerations*. Also worth mentioning are a selection from Staël's rich correspondence compiled by George Solovieff (Springer Publishing, 2000); the new translation of *Ten Years of Exile* by Avriel H. Goldberger (Northern Illinois University Press, 2000); *An Extraordinary Woman: Selected Writings of Germaine de Staël*, edited and translated by Vivian Folkenflick (Columbia University Press, 1987); and the collection of essays in *Germaine de Staël: Crossing the Borders*, edited by Madelyn Gutwirth, et al. (Rutgers University Press, 1991).

political works by many feminists, a regrettable oversight that it is hoped will be corrected in the years ahead. Her works shed original light on the central role played by women in French cultural and political life and suggest a novel way of thinking about the role of women in society that challenges some of the assumptions espoused by contemporary feminist writers in the Anglo-American world.[2]

The Liberty Fund edition of *Considerations on the Principal Events of the French Revolution* seeks to fill this important gap. Its purpose is to familiarize English-speaking readers with a writer whose unique and seductive voice retains a significant relevance today. Few titles are better suited to promote the principles of political freedom, responsibility, and open society than *Considerations*. By reprinting a substantially revised and corrected English translation of *Considerations,* we are making accessible to a large audience a neglected classic of political thought that will contribute to contemporary debates on constitutionalism, representative government, and political moderation. Madame de Staël's work sheds light on what it takes to build a society of free and responsible individuals and explores other important related issues such as the prerequisites of liberty, limited power and the rule of law, the relation between social order and political order, the dependence of liberty on morality and religion, and the institutional foundations of a free regime. Her political writings offer a powerful critique of fanaticism and remind us that moderation and reason should always be allied with responsibility, respect for individual rights, and decency.[3]

Considerations on the Principal Events of the French Revolution was originally published in French in 1818. The two editions printed that year were followed by four others, in 1820, 1843, 1862, and 1881. The book was also reedited in Madame de Staël's *Oeuvres complètes* in 1820, 1836, and 1838. No other French editions of the book appeared between 1881 and 1983,

2. A splendid account of Madame de Staël's contribution to feminist debates may be found in Mona Ozouf, *Women's Words: Essay on French Singularity* (Chicago: University of Chicago Press, 1997), a work which, unfortunately, has been ignored in the United States.

3. Staël wrote that "reason is not a shade of meaning between extremes, but the primary color given off by the purest rays of the sun." (Berger, ed., *Politics, Literature, and National Character,* 136)

when historian Jacques Godechot published a new edition (Paris: Tallandier Publishing House, 1983) that contains an introduction, a bibliography, and a chronology.

The story behind the writing and publication of *Considerations* is not devoid of interesting ambiguities and speculations. We know that Madame de Staël had revised the first two volumes, but not the third one (containing parts V and VI), prior to her untimely death in 1817. Although the two French editors claimed that the published text of *Considerations* was "perfectly conformable" with Staël's corrected manuscript, scholars agree that the original manuscript was altered extensively. The exact nature of the changes remains unclear and poses a considerable challenge to any interpreter of Staël's work. As the late Simone Balayé pointed out, a considerable number of manuscripts of *Considerations* can be found in different archives. A critical edition of the book comparing the different versions of the manuscript, similar to the two critical editions of *De l'Allemagne* and *Dix d'années d'exil* coordinated by the Comtesse de Pange and Simone Balayé, is long overdue.[4]

Although the Liberty Fund edition follows the text of the 1818 English translation (which was originally published in three volumes),[5] it is a *substantially* revised version that seeks to correct the errors and archaisms of the original translation. As editor, I have made numerous changes in the translation with a view to offering a more faithful version of the original text. In doing so, I have followed the French text of the 1983 Godechot edition, published by Tallandier. The notes of the Tallandier edition were valuable in preparing my own notes. In the present work, the original footnotes of both Madame de Staël and the first French editors (Auguste de Staël and Victor de Broglie) appear at the bottom of the page preceded by an asterisk. My explanatory footnotes, preceded by an arabic number to distinguish them from those of the author and original French editors,

---

4. For more information about the differences between the original manuscript and the published one, see the account given by Chinatsu Takeda, "Présentation des documents," in *Revue française d'histoire des idées politiques*, 18 (no. 2): 2003, 355–61.

5. Both the 1818 French edition and the 1818 English translation were published in three volumes (vol. 1: pts. 1 and 2; vol. 2: pts. 3 and 4; vol. 3: pts. 5 and 6). The name of the English translator was not disclosed.

are meant to provide a minimal historical background to the general English-speaking reader. Typographical errors and archaic punctuation in the original translation have been corrected silently; English spellings have been Americanized. The English translators occasionally broke Staël's extremely long paragraphs for clarity; for the most part, we have kept the format of the original translation. In addition, the editors of the 1818 English translation added quotation marks to ambiguous quotations from various authors that were not identified in the original French. I have attempted to give the proper citations where possible and eliminated the quotation marks if a proper citation could not be found.

I am deeply indebted to the Liberty Fund staff for their invaluable assistance, support, and encouragement in bringing this difficult and long project to fruition. Special thanks are due to Laura Goetz and Diana Francoeur, whose editorial help has been much appreciated. I should also like to thank Henry Clark, John Isbell, Jeremy Jennings, Vladimir Protopopescu, and Jean-Bertrand Ribat for their suggestions on the introduction, notes, and translation.

A. C.

*Considerations
on the Principal
Events of the
French Revolution*

CONSIDERATIONS

ON THE

PRINCIPAL EVENTS

OF

THE FRENCH REVOLUTION

POSTHUMOUS WORK OF

THE BARONESS DE STAËL.

EDITED BY

THE DUKE DE BROGLIE, AND THE BARON DE STAËL.

Les Révolutions qui arrivent dans les grands
états ne sont point un effet du hazard, ni du
caprice de peuples.   MEMOIRES DE SULLY.[1]

TRANSLATED FROM THE ORIGINAL MANUSCRIPT.

LONDON:

PRINTED FOR BALDWIN, CRADOCK, AND JOY,

PATERNOSTER-ROW.

1818.

---

1. "Revolutions that occur in large countries are neither the result of chance nor the
whim of the people."

Notice by the Editors[1]

In executing the task which Madame de Staël has condescended to confide to us, it is our particular duty to make known the exact condition in which we found the manuscript entrusted to our care.

Madame de Staël had traced out for all her compositions a system of labor from which she never deviated. She sketched off at once the complete outline of the work of which she had previously conceived the plan, without referring back, without interrupting the course of her thoughts, unless it were to make researches which her subject rendered necessary. This first composition completed, Madame de Staël transcribed it entire with her own hand; and then, not concerning herself with the correction of the style, she modified the expression of her ideas, classing them frequently in a new order. This second performance was then fairly copied out by a secretary, and it was only on this second copy, often even on the proofs of the printed sheets, that Madame de Staël completed the niceties of her diction; being more anxious to convey to her readers all the shades of her thoughts, all the emotions of her soul, than to attain that minute correctness, which may be acquired by mere mechanical labor.

Madame de Staël had completed, early in 1816, the composition of the work we now present to the public. She had devoted a whole year to the revisal of the first two volumes, and a part of the third. She returned to Paris to complete those passages relating to recent events of which she had not been personally a witness, and upon which more precise inquiries might have the effect of modifying some of her opinions. In short, the *Considerations on the Principal Events of the French Revolution* (for such is the title chosen by Madame de Staël herself) would have appeared at the

---

1. The two editors were Victor de Broglie and Auguste de Staël. They were assisted by August Wilhelm von Schlegel, the former teacher of Auguste and close friend of Germaine de Staël.

conclusion of last year if she, who constituted our glory and our happiness, had been preserved to us.

The first two volumes and several chapters of the third were found in the state in which they were intended for the press. Some other chapters were transcribed but not revised by the Author; but others were only composed in the outline, with marginal notes written or dictated by Madame de Staël, indicating the points on which she proposed to dilate.

The first feeling, as the first duty of her children, has been to evince the most sacred respect for the slightest indications of her thoughts; and it is almost superfluous to say that we have permitted ourselves to make not only no addition, but no change, and that the work about to be read is perfectly conformable to the corrected manuscript of Madame de Staël.

The labor of the Editors has been therefore confined entirely to the revisal of the proofs, and to the correction of those slight inaccuracies of style which escape observation even in manuscripts the most carefully revised. This has been performed under the eye of M. A. W. de Schlegel, whose rare superiority of parts and knowledge justifies the confidence with which Madame de Staël consulted him in all her literary labors, as his most honorable character merits the esteem and friendship which she constantly entertained for him during an intimacy of thirteen years.

Mr. de Staël hereafter proposes to fulfill intentions most sacred to him in publishing a complete edition of the works of his mother, and of those of Mr. Necker. The works of Madame de Staël will comprise some inedited compositions; amongst others, the fragments of a work begun under the title *Ten Years of Exile*. A Biographical Notice will precede each collection; but a feeling, which those who knew Madame de Staël will appreciate with indulgence, has not yet permitted her children to commence an undertaking which comes so home to their dearest as to their most sorrowful recollections.

Advertisement of the Author

I began this work with an intention of confining it to an examination of the political actions and writings of my father. But, as I advanced in my labor, I was led by the subject itself to trace, on one hand, the principal events of the French Revolution and to present, on the other, a picture of England, as a justification of the opinion of M. Necker relative to the political institutions of that country. My plan being therefore enlarged, I judged it proper to alter the title, although I had not changed the object. Nevertheless, there will remain in this work more details relative to my father, and even to myself, than I should have inserted if I had originally conceived it in a general point of view; but, perhaps, circumstances of a private nature are conducive to a clearer knowledge of the spirit and character of the times we are about to describe.

Contents[1]

1. The page numbers given in the Contents are those of the Liberty Fund edition.

PART II.

PART III.

PART IV.

PART V.

PART VI.

CHAPTER I

General Reflections.

The Revolution of France is one of the grand eras of social order. Those who consider it as the result of accidental causes have reflected neither on the past nor on the future; they have mistaken the actors for the drama; and, in seeking a solution agreeable to their prejudices, have attributed to the men of the day that which had been in a course of preparation for ages.[1]

It would have sufficed, however, to cast a glance on the critical periods of history, to be convinced, that they were all unavoidable when they were connected in any degree with the development of ideas; and that, after a struggle and misfortunes, more or less prolonged, the triumph of knowledge has always been favorable to the greatness and the amelioration of mankind.

My ambition shall be to speak of the age in which we have lived, as if it were already remote. It will belong to the enlightened part of mankind—to those who, in thought, can render themselves contemporary with future ages—to judge if I have been able to attain the complete impartiality at which I have aimed.

In this chapter I shall confine myself to some general remarks on the political progress of European civilization, restricting myself, however,

---

1. Many historical writings published during the Bourbon Restoration had a covert political agenda that must be placed in the larger context of that epoch. Madame de Staël's point that the French Revolution had been long in the making was developed a decade later by Guizot in his influential *History of Civilization in Europe* (1828).

to its connection with the Revolution of France; for it is to this subject, in itself sufficiently extensive, that this work is devoted.

The two nations of antiquity, whose literature and history still form the principal portion of our intellectual treasure, were indebted for their astonishing superiority entirely to the enjoyment of a free country. But slavery existed among them, and, consequently, those rights and those motives to emulation, which ought to be common to all men, were the exclusive lot of a few. The Greek and Roman nations disappeared from the world in consequence of what was barbarous, that is, of what was unjust, in their institutions. The vast regions of Asia are lost in despotism; and, for centuries past, whatever has remained there of civilization is stationary. Thus, then, the great historical revolution, whose results admit of application to the present state of modern nations, begins from the invasion by the northern tribes; for the public law of most countries in Europe is still founded on the law of conquest.

Nevertheless, that circle of men, who alone were allowed to consider themselves as such, was increased under the feudal system. The condition of the serfs was less hard than that of slaves; there were several methods of escaping from it, and from that time various classes have begun to emancipate themselves by degrees from the fate of the vanquished. It is to the gradual increase of this circle of society that our attention ought to be turned.

The absolute government of one is the worst form of political combinations. Aristocracy is better, for in it several at least are of importance; and the moral dignity of man is recovered in the relation of the great lords with their chief. Social order, which admits all our fellow creatures to equality before the law, as before God, is as much in harmony with the Christian religion as with true liberty: both the one and the other, in different spheres, should follow the same principles.

Since the nations of the North and of Germany overthrew the Western Empire, the laws introduced by them have undergone a variety of modifications; for time, as Bacon says, is the greatest of innovators. It would be very difficult to fix with precision the dates of the successive changes; for, in tracing the leading facts, we find that one event encroaches on another. I think, however, that our attention may be fixed on four eras, in which these changes, previously announced, became particularly conspicuous.

The first political period was that in which the nobles, that is to say the conquerors, considered themselves as co-partners in the royal power of their chief, while the nation was divided among the different lords, who disposed of it as they pleased.

There was then neither education, industry, nor trade: landed property was almost the only kind known; and Charlemagne himself was occupied in his *capitularia*[2] with the rural economy of the royal demesnes. The nobles went to war in person, leading their armed force: thus the sovereigns had no occasion to levy taxes, as they supported neither military nor civil establishments. Everything demonstrates that, at this time, the great lords were very independent of kings; they maintained liberty for themselves, if indeed they can be free themselves who impose servitude on others. Hungary in its present state may convey an idea of this form of government, which must be allowed to possess grandeur for those who participate in it.[3]

The Champs-de-Mai,[4] so often referred to in the history of France, might be called the democratic government of the nobility, such as has existed in Poland. Feudality was established later. Hereditary succession to the crown, without which there can be no tranquillity in monarchies, was not regularly established until the third race of the kings of France: during the second, the nation, that is, the barons and clergy, chose a successor among the individuals of the reigning family. Primogeniture was happily recognized with the third race. But up to the consecration of Louis

2. Written administrative and legislative commands of the Carolingian kings. They were formally divided into sections called *capitula* and were seen as the chief written instrument of royal authority.

3. The accuracy of this historical account must be taken with a grain of salt. Here, Madame de Staël follows an older tradition of interpretation that goes back to Fénélon and Boulainvilliers.

4. The same as the Champs-de-Mars. Napoléon I revived these meetings during the "Hundred Days." Originally the term designated the March meetings held as pageants by Clovis and his followers for the amusement of the freemen who came to offer homage to their lords or to conduct business.

XVI inclusively, the consent of the people has always been laid down as the basis of the rights of the sovereign to the throne.

There was already, under Charlemagne, something which bore a greater resemblance to the English peerage than the institution of the *noblesse*, such as we have seen it in France for the last two centuries. I make this remark, however, without attaching much importance to it. Doubtless it were better that Reason in politics should be of ancient origin; but although she be but of yesterday, still we should bid her welcome.

The feudal system was much more advantageous to the nobles than the situation of courtiers to which royal despotism has condemned them. It is now merely a speculative question, whether mankind would be the gainers from the independence of one class only, or from the exercise of a gentle, but equal, oppression upon all. We have only to remark that the nobles, in the time of their splendor, enjoyed a species of political independence, and that the absolute power of the kings has been established against them with the support of the people.

In the second political period, that of partial enfranchisements, the *bourgeois* of the towns laid claim to certain rights; for, when men unite together, they gain by their union, at least as much in wisdom as in power. The republics of Germany and Italy, the municipal privileges of the rest of Europe, date from this time. The walls of each town afforded protection to its inhabitants. We still see, particularly in Italy, remarkable traces of those individual defenses against the collective powers: castles multiplied in each domain; fortified palaces; in short, attempts ill-combined but worthy of esteem, since they were all directed to increase the importance and energy of each citizen. It is impossible, nevertheless, to deny that these attempts of petty states to ensure their independence, being ill-regulated, have often led to anarchy; but Venice, Genoa, the Lombard League, the Tuscan Republics, Switzerland, the Hanse Towns, established at this time their liberty on an honorable basis. The institutions of these republics have ever borne marks of the period in which they were established; and the rights of individual liberty, such as ensure the exercise and development of the faculties of every class of men, were not secured by them. Holland, become a republic at a later period, approached to the true principles of social order, an advantage for which she was more particularly indebted to the Reformation. The period of partial enfranchisements, of which I have treated, is no longer clearly to be traced, except in free towns and in the republics which have subsisted to the present day. In the history of the great modern states, therefore, only three eras, entirely distinct, ought to be admitted: the feudal system, despotism, and representative government.

For about five centuries, independence and the improvement of knowledge have been operating in every way and almost at random; yet regal power has constantly increased from different causes and by different means. Kings, having often much to apprehend from the arrogance of the nobles, sought support in a closer connection with the people. Regular troops rendered the assistance of the nobles less requisite; the necessity of imposts, on the other hand, forced the sovereigns to have recourse to the commons; and, in order to obtain from them direct contributions, it was necessary to disengage them, more or less, from the influence of the barons. The revival of letters, the invention of the art of printing, the Reformation, the discovery of the new world, and the progress of commerce taught mankind that a military power was not the only one which could possibly exist; and they have since learned that the profession of arms is not the exclusive privilege of birth.

In the Middle Ages, learning was exclusively confined to the priests, who, during the Dark Ages, had rendered important services to mankind. But when the clergy found themselves attacked by the Reformation, they opposed instead of promoting the progress of the human mind.[5] The second class of society then took possession of the sciences and literature, the study of the law, and of commerce; and thus its importance daily increased. On the other hand, states became more concentrated, the resources of government were increased, and kings, by availing themselves of the lower orders against the barons and the higher clergy, established their own despotism; that is, the union of the executive and legislative powers in the hands of one individual.

Louis XI was the first who made a regular trial of this fatal system in France, and the inventor was truly worthy of the invention. Henry VIII

---

5. It is worth pointing out that Madame de Staël's views on this issue were undoubtedly influenced by her Protestantism.

in England, Philip II in Spain, Christian in the North,[6] labored, under different circumstances, upon the same plan. But Henry VIII in preparing the Reformation became the involuntary instrument of conferring liberty on his country. Charles the Fifth might perhaps, for a time, have accomplished his project of universal monarchy if, in spite of the fanaticism of his southern states, he had supported himself by the reforming spirit of the time, by accepting the confession of Augsburg. It is said that he had the intention, but this ray of his genius disappeared under the gloomy power of his son; and the stamp of the terrible reign of Philip II still presses with all its force upon the Spanish nation—there the Inquisition has undertaken to preserve the inheritance of despotism.

Christian II attempted to render Sweden and Denmark subject to the same uncontrolled sway; but he was baffled by the independent spirit of the Swedes. The history of that people exhibits several periods similar to those that we have traced in other countries. Charles XI[7] struggled hard to triumph over the nobles by means of the people; but Sweden already possessed a constitution, in virtue of which the deputies of the citizens and peasantry composed the half of the Diet: they were sufficiently enlightened to know that privileges are to be relinquished only when rights are to be confirmed and that an aristocracy, with all its faults, is less degrading than despotism.

The Danes have afforded the most scandalous political example which history records. In the year 1660, weary of the power of the nobles, they declared their king, not only sole legislator and sovereign master of their lives and fortunes, but they invested him with every power, except that of repealing the act which constituted him a despot; and, after completing this surrender of themselves, they added that if the king of any other country possessed prerogatives beyond what they had conferred, they granted these to their monarchs in advance, and at all risks; yet this unprecedented decision was nothing more than an open avowal of what in other countries was proceeding with greater reserve. The Protestant religion, and still

6. Christian II, King of Denmark, Norway, and Sweden (1481–1523).
7. Charles XI, King of Sweden (1655–97). Crowned in 1660, he became one of the greatest Swedish monarchs.

more the liberty of the press, have since created in Denmark a degree of independence, in point of thinking, which opposes a moral limit to the abuse of prerogative.

Russia, however different from the rest of Europe in its institutions and in its Asiatic manners, underwent, under Peter I, the second crisis of European monarchies, the humiliation of the nobles by the sovereign.

Europe should be summoned before the bar of Poland for the long train of injuries of which that country had been the victim until the reign of the Emperor Alexander. But without dwelling at present on those troubles, which necessarily arose out of the unhappy coincidence of servitude on the part of the peasants and lawless independence on that of the nobles—out of a proud patriotic feeling, on the one hand, and an exposure, on the other, to the pernicious ascendancy of foreign influence—we shall be content with observing that the constitution of 1792, that constitution for which Kosciusko so nobly fought, contained a number of equally wise and liberal provisions.[8]

Germany, considered as a political body, still belongs, in several respects, to the earliest of the periods of modern history—that of the feudal system; although the spirit of the age has evidently penetrated through her antique institutions. France, Spain, and Britain have, all along, aimed at constituting each a political whole: Germany has maintained her subdivisions, from a spirit partly of independence, partly of aristocratic feeling. The treaty of Westphalia, by acknowledging the Protestant religion throughout half the empire, brought in contact two parts of the same nation who had been taught a mutual awe by their long warfare. This is not the place for enlarging on the political and military advantages that would have resulted from a closer union. Germany now possesses strength enough to maintain her national independence, without relinquishing her federal form; and the interest of enlightened men can never be conquest abroad, but liberty at home.

Poor rich Italy, having constantly been the prey of foreigners, the progress of the human mind is traced with more difficulty in her history than

---

8. Madame de Staël refers here to the Polish Constitution of May 3, 1791, which included many liberal provisions.

in that of the rest of Europe. Yet the second period, that of the enfranchisement of towns, which we have described as blending itself with the third, was marked more distinctly here than in other countries, because it gave rise to several republics, which claim our admiration, at least by the distinguished individuals whom they produced. Among the Italians arbitrary power has arisen only in consequence of political division; their situation, in this respect, is very different from that of the Germans. Every patriotic feeling in Italy ought to point to the union of its various states. Foreigners being incessantly brought among them by the attractions of the country, the Italians can never form a people without a national consolidation. It has hitherto been prevented by the influence of the papal government: not that the popes have been the partisans of foreigners; on the contrary, they would have wished to repel them; but, from their priestly character, they were incapable of defending the country, while at the same time they prevented any other power from undertaking it.

England is the only great European Empire that has yet attained what, in our present state of political knowledge, appears the perfection of social order. The middling class, or, in other words, the nation (as elsewhere), co-operated with the Crown, under Henry VII, in reducing the influence of the nobles and clergy, and increased its own at their expense. But the nobility of England were, from the beginning, actuated by a more liberal spirit than the nobility of other countries; for so far back as *Magna Charta*, we find the barons making stipulations in behalf of the people. The revolutionary period of England may be said to have lasted nearly fifty years, if we reckon from the beginning of the civil wars under Charles I to the accession of William III in 1688; and the efforts of these fifty years had no other real and permanent object than the establishment of the existing constitution; that is, of the finest monument of justice and moral greatness existing in Europe.[9]

The same movement in the minds of men which brought about the revolution in England was the cause of that of France in 1789. Both belong

9. Madame de Staël strongly admired the English constitution, which she considered the best in Europe. It is worth pointing to the similarities between her explanation of the success of liberty in England and Tocqueville's account of the singularity of England in *The Old Régime and the Revolution*.

to the third era in the progress of social order—the establishment of representative government—a point toward which the human mind is directing itself from all parts.[10]

Let us now proceed to examine the circumstances peculiar to France—to a country the scene of those gigantic events which in our days have been the source of so much hope and so much fear.

---

10. This thesis would also play a seminal role in Guizot's *History of Civilization in Europe*, lectures XIII and XIV. It is in stark contrast to Burke's account of the French Revolution.

CHAPTER II

Considerations on the History of France.

Men are seldom familiar with any history but that of their own time; and in reading the declamations so frequent in our days, one would be led to think that the eight centuries of monarchical government which preceded the Revolution had been ages of tranquillity; and that the French nation had reposed during that time on a bed of roses. We forget the burning of the Knights Templars under Philip the Fair; the victories of the English under the kings of the Valois race; the civil war of La Jacquerie;[1] the assassination of the Duke of Orléans,[2] and of the Duke of Burgundy;[3] the treacherous cruelty of Louis XI; the condemnation of the French Protestants to frightful punishments under Francis I, at the very time, too, when he was in alliance with their brethren in Germany;[4] the horrors of

1. Rural uprising in the regions of Island-of-France, Picardy, Champagne, Artois, and Normandy in May–June 1358.

2. The Duke of Orléans was assassinated in 1407 at the order of the Duke of Burgundy, known as John the Fearless.

3. The Duke of Burgundy was assassinated in September 1419 at Montereau, where he was to attend a meeting with the dauphin (the future Charles VII). He first distinguished himself in the battle at Nicopolis, where he led a French army that helped the besieged King of Hungary to battle the Turkish forces under Bajazet (the Thunderbolt). After he became duke, he clashed with his father's brothers, particularly Louis, Duke of Orléans. Tensions mounted between Burgundy and Orléans, and the Duke took the initiative and planned the assassination of Louis in 1407.

4. Francis I (1494–1547), crowned King of France in 1515, distinguished himself as a devoted patron of the arts, although his reign was clouded by rifts and tensions within the Christian church. Martin Luther's denunciation of the corruption of the Roman Catholic Church in 1519 triggered the Protestant movement. At first, Francis tolerated the new movement, since many German Protestant princes were turning against his sworn enemy, Charles V, but his later approval of persecutions against the Protestants led to the beginning of a long civil war.

the league, all surpassed by the massacre of St. Bartholomew;[5] the conspiracies against Henri IV and his assassination, that frightful act of the league; the scaffolds raised by the arbitrary Richelieu; the military executions, long remembered under the name of *dragonnades;*[6] the repeal of the Edict of Nantes; the expulsion of the Protestants, and the war of the Cevennes under Louis XIV;[7] and, finally, the less terrific but not less important struggles of the parliaments under Louis XV.

Troubles without end have arisen in France to obtain what was considered to be liberty, at different periods, whether feudal, religious, or representative; and, if we except the reigns of those kings who, like Francis I and, above all, Louis XIV, possessed the dangerous art of occupying the nation by war, we shall not find, in the space of eight centuries, an interval of twenty-five years without a conflict of nobles against the sovereign, of peasants against nobles, of Protestants against Catholics, or, finally, of parliaments against the court—all struggles to escape from that arbitrary power which forms the most insupportable of burdens on a people. The civil commotions, as well as the violent measures adopted to stifle them, are an evidence that the French exerted themselves as much as the English to obtain that liberty confirmed by law, which alone can ensure to a people peace, emulation, and prosperity.[8]

5. The St. Bartholomew's Day massacre unleashed a wave of Catholic mob violence against the Huguenots. The violence started on August 24, 1572, with the assassination of Admiral Gaspard de Coligny, the most respected Huguenot leader, and quickly spread throughout France, lasting for several months.

6. The *dragonnades* were a form of persecution of French Protestants (Huguenots) before and after Louis XIV revoked the Edict of Nantes in 1685. The Edict of Nantes of 1598, promulgated by King Henri IV to restore internal peace in a France torn by the Wars of Religion, defined and secured the rights of the French Protestants. In 1685 Louis XIV declared that the majority of Protestants had converted to Catholicism and annulled the edict of 1598, which, he claimed, had become superfluous.

7. The revocation of the Edict of Nantes by Louis XIV renewed the persecution of Protestants and triggered the so-called War of Camisards in the region of Cevennes from 1702 to 1705; the war ended with a large fire.

8. Madame de Staël offers here an interpretation of the history of France through liberal lenses. Her emphasis on the struggle against arbitrary power is meant to highlight the antecedents of representative institutions and principles in France that found their guarantees in Louis XVIII's Charter of 1814.

It is of importance to repeat to those who are the advocates of rights founded on the past, that it is liberty which is ancient, and despotism which is modern.[9] In all the European states founded at the commencement of the middle age, the power of the king was limited by that of the nobles. The Diets in Germany, in Sweden, in Denmark before its charter of servitude, the Parliaments in England, the Cortes in Spain, the intermediate bodies of all kinds in Italy, prove that the northern tribes brought with them institutions which confined the power to one class, but which were in no respect favorable to despotism. The Franks never acknowledged uncontrolled power in their chiefs; for it is incontrovertible that, under the first two races of their kings, all who had the right of a citizen, that is, the nobles, and the nobles were the Franks, participated in the government. "Every one knows," says M. de Boulainvilliers,[10] who certainly was no philosopher, "that the French were a free people, who elected their chiefs, under the title of kings, to execute the laws which they themselves had enacted, or to command them in war; and that they were very far from considering their kings as legislators who could order everything according to their pleasure. There remains no act of the first two races of the monarchy which is not characterized by the consent of the general assemblies of the Champs de Mars or Champs de Mai, and even no war was then undertaken without their approbation."

The third race of the kings of France was established on the principles of the feudal system; the two preceding races rested more on the law of conquest. The first princes of the third race styled themselves "kings, by the grace of God, and the consent of the people"; and the form of their coronation oath afterward contained a promise to preserve the laws and

9. Madame de Staël had already made this claim in her book *Des circonstances actuelles qui peuvent terminer la Révolution française*, written in 1797–98 (the complete text was first published in 1979 by Lucia Omacini).

10. Henri de Boulainvilliers (1658–1722), French historian and author of *Histoire de l'ancien gouvernement de la France; Etat de la France, avec des memoires sur l'ancien gouvernement; Histoire de la pairie de France;* and *Essais sur la noblesse de France, contenans une dissertation sur son origine & abaissement.* All these books were published posthumously in Holland and England.

rights of the nation. The kings of France, from St. Louis to Louis XI,* did not arrogate to themselves the right of making laws without the consent of the Estates General; but the disputes of the three orders, which could never agree together, obliged them to have recourse to the sovereigns as mediators; and the ministers of the Crown did not fail to profit by this necessity either to avoid the convocation of the Estates General or to render their deliberations ineffectual. At the time of the invasion of France by Edward III of England,[11] that prince declared, in his proclamation, that he "came to restore to the French the rights of which they had been deprived."

The four best kings of France, Saint Louis (Louis IX),[12] Charles V, Louis XII, and above all Henri IV, endeavored to establish the empire of the laws, each according to the prevailing ideas of his age. The Crusades prevented Louis IX from devoting his whole time to the welfare of his subjects. The war with England and the captivity of John[13] absorbed those resources which would have been turned to account by the wisdom of his son Charles V.[14] The unfortunate invasion of Italy, ill begun by Charles VIII[15]

---

* From 1270 to 1461.

11. Edward III (1312–77), among the most famous kings of England, consolidated England's military power during his long reign by asserting its sovereignty over Scotland. He declared himself rightful heir to the French throne in 1337 as the only living male descendant of his grandfather Philip IV and thereby started the Hundred Years' War.

12. Louis IX (1215–70), King of France 1226–70, also known as St. Louis, canonized in 1297 by Pope Boniface VIII. He was a great patron of the arts and built the famous Saint Chapelle in Paris. A devout Christian, he was seen as the model of the Christian monarch and participated in two crusades (1248 and 1270). He died in 1270 near Tunis.

13. John II of France (1319–64), known as John the Good. In 1356, after losing the battle at Poitiers, he was captured and taken to London. Four years later, the Treaty of Brétigny released the French king from captivity on the condition that France pay a hefty ransom and that two of his sons, John and Louis, take his place in London to guarantee the payment of the ransom. After Louis escaped in 1363, John the Good, obeying the laws of honor, turned himself over to the English; he died in London in 1364.

14. Charles V, King of France 1364–80, son of John the Good. His reign marked the end of the Hundred Years' War.

15. Charles VIII, King of France 1483–98, son and successor of Louis XI. He invaded Italy in 1494 and reached as far south as Naples but was forced to retreat when Milan, Venice, Spain, the Holy Roman Emperor Maximilian I, and Pope Alexander VI formed a powerful league against him. Eventually, the French troops were defeated.

and ill continued by Louis XII,[16] deprived France of a part of the advantages which the latter intended for her; and the League, the atrocious League, composed of foreigners and fanatics, bereaved the world of Henri IV, the best of men and the greatest and most enlightened prince that France ever produced.[17] Yet in spite of the singular obstacles which obstructed the progress of these four sovereigns, far superior to all the others, they were occupied during their reigns in acknowledging the existence of rights which limited their own.

Louis IX (St. Louis) continued the enfranchising of the boroughs begun by Louis le Gros;[18] he made laws for the independence and regular attendance of the judges; and, what deserves to be recorded, when chosen by the English barons to arbitrate between them and their king Henry III, he censured the rebel lords, but declared that their prince ought to be faithful to the charter for which he had pledged his oath. Could any other conduct be expected from him who consented to remain prisoner in Africa[19] rather than break his oaths? "I would rather," said he, "that a foreigner from the extremest point of Europe, even from Scotland, should obtain the throne of France than my son, if he is not to be wise and good." Charles V, when only regent, convoked in 1355 the Estates General, and

16. Louis XII, King of France 1498–1515, son of Charles, Duke of Orléans, and cousin of Charles VIII, whom he succeeded on the throne of France. He attempted to impose French domination over Italy. By the treaties of Blois (1504), Louis attempted a compromise with Spain and Holy Roman Emperor Maximilian I. Ultimately, the compromise did not work out and he had to fight the armies of Maximilian, Pope Julius II, and Henry VIII of England.

17. Henri IV (1553–1610), the first Bourbon monarch in France and one of the most popular French kings. He was born into a Catholic family but was raised as a Huguenot. Before ascending to the throne in 1589 he was involved in the Wars of Religion. His marriage to Marguerite de Valois, sister of King Charles IX, was instrumental in bringing much-needed peace between Catholics and Protestants. He restored prosperity to his country, which had been ravaged by religious and civil wars. In 1598, Henri IV enacted the Edict of Nantes, which guaranteed religious liberty to Protestants.

18. Louis VI of France, known as Louis the Large One (1081–1137), reigned as King of France from 1108 until his death. He encouraged the communal movements and the development of social or religious trade associations by granting the inhabitants of various cities tax advantages and the right to govern their local affairs.

19. Allusion to the captivity of St. Louis following his participation in the seventh crusade. He was taken prisoner in Egypt in 1250.

that Assembly proved the most remarkable in the history of France, for the demands which they made in favor of the people. The same Charles V, after succeeding to the throne, convoked that Assembly in 1369 to obtain their sanction to the *gabelles,* or salt tax, then imposed for the first time; he granted a power to the inhabitants of Paris to become the purchasers of fiefs. But, as foreign troops were in possession of a considerable part of the kingdom, his first object was to expel them, and the hardship of his situation caused him to levy certain imposts without the consent of the nation. But, at his dying hour, this prince declared that he regretted the act and acknowledged that he had gone beyond his powers.

The continuance of intestine troubles, and of invasions from England, made for a long time the regular functioning of government very difficult. Charles VII[20] was the first who kept on foot a standing force—a fatal era in the history of nations! Louis XI,[21] whose name recalls the same impressions as those of Tiberius or Nero, attempted to invest himself with absolute power. He made a certain progress in that track which Cardinal Richelieu afterward knew so well how to follow; but he encountered a spirited opposition from his parliaments. These bodies have in general labored to give consistence to the laws in France, and their records scarcely exhibit a remonstrance in which they do not remind the kings of their engagements with the nation. But Louis XI was far from considering himself an unlimited ruler; and in the instructions which he dictated on his deathbed to his son Charles VIII, he said, "When kings or princes cease to respect the laws, they bring their people to servitude, and strip themselves of the name of king; for he only is king who reigns over freemen. It is the nature of freemen to love their rulers;[22] but men in servitude must hate them, as a slave hates his oppressor." So true is it that, in a testa-

20. Charles VII (1403–61), King of France 1422–61. When he became monarch, France had no organized army. The English strengthened their grip over France until 1429, when Joan of Arc urged Charles to raise an army to liberate France from the English.

21. Louis XI (1423–83), King of France 1461–83. A skillful administrator, Louis set up an efficient central administration and used commissions and the Estates General to give his acts the appearance of popular approval. He also diminished the prestige of the courts.

22. The original French text reads as follows: "Car nul ne doit être roi fors celui qui règne et a seigneurie sur les Francs. Les Francs de nature aiment leur seigneur" (72). The use of the word "Francs" was meant to emphasize the contrast between serfs and freemen.

mentary disposition, at least, even tyrants cannot refrain from affixing a stigma upon despotism.

Louis XII, surnamed the "father of his people," submitted to the decision of the Estates General the marriage of his daughter Claude with the Count of Angoulême (afterward Francis I), and the nomination of that prince as his successor. The continuation of the war in Italy was not a good political decision for Louis, but as he lessened the pressure of taxation by the order introduced in his finances, and as he sold his own demesnes to provide a fund for the public wants, the people suffered less from the expense of this expedition than they would have done under any other prince. In the council assembled at Tours, the clergy of France made, at his desire, a declaration "that they did not owe implicit obedience to the pope." And when certain comedians presumed to act a play in ridicule of the king's meritorious parsimony, he would not allow them to be punished, but made use of these remarkable words, "These men may teach us some useful truths; let them proceed in their amusement so long as they respect female honor. I shall not regret its being known that, under my reign, they took this liberty with impunity." Do not these words amount to an acknowledgment of the liberty of the press in all its extent? For in these days the publicity of a theatrical performance was much greater than the publicity of a printed work. Never did a truly virtuous prince find himself in the possession of sovereign power without desiring rather to moderate his own authority than encroach on the rights of the people. Every enlightened king has a wish to limit the power of his ministers and his successors. A spirit of enlightenment, according to the nature of the age, must find its way to all public men of the first rank by the influence either of reason or of feeling.

The early part of the sixteenth century witnessed the progress of the Reformation in the most enlightened states of Europe: in Germany, in England, and, soon after, in France. Far from concealing that liberty of conscience is closely linked to political liberty, the Protestants ought, in my opinion, to make a boast of the alliance. They always have been, and always will be, friends of liberty;[23] the spirit of inquiry in religious points

23. Madame de Staël's Protestantism is again visible in her strong emphasis on the con-

leads necessarily to the representative government and its political institutions. The proscription of Reason is always conducive to despotism, and always subservient to hypocrisy.

France was on the point of adopting the Reformation at the time that it was established in England; the principal nobility of the country, Condé, Coligni, Rohan, and Lesdiguieres, professed the Protestant faith. The Spaniards, guided by the diabolical spirit of Philip II, supported the League in France in conjunction with Catherine of Médicis. A woman of her character must have desired boundless command, and Philip II wanted to make his daughter queen of France, to the exclusion of Henri IV—a proof that despotism does not always respect legitimacy. In the interval from 1562 to 1589, the parliaments refused their sanction to a hundred royal edicts; yet the Chancellor de l'Hôpital found a greater disposition to support religious toleration in such of the Estates General as he could get together, than in the parliament. This body of magistracy, like all corporate establishments, firm in the maintenance of ancient laws, did not partake of the enlightenment of the age. None but deputies elected by the nation can enter into all its wants and desires at every different period.

Henri IV, after being long the head of the Protestants, found himself at last obliged to yield to the prevailing opinion, notwithstanding its being that of his adversaries. Such, however, was the wisdom and magnanimity of his sway, that the impression of that short reign is, at the present day, more fresh in the hearts of Frenchmen than that of the two centuries which have since elapsed.

The Edict of Nantes, promulgated in 1598, founded that religious toleration, the struggle for which is not yet at a close. This edict opposed a potent barrier to arbitrary power; for when a government is obliged to keep the balance even between two rival parties, it can do so only by a continued exercise of reason and justice. Besides, how could such a character as Henri IV have been ambitious of absolute power? he who had taken up arms against the tyranny of Medicis and Guise; he who had fought to deliver his country from them; he whose generous nature was

---

nection between Reformation and liberty. Guizot, himself a Protestant, also highlighted this connection in his *History of Civilization in Europe,* lecture XI.

so much more gratified by the free gift of admiration than by a servile obedience. Sully brought his finances into a state which might have rendered the royal authority entirely independent of the people, but Henry did not make this culpable use of the virtue of economy. He convoked the Assembly of the Notables at Rouen,[24] and declared that the elections should be wholly uninfluenced by the Crown. The civil commotions were still recent, and he might have availed himself of them as a pretext for absorbing all power in his own hands; but true liberty carries with it the most effectual remedy for anarchy. Every Frenchman knows by heart the noble expressions of Henry on opening the Assembly. His conduct was in conformity with his declaration; he acquiesced in their demands, however imperious, because he had given his promise to comply with the desires of the delegates of the people. Finally, in his caution against flattery, expressed to Matthieu, the writer of his history, he gave a proof of the same solicitude for the dissemination of truth which had been already shown by Louis XII.

In the age of Henri IV, religious liberty was the only object which occupied the public mind; he flattered himself with having ensured it by the Edict of Nantes; but that edict owed its origin to him personally, and might be overthrown by a successor. How strange that Grotius,[25] in one of his works published in the reign of Louis XIII, should have predicted that the Edict of Nantes being a royal concession and not a mutual compact, a succeeding sovereign might take on him to annul the work of Henri IV. Had that great prince lived in our days, he would not have allowed the boon conferred on France to rest on a foundation so precarious as his life; he would have strengthened, by the aid of political guarantees, that toleration, of which, after his death, France was so cruelly deprived.

Henry is said to have conceived, shortly before his death, the grand idea of consolidating the independence of the different states of Europe

24. The Assembly was convoked in 1596. It is possible that the King made a number of promises to the nobles because he needed their approval for royal subsidies.

25. Hugo Grotius (1583–1645), eminent Dutch jurist, humanist, and author. Among his major works was the highly influential *Concerning the Law of War and Peace*, originally published in 1625 and considered the first major text on international law.

by a Congress. Be this as it may, his principal object certainly was to support the Protestants in Germany; and the fanaticism which led to his assassination was not mistaken in regard to his intentions.

Thus fell the king the most truly French who ever reigned over France. Often have our sovereigns derived a tinge of foreign habits from their maternal parentage; but Henri IV was in every respect the countryman of his subjects. When Louis XIII evinced that he inherited the habit of dissimulation from his Italian mother, the people no longer recognized the blood of the father in the son. Who would have thought it possible that Madame d'Ancre[26] could have been burned on a charge of sorcery in the presence of that nation who, twenty years before, had received the Edict of Nantes with applause? There are eras in history when the course of national feeling is dependent on a single man—but unfortunate are such times, for nothing durable can be accomplished without the impulse of general concurrence.

Cardinal Richelieu[27] aimed at oversetting the independence of the great nobles, and induced them to reside at Paris that he might convert the lords of the provinces into courtiers. Louis XI had formed the same plan; but in his days the capital offered few attractions in point of society, and the court still fewer. Several men of rare talents and high spirit, such as d'Ossat, Mornay, Sully,[28] had become conspicuous under Henri IV; but after his time, we look in vain for those chivalrous characters whose names form still the heroic traditions of the history of France. The despotic sway

26. Reference to Léonora Dori (1568–1617), the wife of Marshal d'Ancre. Of modest origin, she was the foster sister of Marie de Médicis and became one of the most powerful and richest women in France. Accused of practicing exorcism and exercising a nefarious influence on Marie de Médicis, she was decapitated in 1617.

27. Richelieu (1585–1642), famous cardinal and prominent French statesman, represented the clergy of Poitou in the Estates General of 1614, where his political career began. A famous patron of arts and letters, Richelieu became secretary of state in 1616 and consolidated royal authority and centralization. In so doing, he aimed at limiting the power of the nobles and suppressing political opposition. During the Thirty Years' War, Richelieu allied France with Protestant powers, thus causing problems in the relations with Rome. He died in 1642 and was succeeded by Mazarin.

28. Arnaud d'Ossat (1536–1604) was instrumental in bringing about the reconciliation between Henri IV and the Holy See. Philippe Duplessis-Mornay (1549–1623), whose nickname was "the Pope of the Huguenots," was a favorite adviser to Henri IV.

of Cardinal Richelieu destroyed entirely the originality of the French character—its loyalty, its candor, its independence. That priestly minister has been the object of much encomium because he upheld the political greatness of France, and in this respect we cannot deny his superior talents; but Henri IV accomplished the same object by governing in the spirit of truth and justice. Superiority of mind is displayed not only in the triumph obtained, but in the means employed to accomplish it. The moral degradation impressed on a people accustomed to crime will, sooner or later, prove to be more harmful to it than the effect of temporary success.

Cardinal Richelieu caused a poor innocent curate of the name of Urbain Grandier to be burned on a charge of sorcery, and thus yielded a mean and perfidious acquiescence to that blind superstition from which he was personally exempt. He confined, in his own country house at Ruelle, Marshal de Marillac, whom he hated, that he might with greater certainty be sentenced to death under his own eyes. M. de Thou was brought to the scaffold because he had not denounced his friend. No political crime was legally judged under the ministry of Cardinal Richelieu, and special commissions were always nominated to decide the fate of the victims. And yet the memory of this man has been applauded even in our days! He died indeed in the fullness of power; a safeguard of the first importance to those tyrannical rulers who hope to have a great name in history. The French may in several respects consider this cardinal as a foreigner; his clerical profession, and his Italian education, separate him from the true French character. The magnitude of his influence admits thus of an easier explanation, for history affords various examples of foreigners who have ruled over Frenchmen. That nation has, in general, too much vivacity to counteract the perseverance which is necessary to arrive at arbitrary power; but the man who possesses this perseverance is doubly formidable in a country where, law having never been properly established, the people judge of things only by the event.

Cardinal Richelieu, by inducing the grandees to live in Paris, deprived them of their weight in the country and created that influence of the capital over the rest of France which has never ceased since that day. A court has naturally much ascendancy over the city where it resides, and nothing can be more convenient than to govern an empire by means of a small assemblage of men; I mean convenient for the purposes of despotism.

Many persons are of the opinion that Richelieu laid the foundation of the wonders of the age of Louis XIV, an age which has been often compared to those of Pericles and Augustus. But periods similar to these brilliant eras are found in the histories of several nations under different combinations of circumstances—at the moment when literature and the fine arts appear for the first time, after a long continuance of war, or after the close of civil dissensions. The great phases of the human mind are much less the work of an individual than of the age; for they are all found to bear a resemblance to each other, however different may be the character of the contemporary chiefs.

After the death of Richelieu, and during the minority of Louis XIV, we find some serious political ideas intermixed with the general frivolity of the days of the *Fronde*. We find, for instance, parliament demanding of the Crown that no subject of the realm should be liable to imprisonment without being brought before his natural judges. There was also an attempt made to limit the power of ministers, and the odium against Mazarin[29] might perhaps have led to the acquisition of a certain degree of liberty. But the time soon came when Louis XIV displayed the manners of a court in all their dangerous splendor; flattering the pride of his subjects by the success of his armies, and repelling, by his Spanish gravity, that familiarity which would presume to pass judgment on him. But he made the nobles descend still lower than in the preceding reign. For under Richelieu they were at least important enough to be persecuted, while under Louis XIV they were distinguished from the rest of the nation only by bearing the yoke nearer the presence of their master.

This king, who thought that the property of his subjects was his own,

---

29. Cardinal Mazarin (1602–61), born in southern Italy and educated in Rome, gained rich military and diplomatic experience serving the papal court before becoming papal vice-legate at Avignon (1632) and nuncio extraordinary in France (1634). Eight years later he succeeded his mentor, Cardinal Richelieu, and became chief minister of France, a position he retained until his death. His policy aimed at strengthening royal power eventually led to the civil war known as la Fronde (1648–53).

and who committed arbitrary acts of all descriptions; in short, he who (can we venture to say it, and is it possible to forget it?) came, whip in hand, to prohibit, as an offense, the exercise of the slender remnant of a right—the remonstrances by parliament; this king felt respect for no one but himself, and was never able to conceive what a nation is and ought to be. All the errors that he has been charged with were the natural result of that superstitious idea of his power, in which he had been nurtured from his infancy. How can despotism fail to produce flattery, and how can flattery do otherwise than pervert the ideas of every human being who is exposed to it? What outstanding man has ever been heard to utter the hundredth part of the praises lavished on the weakest princes? And yet these princes, for the very reason that they deserve not those praises, are the more easily intoxicated by them.

Had Louis XIV been a private individual, he would probably never have been noticed, as he possessed no exceptional talents; but he perfectly understood how to cultivate that artificial dignity which imposes an uncomfortable awe on the mind of others. Henri IV was in the habit of familiar intercourse with his subjects, from the highest to the lowest; Louis XIV was the founder of that extreme etiquette which removed the kings of his family, in France as well as in Spain, from a free and natural communication with their subjects: he was in consequence a stranger to their feelings whenever public affairs assumed a threatening aspect. One minister (Louvois) engaged him in a sanguinary contest, from having been vexed by him about the windows of a castle; and, of the sixty-eight years of his reign, Louis XIV, without possessing any military talent, passed fifty-six in a state of war. It was under him that the Palatinate[30] was desolated and that atrocious executions took place in Brittany. The expulsion of 200,000 Protestants from France, the *dragonnades,* and the war of the Cevennes are yet not equal to the cold-blooded horrors to be found in the various *ordonnances* passed after the repeal of the Edict of Nantes, in 1685. The code enacted at that time against the Protestants may be, in

---

30. In September 1688, Louis XIV invaded the Palatinate (in Germany) and occupied Cologne. A nine-year war ensued that ended with the Treaty of Ryswick (1697), by which Louis gave up all lands, including the Palatinate, that he had seized except Strasbourg.

all respects, compared to the laws of the Convention against the emigrants, and bears the same characteristics. The enjoyment of civil rights was refused to them; for their children were not legitimate, in the eye of the law, until the year 1787, when the Assembly of Notables obtained that point from the justice of Louis XVI. Not only was their property confiscated, but it was bestowed on those who informed against them; and their children were forcibly taken from them to be educated in the Catholic faith. Persons officiating as Protestant clergymen, or those who incurred the charge of "relapsing" into heresy, were liable to be sent to the galleys or to the scaffold; and, as it had been at last declared by authority that there were no more Protestants in France, it was easy to consider any of them as relapsed, when there was an object in such treatment.

Injustice of every kind marked that reign of Louis XIV, which has been the object of so many fulsome effusions; and no one remonstrated against the abuses of that authority which was itself a continual abuse. Fénélon alone dared to raise his voice against it,[31] and an appeal from him is conclusive in the eyes of posterity. Besides, this King, who was so scrupulous in regard to the dogmas of religion, was very different in point of morals; and it was only in the day of adversity that he displayed any real virtues. We have no sympathy with him until he was forsaken by fortune; his soul at that time displayed its native grandeur.

Everybody praises the beautiful edifices erected by Louis XIV; but we know, by experience, that in countries where the national representatives do not control the public expenditure, it is easy to have money for any purpose. The pyramids of Memphis cost more labor than the embellishments of Paris; yet the despots of Egypt found no difficulty in employing their slaves to build them.

Had Louis XIV the merit of drawing forth the great writers of his age? He persecuted the seminary of Port Royal, of which Pascal was the head; he made Racine die of grief; he exiled Fénélon; he constantly opposed the honors which others were desirous of conferring on La Fontaine; and

---

31. François Fénélon (1651–1715), famous French bishop and writer, best remembered as the author of *Les aventures de Télémaque, Examen de conscience d'un roi,* and *Tables de Chaulnes.*

confined his admiration to Boileau alone. Literature, in extolling him to the skies, has done much more for him than he had done for it. Pensions granted to a few men of letters will never have much influence over men of real talents. Genius aims only at fame, and fame is the offspring of public opinion alone.

Literature shone with equal luster in the succeeding century, although it had a more philosophic tendency; but that tendency began not until the latter part of the reign of Louis XIV. A reign of more than sixty years was the cause of giving his name to the age; but the ideas of the period had no connection with him; and, if we except Bossuet, who, unfortunately for us and for himself, allowed his talents to be subservient to fanaticism and despotism, almost all the writers of the seventeenth century made very striking advancement in that path in which those of the eighteenth have made such progress. Fénélon, the most respectable of men, showed himself, in one of his works, capable of appreciating the excellence of the English constitution only a few years after its establishment; and, toward the end of Louis XIV's reign, the human mind was visibly advancing in all directions.

Louis XIV extended France by the conquests of his generals; and, as a certain extent of territory is necessary to the independence of a country, he had, in this respect, a title to the national gratitude. But he left the interior of the country in a state of disorder, which continued not only during the regency, but during the reign of Louis XV. At the death of Henri IV the finances, and all the branches of administration, were left in the most perfect order, and France maintained herself for a number of years merely by the strength which she owed to him. At the death of Louis XIV the finances were exhausted to such a degree that they could not be restored until the accession of Louis XVI. The people insulted the funeral procession of Louis XIV and the parliament canceled his will. The blind superstition under which he had bent in his latter years, had so wearied the public that even the licentious practices of the regency were excused, as forming a relief to the burden of an intolerant court. Compare the death of Louis with that of Henri IV—of him who was so unaffected although a sovereign, so mild although a warrior, so intelligent, so cheerful, so wise—of him who knew so well that to cultivate familiarity with men is the means, when one is truly great, of rising in their esteem, that every Frenchman seemed to feel at his heart the stroke of the poignard which cut short his splendid life.

We ought never to form an opinion of absolute princes by those temporary successes which proceed frequently from the intense exercise of their authority. It is the condition in which they leave their country at their death, or at their fall; it is the part of their reign which survives them, that discloses their real character. The political ascendancy of the nobles and the clergy ended in France with Louis XIV; he had made them mere instruments of his power; at his death they found themselves without a connecting link with the people, whose political importance was increasing every day.[32]

Louis XV, or, to speak more properly, his ministers, were in a state of perpetual contention with the *parlements,* who acquired popularity by refusing their sanction to taxes; these *parlements* belonged to the Third Estate, at least in a great degree. The writers of the age, most of whom also belonged to this class, conquered by their talents that liberty of the press which was not accorded by statute. The example of England acquired more and more influence on the public mind; and people were at a loss to comprehend that a narrow channel of only seven leagues sufficed to separate a country where the people were everything, from one in which they were nothing.

Public opinion and public credit, which is nothing more than public opinion applied to financial questions, became daily more essential to government. The bankers[33] have more influence in this respect than the great landholders themselves, and the bankers live in Paris, where they are in the habit of discussing freely all the public questions which affect their personal calculations.

---

32. Madame de Staël describes here the process of social atomization that led to what Tocqueville called in *The Old Régime and the Revolution* collective (group) individualism. The growth of royal absolutism fueled the separation between classes and fostered political apathy. She makes the same critique against Napoléon in parts IV and V of *Considerations.*

33. The original word, "*capitalistes,*" can be translated as bankers, creditors, capitalists, those who use capital. The old English translation used the archaic phrase "monied interests."

The weak character of Louis XV, and the endless errors resulting from that character, naturally strengthened the spirit of resistance. People saw on the one hand Lord Chatham[34] at the head of England, surrounded by parliamentary speakers of talent, all ready to acknowledge his preeminence, while, in France, the meanest of the royal mistresses obtained the appointment and removal of ministers. Public spirit was the ruling principle in England; accident and miserable intrigues decided the fate of France. Yet Voltaire, Montesquieu, Rousseau, Buffon, profound thinkers and superior writers, belonged to the country that was thus governed; and how could the French avoid envying England, when they might say with truth, that it was to her political institutions that she owed her superiority?[35] For they saw among themselves as many men of talent as their neighbors, although the nature of their government prevented them from turning these talents to so much account.

It has been justly said by a man of ability, that the literature of the age is an expression of the feelings of society; if that be true, the censures cast on the writers of the eighteenth century ought to be pointed at the society in which they lived. The writers of that day were not desirous of flattering government; therefore they must have aimed at pleasing the public; for the majority of literary men must follow one or the other of these paths: they stand too much in need of encouragement to bid defiance to both government and the public. The majority of the French in the eighteenth century began to desire the suppression of feudal rights, the imitation of the institutions of England, and, above all, toleration in religion. The influence of the clergy in temporal matters was generally revolting; and, as the spirit of true religion is foreign to intrigue and political ambition, all confidence was withdrawn from those who made use of it as an instrument for temporal purposes. Several writers, above all Voltaire, were highly reprehensible in not respecting Christianity when they attacked superstition; but some allowance is to be made on account of the circumstances

34. William Pitt, First Earl of Chatham (1708–78), was an eminent Whig statesman who became prime minister of England toward the end of his life.

35. For an analysis of the image (and symbol) of England in modern French political thought, see Jennings, "Conceptions of England and Its Constitution in Nineteenth-Century French Political Thought," *Historical Journal* 29, no. 1, 65–85.

under which Voltaire lived. He was born in the latter part of the age of Louis XIV, and the atrocious injustice inflicted on the Protestants had impressed his imagination from his earliest years.

The antiquated superstitions of Cardinal Fleuri,[36] the ridiculous contests between the *parlement* and the archbishop of Paris in regard to *billets de confession*, the *convulsionnaires*,[37] the Jansenists and Jesuits; all puerile in themselves but capable of leading to the effusion of blood, naturally impressed Voltaire with the dread of the renewal of religious persecution. The trials of Calas, of Sirven, of the Chevalier de la Barre, etc. confirmed him in this impression, and the existing laws against the Protestants were still allowed to remain in the barbarous state in which they had been plunged after the repeal of the Edict of Nantes.

I must not, however, be understood as attempting the justification of Voltaire, or of the writers of the age who followed his steps; but it must be admitted that irritable characters (and all men of talents are irritable) feel almost always a desire to attack the stronger party: it is in such attacks only that we recognize the impulse of a bold and ardent mind. In the Revolution we have been exposed only to the evils of unbelief, and to the atrocious violence with which it was propagated. But the same generous feelings which made people detest the proscription of the clergy toward the end of the eighteenth century had inspired, fifty years earlier, the hatred of its intolerance. Both actions and writings should be estimated according to the time of their occurrence.

We shall treat elsewhere the great question of the state of national feeling in France on the subject of religion. In regard to this, as in regard to politics, we must beware of bringing charges against a population of twenty-five million, for that would be little else than quarreling with mankind at large. Let us examine how it has happened that this nation has not

36. André-Hercule Cardinal de Fleuri, Bishop of Fréjus (1653–1743), chief minister of Louis XV.

37. Reference to the group who claimed to possess paranormal qualities and gathered around the tomb of François de Pâris, in the cemetery of the Saint Médard's Day Church in Paris, between 1727 and 1732. Miraculous cures occurred, along with moments of intense devotion resulting in body convulsions.

been molded according to the will of some individuals, by ancient usages, which certainly lasted a sufficient time to exercise their influence. Let us examine also what sentiments are at present in harmony with the hearts of men; for the sacred fire is not and never will be extinct; but it can reappear only by the full light of truth.

CHAPTER III

On the State of Public Opinion in France at the Accession of Louis XVI.

There is extant a letter of Louis XV to the Duchess of Choiseul, in which he says: "I have had a great deal of trouble with the *parlements* during my reign; but let my grandson be cautious of them, for they may put his crown in danger." In fact, in following the course of events during the eighteenth century, we easily perceive that it was the aristocratic bodies in France that first attacked the royal power; not from any intention of overturning the throne, but from being pressed forward by public opinion, which acts on men without their knowing it, and often leads them on in contradiction to their interest. Louis XV bequeathed to his successor a general spirit of discontent among his subjects, the necessary consequence of his endless errors. The finances had been kept up only by bankrupt expedients: the quarrels of the Jesuits and Jansenists had brought the clergy into disrepute. Banishments and imprisonments, incessantly repeated, had failed in subduing the opposition of the *parlement,* and it had been necessary to substitute for that body, whose resistance was supported by public opinion, a magistracy without respectability, and under the presidency of a disreputable chancellor, M. de Maupeou.[1] The nobility, so submissive under Louis XIV, now took part in the general discontent. The great lords, and even the princes of the blood, showed attention to M. de

---

1. Maupeou (1714–92), chancellor of France 1768–74, was instrumental in helping King Louis XV assert his domination over the *parlements* that opposed the fiscal measures proposed by the monarch. In 1771, Maupeou dissolved the *parlements* and exiled the magistrates from Paris, creating in their place a new high court and a system of superior courts. The nobles came to dislike Maupeou and eventually convinced Louis XVI to dismiss him and restore the old *parlements.*

Choiseul,[2] exiled on account of his resistance to the despicable ascendancy of a royal mistress. Modifications of the political organization were desired by all orders of the state; and never had the evils of arbitrary power been more severely felt than under a reign which, without being tyrannical, presented a perpetual succession of inconsistencies. No course of reasoning can so fully demonstrate the misery of depending on a government which is influenced in the first instance by mistresses, and afterward by favorites and relations of mistresses, down to the lowest class of society. The process against the existing state of things in France commenced under Louis XV in the most regular form before the eyes of the public; and whatever might be the virtues of the next sovereign, it would have been difficult for him to alter the opinion of reflecting men that France should be relieved by fixed institutions from the hazards attending hereditary succession. The more conducive hereditary succession is to the public welfare, the more necessary it is that the stability of law, under a representative government, should preserve a nation from the political changes which would otherwise be the unavoidable results of the different character of each king, and still more of each minister.

Certainly if it were necessary to commit entirely the fate of a nation to the will of a sovereign, Louis XVI merited more than anyone else that which no man can deserve. But there was reason to hope that a prince, so scrupulously conscientious, would feel a pleasure in associating the nation in some way or other with himself in the management of public affairs. Such would doubtless have been all along his way of thinking, if, on the one hand, the opposition had begun in a more respectful form, and if, on the other, in every age, certain writers had not been willing to make kings consider their authority as sacred as their creed. The opponents of philosophy endeavor to invest royal despotism with all the sacredness of a religious dogma, in order to avoid submitting their political views to the test of reasoning; the most effectual way certainly to avoid it.

The Queen, Marie Antoinette, was one of the most amiable and gracious persons who ever occupied a throne: there was no reason why she

2. Étienne-François, Duke of Choiseul (1719–85), French military officer, diplomat, and statesman.

should not preserve the love of the French, for she had done nothing to forfeit it. As far, therefore, as personal qualities went, the King and Queen might claim the hearts of their subjects; but the arbitrary form of the government, as successive ages had molded it, accorded so ill with the spirit of the times, that even the virtues of the sovereigns were overlooked amid the accumulation of abuses. When a nation feels the want of political reform, the personal character of the monarch is but a feeble barrier against the impulse. A sad fatality placed the reign of Louis XVI in an era in which great talents and profound knowledge were necessary to contend with the prevailing spirit, or, what would have been better, to make a fair compromise with it.[3]

The aristocratic party, that is, the privileged classes, are persuaded that a king of a firmer cast of character might have prevented the Revolution. These men forget that it was from their ranks that the first attacks were directed, and directed with courage and reason, against the royal power; and how could this power have resisted them since the nation was supporting them at that time? Have they any right to complain that, after having proved too strong for the Crown, they were too weak for the people? Such ought to have been the result.

We cannot too often repeat that the last years of Louis XV had brought the government into disrepute; and, unless a military prince had sprung up to direct the minds of the French to foreign conquest, nothing could have diverted the various classes of the community from the important claims which all considered they had a right to urge. The nobles were tired of being nothing more than courtiers; the higher clergy were eager for a still larger share in the management of public affairs; the *parlements* had too much, and too little, political weight to remain in the passive attitude of judges; and the nation at large, which comprised the writers, the merchants, the bankers, a great number of landholders, and of persons in public employments, made an indignant comparison between the government of England, where ability was the path to power, and that of

3. On public opinion in eighteenth-century France, see Ozouf, "L'opinion publique," 420–34. Also see Ozouf's entry on public opinion in *A Critical Dictionary of the French Revolution*, 771–79.

France, where all depended on favor or on birth. Thus, then, every word and every action, every virtue and every passion, every feeling and every vanity, the public mind and the fashion of the day, tended alike to the same object.

It is in vain to speak with contempt of the national spirit of the French: whatever they wish, they wish strongly. Had Louis XVI been a man of outstanding qualities, some say, he would have put himself at the head of the Revolution; he would have prevented it, say others. But what purpose is served by such suppositions? For outstanding qualities cannot be hereditary in any family, and that government which has nothing but the superior ability of its chief to oppose to the concurrent wishes of the people, must be in incessant danger of falling.

Faults, it is true, may be found in the conduct of Louis XVI, whether he be blamed by some for an unskillful defense of his unlimited power, or accused by others of not embracing with sincerity the improved views of the age. But these faults were so interwoven with the course of circumstances that they would be renewed almost as often as the same external combinations occurred.

The first choice of a prime minister made by Louis XVI was M. de Maurepas.[4] This veteran courtier was certainly anything but an innovating philosopher. During forty years of exile, he had never ceased to regret that he had not been able to prevent his loss of place. He had incurred this loss by no act of courage; for the failure of a political intrigue was the only recollection that he had carried into his retirement, and he came back with as frivolous notions as if he had never quitted a court, which was the only object of his thought. Respect for advanced years, a feeling very honorable in a young king, was the only reason why Louis XVI chose M. de Maurepas.

To this man even the terms which designate the progress of information or the rights of the people were unknown; yet so strongly, although unconsciously, was he led on by public opinion, that his first advice to the

4. Jean-Frédéric Phélypeaux, Count of Maurepas (1701–81), lost his position as secretary of state for the navy in 1749 because he was suspected of having written a pamphlet against Madame de Pompadour, the mistress of the King. Louis XVI appointed him minister of state in 1774.

King was the recall of the ancient *parlements*, dissolved for opposing the abuses of the preceding reign. But these *parlements*, more impressed with their own importance by their recall, constantly opposed the ministers of Louis XVI, and continued to do so until they saw that their own political existence was endangered by the ferment which they had been instrumental in exciting.[5]

Two ministers of distinguished merit, M. de Turgot and M. de Malesherbes,[6] were likewise appointed by Maurepas, who certainly had not a single idea in common with them; but their popularity called them to distinguished stations, and public opinion was obeyed in this point again, although not represented by the medium of regular assemblies.

Malesherbes was desirous of the revival of the edict of Henri IV in favor of the Protestants, the abolition of *lettres de cachet*,[7] and the suppression of the censorship which destroyed the liberty of the press. Such were the principles supported more than forty years ago by M. de Malesherbes; and had they been then adopted, the way would have been paved by wisdom, to that point which has since been obtained by violence.

M. Turgot, a minister equally humane and equally intelligent with Malesherbes, abolished the *corvée;*[8] proposed that, with regard to taxes, there should be no difference between one province and another; and advanced courageously the opinion that the clergy and nobility should pay taxes in the same proportion as the rest of the nation. Nothing could be

---

5. It will be recalled that the *parlements* were courts of justice rather than legislative assemblies. The previous meeting of the Estates General was held in 1614.

6. Anne Robert Jacques Turgot (1727–81), French economist and comptroller general of finances 1774–76, wrote on economic subjects (*Réflexions sur la formation et la distribution des richesses*) and advocated free trade and free competition. Guillaume-Chrétien de Lomoignon de Malesherbes (1721–94), eminent French royal administrator and lawyer, was a relative of Tocqueville. He served as counselor in the *Parlement of Paris* in 1744, director of the press (1750–63), and in 1775 as secretary of state for the royal household. He helped conduct the defense of Louis XVI in 1792 and was arrested a year later, tried for treason, and guillotined. A collection of his political writings can be found in Wyrwa, ed., *Malesherbes, le pouvoir et les Lumières*.

7. Under the Old Regime, the French kings issued *lettres de cachet* ("letters with a seal") to eliminate enemies of the state, via imprisonment or exile, without allowing recourse to a court of law.

8. Compulsory labor of the peasants in the service of their lords.

more equitable and popular than this proposal, but it gave offense to the upper ranks, and Turgot was sacrificed to them. He was of a systematic and inflexible disposition, while Malesherbes was yielding and conciliating. Yet both these generous citizens, alike in opinion, though different in demeanor, experienced the same fate; and the King, who had called them to office, in a short time dismissed the one and discouraged the other, at a moment, too, when the nation was most strongly attached to the principles of their administration.

It was certainly bad policy to excite the expectations of the public by a good choice and to follow this up by disappointment; but Maurepas appointed or removed ministers in compliance with the prevailing language at court. His plan of governing consisted in influencing the mind of the sovereign, and in satisfying those who stood immediately around him. General views of any kind were quite foreign to him; he knew only the obvious truth, that money is indispensable to sustain the expenses of the state, and that the *parlements* became daily more difficult to manage in regard to new taxes.

Doubtless, what in France was then the constitution, that is, the authority of the King, overturned all barriers, since it silenced, whenever it thought proper, the opposition of *parlement* by a *lit de justice*.[9] The government of France has been always arbitrary, and, at times, despotic; but it now became prudent to economize the use of this depotism, as of other resources; for appearances indicated that it would be soon expended.[10]

Taxes, and that credit which can accomplish in one day as great an effort as taxation in a year, were now become so necessary to France that whatever stood in their way was a primary object of apprehension. In England the House of Commons has been frequently known to join a bill relative

9. The *lit de justice* (literally "bed of justice") was a formal session of the *Parlement de Paris*, called by the king, in order to quell *parlementary* remonstrances and impose the registration of royal edicts. It was meant to reassert the power of the monarch against any opposition to his will.

10. The existence of a genuine constitution under the Old Regime is the subject of chapter 8 of Joseph de Maistre's *Considerations on France*, in which he argued that the monarch reigned only through the fundamental laws of the kingdom. Madame de Staël returns to this important issue later in part I, chapter xi: "Did France Possess a Constitution Before the Revolution?"

to the national rights to a bill of consent to subsidies. In France a similar course was attempted by the judiciary assemblies: when asked to register a new tax, they (although aware that the Crown could compel the registry) frequently accompanied their acquiescence, or refusal, with remonstrances on the conduct of ministers, having the support of public opinion. This new power was daily on the increase, and the nation was advancing along the path of liberty by its own exertions. So long as the privileged classes were the only persons of importance, the country might be governed, like a court, by a skillful management of the passions or interests of a few individuals; but no sooner had the middling ranks,[11] the most numerous and most active of all, become aware of their importance, than the knowledge and the adoption of a wider range of policy became indispensable.

From the time that battles ceased to be fought by the followers of the great vassals, and that the kings of France required a revenue to maintain their army, the disorder of the finances has always been the source of the troubles of the kingdom. Toward the end of the reign of Louis XV, the *Parlement of Paris* began to declare that it was not empowered to vote away the public money, and their conduct was applauded by the people; but all returned to the quiet and obedience to which the French had been so long accustomed as soon as the machine of government rolled on without fresh demands on any public body which could believe itself independent of the throne. The want of money was thus evidently the greatest source of danger to the royal prerogative, under the existing circumstances; and it was with this conviction that M. de Maurepas proposed to put M. Necker at the head of the treasury.

A foreigner and a Protestant, M. Necker was quite out of the ordinary line of election to the cabinet; but he had shown so much financial ability in the affairs of the East India Company, of which he was a member; in mercantile business on his own account, which he had carried on for twenty years; in his writings,[12] and, finally, in the different transactions

---

11. Madame de Staël refers here to the bourgeoisie, which was far from being the "most numerous and most active" of all classes. On the eve of the Revolution, the peasants formed approximately 85 percent of the French population, the nobles and clergy approximately 2 percent.

12. A full bibliography of Necker's political writings can be found in Grange, *Les idées de Necker*, 621–34; also see Egret, *Necker, ministre de Louis XVI*.

which he had had with the ministers, from the time of the Duc de Choiseul down to 1776, when he was appointed, that M. de Maurepas made choice of him only to produce an influx of money into the treasury. But M. de Maurepas had not reflected on the connection between public credit and the important measures of administration; and he imagined that M. Necker might re-establish the credit of the state by fortunate speculations, in the same way as that of a banking house. Could anything be more superficial than this mode of reasoning on the finances of a great empire? The revolution which was taking place in the public mind could not be removed from the very center of business without satisfying the nation by all the reform it required; it was necessary to meet public opinion halfway, lest it might press forward too rudely. A minister of finance cannot be a juggler, who passes and repasses money from one box to another, without any effectual means of increasing the receipts or reducing the expenditure. Retrenchment, taxes, or credit, were indispensable to re-establish the deranged balance of the French treasury; and, to render any of these resources available, was a task that required the support of public opinion. Let us now proceed to examine the course to be followed by a minister who aims at obtaining that support.

CHAPTER IV

Of the Character of M. Necker
as a Public Man.

M. Necker, a citizen of the republic of Geneva, had cultivated literature from his earliest years with great attention; and, when called by circumstances to dedicate himself to business and financial transactions, his earlier taste for literature mixed dignified sentiments and philosophical views with the positive interests of life. Madame Necker, certainly one of the most enlightened women of her day, was in the habit of receiving at her house all the eminent men of the eighteenth century, so rich in distinguished and eminently talented individuals.[1] At the same time her extreme strictness in point of religion rendered her inaccessible to every doctrine at variance with the enlightened creed in which she had happily been born. Those who knew her are unanimous in declaring that she passed over all the opinions and all the passions of her age, without ceasing to be a Protestant in the true Christian spirit, equally remote from irreligion and intolerance. M. Necker was actuated by similar impressions: in fact, no exclusive system could be acceptable to his mind, of which prudence was one of the distinguishing features. He took no pleasure in changes, as far as regarded their novelty; but he was a stranger to those prejudices of habit to which a superior mind can never subject itself.

His first literary essay was a "Eulogy on Colbert," which obtained the prize from the French Academy. He was blamed by the philosophers of the day for not applying, in all its extent, to commerce and finances the

---

1. Madame Necker married Jacques Necker in November 1764. She received, among others, Voltaire, Diderot, Holbach, Helvétius, Grimm, d'Alembert, Gibbon, Hume, and Walpole.

system which they wished to impose on the mind. The philosophic fanaticism[2] which proved one of the evils of the Revolution had already begun to show itself. These men were desirous of attributing to a few principles that absolute power which had hitherto been absorbed by a few individuals; as if the domain of inquiry admitted of restriction or exclusion.

M. Necker, in his second work, *On the Corn Trade and Corn Laws*, admitted the necessity of certain restrictions on the export of corn: restrictions required by the daily and pressing wants of the indigent classes. It was on this occasion that M. Turgot and his friends came to a rupture with M. Necker: a popular commotion caused by the high price of bread took place in the year 1775,[3] when his book was published, and, from his having dwelt on the bad decisions which led to the tumult, the more enthusiastic part of the "Economistes" threw the blame of it on his publication. But the blame was evidently absurd; for a tract founded on purely general views can influence, at least in the outset, none but the upper classes.

M. Necker, having been, during life, accustomed to real transactions, was capable of accommodating himself to the modifications which they required. This, however, by no means led him to disdainfully reject general principles, for none but inferior minds place theory and practice in opposition to each other. The one ought to be the result of the other; both are found to aid and extend each other.

A few months before his appointment to the cabinet, M. Necker made a journey to England. He came back with a profound admiration of most of the institutions of that country; but what particularly fixed his attention was the great influence of publicity on national credit and the immense means conferred by the mere existence of a representative assembly for renewing the financial resources of the state. He had not, however, at that time, the slightest idea of proposing a change in the political organization of France. And had not imperious circumstances afterward driven the King to such a change, M. Necker would never have thought himself au-

2. On this issue Madame de Staël is in agreement with Burke's critique of the philosophical radicalism of the French Revolution and its inclination to abstract thought.

3. The revolt, known as *la guerre des farines*, developed and manifested itself mostly in the region of Paris.

thorized to take part in it. His rule was to apply, above all things, to the direct and special duty of his situation; and, though amply convinced of the advantages of a representative body, he would never have conceived that a minister, named by the King, ought to make such a proposal without the positive authorization of his sovereign. It was, moreover, in his character to await the course of circumstances and to avoid proposing measures which might be brought forward by the operation of time. Though a decided opponent of such privileges as the feudal rights and exemption from taxes, his plan was to treat with the possessors of such privileges on the principle of never sacrificing, without an equivalent, a present right for a prospective advantage. He induced the King to abolish, throughout the royal demesnes, the remains of feudal servitude, the mortmain,[4] &c.; but the act which enforced this contained no injunction of a similar conduct on the part of the great nobles. He trusted entirely to the influence of his example.[5]

M. Necker disapproved highly of the existing inequality in the mode of paying taxes; he felt that the higher ranks ought not to bear a smaller proportion of the burden than the other citizens of the state; yet he avoided pressing any measure in that respect on the King. The appointment of the provincial councils was, as we shall see in a subsequent chapter, the best method, in his opinion, for obtaining the voluntary assent of the clergy and nobility to the sacrifice of this inequality of taxation, which was more revolting to the mass of the nation than any other distinction. It was not till his second ministry, in 1788, when the King had already promised to assemble the Estates General, and when financial disorders, caused by a bad choice of ministers, had reached such a height as to put the Crown again in a state of dependence on the *parlements*—it was not, I say, till then that M. Necker tackled the fundamental questions regarding the political organization of France: so long as he had the means of governing by prudent measures, he recommended no other.

The defenders of despotism, who would gladly have seen a Richelieu

4. The term, which originally denoted tenure by a religious corporation, derives from medieval French (literal meaning, "dead hand"). Mortmain refers to the "sterilization" of ownership of property by vesting it perpetually in a corporation.

5. This edict was passed in 1779.

in the person of the King's prime minister, were much dissatisfied with M. Necker; while, on the other hand, the ardent advocates of liberty have complained of his perseverance in defending not only the royal authority, but even the undue advantages of the privileged classes, when he proposed to redeem them by compromise instead of extinguishing them without an equivalent. M. Necker found himself placed, by a concurrence of circumstances, like the Chancellor de l'Hôpital[6] between the Catholics and Protestants; for the political contests in France, in the eighteenth century, have many points in common with the religious dissensions of the sixteenth; and M. Necker, like de l'Hôpital, endeavored to unite all parties at that altar of reason which was at the bottom of his heart. Never did anyone combine, in a more striking manner, prudence in the means with ardor for the end.

M. Necker never adopted a measure of importance without long and serious consideration, in which he consulted alternately his conscience and his judgment, but never his personal interest. To meditate was for him to make an abstraction from himself, and whatever opinion may be formed on his different measures, their origin is to be sought in motives different from those that actuate most men. Scruples were as predominant with him as passions are with others. The extent of his mind and of his imagination sometimes exposed him to the evil of hesitation; and he was particularly alive to self-reproach, to such a degree, indeed, as often to blame himself unjustly. These two noble inconveniences strengthened his attachment to morality: it was in that only that he found decision for the present, and tranquillity for the past. Every impartial man who examines the public conduct of M. Necker in the smallest details will always find it actuated by an impulse of virtue. I do not know whether that is called being no statesman; but, if he is to be blamed on this ground, let the blame be cast on the delicacy of his consciousness: for it was a rule with him that morality is still more necessary in a public than in a private capacity, because the management of extensive and durable interests is more evidently sub-

---

6. Michel de l'Hôpital (1505–73), chancellor of France under Catherine de Médicis, 1560–68, was instrumental in promoting a number of important judicial reforms and religious toleration.

jected, than that of lighter matters, to the principles of probity implanted in us by the Creator.

During his first administration, when public opinion was not yet perverted by party spirit, and when the business of government proceeded on a regular plan, the admiration inspired by his character was general, and his retirement from office was regarded by all France as a public calamity. Let us stop awhile to examine him in this first ministry, before we proceed to those hard and cruel circumstances which created enmity and ingratitude in the judgment of the people.[7]

7. Needless to say, the portrait of Necker drawn by Madame de Staël is far from objective.

CHAPTER V

M. Necker's Plans of Finance.

The principles adopted by M. Necker in the management of the finances are so simple that their theory is within the reach of every person, although their application be very difficult. It is easy to say to statesmen "be just and firm," as to writers "be ingenious and profound": this advice is perfectly clear, but the qualities which enable us to follow it up are very rare.

M. Necker was persuaded that economy, and publicity,[1] the best guarantee of fidelity in our engagements, form the only foundations of order and credit in a great empire. As in his opinion public morality ought not to differ from private, so he conceived that the affairs of the state might, in many respects, be conducted on the same principles as those of each private family. To equalize the receipt and expenditure; to arrive at that desired point rather by a reduction of expense than by an increase of taxation; and, when war unfortunately became necessary, to meet its extra expense by loans, the interest of which should be provided for either by a new tax or by a new retrenchment—such were the great and leading principles from which M. Necker never deviated.

No people can carry on a war without other aid than their ordinary revenue; it becomes therefore indispensable to borrow, that is, to throw on future generations a part of the pressure of a contest supposed to be

1. Toward the end of the eighteenth century, public opinion gradually acquired the status of a universal tribunal before which citizens, magistrates, and governments were held accountable. During the Bourbon Restoration, French liberals regarded publicity as playing a key role in limiting and moderating political power and considered it a pillar of representative government along with elections and freedom of the press. Like Constant and Guizot, Madame de Staël viewed publicity and public debates as essential to creating a public sphere partly similar to the economic market based on free competition of interests and ideas.

undertaken for their welfare. We might suppose the existence of an accumulated treasure, such as that which Frederick the Great possessed; but, besides that there was nothing of the kind in France, it is only a conqueror or those who aim at becoming conquerors that deprive their country of the advantages attached to the circulation of money and the maintenance of credit.

Arbitrary governments, whether revolutionary or despotic, have recourse, for their military expenses, to forced loans, extraordinary contributions, or the circulation of paper; for no country either can or ought to make war with its ordinary revenue. Credit is then the true modern discovery which binds a government to its people; it obliges the executive power to treat public opinion with consideration: and, in the same way that trade has had the effect of civilizing nations, credit, which is the offspring of trade, has rendered the establishment of constitutional forms of some kind or another necessary to give publicity to financial transactions and guarantee contracts. How was it practicable to found credit on mistresses, favorites, or ministers, who are in a course of daily change at a royal court? What father of a family would place his fortune in such a lottery?[2]

Nonetheless, M. Necker was the first and only minister in France who succeeded in obtaining credit without the benefit of any new institution. His name inspired so much confidence that capitalists in various parts of Europe came forward, even to a degree of imprudence, with their funds, reckoning on him as on a government, and forgetting that he could lose his place at any moment. It was customary in England, as in France, to quote him before the Revolution as the best financial head in Europe; and it was considered as a miracle, that war should have been carried on during five years without increasing the taxes, or using other means than providing for the interest of the loans by progressive retrenchments. But when the time came that party spirit perverted everything, his plan of finance was charged with charlatanism—a singular charlatanism, truly; to carry the austerity of private life into the cabinet, and to forgo the pleasure of

---

2. Worth noting is the connection between commerce, credit, and the rule of law, a recurrent topic in Necker's political writings.

making friends and partisans by a lavish distribution of the public money! The true judges of the talents and honor of a finance minister are the public creditors.

During M. Necker's administration, the public funds rose and the interest of money fell, to a degree of which there had been no example in France. The English funds, on the other hand, experienced a considerable fall; and the capitalists of all countries subscribed eagerly to the loans opened at Paris, as if the virtues of an individual could supply the place of the stability of law.

M. Necker has been blamed for the system of loans, as if that system were necessarily ruinous. But what means has England employed to arrive at that degree of wealth which has enabled her to sustain with such vigor twenty-five years of a most expensive war?[3] Loans, of which the interest is not secured, would, no doubt, be ruinous if they were practicable; but, fortunately, they are not practicable, for creditors are very cautious in their transactions, and will make no voluntary loans without a satisfactory pledge. M. Necker, to secure the interest and the sinking fund necessary as a guarantee, balanced each loan with a corresponding reform, and the result was a lowering of expense more than sufficient for the payment of the interest. But this plain method of reducing expenditure to increase disposable revenue does not appear to be ingenious enough to the writers, who aim at being profound when they treat of politics.

It has been alleged that the life annuities granted by M. Necker for the loan of money had a tendency to induce fathers of families to encroach on that property which they ought to leave to their children. Yet it will be found that a life interest, on the plan combined by M. Necker, is as fair and prudent an object of speculation as interest on a perpetuity. The most cautious fathers of families were in the habit of advancing money on the thirty livres at Geneva, in the hope of an eventual increase of capital. There are tontines[4] in Ireland, and they have long existed in France. Different modes of speculation must be adopted to attract capitalists of different

3. Reference to the American War of Independence.

4. Madame de Staël refers here to various onerous forms of financial speculations that were used in the epoch to increase capital. The tontines were invented by an Italian banker named Tonti and were introduced in France in 1653.

views. But no one can doubt that a father of a family, if he wants to bring his expenses in order, may accomplish a great increase of capital by placing out a portion of his funds at a very high interest rate and by saving yearly a portion of this interest. I should be almost ashamed to dwell on arrangements so familiar to bankers in Europe. But in France, when the ignorant oracles of the saloons have caught, on a serious subject, a phrase of which the turn is plain to everybody, they are in the habit of repeating it on all occasions, and this rampart of folly it is very difficult to overturn.

Must I also answer those who blame M. Necker for not having changed the mode of taxation and suppressed the *gabelles*[5] by imposing a uniform salt tax on those parts of the kingdom which enjoyed exemption from it? But local privileges were so fondly cherished that nothing short of a revolution could destroy them. The minister who should have ventured to attack them would have provoked a resistance pernicious to the royal authority without succeeding in his object. Privileged persons of one class or other were all powerful in France forty years ago, and the national interest alone was devoid of strength. Government and the people, who form, however, two main parts of the state, were unable to cope with a particular province or a particular body; and motley rights, the inheritance of the past, prevented even the King from taking measures for the general good.

M. Necker, in his treatise *On the Administration of the Finances of France*,[6] has pointed out all the evils of unequal taxation in France; but it was a further proof of his judgment to attempt no change in this respect during his first ministry. The incessant demands of the war[7] made it wholly unadvisable to incur the risk of domestic contention. A state of peace was indispensable to the introduction of any material change in finance, that the people might at least have the satisfaction of not finding their burdens increased at the time the mode of levying them was about to be altered.

While one class of persons have blamed M. Necker for leaving the system of taxation untouched, another have charged him with too much

---

5. Salt taxes.

6. Necker's *De l'administration des finances de la France* was first published in 1784.

7. A reference to the American War of Independence.

boldness in sending to the press his *Compte Rendu,* or official report to the King on the state of the finances.[8] But he was, as has been already mentioned, in much the same circumstances as the Chancellor de l'Hôpital, and could not take a single step of consequence without being censured for prudence by the innovators, or for rashness by the partisans of the old abuses. The study of his two administrations is therefore, perhaps, the most useful that can occupy a statesman. He will trace in it the road marked out by reason between contending factions, and will discover efforts incessantly renewed to accomplish a pacific compromise between the innovators and their opponents.[9]

The publication of the *Compte Rendu* was intended to answer, in some measure, the purpose so amply attained in England by *parlementary* debates, that of apprising the nation at large of the true state of the finances. This, however, said some, was derogatory to the royal authority by informing the nation of the state of its affairs. A continuance of such mystery might have been possible if the Crown had had no demands to make on the public purse; but the general discontent had by this time reached a height, which rendered the further collection of taxes a most difficult matter, unless the nation had the satisfaction of knowing the use that had been made, or was intended to be made, of them. The courtiers exclaimed against a system of publicity in finance, which alone can constitute a basis of credit; while they solicited with equal vehemence, both for themselves and their connections, all the money which even such a credit could be

8. Reference to Necker's *Compte rendu,* published in 1781, eight years before the French Revolution. Necker became famous as Louis XVI's finance minister when he made public the state budget for the first time in the history of the French monarchy, which had always kept the state of finances a secret. Necker thought this practice both illegitimate and ineffective and pointed out that public opinion had become "an invisible power which, without any treasury, guard, or army, legislates over the city, the court, and even the king's palaces" (Necker as quoted in Baker, *Inventing the French Revolution,* 193). The public success was tremendous: more than three thousand copies of this document were sold the first day of its publication. On the financial crisis during the last two decades of the Old Regime, see Doyle, *Origins of the French Revolution,* 45–53, 91–107.

9. In this passage Madame de Staël highlights Necker's moderation by portraying him as a representative of an older tradition of political moderation in France, which also included Montesquieu and, a few decades later, the so-called *juste milieu* (middle-of-the-road) liberals such as Guizot, Royer-Collard, and Cousin.

made to supply. This inconsistency may, however, be explained by their just dread of exposing to the public eye the expenditure in which they were concerned; for the publication of the state of the finances had the very material advantage of giving the minister the support of public opinion for the various budget cuts that had to be made. To a resolute character like M. Necker the resources offered in France by a plan of economy were very considerable. The King, although personally the reverse of expensive, was of so complying a disposition as to refuse nothing to those who surrounded him; and the grants of every kind under his reign, strict as was his own conduct, exceeded the expenses even of Louis XV. To accomplish a reduction of such grants appeared to M. Necker both the first duty of a minister and the best resource of the state: by acting firmly on this plan he made himself a number of enemies at court, and among persons in the finance department; but he fulfilled his duty, for the people were at that time reduced by taxes to great distress, and he was the first to make that distress the object of examination and relief. To sacrifice himself for those whom he knew not, and to resist the applications of those whom he knew, was a painful course; but it was prescribed by conscience to him who always took conscience for his guide.

At the time of M. Necker's first ministry the most numerous part of the population was loaded with tithes and feudal burdens, from which the revolution has delivered it; the *gabelles* and other local taxes, the general inequalities arising from the exemption of the nobility and clergy, all concurred to render the situation of the people much more uneasy than it is at present. Each year, the intendants decided to sell the last pieces of furniture of the poor, who found themselves incapable of paying the taxes that were demanded from them; in short, in no country in Europe were the people exposed to so harsh a treatment. To the sacred claim of this numerous body was joined that of the Crown, which ought, if possible, to be spared the odium arising from the opposition of *parlements* to the registry of new taxes. All this shows how signal a service M. Necker rendered to the King, by keeping up the public credit and by meeting the expense of war with progressive retrenchments; for the imposition of new burdens would have irritated the people, and given popularity to the *parlement* by affording it the opportunity of opposing them.

A minister who can prevent a revolutionary convulsion by doing good has a plain road to follow, whatever may be his political opinions. M. Necker cherished the hope of postponing, at least for some years, the crisis that was approaching, by introducing order into the finances; and had his plans been adopted, it is not impossible that this crisis might have terminated in a just, gradual, and salutary reform.

CHAPTER VI

M. Necker's Plans of Administration.

A finance minister, before the Revolution, was not confined to the charge of the public treasury; his duties were not restricted to a mere adjustment of receipt and expenditure; the whole administration of the kingdom was in his department; and in this relation the welfare of the country in general stood in a manner under the jurisdiction of the General Controller [of Finances].[1] Several branches of administration were strangely neglected. The principle of absolute power was seen in conjunction with obstacles incessantly arising from the application of that power. There were everywhere historical traditions which the provinces attempted to erect into rights, and which the royal authority admitted only as customs. The management of the revenue was little else than a continued juggle, in which the officers of the Crown attempted to extort as much as possible from the people to enrich the King, as if the King and his people could be considered as adversaries.

The disbursements for the army and the Crown were regularly supplied; but in other respects the penury of the treasury was such that the most urgent claims of humanity were postponed or neglected, from mere inadequacy of means. It is impossible to form an idea of the state in which M. and Madame Necker found the prisons and hospitals in Paris. I mention Madame Necker because she devoted all her time, during her husband's ministry, to the improvement of charitable establishments, and because the principal changes that took place in this respect were effected by her.

1. In October 1776, Necker was appointed general director of the royal treasury. As a foreign citizen (he was both Swiss and Protestant), he could not be officially entrusted with the control of the kingdom's finances. The official title of general controller of finances was reserved for Taboureaux des Réaux. Not surprisingly, Taboureaux des Réaux resigned a few months later and Necker was officially appointed general director of finances.

But M. Necker felt more than anyone how little the personal benefi-cence of a minister can effect in respect of so large and so ill-governed a country as France: this led him to desire the establishment of provincial assemblies, that is, of councils composed of the principal landholders, for the purpose of discussing the fair repartition of taxes and other matters of local interest.[2] M. Turgot had conceived this plan, but no minister before M. Necker had had the courage to expose himself to the resistance to be expected to an institution of this kind, for it was clear that the parliaments and the courtiers, seldom in unison, would now unite to oppose it.

Those provinces, such as Languedoc, Burgundy, Brittany, &c. which had been the latest united to the Crown of France, were called *pays d'états* because they had stipulated a right to be governed by assemblies composed of the three orders of the province. The King fixed the total sum which he required in the shape of taxes, but he was obliged to leave its assessment to the provincial assembly. These assemblies persisted in their refusal of imposing certain duties, and asserted that they were exempt from them in virtue of treaties concluded with the Crown. Hence arose inequality in the plan of taxation; multiplied facilities for a contraband traffic between one province and another; and the establishment of custom-houses in the interior.

The *pays d'états* enjoyed great advantages. They not only paid less, but the sum required was allotted by a board of proprietors acquainted with local interests, and active in promoting them. The roads and public es-tablishments were much better kept up in these provinces, and the col-lection of taxes managed with less severity. The King had never admitted that these assemblies possessed the right of refusing his taxes, but they acted as if in reality they had possessed it; not refusing the money required of them, but qualifying their contributions by calling them a *free gift*. In every respect, their plan of administration was better than that of the other provinces, which, however, were much more numerous and not less en-titled to the attention of government.

2. Necker was instrumental in creating four such provincial assemblies from 1778 to 1780—in Dauphiné, Haute-Guyenne, Bourbonnais, and Berry.

Intendants were appointed by the King to govern the thirty-two *généralités* into which the kingdom was divided.[3] The chief opposition experienced by intendants took place in the *pays d'états*, and sometimes in one or other of the twelve provincial *parlements* (the *Parlement of Paris* was the thirteenth);[4] but in the greater part of the kingdom the intendant was the sole director of public business. He had at his command an army of fiscal retainers, all objects of detestation to the people, whom they were perpetually tormenting to pay taxes disproportioned to their means; and when complaints against the intendant or his subordinates were transmitted to the minister of finance in Paris, the practice was to return these complaints to the intendant, on the ground that the executive power knew no other medium for communicating with the provinces.

Foreigners, and the rising generation too young to have known their country before the Revolution, who form their estimate from the present condition of the people, enriched as they are by the division of the large estates and the suppression of the tithes and feudal burdens, can have no idea of the situation of the country when the nation bore all the burdens resulting from privilege and inequality. The advocates of colonial slavery have often asserted that a French peasant was more to be pitied than a negro—an argument for relieving the whites but not for hardening the heart against the blacks. A state of misery is productive of ignorance, and ignorance aggravates misery. If we are asked why the French people acted with such cruelty in the Revolution, the answer will at once be found in their unhappy state, and in that want of morality which is its result.

It has been in vain attempted, during the last twenty-five years, to produce scenes in Switzerland or Holland similar to those which have occurred in France; the good sense of these people, formed by the long enjoyment of liberty, prevented everything of the kind.

---

3. In 1789 there were thirty-two *généralités* in France.

4. In 1789 there were thirteen *parlements* in France: in Paris, Toulouse, Grenoble, Bordeaux, Dijon, Rouen, Aix, Rennes, Pau, Metz, Besançon, Douai, and Nancy. Moreover, there were four other "sovereign councils" (similar to the *parlements*) in Perpignan, Arras, Colmar, and Ajaccio (in Corsica). For more information, see Hurt, *Louis XIV and the Parlements*. For a brief overview of the role of *parlements*, see Doyle, *Origins of the French Revolution*, 68–70.

Another cause of the excesses of the Revolution is to be sought in the surprising influence of Paris over the rest of France. This would have naturally been lessened by the establishment of provincial assemblies, since the great landholders, engaged by the business in which they were occupied at home, would have had motives for quitting Paris and residing in the country. The grandees of Spain are not at liberty to withdraw from Madrid without the king's leave: to convert nobles into courtiers is an effectual means of despotism, and consequently of degradation. Provincial assemblies would have given a political consistency to the higher nobility of France. And the contests which burst forth so suddenly between the nation and the privileged classes would perhaps never have had existence, had the three orders come in contact with each other by discussing their respective rights and interests in provincial assemblies.[5]

M. Necker composed the provincial administrations established under his ministry on the plan afterward adopted for the Estates General, viz. one-fourth of nobility, one-fourth of clergy, and half of Third Estate, dividing the latter into deputies of towns and deputies of the country. They proceeded to deliberate together, and such was their harmony at the outset that the two first orders spoke of making a voluntary renunciation of their privileges in regard to taxes; and the reports of their sittings were to be printed, that their labors might receive the support of public approbation.

The French nobility were very deficient in education because they had no motives to be otherwise. The graces of conversation, which rendered them acceptable at court, were the surest means of arriving at public honors. This superficial education proved one of the causes of the fall of the nobility: they were found unable to contend with the intelligence of the Third Estate; their object should have been to surpass them. Provincial assemblies would gradually have led them to take a lead by their ability in administration, as they formerly did by their sword; and public spirit in France would have preceded the establishment of free institutions.

The existence of provincial assemblies would have been no bar to the eventual convoking of the Estates General; and when a representative

5. Note the similarity between Madame de Staël's analysis and Tocqueville's account of the internal crisis of the Old Regime.

assembly came to be formed, the first and second classes, accustomed previously to discuss public affairs, would not have met each other with sentiments of decided opposition—the one full of horror at equality, the other all impatient for it.

The Archbishop of Bourges and the Bishop of Rhodez were chosen the respective presidents of the local assemblies established by M. Necker. That Protestant minister showed, on all occasions, a considerable deference for the clergy of France, because they consisted of very wise men in all matters that did not concern their privileges as a body. But since the Revolution, the rancor of party spirit and the nature of the government have necessarily kept the clergy out of public employment.

The *parlements* were dissatisfied at the appointment of provincial assemblies likely to give the King a force of opinion independent from theirs. M. Necker's view was that the provinces should not be altogether dependent on the authorities habitually assembled at Paris; but, far from desiring to destroy what was truly useful in the political power of *parlements,* their power of opposing an extension of taxes, it was he who prevailed on the King to submit to them the increase of the *taille,* an arbitrary tax, of which the ministry alone fixed the amount. M. Necker was desirous of limiting the power of ministers, because he knew from experience that a person overloaded with business, and placed at such a distance from those upon whose interest he is called on to decide, acquires the habit of referring for information from one public officer to another, till at last the matter falls into the hands of subalterns, who are quite incapable of judging the motives that must influence such important decisions.

And here it may be alleged that M. Necker, temporarily filling the place of minister, was very willing to set limits to ministerial power; but that by such conduct he jeopardized the permanent authority of the King. I will not discuss here the great question, whether the king of England does not possess as much and more power than did a king of France. The former, provided he fulfill the indispensable condition of governing according to the public opinion, is sure of uniting the strength of the people to the power of the Crown; but an absolute prince, not knowing how to collect their opinion, which his ministers do not represent to him faithfully, meets at every step with unforeseen obstacles, of which he cannot calculate the dangers. But without anticipating a result which will, I trust, receive some light from the present work, I confine myself at present to the provincial administrations, and I ask whether those were the true servants of the King who sought to persuade him that these assemblies would operate in diminution of his authority?

Their powers did not go the length of deciding the *amount* of the sum to be levied on their particular province; their business was merely to make the *assessment* of the amount already decided upon. Was it then an advantage to the Crown that a tax imposed by an injudicious intendant was the cause of greater suffering and discontent to the people than a larger levy, when allotted with prudence and impartiality by the representatives of the province? Every public officer was in the habit of appealing to the King's will, even in petty matters of detail. The French indeed are never satisfied except when they can, upon every occasion, support themselves by the royal wish. Habits of servility are inveterate among them; while in a free country ministers found their measures only on the public good. A long time must yet pass before the inhabitants of France, accustomed for centuries to arbitrary power, learn to reject this courtiers' language, which ought never to be heard beyond the precincts of the palaces to which it owes its origin.

No controversy occurred between the King and the *parlements* during the ministry of M. Necker. That, some will say, is not to be wondered at, since the King, during that period, required no new taxes and abstained from all arbitrary acts. This was exactly what constituted the merit of the minister; since it would be imprudent for a king, even in a country in which the constitution does not limit his power, to make the experiment to what extent the people will bear with his faults. Power ought not to be stretched to the utmost under any circumstances, but particularly on so frail a foundation as that of arbitrary authority in an enlightened country.

M. Necker's conduct during his first ministry was marked more by an adherence to public probity, if I may so express it, than by a predilection for liberty, because the nature of the existing government admitted the one more than the other; but he was at the same time desirous of institutions calculated to place the public welfare on a more stable foundation than the character of a king, or the still more precarious one of a minister.

The two provincial administrations, which he had established in Berri and Rouergue, succeeded extremely well; others were in a course of preparation; and the impulse necessary to the public mind, in a great empire, was directed toward these partial improvements. There were at that time only two methods of satisfying the anxiety which was already much excited upon the state of affairs in general: the establishment of provincial assemblies and the publication of a fair statement of the finances. But why, it may be asked, should the public opinion be satisfied? I will not enter on the answers which the friends of liberty would make to this singular question; I will merely add that, even for the purpose of eluding the demand of a representative government, the wisest plan was to grant at once what would have been expected from that government, that is, order and stability in the administration. Finally, credit, or, in other words, a supply of money, was dependent on public opinion; and as money was indispensable, the wish of the nation ought at least to have been treated with consideration out of interest, if not from a sense of duty.

CHAPTER VII

Of the American War.

In judging of the past from our knowledge of the events that have ensued, most people will be of the opinion that Louis XVI did wrong in interfering between England and America.[1] Although the independence of the United States was desired by all liberal minds, the principles of the French monarchy did not permit of encouraging what, according to these principles, must be pronounced a revolt. Besides, France had at that time no cause of complaint against England; and, to enter on a war solely on the ground of the habitual rivalship of the two countries, is bad policy in itself, and more detrimental to France than to England; for France, possessing greater natural resources, but being inferior in naval power, is sure of acquiring additional strength in peace, and as sure of being weakened by a maritime war.

The cause of America, and the parliamentary debates on that subject in England, excited the greatest interest in France. All the French officers sent to serve under Washington came home with an enthusiasm for liberty, which made it no easy task for them to resume their attendance at Versailles without wishing for something beyond the honor of being presented at court. Must we then accede to the opinion of those who attribute the Revolution to the political fault of the French government in taking part in the American war? The Revolution must be attributed to everything, and to nothing: every year of the century led toward it by every path; it was a matter of great difficulty to remain deaf to the call of Paris in favor of American independence. Already the Marquis de la Fayette,[2]

1. France intervened in the American War of Independence by siding with the Americans against the English.
2. La Fayette (Marie-Joseph-Paul-Yves-Roch-Gilbert Du Motier, Marquis de La Fa-

a French nobleman, eager for fame and liberty, had gained general approbation by proceeding to join the Americans, even before the French government had taken part with them. Resistance to the King's will, in this matter, was encouraged by the public applause; and when the royal authority has lost ground in public opinion, the principle of a monarchical government, which places honor in obedience, is attacked at its basis.

What was then the course to be adopted by the French government? M. Necker laid before the King the strongest motives for a continuance of peace, and he who has been charged with republican sentiments declared himself hostile to a war of which the object was the independence of a people. I need not say that he, on his part, wished success to the colonists in their admirable cause; but he felt, on the one hand, that war never ought to be declared without positive necessity, and, on the other, that no possible concurrence of political results could counterbalance to France the loss she would sustain of the advantages she might derive from her capital wasted in the contest. These arguments were not successful: the King decided on the war. There were, it must be allowed, very strong motives for it, and government was exposed to great difficulties in either alternative. Already was the time approaching when we might apply to Louis XVI what Hume said of Charles I: "He found himself in a situation where faults were irreparable; a condition too rigorous to be imposed on weak human nature."[3]

---

yette, 1757–1834) was a distinguished French military officer who became famous in both France and the United States for his participation in the American Revolution, in which he served as both a general and a diplomat. Ignoring the King's interdiction, he left for America and landed in Charleston, South Carolina, in June 1777. He returned to France in 1779 and came back to America on three other occasions, the last time in 1824–25. See Gottschalk and Maddox, *La Fayette in the French Revolution*, vol. 1: *Through the October Days*.

3. Hume examines the reign of Charles I in *History of England*, vol. V, chaps. l–lix, pp. 156–548. Charles I's character is discussed on pp. 542–48. Humes's exact words are as follows: "Unhappily, his fate threw him into a period, when the precedents of many former reigns favoured strongly of arbitrary power, and the genius of the people ran violently towards liberty. . . . Exposed, without revenue, without arms, to the assalt of furious, implacable, and bigotted factions, it was never permitted him, but with the most fatal consequences, to commit the smallest mistake; a condition too rigorous to be imposed on the greatest human capacity." (p. 543)

CHAPTER VIII

M. Necker's Retirement
from Office in 1781.

M. Necker had no other object in his first ministry than to prevail on the King to adopt, of his own accord, the measures of public utility required by the nation, and for which it afterward demanded a representative body. This was the only method of preventing a revolution during the life of Louis XVI; and never have I known my father to deviate from the opinion that then, in 1781, he might have succeeded in that object. The most bitter reproach which he ever cast on himself was that of not supporting everything rather than give in his resignation. But he could not then foresee the extraordinary course of events; and, although a generous feeling attached him to his place, there exists in a lofty mind a delicate apprehension of not withdrawing easily from power when a feeling of independence suggests it.

The second class of courtiers declared itself averse to M. Necker. The higher nobility, being exempt from disquietude in regard to their situation and fortune, have, in general, more independence in their manner of viewing things, than that ignoble swarm which clings to court favor in the hope of obtaining fresh gifts on every new occasion. M. Necker had made retrenchments in the royal household, in the pension list, in the charges of the finance department, and in the emoluments arising to court dependents from these charges; a system far from agreeable to all who had been in the habit of receiving the pay of government, and of constantly soliciting favors and money for a livelihood. In vain had M. Necker, for the sake of giving additional weight to his measures of reform, with a personal disinterestedness till then unheard of, declined all the emoluments of his situation. What signified this disinterestedness to those who were far from imitating such an example? Such generous conduct did not disarm the anger of the courtiers of both sexes, who found in M. Necker an obstacle to abuses which had become so habitual that their suppression seemed to them an act of injustice.

Women of a certain rank used to interfere with everything before the revolution. Their husbands or their brothers were in the habit of employing them on all occasions as applicants to ministers; they could urge a point strongly with less apparent impropriety; could even outstep the proper limits, without affording an opening to complaint: and all the insinuations, which they knew how to employ, gave them considerable influence over men in office. M. Necker used to receive them with great politeness; but he had too much sagacity not to see through these verbal tricks which produce no effect on a frank and enlightened mind. These ladies used then to assume a lofty tone, to call to mind, with a careless air, the illustrious rank of their families and demand a pension with as much confidence as a marshal of France would complain of being superseded. M. Necker always made it a rule to adhere to strict justice and never to lavish the money obtained by the sacrifices of the people. "What are three thousand livres to the King?" said these ladies: "three thousand livres," replied M. Necker, "is the taxation of a village."

The value of these sentiments was felt only by the most respectable persons at court. M. Necker could also reckon on friends among the clergy, to whom he had always shown great respect; and among the nobility and great landholders, whom he was desirous of introducing, by the medium of provincial administrations, to the knowledge and management of public business. But the courtiers of the princes and the persons employed in the finance department exclaimed loudly against him. A memorial transmitted by him to the King, on the advantage of provincial assemblies, had been indiscreetly published; and the parliaments had read in it, that one of the arguments used by M. Necker for these new appointments was the support of public opinion which might subsequently be used against the parliaments themselves, if the latter should act the part of ambitious corporations instead of following the wish of the nation. This was enough to make the members of these bodies, jealous as they were of their contested political influence, boldly represent M. Necker as an innovator. But of all innovations, economy was the one most dreaded by the courtiers and persons in the finance departments. Such enemies, however, would not have accomplished the removal of a minister to whom the nation showed more attachment than to anyone since the administration of Sully and of Colbert, if the Count of Maurepas had not adroitly found out the means of displacing him.

He was dissatisfied with M. Necker for having obtained the appointment of the Marechal de Castries to the ministry of marine, without his participation. Yet no man was more generally respected than M. de Castries, or was better entitled to respect; but M. de Maurepas could not bear that M. Necker, or, in fact, anyone, should think of exercising a direct influence over the King. He was jealous even of the Queen; and the Queen was at that time very favorably disposed toward M. Necker. M. de Maurepas was always present at conferences between the King and his minister; but, during one of his attacks of gout, M. Necker, being alone with the King, obtained the removal of M. de Sartines and the appointment of M. de Castries to the ministry of marine.

M. de Sartines was a specimen of the selection made for public offices in those countries where neither the liberty of the press, nor the vigilance of a representative body, obliges the court to have recourse to men of ability. He had acquitted himself extremely well in the capacity of *Lieutenant de Police*, and had arrived, by some intrigue or other, at the ministry of marine. M. Necker called on him a few days after his appointment and found that he had got his room hung round with maps; and he said to M. Necker, while he walked up and down the room, "See what progress I have already made; I can put my hand on this map and point out to you, with my eyes shut, each of the four quarters of the world." Such wonderful knowledge would not have been considered as a sufficient qualification in the First Lord of the Admiralty in England.

To his general ignorance M. de Sartines added an almost incredible degree of inefficiency in regard to the accounts and money transactions of his department; the finance minister could not remain a stranger to the disorders prevalent in this branch of public expenditure. But, weighty as were these reasons, M. de Maurepas could never forgive M. Necker for having spoken directly to the King; and he became, from that day forward, his mortal enemy. What a singular character is an old courtier when minister! The public benefit passed for nothing in the eyes of M. de Maurepas: he thought only of what he called the King's service, and this *service du Roi* consisted in the favor to be gained or lost at court. As to business, even the most important points were all inferior to the grand object of managing the royal mind. He thought it necessary that a minister should possess a certain knowledge of his department, that he might not appear ignorant in his conversations with the King; also that he should possess the good opinion of the public, so far as to prevent an unusual share of criticism from reaching the King's ears; but the spring and object of all was to please his royal master. M. de Maurepas labored accordingly to preserve his favor by a variety of minute attentions, that he might surround the sovereign as in a net, and succeed in keeping him a stranger to all information in which he might be likely to hear the voice of sincerity and truth. He did not venture to propose to the King the dismissal of so useful a minister as M. Necker; for, to say nothing of his ardor for the public welfare, the influx of money into the treasury by means of his personal credit was not to be despised. Yet the old minister was as imprudent in respect to the public interest, as cautious in what regarded himself; for he was much less alarmed at the apprehension of financial embarrassment than at M. Necker presuming to speak, without his intervention, to the King. He could not, however, go the length of saying to that King, "You should remove your minister, because he has taken on him to refer to you without consulting me." It was necessary to await the support of other circumstances; and, however reserved M. Necker was, he had a certain pride of character and sensibility of offense; a degree of energy in his whole manner of feeling that could hardly fail, sooner or later, to lead him into faults at court.

In the household of one of the princes there was, in the capacity of intendant or steward, a M. de Sainte Foix, a man who made little noise, but who was persevering in his hatred of all elevated sentiments. This man, to his latest day, and when his gray hairs appeared to call for graver thoughts, was still in the habit of repairing to the ministers, even of the Revolution, in quest of a dinner, official secrets, and pecuniary benefits. M. de Maurepas employed him to circulate libels against M. Necker; and, as the liberty of the press did not then exist in France, there was something altogether new in pamphlets against a member of the cabinet, encouraged by the prime minister, and hence publicly distributed.

The proper way, as M. Necker repeatedly said afterward, would have been to treat with contempt these snares laid for his temper; but Madame Necker could not bear the chagrin excited by these calumnies circulated against her husband. She thought it a duty to withhold from him the first libel that came into her hands, that she might spare him a painful sensation; but she took the step of writing, without his knowledge, to M. de Maurepas, complaining of the offense and requesting him to take measures against these anonymous publications: this was appealing to the very person who secretly encouraged them. Although a woman of great talents, Madame Necker, educated among the mountains of Switzerland, had no idea of such a character as M. de Maurepas—of a man who, in the expression of sentiments, only sought an opportunity to discover the vulnerable side. No sooner did he become aware of M. Necker's sensitive disposition by the mortification apparent in his wife's complaint, than he secretly congratulated himself on the prospect of impelling him, by renewed irritation, to give in his resignation.

M. Necker, on learning the step taken by his wife, expressed displeasure at it, but was at the same time much concerned at its cause. Next to the duties enjoined by religion, the esteem of the public was his highest concern; he sacrificed to it fortune, honors, all that the ambitious desire; and the voice of the people, not yet perverted, was to him almost divine. The slightest taint on his reputation caused him greater suffering than anything else in this world could ever bring about. The motive of all his actions, as far as that motive was temporal, the breeze which propelled his bark, was the love of public esteem. Add to this, that a cabinet minister in France had not, like an English minister, a power independent of the court: he had no opportunity of giving, in the House of Commons, a public vindication of his motives and conduct; and there being no liberty of the press, clandestine libels were all the more dangerous.[1]

1. The main author of the anonymous libels against Necker seems to have been Augeard,

M. de Maurepas circulated underhandedly that attacks on the finance minister were by no means unpleasant to the King. Had M. Necker requested a private audience of the King and submitted to him what he knew in regard to his prime minister, he might perhaps have succeeded in getting him removed from office. But the advanced years of this man, frivolous as he was, had a claim to respect; and besides, M. Necker could not overcome a feeling of grateful recollection toward him who had placed him in the ministry. M. Necker determined therefore to content himself with requiring some mark of his sovereign's confidence that would discourage the libelers: he desired that they might be removed from their employments in the household of the Count d'Artois, and claimed for himself a seat in the cabinet (*conseil d'état*) to which he had not as yet been admitted on account of being a Protestant. His attendance there was decidedly called for by the public interest; for a finance minister, charged with levying on the people the burdens of war, is certainly entitled to participate in deliberations relating to the question of peace.

M. Necker was impressed with the idea that unless the King gave a decided proof of his determination to defend him against his powerful enemies, he would no longer possess the weight necessary to conduct the finance department on the strict and severe plan that he had prescribed to himself. In this, however, he was mistaken: the public attachment to him was greater than he imagined, and had he waited until the death of the first minister, which took place six months later, he would have kept his place. The reign of Louis XVI might probably have been passed in peace, and the nation been prepared by good government for the emancipation to which it was entitled.

M. Necker made an offer of resigning unless the conditions that he required were complied with. M. de Maurepas, who had stimulated him to this step, knew perfectly well what would be the result; for the weaker kings are, the more attachment do they show to certain rules of firmness impressed on them from their earliest years, of which one of the first, no doubt, is that a king should never decline an offer of resignation or sub-

---

who served as financial adviser to Maurepas. The libels attacked Necker's religion (he was a Protestant) and accused him of not being French (he was born in Switzerland).

scribe to the conditions affixed by a public functionary to the continuance of his services.

The day before M. Necker intended to propose to the King the alternative of resigning, if what he wished was not complied with, he went with his wife to the hospital at Paris which still bears their name.[2] He often visited this respectable asylum to recover the firmness requisite to support the hard trials of his situation. Sœurs de la Charité, the most interesting of the religious communities, attended the sick of the hospital: these nuns take their vows only for a year, and the more beneficent their conduct, the less it is marked by intolerance. M. and Madame Necker, though both Protestants, were the objects of their affectionate regard. These holy sisters came to meet them with flowers and sung to them verses from the Psalms, the only poetry that they knew; they called them their benefactors, because they contributed to the relief of the poor. My father, as I still remember, was that day more affected than he had ever been by these testimonies of their gratitude: he no doubt regretted the power he was about to lose, that of doing good to France. Alas! who at that time would have thought it possible that such a man should be one day accused of being harsh, arrogant, and factious? Ah! never did a purer heart encounter the conflict of political storms: and his enemies, in calumniating him, commit an act of impiety; for the heart of a virtuous man is the sanctuary of the Divinity in this world.

Next day, M. Necker returned from Versailles, and was no longer a minister. He went to my mother's apartment, and, after half an hour of conversation, both gave directions to the servants to have everything ready in the course of twenty-four hours for removing to St. Ouen, a country house belonging to my father, two leagues from Paris. My mother sustained herself by the very exaltation of her sentiments; my father continued silent, and as for me, at that early age, any change of place was a source of delight; but when, at dinner, I observed the secretaries and clerks of the finance department silent and dispirited, I began to dread that my

2. The hospital, which still carries Necker's name, was built in 1778. Madame Necker played a key role in its construction.

gaiety was unfounded. This uneasy sensation was soon removed by the innumerable attentions received by my father at St. Ouen.

Everybody came to see him; noblemen, clergy, magistrates, merchants, men of letters, all flocked to St. Ouen. More than five hundred letters,* received from members of the provincial boards and corporations, expressed a degree of respect and affection which had, perhaps, never been shown to a public man in France. The Memoirs of the time, which have already been published, attest the truth of all that I have stated.† A good

---

* These letters, which are a family treasure, are in my possession at our seat at Coppet.

† *Correspondance littéraire, philosophique et critique, adressé à un souverain d'Allemagne, par le baron de Grimm, et par M. Diderot.* (Vol. v, p. 297, May 1781)

It was only on Sunday morning, the 20th of this month, that the people of Paris were apprised of M. Necker's resignation, sent in the evening before; they had been long prepared for it by the rumor of the town and court, by the impunity of the most offensive libels, and by a kind of patronage extended by a powerful party, by every means open and secret, to those who were shameless enough to circulate them. Yet, to judge from the general surprise, one would have said that no intelligence had ever been so unexpected: consternation was stamped on every countenance; those who felt differently were few in number, and would have been ashamed to show it. The walks, the coffee-houses, and all the places of public resort were crowded with people, but there prevailed an extraordinary silence. They looked at each other and shook hands in despondence, I should say, as at the sight of a public calamity; if these first moments of distress might not rather be compared to the state of a disconsolate family which has just lost the object and support of its hopes.

It happened that they acted, on that evening, at the Theatre Français, the *Partie de Chasse de Henri IV.* I have often seen at the Paris theaters a surprising quickness in applying passages of a play to momentary circumstances, but I never saw it done with so lively and general an interest. The name of Sully was never introduced without bringing forth a shout of applause, marked each time by a particular character, by a shade belonging to the feeling with which the audience were penetrated, being actuated one moment by regret and grief, at another by gratitude and respect; all so true, so just, and so distinctly marked, that language itself could not have given these emotions a more lively or interesting expression. Nothing that could, without difficulty, be applied to the public feeling toward M. Necker was overlooked; often the rounds of applause burst forth in the midst of an actor's speech, when the audience foresaw that the end of it would not admit of so clear, so natural, and flattering an application. In short, seldom has there been a more evident or delicate concurrence of feeling; or one, if I may so express myself, more spontaneously unanimous. The comedians thought it incumbent on them to apologize to the *lieutenant de police* for having been the cause of this touching scene, with which, however, they could not be reproached; they had no difficulty in

minister was, at that time, all that the French desired. They had become successively attached to M. Turgot, to M. de Malesherbes, and particularly to M. Necker, because he was much more of a practical man than the others. But when they saw that even under so virtuous a king as Louis XVI no minister of austerity and talent could remain in office, they felt that nothing short of settled institutions could preserve the state from the vicissitudes of courts.

Joseph II, Catherine II, and the Queen of Naples all wrote to M. Necker, offering him the management of their finances; but his heart was too truly French to accept such an indemnification, however honorable it might be. France and Europe were impressed with consternation at the resignation of M. Necker: his virtue and talents gave him a right to such an homage; but there was, moreover, in this universal sensation, a confused dread of the political crisis with which the public were threatened, and which a wise course, on the part of the French ministry, could alone retard or prevent.

The public under Louis XIV would certainly not have ventured to shower attention on a dismissed minister, and this new spirit of independence ought to have taught statesmen the growing strength of public opinion. Yet, so far from attending to it during the seven years that elapsed between the retirement of M. Necker and the promise of convoking the Estates General, given by the Archbishop of Sens, ministers committed all kinds of faults, and did not scruple to irritate the nation without having in their hands any real power to restrain it.

---

exculpating themselves, as the piece had been in preparation for a week. The police thought proper to take no notice of it, and merely forbade the newspaper writers from mentioning, in future, M. Necker's name with either praise or censure.

No minister ever carried a more spotless fame into retirement; none ever received more marks of the public confidence and admiration. For several days after his leaving Paris, the road to his country house at St. Ouen exhibited a continued procession of carriages. Men of all ranks and conditions hastened to show him marks of their sensibility and regret. In the number were to be seen the most respectable persons of the town and court; the prelates most distinguished by their birth and piety, the Archbishop of Paris at their head; the Birons, the Beauvaux, the Richelieus, the Choiseuls, the Noailles, the Luxembourgs; in short, the most respected names in France, not omitting even M. Necker's official successor, who thought the best way of giving to the public confidence in his administration was to express the greatest admiration of that of M. Necker, and congratulate himself on having only to follow the path he found so happily traced.

The Circumstances That Led to the Assembling of the Estates General.— Ministry of M. de Calonne.

M. Turgot and M. Necker owed their loss of place in a great degree to the influence of the parliaments, who were adverse both to the suppression of exemptions from taxes and to the establishment of provincial assemblies. This made the King think of choosing a finance minister from among the members of the parliament, as a method of disarming the opposition of that body when new taxes came under discussion. The consequence was the appointment, successively, of M. Joly de Fleury and M. d'Ormesson; but neither of these had the least idea of finance business, and their ministries may be considered, in this respect, as periods of anarchy. Yet the circumstances in which they were placed were much more favorable than those with which M. Necker had had to struggle. M. de Maurepas was no more, and the war had been brought to a close. What improvements would not M. Necker have made under such auspicious circumstances! But it was part of the character of these men, or rather of the body to which they belonged, to admit of no improvements of any kind.

Representatives of the people receive information every year, and particularly at each election, from the progress that knowledge makes in all directions; but the *Parlement of Paris* was, and would always have been, unacquainted with new ideas. The reason is perfectly plain; a privileged body derives its patent from history; it possesses strength today only because it has existed for ages. The consequence is, that it attaches itself to the past and is suspicious of innovation. The case is quite different with elected deputies, who participate in the revived and increasing spirit of the nation which they represent.

The choice of finance ministers from among the *Parlement of Paris* not having succeeded, the only remaining field for selection was from among the intendants, or provincial administrators appointed by the King. M. Senac de Meilhan, a superficial writer, whose only depth lay in his vanity, could not pardon M. Necker for having been appointed to his situation, for he considered the finance ministry as his right; but it was in vain that he cherished hatred or indulged in calumny; he did not succeed in drawing the public opinion to himself. Among the candidates, there was only one that had the reputation of great talent—M. de Calonne: the world gave him credit for great abilities, because he treated with levity things of the greatest importance, including virtue. The French are but too apt to fall into the great mistake of ascribing wonderful powers to immoral men. Faults caused by passion may often be taken as a sign of distinguished faculties; but a disposition to venality and intrigue belongs to a kind of mediocrity, the possessor of which can be useful in nothing but for his own good. We should be nearer the truth in setting down as incapable of public business any man who has devoted his life to an artful management of persons and circumstances. Such was M. de Calonne; and, even in this light, the frivolity of his character followed him, for when he meant to do mischief, he did not do it with ability.[1]

His reputation, founded on the report of the women in whose society he was in the habit of passing his time, pointed him out for the ministry. The King was long averse to an appointment at variance with his conscientious feelings; the Queen, although surrounded by persons of a very different way of thinking, partook of her husband's repugnance; and one is almost tempted to say that both had a presentiment of the misfortunes into which such a character was likely to involve them. No single man, I repeat it, can be considered the author of the French Revolution; but if we want to attribute a certain worldly event to a particular individual, then the blame should rest with M. de Calonne's actions. His object was to make himself acceptable at court by lavishing the public money; he

1. Calonne became controller general of finances in November 1783 and held this position until April 1787. For more information on Calonne, see Doyle, *Origins of the French Revolution*, 45–53.

encouraged the King, the Queen, and the princes to dismiss all restraint in regard to their favorite objects of expense, giving them the assurance that luxury was the source of national prosperity. Prodigality, according to him, was an enlarged economy. In short, his plan was to be easy and accommodating in everything, that he might form a complete contrast to the austerity of M. Necker. But if M. Necker was more virtuous, it is equally true that he also was superior in spirit. The paper controversy that took place some time after between them in regard to the deficit in the revenue showed that, even in point of wit, all the advantage was on M. Necker's side.[2]

M. de Calonne's levity was apparent rather in his principles than in his manners; he thought there was something brilliant in making light of difficulties, as in truth there would be if we overcame them; but when they prove too strong for him who pretends to control them, his negligent confidence tends merely to make him more ridiculous.

M. de Calonne continued during peace the system of loans, which, in M. Necker's opinion, was suitable only to a state of war. The credit of the minister experiencing a visible decline, he was obliged to raise the rate of interest to get money, and thus disorder grew out of disorder. It was about this time that M. Necker published his *Administration des Finances*, which is now considered a standard book, and had from its first appearance a surprising effect; the sale extended to 80,000 copies. Never had a work on so serious a subject obtained such general success. The people of France already began to give much attention to public business, although not aware of the share that they might soon take in it.

This work contained all the plans of reform subsequently adopted by the Constituent Assembly in regard to taxes; and the favorable effect produced by these changes on the circumstances of the people has afforded ample evidence of the truth of M. Necker's constant opinion advanced in his works of the extent of the natural resources of France.

M. de Calonne was popular only among the courtiers; and such was

2. The paper controversy was originally triggered by Calonne's critique of Necker's ideas in *On the Administration of the Finances of France* (1784). Calonne gave a discourse in the Assembly of Notables on February 22, 1787, followed by *Necker's Response to the Discourse Pronounced by Mr. de Calonne* (Paris, 1787).

the financial distress caused by his prodigality and carelessness, that he was obliged to have recourse to a measure—the equalization of taxes among all classes, which originated with M. Turgot, a statesman as different from him as possible in every respect. But to what obstacles was not this new measure exposed, and how strange the situation of a minister, who, after dilapidating the treasury to make friends among the privileged orders, found himself obliged to displease that body at large by imposing a burden on the whole to meet the largesses made to individuals.

M. de Calonne was aware that the *Parlement of Paris* would not give its consent to new taxes, and likewise, that the King was averse to recurring to the expedient of a *lit de justice*—an expedient which showed the arbitrary power of the Crown in a glaring light, by annulling the only resistance provided by the constitution of the state. On the other hand, the weight of public opinion was daily on the increase, and a spirit of independence was manifesting itself among all classes. M. de Calonne flattered himself that he should find a support from this opinion against the *parlement*, whereas it was as much adverse to him as to that body. He proposed to the King to summon an Assembly of the Notables, a measure never adopted since the reign of Henri IV, a king who might run any risk in regard to authority, because assured of regaining everything by affection.[3]

These Assemblies of Notables had no power but that of giving the King their opinion on the questions which ministers thought proper to address to them. Nothing could be more ill-adapted to a time of public agitation than the assembling of bodies of men whose functions are confined to speaking: their opinions are carried to a higher state of excitement because they find no issue. The constitution placed the right of sanctioning taxes solely in the Estates General, the last convocation of which had taken place in 1614; but as taxes had been imposed unceasingly during an interval of 175 years, without a reference to this right, the nation had not the habit of remembering it, and at Paris they talked much more of the constitution

3. In fact, Assemblies of Notables had been convoked after the death of Henri IV and again in 1617, 1625, and 1626. Necker's account of the Assembly of Notables of 1787 is in Necker, *De la Révolution française*, pt. I, 60–64. Also see Furet, *Revolutionary France*, 41–45; and Baker, ed., *The Old Régime and the French Revolution*, 124–35.

of England than of that of France. The political principles laid down in English publications were much better known to Frenchmen than their ancient institutions, disused and forgotten for nearly two centuries.[4]

At the opening meeting of the Assembly of Notables in 1787, M. de Calonne confessed, in his statement of the finances, that the national expenditure exceeded the receipt by 56,000,000 livres a year;* but he alleged that this deficiency had commenced long before him, and that M. Necker had not adhered to truth when he asserted in 1781 that the receipt exceeded the expenditure by 10,000,000 livres.[5] No sooner did this assertion reach the ears of M. Necker than he refuted it in a triumphant memorial, accompanied by official documents, of the correctness of which the Notables were capable of judging at the time. His two successors in the ministry of finance, M. Joly de Fleury and M. d'Ormesson, attested the truth of his assertions. He sent a copy of this memorial to the King, who seemed satisfied of its truth but required of him not to print it.

In an arbitrary government, kings, even the best, have difficulty in conceiving the importance which every man naturally attaches to the good opinion of the public. In their eyes the court is the center of everything, while they themselves are the center of the court. M. Necker felt himself under the necessity of disobeying the King's injunction: to oblige a minister in retirement to keep silence, when accused by a minister in office of a falsehood in the face of the nation, was like forbidding a man to defend his honor. A sensibility to reputation less keen than that of M. Necker would have prompted a man to repel such an offense at all hazards. Ambition would, no doubt, have suggested a submission to the royal commands; but, as M. Necker's ambition pointed to fame, he published his work, although assured by everybody that by so doing he exposed himself, at the least, to exclusion forever from the ministry.[6]

* In English money 2,300,000*l.* sterling.

4. For the image of England in France, see p. 42n35 of the present volume.

5. The historians who questioned the accuracy of Necker's account concluded that the ten-million-livre budget surplus Necker announced in his *Compte rendu* was an exaggerated figure. For more information, see Egret, *Necker, ministre de Louis XVI*, 201–15.

6. In his book, Necker answered Calonne's criticism and defended his policy. The King, who was displeased with Necker's decision to publish the book, initially wanted to send

One evening in the winter of 1787, two days after the answer to M. de Calonne's attack had appeared, a message was brought to my father, while in the drawing room along with his family and a few friends. He went out, and having first sent for my mother, and, some minutes afterward, for me, he told me that M. Le Noir, the Lieutenant de Police, had just brought him a *lettre de cachet*, by which he was exiled to the distance of forty leagues from Paris. I cannot describe the state into which I was thrown by this news; it seemed to me an act of despotism without example; it was inflicted on my father, of whose noble and pure sentiments I was fully aware. I had not yet an idea of what governments are, and the conduct of the French government appeared to me an act of the most revolting injustice. I have certainly not changed my opinion in regard to the punishment of exile without trial; I think, and shall endeavor to prove, that of all harsh punishments it is the one most liable to abuse. But at that time, *lettres de cachet*, like other irregularities, were considered as ordinary things; and the personal character of the King had the effect of softening the abuse of them as much as possible.

But M. Necker's popularity had the effect of changing persecutions into triumph. All Paris came to see him during the twenty-four hours that he required to get ready for his journey. The Archbishop of Toulouse, patronized by the Queen, and on the eve of succeeding M. de Calonne, thought it incumbent on him, even on a calculation of ambition, to pay a visit to the exile. Offers of residences were made on all hands to M. Necker; all the castles at the distance of forty leagues from Paris were placed at his disposal. The evil of a banishment, known to be temporary, could not be very great, and the compensation for it was most flattering. But is it possible that a country can be governed in this manner? Nothing is so pleasant, for a certain time, as the decline of a government, for its weakness gives it an air of mildness; but the fall that ensues is dreadful.

The exile of M. Necker had by no means the effect of rendering the Notables favorable to M. de Calonne: they were irritated at it, and the assembly made more and more opposition to the plans of the minister.

Necker into exile, but at the intervention of the Queen ordered him to leave Paris and remain forty leagues from the capital. The Necker family eventually settled close to Fontainebleau.

His proposed taxes were all founded on the abolition of pecuniary privileges; but, as they were alleged to be very ill planned, the Notables rejected them under this pretext. This body, composed almost entirely of nobility and clergy,[7] was certainly not disposed (with some exceptions) to admit the principle of equalization of taxes; but it was cautious in expressing its secret wish in this respect; and, connecting itself with those whose views were entirely liberal, the result was its concurrence with the nation, which dreaded indiscriminately all new taxes of whatever nature.

The unpopularity of M. de Calonne was now so great, and the Assembly of the Notables afforded so imposing a medium for expressing this unpopularity, that the King felt himself obliged not only to remove M. de Calonne from office, but even to punish him. Now, whatever might be the faults of the minister, the King had declared to the Notables, two months before, that he approved his plans: there was consequently as great a loss of dignity in thus abandoning a bad minister as in previously removing a good one. But the great misfortune lay in the incredible choice of a successor; the Queen wished for the Archbishop of Toulouse; but the King was not disposed to appoint him. M. de Castries, who was then Minister of Marine, proposed M. Necker; but the Baron de Breteuil, who dreaded him, stimulated the King's pride by pointing out to him that he could not choose as minister one whom he had so lately exiled. Those kings who possess the least firmness of character are of all others the most sensitive when their authority is in question; they seem to think that it can go on of its own accord, like a supernatural power, entirely independent of means and circumstances. The Baron de Breteuil succeeded in preventing the appointment of M. Necker; the Queen failed in regard to the Archbishop of Toulouse; and the parties united for an instant on ground certainly very neutral, or rather no ground at all, in the appointment of M. de Fourqueux.[8]

Never had the wig of a counselor of state covered a poorer head: the man seemed at first to form a very proper estimate of his abilities, and

7. Of the 144 members of the Assembly of 1787, 106 notables represented the nobles and the clergy, and 38 represented the Third Estate.

8. Bouvard de Fourqueux proved to be a competent public official, although perhaps not physically fit for the new office.

wanted to refuse the position he was incapable of filling. But so many entreaties were made for his acceptance of it, that, at the age of sixty,[9] he began to conceive that his modesty had till then prevented him from being aware of his own talents, and that the court had at last discovered them. Thus did the well-wishers of M. Necker, and the Archbishop of Toulouse, fill the ministerial chair for an interval, as a box in a theater is kept by a servant till the arrival of his masters. Each party flattered itself with gaining time so as to secure the ministry for one of the two candidates, who alone had now a chance of it.

It was still perhaps not impossible to save the country from a revolution, or at least to preserve to government the control of public proceedings. No promise had as yet been given to convene the Estates General; the old methods of doing public business were not yet abandoned; perhaps the King, aided by the great popularity of M. Necker, might still have been enabled to accomplish the reforms necessary to straighten out the finances. Or, that department of government, bearing directly on public credit, and the influence of *parlements,* might with propriety be called the keystone of the arch. M. Necker, exiled at that time forty leagues from Paris, felt the importance of the crisis; and before the messenger who brought him the news of the appointment of the Archbishop of Toulouse had left the room, he expressed himself to me in these remarkable words: "God grant that the new minister may succeed in serving his king and country better than I should have been able to do; circumstances are already of a nature to make the task perilous; but they will soon be such as to surpass the powers of any man."

9. Fourqueux was sixty-eight (b. 1719), not sixty, when he assumed this office.

CHAPTER X

Sequel of the Preceding.—Ministry of the Archbishop of Toulouse.

M. de Brienne, Archbishop of Toulouse, had almost as little seriousness of character as M. de Calonne; but his clerical dignity, coupled with a constant ambition to attain a seat in the cabinet, had given him the outward gravity of a statesman; and he had the reputation of one, before he was placed in a situation to undeceive the world. He had labored during fifteen years, through his subordinates, to acquire the esteem of the Queen; but the King, who had no opinion of clerical philosophers, had always refused to admit him to the ministry. He gave way at last, for Louis XVI had not much confidence in himself; no man would have been happier had he been born King of England; for by being able to acquire a clear knowledge of the national wish, he would then have regulated his measures by that unfailing standard.

The Archbishop of Toulouse was not sufficiently enlightened to act the part of a philosopher, nor sufficiently firm for that of a despot:[1] he admired at one time the conduct of Cardinal Richelieu, at another the principles of the *"Encyclopedists"*; he attempted arbitrary measures, but desisted at the first obstacle; and, in truth, the things he aimed at were greatly beyond

---

1. Loménie de Brienne (1727–94), French statesman and cardinal of the Roman Catholic Church, was Archbishop of Toulouse (1763–88) and of Sens (1788). Nominated as president of the Assembly of Notables, he criticized the fiscal policy of Calonne, whom he succeeded as head of the treasury in May 1787. Brienne admired Necker and asked the King to bring him back to Paris and offer him a ministerial position. Brienne was forced out of office in August 1788. After the beginning of the Revolution, Brienne was one of the few French prelates to take an oath to the civil constitution of the clergy promulgated in 1790. He was subsequently arrested by the revolutionary government and died in prison in 1794.

the possibility of accomplishment. He proposed several taxes, particularly the stamp tax; the *parlement* rejected it, on which he made the King hold a *lit de justice:* the *parlements* suspended their judicial functions; the minister exiled them; nobody would come forward to take their place, and he conceived the plan of a plenary court, composed of the higher clergy and nobility. The idea was not bad, if meant in imitation of the English House of Peers; but a house of representatives, elected by the people, was a necessary accompaniment, as the plenary court was named by the King. The parliaments might be overturned by national representatives; but not by a body of Peers, extraordinarily convoked by the prime minister! The measure was so unpopular that several even of the courtiers refused to take their places in the assembly.

In this state of things the acts, intended by government as acts of authority, tended only to show its weakness; and the Archbishop of Toulouse, at one time arbitrary, at another constitutional, proved equally awkward in both.

Marshal de Segur had committed the great error of asking, in the eighteenth century, for proofs of nobility as a condition to the rank of officer. It was necessary to have been ennobled for a hundred years to have the honor of defending the country. This regulation irritated the Third Estate, without producing the effect of attaching the nobility "whom it favored more" to the authority of the Crown. Several officers of family declared that, if desired to arrest members of the *parlement,* or their adherents, they would not obey the orders of the King. The privileged classes began the resistance to the royal authority, and the *parlement* pronounced the word upon which hung the fate of France.

The *parlement* called loudly on the minister to produce his account of the national receipt and expenditure, when the Abbé Sabatier, a counselor of *parlement,* a man of lively wit, exclaimed, "You demand, Gentlemen, the states of receipt and expenditure (*états de recette et de depence*), when it is the Estates General (*états generaux*) that you ought to call for."[2] This

2. Sabatier uttered these famous words during a meeting on July 9, 1787. He was arrested in November 1787. On his return to Paris in the fall of 1788, he became a member of the Society of the Thirty, which was instrumental in preparing the elections to the Estates General.

word, although introduced as a pun, seemed to cast a ray of light on the confused wishes of everyone. He who had uttered it was sent to prison; but the *parlement,* soon after, declared that it did not possess the power of registering taxes, although they had been in the habit of exercising that power during two centuries; and, instigated by the ambition to take a lead in the popular ferment, they relinquished at once to the people a privilege which they had so obstinately defended against the Crown. From this moment the Revolution was decided, for there was but one wish among all parties—the desire of convoking the Estates General.

The same magistrates, who some time after gave the name of rebels to the friends of liberty, called for the convocation of the estates with such vehemence that the King thought himself obliged to arrest by his body-guards, in the midst of the assembly, two of their members, MM. d'Esprémenil and de Monsabert.[3] Several of the nobles, subsequently conspicuous as ardent opponents of a limited monarchy, then kindled the flame which led to the explosion. Twelve men of family from Brittany were sent to the Bastille; and the same spirit of opposition, which was punished in them, animated the other nobles of their province.[4] Even the clergy called for the Estates General. No revolution in a great country can succeed unless it take its beginning from the higher orders; the people come forward subsequently, but they are not capable of striking the first blows. By thus pointing out that it was the *parlements,* the nobles, and the clergy who first wished to limit the royal authority, I am very far from pretending to affix any censure to their conduct. All Frenchmen were then actuated by a sincere and disinterested enthusiasm; public spirit had become general; and, among the higher classes, the best characters were the most anxious that the wish of the nation should be consulted in the man-

3. In May 1788, Duval d'Eprésmésnil and Goislard de Monsabert drafted the *remontrances* that invoked the "fundamental laws of the state" and claimed that the Estates General alone had the right to approve new subsidies. Immediately after that, Louis XVI ordered the arrest of his two advisers; they were released in September 1788.

4. The protests and discontent among the nobles were not confined to Brittany; they spread to other regions of France as well. The nobles from Brittany appointed twelve representatives, whom they sent to the King to express their discontent with the judicial reforms of May 1788, which limited the authority of *parlements.* The twelve representatives were arrested and imprisoned at the Bastille in mid-July.

agement of its own concerns. But why should individuals in these higher classes, who however began the revolution, accuse one man, or one measure of that man, as the cause of the revolution? "We were desirous," say some, "that the political change should stop at a given point"; "We were desirous," say others, "of going a little further." True—but the movement of a great people is not to be stopped at will; and, from the time that you begin to acknowledge its rights, you will feel yourself obliged to grant all that justice requires.[5]

The Archbishop of Toulouse now recalled the *parlements*, but found them as untractable under favor as under punishment.[6] A spirit of resistance gained ground on all sides, and petitions for the Estates General became so numerous that the minister was at last obliged to promise them in the King's name; but he delayed the period of their convocation for five years, as if the public would have consented to put off its triumph. The clergy came forward to protest against the five years, and the King gave a solemn promise to convene the assembly in May of the following year.[7]

The Archbishop of Sens (for that was now his title, he not having forgotten, in the midst of all the public troubles, to exchange his archbishopric of Toulouse for a much better one), seeing that he could not successfully play a despotic game, drew near to his old philosopher friends and, discontented with the higher classes, made an attempt to please the nation by calling on the writers of the day to give their opinion on the best mode of organizing the Estates General.[8] But the world never gives a minister credit for his acts when they are the results of necessity; that which renders public opinion so deserving of regard is its being a compound of pene-

---

5. By emphasizing the revolt of the nobles against the arbitrary measures of the King's ministers, Madame de Staël sought to demonstrate the long history of opposition to arbitrary power in France. Seen from this perspective, the events of 1789 appeared both justified and inevitable, an idea at odds with the opinions of the ultraroyalist camp.

6. It was Necker, recalled to power following the resignation of the Archbishop of Toulouse, who reestablished the *parlements* on September 23, 1788.

7. Necker proposed to convoke the Estates General on January 1, 1789, rather than May 1, the date suggested by Brienne.

8. This had significant consequences for freedom of the press in France. Brienne's decision was announced on July 5, 1788.

tration and power: it consists of the views of each individual, and of the ascendancy of the whole.

The Archbishop of Sens had stirred up the Third Estate in the hope of supporting himself against the privileged classes. The Third Estate soon intimated that it would take the place of representative of the nation in the Estates General; but it would not receive that station from the hand of a minister who returned to liberal ideas only after failing in an attempt to establish the most despotic institutions.

Finally, the Archbishop of Sens completely exasperated all classes by suspending the payment of a third of the interest of the national debt. A general cry was now raised against him; even the princes applied to the King to dismiss him, and so pitiable was his conduct that a number of people set him down for a madman. This, however, was by no means the case, he was on the contrary a sensible man in the current acceptation of the word; that is, he possessed the talents necessary to have made him an expert minister in the ordinary routine of a court. But no sooner does a nation begin to participate in the management of its own concerns, than all drawing-room ministers are found unequal to their situation: none will do then but men of firm principles; these alone can follow a steady and decisive course. None but the large features of the mind are capable, like the Minerva of Phidias, of producing effect upon crowds when viewed at a distance. Official dexterity, according to the old plan of governing a country by the rules of ministerial offices, only excites distrust in a representative government.

CHAPTER XI

Did France Possess a Constitution
Before the Revolution?[1]

Of all modern monarchies, France was certainly the one whose political institutions were most arbitrary and fluctuating; and the cause is probably to be sought in the incorporation, at very different periods, of the provinces that compose the kingdom. Each province had different claims and customs; the government skillfully made use of the old against the new ones, and the country became only gradually a whole.

Whatever may be the cause, it is an undoubted fact that there exists no law in France, not even an elementary law, which has not, at some time or other, been disputed—nothing, in short, which has not been the object of difference of opinion. Did, or did not the legislative power reside in the kings? Could they, or could they not impose taxes in virtue of their prerogative and will? Or, the Estates General, were they the representatives of the people, to whom alone belonged the right of granting subsidies? In what manner ought these Estates General to be composed? The

1. This unusually long chapter plays a seminal role in Madame de Staël's analysis of the Old Regime and the roots of the French Revolution. The question whether France did or did not have a true constitution was an old one, and any answer was pregnant with significant political implications. Most famously, Abbé Sieyès answered in the negative, thus justifying his revolutionary claims in *What Is the Third Estate?* (1789). In a surprisingly short (four-page) chapter of his own book, Bailleul pointed to the contradictions in Madame de Staël's analysis in part I, chapter xi. He ironically noted (*Examen critique*, vol. 1, 146–47) that by concluding that France had no genuine constitution under the Old Regime, Madame de Staël was contradicting some of her earlier statements such as the existence of a forceful opposition to royal power coming from local privileges and intermediary bodies. For another critique see Louis de Bonald, *Observations sur l'ouvrage de Madame la baronne de Staël*, chap. I (Paris, 1818).

privileged classes, who possessed two voices out of three, could they consider themselves as essentially distinct from the nation at large, and entitled, after voting a tax, to relieve themselves from its operation, and to throw its burden on the people? What were the real privileges of the clergy, who at one time held themselves to be independent of the king, at another independent of the pope? What were the powers of the nobles, who, at one time, even down to the minority of Louis XIV, asserted the right of maintaining their privileges by force of arms in alliance with foreigners, while, at another time, they would acknowledge that the king possessed absolute power? What ought to be the situation of the Third Estate, emancipated by the kings, introduced into the Estates General by Philip the Fair,[2] and yet doomed to be perpetually in a minority, since it had only one vote in three, and since its complaints could carry little weight, presented as they were to the monarch on the knee?

What was the political influence of the *parlements*, these assemblies, which declared at one time that their sole business was to administer justice, at another that they were the Estates General on a reduced scale, that is, the representatives of the representatives of the people? The same parliaments refused to acknowledge the jurisdiction of the intendants, who were the provincial administrators of the Crown; and the cabinet, on the other hand, contested with the *pays d'états* the right, to which they pretended, of acquiescing in the taxes. The history of France would supply us with a crowd of examples of similar want of consistency in small things as in great; but enough of the deplorable results of this want of principles. Persons accused of state offenses were almost all deprived of a fair trial; and many of them, without being brought before a court at all, have passed their lives in prisons, to which they had been sent by the sole authority of the executive power. The code of terror against Protestants, cruel punishments, and torture, still existed down to the Revolution.[3]

The taxes, which pressed exclusively on the lower orders, reduced them to hopeless poverty. A French jurist, only fifty years ago, continued to call

2. Philip IV was King of France from 1285 to 1314. His nickname, Philip the Fair (*le Bel*), came from his handsome appearance.

3. For a comprehensive analysis of the political institutions of the Old Regime, see Mousnier, *Les institutions de la France sous la monarchie absolue*.

the Third Estate, according to custom, the people taxable, and liable at mercy to seignorial service (*la gent corvéable et taillable à merci et miséricorde*). The power of imprisoning and banishing, after being for some time disputed, became a part of the royal prerogative; and ministerial despotism, a dexterous instrument for the despotism of the Crown, at last carried matters so far as to admit the inconceivable maxim, *Si veut le roi, si veut la loi* (as wills the king, so wills the law), as the only political institution of France.[4]

The English, proud, and with reason, of their own liberty, have not failed to say that if the national character of the French had not been adapted to despotism, they could not have borne with it so long; and Blackstone,[5] the first of the English jurists, printed in the eighteenth century these words: "Kings might then, as in France or Turkey, imprison, dispatch, or exile, any man that was obnoxious to them, by an instant declaration that such is their will and pleasure."* I postpone, till the end of the work, a view of the national character of the French, too much calumniated in these times; but I cannot avoid repeating what I have already said, that the history of France will be found to exhibit as many struggles against despotic power as that of England. M. de Boulainvilliers, the great champion of the feudal system, asserts repeatedly that the kings of France had neither the right of coining money, of fixing the strength of the army, of taking foreign troops into their pay, nor, above all, of levying taxes, without the consent of the nobles. He is, indeed, somewhat concerned, that there should have been formed a second order out of the clergy, and, still more, a third out of the people; and he loses all patience with the kings of France for assuming the right of granting patents of nobility, which he calls enfranchisements; and with reason, because according to the principles of the aristocracy it is a discredit to be recently ennobled: neither is it less offense to the principles of liberty.

M. de Boulainvilliers is an aristocrat of the true kind, that is, without

* Commentaries, book iv, chap. 27, §5.

4. At the core of Madame de Staël's critique of Louis XVI's arbitrary power is her emphasis on the absence of the rule of law under the Old Regime.

5. William Blackstone (1723–80), author of *Commentaries on the Laws of England* (1765–69).

any mixture of the temper of a courtier, the most degrading of all. He considers the nation as confined to the nobility and reckons that, in a population of more than twenty-four million, there are not above one hundred thousand descendants of the Franks; for he excludes, and rightly, according to his system, all families ennobled by the Crown, as well as the clergy of the second rank; and, according to him, these descendants of the Franks being the conquerors, and the Gauls the conquered, the former alone can participate in the management of public business. The citizens of a state have a right to share in making and preserving the laws; but if there are only one hundred thousand citizens in a state, it is they alone who possess this political right.[6] The question, therefore, is, whether the 23,900,000 souls at present composing the Third Estate in France are, in fact, vanquished Gauls, or willing to be treated as such.

So long as the degraded condition of serfs allowed things to go on in this manner, we find everywhere governments in which liberties, if not liberty, have been perfectly acknowledged; that is, where privileges have obtained respect as rights. History and reason concur in showing that if, under the first race of the kings of France, those who possessed the right of citizens had a right to sanction legislative acts; if, under Philip the Fair, the free men of the Third Estate (far from numerous in that age, as the mass of the population still were *serfs*) were associated to the two other orders, it follows that the kings could not make use of them as a political counterpoise without acknowledging them for citizens. The inference is that these citizens were entitled to exercise the same powers, in regard to laws and taxes, as were at first exercised only by the nobles. And when the number of those who have acquired the right of citizens becomes so great that they cannot personally attend at public deliberations, this is when representative government is born.

The different provinces stipulated for certain rights and privileges as they became united to the Crown; and the twelve provincial *parlements* were successively established, partly for the administration of justice, but

6. These ideas can be found in Boulainvilliers' influential books *Histoire de l'ancien gouvernement de France* (1727) and *Essai sur la noblesse* (1732). Henri de Boulainvilliers (1658–1722) was a leading historian of the French monarchy. An analysis of his writings can be found in Ellis, *Boulainvilliers and the French Monarchy*.

particularly for ascertaining whether the royal edicts, which they had the right to promulgate or not, were or were not in unison with the provincial privileges, or with the fundamental laws of the kingdom. Yet their authority in this respect was very precarious. In 1484, when Louis XII, then Duke of Orléans, made a complaint to them of want of attention to the demands of the last Estates, they answered that they were men of study, whose business related not to matters of government, but to the administration of justice. They soon after, however, advanced much higher claims, and their political power was such that Charles V sent two ambassadors to the *parlement* of Toulouse, to ascertain if they had ratified his treaty with Francis I.[7] The *parlements* seemed therefore to have been intended as a habitual limitation of the royal authority; and the Estates General, being superior to *parlements*, should be considered as a still more powerful barrier. It was customary, in the Middle Ages, to mix the judicial with the legislative power; and the double power of the English peers, as judges in some cases, and legislators in all, is a remnant of this ancient conjunction. Nothing can be more natural in an uncivilized age, than that particular decisions should be antecedent to general laws. The respectability of the judges was in these days such as to make them considered the fittest persons to mold their own decisions into general laws. St. Louis was the first, as is believed, who erected the *parlement* into a court of justice;[8] before his time it appears to have been only a royal council; but this sovereign, enlightened by his virtues, felt the necessity of giving strength to the institutions which could serve as a guarantee of the rights of his subjects.

The Estates General had no connection with the administration of justice: we thus recognize in the monarchy of France two powers, which, though badly organized, were each of them independent of the royal authority: the Estates General and the *parlements*. The ruling policy of the third race of kings was to extend immunities to the towns and to the inhabitants of the country, that they might gradually bring forward the Third Estate as a counterpoise to the great lords. Philip the Fair introduced

7. Reference to the peace treaty signed by Francis I, prisoner of Charles V, on January 14, 1526. The treaty had to be ratified by the Estates General and other sovereign courts of France.

8. This development occurred around 1250 under the reign of St. Louis.

the national deputies into the Estates General as a third order; because he stood in need of money, and because he dreaded the ill-will which his character had produced, and felt the want of support, not only against the nobles, but against the pope, by whom he was then persecuted. From this time forward (in 1302), the Estates General had, in right if not in fact, equal legislative powers with the English parliament. Their decrees (*or-donnances*) of 1355 and 1356[9] were as much in the spirit of liberty as the *Magna Charta* of England; but there was no provision for the annual con-vocation of this assembly, and its separation into three orders, instead of into two chambers, gave the King much greater means of setting them in opposition to one another.

The confusion of the political authority of the *parlement*, which was perpetual, and of that of the Estates General, which approached more to the elective form, is conspicuous in every reign of the kings of France of the third race. During the civil wars which took place, we find the king, the Estates General, and the *parlement*, each bringing forward different pretensions; but whatever were the avowed or concealed attempts of pre-ceding monarchs, no one before Louis XIV ever openly advanced the doctrine of absolute power. All the strength of the *parlements* lay in their privilege of registry, since no law could be promulgated or subsequently executed without their consent. Charles VI was the first king who at-tempted to change the *lit de justice*, which formerly meant nothing but the presence of the king at a *parlementary* sitting, into an order to register, by express command, and in spite of remonstrance. The Crown was soon after obliged to cancel the edicts which the *parlement* had been made to accept by force; and a counselor of Charles VI, who, after having approved of these edicts, supported the canceling of them, being asked by a member of *parlement* his motive for such a change, replied: "Our rule is to desire what the King desires; we are regulated by the circumstances of the time; and find, by experience, that, in all the revolutions of courts, the best way

---

9. A reference to the 1355–56 ordinances King John was forced to sign during a meeting of the Estates General giving the latter some control over the collection of taxes and limiting their duration to one year. It was not uncommon for commentators to compare these or-dinances with the Magna Carta.

to maintain our footing is to range ourselves on the stronger side." Really, in this respect, one could deny the perfectibility of the human species.

Henri III put a stop to the practice of inserting at the top of official edicts, "*by express command,*" lest the people should refuse to obey them. Henri IV, who came to the crown in 1589, declared, himself, in one of his speeches, quoted by Joly, that *parlementary* registration was necessary for the validation of royal edicts. The *Parlement of Paris,* in its remonstrances against Mazarin's ministry, recalled the promises made by Henri IV and quoted his own words upon the subject: "The authority of kings destroys itself in endeavoring to establish itself too firmly."

Cardinal Richelieu's political system entirely consisted in overthrowing the power of the nobles by aid of the people; but before and even during his ministry, the magistrates of *parlement* always professed the most liberal maxims. Pasquier, under Henri III, said that monarchy was one of the forms of the republic; meaning, by that word, the government whose object is the welfare of the people. The celebrated magistrate Talon thus expressed himself under Louis XIII: "In former years, the orders of the king were not received or executed by the people, unless signed in the original by the grandees of the kingdom, the princes, and higher officers of the crown. This political jurisdiction has now devolved on the *parlements.* We enjoy this second power, which the authority of time sanctions, which subjects suffer with patience, and honor with respect."[10]

Such were the principles of the *parlements;* they admitted, like the constitutionists of the present day, the necessity of the consent of the nation; but they declared themselves its representatives, without, however, having the power to deny that the claims of the Estates General were, in this respect, superior. The *Parlement of Paris* took it amiss that Charles IX should have declared himself arrived at majority at Rouen, and that Henri IV should have convened the Notables. This *parlement,* being the only one in which the peers of France occupied seats, could alone allege a title to political interference; yet every *parlement* in the kingdom made similar claims. A strange idea, that a body of judges, indebted for their

---

10. This statement of Jacques Talon, *avocat général* of the *Parlement of Paris,* was made in 1631.

office either to the king's appointment or to the practice of purchasing their situations, should come forward and call themselves the representatives of the nation! Yet, singular as was the foundation of their claims, its practical exercise sometimes served as a check to arbitrary power.

The *Parlement of Paris* had, it must be confessed, all along persecuted the Protestants: horrible to say, it had even instituted an annual procession of thanks for the dreadful day of St. Bartholomew: but in this it was the instrument of party; and no sooner was fanaticism appeased, than this same parliament, composed of men of integrity and courage, often resisted the encroachments of the throne and the ministers. But of what avail was their opposition, when, after all, silence might be imposed on them by a *lit de justice* held by the king? In what, then, could the French constitution be said to consist? in nothing but the hereditary nature of the royal power. Undoubtedly this is a very good law, since it is conducive to the tranquillity of nations, but it is not a constitution.[11]

The Estates General were convened only eighteen times between 1302 and 1789: that is, during nearly five centuries. Yet with them alone rested the power of sanctioning a tax; and if all had been regular, their assembling should have taken place each time that new taxes were imposed, but the kings often disputed their power in this respect, and acted in an arbitrary manner without them. The *parlements* intervened in the sequel between the kings and the Estates General—not denying the unlimited power of the Crown, and yet maintaining that they were the guardians of the laws of the kingdom. But what law can there be in a country where the royal power is unlimited? The *parlements* made remonstrances on the edicts laid before them; the king then sent them a positive order to register these edicts, and to be silent. To have disobeyed would have been an inconsistency; since, after acknowledging the supremacy of the royal power, what were they themselves, or what could they say, without the permission of that very monarch whose power they were supposed to limit? This circle

---

11. The question to be decided was whether France had to create an entirely new constitution (having arguably had none) or was supposed only to restore (reform) an existing one. The answer to this question was bound to have major political implications, as the course of subsequent events plainly demonstrated. For more information, see Baker, *Inventing the French Revolution*, 255–305.

of pretended oppositions always ended in servitude, and its fatal mark has remained on the face of the nation.

France has been governed by custom, often by caprice, and never by law. There is not one reign like another in a political point of view; everything might be supported, and everything forbidden, in a country where the course of circumstances alone was decisive of what everyone called his right. Will it be alleged that some of the *pays d'états* maintained their treaties with the Crown? They might found a course of argument on such treaties, but the royal authority cut short all difficulties, and the remaining usages were little else than mere forms, maintained or suppressed according to the will and pleasure of ministers. Did the nobles possess privileges beyond that of exemption from taxes? Even that privilege a despotic king had it in his power to abolish. In fact, the nobles neither could nor ought to boast the possession of a single political right: for, priding themselves in acknowledging the royal authority to be unlimited, they could not complain, either of those special commissions which have sentenced to death the first lords in France, or of the imprisonment, or the exiles which they suffered.[12] The king could do everything, what objection was it then possible to make to anything?

The clergy who acknowledged the power of the pope, and derived from it the power of the king, were alone entitled to make some resistance. But it was themselves who maintained the divine right on which despotism rests, well knowing that this divine right cannot be permanently supported without the priesthood. This doctrine, tracing all power from God, interdicted men from attempting its limitation. Such certainly are not the precepts of the Christian faith; but we speak at present of the language of those who wish to convert religion to their own purposes.

We thus see that the history of France is replete with attempts on the part of the nation and nobles, the one to obtain rights, the other privileges; we see in it also continual efforts of most of the kings to attain arbitrary power. A struggle, similar in many respects, is exhibited in the history of England; but as, in that country there all along existed two houses of Par-

---

12. For example, special commissions for punishing those involved in the trafficking of salt and cigarettes were instituted in Valence (1733), Saumur (1742), and Reims (1765).

liament,[13] the means of resistance were better, and the demands made on the Crown were both more important in their objects and more wisely conducted than in France. The English clergy not being a separate political order, they and the peers together composed almost half of the national representation, and had always much more regard for the people than in France. The great misfortune of France, as of every country governed solely by a court, is the domineering influence of vanity. No fixed principle gains ground in the mind; all is absorbed in the pursuit of power, because power is everything in a country where the laws are nothing.

In England, the Parliament combined in itself the legislative power, which, in France, was shared between the *parlements* and the Estates General. The English Parliament was considered permanent, but as it had little to do in the way of the administration of justice, the kings abridged its session or postponed its meeting as much as possible. In France the conflict between the nation and the royal authority assumed another aspect: resistance to the power of ministers proceeded with more constancy and energy from those *parlements* which did the duty of judicial bodies, than from the Estates General. But as the privileges of French *parlements* were undefined, the result was, that the king was at one time kept in tutelage by them, and they, at another, were trampled underfoot by the king. Two houses, as in England, would have done much less to clog the exercise of the executive power, and much more to secure the national liberty. The Revolution of 1789 had then no other object than to give a regular form to the limitations which have, all along, existed in France.[14] Montesquieu

13. The two houses in England were established in the fourteenth century.

14. Fixing the French constitution was a highly contested topic in 1789. Some members of the Constituent Assembly sought to give a more regular form to the old limits to absolute power; others wanted to make a tabula rasa of the past and devise an entirely new constitution. Necker commented on the difficult task of amending the old French constitution in *De la Révolution française*, pt. I, 41–45, 203–5. In Necker's opinion, there was a clear tension between the social and political orders of France on the eve of the Revolution. Public opinion demanded the elimination of the significant financial privileges enjoyed by the nobles and the clergy. For an overview of the debates on amending the French constitution, see Baker, *Inventing the French Revolution*, 252–305, and Valensise, "The French Constitution in Pre-revolutionary Debate," 22–57. For an overview of the projects for reform in the last years of the Old Regime, see Furet, *Revolutionary France*, 17–27, 33–40, and Doyle, *The Oxford History of the French Revolution*, 86–111.

pronounced the rights of intermediate bodies the strength and freedom of a kingdom. Now what intermediate body is the most faithful representative of all the national interests? The two houses of Parliament in England; and even, were it not absurd in theory to entrust a few privileged persons, whether of the magistracy or nobles, with the exclusive discussion of the interests of a nation which has never been able to invest them legally with its powers, the recent history of France, presenting nothing but an almost unbroken succession of disputes relative to the extension of power and of arbitrary acts committed in turn by the different parties, sufficiently proves that it was high time to seek an improved form of national representation.

In regard to the right of the nation to be represented, this right has, ever since France existed, been acknowledged by the kings, the ministers, and the magistrates, who have merited the national esteem. The claim of unlimited royal power has had, undoubtedly, a number of partisans; so many personal interests are involved in that opinion! But what names stand averse to each other in this cause! Louis XI must be opposed to Henri IV; Louis XIII to Louis XII; Richelieu to De l'Hôpital; Cardinal Dubois to M. de Malesherbes; and, if we were to quote all the names preserved in history, we might assert at a venture that, with few exceptions, wherever we meet with an upright heart or an enlightened mind, no matter in what rank of society, we shall there find a friend to liberty; while unlimited power has hardly ever been defended by a man of genius, and still less by a man of virtue.

The *Maximes du Droit public François,*[15] published in 1775 by a magistrate of the *Parlement of Paris,* are perfectly accordant with those of the Constituent Assembly on the expediency of balancing the different powers

---

15. The authors of *Maximes du droit public françois* (Amsterdam, 1775), 2 vols., were Claude Mey and Gabriel-Nicolas Maultrot, jurists in the natural-law tradition who may have been influenced on certain points by Hobbes and Rousseau. A useful analysis of this work can be found in Echeverria, "The Pre-revolutionary Influence of Rousseau's *Contrat Social,*" 551–52; and Van Kley, "New Wine in Old Wineskins," 447–65. The latter suggests that the work arose out of the attack upon the despotism of the Maupeou judicial revolution of 1771–74; one of Maultrot's other works was reprinted to similar effect in the 1787–89 antidespotism campaign.

of the state, on the necessity of obtaining the consent of the people to taxes, on their participation in legislative acts, and on the responsibility of ministers. In every page the author recalls the existing contract between the king and the people, and his reasonings are founded on historical facts.

Other respectable members of the French magistracy maintain that there once were constitutional laws in France, but that they had fallen into disuse. Some say that they have ceased to be in vigor since the time of Richelieu, others since Charles V, others since Philip the Fair, while a last party go as far back as Charlemagne. It was assuredly of little importance that such laws had ever existed, if they had been consigned to oblivion for so many ages. But it is easy to close this discussion. If there are fundamental laws, if it be true that they contain all the rights secured to the English nation, the friends of liberty will then be agreed with the partisans of the ancient order of things; and yet the treaty seems to me still a matter of difficult arrangement.

M. de Calonne, who had declared himself averse to the Revolution, published a book to show that France had no constitution.[16] M. de Monthion, chancellor to the Comte d'Artois, published a reply to M. de Calonne and entitled his work *A Report to His Majesty Louis XVIII* in 1796.

He begins by declaring that if there were no constitution in France, the Revolution was justified, as every people possess a right to a political constitution. This assertion was somewhat hazardous, considering his opinions; but he goes on to affirm, that by the constitutional statutes of France, the King did not have the right of making laws without the consent of the Estates General; that Frenchmen could not be brought to trial but before their natural judges; that every extraordinary tribunal was contrary to law; that, in short, all *lettres de cachet,* all banishments, and all imprisonments founded merely on the King's authority were illegal. He added that all Frenchmen had a right to be admitted to public employments, that the military profession conferred the rank of gentleman on all who followed it; that the forty thousand municipalities of the kingdom had the right of

16. The title of Calonne's book (published in London in 1796) is *Tableau de l'Europe jusqu'au commencement de 1796.* He also published an answer to Monthion's critique, *Lettre de M. de Calonne au citoyen autour du prétendu rapport fait à S. M. Louis XVIII.*

being governed by administrators of their choice, with whom rested the assessment of the taxes imposed; that the King could order nothing without his council, which implied the responsibility of ministers; that there existed a material distinction between the royal ordinances (*ordonnances*) or laws of the King and the fundamental laws of the state; that the judges were not pledged to obey the King's orders if at variance with the latter; and that the military force could not be employed in the interior, except to put down insurrection or in fulfillment of the mandates of justice. He added that the assembling at stated periods of the Estates General forms part of the French constitution, and concluded by saying, in the presence of Louis XVIII, that the English constitution is the most perfect in the world.

Had all the adherents of the old government professed such principles, the Revolution would have been without apology, since it would have been unnecessary. But the same writer has inserted in his work, in a solemn address to the King, the following sketch of the abuses existing in France before the Revolution.*

> The most essential right of citizenship, the right of voting on the laws and taxes, had, in a manner, become obsolete; and the Crown was in the habit of issuing, on its sole authority, those orders in which it ought to have had the concurrence of the national representatives.
>
> The right in question, though belonging essentially to the nation, seemed transferred to the *parlements;* and the freedom even of their suffrages had been encroached on by arbitrary imprisonments and *lits de justice.*
>
> It frequently happened that the laws, regulations, and general decisions of the King, which ought to have been deliberated in council, and which made mention of the concurrence of the council, had never been laid before that body: and in several departments of business this official falsehood had become habitual. Several clerical dignitaries infringed the laws, both in letter and spirit, by holding a plurality of livings, by nonresidence, and by the use that they made of the property of the church. A part of the nobles had received their titles in a manner unbecoming the

---

* M. de Monthion's Report, p. 154 of the London edition.

institution; and the services due by the body had not for a length of time been required.

The exemption of the two first orders from taxes was sanctioned by the constitution, but was certainly not the proper kind of return for the services of these orders.

Special commissions in criminal cases, composed of judges chosen in an arbitrary manner, certainly might alarm the innocent.

Those unauthorized acts which deprived individuals of liberty, without a charge and without a trial, were so many infractions on the security of the rights of citizens. The courts of justice, whose stability was all the more important as, in the absence of a national representation, they constituted the only defense of the nation, had been suppressed and replaced by bodies of magistrates who did not possess the confidence of the people: and, since their re-establishment, innovations had been attempted on the most essential points of their jurisdiction.

But it was in matters of finance that the law had been most glaringly violated. Taxes had been imposed without the consent of the nation, or of its representatives.

They had also been collected after the expiration of the time fixed by government for their duration.

Taxes, at first of small amount, had been carried by degrees to an irregular and prodigious height; a part of the taxes pressed more on the indigent than the rich.

The public burdens were assessed on the different provinces without any correct idea of the relative means of each. There was reason sometimes to suspect that deductions had been made in consequence of the resistance opposed to them; so that the want of patriotism had proved a cause of favorable treatment.

Some provinces had succeeded in obtaining tax settlements,[17] and, bargains of this kind being always in favor of the provinces, it was an indulgence to one part of the kingdom at the expense of the rest.

The sums stipulated in these tax settlements remained always the same, while the other provinces were subject to official inquiries which annually increased the tax: this was another source of inequality.

---

17. In French, *abonnement d'impôts*. Before 1789 (when it first seems to have taken on that meaning) the term had both feudal and fiscal connotations, and it meant fixing in advance the returns or the taxes on this or that property.

Another abuse consisted in assessing by officers of the Crown, or even by their commissioners, taxes of which the assessment should have been left to persons chosen from among those who were to pay them.

Of some taxes the kings had made themselves judges in their council: commissions were to be established to decide on fiscal questions, the cognizance of which belonged properly to the courts of justice. The public debt which bore so hard on the nation had been contracted without its consent; the loans, to which the *parlements* had given an assent which they had no right to give, had been exceeded by means of endless irregularities, which were so many acts of treachery at once to the courts of justice, whose sanctions were thus illusory; to the public creditors, who had competitors of whose existence they were ignorant; and to the nation, whose burdens were increased without its knowledge. The public expenditure was in no respect fixed by law.

The funds meant to cover the personal expenses of the king, the funds intended for the payment of the public dividends, and the expenses of government were distinguished only by a particular and secret act of the king's will.

The personal expenses of our kings had been carried to an enormous amount; the provisions made for guaranteeing some portions of the public debt had been eluded; the king might quicken or delay, as he thought proper, the payments in various parts of the expenditure.

In the pay of the army the sum appropriated to the officers was almost as great as that appropriated to the soldiers.

The salaries of almost all government officers, of whatever description, were too high, particularly for a country where honor ought to be the principal, if not sole reward of services rendered to the state.

The pension list had been carried to a much higher amount than that of other countries in Europe, keeping in view the relative amount of revenue.

Such were the points on which the nation had just ground of complaint, and if we are to censure government for the existence of these abuses, we are likewise to censure the constitution which made their existence possible.

If such was the situation of France, and we can hardly refuse the evidence of a chancellor of the Comte d'Artois, especially when laid officially before the King; if, then, such was the situation of France, even in the opinion of those who asserted that she possessed a constitution, who can deny that a change was necessary, either to give a free course to a constitution hitherto perpetually infringed; or to introduce those guarantees which might give the laws of the state the means of being maintained and obeyed?[18]

18. Madame de Staël's emphasis on the inevitability of the Revolution evokes the similar approach of Tocqueville in *The Old Régime and the Revolution*, vol. 1, bk. 1, chap. 5: "What Did the Revolution Really Accomplish?"

CHAPTER XII

On the Recall of M. Necker in 1788.

Had M. Necker, when he was minister, proposed to convene the Estates General, he might have been accused of a dereliction of duty, since, with a certain party, it is a settled point that the absolute power of kings is sacred. But at the time when the public opinion obliged the Court to dismiss the Archbishop of Sens, and to recall M. Necker, the Estates General had been solemnly promised:[1] the nobles, the clergy, and the *parlement* had solicited this promise; the nation had received it; and such was the weight of universal opinion on this point, that no force, either civil or military, would have come forward to oppose it. I consign this assertion to history; if it lessens the merit of M. Necker by showing that he was not the cause of convening the Estates General, it places in the proper quarter the responsibility for the events of the Revolution. Would it have been possible for such a man as M. Necker to propose to a virtuous sovereign, to Louis XVI, to retract his word? And of what use would have been a minister whose strength lay in his popularity, if the first act of that minister had been to advise the King to fail in the engagements that he had made with the people?

That aristocratical body which finds it so much easier to cast calumny on a man than to confess the share that it bore itself in the general ferment, that very aristocracy, I say, would have been the first to feel indignant at the perfidy of the minister: he could not have derived any political advantage from the degradation to which he would have consented. When a measure, therefore, is neither moral nor useful, what madman, or what pretended sage, would come forward to advise it?

1. The promise to convoke the Estates General (at the latest in 1792) was first made by Brienne in November 1787.

M. Necker, at the time when public opinion brought him back to the ministry, was more alarmed than gratified by his appointment. He had bitterly regretted going out of office in 1781, as he thought himself sure at that time of doing a great deal of good. On hearing of the death of M. de Maurepas, he reproached himself with having, six months before, given in his resignation, and I have always present to my recollection his long walks at St. Ouen, in which he often repeated that he tormented himself with his reflections and with his scruples. Every conversation that revived the recollection of his ministry, every encomium on that subject, gave him pain. During the seven years which elapsed between his first and second ministry, he was in a state of perpetual chagrin at the overthrow of his plans for improving the situation of France. At the time when the Archbishop of Sens was called to office, he still regretted his not being appointed; but in 1788, when I came to apprise him, at St. Ouen, of his approaching nomination, he said to me, "Ah! why did they not give me those fifteen months of the Archbishop of Sens? Now it is too late."

M. Necker had just published his work upon the importance of religious opinions.[2] His rule throughout life was to attack a party when in all its strength; his pride led him to that course. It was the first time that a writer, sufficiently enlightened to bear the name of a philosopher, came forward to mark the danger arising from the irreligious spirit of the eighteenth century; and this work had filled its author's mind with thoughts of a much higher nature than can be produced by temporal interests, even of the highest kind. Accordingly he obeyed the King's orders with a feeling of regret, which I was certainly far from sharing: on observing my delight, he said, "The daughter of a minister feels nothing but pleasure; she enjoys the reflection of her father's power; but power itself, particularly at this crisis, is a tremendous responsibility." He judged but too well—in the vivacity of early youth, talent, if it be possessed, may enable the individual to speak like one of riper years; but the imagination is not a single day older than ourselves.

In crossing the Bois de Boulogne at night to repair to Versailles, I was in great terror of being attacked by robbers; for it appeared to me that the

2. Necker's book was entitled *De l'importance des opinions religieuses* (1788).

happiness which I felt at my father's elevation was too great not to be counterpoised by some dreadful accident. No robbers came to attack me, but the future but too fully justified my fears.

I waited on the Queen according to custom on the day of St. Louis: the niece of the Archbishop of Sens, who had that morning been dismissed from office, was also at the levee; and the Queen showed clearly, by her manner of receiving the two, that she felt a much stronger predilection for the removed minister than for his successor. The courtiers acted differently; for never did so many persons offer to conduct me to my carriage. Certainly, the disposition of the Queen proved, at that time, one of the great obstacles that M. Necker encountered in his political career; she had patronized him during his first ministry, but in the second, in spite of all his efforts to please her, she always considered him as appointed by public opinion; and in arbitrary governments, sovereigns are, unfortunately, in the habit of considering public opinion as their enemy.

M. Necker, on entering on office, found only two hundred and fifty thousand francs in the public treasury; but the next day the bankers brought him considerable sums. The stocks rose thirty percent in one morning; such an effect on public credit, resulting from confidence in a single man, is wholly without example in history.[3] M. Necker obtained the recall of all the exiles, and the deliverance of all persons imprisoned for matters of opinion; among others, of the twelve gentlemen from Brittany, whom I have already mentioned. In short, he did all the good, in regard to individuals and matters of detail, which could be effected by a minister; but by this time the importance of the public had increased, and that of men in office was in consequence proportionally lessened.

---

3. This was the outcome of Necker's proposal (September 14, 1788) to revoke Brienne's decision of August 16 ordering the payment in paper money of a part of salaries and rents.

CHAPTER XIII

Conduct of the Last Estates General, Held at Paris in 1614.

The aristocratical party, in 1789, were perpetually demanding the adoption of ancient usages. The obscurity of time is very favorable to those who are not disposed to enter on a discussion of truth on its own merits. They called out incessantly, "Give us 1614, and our last Estates General; these are our masters, these are our models."

I shall not stop to show that the Estates General held at Blois in 1576 were almost as different, in point both of composition and form of proceeding, from the Paris assembly of 1614, as from their predecessors under King John and Louis XII. No meeting of the three orders having been founded on clear principles, none had led to permanent results. It may, however, be interesting to recall some of the principal characteristics of the last Estates General, brought forward, as they were, after a lapse of nearly two centuries, as a guide to the assembly of 1789. The Third Estate proposed to declare that no power, spiritual or temporal, had a right to release the king's subjects from their allegiance to him. The clergy, through the medium of Cardinal du Perron, opposed this,[1] making a reservation of the rights of the Pope; the nobles followed the example, and received, as well as the clergy, the warm and public thanks of His Holiness. Those who speak of a compact between the nation and the Crown are liable, even in our days, to be considered Jacobins; but in those times, the

---

1. After the meeting of the Estates General in Blois in 1576, Du Perron tried to find a conciliatory solution and convinced the Pope to revoke the excommunication of Henri IV. In 1614, Du Perron represented the clergy at the meeting of the Estates General and pronounced himself against the independence of the Crown from the Holy See.

argument was, that the royal authority was dependent on the head of the church.

The Edict of Nantes had been promulgated in 1598, and the blood of Henri IV, shed by the adherents of the League, had hardly ceased to flow when the Protestants among the nobles and Third Estate demanded, in 1614, in the declaration relative to religion, a confirmation of the articles in the edict of Henri, which established the toleration of their form of religion; but this request was rejected.

M. de Mesme, *lieutenant civil,* addressing the nobles on the part of the Third Estate, declared that the three orders ought to consider themselves as three brothers, of whom the Third Estate was the youngest. Baron de Senneci answered in the name of the nobles that the Third Estate had no title to this fraternity, *being neither of the same blood nor of equal virtue.*[2] The clergy required permission to collect tithes in all kinds of fruit and corn, and an exemption from the excise duties paid on articles brought into the towns, as well as from contributing to the expense of the roads; they also required further restraints on the liberty of the press. The nobles demanded that the principal offices of state should be bestowed on men of family only, and that the commoners (*roturiers*) should be forbidden the use of arquebuses, pistols, and even of dogs, unless houghed, to prevent their being employed in the chase. They required, also, that the commoners should pay further seignorial duties to the proprietors of fiefs; that all pensions granted to the Third Estate should be suppressed, while their own body should be exempt from personal arrest and from all taxes on the product of their lands. They asked, further, a right to receive salt from the king's granaries at the same price as the merchants; and, finally, that the Third Estate should be obliged to wear a different dress from that of persons of family.

I abridge this extract from the Minutes of the Assembly of 1614, and could point out a number of other ridiculous things, were not our attention wholly required by those that are revolting. It is, however, quite enough to prove that the separation of the three orders served only to give oc-

2. The Baron of Senneci (or Senecey) was one of the most respected members of the nobility at the meeting of the Estates General in 1576.

casion to the constant demands of the nobles to escape taxes, to secure new privileges, and to subject the Third Estate to all the humiliations that arrogance can invent. A claim of exemption from taxes was made in like manner by the clergy, and accompanied with all the vexatious demands of intolerance. As to the public welfare, it seemed to affect only the Third Estate, since the weight of taxation fell totally upon them. Such was the spirit of that assembly, which it was proposed to revive in the Estates General of 1789; and M. Necker is to this day censured for having desired to introduce modifications into such a course of proceeding.[3]

3. Madame de Staël's description of the separation between the three orders is similar to Tocqueville's analysis in *The Old Régime and the Revolution*, vol. 1.

CHAPTER XIV

The Division of the Estates General into Orders.

The Estates General of France were, as I have just mentioned, divided into three orders—the clergy, the nobility, and the Third Estate—and accustomed to deliberate separately, like three distinct nations: each presented its grievances to the King, and each confined itself to its particular interests, which had, according to circumstances, more or less connection with the interests of the public at large. In point of numbers, the Third Estate comprised almost the whole nation, the two other orders forming scarcely a hundredth part of it. Having gained greatly in relative importance in the course of the last two centuries, the Third Estate demanded, in 1789, that the mercantile body, or the towns, without reference to the country, should have enough deputies to render the number of the representatives of their body equal to that of the two other orders together; and this demand was supported by motives and circumstances of the greatest weight.

The chief cause of the liberty of England has been the uniform practice of deliberating in two chambers instead of three. In no country where the three orders have remained separate has a free form of government as yet been established. The division into four orders, as is at present the case in Sweden, and was formerly in Aragon, is productive of delay in public business; but it is much more favorable to liberty.[1] The order of peasants in Sweden, and in Aragon the equestrian order, gave two equal shares to the representatives of the nation, and to the privileged classes of the first

---

1. In Sweden, the four estates were the nobility, the clergy, the bourgeoisie, and the peasants. The Cortés of Aragon comprised the nobility, the knights, the clergy, and the "people."

rank; for the equestrian order, which may be compared to the House of Commons in England, naturally supported the interests of the people. The result, therefore, of the division into four orders was that in these two countries, Sweden and Aragon, liberal principles were early introduced and long maintained. Sweden has still to desire that her constitution be assimilated to that of England; but we cannot fail to respect that feeling of justice which, from the earliest time, admitted the order of peasants into the Diet. The peasantry of Sweden are accordingly enlightened, happy, and religious, because they have enjoyed that sentiment of tranquillity and dignity which can arise only from free institutions. In Germany the clergy have had seats in the upper house, but without constituting a separate order, and the natural division into two chambers has been always maintained. Three orders have existed only in France and in a few states, such as Sicily, which did not form a separate monarchy. This unfortunate division, having had the effect of giving always a majority to the privileged classes against the nation, has often induced the French people to prefer arbitrary power in the Crown to that dependence on the aristocratic orders, in which they were placed by such division in three orders.

Another inconvenience in France arose from the number of gentry of the second order, ennobled but yesterday, either by the letters of *noblesse* granted by the kings, as a sequel to the enfranchisement of the Gauls, or by purchased offices, such as that of secretary to the King, &c. which had the effect of associating new individuals to the rights and privileges of the old nobility. The nation would have willingly submitted to the preeminence of the families whose names are distinguished in history, and who, I can affirm, without exaggeration, do not in France exceed two hundred. But the hundred thousand nobles, and the hundred thousand clergy, who laid their claim for privileges equal to those of MM. de Montmorency, de Grammont, de Crillon, &c., created general discontent; for merchants, capitalists, and men of letters were at a loss to understand the superiority granted to a title acquired by money or obsequiousness, and to which a term of twenty-five years was deemed sufficient to give admittance to the chamber of nobles, and to privileges of which the most respected members of the Third Estate were deprived.

The House of Peers in England is an assemblage of patrician magistrates, indebted for its origin, no doubt, to the ancient recollections of chivalry; but entirely associated with institutions of a very different nature. Admission into it is daily obtained by eminence, sometimes in commerce, but particularly in the law; while the duty of national representatives, discharged by the peers in the state, affords the nation an assurance of the utility of the institution. But what advantage could the French derive from those Viscounts of the Garonne, or those Marquisses of the Loire, who not only did not pay their proportion of taxes to the state, but could not even be received at court, since for that purpose a proof of nobility for more than four centuries was necessary, and most of them could go hardly fifty years back? The vanity of this class of people could be displayed only on their inferiors, and these inferiors were twenty-four million in number.

It may be conducive to the dignity of an established church that there be archbishops and bishops in the Upper House, as in England. But what improvement could be ever accomplished in a country where the Catholic clergy composed a third of the representation and had an equal voice with the nation itself, even in legislative measures? Was it likely that this clergy would give its consent to religious toleration, or to the admission of Protestants to public offices? Did it not obstinately refuse the equalization of taxes, that it might keep up the form of free gifts, which increased its importance with government? When Philip the Tall[2] dismissed churchmen from the *Parlement of Paris,* he said "that they ought to be too much occupied with spiritual matters to have time for temporal ones." Why have they not all along submitted to this wise maxim?

Never was there any thing decisive done by the Estates General, merely from their unfortunate division into three instead of two orders. The Chancellor de l'Hôpital could not obtain his edict of peace, even temporarily, except from a convocation at St. Germains, in 1562, in which, by a rare accident, the clergy were not present.

The Assemblies of Notables, called together by the kings, almost all

---

2. Philip the Tall (Philip V), King of France (from 1316) and King of Navarre (as Philip II, from 1314), who largely succeeded in restoring the royal power to what it had been under his father, Philip IV, did not convoke the clergy to all the sessions of the *Parlement of Paris.*

decided by individual votes; and the parliament, which in 1558 had at first consented to form a fourth and separate order, required in 1626 to vote individually in an Assembly of Notables, that they might not be distinguished from the nobility.[3] The endless fluctuations exhibited in all the usages of France are more conspicuous in the composition of the Estates General than in any other political institution. Were we to insist obstinately on the past, as forming an immutable law for the present, we should be immersed in endless disputes, and should find that the past, which is brought forward as our guide, was itself founded on an alteration of an earlier "past." Let us return then to matters that are less equivocal; the events of which we have been eyewitnesses.

The Archbishop of Sens, acting in the King's name, invited the eminent writers of the day to publish their opinion on the mode of convening the Estates General. Had there existed constitutional laws decisive of the question, would the minister of the Crown have consulted the nation in this respect, through the medium of the press? The Archbishop of Sens, in establishing provincial assemblies, had not only rendered in them the number of deputies of the Third Estate equal to that of the two other orders collectively, but he had determined in the King's name, that the voting should take place individually. The public mind was thus strongly prepared, both by the measures of the Archbishop of Sens and by the strength of the Third Estate itself, to obtain for the latter, in 1789, a larger share of influence than in antecedent assemblies of the Estates General. There was no law to fix the number of the three orders; the only established principle was that each order should have one voice. Had not a legal provision been made for a double representation of the Third Estate, it was undoubted that the nation, irritated at the refusal of its demand, would have sent a still greater number of deputies to the Estates General. Thus, all those symptoms of a political crisis, of which it is the part of a statesman to take cognizance, indicated the necessity of giving way to the spirit of the age.

3. The Assembly of Notables of 1558 comprised the three traditional orders and the presidents of the *parlements* of the kingdom, which formed a special order in itself. The Assembly of Notables that met in 1626 addressed the serious budgetary problems facing France at that time.

Yet M. Necker did not take on himself to follow the course, which, in his own judgment, would have been the best; and confiding, it must be admitted, too much in the power of reason, he advised the King to assemble once more the Notables already convoked by M. de Calonne. The majority of these Notables, consisting of the privileged classes, were adverse to doubling the representatives of the Third Estate. One division only of the Assembly gave an affirmative opinion, and that division was under the presidency of Monsieur (now Louis XVIII). It is gratifying to think that a king, the first author of a constitutional charter proceeding from the throne,[4] was at that time in unison with the people on the important question which the aristocrats still seek to represent as the cause of the overthrow of the monarchy.

M. Necker has been blamed for consulting the Notables without following their opinion—his fault lay in consulting them at all; but could anyone imagine that those privileged members of that Assembly, which had lately shown itself so adverse to the abuse of royal authority, should so soon defend the unjust claims of their own, with a pertinacity so much at variance with the opinion of the nation?

Yet M. Necker suspended the decision of the question of doubling the Third Estate as soon as he saw that a majority of the Notables differed from him; and there elapsed more than two months between the close of their Assembly and the decision of the council on 27th December, 1788. During this interval, M. Necker studied constantly the public feeling as the compass which, on this point, ought to guide the decisions of the King. The unanimity of the provinces was positive in regard to the necessity of granting the demands of the Third Estate, for the party of the unmixed aristocrats (*aristocrats purs*) was, as it had ever been, far from numerous; many of the nobles and clergy of the class of *curés* had gone over to the public opinion. The province of Dauphiny assembled, at Romans, its ancient states, whose meetings had long been discontinued, and admitted there not only the doubling of the deputies of the Third Estate, but the voting individually. A number of officers of the army discovered a dis-

---

4. Allusion to the Charter of 1814 granted by Louis XVIII on his return to the throne of France in 1814.

position to favor the popular wish. All, whether men or women, who in the higher circles exercised influence on the public opinion, spoke warmly in favor of the national cause. Such was the prevailing fashion; it was the result of the whole of the eighteenth century; and the old prejudices, which still favored antiquated institutions, had at that time much less strength than at any other period during the twenty-five years that ensued. In short, the ascendancy of the popular wish was so great that it carried along with it the parliament itself. No body ever showed itself more ardent in the defense of ancient usages than the *Parlement of Paris;* every new institution seemed to it an act of rebellion, because, in fact, its own existence could not be founded on the principles of political liberty. Offices that were purchased by the occupants, a judicial body pretending to a right to pass bills for taxes, yet renouncing that right at the command of the King; all these contradictions, which could only be the result of chance, were ill calculated to bear discussion; consequently, they appeared singularly suspicious in the French magistracy. All requisitions against the liberty of the press proceeded from the *Parlement of Paris;* and if they opposed a limit to the active exercise of the royal authority, they, on the other hand, encouraged that kind of ignorance, which is of all things most favorable to absolute power. A body so strongly attached to ancient usages, and yet composed of men entitled by their virtues in private life to much esteem, decided the question naturally enough, by declaring that, as the number of the deputies of each order was not fixed by any usage or any law, it remained to be regulated by the wisdom of the King. This took place in the beginning of December, 1788, two months after the Assembly of the Notables.*

---

* Extract of the decree of Parlement of 5th Dec. 1788, the peers being present.

Considering the actual situation of the nation, &c., this court declares that, in distinguishing in the Estates General of 1614, the convoking, the composition, and the number:

In regard to the first point the court must call for the form established at that period; that is, convoking by bailiwicks and senechalships, not by governments or *généralités;* this form, sanctioned century after century by many examples, and by the last Estates, being the only method to obtain a complete assemblage of the electors in the legal form before officers independent from their situation.

In regard to the composition of the Assembly, the court neither could nor ought to infringe in the slightest manner on the right of the electors; a right founded in nature,

What! could the body that was considered as the representative of the past, yielding to the opinion of the day, relinquish indirectly on this oc-

---

in the constitution, and hitherto respected—that of committing their powers to the citizens whom they judge most deserving of them.

In respect to the number, that of the respective deputies not being determined by any law, or any usage, for any of the orders, it has not been within the powers or intention of this court to decide it; the said court can only trust to the wisdom of the King for the measures necessary to arrive at that course which reason, liberty, justice, and the general wish shall point out. The said *Parlement* has further decreed that the said Lord the King should be most humbly entreated to permit no longer delay in assembling the Estates General, and to take into his consideration, that there would be no cause for agitation in the public mind or disquietude in the orders, if he were pleased, on calling together that assembly, to declare as sacred

The future assembling of the Estates General;

Their right to assign, as a security, certain fixed taxes to the public creditors; their duty to the people to grant no other tax without defining it both as to amount and duration; their right to fix and appropriate freely the funds of each department at the demand of the King;

The resolution of our said Lord the King to take steps to suppress all taxes which constitute a distinction between the higher orders and the class which alone supports them, and to replace them by taxes payable equally by the kingdom at large;

The responsibility of ministers;

The right of the Estates General to bring actions before the courts of justice in all cases that directly interest the nation at large, without prejudicing the rights of the King's *procureur general* in similar cases;

A connection between the Estates General and the higher courts of justice, of such a nature that the courts ought not, and cannot, suffer the collection of any tax unless legally voted, nor further the execution of any law not passed by the Estates General;

The individual liberty of citizens by the obligation to bring every man detained in a royal prison forthwith before his natural judges;

And the legitimate liberty of the press, the only prompt and sure resource of men of character against the licentiousness of the worthless; leaving, however, the author or publisher answerable for his writings after they are printed.

By means of these preliminary arrangements, which are from this moment in the hands of His Majesty, and without which there cannot exist a truly national assembly, it appears to this court that the King would afford the members of the magistracy the most gratifying return for their zeal, by procuring to the nation, by means of well-established liberty, all the happiness to which it is entitled.

Decrees, consequently, that the motives, the principles, and the wishes of this decree shall be laid before our Lord the King, through the medium of very humble and respectful supplication.

casion the maintenance of ancient customs![5] and could the minister, whose whole strength lay in his respect for the nation, have taken on himself to refuse that nation what in his conscience he thought equitable; what in his judgment he deemed necessary!

But this is not all. At that time the adversaries of the King's authority were the privileged orders, while the Third Estate were desirous of rallying round the Crown; and had not the King withdrawn himself from the representatives of the Third Estate after the opening of the Estates General, there is not a doubt that they would have supported his prerogative. When a sovereign adopts a system in politics, he ought to follow it with constancy, for changes bring on him the disadvantages of all the opposing parties. "A great revolution," said Monsieur (Louis XVIII) to the municipality of Paris, in 1789, "is at hand; the King, by his views, his virtues, and his supreme rank, ought to be at its head." All that wisdom could suggest on the occasion is contained in these words.

M. Necker, in the report accompanying the result of the council of 27th December, announced in the King's name, that his Majesty would grant the suppression of the *lettres de cachet,* the liberty of the press, and the reassembling of the Estates General at stated periods for the revision of the finances.[6] He endeavored to snatch from the future deputies the good they were desirous of doing, that he might engross the affection of the people for the King. And no resolution, that ever proceeded from a throne, was productive of such enthusiasm as the result of the council. Addresses of congratulation arrived from all parts of the kingdom; and among the numberless letters received by M. Necker, two of the most remarkable were those from the Abbé, afterward Cardinal, Maury, and from M. de Lamoignon. The royal authority had at that time more power over the public mind than ever; the nation admired that strength of reason, and that can-

5. In its session of September 25, 1788, the members of the *Parlement of Paris* voted in favor of upholding the forms of the 1614 meeting of the Estates General. Public opinion forced them to change their view three months later.

6. The council of December 27, 1788, that established the number of deputies of the Third Estate made no decision on the seminal issue of voting by order or by head. Necker's comments on this issue can be found in *De la Révolution française*, pt. I, 64–67. On this issue, also see Doyle, *The Oxford History of the French Revolution*, 92–94.

dor, which made the King anticipate the reforms demanded by it; while the Archbishop of Sens had placed him in the most precarious situation by advising him to refuse today what he was obliged to grant tomorrow.

To profit, however, by this popular enthusiasm, it was necessary to proceed firmly in the same road. But six months after, the King followed a perfectly opposite plan; why, then, should M. Necker be accused of events which resulted from the rejection of his opinion and the adoption of that of the opposite party? When an unskillful commander loses a campaign victoriously begun by another, is it ever said that the victor of the early part is answerable for the defeat of a successor, whose manner of seeing and acting is entirely different? Some, however, will ask, was not the voting individually, instead of by orders, the natural result of doubling the representatives of the Third Estate; and have we not seen the consequence of the union of the three orders in one assembly? The natural consequence of the doubling of the Third Estate would have been deliberating in two chambers; and far from fearing such a result, it ought to have been desired. Why, then, will M. Necker's adversaries say, did not he make the King express a resolution on this point at the time that the royal consent was given to doubling the deputies? He did not do it because he thought that a change of such a nature ought to be concerted with the representatives of the nation; but he proposed it as soon as these representatives were assembled. Unfortunately, the aristocratic party opposed it, and ruined France in ruining themselves.

A scarcity of corn, such as had not for a long time been felt in France, threatened Paris with famine in the winter of 1788, 1789. The infinite exertions of M. Necker, and the deposit of his own fortune, the half of which he had placed in the treasury, were the means of preventing incalculable calamities. Nothing excites so strong a disposition to discontent among the people as a dread of scarcity; yet, such was their confidence in the administration, that no tumult whatever occurred.

The Estates General bade fair to meet under favorable auspices; the privileged orders could not, from their situation, abandon the throne, although they had shaken it; the deputies of the Third Estate were grateful for the attention shown to their demands. There still remained, it is true, very serious subjects of contention between the nation and the privileged classes; but the King was so placed as to act the part of arbiter, by reducing his own power to a limited monarchy: if indeed the name of reduction can be given to the erection of barriers, which defend you from your own errors, and still more from those of your ministers. A monarchy wisely limited may be compared to an honest man, in whose soul conscience always presides over conduct.

The act of the council of 27th December was adopted by the ablest ministers of the Crown, such as MM. de St. Priest, de Montmorin, and de la Luzerne; the Queen herself thought proper to be present at the debate on doubling the members of the Third Estate. It was the first time that she appeared at council; and the approbation given spontaneously by her to the measure proposed by M. Necker might be considered in the light of an additional sanction; but M. Necker, acting in fulfillment of his duty, necessarily took the responsibility on himself. The whole nation, with the exception of perhaps a few thousand individuals, were at that time of his opinion; since then, none but the friends of justice and of political liberty, such as it was understood on the opening of the Estates General, have remained consistent during twenty-five years of vicissitude. They are few in number, and death thins them daily; but death alone has the power of diminishing this faithful army; for neither corruption nor terror would be able to detach the most obscure combatant from its ranks.

CHAPTER XV

What Was the Public Feeling of Europe at the Time of Convening the Estates General?

Philosophic views, that is, the appreciation of things from reason, and not from habit, had made so much progress in Europe that the possessors of privileges, whether kings, nobles, or clergy, were the first to confess the unfairness of the advantages they enjoyed. They wished to preserve them, but they laid claim to the honor of being indifferent about them; and the more dexterous among them flattered themselves that they could lull the public opinion so as to prevent its contesting the retention of that which they had the appearance of disdaining.

The Empress Catherine professed to follow Voltaire; Frederic II was almost his rival in literature; Joseph II was the most decided philosopher in his dominions; the King of France had twice taken, in America and in Holland, the part of the subjects against their prince;[1] his policy had led him to support the one against their king, the other against their Stadtholder. In England the state of feeling, on all political principles, was quite in harmony with the constitution; and, before the French Revolution, there was certainly a stronger spirit of liberty in England than at present.

M. Necker was then perfectly right when he said, in the act of council of 27th December (1788), that the voice of Europe invited the King to consent to the wishes of the nation. The English constitution, which it then desired, it again calls for at the present day.[2] Let us examine, with impartiality, what are the storms which drove her from that haven, in which alone she can find a secure retreat.

1. It will be recalled that France supported not only the Americans in their War of Independence against England but also the Dutch patriots (1783–87).
2. This passage was most likely written during Napoléon's reign, before the Charter of 1814, which took inspiration from the unwritten English constitution. For more information, see Furet, *Revolutionary France*, 211–66.

CHAPTER XVI

Opening of the Estates General
on the 5th of May, 1789.

I shall never forget the hour that I saw the twelve hundred deputies of France[1] pass in procession to church to hear mass, the day before the opening of the assembly. It was a very imposing sight, and very new to the French; all the inhabitants of Versailles, and many persons attracted by curiosity from Paris, collected to see it. This new kind of authority in the state, of which neither the nature nor the strength was as yet known, astonished the greater part of those who had not reflected on the rights of nations.

The higher clergy had lost a portion of its influence with the public, because a number of prelates had been irregular in their moral conduct, and a still greater number employed themselves only in political affairs. The people are strict in regard to the clergy, as in regard to women; they require from both a close observance of their duties. Military fame, which is the foundation of reputation to the nobility, as piety is to the clergy, could now only appear in the past. A long peace had deprived those noblemen who would have most desired it of the opportunity of rivaling their ancestors; and all the great lords of France were now illustrious obscures. The nobility of the second rank had been equally deprived of opportunities of distinction, as the nature of the government left no opening to nobles but the military profession. The nobles of recent origin were seen in great numbers in the ranks of the aristocracy; but the plume and sword did not become them; and people asked why they took their station with the first class in the country, merely because they had obtained an

1. The Estates General consisted of twelve hundred deputies. For more information, see Doyle, *The Oxford History of the French Revolution*, 93–111.

exemption from their share of the taxes; for in fact their political rights were confined to this unjust privilege.

The nobility having fallen from its splendor by its courtier habits, by its intermixture with those of recent creation, and by a long peace; the clergy possessing no longer that superiority of information which had marked it in days of barbarism, the importance of the deputies of the Third Estate had augmented from all these considerations. Their black cloaks and dresses, imposing numbers, and confident looks fixed the attention of the spectators. Literary men, merchants, and a great number of lawyers formed the chief part of this order.[2] Some of the nobles had got themselves elected deputies of the Third Estate, and of these the most conspicuous was the Comte de Mirabeau.[3] The opinion entertained of his talents was remarkably increased by the dread excited by his immorality; yet it was that very immorality that lessened the influence which his surprising abilities ought to have obtained for him. The eye that was once fixed on his countenance was not likely to be soon withdrawn: his immense head of hair distinguished him from amongst the rest, and suggested the idea that, like Samson, his strength depended on it; his countenance derived expression even from its ugliness; and his whole person conveyed the idea of irregular power, but still such power as we should expect to find in a tribune of the people.

His name was as yet the only celebrated one among the six hundred deputies of the Third Estate; but there were a number of honorable men, and not a few that were to be dreaded. The spirit of faction began to hover over France, and was not to be overcome but by wisdom or power. If therefore public opinion had by this time undermined power, what was to be accomplished without wisdom?

2. The reader may find it interesting to compare Madame de Staël's ideas on this topic with Burke's sarcastic description of the nefarious role played by lawyers in the Constituent Assembly.

3. Honoré Gabriel Riqueti, Comte de Mirabeau (1749–91), was a prominent French orator and statesman who played a leading role in the debates of the Constituent Assembly until his untimely death in April 1791. For an excellent selection of his political writings (discourses and notes), see Chaussinand-Nogaret, ed., *Mirabeau entre le roi et la Révolution.*

I was placed at a window near Madame de Montmorin, the wife of the Minister of Foreign Affairs, and I confess I gave myself up to the liveliest hope on seeing national representatives for the first time in France. Madame de Montmorin, a woman nowise distinguished for capacity, said to me, in a decided tone and in a way which made an impression upon me, "You do wrong to rejoice; this will be the source of great misfortunes to France and to us." This unfortunate woman perished on the scaffold along with one of her sons; another son drowned himself; her husband was massacred on the 2d of September;[4] her eldest daughter died in the hospital of a prison; and her youngest daughter, Madame de Beaumont, an intelligent and generous creature, sank under the pressure of grief before the age of thirty.[5] The family of Niobe was not doomed to a more cruel fate than that of this unhappy mother; one would have said that she had a presentiment of it.

The opening of the Estates General took place the next day; a large hall had been hastily erected in the avenue of Versailles to receive the deputies.[6] A number of spectators were admitted to witness the ceremony. A platform floor was raised to receive the King's throne, the Queen's chair of state, and seats for the rest of the royal family.

The Chancellor, M. de Barentin, took his seat on the stage of this species of theater; the three orders were, if I may so express myself, in the pit, the clergy and nobility to the right and left, the deputies of the Third Estate in front. They had previously declared that they would not kneel on the entrance of the King, according to an ancient usage still practiced on the last meeting of the Estates General. Had the deputies of the Third Estate put themselves on their knees in 1789, the public at large, not excepting the proudest aristocrats, would have termed the action ridiculous, that is, wholly inconsistent with the opinions of the age.

When Mirabeau appeared, a low murmur was heard throughout the assembly. He understood its meaning; but stepping along the hall to his

4. Reference to the massacres of September 2, 1792.

5. In reality, at thirty-five, not thirty.

6. Reference to La Salle des Menus Plaisirs, Avenue de Paris, at Versailles, an older store transformed to accommodate the Assembly of Notables in 1787. It was reshaped to accommodate the meeting of the Estates General.

seat with a lofty air, he seemed as if he were preparing to produce sufficient trouble in the country to confound the distinctions of esteem as well as all others. M. Necker was received with bursts of applause the moment he entered; his popularity was then at its height; and the King might have derived the greatest advantage from it, by remaining steadfast in the system of which he had adopted the fundamental principles.

When the King came to seat himself on his throne in the midst of this assembly, I felt, for the first time, a sensation of fear. I observed that the Queen was much agitated; she came after the appointed time, and her color was visibly altered. The King delivered his discourse in his usual unaffected manner; but the looks of the deputies were expressive of more energy than that of the monarch, and this contrast was disquieting at a time when, nothing being as yet settled, strength was requisite to both sides.

The speeches of the King, the Chancellor, and M. Necker all pointed to the reinstatement of the finances. That of M. Necker contained a view of all the improvements of which the administration was capable; but he hardly touched on constitutional questions; and confining himself to cautioning the Assembly against the precipitation of which it was too susceptible, he made use of a phrase which has since passed into a proverb, "*Ne soyez pas envieux du temps*"—"do not expect to do at once that which can be accomplished only by time." On the rising of the Assembly, the popular party, that is, the majority of the Third Estate, a minority of the nobility, and several members of the clergy, complained that M. Necker had treated the Estates General like a provincial administration, in speaking to them only of measures for securing the public debt and improving the system of taxation. The grand object of their assembling was, doubtless, to form a constitution; but could they expect that the King's minister should be the first to enter on questions which it belonged to the representatives of the nation to introduce?

On the other hand, the aristocratic party, having seen from M. Necker's speech that in the course of eight months he had sufficiently reinstated the finances to be able to go on without new taxes, began to blame the minister for having convened the Estates General, since there was no imperious call for them on the score of money. They no doubt forgot that the promise of convening them had been given by the Crown before the recall of M. Necker. In this, as in almost every other point, he observed a medium; for he would not go the length of saying to the representatives of the people, "Employ yourselves only on a constitution"; and still less would he consent to relapse into the arbitrary system, by contenting himself with momentary resources, that would neither have given a stable assurance to the public creditors, nor have satisfied the people in regard to the appropriation of its sacrifices.[7]

7. The importance of finding a middle way between the extremes was also emphasized by Necker in *De la Révolution française*, pt. I, 34–35, 137–38.

Of the Resistance of the Privileged Orders to the Demands of the Third Estate in 1789.

M. de la Luzerne, Bishop of Langres, one of the soundest minds in France, wrote, on the opening of the Estates General, a pamphlet to propose that the three orders should form themselves into two chambers, the higher clergy uniting with the Peers, and the lower with the Commons.[1] The Marquiss of Montesquiou, afterward a general, made a motion to this effect in the Chamber of the nobility, but in vain. In short, all enlightened men felt the necessity of putting an end to this manner of deliberating in three bodies, each of which could impose a *veto* upon the other; for, to say nothing of its injustice, it rendered the public business interminable.

In social, as in natural order, there are certain principles from which we cannot depart without creating confusion. The three powers, monarchy, aristocracy, and democracy, are in the essence of things; they exist in all governments, as action, preservation, and renewal exist in the course of nature.[2] If you introduce into the political organization a fourth power, the clergy, who are all or nothing, according as they are considered, you can no longer establish definite reasoning on the laws necessary for the

---

1. A reference to *Forme d'opiner aux États généraux* (Paris, 1789), to which Mirabeau responded.

2. For a history of the concept of mixed government, see Blythe, *Ideal Government and the Mixed Constitution in the Middle Ages.* Blythe pointed out that "a mixed government in its broadest sense is any one in which power is shared by at least two of these groups, or one in which there is a combination of two or more simple forms of government. The sharing or combination may be accomplished institutionally or by incorporating procedures thought to characterize various forms" (11).

public welfare, because you are embarrassed by secret authorities, where you ought to admit no guidance but the public interest.

France, at the time the Estates General were assembled, was threatened by two great dangers, financial bankruptcy and famine; and both required speedy relief. How would it have been possible to adopt expeditious measures while each order had its *veto?* The two first would not consent to an unconditional equality of taxes, while the nation at large demanded that this measure should be employed, before any other, for the re-establishment of the finances. The privileged classes had indeed said that they would accede to this equality, but they had taken no formal resolution to that effect; and they had still the power of deciding on what concerned them, according to the ancient plan of deliberating. The mass of the nation had thus no decisive influence, although it bore the great proportion of the burdens. This made the deputies of the Third Estate insist on voting individually, while the nobility and clergy argued for voting by the order.[3] The dispute on this point began from the moment that the powers were verified; and from that moment also, M. Necker proposed a plan of reconciliation which, though very favorable to the higher orders, might have been accepted by the Third Estate, as the question was still under negotiation.[4] To all the obstacles inherent in the plan of deliberating in three orders, we are to add the imperative orders (*mandats impératifs*), that is, instructions from the electors, imposing on the deputies the necessity of conforming their opinions to the will of their constituents on the principal subjects discussed in the Assembly.[5] This antiquated usage was suitable

3. For more details on voting procedures in the Estates General, see Doyle, *The Oxford History of the French Revolution*, 96–111. Mousnier's *Les institutions de la France sous la monarchie absolue* also contains valuable information.

4. On June 4, 1789, Necker proposed that the verification of powers be done by each order and that results be communicated by each order to the two others. The contested deputies were supposed to be examined by a committee consisting of members of all three orders and, if necessary, by the King himself.

5. For more information on the debate on imperative mandates, see Carré de Malberg, *Contribution à la théorie générale de l'État*. It will be recalled that in *Considérations sur le gouvernement de Pologne*, Rousseau acknowledged the need for a mandate-based system of representation and made an important distinction between representatives and deputies. He insisted that the deputies of the people ought to be subject to imperative mandates. In his

only to the infancy of a representative government. Public opinion had hardly any weight in an age when the communication between one province and another was a matter of difficulty, and particularly when there were no newspapers, either to suggest ideas or communicate intelligence. But to oblige deputies in our days to adhere strictly to provincial instructions would have been to make the Estates General an assembly with little other power than that of laying petitions on the table. The information acquired in debate would have been fruitless, since they would have had no power to deviate from their previous instructions. Yet it was on these imperative orders that the nobles rested their chief arguments for refusing to vote individually. But one part of them, those of Dauphiny, had brought a positive instruction never to deliberate by order.

A minority of the nobility, that is, more than sixty members, whose families were most illustrious, but who, by their information, were fully on a level with the spirit of the age, were desirous that, as far as regarded the plan of a constitution, the mode of voting should be individually; but the majority of their order, supported by a portion of the clergy (although the latter were comparatively moderate), showed an inveterate objection to any mode of conciliation. They declared themselves ready to give up their privilege of exemption from taxes; but instead of taking a formal resolution to that effect on the opening of the meetings, they wanted to make that an object of negotiation which the nation regarded as a right. Time was thus lost in caviling, in polite refusals, and in new difficulties. When the Third Estate raised their tone and showed their strength, supported by the wish of the nation, the nobles of the court gave way, accustomed, as they were, to yield to power; but no sooner did the crisis appear to be solved than they resumed their arrogance and seemed to despise the Third Estate, as in the days when vassals solicited enfranchisement from their lords.

---

political writings, Sieyès opposed imperative mandates in categorical terms: "For the deputy there is, and can be, no imperative mandate, or indeed no positive will, except that of the national will. He needs to defer to the councils of those who directly elect him only in so far as these councils are in conformity with the national will. And where else can this will exist, where else can it be recognized except in the National Assembly itself?" (Sieyès as quoted in Forsyth, *Reason and Revolution,* 138)

The provincial nobility was still less tractable than the nobility of the first rank. The latter were certain of preserving their existence—they were guaranteed by historical recollections; but the petty nobles, whose titles were known only to themselves, saw themselves in danger of losing distinctions which no longer obtained respect from anyone. These personages spoke about their rank with as much presumption as if it had existed before the creation of the world, although it had been only lately acquired. They considered their privileges, which were of no use but to themselves, like that right of property which forms the basis of general security. Privileges are sacred only when conducive to the general advantage; it requires, then, some argument to support them, and they cannot be said to be truly solid, except when sanctioned by public utility. But the chief part of the *noblesse* entrenched themselves in the assertion, "So it was heretofore"— "*C'étoit ainsi jadis.*" Nonetheless, they were told, particular circumstances produced that state of things, and these circumstances are entirely changed: in vain—nothing could operate conviction on them. They were actuated by a certain aristocratic foppery, of which an idea can be formed only in France; a mixture of frivolity in manner and of pedantry in opinion; the whole united to a profound disdain for knowledge and spirit, unless enlisted in the ranks of folly, that is, employed in giving a retrograde course to reason.

In England, the eldest son of a peer is generally a member of the House of Commons, until at his father's death he enters the upper house; the younger sons remain in the body of the nation and form a part of it. An English peer said ingeniously, "I cannot become an aristocrat, for I have constantly beside me representatives of the popular party; these are my younger sons." The ordered arrangement of the different ranks of society is one of the admirable beauties of the English constitution. But in France the effect of custom had been to introduce two things directly contradictory—one, ascribing such a respect to antiquity that a member of the nobility could not step into one of the king's carriages without proofs verified by the court genealogist, and prior in date to the year 1400, that is, prior to the time the kings began to grant nobility by letters patent; while, on the other hand, the greatest importance was attached to the royal prerogative of ennobling by patent. No human power can make a true noble, in the sense implied by that epithet in France; it would imply the power of disposing of the past, which seems impossible even to the Divinity. Yet nothing was easier in France than to become a privileged person, although it was entering into a separate caste, and acquiring, if I may say so, a right to injure the rest of the nation by swelling the number of those who escaped the public burdens, and who thought themselves particularly entitled to government favors. Had the French nobility continued strictly military, the public might long have submitted, from a sentiment of admiration and gratitude, to the continuance of its privileges; but for a century back a *tabouret* at court had been the object of as much solicitation as a regiment in the army. The French nobles were neither members of the legislature as in England, nor sovereign lords as in Germany.[6] What were they, then? They unluckily resembled the *noblesse* of Spain and Italy, and they escaped from the mortifying comparison only by the elegant manners and the information of a certain part of their number; but these persons, in general, renounced the doctrine of their order, and ignorance alone remained to watch over prejudice.

What orators could support this party, abandoned by its most distinguished members? The Abbé Maury, who was far from occupying a conspicuous rank among the French clergy, defended his abbeys under the name of the public good; and M. de Casalès, a captain of cavalry, whose nobility was dated only twenty-five years back, was the champion of the privileges of the nobility in the Constituent Assembly. This man was subsequently one of the first to attach himself to the dynasty of Bonaparte; and Cardinal Maury seemed to do the same with no little readiness.[7] We are thus led to conclude, from these as from other examples, that in our days the advocates of prejudice are by no means slow in bargaining for

6. It would be worth comparing Madame de Staël's ideas on the decline of the French nobility with the thesis of Guizot as outlined in his *History of Civilization in France*, which had an important impact on his famous disciple Tocqueville.

7. Abbé Maury (1746–1817), a member of the French Academy (elected in 1785), served as deputy of the clergy in the Estates General. He went into exile in 1792 and was appointed cardinal two years later. In 1810 Napoléon appointed him Archbishop of Paris. Cazalès (1758–1805) represented the nobility in the Estates General. He went into exile in 1792 and returned to France eleven years later.

their personal interest. The majority of the nobles finding themselves abandoned in 1789 by men of talents and information, proclaimed indiscreetly the necessity of employing force against the popular party. We shall soon see if that force was in existence; but we may venture to say at once, that if it was not in existence, the menace was extremely imprudent.

Conduct of the Third Estate During the First Two Months of the Session of the Estates General.

Several individuals among the nobility and clergy, the first persons in the country, inclined strongly, as we have already said, to the popular party, and there was a great number of intelligent men among the deputies of the Third Estate. We must not form an opinion of the France of that time judging by the France of the present day: twenty-five years of continual danger, of every kind, have unfortunately accustomed the French to employ their faculties only for their personal defense or interest; but in 1789 the country contained a great number of intelligent and philosophic minds.[1] Why, it may be asked, could they not adhere to the government under which they had been thus formed? It was not the government, it was the advanced knowledge of the age which had developed all these talents, and those who felt they possessed them felt also the necessity of exercising them. Yet the ignorance of the people in Paris, and still more in the country, that ignorance which results from the long oppression and

---

1. Madame de Staël refers here to the civic apathy during the First Empire and the first years of the Bourbon Restoration. A similar warning can be found in Benjamin Constant's well-known speech, "The Liberty of the Ancients Compared to That of the Moderns," given at the Athénée Royal in Paris in 1819; the English translation is in Benjamin Constant, *Political Writings*, 309–28. In his turn, Tocqueville also admired the people of 1789 for having real convictions and pursuing noble ideals: "Everybody followed his own convictions boldly, passionately. . . . I have never met with a revolution where one could see at the start, in so many men, a more sincere patriotism, more disinterest, more true greatness. . . . This is 1789, a time of inexperience doubtless, but of generosity, of enthusiasm, of virility, and of greatness, a time of immortal memory." (*The Old Régime and the Revolution*, vol. I, 208, 237, 244)

neglected education of the lower orders, contained the seeds of all those misfortunes which afterward overpowered France.[2] Of distinguished men the country contained perhaps as many as England; but the stock of good sense that belongs to a free nation did not exist in France. Religion founded on inquiry, education generally diffused, the liberty of the press, and the right of voting at public elections, are sources of improvement which had been in operation in England for more than a century. The Third Estate desired that France should be enriched by a part of these advantages; the national wish strongly supported that desire; but the Third Estate, being the strongest party, could have only one merit, that of moderation, and unfortunately it was not in a disposition to adopt it.

There were two parties among the deputies of the Third Estate; the leaders of the one were Mounier and Malouet[3]—of the other Mirabeau and Sieyès.[4] The former aimed at a constitution in two chambers, and were in hopes of obtaining this change from the nobles and the King by amicable means; the other was superior in point of talent, but unfortunately more guided by passion than opinion.

Mounier had been the leader of the calm and well-planned revolution in Dauphiny. He was a man passionately devoted to reason and moderation. He was enlightened rather than eloquent, but consistent and firm

2. According to Jacques Godechot, on the eve of the Revolution the literacy rate in France was 50 percent for men and only 20 percent for women.

3. Mounier and Malouet belonged to the *monarchiens,* a group that also included Lally-Tollendal and Clermont-Tonnerre. Proponents of a moderate form of monarchy in 1789, they endorsed the initial demands of the Third Estate and demanded that France adopt the principles of constitutionalism of England. In the footsteps of Montesquieu, the *monarchiens* put forward a moderate plan of reform that sought to create a constitutional monarchy in France by reconciling the rights of the monarch with those of the nation. Unfortunately, their middling political project was defeated soon after the fall of the Old Regime and the *monarchiens* slipped into obscurity. For detailed biographical notes about them, see Furet and Halévi, *Orateurs de la Révolution française,* vol. I: *Les Constituants,* 1256–61, 1311–16, 1356–62, 1496–1502. For an analysis of their political thought, see Griffith's *Le Centre perdu: Malouet et les "monarchiens" dans la Révolution française.* For a brief presentation of the *monarchiens,* see Ran Halévi's entry in *A Critical Dictionary of the French Revolution,* 370–79.

4. For a recent English translation, see Emmanuel Joseph Sieyès, *Political Writings.* For Mirabeau's discourses, see the selection edited by Chaussinand-Nogaret, *Mirabeau entre le roi et la Révolution.*

in his path, so long as it was in his power to choose one.[5] Malouet, whatever might be his situation, was always guided by his conscience. Never did I know a purer mind, and if he lacked anything that prevented him from acting efficiently, it was the fact that in his actions he did not engage enough with other people, trusting always to the self-evidence of truth without sufficiently reflecting on the means of bringing it home to the conviction of others.[6]

Mirabeau, who knew and who foresaw everything, was determined to make use of his thundering eloquence only to gain himself a place in the first rank, from which he had been banished by his immorality. Sieyès was the mysterious oracle of approaching events; he has, undoubtedly, a mind of the greatest compass and strength, but that mind is governed by a very wayward temper; and as it was a matter of difficulty to extort a few words from him, these, from their rarity, passed for little less than orders or prophecies. While the privileged classes were employed in discussing their powers, their interests, their ceremonials; in short, whatever concerned only themselves; the Third Estate invited them to join in a deliberation on the scarcity of provisions and state of the finances. What advantageous ground did the deputies of the people choose, when soliciting a union for such purposes! At last the Third Estate grew weary of these unavailing efforts, and the factious among them rejoiced that the inutility of these attempts seemed to prove the necessity of more energetic measures.

Malouet required that the chamber of the Third Estate should declare itself the assembly of the representatives of the majority of the nation. Nothing could be said against this incontestable title. Sieyès proposed to constitute themselves purely and simply the "National Assembly of France"; and to invite the members of the two orders to join them. A decree passed to this effect, and that decree constituted the Revolution.[7] How important would it have been to have prevented it! But such was the success of this measure that the deputies of the nobility from Dauphiny,

5. For an interesting self-portrait of Mounier, see his preface to *Considérations sur les gouvernements* (Paris, 1789), 4.

6. For more information, see Malouet, *Mémoires*.

7. The debates on this issue had more than a purely symbolical import and paved the way for the Assembly declaring itself the Constituent Assembly on June 20, 1789.

and some of the clergy, acceded immediately to the invitation; the influence of the assembly gained ground every hour. The French are more prompt than any other people in perceiving where strength lies; and partly by calculation, partly by enthusiasm, they press on toward power, and give it additional impulse by rallying under its banners.

The King, as will appear from the next chapter, was much too tardy in interfering in this critical state of things; and, by a blunder, not unfrequent on the part of the privileged classes, who, though always weak, are full of confidence, the grand master of the ceremonies thought proper to shut up the hall of meeting of the Third Estate, that the platform, the carpeting, and other preparations for the reception of the King might be completed. The Third Estate believed, or professed to believe, that they were forbidden to continue their meetings; the troops that were now advancing from all directions to Versailles placed the deputies decidedly on the vantage ground. The danger was sufficiently apparent to give their resistance an air of courage, while it was not so real as to keep back even the timid among them. Accordingly all the members of the Assembly concurred in meeting in the tennis court (*salle du jeu de Paume*) at Versailles, and bound themselves by an oath to maintain the national rights. This oath was not without dignity, and if the privileged classes had been stronger when they were attacked, and the national representatives had made a more moderate use of their triumph, history would have consecrated that day as one of the most memorable in the annals of liberty.[8]

8. The event occurred on June 20, 1789.

CHAPTER XIX

Means Possessed by the Crown in 1789
of Opposing the Revolution.

The true public opinion, which rises superior to faction, has been the same in France for twenty-seven years; and every other direction given to it, being artificial, could have only a temporary influence.

There was at this time no intention of overturning the throne, but a decided determination that laws should not be passed by those who were to execute them; for it was not in the hands of the King, but of his ministers, that the authority of the former arbitrary governments was vested. The French did not, at that time, willingly submit to the singular humility which they are at present required to practice—that of believing themselves unworthy of exercising, like the English, an influence on their own fate.[1]

What objection could be made to this, the almost unanimous wish of France, and to what length ought a conscientious king carry his refusal? Why take on himself alone the responsibility of government, and why should not the information that would accrue to him from an assembly of deputies, composed like the English parliament, be of equal avail to him, as that which he derived from his council or his court? Why substitute for the mutual duties of subject and sovereign, the revived theory of the Jews on divine right? Without at present entering into a discussion, it cannot be denied at least that force is necessary to maintain that theory, and that "divine right" requires a human army to make it manifest to the incredulous. And what were at that time the means of which the royal authority could avail itself?

1. These lines were written during Napoléon's reign.

There seemed only two courses to follow—to triumph over public opinion or to enter into treaty with it. Force! force! is the cry of those men who imagine that they acquire it by pronouncing this word. But in what consists the force of a sovereign unless in the obedience of his troops? Now the army, so early as 1789, was, in a great measure, attached to the popular opinion, against which, on this supposition, it would have had to act. It had hardly been engaged in the field for twenty-five years; it was thus an army of citizens imbrued with the feelings of the nation and proud of being associated with it. Had the King, say some, put himself at its head, he would have carried it along with him. The King had not received a military education, and all the ministers in the world, without excepting such a man as Cardinal Richelieu, are incapable of supplying, in this respect, the personal agency of a monarch. Others may write for him, but they cannot command an army in his stead, particularly when it is to be employed in the interior. Royalty cannot be performed, like certain theatrical exhibitions, where one actor does the gestures while another pronounces the words. Had even the most decided character of modern times, Bonaparte himself, been on the throne, his will would have failed in the contest with popular opinion at the time of the opening of the Estates General. Politics were then a new field for the imagination of Frenchmen; everyone flattered himself with acting a part, everyone saw a personal object in the chances opening in all directions. The course of events, and the spirit of literary publications, for a century back, had prepared the mind of the nation for countless advantages which it thought itself ready to seize.[2] When Napoléon established despotism in France, circumstances were favorable to such a plan; the public was weary of trouble, awed by the remembrance of dreadful misfortunes, and apprehensive of their return by a revival of faction. Besides, the public ardor was turned toward military fame; the war of the Revolution had raised the national pride. Under Louis XVI, on the contrary, the current of public opinion was directed to objects purely philosophical; it had been formed by books, which proposed a number of improvements in the administration of justice and other branches of civil government. The nation had long enjoyed pro-

---

2. Tocqueville and Burke also criticized the "literary style" in politics.

found peace, and war had been, in a manner, out of fashion since the time of Louis XIV. All the activity of the popular mind pointed to a desire of exercising political rights, and all the skill of a statesman consisted in the art of dealing tactfully with this opinion.

So long as it is practicable to govern a country by military force, the task of ministers is easy, and great talents are not necessary to ensure obedience; but if, unfortunately, recourse be had to force, and it fails, the other resource, that of winning the public opinion, is no longer available; it is lost forever from the time that an attempt was made to constrain it. Let us examine on this principle the plans proposed by M. Necker, and those which the King was persuaded to adopt in sacrificing this minister.

CHAPTER XX

The Royal Session of 23d June, 1789.

The secret council of the King was altogether different from his ostensible ministry; a few of the latter shared the opinion of the former; but the acknowledged head of administration, M. Necker, was the very person against whom the privileged classes directed their efforts.

In England the responsibility of ministers is a bar to this double government, by official agents and secret advisers. No act of the royal power being executed without the signature of a minister, and that signature involving a capital punishment to whoever abuses it, even were the king surrounded by chamberlains preaching the doctrine of absolute power, there is no danger that any of them would run the risk of performing as a minister what he might support as a courtier. In France the case was different. Orders were given, without the knowledge of the prime minister, to bring forward regiments of Germans, because dependence could not be placed on the French regiments; it was expected that, with this foreign band, public opinion could be controlled in such a country as was then illustrious France.

The Baron de Breteuil,[1] who aspired to succeed to M. Necker's station, was incapable of understanding anything but the old form of government; and, even in the old form, his ideas had never extended beyond the precincts of a court, either in France or in the foreign countries where he had been sent as ambassador. He cloaked his ambition under an aspect of good nature; he was in the habit of shaking hands in the English manner with all he met, as if he would say, "I should like to be minister; what harm

---

1. Baron Louis Auguste Le Tonnelier de Breteuil (1730–1807). After his fall from power in 1789, he emigrated and served as the King's emissary abroad. He returned to France in 1802.

will that do you?" By dint of repeating that he wished to be minister, he had been introduced into the cabinet, and he had governed as well as another so long as there was nothing to do but subscribe his name to the official papers brought to the minister in a finished state by the clerks. But in the great national crisis on which we are about to enter, his councils caused terrible harm to the cause of the King. His rough voice conveyed an idea of energy; in walking he pressed the ground with a ponderous step, as if he would call an army from below—and his imposing presence deluded those who put all their hopes in their own desires.

When M. Necker asked the King and Queen, "Are you certain of the obedience of the army?" some interpreted the doubt implied in the question as the sign of a factious disposition; for one of the characteristics of the aristocratic party in France is to look with a suspicious eye on a knowledge of facts. These facts are obstinate, and have in vain risen up ten times against the hopes of the privileged classes: they have always attributed them to those who foresaw them, and never to the nature of things. A fortnight after the opening of the Estates General, and before the Third Estate had constituted itself the National Assembly, while the two parties were ignorant of their mutual strength, and while each was looking to government for support, M. Necker laid before the King a sketch of the situation of the kingdom. "Sire," he said,

> I am afraid that you are led into error in regard to the temper of the army: our correspondence with the country makes us conclude that it will not act against the Estates General. Do not then make it draw near to Versailles, as if you intended to make a hostile use of it against the deputies. The popular party does not know yet with certainty the disposition of this army. Make use of this very uncertainty to keep up your authority with the public; for, if the fatal secret of the insubordination of the troops were known, how would it be possible to restrain the factious? The point at present, Sire, is to accede to the reasonable wishes of France; deign to resign yourself to the English constitution; you, personally, will not experience any restraint by the empire of law, for never will it impose on you such barriers as your own scruples; and in thus volunteering to meet the wish of your people, you will grant today as a boon, what they may exact tomorrow as a right.

After making these observations, M. Necker transmitted the sketch of a declaration, which was to have been made by the King a month before the 23d June; that is, long before the Third Estate had declared itself the National Assembly, before the oath at the tennis court, in short, before the deputies had embraced any hostile measure. Concessions on the part of the King would then have had more dignity. The declaration, as composed by M. Necker, was almost word for word similar to the one issued by Louis XVIII at St. Ouen,[2] on the 2d May, 1814, twenty-five years after the opening of the Estates General.* May we not be allowed to believe that the bloody cycle of the last twenty-five years would have been avoided if the executive power had from the first day consented to what the nation then wished, and will always continue to wish?

The success of M. Necker's proposition was to have been secured by an ingenious plan. The King was to order the deputies to vote individually in what related to taxes, while in regard to the privileges, interests, or other matters peculiar to each order, they should continue to deliberate separately, until the settlement of the constitution. The Third Estate, being not sure of carrying the point of individual voting, would have been grateful for obtaining it, in regard to taxes; and this was what justice required, for what Estates General would those be in which a majority, that is, the two orders, who paid comparatively little or nothing, should have decided on burdens to be borne almost entirely by the minority, the Third Estate? The project of M. Necker contained, further, a declaration that the King would, in future, sanction the Estates General in no other shape than as a legislative body in two chambers. This was followed by several popular propositions in regard to legislation and finance, which would have entirely gained the public favor to the declaration. The King adopted it in all its extent, and it is certain that at the first moment it had his approbation. M. Necker was now at the summit of his hopes; for he flattered himself with prevailing on the majority of the deputies of the Third Estate to

* On this spot, St. Ouen, my father passed a great part of his life; and puerile as it may seem, I cannot help being struck with the singular coincidence.

2. In the Declaration of St. Ouen (a suburb of Paris) on May 2, 1814, Louis XVIII endorsed the principles of constitutional monarchy and promised to grant a new constitution. The Charter of 1814 was made public a month later.

accept this well-combined plan, although the more ardent of them were inclined to reject whatever proceeded from the court.[3]

While M. Necker was willingly risking his popularity by coming forward as the defender of an Upper House of Parliament,[4] the aristocratic body, on the other hand, thought themselves robbed of their rights by such a proposition. Each party, during twenty-five years, has, in its turn, rejected and desired the English constitution, according as it was victor or vanquished. In 1792, the Queen said to the Chevalier de Coigny, "I would that I had lost an arm, and that the English constitution had been established in France." The nobility unceasingly wished for it after they had been stripped of their power and property; and under Bonaparte the popular party would, no doubt, have been very well satisfied to have obtained it. It may be said that the English constitution, or, in other words, reason in France, is like the fair Angelica in the comedy of the "Gambler"—he implores her in his distress and neglects her when he is fortunate.[5]

M. Necker was extremely anxious that the King should not lose an instant in interposing his mediation in the debates of the three orders. But the King rested tranquil in the popularity of his minister, and believed that if the proposed interference were necessary, any time might suffice for it. This was a great error. M. Necker had the power of going a certain length; he could put a limit to the claims of the deputies of the Third Estate by granting them a particular point which they were not otherwise sure of obtaining; but if he had renounced that which constituted his strength, I

3. Necker gave a full account of the June 23, 1789, royal council in *De la Révolution française*, pt. I, 175–215. Necker emphasized time and again the errors committed by some of Louis XVI's advisers, who convinced the monarch to reject the necessary compromises demanded by the configuration of political forces in May and June 1789. The King's greatest error was his refusal to accept the reunion of the three orders and his injunction to continue the deliberations separately. This course of action, Necker pointed out, was both imprudent and unwise, because the legitimate demands of the Third Estate, backed by public opinion, were accepted a few days later by a monarch whose authority and power were severely diminished by his inability to make timely concessions.

4. The *monarchiens* also favored an upper house based on the English model, but such a proposal had no chance of swaying public opinion in 1789.

5. Comedy in five acts in verses by Regnard (1696).

mean the essence of his opinions, his influence with them would have sunk lower than that of any other man.

One party among the deputies of the Third Estate, that of which Mounier and Malouet were the leaders, was in concurrence with M. Necker: but the other party aimed at a revolution, and was not contented to accept what it preferred to conquer. While M. Necker was contending with the court for the cause of liberty, he defended the royal authority, and even the nobility, against the Third Estate! All his hours, and all his faculties, were employed to guard the King against the courtiers, and the deputies against the factious.

All this, some will say, does not matter since M. Necker was not successful; the inference is that he lacked ability. For the space of thirteen years, five passed in office and eight in retirement, M. Necker had stood at the summit of popular favor; he still possessed it to such a degree that all France was indignant at the news of his banishment.[6] What, then, can he be said to have lost by his fault? and how, I must repeat it, is a man to be made answerable for misfortunes that occurred because his advice was not followed? If monarchy was overturned in consequence of the adoption of a system contrary to his, is it not likely that it would have been preserved if the King had adhered to the path followed for some time after the return of M. Necker to the ministry?

Not long after that, a day had been fixed for holding a royal session when the secret enemies of M. Necker induced the King to make a journey to Marly, a residence where the voice of the public was heard still less than at Versailles. Courtiers generally place themselves between the prince and the nation, like a deceitful echo, which alters what it repeats. M. Necker relates that, in the evening of the cabinet meeting at which the royal session was to be fixed for the next day, a note from the Queen induced the King to quit the council room; the deliberation was adjourned till next day. By that time two other members were admitted to the council, as well as the King's two brothers.[7] The two members knew no forms

6. The King dismissed Necker on July 11, 1789, and recalled him a few days later.

7. Reference to the future monarchs Louis XVIII and Charles X. Meetings were held at Marly and Versailles, but Necker attended only the first one; his plans were criticized by

but the ancient; and the princes, who were then young, confided too much in the army.

The party which came forward to defend the throne spoke with much disdain of the nature of royal authority in England; they wished to affix something criminal to the idea of reducing a king of France to the hard condition of a British monarch. This view of things was not only erroneous, but the result, perhaps, of selfish calculation; for, in truth, it was not the King, but the nobles, and particularly the nobles of the second class, who were likely, according to their mode of thinking, to lose by becoming the citizens of a free country.

The adoption of the English institutions would neither have lessened the enjoyments of the King, nor the authority which he would and could have exerted. Nor would these institutions have at all lessened the dignity of the great and ancient families of France; so far from that, placing them in the House of Peers, they received a more assured prerogative and were more clearly discriminated from the rest of their order. It was then only the privileges of the second class of nobility and the political influence of the higher clergy which it was necessary to sacrifice. The *parlements* also were apprehensive of losing those long-contested powers, which they had of themselves renounced, but which they still regretted; they perhaps saw, by anticipation, the institution of juries, that safeguard of humanity in the administration of justice. But, once for all, the interest of these orders was not identified with that of the Crown, and, by wishing to make them inseparable, the privileged classes involved the throne in their own fall. Not that their intention was to overturn monarchy; but they desired that monarchy should triumph with them and by them; while matters had come to such a pass that it was unavoidable to sacrifice, sincerely and unequivocally, that which it was impossible to defend, for the sake of preserving the remainder.

Such was the opinion of M. Necker; but it was not that of the new members of the King's council. They proposed various changes, all in conformity with the passions of the majority of the privileged classes. M. Necker combated these new adversaries, during several days, with an en-

---

Chaumont de la Galasière during the second meeting. Necker's account of the royal councils held at Marly and Versailles can be found in *De la Révolution française*, pt. I, 198–201.

ergy surprising in a minister who was certainly desirous of pleasing the King and the royal family. But he was so fully persuaded of the truth of what he affirmed that he discovered in this point a resolution not to be shaken. He foretold the defection of the army if it were employed against the popular party; he predicted that the King would lose all his ascendancy over the Third Estate, by the tone in which it was proposed to compose the declaration; finally, he signified, in respectful terms, that he could not give his support to a plan which was not his, and the consequence of which would, in his opinion, be disastrous.

The court was not disposed to listen to this advice; but they desired M. Necker's attendance at the royal session, for the sake of persuading the deputies of the people that the declaration had his approbation. This M. Necker refused, and sent in his resignation. Yet, said the aristocrats, a part of his plan was retained; true, there remained in the declaration of the 23d June, several of the concessions desired by the nation, such as the suppression of the personal tax (*taille*), the abolition of privileges in regard to taxes, the admission of all citizens to civil and military employments, &c. But things had changed greatly in the course of a month; the Third Estate had acquired a degree of importance which prevented it from feeling grateful for concessions which it was sure of obtaining. M. Necker wished the King to grant the right of individual voting in regard to taxes, in the very outset of his speech; the Third Estate would then have concluded that the object of the royal session was to support its interest, and that would have gained their confidence. But, in the newly modeled plan pressed on the King, the first article invalidated all the resolutions which the Third Estate had taken in its character of National Assembly, and which it had rendered sacred by the oath at the tennis court. M. Necker had proposed the royal session before the deputies had come under such engagements to public opinion. Was it prudent to offer them so much less after their power had become still greater in the interval which the court had lost in vacillation?

Acting in an appropriate and timely manner is the nymph Egeria[8] of

---

8. Egeria was a fountain nymph who advised Numa Pompilius, one of the founders of Rome, in their frequent secret meetings. She subsequently became a byword for wise secret counsel.

all statesmen, generals, and all those who have to do with the ever-changing character of human nature. An authoritative measure against the Third Estate was no longer practicable on the 23d of June; and it was rather the nobles whom the King should have aimed at commanding: for obedience may be a point of honor with them, since it is one of the statutes of ancient chivalry to submit to kings as to military commanders; but implicit obedience on the part of the people is nothing short of subjection, and the spirit of the age ran no longer in that direction. In our days the throne cannot be solidly established but on the power of law.

The King ought by no means to have sacrificed the popularity which he had lately acquired by granting a double number of deputies to the Third Estate. This popularity was of more consequence to him than all the promises of his courtiers. He lost it, however, by his address to the Assembly on the 23d of June; and, although that address contained some very good points, it failed entirely in its effect. Its very outset was repulsive to the Third Estate, and, from that moment forward, that body refused to listen to things which it would have received favorably, could it have been persuaded that the King was inclined to defend the nation against the claims of the privileged classes, and not the latter against the nation.[9]

9. The King's declaration of June 23, 1789, endorsed the old division in three orders and declared void the decisions previously taken by the representatives of the Third Estate. According to Necker, this was an unwise and imprudent decision on the part of the monarch and his closest advisers.

CHAPTER XXI

Events Caused by the Royal Session
of 23d June, 1789.

The predictions of M. Necker were but too fully realized; and that royal session, against which he had said so much, produced consequences still more unfortunate than he had calculated. Hardly had the King left the hall, when the Third Estate, who had continued there after the other orders had withdrawn, declared that it would pursue its deliberations without any attention to what they had just heard. The impulse was given; the royal session, far from attaining the hoped for object, had given new vigor to the Third Estate, and had afforded them the opportunity of a new triumph.

The rumor of M. Necker's resignation now spread abroad, and all the streets of Versailles were instantly filled with the inhabitants, who proclaimed his name. The King and Queen sent for him to the palace on that very evening, and both urged him, in the name of the public safety, to resume his place; the Queen added that the safety of the King's person depended on his continuing in office. How could he decline obeying? The Queen promised solemnly to follow henceforth his council; such was her determination at the time, because she was alarmed by the popular movement: but as she was always under the impression that any limit imposed on the royal authority was a misfortune, she necessarily fell again under the influence of those who viewed matters in the same light.

The King, it cannot be too often repeated, possessed all the virtues necessary for a constitutional monarch; for such a monarch is rather the first magistrate than the military chief of his country. But, though he was very well informed, and read the English historians, in particular, with attention, the descendant of Louis XIV felt a difficulty in relinquishing the doctrine of divine right.[1] That doctrine is considered as a crime of *lèse-majesté* in England, since it is in virtue of a compact with the nation that the present dynasty occupies the throne.[2] But although Louis XVI was by no means stimulated by his disposition to aim at absolute power, that power was the object of a disastrous prejudice, which unfortunately for France and for himself he never wholly renounced.

M. Necker, won by the entreaties which the King and Queen condescended to make to him, promised to continue minister, and spoke only of the future: he by no means disguised the extent of existing danger; but added that he hoped yet to remedy it, provided orders were not given to bring troops around Paris unless the Crown were certain of their obedience. In such a case he must make a point of retiring, and of being satisfied with indulging in private his wishes for the welfare of the King.

There remained only three means of preventing a political catastrophe: the hope which the Third Estate still founded on the personal disposition of the King; the uncertainty of the course which the military might take, an uncertainty which might still keep back the factious; and finally, the popularity of M. Necker. We shall soon see how these resources were lost in the course of a fortnight, by the advice of the committee to which the court gave itself up in private.

On returning from the palace to his house, M. Necker was carried in triumph by the people. Their lively transports are still present to my recollection, and revive in me the emotion which they caused in the joyous season of youth and hope. All the voices which repeated my father's name seemed to me those of a crowd of friends, who shared in my respectful affection. The people had not as yet stained themselves by any crime; they loved their King; they looked on him as deceived, and rallied with friendly

1. Madame de Staël's claim that Louis XVI possessed all the virtues necessary for a constitutional monarch is contradicted by her later statement that he was reluctant to relinquish the doctrine of divine right. It can be argued that Louis XVI was never fully prepared to become a constitutional monarch *à l'anglaise*. Under the influence of his advisers, the King made a number of unfortunate choices (including the flight to Varennes) that contributed significantly to the events of 1789–91.

2. Reference to the Declaration of Rights accepted by William III and Mary II in 1689, inserted later into the Bill of Rights, and ratified by the House of Commons and the House of Peers in October 1689.

warmth around the minister whom they considered as their defender: all was true and upright in their enthusiasm. The courtiers circulated that M. Necker had planned this scene; but, supposing him to have been capable of this, how could anyone succeed in producing, by underhand means, a movement in so vast a multitude? All France took part in it; addresses arrived from every quarter of the country, and in these days addresses expressed the general wish. But one of the great misfortunes of those who live in courts is to be unable to understand rightly what a nation is. They attribute everything to intrigue, yet intrigue can accomplish nothing on public opinion. In the course of the Revolution, we have seen factious men succeed in stirring up this or that party; but in 1789, France was almost unanimous; to attempt struggling against this colossus, with the mere power of aristocratic dignities, was like fighting with toys against real weapons.

The majority of the clergy, the minority of the nobility, and all the deputies of the Third Estate repaired to M. Necker on his return from the palace; his house could hardly contain those who had gathered there, and it was there that we saw the truly amiable traits of the French character; the vivacity of their impressions, their desire to please, and the ease with which a government may win or offend them, according as it addresses itself, well or ill, to that particular kind of imagination of which they are susceptible. I heard my father entreat the deputies of the Third Estate not to carry their claims too far. "You are now," he said, "the strongest party; it is on you then that moderation is incumbent." He described to them the situation of France and the good which they might accomplish; several of them were moved to tears and promised to be guided by his councils; but they asked him, in return, to be responsible to them for the intentions of the King. The royal power still inspired not only respect but a certain degree of fear: these were the sentiments which ought to have been preserved.

One hundred and fifty deputies of the clergy, among whom were several of the higher prelates, had by this time gone over to the National Assembly; forty-seven members of the nobility, most of them placed in the first rank both by birth and talent, had followed them; above thirty others waited only for leave from their constituents to join them. The people called loudly for the union of the three orders, and insulted those of the clergy and nobles who repaired to their separate chamber. M. Necker then proposed to the King to issue an order to the clergy and nobility to deliberate along with the Third Estate, that he might spare them the painful anxiety under which they labored and the vexation of appearing to yield to the power of the people. The King complied, and the royal injunction still produced a surprising effect on the public mind.[3] The nation was grateful to its sovereign for his condescension, although the measure was almost the result of necessity. The majority of the chamber of nobles were favorably received on their junction, although it was known that they had made a protest against the very step which they had taken. The hope of doing good revived; and Mounier, the chairman of the constitutional committee, declared that they were about to propose a political system similar, in almost everything, to that of the English monarchy.

In comparing this state of things and of the popular mind to the dreadful ferment of the evening of the 23d of June, it cannot be denied that M. Necker had a second time placed the reins of government in the King's hands, as he had done after the dismission of the Archbishop of Sens. The throne was doubtless shaken, but it was still possible to strengthen it by taking care, above all, to avoid an insurrection, as an insurrection must evidently prove too strong for the means which government still had to resist it. But the failure of the royal session of 23d June by no means discouraged those who had caused it; and the secret advisers of the King, while they allowed M. Necker to guide the external actions of the King, advised His Majesty to give a feigned acquiescence to everything until the German troops, commanded by Marshal Broglio, should approach Paris. They took good care to conceal from M. Necker that the order for their approach had been given with a view to dissolve the Assembly: when the measure could be no longer kept private, it was said to have been adopted to quell the partial troubles that had occurred in Paris, and in which the French guards, when commanded to interfere, had shown the most complete insubordination.[4]

3. June 25, 1789.
4. Such examples of insubordination occurred on June 24 and 28, 1789.

M. Necker was not ignorant of the true motive for the approach of the troops, although attempts were made to conceal it from him. The intention of the Court was to assemble at Compiègne all the members of the three orders who had not shown themselves favorable to innovation, and to make them give there a hasty consent to the loans and taxes they stood in need of, after which the Assembly was to be dissolved. As such a project could not be seconded by M. Necker, it was proposed to dismiss him as soon as the troops arrived. Every day, he was well informed of his situation and could not have any doubt about it; but, having seen the violent effects produced on the 23d of June by the news of his resignation, he was determined not to expose the public welfare to a fresh shock; for what he dreaded, of all things, was obtaining a personal triumph at the expense of the royal authority. His partisans, alarmed at the enemies by whom he was surrounded, entreated him to resign. He knew some people thought of sending him to the Bastille; but he knew also that, under existing circumstances, he could not resign without giving a confirmation to the rumor circulated about the violent measures in preparation at Court. The King having resolved on these measures, M. Necker was determined not to participate in them, but he decided also on not giving the signal of opposition: he remained like a sentinel left at his post to conceal maneuvers from the enemy.

The popular party understanding very well the measures planned against them, and being by no means disposed, like M. Necker, to become the victims of the Court, embraced the proposition of Mirabeau, which led to the famous address for sending back the troops.[5] It was the first time that France heard that popular eloquence, the natural power of which was increased by the grandeur of the circumstances. Respect for the personal character of the King was still remarkable in this tribunitian harangue. "And in what manner, Sire," said the orator of the chamber,

> do they act to make you doubt the attachment and affection of your subjects? Have you been lavish of their blood? Are you cruel, implacable? Have you made an abuse of justice? Does the people charge its misfortunes on you? Does it name you in its calamities? . . . Do not put faith

5. On July 8, 1789.

in those who speak to you with levity of the nation, and who represent it to you only according to their views, at one time as insolent, rebellious, seditious—at another submissive, docile to the yoke, and ready to bow the head to receive it. Each of these descriptions is equally unfaithful.

Always ready, Sire, to obey you, because you command in the name of the law, our fidelity is without bounds, and without reproach.

Sire, we entreat you in the name of our country, in the name of your happiness and your fame; send back your soldiers to the stations whence your advisers have drawn them; send back that artillery which is destined to cover your frontiers; send back, above all, the foreign troops, those allies of the nation whom we pay for defending, and not for disquieting our homes. Your Majesty has no need for them; why should a monarch, adored by twenty-five million Frenchmen, call, at a heavy expense, around his throne a few thousand foreigners? Sire, in the midst of your children be guarded by their affection.

These words are the last gleam of attachment which the French showed to their King for his personal virtues. When the military force was tried, and tried in vain, the affection of the people seemed to disappear with the power of the Court.

M. Necker continued to see the King daily; but nothing of serious import was communicated to him. Such silence toward the prime minister was very disquieting, when foreign troops were seen to arrive from various points and take their station around Paris and Versailles. My father told us in confidence every evening that he expected being put under arrest next day; but that the danger to which the King was exposed was, in his opinion, so great that he deemed it his duty to remain in office, that he might not appear to suspect what was going on.

On the 11th of July, at three in the afternoon, M. Necker received a letter from the King, ordering him to quit Paris and France, and only enjoining him to conceal his departure from everyone. The Baron de Breteuil had advised, in the committee, the arrest of M. Necker, as his dismissal might cause a tumult. "I will answer," said the King, "that he will obey strictly my injunction in regard to secrecy." M. Necker was affected by this mark of confidence in his probity, although accompanied by an order for exile.

He was informed in the sequel that two officers of the life guards had followed him to secure his person if he had not complied with the injunction of the King. But they could hardly reach the frontiers so soon as M. Necker himself. Madame Necker was his sole confidante; she set out, on quitting her saloon, without any preparation for the journey, with the precautions which a criminal would take to escape his sentence; and this sentence, so much dreaded, was the triumph which the people would have prepared for M. Necker had he been willing to accept it. Two days after his departure, and as soon as his removal from office was known, the theaters were shut as for a public calamity. All Paris took up arms;[6] the first cockade worn was green, because that was the color of M. Necker's livery: medals were struck with his effigy; and had he thought proper to repair to Paris instead of quitting France by the nearest frontier, that of Flanders, it would be difficult to assign a limit to the influence that he might have acquired.

Duty, doubtless, required obedience to the King's order: but what man is there who, even in yielding obedience, would not have allowed himself to be recognized, and would not have consented to have been brought back in spite of himself, by the multitude? History does not perhaps offer an example of a man shunning power, with all the precautions which he would have taken to escape from proscription. It was necessary, to be the defender of the people, to incur banishment in this manner; and, at the same time, the most faithful subject of his monarch, to sacrifice to him so scrupulously the homage of an entire nation.

6. Necker's dismissal became publicly known on July 12, 1789; this date marked the beginning of the insurrection in Paris. The Bastille fell two days later.

CHAPTER XXII

Revolution of the 14th of July (1789).

Two other ministers were removed at the same time as M. Necker, M. de Montmorin, a man personally attached to the King from his infancy, and M. de St. Priest, who was remarkable for the soundness of his judgment. But what will appear almost incredible to posterity is, that in adopting a resolution of such importance, no measure was taken to ensure the personal safety of the Sovereign in case of misfortune. The advisers of the Crown thought themselves so sure of success, that no troops were assembled around Louis XVI to accompany him to a certain distance in the event of a revolt of the capital. The soldiers were encamped in the plains near the gates of Paris, which gave them an opportunity of communicating with the inhabitants; the latter came to them in numbers, and made them promise not to make use of their arms against the people. Thus, with the exception of two German regiments,[1] who did not understand French, and who drew their sabers in the gardens of the Tuileries almost as if they had wished to afford a pretext for insurrection, all the troops on which dependence was made participated in the feeling of the citizens, and complied in no respect with what was expected from them.

As soon as the news of M. Necker's departure was spread abroad in Paris, the streets were barricaded, and all the inhabitants formed themselves into national guards, assuming some sort of military dress and laying hold of whatever weapon first offered, whether musket, saber, or scythe. Multitudes of men of the same opinion embraced each other in the streets like brothers; and the army of the people of Paris, consisting of more than a hundred thousand men, was formed in an instant, as if by a

---

1. In reality, there was only one German regiment in Paris at that time.

miracle.[2] The Bastille, that citadel of arbitrary power, was taken on the 14th of July, 1789. The Baron de Breteuil, who boasted that he would put an end to the crisis in three days, remained only that number of days in office—long enough, however, to contribute to the overthrow of the royal power.

Such was the result of the advice of the adversaries of M. Necker. How can minds of such a cast still take on them to give an opinion on the affairs of a great people? What resources were prepared against the danger which they themselves had created? And did the world ever see men, who would not hear reason, acquit themselves so ill in the application of force?

The King in such circumstances could inspire no feeling but one of profound interest and compassion. Princes educated to rule in France have never been accustomed to look the realities of life in the face; there was held up to them an artificial world, in which they lived from the first to the last day of the year; and misfortune necessarily found them without defense in themselves.

The King was brought to Paris for the purpose of adopting, at the Hotel de Ville, that revolution which had just taken place against his power. His religious tranquillity preserved his personal dignity in this, as in all ensuing occasions; but his authority was at an end: and if the chariots of kings ought not to drag nations in their train, it is no more appropriate for a nation to make a king the ornament of its triumph. The apparent homage rendered on such an occasion to a dethroned sovereign is revolting to generous minds. Never can liberty be established when either the monarch or people are in a false situation. Each, to be sincere, must be in possession of his rights. Moral constraint imposed on the head of a government can never be the basis of the constitutional independence of a country.

The 14th of July, although marked by bloody assassinations on the part

2. The citizens' militias were formed on July 13, 1789. It is somewhat surprising that Madame de Staël did not give a detailed account of the fall of the Bastille. She mentions only a few "bloody assassinations" that took place on July 14 and refrains from dwelling on the violent episodes that marked the fall of the Bastille, preferring instead to point out the general enthusiasm of the population.

of the populace, was yet a day of grandeur: the movement was national; no faction, either foreign or domestic, would have been able to excite such enthusiasm. All France participated in it, and the emotion of a whole people is always connected with true and natural feeling. The most honorable names, Bailly, La Fayette, Lally, were proclaimed by the public opinion; the silence of a country governed by a court was exchanged for the sound of the spontaneous acclamations of all the citizens. The minds of the people were exalted; but as yet there was nothing but goodness in their souls; and the conquerors had not had time to contract those haughty passions from which the strongest party in France is scarcely ever able to preserve itself.

CHAPTER XXIII

Return of M. Necker.

M. Necker, on arriving at Brussels, remained two days to take rest before proceeding to Switzerland by way of Germany. His greatest subject of disquietude at this time was the scarcity that threatened Paris. In the preceding winter his indefatigable exertions had preserved the capital from the misfortune of famine; but the bad harvest rendered it more and more necessary to have recourse to foreign arrivals and to the credit of the great mercantile houses of Europe. He had consequently written in the beginning of July to Messrs. Hope, the celebrated Amsterdam merchants; and apprehensive that, in the existing posture of affairs, they might be averse to undertake the purchase of corn for France, unless he personally guaranteed the payment, he had offered them security to the extent of a million livres on his private fortune. On arriving at Brussels, M. Necker recalled this guarantee to his mind. He had reason to fear that, in the crisis of a revolution, the duties of government might be neglected, or that the news of his departure might be prejudicial to the public credit. Messrs. Hope, in particular, might presume that, under such circumstances, M. Necker would withdraw his security; but he even wrote to them from Brussels that he was exiled from France, but that they were to consider the personal engagement he had taken as unaltered.

The Baron de Breteuil, during the few days that he was minister, received the answer of Messrs. Hope to M. Necker's first letter, which contained an offer to guarantee their purchases by his private fortune. M. Dufresne de Saint-Léon,[1] chief clerk in the finance department, a man of

---

1. Dufresne de Saint-Léon had collaborated with Necker on the publication of the *Compte rendu* in 1781. On July 17, 1789, he was charged with the mission of bringing Necker back to Paris. They met in Basel six days later.

penetration and decision, gave this letter to the Baron de Breteuil, who treated the whole as folly: "What," said he, "can the private fortune of a minister have to do with the public interest?" He might as well have added, "Why does this foreigner interfere at all with the affairs of France?"

During the interval that M. Necker was traveling along the German frontier, the Revolution of the 14th of July took place at Paris. Madame de Polignac,[2] whom he had left at Versailles all powerful by the Queen's favor, sent for him to his great surprise in an inn at Basel and apprised him that she had fled in consequence of the events that had occurred. M. Necker could not conceive the possibility of proscriptions, and he was long in comprehending the motives that had led to the departure of Madame de Polignac. Letters brought by couriers, orders from the King, and invitations from the Assembly, all pressed him to resume his situation. "M. Necker," says Burke, in one of his writings, "was recalled, like Pompey, to his misfortune, and, like Marius, he sat down on ruins."[3] M. and Madame Necker saw the matter in this light, and it will appear from the details that I have given in the private life of my father,[4] how much it cost him to take the determination of returning.

All the flattering circumstances attending his recall could not blind him in regard to the actual state of things. Murders had been committed by the people on the 14th of July, and M. Necker, at once religious and philosophic in his manner of viewing things, abandoned all hope of the success of a cause already marked by bloodshed. Nor could he flatter himself with possessing the confidence of the King, since Louis recalled him only from dread of the danger to which his absence exposed him. Had he been actuated merely by ambition, nothing was easier than to return in triumph, supporting himself on the strength of the National Assembly; but it was

2. Yolande Martine Gabrielle de Polastron, Duchess of Polignac, was a close friend of the Queen. The duchess went into exile and died in Vienna in 1793.

3. Staël does not indicate the exact source. In *Reflections on the Revolution in France*, Burke refers favorably to Necker and draws heavily upon Necker's *De l'administration des finances de la France* (1784).

4. The title of the original text edited by Madame de Staël was *Manuscrits de M. Necker publiés par sa fille* (Geneva, 1795). A second edition was published two decades later under the title *Mémoires sur la vie privée de mon père par Mme la baronne de Staël-Holstein, suivies des mélanges de M. Necker* (Paris and London, 1818).

only to sacrifice himself to the King, and to France, that M. Necker consented to resume his position after the Revolution of the 14th of July. He thought to serve the country by lavishing his popularity in the defense of the royal authority, now too much weakened. He hoped that a man exiled by the aristocratic party would be heard with the same favor when he pleaded their cause. A distinguished citizen in whom twenty-seven years of revolution daily discovered new virtues, an admirable orator whose eloquence has defended the cause of his father, of his country, and of his King, Lally Tollendal,[5] combining both reason and emotion—one who is never led away from truth by enthusiasm, expressed himself thus on M. Necker's character and conduct, at the time of his removal:

> We have just learned, Gentlemen, the deception practiced on the confidence of a King whom we love, and the wound given to the hopes of the nation whom we represent.
>
> I will not now repeat all that has been said to you, with as much justice as energy; I will lay before you a plain sketch, and ask of you to accompany me back to the month of August of last year.
>
> The King was deceived.
>
> The laws were without administrators, and a population of twenty-five million without judges;
>
> The treasury without money, without credit, without the means of preventing a general bankruptcy, which in fact would have taken place in the course of a few days;
>
> Those in power had neither respect for the liberty of individuals, nor strength to maintain public order; the people without any resource but the convocation of the Estates General, yet hopeless of obtaining it, and distrustful even of the promise of a King whose probity they revered,

---

5. Trophime-Gérard de Lally-Tollendal (1751–1830) was a follower of Montesquieu and a prominent member of the French *monarchiens*. During the Revolution, he emerged as one of the most eloquent defenders of constitutional monarchy and was one of forty-seven nobles who joined the National Assembly a few days after the Royal Council of June 23, 1789. On August 31, 1789, Lally gave a famous speech on the relationship between the executive and legislative powers and the royal veto (republished in *Orateurs de la Révolution française*, 364–92). He had an interesting correspondence with Burke and spent some time in England, where he fled after being imprisoned briefly in August 1792. He returned to France under the Consulate and became active in politics again under the Restoration, when he was also elected to the French Academy.

because they persisted in believing that the ministers of the day would elude compliance.

To these political afflictions Providence, in its anger, had joined others; ravage and desolation was spread through the country; famine appeared in the distance, threatening a part of the kingdom.

The cry of truth reached the King's ears; his eye fixed itself on this distressing picture; his pure and upright heart was moved; he yielded to the wish of the people; he recalled the minister whom the people demanded.

Justice resumed its course.

The public treasury was filled; credit reappeared as in times of the greatest prosperity; the infamous name of bankruptcy was no longer pronounced.

The prisons were opened, and restored to society the victims whom they contained.

The insurrections, of which the seeds had been sown in several provinces, and which were likely to lead to the most dreadful results, were confined to troubles certainly afflicting in their nature, but temporary, and soon appeased by wisdom and leniency.

The Estates General were once more promised: no one was now doubtful of their meeting, when they saw a virtuous King confide the execution of his promise to a virtuous minister. The King's name was covered with benedictions.

The season of scarcity came. Immense exertions, the sea covered with ships, all the powers of Europe applied to, the two hemispheres put under contribution for our subsistence, more than fourteen hundred thousand quintals of corn and flour imported among us, more than twenty-five million taken out of the royal treasury, an active, efficacious, unremitted concern applied every day, every hour, in every place succeeded in warding off this calamity; and the paternal disquietude, the generous sacrifices of the King, published by his minister, excited in the hearts of all his subjects new feelings of love and gratitude.

Finally, in spite of numberless obstacles, the Estates General were assembled. The Estates General assembled! How many things, Gentlemen, are comprised in these few words! how many benefits do they suggest! to what a degree ought the gratitude of Frenchmen to be fixed on them! Certain divisions appeared at the outset of this memorable assembly; let us beware of reproaching each other with it, and let none of us pretend to be wholly innocent. Let us rather say for the sake of peace, that every one of us may have allowed himself to fall into some venial errors; let us say that the last moment of prejudice is like the last moment of him whom it torments—that at the instant it is about to expire, it acquires a temporary animation and shows a final gleam of existence. Let us acknowledge that, as far as human exertions could go, there was not one conciliating measure which the minister did not attempt with the most strict impartiality, and that where he did not succeed, the fault lay in the force of circumstances. But amidst diversity of opinion a patriotic feeling animated every heart; the pacifying efforts of the minister, the reiterated invitations of the King, were at last successful. A reunion took place: every day removed some principle of division; every day produced a motive for reconciliation: a plan of a constitution, sketched by an experienced hand, conceived by an intelligent mind and an upright heart [by Mounier], rallied all our minds and all our hearts. We were now making a real progress: we now entered effectually on our task, and France was beginning to respire.

It is at this instant, after overcoming so many obstacles, in the midst of so many hopes and so many wants, that perfidious advisers removed from the most just of kings, his most faithful servant, and, from the nation, the citizen minister in whom she had placed her confidence.

Who then are his accusers before the throne? certainly not the parliaments, whom he recalled; certainly not the people, whom he saved from famine; nor the public creditors, whom he paid; nor the upright citizens, whose wishes he has seconded. Who are they then? I do not know, but some there must be; the justice, the well-known goodness of the King do not allow me to doubt it—whoever they are, their guilt is serious.

If we cannot trace the accusers, let us endeavor to find the crimes which they may have laid to his charge. This minister, whom the King had granted to his people as a gift of his love, in what manner has he become all at once the object of ill will? what has he done for the last year? we have just seen it, I have said it, and I now repeat it: when there was no money in the treasury, he paid us; when we had no bread, he fed us; when there was no authority left, he calmed those who revolted. I have heard him accused alternately of shaking the throne, and of rendering the King despotic; of sacrificing the people to the nobility, and the nobility to the people. I considered these accusations the ordinary lot of the just and impartial, and the double censure appeared to me a double homage.

I recollect further having heard him called a factious man; I asked myself the meaning of this expression. I asked what other minister had ever been more devoted to the master whom he served, what other had been more eager to publish the virtues and good actions of the King, what other had given or procured to him a larger share of benedictions, of testimonies of love, and of respect.

Members of the Commons! whose noble sympathy made you rush before him on the day of his last triumph; that day, when after fearing you would lose him, you believed that he was restored to you for a longer time; when you surrounded him, when in the name of the people, of whom you are the august representatives, in the name of the King, whose faithful subjects you are, you entreated him to remain the minister of both, while you were shedding your virtuous tears on him; ah! say if it was with a factious look, or with the insolence of the leader of a party, that he received all these testimonies of your affection? Did he say to you, or did he ask you *anything but to put your confidence in the King, to love the King, and to render this assembly dear to the King?* Members of the Commons, answer me, I entreat you, and if my voice presumes to give publicity to a falsehood, let yours arise to confound me.

And his manner of retiring, Gentlemen, did it bear in any respect the appearance of a factious mind? His most trusted servants, his most affectionate friends, even his family, remained ignorant of his departure. He professed that he was going to the country; he left a prey to anxiety all who were connected with him, all who were attached to him; a night was passed in seeking him in all directions. Such behavior would be perfectly natural in the case of a prevaricator eager to escape the public indignation; but when you consider that he did it to withdraw from its homage, from expressions of regret which would have followed him along his way, and which might have soothed his misfortunes; that he should have deprived himself of this consolation, and suffered in the persons of all whom he loved, rather than be the cause of a moment's disorder or popular commotion; that in short the last feeling that he experienced, the last duty that he prescribed to himself in quitting that France from which he was banished, consisted in giving the King and the nation this proof of respect and attachment—we must either not believe in the existence of virtue, or confess that virtue is here displayed in as pure a form as she ever exhibited on earth.

All that I had hitherto seen—the transports of the people which I had witnessed, my father's carriage drawn by the citizens of the towns through which we passed—women on their knees when they saw him pass along the road—nothing made me experience so lively an emotion as such an opinion pronounced by such a man.

In less than a fortnight two million national guards were under arms in France. The arming of this militia was, no doubt, quickened by the dexterous circulation of a rumor in every town and village that the arrival of the brigands was imminent;[6] but the unanimous feeling that drew the people from a state of tutelage was inspired by no artifice and directed by no party; the ascendency of the privileged bodies, and the strength of regular troops, disappeared in an instant. The nation took the place of all; it said, like the Cid, "We now arise"; and to show itself was to accomplish the victory. But alas! it also, in a short time, was depraved by flatterers, because it had become a power.

In the journey from Basel to Paris, the newly constituted authorities came out to address M. Necker as he passed through the towns; he recommended to them respect for property, attention to the clergy and nobility, and love for the King. He prevailed on them to grant passports to several persons who were quitting France. The Baron de Besenval, who had commanded a part of the German troops, was arrested at the distance of ten leagues from Paris, and the municipality of the capital had ordered him to be brought thither. M. Necker took on himself to suspend the execution of this order, in the dread, for which there were but too strong reasons, that the populace of Paris would have massacred him in its rage. But M. Necker felt all the danger that he incurred, in acting thus on the mere ground of his popularity. Accordingly, the day after his return to Versailles, he repaired to the Hotel de Ville of Paris to give an explanation of his conduct.

Let me be permitted to dwell once more on this day, the last of pure

6. A reference to the Great Fear (July 20–August 6, 1789).

happiness in my life, which, however, had hardly begun its course. The whole population of Paris rushed in crowds into the streets; men and women were seen at the windows, and on the roofs, calling out *Vive M. Necker.* As he drew near the Hotel de Ville the acclamations redoubled, the square was filled with a multitude animated by one feeling, and pressing forward to receive a single man, and that man was my father. He entered the hall of the Hotel de Ville, explained to the newly elected magistrates the order that he had given to save M. de Besenval; and urging to them, with his accustomed delicacy, all that pleaded in favor of those who had acted in obedience to their sovereign, and in defense of a state of things that had existed during several centuries, he asked an amnesty for the past, whatever it might be, and reconciliation for the future. The confederates of Rutli,[7] in the beginning of the fourteenth century, when they swore to deliver Switzerland, swore at the same time to be just toward their adversaries; and it was doubtless to this noble resolution that they were indebted for their triumph. Hardly had M. Necker pronounced the word *amnesty,* than it came home to every heart; the people collected in the square were eager to participate in it. M. Necker then came forward on the balcony, and proclaiming in a loud voice the sacred words of peace among Frenchmen of all parties, the whole multitude answered him with transport. As for me, I saw nothing after this instant, for I was bereft of my senses by joy.

Amiable and generous France, adieu! Adieu, France, which desired liberty, and which might then so easily have obtained it! I am now doomed to relate first your faults, next your crimes, and lastly your misfortunes: gleams of your virtues will still appear; but the light which they cast will serve only to show more clearly the depth of your miseries. Yet you have ever possessed such titles to be loved, that the mind still cherishes the hope of finding you what you were in the earliest days of national union. A friend returning after a long absence would be welcomed more kindly for the separation.

7. A reference to an important moment in the history of Switzerland. In 1291 people from Uri, Schwyz, and Unterwalden feared that the counts of Habsburg would try to regain influence in their territories. As a result, they met and swore to help each other against anyone attempting to subject them. This is the historical background of the legend of the *Oath on Rütli* (a meadow on the western shore of Lake Lucerne).

CHAPTER I

Mirabeau.

One would almost say that in every era of history there are personages who should be considered as the representatives of the good and of the wicked principle. Such, in Rome, were Cicero and Catiline; such, in France, were M. Necker and Mirabeau. Mirabeau, gifted with the most comprehensive and energetic mind, thought himself sufficiently strong to overthrow the government, and to erect on its ruins a system, of some kind or other, that would have been the work of his own hands. This gigantic project was the ruin of France, and the ruin of himself; for he acted at first in the spirit of faction, although his real manner of judging was that of the most reflecting statesman. He was then of the age of forty, and had passed his whole life in lawsuits, abduction of women, and in prisons; he was excluded from good society, and his first wish was to regain his station in it. But he thought it necessary to set on fire the whole social edifice, that the doors of the Paris saloons might be opened to him. Like other immoral men, Mirabeau looked first to his personal interest in public affairs, and his foresight was limited by his egoism.[1]

1. Madame de Staël's view of Mirabeau was hardly objective because the latter was a powerful rival of Staël's father. Bailleul was among the first to criticize Madame de Staël's views of Mirabeau (*Examen critique de l'ouvrage posthume de Mme. la Bnne. de Staël*, vol. I, 239–75). For another opinion on Mirabeau, see chap. X of Lord Acton's *Lectures on the French Revolution*. "Odious as he was and foredoomed to fail," wrote Acton, "he [Mirabeau] was yet the supreme figure of the time. . . . As a Minister, he might have saved the Constitution. . . . If Mirabeau is tried by the test of public morals, . . . the verdict cannot be

An unfortunate deputy of the Third Estate, a well-intentioned but a very weak man, gave the Constituent Assembly an account of what had passed at the Hotel de Ville, and of the triumph obtained by M. Necker over the emotions of hatred which some persons had attempted to excite among the people. This deputy hesitated so much, expressed himself with so much coldness, and still showed such a desire to be eloquent, that he destroyed all the effect of the admirable recital which he had taken on himself. Mirabeau, his pride deeply wounded at the success of M. Necker, promised himself to defeat the outcome of enthusiasm by throwing out ironical insinuations in the Assembly, and suspicions among the people. He repaired on that very day to all the sections of Paris, and prevailed on them to retract the amnesty granted the day before. He endeavored to excite exasperation against the late projects of the court, and alarmed the Parisians by the dread of passing for the dupes of their good nature, an apprehension that operates very potently on them, for they aim above all things at being considered quick-sighted and formidable. Mirabeau, by snatching from M. Necker the palm of domestic peace, struck the first blow at his popularity; but this reverse was bound to be followed by a number of others; for from the time that the popular party were urged to persecute the vanquished, M. Necker could no longer make common cause with the victors.

Mirabeau proceeded to circulate doctrines of the wildest anarchy, although his intellect, when viewed apart from his character, was perfectly sound and luminous. M. Necker has said of him in one of his writings that he was a demagogue by calculation and an aristocrat by disposition.[2] There cannot be a more correct sketch of the man; not only was his mind too enlightened to avoid perceiving the impossibility of a democratic gov-

---

doubtful. His ultimate policy was one vast intrigue, and he avowedly strove to do evil that good might come. . . . The answer is different if we try him by a purely political test, and ask whether he desired power for the whole or freedom for the parts. Mirabeau was not only a friend of freedom . . . but a friend of federalism. . . . If in this he was sincere, he deserves the great place he holds in the memory of his countrymen." (*Lectures on the French Revolution*, 136–37)

2. The French text contains some quotations that are not properly referenced, and I have thus removed the quotation marks.

ernment in France, but he would not have desired it had it been practicable. He was vain in attaching a high price to his birth, and could not speak of the day of St. Bartholomew without saying, "Admiral Coligni, who, by the way, was a relation of my family." So desirous was he of reminding people on all occasions of his noble descent.

His expensive habits made money extremely necessary to him, and M. Necker has been blamed for not having given him money on the opening of the Estates General. But other ministers had undertaken this kind of business, for which M. Necker was by no means calculated. Besides, Mirabeau, whether he accepted the money of the court or not, was determined to render himself not the instrument but the master of the court, and he never would have been willing to renounce his power as a demagogue until that power had raised him to the head of the government. He urged the union of all power in a single assembly, although perfectly aware that such a plan was hostile to the public good; but he flattered himself that France would thus fall into his hands, and that, after having precipitated her into confusion, he should have the power of saving her when he thought proper. Morality is the first of sciences, even in the light of calculation! There are always limits to the intellect of those who have not felt the harmony that exists between the nature of things and the duties of man. "*La petite morale tue la grande*—morality in small things destroys morality in great," was a frequent remark of Mirabeau; but an opportunity of exercising the latter hardly occurred, according to his views, in the course of a life.

He possessed a larger share of intellect than of talent, and he was never fully at ease when speaking extemporaneously at the tribune. A similar difficulty in composing made him have recourse to the assistance of friends in all his works;[3] yet not one of them after his death would have been capable of writing what he had found means to inspire into them. In speaking of the Abbé Maury he used to say, "When he is on the right side of the question, we debate; when he is on the wrong, I crush him"; but the

---

3. An allusion to the "Mirabeau workshop" composed of friends (such as Clavière, du Roveray, Reybaz, and Dumont) who helped Mirabeau compose his works. For more details, see Bénétruy, *L'atelier de Mirabeau.*

truth was, that the Abbé Maury often defended even a good cause with that kind of eloquence which does not proceed from real emotion of the heart.[4]

Had ministers been allowed to sit in the Assembly, M. Necker, who was capable of expressing himself with the greatest warmth and force, would, I believe, have triumphed over Mirabeau. But he could not enter on debate, and was obliged to confine himself to the transmission of memorials. Mirabeau attacked the minister in his absence, while also praising his goodness, his generosity, his popularity, the whole expressed with a deceitful respect that was particularly dangerous. Yet he had a sincere admiration for M. Necker, and acknowledged it to his friends; but he well knew that so scrupulous a character would never coalesce with his own, and his grand object was to destroy his influence.

M. Necker was reduced to acting on the defensive; the other assailed with the more confidence, that neither the success nor the responsibility of administration was his concern. M. Necker, by defending the royal authority, necessarily sacrificed his favor with the popular party. He knew besides, by experience, that the King had secret counselors[5] and private plans, and he was by no means certain of prevailing on him to follow the course that he thought best. Obstacles of every kind impeded his measures; he was not at liberty to speak openly on any subject; the line, however, which he invariably followed was that which was pointed out to him by his duty as minister. The nation and the King had exchanged places: the King had become by much, far too much, the weaker party. It was thus incumbent on M. Necker to defend the throne against the nation, as he had defended the nation against the throne. But Mirabeau was not to be restrained by those generous sentiments; he put himself at the head of a party that aimed at political importance regardless of the cost; and the most abstract principles were in his hands nothing but instruments of intrigue.

Nature had effectually seconded him by giving him those defects and

---

4. For Abbé Maury, see pt. I, chap. xvii, note 7.

5. Mirabeau had a secret correspondence with Louis XVI. His notes to the King were published in Chaussinand-Nogaret, ed., *Mirabeau entre le roi et la Révolution.*

advantages that operate on a popular assembly: sarcasm, irony, force, and originality. The moment he rose to speak, the moment he stepped to the tribune, the curiosity of all was excited; nobody esteemed him, but the impression of his talents was such that no one dared to attack him, if we except those members of the aristocratic body, who, declining a conflict in debate, thought proper to send him challenge after challenge to meet them with the sword. He always refused these challenges, and merely noted the names of the parties in his pocket book, with a promise that they should be answered at the dissolution of the assembly. It is not fair, he said, in speaking of an honest country gentleman, of I do not know what province, to expose a man of talent like me against a blockhead like him. And, what is very extraordinary in such a country as France, this behavior had not the effect of bringing him into contempt; it did not even make his courage suspected. There was something so martial in his mind, and so bold in his manner, that no one could impute cowardice in any way to such a man.

CHAPTER II

Of the Constituent Assembly
After the 14th of July.

The Third Estate, and the minority of the nobility and clergy, formed the majority of the Constituent Assembly; and this Assembly disposed of the fate of France. After the 14th of July, nothing could be more striking than the sight of twelve hundred deputies, listened to by numerous spectators, and stirred up at the very name of those great truths which have occupied the human mind since the origin of society on earth. This Assembly partook of the passions of the people; but no collection of men could present such an imposing mass of information.[1] Thoughts were communicated there with electric rapidity, because the action of man on man is irresistible, and because nothing appealed more strongly to the imagination than that unarmed will bursting the ancient chains, forged originally by conquest and now suddenly disappearing before the simplicity of reason. We must carry ourselves back to 1789, when prejudice had been the only cause of mischief, and when unsullied liberty was the idol of enlightened minds. With what enthusiasm did one contemplate such a number of persons of

---

1. The reader might find it interesting to compare Madame de Staël's views on this issue with Burke's. Staël opposed the idea that the representatives of the people are depositories of a power without limits. Burke argued: "That Assembly, since the destruction of the orders, has no fundamental law, no strict convention, no respected usage to restrain it. . . . Nothing in heaven or upon earth can serve as a control on them." (*Reflections*, 135) Benjamin Constant insisted that since "no authority upon earth is unlimited," even the authority of the democratically elected representatives of the people must be properly limited. He added: "The abstract limitation of sovereignty is not sufficient. We must find for political institutions which combine the interest of the different holders of power." (*Principles of Politics*, 180, 182) Taine's judgment on this issue can be found in Taine, *The French Revolution*, vol. I, 159–216.

different classes, some coming to make sacrifices, others to enter on the possession of their rights. Yet there were symptoms of a certain arrogance of power among those sovereigns of a new kind, who considered themselves depositories of a power without limits, the power of the people. The English had proceeded slowly in forming a new political constitution; the French, seeing it had stood its ground firmly for more than a century, ought to have been satisfied with its imitation.

Mounier, Lally, Malouet, Clermont-Tonnerre, came forward in support of the royal prerogative as soon as the Revolution had disarmed the partisans of the Old Regime.[2] This course was dictated not only by reflection, but by that involuntary sympathy which we feel for the powerful in a state of misfortune, particularly when surrounded by august recollections. This generous feeling would have been that of the French at large, if the necessity of applause did not with them rise pre-eminent to every other impulse; and the spirit of the time inspired the maxims of demagogues into those very persons who were afterward to become the apologists of despotism.

A man of talent said some time ago, "Whoever may be named finance minister, may consider me beforehand as his friend, and even as, in some degree, his relative." In France, on the other hand, it is a duty to befriend the vanquished party, be it what it may; for the possession of power produces a more depraving effect on the French than on any other nation. The habit of living at court, or the desire of getting there, forms their minds to vanity; and in an arbitrary government, people have no idea of any doctrine but that of success. It was the faults generated and brought forth by servility which were the cause of the excesses of licentiousness.

Every town, every village, sent its congratulations to the Assembly; and whoever had composed one of these forty thousand addresses began to think himself a rival to Montesquieu.

The crowd of spectators admitted into the galleries stimulated the speakers to such a degree that each endeavored to obtain a share in those

---

2. According to Acton, "Mounier, with some of his friends, deserves to be remembered among the men, not so common as they say, who loved liberty sincerely; I mean, who desired it, not for any good it might do them, but for itself, however arduous, or costly, or perilous its approach might be." (Acton, *Lectures on the French Revolution*, 98)

peals of applause, which were so new and so seductive to the self-love of the individual. In the British Parliament it is a rule not to read a speech, it must be spoken; so that the number of persons capable of addressing the house with effect is necessarily very small. But, as soon as permission is given to read either what we have written for ourselves or what others have written for us, men of eminence are no longer the permanent leaders of an assembly, and we thus lose one of the great advantages of a free government—that of giving talent its place and, consequently, prompting all men to the improvement of their faculties. When one can become a courtier of the people with as little exertion as makes one a courtier of a prince, the cause of mankind gains nothing by the change.

The democratic declamations which obtained success in the assembly were transformed into actual outrage in the country; country-seats were burned in fulfillment of the epigrams pronounced by the popular speakers, and the kingdom was thrown into confusion by a war of words.

The Assembly was seized with a philosophic enthusiasm, proceeding, in part, from the example of America. That country, new as yet to history, had nothing in the shape of ancient usage to preserve, if we except the excellent regulations of English jurisprudence, which, long ago adopted in America, had there implanted a feeling of justice and reason. The French flattered themselves with the power of adopting for the basis of their government the principles that suited a new people; but, situated in the midst of Europe, and having a privileged caste, whose claims it was necessary to quiet, the plan was impracticable; besides, how were they to conciliate the institutions of a republic with the existence of a monarchy? The English constitution offered the only example of the solution of this problem. But a mania of vanity, something like that of a man of letters, prompted the French to innovate in this respect; they had all the fastidious apprehension of an author who refuses to borrow either character or situations from existing works. Now, as far as fiction goes, we do well to aim at originality; but when real institutions are in question, we are fortunate in having before us a practical proof of their utility.[3] I should cer-

3. Burke made a similar point in his *Reflections on the Revolution in France.*

tainly be ashamed at this time,[4] more than any other, to take part in declamations against the first representative assembly of France: it contained men of the greatest merit, and it is to the reforms introduced by it that the nation is still indebted for the stock of reason and liberty which it will, and ought to, preserve, at whatever sacrifice. But if this assembly had added to its shining talents a more scrupulous regard to morality, it would have found the happy medium between the two parties, who, if we may use the expression, contested with each other the theory of politics.

4. During the first years of the Bourbon Restoration.

CHAPTER III

General La Fayette.

M. de la Fayette, having fought from his early youth for the cause of America, had early become imbued with the principles of liberty which form the basis of that government. If he made mistakes in regard to the French Revolution, we are to ascribe them all to his admiration of the American institutions, and of Washington, the hero citizen who guided the first steps of that nation in the career of independence. La Fayette, young, affluent, of noble family, and beloved at home, relinquished all these advantages at the age of nineteen to serve beyond the ocean in the cause of that liberty, the love of which has decided every action of his life. Had he had the happiness to be a native of the United States, his conduct would have been that of Washington: the same disinterestedness, the same enthusiasm, the same perseverance in their opinions, distinguished each of these generous friends of humanity. Had General Washington been, like the Marquis de la Fayette, commander of the national guard of Paris, he also might have found it impossible to control the course of circumstances; he also might have seen his efforts baffled by the difficulty of being at once faithful to his engagements to the King, and of establishing at the same time the liberty of his country.

M. de la Fayette, I must say, has a right to be considered a true republican; none of the vanities of his rank ever entered his head; power, the effect of which is so great in France, had no ascendancy over him; the desire of pleasing in drawing-room conversation did not with him influence a single phrase; he sacrificed all his fortune to his opinions with the most generous indifference. When in the prisons of Olmütz,[1] as when at

---

1. After his surrender to the Austrians (August 19, 1792), La Fayette was imprisoned at Olmütz from May 1794 to October 1797.

the height of his influence, he was equally firm in his attachment to his principles. His manner of seeing and acting is open and direct. Whoever has marked his conduct may foretell with certainty what he will do on any particular occasion. His political feeling is that of a citizen of the United States, and even his person is more English than French. The hatred of which M. de la Fayette is the object has never embittered his temper, and his gentleness of soul is complete; at the same time nothing has ever modified his opinions, and his confidence in the triumph of liberty is the same as that of a pious man in a future life. These sentiments, so contrary to the selfish calculations of most of the men who have acted a part in France, may appear pitiable in the eyes of some persons—"It is so silly," they think, "to prefer one's country to oneself, not to change one's party when that party is vanquished; in short, to consider mankind not as cards with which to play a winning game, but as the sacred objects of unlimited sacrifices." If this is to form the charge of silliness, would that it were but once merited by our men of talents!

It is a singular phenomenon that such a character as that of M. de la Fayette should have appeared in the foremost rank of French nobles; but he can neither be censured nor exculpated with impartiality, without being acknowledged to be such as I have described him. It then becomes easy to understand the different contrasts which naturally arose between his disposition and his situation. Supporting monarchy more from duty than taste, he drew involuntarily toward the principles of the democrats whom he was obliged to resist; and a certain kindness for the advocates of the republican form was perceptible in him, although his reflection forbade the admission of their system into France. Since the departure of M. de la Fayette for America, now forty years ago,[2] we cannot quote a single action or a single word of his which was not direct and consistent; personal interest never blended itself in the least with his public conduct. Success would have displayed such sentiments to advantage; but they deserve all the attention of the historian, in spite of circumstances, and in spite even of faults which might serve as weapons for opponents.

2. La Fayette left for America in 1777. Madame de Staël wrote these lines forty years later, in 1817.

On the 11th of July, before the Third Estate had obtained their triumph, M. de la Fayette addressed the Constituent Assembly and proposed a declaration of rights, nearly similar to that which the Americans placed at the head of their constitution, after conquering their independence.[3] The English, likewise, after excluding the Stuarts and calling William III to the crown, made him sign a bill of rights, on which their present constitution is founded. But the American declaration of rights being intended for a people where there were no pre-existing privileges to impede the pure operation of reason, a number of universal principles regarding political liberty and equality were placed at the beginning of this declaration altogether in conformity with the state of knowledge already diffused among them. In England the bill of rights did not proceed on general ideas; it confirmed existing laws and institutions.[4]

The French declaration of rights in 1789 contained the best part of those of England and America; but it would have perhaps been better to have confined it, on the one hand to what was indisputable and on the other to what would not have admitted of any dangerous interpretation. There can be no doubt that *distinctions in society can have no other object than the general good; that all political power takes its rise from the interest of the people; that men are born and remain free and equal in the eye of the law;* but there is ample space for sophistry in so wide a field, while nothing is more clear or undoubted than the application of these truths to individual liberty, the establishment of juries, the freedom of the press, popular

3. An inaccurate description. The American Constitution is not prefaced by a declaration of rights. The first ten amendments to the U.S. Constitution—the famous Bill of Rights—were adopted within three years of the Constitution's ratification and resulted from political negotiations during the state ratifying conventions that were called to accept or reject the draft produced by the 1787 Constitutional Convention in Philadelphia. It is likely that the source of La Fayette's inspiration might have been Virginia's famous 1776 Declaration of Rights. For more information on this topic, see Hoffman and Albert, *The Bill of Rights: Government Proscribed*, especially the essay by Akhil Reed Amar, "The Bill of Rights as a Constitution," 274–386.

4. The Bill of Rights had been signed on October 23, 1689. Madame de Staël seems to confound here the Declaration of Independence (1776) and the first ten amendments to the Constitution (September 1789–December 1791).

elections, the division of the legislative power, the sanctioning of taxes, etc.[5] Philip the Tall said that "every man, in particular every Frenchman, was born, and remained free"; he was, it is well known, very far from imposing any restraint on himself from the consequences of this maxim. A nation, however, is likely to take words of this nature in a much more extensive sense than a king. When the declaration of the rights of man appeared in the Constituent Assembly, in the midst of all those young nobles who so lately had figured as courtiers, they brought to the tribune, one after the other, their philosophical phrases; entering with self-complacency into minute discussions on the mode of expressing this or that maxim, the truth of which, however, is so evident that the plainest words in any language are equally capable of conveying it. It was then foreseen that nothing durable could be produced by a mode of debating into which vanity, at once frivolous and factious, had so soon found its way.

5. On the *Declaration of Rights of Man and of Citizen*, see Marcel Gauchet's entry on the rights of man in *A Critical Dictionary of the French Revolution*, 818–28, and also see Gauchet, *La Révolution des droits de l'homme*.

CHAPTER IV

Of the Good Effected by
the Constituent Assembly.

Before entering on the distressing events which have disfigured the French Revolution, and lost, perhaps for a considerable time, the cause of reason and liberty in Europe, let us examine the principles proclaimed by the Constituent Assembly and exhibit a sketch of the advantages which their application has produced, and still produces in France, in spite of all the misfortunes that have pressed on that country.

The use of torture still subsisted in 1789; the King had abolished only the rack before trial; punishments, such as straining on the wheel, and torments similar to those which during three days were inflicted on Damiens, were, in certain cases, still admitted. The Constituent Assembly abolished even the name of these judicial barbarities. The penal laws against the Protestants, already modified in 1787 by the predecessors of the Estates General, were replaced by the most complete liberty of public worship.

Criminal processes were not carried on in public, and not only were a number of irreparable mistakes committed, but a much greater number were supposed; for whatever is not public in the administration of justice is always accounted unfair.

The Constituent Assembly introduced into France all the criminal jurisprudence of England, and perhaps improved it in several respects, as they were not checked in their labors by ancient usages. M. de la Fayette, from the time that he was placed at the head of the armed force of Paris, declared to the magistrates of that city that he could not take upon himself to arrest anyone unless the accused were to be provided with counsel, a copy of the charge, the power of confronting witnesses, and publicity given to the whole procedure. In consequence of this demand, equally liberal and rare on the part of a military man, the magistrates asked and obtained from the Constituent Assembly that those precious securities should be in force till the establishment of juries should prevent all anxiety about the equity of the decisions.

The *parlements* of France were, as is apparent from their history, bodies possessing certain privileges and acting frequently as the instruments of political passions; but from their having a certain independence in their constitution, and preserving a strict respect for forms, the King's ministers were almost always in a state of altercation with them. Since the commencement of the French monarchy there has, as we have already remarked, hardly existed a state offense, the knowledge of which has not been withdrawn from the ordinary courts, or in the decision of which the forms enjoined by law were preserved. In examining the endless list of ministers, noblemen, and citizens condemned to death on political grounds during several centuries, we see, and it is to the honor of the established judges that we say it, that government was obliged to commit the trials to extraordinary commissions when it wished to secure a conviction.[1] These commissions were, it is true, usually composed of men who had been judges, but they were not formed on the established plan; and yet government had but too much reason to reckon with confidence on the spirit of the courts. Criminal jurisprudence in France was entirely adapted to avenge the wrongs of government, and did not protect individuals at all. In consequence of the aristocratic abuses which oppressed the nation, civil actions were conducted with much more equity than the criminal, because the higher ranks were more interested in them. In France, even at present, very little difference is made between a man brought to trial and a man found guilty; while in England, the judge himself apprises the accused of the importance of the questions he is about to put to him, and of the danger to which he may expose himself by his answers. To begin with the commissaries of police and end with the application of torture, we find that there scarcely exists a method that has not been employed by the old jurisprudence, and by the tribunals of the Revolution, to ensnare

---

1. Reference to the special commissions instituted for the punishment of those involved in black market or various political activities.

the man brought to trial; the man for whom society ought to provide the means of defense because it considers itself to have the sad right of taking away his life.

Had the Constituent Assembly abolished the punishment of death, at least for political offenses, perhaps the judicial assassinations which we have witnessed would not have taken place.[2] The Emperor Leopold II, in his capacity of Grand Duke of Tuscany, abolished the punishment of death in his territories, and so far from increasing offenses by the mildness of his legislation, the prisons were empty during several months successively, a thing never before known in that country. The National Assembly substituted for the parliaments, composed of men who had purchased their places, the admirable institutions of juries, which will be daily more venerated as the public becomes more sensible of its advantages.[3] Particular circumstances of rare occurrence may intimidate jurymen when both government and the people unite to alarm them; but we have seen most of the factions which have succeeded to power distrust these equitable tribunals and replace them by military commissions, and by prevôtal or by special courts,[4] which are merely so many names to disguise political murders. The Constituent Assembly, on the other hand, limited, as much as it possibly could, the competency of courts-martial, confining their jurisdiction to trespasses committed by soldiers in time of war, and out of the territory of France; it deprived the prevôtal courts of those powers which it has since unluckily attempted to renew and even to extend.

Lettres de cachet enabled the King, and consequently his ministers, to exile, transport, or imprison for life any man without even the form of trial. A power of this nature, wherever it exists, is equivalent to despotism:

2. Robespierre proposed the elimination of the death penalty in May 1791. It was finally abolished in February 1848, but the decree was not implemented before 1871.

3. Judgment by jury was a major topic in the political debates of the Bourbon Restoration, when it was defended by all French liberals from Constant to Royer-Collard. In volume 1 of *Democracy in America*, Tocqueville drew a long list of the advantages of juries for the democratic education of citizens, insisting on the seminal role played by the juries in the apprenticeship of civil and political liberties.

4. This occurred during the Consulate and the Empire. On prevotal and martial courts in France, see Jacques Godechot, *Les institutions de la France sous la révolution et l'empire.*

it ought to have fallen from the first day that the deputies of the French nation were assembled.

The Constituent Assembly, by proclaiming complete liberty of worship, replaced religion in its sanctuary—the conscience; and twelve centuries of superstition, hypocrisy, and massacre, no longer left any traces, thanks to the short interval in which the power of legislation was placed in the hands of enlightened men.

Religious vows were no longer deemed obligatory in law; every individual, of either sex, was left at liberty to impose on themselves the most singular privations if they thought that such was the mode of pleasing the author of all pure and virtuous enjoyments; but society no longer took on itself to force either monks or nuns to remain in their secluded abodes if they repented the unfortunate promises made in a moment of enthusiasm. The younger sons of families, frequently obliged to enter the ecclesiastical state, were now freed from their chains, and were afterward set still more at liberty when the property of the clergy became the property of the country.[5]

A hundred thousand nobles were exempt from the payment of taxes.[6] They were not accountable for an insult committed on a citizen or on a soldier of the Third Estate, because they were considered as of a different race. Officers could be appointed only from among those privileged persons, with the exception of the artillery and engineer departments, in which there was required a larger share of information than was in general

---

5. On this issue, see Acton, *Lectures on the French Revolution*, 143–50. In August 1789, it was decided that the clergy, once a powerful and privileged order, would become salaried functionaries of the state. On November 26, 1789, the majority of the representatives (568 to 346) voted to place the possessions of the clergy at the disposal of the French state. After the property of the church became the property of the state, the Constituent Assembly passed the so-called Civil Constitution of the Clergy (July 12, 1790), which regulated the relations between church and state under the new political circumstances. Pope Pius VI condemned the document as heretical in the spring of 1791. The text of the Civil Constitution can be found in Baker, ed., *The Old Regime and the French Revolution*, vol. 7, 239–42. For more information, see *A Critical Dictionary of the French Revolution*, 449–57.

6. The nobles were exempt from the payment of the *taille*. At the same time they did not pay the other direct taxes according to their wealth.

possessed by the provincial nobles.[7] Regiments were, however, given to young men of rank incapable of commanding them, because, their birth preventing them from following any other than the military profession, it became incumbent on government to provide for their support. The consequence was that, with the exception of personal courage, the French army under the Old Regime was becoming daily less and less respectable in the eyes of foreigners. What emulation, and what military talents, has not the equality of the citizens drawn forth in France! It is thus that we owe to the Constituent Assembly that glory of our arms of which we had reason to be proud, so long as it did not become the property of one man.[8]

The unlimited power of the King enabled him, by a *lettre de cachet*, to shield a man of rank from prosecution when he had been guilty of a crime. Of this the Comte de Charalois[9] was a striking example in the last century, and many others of the same nature might be quoted. Yet, by a singular contrast the relatives of the nobility lost none of their respectability when one of their number underwent a capital punishment, while the family of a man of the Third Estate was dishonored if he was condemned to the infamous death of hanging, from which the nobles alone were exempt.

All these prejudices vanished in a day. The power of reason is immense, as soon as it can show itself without obstruction. The efforts made in the last fifteen years have been in vain: it will be impossible to bring back the nation to the endurance of those abuses which force alone had maintained.

We are indebted to the Constituent Assembly for the suppression of the privileged castes in France, and for civil liberty to all; at least, we owe to them liberty, such as it exists in their decrees; for it has been always found necessary to deviate from these decrees when attempts were made to re-establish suppressed abuses either under new or old names.

Law in France was so varied and multiform that not only were the different orders of the state governed by different laws, but almost each

---

7. After the changes introduced by Count de Saint-Germain and the Marshal de Ségur in 1776–77 and 1781, all the officers were required to prove that they had a certain noble origin.

8. Reference to Napoléon, the archenemy of Madame de Staël.

9. The brother of the Duke of Bourbon, the Count of Charalois, was known for his extravagant behavior and numerous conflicts with the authorities (he was arrested and freed). His land was annexed by France after his death in 1761.

province, as we have already remarked, had its distinct privileges. The Constituent Assembly, by dividing France into eighty-three departments, effaced these ancient separations: it suppressed the taxes on salt and tobacco, taxes equally expensive and vexatious, which exposed to the severest punishment a number of fathers of families who were tempted, by the facility of contraband, to violate unjust laws. The taxes were rendered uniform, and this advantage, at least, is secured forever.

Distinctions of all kinds were invented by the nobles of the second order to protect them from that equality with which they are in truth very closely threatened. The privileged of yesterday aimed, above all things, to escape being confounded with the people of whom they were so lately a part. The tithes and feudal services pressed heavily on the poor; compulsory service, such as that of the *corvée,* and other relics of feudal barbarism were still general. The game laws contained provisions ruinous to the farmers, and the insolent tone of these laws was at least as revolting as the actual evil that resulted from them.

If we are surprised that France should still have so many resources in spite of her misfortunes; if, notwithstanding the loss of her colonies, commerce has opened new paths; if the progress of agriculture is wonderful in spite of the conscription and the invasion of foreign troops, it is to the decrees of the Constituent Assembly that we are to attribute it. France under the old form would have sunk under the thousandth part of the disasters which France of the present day has supported.

The division of properties, by the sale of the church lands, has relieved a very numerous class of society from a state of misery. It is to the suppression of the rights of corporations and wardenships, and to the removal of all restraints on industry, that we are to attribute the increase of manufactures and the spirit of enterprise which has shown itself in all directions. In short, a nation long fixed to the soil has come forth in a manner from underground; and we are astonished, after all the scourges of civil discord, at the store of talent, wealth, and emulation in a country delivered from the threefold fetters of an intolerant church, a feudal nobility, and an unlimited monarchy.[10]

---

10. In spite of their many political affinities, Madame de Staël and Burke differed significantly in their views on the Constituent Assembly. Burke ended up rejecting the entire

The finances, which seemed so complicated a labor, assumed regularity almost of themselves as soon as it was decided that the taxes should await the sanction of the representatives of the people, and that publicity should be given to the accounts of revenue and expenditure. The Constituent Assembly is perhaps the only one in France that fully represented the national wish; and it is on that account that its strength was incalculable.

Another aristocracy, that of the capital, had also an imperious sway. Everything was done at Paris, or rather at Versailles; for all power was concentrated in the ministers and in the court. The Constituent Assembly easily accomplished what M. Necker had attempted in vain, the establishment of provincial assemblies. One was constituted in each department,[11] and municipalities were appointed for each town. Local business was thus committed to magistrates who took a real interest in it, and who were personally known to those whose affairs they administered. On all sides were diffused life, emulation, and intelligence: there was a France instead of a capital, a capital instead of a court. The voice of the people, so long called the voice of God, was at last consulted by government; and it would have supplied a wise rule of guidance had not, as we are condemned to remember, the Constituent Assembly proceeded with too much precipitation in its reform, from the very commencement of its power; and had it not soon after fallen into the hands of factious men, who, having nothing more to reap in the field of beneficence, endeavored to excite mischief, that they might enter on a new career.

The establishment of a national guard is another very great benefit derived from the Constituent Assembly. No liberty can exist in that country where arms are borne only by soldiers, and not by citizens. Finally, this Assembly, in proclaiming the renunciation of conquests, seemed inspired by prophetic dread; wishing to turn the vivacity of the French toward internal improvement and raise the dominion of thought above that of arms. All inferior men are ready to call the bayonet to their assistance

---

work of the Assembly, while Staël espoused a much more nuanced position in line with that of other French liberals.

11. As Godechot pointed out, the Assembly was instrumental in the creation of *conseils généraux des departements*, whose attributions were different from those of the provincial assemblies.

against the arguments of reason, that they may act by means just as mechanical as their own understanding; but superior minds desire nothing but the free exercise of thought, and are aware how much a state of war is unfavorable to it.[12] The good produced by the Constituent Assembly in France doubtless inspired the nation with that energetic feeling which made it defend by arms the rights it had acquired; but we are bound, in justice, to say that the principles of this Assembly were perfectly pacific. It felt no envy toward any portion of Europe; and if it had been shown, in a magic mirror, France losing her liberty by her victories, it would have endeavored to combat this impulse of the blood by the more lofty impulse of the understanding.

12. An indirect critique of Napoléon, who shrewdly used the army and censorship to strengthen his personal power.

Liberty of the Press, and State of the Police, During the Time of the Constituent Assembly.

Not only does the Constituent Assembly claim the gratitude of the French people for the reform of the abuses by which they were oppressed; but we must render it the further praise of being the only one of the authorities which have governed France before and since the Revolution which allowed, freely and unequivocally, the liberty of the press. This it no doubt did more willingly from the certainty of its having public opinion in its favor; but there can be no free government except on that condition. Moreover, although the great majority of publications were in favor of the principles of the Revolution, the newspapers on the aristocratic side attacked, with the greatest bitterness, individuals of the popular party, who could not fail to be irritated by it.[1]

Previous to 1789, Holland and England were the only countries in Europe that enjoyed the liberty of the press secured by law. Political discussions in periodical journals began at the same time with representative governments; and these governments are inseparable from them. In absolute monarchies, a court gazette suffices for the publication of official

1. Madame de Staël's statement must be interpreted in the historical context of the first years of the Bourbon Restoration, during which time the issue of the liberty of the press, one of the pillars of representative government, was widely debated in the Chamber of Deputies. Staël's friend Benjamin Constant was one of the most important and eloquent defenders of liberty of the press against its critics. Staël favored absolute liberty for books but defended the need for censorship of journals. For more information, see Hatin, *Histoire politique et littéraire de la presse en France*, vol. 8. For more information about freedom of the press in France since 1789, also see Avenel, *Histoire de la presse française depuis 1789 à nos jours;* and Livois, *Histoire de la presse française. I: Des origines à 1881.*

news; but that a whole nation may read daily discussions on public affairs, it is necessary that it should consider public affairs as its own. The liberty of the press is then quite a different matter in countries where there are assemblies whose debates may be printed every morning in the newspapers, and under the silent government of unlimited power. The *censure préalable,* or examination before printing, may, under the latter government, either deprive us of a good work or preserve us from a bad one. But the case is not the same with newspapers, the interest of which is momentary: these, if subjected to previous examination, are necessarily dependent on ministers; and there is no longer a national representation from the time that the executive power has in its hands, by means of newspapers, the daily molding of facts and reasonings: this makes it as much master of the public opinion as of the troops in its pay.

All persons are agreed on the necessity of repressing by law the abuses of the liberty of the press; but if the executive power alone has the right of giving a tone to the newspapers, which convey to constituents the speeches of their delegates, the censorship is no longer defensive, it is imperative; for it must prescribe the spirit in which the public papers are to be composed. It is not then a negative but a positive power, that is conferred on the ministers of a country when they are invested with the correction, or rather the composition of newspapers. They can thus circulate whatever they want about an individual, and prevent that individual from publishing his justification. At the time of the revolution of England, in 1688, it was by sermons delivered in the churches that public opinion was formed. The case is similar in regard to newspapers in France: had the Constituent Assembly forbidden the reading of "the Acts of the Apostles,"[2] and permitted only the periodical publications adverse to the aristocratic party, the public, suspecting some mystery because it witnessed constraint, would not have so cordially attached itself to deputies whose conduct it could not follow nor appreciate with certainty.

Absolute silence on the part of newspapers would, in that case, be infinitely preferable, since the few letters that would reach the country

2. The main authors were Rivarol and Peltier. Also see Belanger et al., *Histoire générale de la presse française,* vol. 1, 475–79.

would convey, at least, some pure truths. The art of printing would bring back mankind to the darkness of sophistry were it wholly under the management of the executive power, and were governments thus enabled to counterfeit the public voice. Every discovery for the improvement of society is instrumental to a despotic purpose if it is not conducive to liberty.

But the troubles of France were caused, it will be alleged, by the licentiousness of the press. Who does not now admit that the Constituent Assembly ought to have left seditious publications, like every other public offense, to the judgment of the courts? But if for the purpose of maintaining its power it had silenced its adversaries, and confined the command of the press only to its adherents, the representative government would have been extinguished. A national representation on an imperfect plan is but an additional instrument in the hands of tyranny. The history of England shows how far obsequious parliaments go beyond even ministers themselves in the adulation of power. Responsibility has no terrors to a collective body; besides, the more admirable a thing is in itself, whether we speak of national representation, oratory, or the talent of composition, the more despicable it becomes when perverted from its natural destination; in that case, that which is naturally bad proves the less exceptionable of the two.

Representatives form by no means a separate caste; they do not possess the gift of miracles; they are of importance only when supported by the nation; but as soon as that support fails them, a battalion of grenadiers is stronger than an assembly of three hundred deputies. It is then a moral power which enables them to balance the physical power of that authority which soldiers obey; and this moral power consists entirely in the action of the liberty of the press on the public mind. The power which distributes patronage becomes everything as soon as the public opinion, which awards reputation, is reduced to nothing.

But cannot this right, some persons may say, be suspended for some time? And by what means should we then be apprised of the necessity of re-establishing it? The liberty of the press is the single right on which all other rights depend; the security of an army is in its sentinels. When you wish to write against the suspension of that liberty, your arguments on such a subject are exactly what government does not permit you to publish.

There is, however, one circumstance that may necessitate the submitting of newspapers to examination, that is, to the authority of the government which they ought to enlighten: I mean, when foreigners happen to be masters of a country. But in that case, there is nothing in the country, do what you will, that can be compared to regular government. The only interest of the oppressed nation is then to recover, if possible, its independence; and, as in a prison, silence is more likely to soften the jailor than complaint, we should be silent so long as chains are imposed at once on our thoughts and our feelings.

A merit of the highest kind which belonged, beyond dispute, to the Constituent Assembly was that of always respecting the principles of freedom, which it proclaimed. Often have I seen sold at the door of an assembly more powerful than ever was a king of France, the most bitter insults to the members of the majority, their friends, and their principles. The Assembly forebore likewise to have recourse to any of the secret expedients of power, and looked to no other support than the general adherence of the country. The secrecy of private correspondence was inviolate, and the invention of a ministry of police did not then figure in the list of possible calamities.[3] The case in regard to the police is the same as in regard to the restraint on newspapers: the actual state of France, occupied by foreign troops,[4] can alone give a proper conception of its cruel necessity.

When the Constituent Assembly, removed from Versailles to Paris, was, in many respects, no longer mistress of its deliberations, one of its

3. Such a ministry of police was created under the Directory in 1796.

4. Humiliated by its defeat at Waterloo in 1814, France was placed under the supervision of the League of the Holy Alliance represented by Russia, Austria, and Prussia, which had the right to interfere in the domestic affairs of all other European countries. The Allies demanded that France surrender a considerable piece of its territory (including three key cities: Lille, Metz, and Strasbourg), pay an indemnity of 700 million francs, and accept a five-year military occupation (later reduced to three years). As a result of the Treaty of November 1815, France lost at least 500,000 inhabitants and was required to accommodate some 800,000 foreign soldiers, who had to be supplied by means of requisitions.

committees thought proper to take the name of Committee of Inquiries, appointed to examine into the existence of some alleged conspiracies denounced in the Assembly. This committee was without power, as it had no spies or agents under its orders, and the freedom of speech was besides wholly unlimited. But the mere name of Committee of Inquiries, analogous to that of the inquisitorial institutions adopted by tyrants in church and state, inspired general aversion;[5] and poor Voydel, who happened to be president of this committee, although perfectly inoffensive, was not admitted into any party.

The dreadful sect of Jacobins pretended, in the sequel, to found liberty on despotism, and from that system arose all the crimes of the Revolution. But the Constituent Assembly was far from adopting that course; its measures were strictly conformable to its object, and it was in liberty itself that it sought the strength necessary to establish liberty. Had it combined with this noble indifference to the attacks of its adversaries, for which public opinion avenged it, a proper severity against all publications and meetings which stimulated the populace to disorder; had it considered that the moment any party becomes powerful, its first duty is to repress its own adherents, this Assembly would have governed with so much energy and wisdom that the work of ages might have been accomplished, perhaps, in two years. One can scarcely refrain from believing that that fatality, which so often punishes the pride of man, was here the only obstacle: for, at that time, everything appeared easy, so great was the union of the public and so fortunate the combination of circumstances.

5. The formation of the Committee of Inquiries was followed by the creation of a Committee of General Security in 1792.

CHAPTER VI

Of the Different Parties Conspicuous in the Constituent Assembly.

There was one general disposition among all the popular party, for all aimed at liberty; but there were particular divisions in the majority as in the minority of the Assembly, and most of these divisions were founded on the personal interests which now began to prevail. When the influence of an assembly ceases to be confined within the limits of legislating, and when a great share of the public patronage falls into its hands, the danger in any country, but particularly in France, is that general views and principles generate only sophisms, which make general truths dexterously subservient to the purposes of individuals.

The aristocratic part of the Assembly, called the right side (*coté droit*), was composed almost entirely of nobles, prelates, and members of the old parliament: scarcely thirty members of the Third Estate had joined them. This party, which had protested against all the resolutions of the Assembly, continued to attend it only from motives of prudence: all that passed there appeared to it insolent and unimportant; so ridiculous did they think that discovery of the eighteenth century—*a nation*—while, till then, nothing had been heard of but nobility, priests, and people. When the members of the right side condescended to drop their ironical strain, it was to treat as impious every encroachment made on old institutions; as if the social order alone, in the course of nature, ought to be doomed to the double infirmity of infancy and old age, and to pass from the formlessness of youth to the decrepitude of old age without receiving any real strength from the knowledge acquired over time. The privileged orders made use of religion as a safeguard for the interest of their caste; and it was by thus confounding privileges and dogmas that they greatly impaired the influence of true Christianity in France.

The orator of the nobles, as I have already remarked, was M. de Casalès, who had been ennobled within the last twenty-five years; for most of the men of talent among the families of real antiquity had sided with the popular party. The Abbé Maury, the orator of the clergy, often supported the good cause, because he was on the side of the vanquished, a circumstance which contributed more to his success than even his talents. The Archbishop of Aix, the Abbé de Montesquiou, and other acute defenders of their orders sometimes endeavored, like Casalès, to win the favor of their adversaries, that they might obtain, not an acquiescence in their opinions but a vote of confidence on their talents. The other aristocrats were in the habit of using abusive language to the deputies of the people; and, always unwilling to yield to circumstances, imagined that they were doing good when they were only aggravating the evil. Wholly occupied in justifying their reputation as prophets, they even desired misfortune, that they might enjoy the satisfaction of having predicted truly.[1]

The two extreme parties in the assembly were in the habit of placing themselves as at the two ends of an amphitheater, and of occupying the highest seats on each side. On the right side,[2] coming down, were the party called *la plaine,* or *le marais;* that is, the moderates, for the most part advocates of the English constitution. I have already named their chiefs, Malouet, Lally, and Mounier;[3] they were the most conscientious men in the Assembly. But although Lally possessed the most impressive eloquence, though Mounier was a political writer of the greatest judgment, and Malouet a practical man of first rate energy; although out of doors they were supported by ministers, with M. Necker at their head, and although in the Assembly several men of talent rallied under their opinions,

---

1. On the role of Maury and Casalès in the constitutional debates of 1789, see Acton, *Lectures on the French Revolution,* 95. Acton rightly reproached the conservatives for their refusal of bicameralism out of fear that an upper chamber would be used as a reward for those who defected their ranks (106).

2. This is the origin of the terms "left" and "right," which originally designated the progressive and conservative groups, respectively, in the Assembly.

3. Acton held a similar view; see, especially, *Lectures on the French Revolution,* 98–103.

the two extreme parties threw in the background those voices, the most pure and courageous of all. They were still heard in the midst of a misled multitude; but the proud aristocrats could not have patience with men desirous of establishing a wise, free, and, consequently, durable constitution; and they were often seen to prefer joining the violent democrats, whose folly threatened France and themselves with a frightful anarchy. Such are the characteristics of party spirit, or rather of that extreme self-love which does not allow men to tolerate any other ideas than their own.

Next to the moderate or impartial members were the popular party, which, although united on questions of great importance, were divided into four sections, each marked by clear shades of distinction. M. de la Fayette, as commander of the National Guard, and the most disinterested and ardent friend of liberty, was much esteemed by the Assembly; but his scrupulous opinions did not allow him to influence the deliberations of the representatives of the people; and it was, perhaps, too great a sacrifice to him to risk his popularity out of the Assembly by debates, in which he would have had to support the royal prerogative against democratic principles. He preferred the passive course that is suitable to a military man.[4] At a subsequent time he made a courageous sacrifice of this love of popularity, the favorite passion of his soul; but in the time of the Constituent Assembly he lost part of his credit with the deputies because he made use of it too seldom.

Mirabeau, who was known to be corruptible, had with him personally only those who aimed at sharing the chances of his fortune. But although he had not what can be called a party, he exercised ascendancy over all when he made use of the admirable power of his mind. The men of influence on the popular side, with the exception of a few Jacobins, were Duport,[5] Barnave, and some young men of the court who had become democrats; men perfectly pure in a pecuniary sense, but very desirous of acting a part of consequence. Duport, a counselor of *parlement*, had been

---

4. On La Fayette as commander of the National Guard, see ibid., 75–76.

5. Adrien Duport (1759–98) represented the nobles in the Estates General and joined the Third Estate in June 1789. He was one of the founders of the Feuillants, the Revolution's last moderates. For more information on the latter, see *A Critical Dictionary of the French Revolution*, 343–50.

during his whole life impressed with the defects of the institution to which he belonged; his profound knowledge of the jurisprudence of different countries gave him a claim, in that respect, to the confidence of the Assembly.

Barnave,[6] a young counselor from Dauphiny of the greatest merit, was more fitted by his talents than almost any other deputy to figure as a speaker in the English manner. He lost himself with the aristocratic party by one unlucky expression. After the 14th of July, great and just indignation was expressed at the death of three victims assassinated in the tumult. Barnave, elated by the triumph of that day, could not hear with patience charges which seemed directed against the people at large. In speaking of those who had been massacred, he called out, "Was then their blood so pure?" An unfortunate apostrophe, wholly unsuited to his upright, delicate, and even feeling character: but his career was forever marred by these reprehensible expressions. All the newspapers, all the speakers on the right, stamped them on his forehead, and irritated his pride to such a point as to make it impossible for him to recant without humiliation.

The leaders of the *côté gauche,* or left side of the Assembly, would have succeeded in introducing the English constitution if they had formed a union for this purpose with M. Necker, among the ministers, and with his friends in the Assembly. But, in that case, they would have been but secondary agents in the course of events, while they wished to hold the first rank; they consequently committed the great imprudence of seeking support from the crowds out of doors, which were beginning to prepare a subterranean explosion. They gained an ascendancy in the Assembly by ridiculing the *moderates,* as if moderation were weakness, and they the only men of energy. They were seen, both in the halls and in the seats of the deputies, turning into ridicule whoever ventured to assert that, before

6. Barnave (1761–93) was a representative of the Third Estate in the Estates General of 1789 and a prominent orator in the Constituent Assembly. The discovery of his secret correspondence with Marie Antoinette was the pretext for his imprisonment and execution in November 1793. On Barnave, see Furet's entry in *A Critical Dictionary of the French Revolution,* 186–96. For an English selection from his writings, see Chill, ed., *Power, Property, and History: Barnave's Introduction to the French Revolution and Other Writings.*

their day, there had been such a thing as society, that writers had been capable of thinking, or that England had possessed any share of liberty. One would have said that they were called to hear nursery tales, so impatiently did they listen to them, and so disdainfully did they pronounce certain phrases, extremely exaggerated and emphatic, on the impossibility of admitting a hereditary senate, a senate even for life, an absolute *veto*, property qualifications, in short, anything that, according to them, infringed on the sovereignty of the people. They carried all the foppery of a court into the cause of democracy, and many deputies of the Third Estate were at once dazzled by their manners as fine gentlemen and captivated by their democratic doctrines.

These elegant leaders of the popular party aimed at entering into the government. They were desirous of pushing matters to the point where their assistance would be necessary; but in this rapid descent the chariot did not stop at the stages they intended. They were by no means conspirators, but they were too confident of their influence with the Assembly, and thought themselves capable of restoring the authority of the throne as soon as they had made it come within their reach; but when they became sincerely disposed to repair the mischief already committed, the time was past. How many distresses would have been saved to France if this party of young men had united its forces with the moderates! for, before the events of the 6th of October (1789), when the King had not been removed from Versailles, and while the army, quartered throughout the different provinces, still preserved some respect for the throne, circumstances were such as to admit of establishing in France a reasonable monarchy.[7] Ordinary thinkers are in the habit of believing that whatever has taken place was unavoidable: but of what use would be the reason and the liberty of man if his will were not able to prevent that which that will has so visibly accomplished?

In the first rank on the popular side was seen the Abbé Sieyès, insulated by his peculiar temper, although surrounded by admirers of his mind. Till the age of forty he had led a solitary life, reflecting on political questions

7. In the French text: "une monarchie raisonnable," in other words, a constitutional monarchy.

and carrying great powers of abstraction into that study; but he was ill qualified to hold communication with other men, so easily was he hurt by their caprices, and so ready was he to irritate them in his turn. But as he possessed a superior mind, with a keen and laconic manner of expressing himself, it was the fashion in the Assembly to show him an almost super-stitious respect. Mirabeau had no objection to hear the silence of the Abbé Sieyès extolled above his own eloquence, for rivalship of such a kind is not to be dreaded. People imagined that Sieyès, that mysterious man, pos-sessed secrets in government, from which surprising effects were expected whenever he should reveal them. Some young men, and even some minds of great compass, professed the highest admiration for him; and there was a general disposition to praise him at the expense of everybody because he on no occasion allowed the world to form a complete estimate of him.[8]

One thing, however, was known with certainty—he detested the dis-tinctions of nobility; and yet he retained, from his professional habits, an attachment to the clerical order, which he showed in the clearest way pos-sible at the time of the suppression of the tithes. "*They wish to be free and do not know how to be just,*" was his remark on that occasion; and all the faults of the Assembly were comprised in these words. But they ought to have been applied equally to those various classes of the community who had a right to pecuniary indemnities. The attachment of the Abbé Sieyès to the clergy would have ruined any other man in the opinion of the pop-ular party; but, in consideration of his hatred of the nobles, the party of the *Mountain* forgave him his partiality to the priests.

The Mountain formed the fourth party on the left side of the Assembly. Robespierre was already in its ranks, and Jacobinism was preparing itself in the clubs. The leaders of the majority of the popular party were in the habit of ridiculing the exaggerations of the Jacobins, and of congratulating themselves on the appearance of wisdom which they could assume when compared with factious conspirators. One would have said that the pre-tended moderates made the most violent democrats follow them, as a huntsman leads his pack, boasting that he knows how to restrain them.

8. For more information about Sieyès and his political activity, see M. Sonnencher's preface to Sieyès, *Political Writings*, vii–lxiv.

It may naturally be asked what part of the Assembly could be called the Orléans party. Perhaps there was no such party; for no one acknowledged the Duke of Orléans as a leader, and he did not at all come forward in that capacity. The court had, in 1788, exiled him for six weeks to one of his estates; it had at times opposed his frequent journeys to England: it is to such contradictions that we are to attribute his irritation. His mind was more actuated by discontent than by projects, more by whims than by real ambition. What gave rise to the belief in the existence of an Orléans party was the idea current at that time among political writers that a deviation from the line of hereditary succession, such as took place in England in 1688,[9] could be favorable to the establishment of liberty, by placing at the head of the constitution a king who should be indebted to it for his throne, instead of one who should look on himself as humiliated by it. But the Duke of Orléans was in all possible points the man the least fitted to act in France the part of William III in England; and without taking into the account the respect entertained for Louis XVI, and so well merited by him, the Duke of Orléans was incapable either of supporting himself or of proving a support to anyone. He had grace, noble manners, and was a spirited presence in society; but his worldly successes made him prone to take principles lightly; and when agitated by the convulsions of the Revolution, he found himself without restraint as without power.[10] Mirabeau probed his moral value in several conversations, and became convinced, after the examination, that no political enterprise could be founded on such a character.

The Duke of Orléans voted always with the popular party in the Constituent Assembly, perhaps in a vague expectation of obtaining the highest prize; but this hope never gained consistency in any other head. He lav-

9. Reference to the so-called Glorious Revolution of 1688 that led to the peaceful replacement of the Stuart dynasty with William of Orange and Mary, daughter of James II. The key to William's success lay in the fact that the new king paid due respect to the constitution and customs of the country while promoting the necessary political changes that brought social and political peace.

10. Philippe d'Orléans, also known as Philippe-Égalité, father of the future King Louis-Philippe (1830–48), voted for the death sentence for Louis XVI before being himself executed in November 1793.

ished money, it is said, to gain the populace; but whether he did so or not, one can have no just conception of the Revolution to imagine that money so given could be productive of any influence. A whole people is not to be put in motion by such means. The great error of the adherents of the court always lay in seeking in matters of detail for the cause of the sentiments expressed by the nation at large.

CHAPTER VII

Of the Errors of the Constituent Assembly in Matters of Administration.

The whole power of government had fallen into the hands of the Assembly, which, however, should have possessed only legislative functions; but the division of parties was the unfortunate cause of confusion in the distribution of power. The distrust excited by the intentions of the King, or rather of the court, prevented him from being invested with the means necessary to re-establish order; and the leaders of the Assembly took no trouble to counteract this distrust, that they might have a pretext for exercising a close inspection on ministers. M. Necker was the natural intermediary between the royal authority and the Assembly. It was well known that he would betray the rights of neither; but the deputies, who continued attached to him notwithstanding his political moderation, believed that the aristocrats were deceiving him and pitied him for being their dupe. This, however, was by no means the case: M. Necker had as much penetration of mind as rectitude of conduct, and he perfectly knew that the privileged orders would be less backward in reconciling themselves to any party than to that of the early friends of liberty. But he performed his duty by endeavoring to restore strength to the government, for a free constitution can never be the result of a general relaxation of ties: the probable consequence is despotism.

The action of the executive power being stopped by several decrees of the Assembly, the ministers could do nothing without being authorized by it. The taxes were no longer discharged, because the people imagined that the Revolution so joyously welcomed was to bring with it the gratification of paying nothing. Public credit, even wiser than public opinion, although apparently dependent on it, was shaken by the faults committed by the Assembly. That body had much more strength than was necessary to bring the finances into order and to facilitate the purchase of corn, rendered necessary by the scarcity with which France was again threatened. But it replied with indifference to the reiterated applications of M. Necker on these points, because it did not wish to be considered, like the old Estates General, assembled merely for financial purposes; it was to constitutional discussions that it attached the highest interest. So far the Assembly was right; but by neglecting the objects of administration it caused disorder throughout the kingdom, and by that disorder all the misfortunes of which it bore itself the pressure.

At a time when France had both famine and bankruptcy to dread, the deputies used to make speeches in which they asserted that "every man has from nature a right and a wish to enjoy happiness; that society began by the father and the son," with other philosophic truths much fitter for discussion in books than in the midst of an assembly. But if the people stood in need of bread, the speakers stood in need of applause, and a scarcity in that respect would have seemed to them very hard to bear.

The Assembly, by a solemn decree, placed the public debt under the safeguard of the honor and loyalty of Frenchmen; but still it took no step to give a substantial effect to these fine words. M. Necker proposed a loan, at an interest of five percent; the Assembly discovered that four and a half was less than five: it reduced the interest accordingly; and the loan failed, for the plain reason that an assembly cannot, like a minister, possess the tact which shows how far the confidence of capitalists may be carried. Credit, in money matters, is almost as delicate as style in literary productions; a single word may disfigure a sentence, as a slight circumstance may overturn a speculation. The matter, it will be said, is in substance the same; but in the one way you captivate the imagination of men, and in the other it escapes from your hold.

M. Necker proposed voluntary gifts, and was the first to pour, by way of example, 100,000 francs of his own fortune into the treasury, although he had been already obliged to dispose of a million of his property in annuities to meet, by increased income, his expense as minister; for in his second, as in his first ministry, he refused all salary. The Constituent Assembly praised his disinterestedness but still declined to take financial matters into its serious consideration. The secret motive of such conduct in the popular party was, perhaps, a wish to find itself forced, by want of money, to a step which it had much at heart, the appropriation of the church property. M. Necker, on the other hand, wished to make the country independent of this resource, and to let its appropriation depend not on the wants of the treasury, but on justice. Mirabeau, who aimed at succeeding M. Necker as minister, availed himself of the jealousy natural to every assembly in regard to its power, to make it take umbrage at the attachment still shown by the nation to the minister of finance. He had an insidious manner of praising M. Necker. "I do not approve his plans," he used to say; "but since public opinion grants him the dictatorship, we must take them on trust." M. Necker's friends were aware with how much art Mirabeau sought to deprive him of the public favor by exhibiting that favor in exaggerated coloring; for nations, like individuals, are less prone to love when they are too often reminded of their affection.

The day when Mirabeau was most eloquent was that in which, in artfully defending a finance decree proposed by M. Necker, he delineated all the horrors of bankruptcy. Three times did he rise to excite terror by this picture; the provincial deputies were not at first much alive to it; but as they did not then know what they have been since so severely taught, to what a degree a nation can support bankruptcy, famine, massacre, executions, civil war, foreign war, and tyranny, they shuddered at the idea of the sufferings portrayed by the orator.[1] I was at a short distance from Mirabeau when he addressed the assembly with so much *éclat;* and, although very distrustful of his intentions, he captivated my admiration during two hours. Nothing could be more *impressive* than his voice; the gestures and the biting sarcasm which he knew so well how to use did not, perhaps, proceed from the soul, that is, from the inward emotion, but there was in his speech a life and power of which the effect was amazing. "What

---

1. A reference to Mirabeau's speeches on finances and bankruptcy given on September 26, 1789. Necker had two days earlier provided an account of the kingdom's finances, to which Mirabeau responded. Mirabeau intervened four times in the September 26, 1789, debates and managed to convince the Assembly to pass a vote of no confidence on Necker's plan. His interventions can be found in Chaussinand-Nogaret, ed., *Mirabeau entre le roi et la Révolution,* 286–95.

would it have been had you seen the *prodigy* (*monstre*)," said Garat, in his lively *Journal de Paris*. The remark of Eschines on Demosthenes[2] could not be more happily applied, and the uncertain meaning of the word (*monstre*) which denotes a prodigy, either in good or evil, added not a little to the point.

It would, however, be unjust to see nothing but faults in Mirabeau; with so much true talent, there always is a portion of good sentiments. But he had no conscience in politics; and this is the great defect which in France may be often charged on individuals as on assemblies. Some aim at popularity, others at honors, several at fortune; while some, and these are the best, at the triumph of their opinions. But where are those who ask themselves conscientiously in what their duty consists, without taking account of the sacrifice, whatever it may be, which the performance of that duty may require at their hands?

2. Eschines (390–314 B.C.), prominent Greek orator and rival of Demosthenes.

CHAPTER VIII

Of the Errors of the National Assembly in Regard to the Constitution.

In the code of liberty we have the means of distinguishing that which is founded on invariable principles from that which belongs to particular circumstances. Imprescriptible rights consist in—equality under the law, individual liberty, the liberty of the press, freedom of religion, the right of admission to public employments, and the grant of taxes by the representatives of the people. But the form of government, whether aristocratic or democratic, monarchical or republican, is but an organization of powers; and powers are themselves nothing but the guarantees of liberty. It does not enter into the natural rights of man that every government should consist of a house of peers, a house of elected deputies, and of a king, whose sanction forms a part of the legislative power. But human wisdom has not even to our days discovered any form of government which in a great country gives more security to the blessings of social order.

In the only revolution within our knowledge which was directed to the establishment of a representative government, the order of succession to the throne was changed, because the English nation were persuaded that James II would not sincerely give up his claims to absolute power in order to exchange it with a legal power. The Constituent Assembly did not go the length of deposing so virtuous a sovereign as Louis XVI, and yet it aimed at establishing a free constitution; the result of this was its considering the executive power as inimical to liberty, instead of rendering it one of its safeguards. It formed a constitution as a general would form a plan of attack.[1] All the mischief proceeded from this fault; for whether the King

1. In its original form, the principle of the separation of powers (Article 16 of the *Dec-*

was or was not resigned in his heart to the restraints required by the interest of the nation, they ought not to have examined his secret thoughts, but have established the royal power, independently of what might be feared or hoped from its actual possessor. Institutions, in the course of time, adapt men to themselves with more facility than men can rid themselves of institutions. To preserve the King, and to strip the office of its necessary prerogatives, was the most absurd and most reprehensible plan of all.[2]

Mounier, a declared friend of the English constitution, did not hesitate to make himself unpopular by professing that opinion: he declared, however, in the Assembly that the fundamental laws of the constitution did not stand in need of the royal sanction, on the broad principle that the constitution was prior to the throne, and that the king existed only by means of it.[3] There must be a compact between king and people, and to deny the existence of such contract would be equally contrary to liberty as to monarchy. But as a kind of fiction is necessary to royalty, the Assembly did wrong in calling the king a public functionary: he is one of the independent powers of the state, participating in the sanction of the fundamental laws, as well as in those of daily enactment. Were he only a simple citizen, he could not be king.

There is in a nation a certain stock of feeling, which should be managed like so much physical power. A republic has its enthusiasm, which Montesquieu calls its principle; a monarchy has also its principle; and even despotism, when, as in Asia, it is a part of the religious creed, is maintained by certain virtues; but a constitution of which one of the elements is the

---

laration of the Rights of Man) had a strong antimonarchical character insofar as it sought to transform the king into a simple magistrate—the head of the executive—entirely dependent on legislative power. At the same time, the skeptical attitude toward the executive power was accompanied by the extreme confidence in the virtues of legislative power.

2. In *Du pouvoir exécutif dans les grands états* (1792), Necker reevaluated the role of executive power and the balance of powers in modern society. Following in the footsteps of her father, Madame de Staël argued that in spite of the controversy surrounding the division of powers the most difficult problem was not their separation but their proper union.

3. Sieyès, otherwise a critic of Mounier, also defended the theory of the superiority of the constituent power vis-à-vis the authority of the monarch.

humiliation of either sovereign or people must necessarily be overturned by the one or the other.

That controlling power of circumstances which decides so many things in France prevented the proposition of a House of Peers. M. de Lally, who wished for it, endeavored to supply it by asking at least a House of Senators holding their places for life; but the popular party was irritated at the privileged orders, who kept themselves perpetually aloof from the nation, and rejected a lasting institution from momentary prejudice.[4] This was a very serious fault, not only because an upper house was a necessary medium between the sovereign and the national deputies, but because there existed no other method of quietly consigning to obscurity the nobility of the second order, so numerous in France; a nobility in no way consecrated by history or recommended by public utility in any shape— and which discovered, much more than its higher brethren, a contempt for the Third Estate because its vanity always made it fear its not attaining sufficient distinction.

The right side of the Constituent Assembly, that is, the aristocrats, could have carried the point of a House of Senators for life by joining M. de Lally and his party. But they preferred voting for a single chamber instead of two, in the hope of obtaining good by the excess of evil; a detestable calculation, which, however, made converts by its apparent depth. Many men imagine that to deceive is a greater compliment to their capacity than to adhere to truth, because the falsehood is their creation: it is, however, an author's vanity very misapplied.

After the cause of the two chambers was lost, the discussions proceeded to the question of the royal sanction to legislative acts.[5] Was the *veto* about

---

4. Lally-Tollendal's report recommending bicameralism was rejected by the Constituent Assembly on September 10, 1789. His colleague, Mounier, was also an eloquent defender of two chambers. For more information, see Furet and Halévi, eds., *Órateurs de la Révolution français*, vol. 1, 882–83.

5. The royal veto was discussed on August 31, September 4, and September 11, 1789. The *monarchiens* and Mirabeau argued in favor of an absolute royal veto. Sieyès opposed any form of royal veto, and Abbé Grégoire opposed the absolute veto and defended the suspensive (provisional) one. The representatives finally voted in favor of a suspensive royal veto on the Assembly's decrees during two legislative sessions. Grégoire's and Mirabeau's speeches of September 4, 1789, can be found in Beik, ed., *The French Revolution*, 97–112.

to be given to the King to be suspensive or absolute? The word "absolute" resounded in the ears of the vulgar, as if despotism were in question; and we now begin to see the disastrous effect of popular clamor on the decisions of enlightened men. It is scarcely possible for a reflecting mind to exercise sufficient deliberation to understand all the questions relative to political institutions; what, then, can be more fatal than to submit such questions to the arguments, and, above all, to the sarcasms of the multitude? They spoke of the *veto* in the streets of Paris as of a monster that would devour little children. Not that we are to draw from this the inference suggested to some persons by a contempt for their species—that the people are unfit to judge of what relates to their concerns. Governments have on their part given surprising proofs of incapacity; and checks are necessary to authority in every shape.

The popular party desired only a suspensive instead of an absolute *veto:* that is, that the King's refusal to sanction a law should, of itself, fall to the ground in the next Assembly, if the same law were again insisted on. The debates became heated: on one side it was argued that an absolute *veto* on the part of the King would be a bar to all improvements proposed by the Assembly: on the other, that the suspensive *veto* would reduce the King, sooner or later, to the necessity of obeying in all points the representatives of the people. M. Necker, in a report in which he treats with uncommon sagacity the most important constitutional questions, pointed out, as a means of accommodation, three stages in legislative progress instead of two; that is, that the King's *veto* should not fall to the ground till after a demand reiterated by the third Assembly. His reasoning on this subject was as follows.

In England, he said, the king very seldom makes use of his right to the *veto*, because the House of Peers almost always spares him that pain; but as it has been unfortunately decided in France that there should be but one chamber, the King and his council find themselves under the necessity of discharging at once the functions of an upper house and of the executive power. The obligation of making a habitual use of the *veto* implies the

Also see Furet, *Revolutionary France*, 76–78. For an overview of the constitutional debates of the summer of 1789, see Acton, *Lectures on the French Revolution*, 95–109.

necessity of rendering it more flexible, just as we require lighter weapons when obliged to employ them frequently. We may also be assured that by the time of a third legislative assembly, that is, three or four years after the vivacity of the French, on whatever subject, will be always calmed; and, in the contrary event, it is equally certain that if three representative assemblies should successively demand the same thing, the public opinion must be too strong to render it advisable for the King to oppose it.

It was improper under existing circumstances to irritate the public by the expression "an absolute *veto*," when, in fact, in every country, the royal *veto* gives way, more or less, before the national wish. The pompous nature of the word might be regretted; but the danger of it also was to be dreaded when the King was placed alone in the presence of a single assembly, and when, being deprived of the gradations of rank, he seemed, if I may so say, face-to-face with the people, and forced to put incessantly in the balance the will of one man against that of twenty-four million. Yet M. Necker in a manner protested against this plan of conciliation even in proposing it: for, while showing how the suspensive *veto* was the necessary result of having only one legislative chamber, he repeated that a single chamber was wholly incompatible with anything sound or permanent.

Efforts Made by M. Necker with the Popular Party in the Constituent Assembly to Induce It to Establish the English Constitution in France.

The King possessing no military strength after the Revolution of the 14th of July, there remained for the minister only the power of persuasion, whether in acting immediately on the deputies, or in finding sufficient support in public opinion to influence the Assembly through that medium. During the two months of tranquillity which were still enjoyed between the 14th of July, 1789, and the frightful insurrection of the 5th of October, the ascendency of the King on the public mind began again to appear. M. Necker recommended to him successively several measures which obtained the approbation of the country.

The suppression of feudal rights, pronounced by the Assembly during the night of the 4th of August, was presented to the sanction of the Monarch: he gave his assent to it,[1] but addressed to the deputation of the Assembly observations which obtained the approbation of all wise people. He blamed the rapidity with which resolutions of such number and importance had been embraced; he made them feel the necessity of a reasonable indemnity to the former proprietors of several of the suppressed

1. The King's consent to the decree of August 4, 1789, came late and was not unqualified. He sanctioned the decrees of August 4 and 11 only three months later, after the October Days. It is worth pointing out that the decree of August 11, passed after a week-long debate in the Assembly, decided which of the feudal rights were to be compensated. On the debates and significance of August 4, 1789, see Acton's *Lectures on the French Revolution*, 82–89.

revenues. The declaration of rights[2] was also offered to the royal sanction, together with several decrees already passed relative to the constitution. M. Necker was of the opinion that the King should answer that he could sanction only the whole, not a separate part, of a constitution; and that the general principles of the declaration of rights, though in themselves extremely just, required a special application that they might be subjected to the ordinary form of decrees. In fact, what signified the royal acquiescence to an abstract declaration of natural rights? But there existed for a length of time in France such a habit of making the King intervene in everything that, in truth, the republicans might as well have asked his sanction of a republic.

The establishment of a single chamber, and several other constitutional decrees which formed a complete deviation from the political system of England, were the cause of great concern to M. Necker, for he saw in this *royal democracy,* as it was then called, the greatest danger for the throne and for liberty. The spirit of party has only one apprehension: wisdom has always two. We may see, in the different publications of M. Necker, the respect which he had for the English government, and the arguments on which he drew when desiring the application of its fundamental principles to France. It was from the popular deputies, at that time all-powerful, that he now met with obstacles as great as those he had previously had to combat in the royal council. Whether as minister or as writer, he has always held the same language in this respect.

The argument urged in common by the two parties, the aristocrats and democrats, against the adoption of the English constitution was that England could do without regular troops, while France, being obliged by her continental position to maintain a great army, liberty would be found unable to resist the preponderance given by that army to the King. The aristocrats did not perceive that this objection turned against themselves; for if the King of France has, from the nature of things, greater compulsory means than the King of England, what inconvenience is there in imposing at least equal limits on his authority?

2. For more information, see Furet and Ozouf, eds., *A Critical Dictionary of the French Revolution,* 818–28, and Acton, *Lectures on the French Revolution,* 89–94.

The arguments of the popular party were more specious because they supported them even on those of their adversaries. The regular army, they said, ensuring more power to the King of France than to the King of England, it is indispensable to restrict his prerogative more, if we aim at obtaining as much liberty as is enjoyed by the English. To this objection, M. Necker replied that in a representative government, that is, one founded on independent elections and maintained by the liberty of the press, public opinion has always so many means of forming and showing itself that it may be equivalent to an army; moreover, the establishment of national guards was a sufficient counterpoise to the *esprit de corps* of the regular troops, even if the army (which is by no means probable in a country where the officers would be chosen not in one class exclusively, but agreeably to their merit) should not feel itself a part of the nation, nor take a pride in sharing its sentiments.

The Chamber of Peers was also, as I have already remarked, displeasing to both parties: to the one as reducing the nobility to a hundred or a hundred and fifty families whose names are known in history; to the other as renewing hereditary institutions to which a great many persons in France are extremely hostile, because the privileges and claims of the nobles have deeply wounded the feelings of the whole nation. Yet M. Necker made vain efforts to prove to the Commons that to change conquering nobles into patrician magistrates was the only method to accomplish a radical extinction of feudal customs; since nothing is effectually destroyed for which we do not provide a substitute. He endeavored also to prove to the democrats that it was a much better way of proceeding to equality, to raise merit to the first rank, than to make a vain effort to degrade the recollections of history, the effect of which is indestructible. These recollections are an ideal treasure, from which advantage may be derived by associating distinguished individuals with their splendor. "We are what your ancestors were," said a brave French General to a nobleman of the old government; hence the necessity of an institution in which the new shoots may blend with the ancient stems: to establish equality by admixture is a much more effectual mode than by attempts at leveling.[3]

3. Necker's account of the Constituent Assembly can be found in part II, chapter 2, of

Yet this wise opinion, though conveyed by such a man as M. Necker, perfectly unaffected and candid in his manner of expressing himself, proved unavailing against those passions which owed their origin to injured pride; and the factious, perceiving that the King, guided by the judicious advice of his minister, was daily regaining a salutary popularity, determined to make him lose this moral influence, after having stripped him of all real power. The hope of a constitutional monarchy was then once more lost for France, at a time when the nation had not yet disgraced itself by great crimes, and while it possessed the esteem both of itself and of Europe.

De la Révolution française (reprinted in *Oeuvres complètes*, vol. 9, 254–300). He summarized his position as follows: "The government of England was at hand to serve as an example to the Constituent Assembly; but the latter aspired to have the honor of inventing something new. It wanted to make people forget the past Numas, the Solons, the Lycurguses; it wanted to extinguish the glory of past, present, and future legislators, and the outcome of such an unreasonable ambition was a series of great evils. What a difference . . . [it] would have made if, instead of allowing so many political speakers, so many novices to err and divagate endlessly, they would have charged a simple clerk to come to the tribune and read from there, in a stentorian voice, the English constitution!" (298–99; my translation).

CHAPTER X

Did the English Government Give Money to Foment Troubles in France?

As the prevailing opinion of French aristocrats has always been that the greatest changes in social order are to be traced to individual circumstances, they were long converts to the notion which had absurdly gained ground, that the English ministry had excited, by means of money, the troubles of the Revolution. The Jacobins, the natural enemies of England, took a lot of delight in pleasing the people by affirming that *all the mischief arose from English gold distributed in France*. But whoever is capable of a little reflection will not believe, for a moment, the absurdity thus circulated. Could a ministry, subject, like the English, to the scrutinizing eye of the representatives of the people, dispose of a considerable sum of money without venturing to acknowledge its use to Parliament? All the provinces of France, rising at the same time, were without leaders, while the proceedings at Paris had been long before prepared by the course of events. Besides, would not any government, and particularly the most enlightened one of Europe, have felt the danger of establishing such contagious anarchy in its own neighborhood? Had not England, and Mr. Pitt in particular, to dread that the revolutionary spark would light on the navy, and among the inferior ranks of society?[1]

The English ministry have often given assistance to the emigrant party; but it was on a plan wholly contrary to that which would have been nec-

1. Fear that the Revolution might spread to England was, in fact, what motivated Burke to write *Reflections of the Revolution in France*. In the first part of the book, he vigorously attacked the revolutionary theories propagated by R. Price and his followers in the Revolutionary Society of London. For more on the impact of the French Revolution in England, see Hampsher-Monk, ed., *The Impact of the French Revolution*.

essary to excite a spirit of jacobinism. How can we suppose that individuals, extremely respectable in their private character, would have taken into pay, from among the lowest class, men who could not at that time interfere with public affairs otherwise than by committing theft or murder? Whatever opinion we may have of the diplomacy of the English government, can we imagine that the heads of a state who, during fifteen years, made no attempt on the life of a man (Bonaparte) whose existence threatened that of their country, should have stooped to a much greater crime by purchasing assassinations at random? Public opinion in England may be altogether misled in regard to foreign politics; but never, if I may so express myself, in regard to Christian morality, that is, in respect to actions which are not subjected to the control or excuse of circumstances. Louis XV generously rejected the Greek fire,[2] the fatal secret of which was offered to him; the English, in like manner, would never have kindled the desolating flames of jacobinism, had it even been in their power to create that new monster who rose up with devouring fury against social order.

To these arguments, which seem to me clearer than even facts themselves, I will add what my father has often declared to me—that, hearing an incessant rumor about pretended secret agents of England, he made every exertion to find them out; and that all the inquiries of the police, ordered and followed up during his ministry, served to prove that the gold of England had nothing to do with the civil troubles of France. Never has it been practicable to discover the slightest trace of connection between the popular party and the English government: in general, the most violent persons in that party have had no connection with foreigners; and, on the other hand, the English government, far from encouraging democracy in France, has made every effort to repress it.

---

2. A mixture of carbon, sulfur, and petrol that could burn even on water and was used to set fire to ships during the Middle Ages.

CHAPTER XI

Events of the 5th and 6th of October, 1789.

Before describing these too disastrous days, we should bring to our recollection that in France at the time of the Revolution, as well as in the rest of Europe, people had enjoyed for nearly a century a kind of tranquillity which conduced, it is true, to relaxation and corruption; but was, at the same time, the cause and effect of very mild manners. Nobody imagined, in 1789, that vehement passions lurked under this apparent tranquillity. The Constituent Assembly accordingly gave itself up without apprehension to the generous wish of ameliorating the lot of the people. They had seen it only in a state of servitude, and they did not suspect what has been since but too well proved—that the violence of revolt being always in proportion to the injustice of slavery, it was necessary to bring about changes in France with a prudence proportioned to the oppression of the old system.

The aristocrats will say that they foresaw all our misfortunes; but prophecies prompted by personal interest have weight with no one. Let us resume, then, the sketch of the situation of France before the occurrence of those early crimes from which all the others proceeded.

The general direction of business at court was the same as before the Revolution of the 14th of July; but the means at the disposal of the royal authority being considerably diminished, the danger of exciting a new insurrection was proportionably augmented. M. Necker was well aware that he did not possess the entire confidence of the King, and this diminished his authority in the eyes of the representatives of the people; but he did not hesitate to sacrifice by degrees all his popularity to the defense of the throne. There are not on earth greater trials for morality than political employments; for the arguments which, in such a situation, may be used to reconcile conscience with interest are innumerable. The principle, however, from which we ought rarely to deviate, is that of bringing assistance to the weaker party: we seldom err in guiding ourselves by such a landmark.[1]

M. Necker was of the opinion that the most perfect sincerity toward the representatives of the people was the soundest calculation for the King; he advised him to make use of his *veto*, to refuse whatever he deemed fit for rejection; to accept only what he approved; and to ground his resolutions on motives which might gradually influence public opinion. Already had this system produced a certain degree of good, and, had it been steadily followed, it would have still prevented many misfortunes. But it was so natural for the King to feel irritated at his situation that he lent too willing an ear to all the projects which accorded with his wishes, and which offered the pretended means of a counter-revolution. It is very difficult for a king, the inheritor of a power which, since Henri IV, had never been disputed, to believe himself without force in the midst of his kingdom; and the devoted attachment of those who surround him must easily excite his hopes and illusions. The Queen was still more alive to these confident conclusions, and the enthusiasm of her bodyguards, and other persons of her court, appeared to her sufficient to repel the popular wave, which pressed forward more and more in proportion to the weakness of the opposing dikes.

Marie Antoinette presented herself then, like Maria Theresa, to the bodyguards at Versailles, to recommend to them her august husband and her children. They replied by acclamations to an appeal which, in fact, should have moved them to the bottom of their souls; but this was quite enough to excite the suspicions of that crowd of men, whose minds were heated by the new prospects opened to them by the state of affairs. It was repeated at Paris, among all classes, that the King wished to leave the country; and that he wanted to make a second attempt to dissolve the Assembly. The Monarch thus found himself in the most dangerous situ-

---

1. A classic example of trimming in politics. The notion of trimming was first conceptualized by the Marquis of Halifax in his essay "The Character of a Trimmer"; see Kenyon, ed., *Halifax. Complete Works*, 50.

ation: he had excited disquietudes as if he had been strong, while, in fact, he was deprived of all means of defending himself.[2]

The rumor spread that two hundred thousand men were preparing to march to Versailles, to bring the King and the National Assembly to Paris. "They are surrounded," it was said, "by enemies to the public welfare; we must bring them amongst the true patriots." No sooner is a tolerably plausible expression invented in a time of trouble, than party men, and particularly Frenchmen, find a singular pleasure in repeating it. The arguments that might be opposed to it have no power on their minds; for their great object is to think and speak like others, that they may make sure of their applause.

On the morning of the 5th of October I learned that the populace were marching to Versailles; my father and mother had their residence there. I immediately set out to join them, but went by a less-traveled road, on which I met nobody. On drawing near to Versailles I saw the huntsmen who had accompanied the King to the chase, and, on arriving, I was told that an express had been dispatched to entreat him to come back. How strange is the power of habit in a court life! The King still did the same things, in the same manner, and at the same hours, as in the most tranquil times: the composure of mind which this implied procured him admiration at a time when circumstances allowed him no other virtues than those of a victim. M. Necker proceeded very quickly to the palace, to be present at the council; and my mother, more and more frightened by the threatening intelligence received from Paris, repaired to the hall which served as an antechamber to the council room, that she might share my father's fate, whatever it might be. I followed her and found the hall filled with a great number of persons, brought thither by very different sentiments.

We saw Mounier pass through to require, in his capacity of president of the Constituent Assembly, but much against his will, the unqualified

---

2. In fact, the King had again called the troops to Versailles. During a banquet given by the King's officers in honor of the recently arrived Flanders Regiment, the officers toasted the royal family and destroyed the *tricolore*. The news of this event reached Paris the next day and triggered the fury of the masses. The latter distrusted the King, who had yet to sign the decrees of the Assembly of August 4 and 11 and the *Declaration of the Rights of Man and of the Citizen*.

sanction of the King to the declaration of rights. The King had, so to speak, made a literal admission of its maxims; but he waited, he said, for their application, that he might affix his consent. The Assembly revolted against this slight obstacle to its will; for nothing is so violent in France as the anger which is felt toward those who presume to resist without being the strongest.

Everyone in the hall where we were assembled asked whether the King would set out or not. We were first told that he had ordered his carriages, and that the people of Versailles had unharnessed them; afterward that he had given orders to the regiment of Flanders, then in garrison at Versailles, to take arms, and that that regiment had refused. It has since been ascertained that the council took into deliberation whether the King should withdraw into the country; but as the royal treasury was empty, as the scarcity of corn was such that no assemblage of troops could be effected, and as no measures had been taken to make sure of the regiments on which reliance was still placed, the King apprehended the greatest eventual hazards from going to a distance; he was, moreover, persuaded that if he left the country, the Assembly would give the crown to the Duke of Orléans. But the Assembly had no such idea even at this time; and when the King consented, eighteen months after, to the journey which ended at Varennes,[3] he had an opportunity of seeing that he had no ground for apprehension in that respect. M. Necker was not of the opinion that the court should set out without such aid as might ensure the success of that decisive step; but he offered to the King to follow him, if he determined on it; being ready to devote to him his fortune and his life, although perfectly aware of what his situation would be in adhering to his principles in the midst of courtiers who, in politics as in religion, know only one thing—intolerance.

The King having eventually fallen at Paris under the sword of the factious, it is natural for those who advised his departure on the 5th of October to make a boast of it: for we may always say what we think proper

---

3. On the night of June 20, 1791, the royal family slipped out of Paris and headed toward the eastern frontier. The King and the Queen were captured the next day at Varennes and brought back to Paris.

of the good effects of an advice that has not been followed. But, besides that it was perhaps already impracticable for the King to quit Versailles, we must not forget that M. Necker, in admitting the necessity of coming to Paris, proposed that the King should thenceforward go hand in hand with the constitution, and seek support in it only; without that determination he would be exposed, do what he might, to the greatest misfortunes.

The King, in deciding on remaining, might still have taken the decision of putting himself at the head of his bodyguards, and of repelling force by force. But Louis XVI felt a religious scruple at exposing the lives of Frenchmen for his personal defense; and that courage, which no person could doubt who witnessed his death, never prompted him to any spontaneous resolution. Besides, at this time, even success would not have accomplished his safety; the public mind was in the spirit of the Revolution, and it is by studying the course of things that we succeed in foreseeing (as much as foresight is granted to the human mind) the events which the vulgar represent as the result of chance, or of the inconsiderate actions of a few individuals.

The King then decided on awaiting the army, or rather multitude, which had already begun its march; and every eye was turned toward the road that fronts the windows of the palace at Versailles. We thought that the cannon might first be pointed against us, which occasioned us much fear; yet not one woman thought of withdrawing in this great emergency.

While this mass was on its march toward us, we were informed of the arrival of M. de la Fayette, at the head of the National Guards, and this was, no doubt, a ground of tranquillity. But he had long resisted the wish of the National Guard, and it was only by an express order of the Commune of Paris that he had marched to prevent, by his presence, the misfortunes that were threatened. Night was coming on, and our dread was increased with the darkness, when we saw M. de Chinon, who, as Duke of Richelieu, has since so justly acquired a high reputation, enter the palace.[4] He was pale, fatigued, and in his dress like a man of the lower orders:

---

4. The Count of Chinon, later Duke de Richelieu (1766–1822), went into exile in Russia and returned to France at the beginning of the Bourbon Restoration. He served as prime minister from 1815 to 1818.

it was the first time that such apparel entered the royal abode, and that a nobleman of the rank of M. de Chinon found himself obliged to put it on. He had walked part of the way from Paris to Versailles, mixed with the crowd, that he might hear their conversation; and he had left them half-way, to arrive in time to give notice to the royal family of what was going on. What a story did he tell! Women and children, armed with pikes and scythes, hastened from all parts. The lowest of the populace were brutalized still more by intoxication than by rage. In the midst of this infernal band, there were men who boasted of having got the name of "headsmen" (*coupe-têtes*), and who promised to make good their title to it. The National Guard marched with order, was obedient to its commander, and expressed no wish but that of bringing the King and the Assembly to Paris. At last M. de la Fayette entered the palace and crossed the hall where we were, to go in to the King. Everyone surrounded him with ardor, as if he had been the master of events, while the popular party was already stronger than its leader; principles were now giving way to factions, or rather were used by them only as pretexts.

M. de la Fayette seemed perfectly calm; he has never been seen otherwise, but his delicacy suffered by the importance of the part he had to act; to ensure the safety of the palace he desired to occupy the posts of the interior: the exterior posts only were given to him. This refusal was natural, as the bodyguards ought not to be removed; but it had almost been the cause of the greatest misfortunes. M. de la Fayette left the palace, giving us the most tranquilizing assurances: we all went home after midnight, thinking that the crisis of the day was over and believing ourselves in perfect security, as is almost always the case after one has experienced a great fright which has not been realized. At five in the morning M. de la Fayette thought that all danger was over and relied on the bodyguards, who had answered for the interior of the palace. A passage which they had forgotten to shut enabled the assassins to get in. A similar accident proved favorable to two conspiracies in Russia,[5] at times when vigilance was at its height and when outward circumstances were most tranquil. It

---

5. Reference to the conspiracies against Tsars Peter III (July 1762) and Paul I (March 1801).

is therefore absurd to censure M. de la Fayette for an event that was so unlikely to occur. No sooner was he informed of it than he rushed forward to the assistance of those who were threatened, with an ardor which was acknowledged at the moment, before calumny had prepared her poison.

On the 6th of October, at a very early hour, a lady far advanced in years, the mother of Comte de Choiseul-Gouffier, author of the delightful *Travels in Greece*,[6] entered my room: she came in a panic to seek refuge among us, although we had never had the honor of seeing her. She informed me that assassins had made their way even to the Queen's antechamber, that they had massacred several of her guards at the door, and that, awakened by their cries, the Queen had saved her life only by flying into the King's room by a private passage. I was told at the same moment that my father had already set out for the palace, and that my mother was about to follow him; I made haste to accompany her.

A long passage led from the contrôle général, where we lived, to the palace: as we approached we heard musket shots in the courts, and as we crossed the gallery we saw recent marks of blood on the floor. In the next hall the bodyguards were embracing the National Guards, with that warmth which is always inspired by emotion in great emergencies; they were exchanging their distinctive marks, the National Guards putting on the belt of the bodyguards, and the bodyguards the tricolored cockade. All were then exclaiming with transport, *Vive la Fayette*, because he had saved the lives of the bodyguards when threatened by the populace. We passed amidst these brave men who had just seen their comrades perish, and were expecting the same fate. Their emotion restrained, though visible, drew tears from the spectators; but, further on, what a scene presented itself!

The people demanded with great clamor that the King and royal family should remove to Paris; an answer in assent had been given on their part, and the cries, and the firing which we heard, were signs of rejoicing from the Parisian troops. The Queen then appeared in the hall; her hair di-

---

6. Choiseul-Gouffier (1752–1817), French diplomat who served as French ambassador to Constantinople from 1784 to 1792. He was the author of the multivolume *Voyage pittoresque en Grèce*.

sheveled, her countenance pale, but dignified; everything in her person was striking to the imagination. The people required that she should appear on the balcony, and, as the whole court, which is called the marble court, was full of men with firearms in their hands, the Queen's countenance discovered her apprehensions. Yet she advanced without hesitation along with her two children, who served as her safeguard.

The multitude seemed affected on seeing the Queen as a mother, and political rage became appeased at the sight: those who that very night had perhaps wished to assassinate her, extolled her name to the skies.

The populace, in a state of insurrection, are, in general, inaccessible to reasoning, and are to be acted on only by sensations rapid as electricity, and communicated in a similar manner. Mobs are, according to circumstances, better or worse than the individuals which compose them; but whatever be their temper, they are to be prompted to crime as to virtue, only by having recourse to a natural impulsion.

The Queen, on returning from the balcony, approached my mother, and said to her, with stifled sobs, "They are going to force the King and me to proceed to Paris, with the heads of our bodyguards carried before us on the point of their pikes." Her prediction was accomplished, nearly as she had said: the King and Queen were taken to their capital. We went to Paris by a different road, which spared us that dreadful sight. It was through the Bois de Boulogne that we went, and the weather was uncommonly fine; the breeze scarcely agitated the trees, and the sun was sufficiently bright to leave nothing gloomy in the prospect: no outward object was in correspondence with our grief. How often does this contrast, between the beauty of nature and the sufferings inflicted by man, renew itself in the course of life!

The King repaired to the Hotel de Ville, and the Queen displayed there a remarkable presence of mind. The King said to the Mayor: "I come with pleasure to my good city of Paris"; the Queen added, "and with confidence." The expression was happy, but the event, alas! did not justify it. Next day the Queen received the diplomatic body and the persons of her court: she could not give vent to one word without sobbing, and we, likewise, were unable to reply to her.

What a spectacle was this ancient palace of the Tuilleries, abandoned for more than a century by its august inhabitants![7] The antiquated appearance of the outward objects acted on the imagination and made it wander into past times. As the arrival of the royal family was in no degree expected, very few apartments were in a habitable state, and the Queen had been obliged to get tent beds put up for her children in the very room where she received us: she apologized for it, and added, "You know that I did not expect to come here." Her physiognomy was beautiful, but irritated; it was not to be forgotten after having been seen.

Madame Elizabeth, the King's sister, appeared at once calm as to her own fate and agitated for that of her brother and sister-in-law. She manifested her courage by her religious resignation; this virtue which suffices not always for a man, is heroism in a woman.[8]

7. The Tuileries Palace, on the right bank of the Seine, was destroyed in 1871. The construction of the palace began under Catherine de Médicis in 1564, and the building was later enlarged so that its southeast corner adjoined the Louvre. Louis XIV resided at the Tuileries Palace while the palace at Versailles was under construction. After the completion of the latter in the 1660s, the royal family virtually abandoned the Tuileries Palace.

8. For more information on the October Days and the march to Versailles, see Acton, *Lectures on the French Revolution*, 110–22; and Necker, *De la révolution française*, part II, 271–82.

CHAPTER XII

The Constituent Assembly at Paris.

The Constituent Assembly, removed to Paris by an armed force, found itself, in several respects, in the same situation as the King: it no longer enjoyed complete liberty. The 5th and 6th of October were, if one may say so, the first days of the accession of the Jacobins; the Revolution then changed its object and its sphere; equality, not liberty, was henceforth its mark, and the lower order of society began from that day to assume an ascendency over that class which is called to govern by virtue of its knowledge and education. Mounier and Lally abandoned the Assembly and France.[1] A just indignation made them commit this error; the result was that the moderate party was without strength. The virtuous Malouet and an orator at once brilliant and serious, M. de Clermont Tonnerre, endeavored to support it; but there were henceforth few debates except between the extreme opinions.

The Constituent Assembly had been mistress of the fate of France from the 14th of July to the 5th of October, 1789; but from the latter date forward, popular force was predominant. We cannot too often repeat that for individuals, as for political bodies, there is but one moment of happiness and power; that moment should be embraced, for the chance of prosperity does not occur twice in the course of the same destiny, and he who has not turned it to account receives in the sequel only the gloomy

---

1. After the events of October 5–6, 1789, Mounier (who had been elected president of the Constituent Assembly in late September) gave up his mandate and returned to Dauphiny on November 15. A month later, he wrote *Exposé de ma conduite dans l'Assemblée Nationale* (in *Orateurs de la Révolution française*, vol. I, 908–97). Lally also presented his resignation in October and withdrew to Lausanne, where he wrote his *Mémoire de M. le comte de Lally-Tollendal*, which recounts his political career during the first phases of the Revolution. He returned to France under the Consulate and became a peer during the Bourbon Restoration.

lesson of adversity. The Revolution naturally descended lower and lower each time that the upper classes allowed the reins to slip from their hands, whether by their want of wisdom or their want of address.

The rumor was circulated that Mirabeau and some other deputies were about to be appointed ministers. Those of the *Mountain*,[2] who were well assured that the choice would not fall on them, proposed to declare the functions of deputy and minister incompatible, an absurd decree which transformed the balance of power into mutual hostility. Mirabeau, on this occasion, proposed very ingeniously that they should confine the exclusion from ministerial employment to him by name, in order that the personal injustice of which he was, as he said, the object, might not lead to the adoption of a measure at variance with the public welfare.[3] He required that the ministers should at least be present at the deliberations of the Assembly if, in contradiction to his opinion, they were prevented from being members of it. The Jacobins exclaimed that the presence of ministers would be enough to influence the opinion of the representatives, and assertions of this nature never failed to be received with enthusiasm by the galleries. One would have said that nobody in France could look at a powerful man, that no member of the Third Estate could approach a person belonging to the court, without feeling himself in subjection. Such are the melancholy effects of arbitrary government and of too exclusive distinctions of rank! The hostility of the lower orders toward the aristocratic class does not destroy its ascendency, even over those by whom it is hated; the inferior classes, in the sequel, inflicted death on their former masters as the only method of ceasing to obey them.

The minority of the nobility, that is, the noblemen who had gone over to the popular party, were infinitely superior, in purity of sentiment, to the extravagant part of the deputies of the Third Estate. These nobles were disinterested in the cause which they supported; and, what is still more honorable, they preferred the generous principles of liberty to the personal advantages which they enjoyed. In all countries where aristocracy pre-

2. The *Mountain* designated the Jacobin club, whose leaders were called *Montagnards* (mountain men) from the high benches they occupied in the Assembly.
3. The debate took place on November 6–7, 1789.

vails, that which lowers the nation gives a proportional elevation to certain individuals who unite the habits of high rank to the information acquired by study and reflection. But it is too costly to limit the range of so many men in order that a minority of the nobility, such as MM. de Clermont-Tonnerre, de Crillon, de Castellane, de la Rochefoucauld, de Toulongeon, de la Fayette, de Montmorency,[4] etc. should be considered the elite of France; for, in spite of their virtues and talents, they found themselves without strength on account of the smallness of their number. From the time that the Assembly held its deliberations in Paris, the people exercised their tumultuous power in all directions; clubs began to be established; the denunciations of the journals, the vociferations from the tribunes, mis-led the public mind; fear was the gloomy muse of most of the speakers, and every day new modes of reasoning and new forms of oratory were invented to obtain the applause of the multitude. The Duke of Orléans was accused of having tampered in the conspiracy of the 6th of October. The tribunal directed to examine the documents relative to the charge discovered no proofs against him; but M. de la Fayette could not bear the idea that even popular violence should be attributed to anything that could be called a conspiracy. He required of the Duke to go to England; and that prince, whose deplorable weakness admits of no qualification, accepted without resistance a mission which was a mere pretext to remove him. After this singular act of condescension, I do not believe that even the Jacobins ever had a notion that such a man was capable of at all in-fluencing the fate of France: the virtues of his family make it incumbent on us to mention him no more.

The country participated in the agitation of the capital, and a zeal for equality put France in motion, in the same way as hatred of popery kindled

---

4. The Marquis de Crillon (1742–1806) was a member of the liberal nobility and a dis-tinguished army officer. The Count de Castellane-Novejean (1758–1837) was also a promi-nent army officer and was elected deputy to the Estates General. The Duke de la Rochefoucauld-Liancourt (1747–1827), famous for his philanthropy, immigrated to Amer-ica in 1792 and returned to France in 1799. The Viscount of Toulongeon (1748–1812) was the author of *Histoire de la France depuis la Révolution de 1789*, published under the Consulate. The Duke de Montmorency-Laval (1767–1826) also represented the liberal no-bility and was a close friend of Madame de Staël's. He served as minister of foreign affairs in 1821–22.

the passions of the English in the seventeenth century. The Constituent Assembly was beaten by the waves in the midst of which it seemed to hold its course. The most conspicuous man among the deputies, Mirabeau, now, for the first time, inspired some esteem; and one could not avoid a sentiment of pity at the constraint imposed on his natural superiority. He was seen incessantly taking in the same speech the side of popularity and that of reason, endeavoring to obtain from the Assembly a monarchical decree in the language of a demagogue, and often venting sarcasms against the royalist party at the very time that he labored at the adoption of some of their opinions; in short, one saw clearly that he kept up a continued struggle between his judgment and his want of popularity. He received money in secret from the ministers for defending the interests of the throne: yet, after he rose to speak, he often forgot the engagements he had taken, and yielded to those peals of applause of which the fascination is almost irresistible. Had he been a conscientious character, he possessed perhaps talents enough to create in the Assembly a party independent of the court and people; but his genius was too much warped by personal interest to allow him its free use. His passions, like the serpents of Laocoön, enveloped him in all directions, and we witnessed his strength in the struggle without venturing to expect his triumph.

CHAPTER XIII

Of the Decrees of the Constituent Assembly in Regard to the Clergy.

The most serious reproach made to the Constituent Assembly is that it had been indifferent to the maintenance of religion in France: hence the declarations against philosophy which succeeded those formerly directed against superstition. The intentions of the Assembly in this respect are to be justified by examining the motives of its decrees. The privileged classes in France embraced a mode of defense common to the majority of mankind, that of attaching a general idea to their particular interests. Thus the nobility maintained that valor was the exclusive inheritance of their order; and the clergy, that religion could not subsist without the possession of property by the church. Both assertions are equally unfounded: battles have been admirably fought in England, and in France since the fall of the nobility as a body; while religion would find its way into the hearts of the French if attempts were not incessantly made to confound the articles of faith with political questions, and the wealth of the upper clergy with the simple and natural ascendency of the curates over the lower orders.

The clergy in France formed a part of the four legislative powers;[1] and from the time that it was judged necessary to change this singular constitution, it became impossible that a third[2] of the landed property of the kingdom should remain in the hands of ecclesiastics: for it was to the clergy, as an order, that these great possessions belonged, and they were

1. The four powers were the king, the clergy, the Estates General, and the *parlements*.
2. According to Godechot, the real figure was approximately 10 percent, with important local variations. See Godechot's notes to the French edition of Staël's *Considérations*, 627.

administered collectively. The property of priests and religious establishments could not be subjected to those civil laws which ensure the inheritance of parents to children; from the moment, therefore, that the constitution of the country underwent a change, it would have been imprudent to leave the clergy in possession of wealth which might enable them to regain the political influence of which it was intended to deprive them. Justice required that the possessors should be maintained in their incomes during life; but what was due to those who had not yet become priests, especially when the number of ecclesiastics greatly surpassed what the public service required? Will it be alleged that we never ought to change what once has been? In what moment then did the famous *"once has been"* become established forever? When did improvement become impossible?

Since the destruction of the Albigenses by fire and sword, since the torturing of the Protestants under Francis I, the massacre of St. Bartholomew, the revocation of the Edict of Nantes, and the war of the Cevennes, the French clergy have always preached, and still preach, intolerance. The free exercise of worship then could not accord with the opinions of the priests, who protest against it, if they were allowed to retain a political existence; or if the magnitude of their property placed them in a condition to regain that political existence the loss of which they will never cease to regret. The church does not become tolerant any more than the emigrants become enlightened; our institutions should be adapted to this.

What! it will be said, does not the church of England own property? The English clergy, being of the reformed faith, were on the side of political reform at the time when the last of the Stuarts wished to re-establish the Catholic religion in England. The case is not the same with the French clergy, who are naturally inimical to the principles of the Revolution.[3] Besides, the English clergy have no influence in state affairs; they are much less wealthy than the old clerical body of France, as England contains neither convents, abbeys, nor anything of the kind. The English clergy marry, and thus become a part of society. Finally, the French clergy hesitated long between the authority of the Pope and that of the King; and

3. It is important to recall that on June 14, 1789, six clergymen joined the Third Estate, thus contributing to the formation of the National Assembly.

when Bossuet[4] supported what is called the liberties of the Gallican church, he concluded, in his *Sacred Politics,* an alliance between the altar and the throne; but he did so by founding it on the maxims of religious intolerance and royal despotism.

When the French clergy quitted a life of retirement to intermeddle with politics, their conduct in the latter was almost always marked by a degree of confidence and artifice very unfavorable to the public interest. The dexterity which distinguishes men early obliged to conciliate two opposite things, their profession and the world, is such that, for two centuries past, they have constantly insinuated themselves into public business, and France has almost always had cardinals or bishops for ministers.[5] The English, notwithstanding the liberal principles which actuate their clergy, do not admit ecclesiastics of the second order into the House of Commons; and there is no example since the Reformation of a member of the higher clergy becoming a minister of state. The case was the same at Genoa, in a country altogether Catholic; and both government and the priesthood found their advantage in this prudent separation.

In what manner would the representative system be compatible with the doctrine, the habits, and the wealth of the French clergy, such as that body formerly was? A striking analogy naturally induced the Constituent Assembly no longer to acknowledge it as entitled to hold property. The kings possessed demesnes considered in former days as unalienable, and these properties were certainly as legitimate as any other paternal inheritance. Yet, in France, as in England, and in every country where constitutional principles are established, kings have a civil list; and it would be considered disastrous to liberty that they should be enabled to possess revenues independent of the national sanction. For what reason, then, should the clergy be better treated in this respect than the Crown? Might not the magistracy lay claim to property with more reason than the clergy,

---

4. Jacques-Bénigne Bossuet was a prominent French bishop and famous orator (1627–1704). He wrote many important books, including *Politics Drawn from the Very Words of Holy Scripture*, in which he defended royal absolutism and the divine right of kings.

5. In fact, only four prime ministers were clergymen: Richelieu, Mazarin, Fleury, and Brienne.

if the object of supporting them by an established land revenue be to exempt those who enjoy it from the ascendancy of government?

What signify, it will be said, the advantages or disadvantages of clerical property? The Assembly did not have a right to take it. This question is exhausted by the excellent speeches pronounced on the subject in the Constituent Assembly:[6] it was there shown that corporate bodies (*corps*) did not hold property by the same title as individuals, and that the state could not maintain the existence of these bodies, but inasfar as they should not be in contradiction to public interest and constitutional laws. When the Reformation was established in Germany, the Protestant princes appropriated a share of the church property either to the public expenditure or to charitable establishments; and a number of Catholic princes have, on various other occasions, made a similar disposal of such property. The decrees of the Constituent Assembly, sanctioned by the King, ought, certainly, to have as much force in law as the will of sovereigns in the sixteenth and following centuries.

The kings of France used to receive the revenues of clerical benefices during the intervals that they were vacant. The religious orders, who in this question are to be distinguished from the secular clergy, have often ceased to exist; and one cannot conceive, as was said by one of the most ingenious speakers whom we heard in the last session[7] of the Chambers, M. de Barante: "One cannot conceive in what manner the property of orders that are no more should belong to those who do not exist." Three-fourths of the property of churchmen were given them by the Crown, that is, by the sovereign authority of the time; not as a personal favor but to ensure divine service. For what reason, then, should not the Estates Gen-

---

6. Reference to the speeches on this issue given, among others, by Thouret, Talleyrand, Le Chapelier, Boisegelin, and Mirabeau (October–November 1789). For more information, see Furet and Halévi, eds., *Orateurs de la Révolution française*, vol. 1, 141–70, 393–94, 511–37, 692–700, 1044–59, 1091–97.

7. Reference to a speech given in 1816 by Baron Prosper de Barante (1782–1866), a prominent member of the French Doctrinaires and author of *Histoire des ducs de Bourgogne* (1824–26) and *Des communes et de l'aristocratie* (1821). Barante was a very close friend of both Madame de Staël's and Constant's. For more information, see Craiutu, *Liberalism Under Siege*, 30.

eral, in conjunction with the King, have had a right to alter the manner of providing for the support of the clergy?

But particular founders, it will be said, having bequeathed their property to ecclesiastics, was it lawful to divert it from this appropriation? What means does man possess to give the stamp of eternity to his resolutions? Are we to search in the darkness of time for titles that are no more, in order to oppose them to living reason? What connection is there between religion and that continued chicanery of which the sale of the national property is the object? In England, particular sects, and, above all, the Methodists, who are very numerous, provide regularly and spontaneously for the expenses of their worship. True, it will be said, but the Methodists are very religious, and the inhabitants of France would make no pecuniary sacrifice for their priests. Is not this incredulity produced entirely by the display of wealth in the church, and of the abuses which wealth brings along with it? The case is the same with religion as with government: when you endeavor to maintain by force what is no longer in consonance with the age, you deprave the human heart instead of improving it. Do not deceive the weak; neither irritate another class of weak men, the Free Thinkers,[8] by rousing political passions against religion; separate entirely the one from the other, and solitary reflection will always lead to dignified thoughts.

A great error, and one which it seemed easier for the Constituent Assembly to avoid, was the unfortunate invention of a constitutional clergy.[9] To exact from ecclesiastics an oath at variance with their conscience, and, on their refusing it, to persecute them by the loss of a pension, and afterward even by transportation, was to degrade those who took the oath, to which temporal advantages were attached.

---

8. In original: "esprit forts." A paraphrase by the English translator.

9. Reference to the division of the clergy triggered by the famous Civil Constitution of the Clergy, voted on July 12, 1790, that obliged all priests to pledge allegiance to the constitution. Some clergymen agreed (hence their name "constitutional"), but the majority refused to do it. It was at this point that the Revolution and the Catholic Church became implacable enemies. The conflict between the two hastened the fall of the monarchy and the civil war. For more information, see Furet's entry in *A Critical Dictionary of the French Revolution*, 449–57; and Acton, *Lectures on the French Revolution*, 145–50.

The Constituent Assembly ought not to have thought of forming a clerical body devoted to it, and thus affording the means, which were afterward embraced, of distressing the ecclesiastics attached to their ancient creed. This was putting political in the place of religious intolerance. A single resolution, firm and just, ought to have been taken by statesmen under those circumstances; they ought to have imposed on each communion the duty of supporting their own clergy.[10] The Constituent Assembly thought that it acted with greater political depth by dividing the clergy, by establishing a schism, and by thus detaching from the court of Rome those who should enroll themselves under the banners of the Revolution. But of what use were such priests? The Catholics would not listen to them, and philosophers did not want them: they were a kind of militia, who had lost their character beforehand, and who could not do otherwise than injure the government whom they supported. The establishment of a constitutional clergy was so revolting to the public mind that it was found necessary to employ force to give it effect. Three bishops were necessary to give consecration to the schismatics, and thus to communicate to them the power of ordaining other priests in their turn. Of these three bishops, on whom the founding of the new clergy depended, two were, at the last moment, ready to renounce their singular undertaking, condemned as it was equally by religion and philosophy.

We cannot too often repeat that it is necessary to act on all great ideas with sincerity, and to be careful how we admit Machiavellian combinations in the application of truth; for prejudices founded on time have more strength than reason herself from the moment that bad means are employed to establish the latter. It was likewise of importance in the contest still subsisting between the privileged classes and the people, never to put the partisans of the old institutions in a situation calculated to inspire any kind of pity; and the Constituent Assembly excited this feeling in favor of the priests from the time it deprived them of their life-hold estates, and thus gave a retroactive effect to the law. Never can the world disregard

10. The duty of supporting their own clergy was decided by the Convention in February 1795.

those who are in a state of suffering; human nature is, in this respect, better than it is thought.

But who, it may be said, will teach children religion and morality if there are no priests in the schools? It was certainly not the higher clergy who fulfilled this duty; and, as to the curates, they are more required for the care of the sick and the dying than even for education, excepting what regards a knowledge of religion: the time in which churchmen were superior to others in point of information is past. Establish and multiply the schools in which, as in England, the children of the poor are taught to read, write, and account: schools of a higher class are necessary for teaching the ancient languages, and universities for carrying still further the study of those beautiful languages and of the higher sciences. But it is political institutions that afford the most effectual means of laying the foundation of morals; they excite emulation and form dignity of character: we cannot teach a man that which he can learn only through himself. The English are not told in any catechism that they must love their constitution; there is no master for patriotism in the schools: public prosperity and domestic life are more effectual in inspiring religion than all that remains of the ancient customs intended for its maintenance.

CHAPTER XIV

Of the Suppression of Titles of Nobility.

The clergy are perhaps still the less unpopular of the two privileged orders in France; for equality being the moving principle of the Revolution, the nation felt itself less hurt by the prejudices of the priests than by the claims of the nobles. Yet we cannot too often repeat that nothing is more unfortunate than the political influence of ecclesiastics in a country, while hereditary magistracy, of which the recollections of birth constitute a part, is an indispensable element in every limited monarchy. But the hatred of the people toward nobles having burst forth in the earliest days of the Revolution, the minority of the nobility in the Constituent Assembly wished to destroy this germ of enmity, and to form a complete union with the nation. One evening then, in a moment of heat, a member proposed the abolition of all titles.[1] No nobleman, of those who had joined the popular party, could refuse to support this without showing ridiculous vanity; yet it would have been very desirable that the former titles should not have been suppressed without being replaced by a peerage, and by the distinctions which emanate from it. A great English writer[2] has said, with truth, that "whenever there exists in a country any principle of life whatever, a legislature ought to take advantage of it." In fact, since nothing is so difficult as to create, it is generally found necessary to engraft one institution on another.

The Constituent Assembly treated France like a colony in which there was no "past";[3] but wherever "a past" has existed, it is impossible to pre-

---

1. On June 19, 1790.
2. That writer is Burke.
3. For a similar critique, see Burke, *Reflections on the Revolution in France*, especially 124–26: "You had all these advantages in your antient states; but you chose to act as if you

vent it from having influence. The French nation was tired of the second order of nobility, but it had, and always will have, respect for the families distinguished in history. It was this feeling which ought to have been used in establishing an upper house, and endeavoring by degrees to consign to disuse all those denominations of Counts and Marquisses which, when they are connected neither with recollection of the past nor with political employments, sound more like nicknames than titles.

One of the most singular propositions of this day was that of renouncing the names of estates, which many families had borne for ages, and obliging them to resume their patronymic appellations. In this way the *Montmorencies* would have been called *Bouchard; La Fayette, Mottié; Mirabeau, Riquetti.* This would have been stripping France of her history; and no man, howsoever democratic, either would or ought to renounce in this manner the memory of his ancestors. The day after this decree was passed, the newspaper writers printed in their accounts of the meeting *Riquetti* the elder instead of *Comte de Mirabeau:* he went up in a rage to the reporters who were taking notes of the debates in the Assembly, and said to them, "You have by your *Riquetti* puzzled Europe for three days." This effusion encouraged everyone to resume the name borne by his father; a course that could not be prevented without resorting to an inquisition quite contrary to the principles of the Assembly, for we should always remember that it never made use of the expedients of despotism to establish liberty.

M. Necker, alone among the members of council, proposed to the King to refuse his sanction to the decree which put an end to nobility without establishing a patrician body in its stead; and his opinion not having been adopted, he had the courage to publish it. The King had determined on sanctioning indiscriminately all the decrees of the Assembly: his plan was to be considered by others, after the 6th of October, as being in a state of captivity; and it was only in compliance with his religious scruples that

---

had never been moulded into civil society, and had everything to begin anew. You began ill because you began by despising everything that belonged to you. You set up your trade without a capital." (*Reflections on the Revolution in France,* 124)

he did not in the sequel affix his name to the decrees which proscribed those of the priests who continued to acknowledge the power of the Pope.

M. Necker, on the other hand, wished the King to use his prerogative sincerely and steadily; he pointed out to him that if he should one day recover all his power, he would still have the power to declare that he had been in a state of imprisonment since his arrival at Paris; but that if he should not recover it, he was losing the respect of, and above all his influence with, the nation, by not making use of his *veto* to stop the inconsiderate decrees of the Assembly; decrees of which that body often repented when the fever of popularity was moderated. The important object for the French nation, as for every nation in the world, is that merit, talent, and services should be the means of rising to the first employments of the state. But to aim at organizing France on the principles of abstract equality[4] was to deprive the country of that source of emulation so congenial to the French character that Napoléon, who applied it in his own way, found it a most effectual instrument of his arbitrary sway. The report published by M. Necker in the summer of 1790, at the time of the suppression of titles, was closed by the following reflections.

> In following all the marks of distinction in their smallest details, we, perhaps, run the risk of misleading the people as to the true meaning of this word "equality," which can never signify, in a civilized nation, and in a society already established, equality of rank or property. Diversity in situation and employment, difference in fortune, education, emulation, industry; differing levels of ability and knowledge, all the disparities that are productive of movement in the social body, necessarily involve an outward inequality; and the only object of the legislator is, in imitation of nature, to point them all toward a happiness that may be equal, though different in its forms and development.
>
> Everything is united, everything is linked together in the vast extent

---

4. In *The Old Régime and the Revolution*, Tocqueville also highlighted the passion for equality (or the hatred of inequality) as the main element of the Revolution: "While the passion for freedom constantly changes its appearance, shrinks, grows, strengthens, and weakens according to events, the passion for equality is always the same, always attached to the same purpose with the same obstinate and often blind ardor, ready to sacrifice everything to those who permit it to satisfy itself" (246).

of social combinations; and those kinds of superiority which, to the first glance of a philosophic eye, appear an abuse, are essentially useful in affording protection to the different laws of subordination; to those laws which it is so necessary to defend, and which might be attacked so powerfully if habit and imagination should ever cease to afford them support.[5]

I shall have occasion in the sequel to remark that in the different works published by M. Necker during the course of twenty years, he invariably predicted the events which afterward occurred: so much penetration was there in his sagacity. The reign of Jacobinism was principally caused by the wild intoxication of a certain kind of equality; it appears to me that M. Necker described this danger when he wrote the remarks which I have just quoted.

5. From *Opinion de M. Necker sur le décret de l'Assemblée Nationale concernant les titres les noms, les armoires* (Paris, 1790); also see Egret, *Necker, ministre du roi,* 422–26.

CHAPTER XV

Of the Royal Authority As It Was
Established by the Constituent Assembly.

It was already a very dangerous matter for the public tranquillity to break all at once the strength that resided in the two privileged orders of the state. But had the means given to the executive power been sufficient, it would have been practicable to replace, if I may so express myself, fictitious by real institutions. But the Assembly, ever distrustful of the intentions of the courtiers, framed the royal authority against the King instead of making it a vehicle for the public good. Government was shackled to such a degree that its agents, though responsible for everything, could act in nothing. The ministry had scarcely a messenger at their disposal; and M. Necker, in his examination of the constitution of 1791,[1] has shown that in no republic, including even the petty Swiss cantons, was the executive power so limited in its constitutional action as the King of France. The apparent splendor and actual inefficiency of the Crown threw the ministers, and the King himself, into a state of anxiety that was perpetually increasing. It is certainly not necessary that a population of twenty-five million should exist for one man; but it is equally unnecessary that one man should be miserable even under the pretext of giving happiness to twenty-five million; for injustice of any kind, whether it reaches the throne

---

1. See Necker's arguments on the role of executive power in *Du pouvoir exécutif dans les grands états*, especially pt. II, chap. xv, 549–57, 575–78. Necker also discussed the Assembly's skepticism toward the executive power in *De la Révolution française*, pt. II, 288–97. On the role and limits of the executive power, also see Burke, *Reflections*, 309–16. A comprehensive analysis of Necker's views on this topic can be found in Grange, *Les idées de Necker*, 279–93.

or the cottage, prevents the possibility of a free, that is, of an equitable, government.

A prince who would not content himself with the power granted to the King of England would not be worthy of reigning; but, in the French constitution, the situation of the King and his ministers was insupportable. The country suffered from it still more than the sovereign; and yet the Assembly would neither remove the King from the throne nor renounce its temporary mistrust, at the time that the formation of a durable system was under discussion.

The eminent men of the popular party, unable to extricate themselves from this uncertainty, always mixed in their decrees a portion of evil with good. The establishment of provincial assemblies had long been desired; but the Constituent Assembly combined them in such a manner as to exclude the ministers altogether from this portion of the administration.[2] A salutary dread of all those wars so often undertaken for the quarrels of kings had guided the Constituent Assembly in the mode of organizing the military force; but it had put so many obstacles to the influence of the executive power in this respect that the army would have been unfit to serve out of the country, so apprehensive were they of its becoming instrumental to oppression at home. The reform of criminal jurisprudence and the establishment of juries brought down blessings on the name of the Constituent Assembly; but it decreed that the judges should owe their appointment to the people instead of the King, and that they should be re-elected every three years. Yet the example of England and the dictates of enlightened reflection concur to show that judges, under whatever government, ought not to be removable, and that in a monarchical state it is fit that their nomination should belong to the Crown. The people are much

2. The Constitution of 1791 provided for an unprecedented extension of the practice of popular election of local officials. According to chapter IV, section 2, "Internal Administration," the administrators of every department enjoyed a certain independence from central power. They were "elected at stated times by the people to perform administrative duties under the supervision and authority of the king." (*Documentary Survey of the French Revolution*, 252) The original text of the Constitution can be found in *Les Constitutions et les principales lois politiques de la France depuis 1789*, 1–32. For more information, see Taine, *The French Revolution*, vol. I, 217–49. Bailleul criticized Madame de Staël's views on the Constitution of 1791 in *Examen critique*, vol. I, 359–92.

less capable of appreciating the qualities necessary for a judge than those necessary for a representative of the people: ostensible merit and extensive information ought to point out to the eyes of all a fit representative,[3] but length of study alone qualifies a man for the duties of the bench. Above all, it is important that judges should be subject neither to removal by the king nor to re-appointment or rejection by the people. If, from the first days of the Revolution, all parties had agreed to show invariable respect to judicial forms, from how many misfortunes would France have been preserved! For it is for extraordinary cases, above all, that ordinary tribunals are established.

One would almost say that justice among us is like a good housewife, who is employed in domestic matters on working days, but who must not be brought forward on solemn occasions; and yet it is on occasions when passion is most excited that the impartiality of law becomes more necessary than ever.

On the 4th of February, 1790, the King had repaired to the Assembly to give, in a very well composed discourse, at which M. Necker had labored, his sanction to the principal laws already decreed by the Assembly. But in this same discourse the King forcefully showed the unhappy state of the kingdom and the necessity of improving and finishing the constitution. Such a course was indispensable, because the secret advisers of the King, representing him always as if he were in captivity, made the popular party distrustful of his intentions. Nothing was less suitable to so moral a character as Louis XVI than a presumed state of continual powerlessness; the pretended advantages of such a system were destructive of the real strength of virtue.

3. In the United States, however, judges are elected.

CHAPTER XVI

Federation of 14th July, 1790.

Notwithstanding the faults which we have pointed out, the Constituent Assembly had produced so much good, and triumphed over so many misfortunes, that it was adored by almost all France. The deficiencies in the work of the constitution were perceptible only to those intimately acquainted with the principles of political legislation, and liberty was actually enjoyed, although the precautions taken for its maintenance were not well combined. The career opened to talents of every kind excited general emulation; the discussions of an Assembly distinguished for talent, the varied movement of the liberty of the press, the publicity given to every matter of importance, delivered from bondage the mind of Frenchmen, their patriotism, in short, all those energetic qualities, the results of which we have since seen sometimes marked with cruelty, but always gigantic. It was like an individual who breathed more freely, whose lungs contained a larger portion of air; the indefinite hope of happiness without alloy had taken possession of the nation in its strength as it takes possession of a man in youth, when under the influence of illusion and devoid of foresight.

The chief uneasiness of the Constituent Assembly arising from the danger to which a standing force might one day expose liberty, it was natural for it to endeavor, by every method, to gain the national militia, considering it with truth as an armed force of citizens; besides, the Assembly was so sure of public opinion in 1790 that it took a pleasure in surrounding itself with the country's soldiers. A standing army is altogether a modern invention, the real object of which is to put into the hands of kings a power independent of their people. It was from the institution of national guards in France that the eventual conquest of continental Europe proceeded; but the Constituent Assembly was then very far from desiring war, for it was too enlightened not to prefer liberty to everything; and this liberty is incompatible with an invading spirit and with military habits.

The eighty-three departments sent deputies from their national guards to take an oath of fidelity to the new constitution. It was not, it is true, as yet completed; but the principles which it declared sacred had obtained universal assent. Patriotic enthusiasm was so strong that all Paris moved in a mass to the "federation of 1790," as it had moved the year before to the destruction of the Bastille.[1]

The assemblage of the national militia was to take place in the Champ de Mars, in front of the Military School, and not far from the Hotel des Invalides. It was necessary to erect around this extensive space mounds of grass to hold the spectators. Women of the first rank were seen joining the crowd of voluntary laborers who came to bear a part in the preparations for the fête. In a line from the Military School, and in front of the Seine, which flows past the Champ de Mars, steps had been raised, with a tent to accommodate the King, Queen, and all the court. Eighty-three spears fixed in the ground, and bearing each the colors of its respective department, formed a vast circle, of which the amphitheater prepared for the royal family made a part. At the other extremity was seen an altar, prepared for mass, which, on this great occasion, was celebrated by M. de Talleyrand, then Bishop of Autun. M. de la Fayette approached this altar to take the oath of fidelity to the nation, the law, and the King; and the oath, and the man who pronounced it, excited a strong feeling of confidence. The spectators felt an intoxication of delight; the King and liberty seemed to them, at that time, completely united. A limited monarchy has always been the true wish of France;[2] and the last movement of a truly national enthusiasm was displayed at this federation of 1790.

Yet those who were capable of reflection were far from giving themselves up to the general joy. I observed a deep anxiety in my father's countenance; at the moment when the public thought it was rejoicing for a triumph, he was perhaps aware that no resource was left. M. Necker hav-

---

1. On the formation of the National Federation, see Taine, *The French Revolution*, vol. I, 253–62.

2. This claim clearly illustrates the liberal intentions and agenda of Madame de Staël.

ing sacrificed all his popularity to the defense of the principles of a free and limited monarchy, M. de la Fayette was, of course, the grand object of popular affection on this day: he inspired the National Guard with an exalted devotion; but, whatever might have been his political opinion, his power would have fallen to the ground if he had ventured to oppose the feeling of the day. Ideas, not individuals, were then all-powerful. The dreadful will of Bonaparte himself would have been unavailing against the direction of the public mind; for the French at that time, far from being fond of military power, would have obeyed an assembly much more willingly than a general.

That respect for national representation which is the first basis of a free government existed in every mind in 1790, as if that representation had lasted a century instead of a year. In fact, if truths of a certain description are self-evident instead of requiring to be taught, it is enough to exhibit them to mankind in order to gain their attachment.

CHAPTER XVII

Of the State of Society in Paris During the Time of the Constituent Assembly.

Foreigners can have no idea of the boasted charms and splendor of Parisian society if they have seen France only in the last twenty years; but it may be said with truth that never was that society at once so brilliant and serious as during the first three or four years of the Revolution, reckoning from 1788 to the end of 1791. As political affairs were still in the hands of the higher classes, all the vigor of liberty and all the grace of former politeness were united in the same persons. Men of the Third Estate, distinguished by their knowledge and their talents, joined those gentlemen who were prouder of their personal merits than of the privileges of their body; and the highest questions to which social order ever gave rise were treated by minds the most capable of understanding and discussing them.

The main causes that take away from the pleasures of English society are the occupations and interests of a country that has long possessed representative government. French society, on the other hand, was rendered somewhat superficial by the leisure of the monarchy. But the vigor of liberty became all at once joined to the elegance of aristocracy: in no country, and at no time, has the art of speaking in every way been so remarkable as in the early years of the Revolution.[1]

In England, women are accustomed to be silent before men when politics form the matter of conversation:[2] in France, women are accustomed

1. On this issue, see Craveri, *The Age of Conversation*.
2. For a more nuanced view of eighteenth-century England, see Brewer, *The Pleasures of the Imagination*.

to lead almost all the conversation that takes place at their houses, and their minds are early formed to the facility which this talent requires. Discussions on public affairs were thus softened by their means, and often intermingled with kind and lively pleasantry. Party spirit, it is true, caused divisions in society; but everyone lived with those of his own side.

At court, the two battalions of good company, one faithful to the old state of things, the other the advocates of liberty, drew up on opposite sides and rarely approached each other. I sometimes ventured, in the spirit of enterprise, to try a mixture of the two parties, by bringing together at dinner the most intelligent men of each side; for people of a certain superiority almost always understand each other; but affairs became too serious to admit of the easy renewal of even this momentary harmony.

The Constituent Assembly, as I have already mentioned, did not suspend the liberty of the press for a single day. Thus those who suffered from finding themselves always in a minority in the Assembly had at least the satisfaction of ridiculing all their opponents. Their newspapers abounded in lively witticisms on the most important matters: it was the history of the world converted into daily gossip. Such is everywhere the character of the aristocracy of courts; yet as the acts of violence that had marked the outset of the Revolution had been soon appeased, and as no confiscation, no revolutionary sentences had taken place, everyone preserved enough of comfort to give himself up to the free exercise of his mind. The crimes with which the cause of patriots has since been sullied did not then oppress their souls; and the aristocrats had not yet suffered enough for the people to dare to get the better of them.

Everything was then in opposition—interests, sentiments, and manner of thinking; but so long as scaffolds were not erected, the use of speech proved an acceptable mediator between the two parties. It was, alas! the last time that the French spirit showed itself in all its splendor; it was the last, and, in some respects, likewise the first time that the society of Paris could convey an idea of that communication of superior minds with each other, the noblest enjoyment of which human nature is capable. Those who lived at that time cannot but acknowledge that they never witnessed in any country so much animation or so much intelligence; we may judge by the number of men of talent drawn forth by the circumstances of the time what the French would become if called on to take part in public business in a path traced by a wise and sincere constitution.

It is possible indeed to introduce into political institutions a kind of hypocrisy which condemns people, from the time they come into society, to be silent or to deceive. Conversation in France has been as much spoiled during the last fifteen years by the sophistry of party spirit and the prudence of pettiness, as it was frank and animated at a time when the most important questions were boldly discussed. At that time there was only one kind of apprehension, that of not being worthy enough of the public esteem; and this apprehension gives extension to the powers of the mind instead of compressing them.

CHAPTER XVIII

The Introduction of Assignats, and Retirement of M. Necker.

The members of the Finance Committee proposed to the Constituent Assembly to discharge the public debt by creating nearly ninety million sterling of paper money, to be secured on church lands, and to be of compulsory circulation.[1] This was a very simple method of bringing the finances in order; but the probability was that in thus getting rid of the difficulties which the administration of a great country always presents, an immense capital would be expended in a few years, and the seeds of new revolutions be sown by the disposal of that capital. In fact, without such vast pecuniary resources, neither the interior troubles of France nor the foreign war could have so easily taken place. Several of the deputies who urged the Constituent Assembly to make this enormous emission of paper money were certainly unconscious of its disastrous effects; but they were fond of the power which the command of such a treasure was about to give them.

M. Necker made a strong opposition to the assignat system; first, because, as we have already mentioned, he did not approve of the confiscation of all the church lands and would always, in accordance with his principles, have excepted from it the archbishoprics, bishoprics, and, above all, the smaller benefices (*presbytères*): for the curates have never been sufficiently paid in France, although, of all classes of priests, they are

---

1. The first *assignats* were issued on December 21, 1789 (worth 400 million francs). Nine months later, in September 1790, the Assembly decided to limit the *assignats* to 1.2 million francs. In his *Reflections* (esp. 348–57), Burke denounced in unambiguous terms this practice, which in his view was both politically irresponsible and financially unsound.

the most useful. The effects of paper money, its progressive depreciation, and the unprincipled speculations to which that depreciation gave rise were explained in M. Necker's report, with an energy too fully confirmed by the event.[2] Lotteries, to which several members of the Constituent Assembly and, in particular, the Bishop of Autun (Talleyrand), very properly declared themselves adverse, are a mere game of chance; while the profit resulting from the perpetual fluctuation of paper money is founded almost entirely on the art of deceiving, at every moment of the day, in regard to the value either of the currency or of the articles purchased with it. The lower class, thus transformed into gamblers, acquire by the facility of irregular gains a distaste for steady labor; finally, the debtors who discharge themselves in an unfair manner are no longer people of strict probity in any other transaction. M. Necker foretold, in 1790, all that has since happened in regard to the assignats—the deterioration of public wealth by the low rate at which the national lands would be sold, and that series of sudden fortunes and sudden failures which necessarily perverts the character of those who gain as of those who lose; for so great a latitude of fear and hope produces agitations too violent for human nature.

In opposing the system of paper money M. Necker did not confine himself to the easy task of attacking; he proposed, as a counter-expedient, the establishment of a bank on a plan of which the principal parts have since been adopted,[3] and in which he was to have introduced as a security, a portion of the church lands sufficient to restore the finances to the most prosperous condition. He also insisted strongly, but without effect, that the members of the Board of Treasury should be admitted into the Assembly, that they might discuss questions of finance in the absence of the minister, who had no right to be there. Finally, M. Necker, before quitting office, made use, for the last time, of the respect that he inspired in directly

---

2. Necker's *Mémoire du Premier Ministre des finances lu à l'Assemblée nationale le 6 mars 1790* and his following *Mémoire du 12 mars* and *Observations sur le rapport fait au nom du Comité des finances* (March 1790) express his deep concern for the financial situation of the country and recommend concrete measures to solve the crisis.

3. The Bank of France, created under Napoléon in January 1800.

refusing to the Constituent Assembly, and in particular to Camus, a member, a communication of the "Red Book."[4]

This book contained the secret expenditure of the state under the preceding reign and under that of Louis XVI. It contained not a single article ordered by M. Necker; yet it was he who encountered a most disagreeable struggle, to prevent the Assembly from being put in possession of a register which bore evidence of the misconduct of Louis XV, and of the too great bounty of Louis XVI: his bounty only—for M. Necker made a point of communicating that in the space of sixteen years, the King and Queen had taken for themselves only eleven million sterling of this secret expenditure; but a number of persons then alive might be exposed by giving publicity to the large sums that they had received. These persons happened to be M. Necker's enemies, because he had blamed the lavishness of the Court toward them: still it was he who ventured to displease the Assembly by preventing the publicity of the faults of his antagonists. So many virtues in so many ways, generosity, disinterestedness, perseverance, had in former times been rewarded by public confidence, and were now more than ever entitled to it. But that which should inspire a profound interest in whosoever has formed an idea of the situation of M. Necker was seeing a man of the finest talents, and highest character, placed between parties so opposite, and duties so different, that the complete sacrifice of himself, his reputation, and his happiness could not succeed in reconciling either prejudices to principles or opinions to interests.

Had Louis XVI allowed himself to be effectually guided by the advice of M. Necker, it would have been the duty of that minister not to retire. But the partisans of the old government advised the King, as they perhaps would do at present, never to follow the counsel of a man who had shown attachment to liberty: that, in their eyes, is a crime never to be forgiven. Besides, M. Necker perceived that the King, dissatisfied with the part allotted to him in the constitution, and weary of the conduct of the Assembly, had determined to withdraw from such a situation. Had he addressed

4. The Red Book contained the secret expenses of the King (both Louis XVI and Louis XV), including the pensions granted to the King's courtiers.

himself to M. Necker, to concert with him his departure, his minister would, no doubt, have felt it incumbent on him to second it with all his means, so cruel and dangerous did the situation of the monarch appear to him! And yet it was extremely contrary to the natural wishes of a man called to his station by the wish of the people, to pass into a foreign territory: but if the King and Queen did not intimate to him their intentions in that point, was it for him to call forth confidential communications? Things had proceeded to such an extremity that a man, to possess influence, must have been either factious or counter-revolutionary, and neither of these characters was suitable to M. Necker.

He took, therefore, the determination of resigning, and, doubtless, it was at this time his only proper course; but always guided by a wish to carry his sacrifices for the public as far as possible, he left two million livres of his fortune[5] as a deposit in the treasury, precisely because he had foretold that the paper money, with which the dividends were about to be paid, would soon be of no value. He was unwilling, as a private individual, to set an example which might be injurious to the operation which he blamed as minister. Had M. Necker possessed very great wealth, this manner of abandoning his property would even then have been very extraordinary; but as these two million formed more than the half of a fortune reduced by seven years of a ministry without salary, the world will perhaps be surprised that a man who had acquired his property by his own exertions should thus feel the necessity of sacrificing it to the slightest sentiment of delicacy.

My father took his departure on the 8th of September, 1790. I was unable to follow him at that time because I was ill; and the necessity of remaining behind was the more painful to me as I was apprehensive of the difficulties he might encounter on his journey. In fact, four days after his departure, a courier brought me a letter from him with notice of his being arrested at Arcis-sur-Aube. The people, persuaded that he had lost his credit in the Assembly only from having sacrificed the cause of the

5. Necker left as a "warranty" his house in Paris, his country house, and his bonds, worth two million livres. Under the Consulate, Madame de Staël attempted to recover a part of Necker's money. At the time of her death, in 1817, her assets were worth five million livres.

nation to that of the King, endeavored to prevent him from continuing his journey. The thing which, of all others, made M. Necker suffer most in this situation was the heart-rending disquietude that his wife felt for him; she loved him with a feeling so sincere and impassioned that he allowed himself, perhaps injudiciously, to speak of her, and of her grief, in the letter which on his departure he addressed to the Assembly. The times, it must be confessed, were not suitable to domestic affection; but that sensibility which a great statesman was unable to restrain in any circumstance of his life was exactly the source of his characteristic qualities—penetration and goodness. He who is capable of true and profound emotion is never intoxicated by power; and it is by this, above all, that we recognize in a minister true greatness of soul.

The Constituent Assembly decided that M. Necker should be allowed to continue his journey. He was set at liberty and proceeded to Basel, but not without still running great hazards: he performed this distressing journey by the same road, across the same provinces where, thirteen months before, he had been carried in triumph. The aristocrats did not fail to make a boast of his sufferings, without considering, or, rather without being willing to allow, that he had put himself into that situation for the sake of defending them, and of defending them solely in the spirit of justice: for he well knew that nothing could restore him to their good opinion; and it was certainly not in any such expectation, but from attachment to his duty, that he made a voluntary sacrifice, in thirteen months, of a popularity of twenty years.

He departed with an anguished heart, having lost the fruits of a long career; nor was the French nation likely perhaps ever to find a minister who loved it with equal feeling. What was there, then, so satisfactory to anyone in such a misfortune? What! the incorrigible will exclaim, was he not a partisan of that liberty which has done us all so much mischief? Assuredly I will not tell you all the good that this liberty would have done you had you been willing to adopt her when she offered herself to you pure and unstained; but if we suppose that M. Necker was mistaken along with Cato and Sydney, with Chatham and Washington, ought such an error, the error of all generous minds during two thousand years, to extinguish all gratitude for his virtues?

CHAPTER XIX

State of Affairs and of Political Parties in the Winter of 1790 – 91.

In all the provinces of France there burst forth troubles, caused by the total change of institutions and by the struggle between the partisans of the old and new regimes.

The executive power lay dormant, according to an expression of a deputy on the left side of the Assembly, because it hoped, though without foundation, that good might follow from excess even in mischief. The ministers were incessantly complaining of the disorders; and although they had but limited means to oppose to them, even these they did not employ, flattering themselves that the unhappy state of things would oblige the Assembly to put more strength into the hands of government. The Assembly, perceiving this plan of proceeding, assumed the control of the whole administration instead of restricting itself to making laws. After M. Necker's retirement, the Assembly demanded the removal of the ministers, and in its constitutional decrees, looking only to the circumstances of the moment, it deprived the King successively of the appointment of all the agents of the executive power.[1] It put its bad humor against this or that person into the shape of a decree, believing, like almost all men in power, in the duration of the present state of things. The deputies of the left side were accustomed to say: "The head of the executive power in England has agents of his own nomination; while the executive power in France, not less strong but more happy, will have the advantage of commanding only persons chosen by the nation, and will thus be more

---

1. All local representatives of the executive power were to be elected rather than nominated.

intimately united with the people." There are phrases for everything, particularly in the French language, which has served so much and so often for different and momentary objects. Nothing, however, was so easy as to prove that one cannot command men over whose fortune one does not possess influence. This truth was avowed only by the aristocratic party, but it went into the opposite extreme in not recognizing the necessity of the responsibility of ministers. One of the greatest beauties of the English constitution is that each branch of government, whether King, Lords, or Commons, is all that it can be. The powers are equal among them, not from weakness but on account of their strength.[2]

In whatever was not connected with the spirit of party the Constituent Assembly gave proofs of the highest degree of reason and information: but there is something in our passions so violent as to burst the links in the chain of reasoning: certain words inflame the blood, and self-love makes the gratification of the moment triumph over all that might be durable.

The same distrust of the King which obstructed the proper functioning of the administration and the judicial branch of government made itself still more felt in the decrees relative to the army. The Assembly willingly fomented a spirit of insubordination in the army at a time when nothing would have been so easy as to repress it; a proof of this was seen in the mutiny of the regiment of Chateauvieux:[3] the Assembly thought proper to repress this revolt, and, in a few days, its orders were carried into effect. M. de Bouillé, an officer of true merit in the old government, at the head of the troops that had remained faithful, obliged the soldiers in insurrection to give up the town of Nancy, of which they had obtained possession. This success, owing in fact only to the ascendancy of the decrees of the Assembly, gave false hopes to the Court; it imagined, and M. de Bouillé did not fail to confirm it in the delusive idea, that the army wanted only to give back to the King his former power; while, in fact, the army, like the nation at large, wanted to assign limits to the will of a single ruler. To

2. The theory of a balanced constitution in England is discussed in Vile, *Constitutionalism and the Separation of Powers*, 58–82.

3. On August 1, 1790.

date from the expedition of M. de Bouillé, in the autumn of 1790, the Court entered into negotiation with him, and hopes were entertained of being able, in some way or other, to bring Mirabeau to enter into concert with that General. The Court conceived that the best means of stopping the Revolution was to gain its leaders; but this revolution had only invisible leaders: these were the truths which were firmly believed, and which no seductive power was capable of shaking. In politics we must treat with principles and not trouble ourselves about individuals, who fall of themselves into their place as soon as we have given a proper shape to the frame into which they are to enter.

However, the popular party on its part became sensible that it had been carried too far, and that the clubs which were establishing themselves out of the Assembly were beginning to dictate laws to the Assembly itself. From the moment that we admit into a government a power that is not legal, it invariably ends by becoming the strongest. As it has no other business than to find fault with what is going on, and has no active duty to discharge, it lies nowise open to censure, and it counts among its partisans all who desire a change in the country. The case is the same with the free-thinkers, who attack religion of every kind, but who know not what to say when asked to substitute a system, of whatever sort, for that which they aim at overturning. We must beware of confounding these self-constituted authorities, whose existence is so pernicious, with the public opinion, which makes itself felt in all directions but never forms itself into a political body. The Jacobin clubs[4] were organized as a government more than the government itself: they passed decrees; they were connected by correspondence in the provinces with other clubs not less powerful; finally, they were to be considered as a mine underground, always ready to blow up existing institutions when opportunities should offer.

The party of the Lameths, Barnave, and Duport, the most popular of all next to the Jacobins, was, however, already threatened by the dema-

---

4. For more information about the organization and ideology of the Jacobin club, see Furet's entry on Jacobinism in *A Critical Dictionary of the French Revolution*, 704–15; also see Kennedy, *The Jacobin Clubs in the French Revolution*.

gogues of the day, most of whom were, in their turn, to be considered in the ensuing year as the next thing to aristocrats. The Assembly, however, always perseveringly rejected the measures proposed in the clubs against emigration, against the liberty of the press, against the meetings of the nobles; never, to its honor (and we shall not be weary of repeating it), did it adopt the terrible doctrine of establishing liberty by means of despotism. It is to that detestable system that we must ascribe the loss of public spirit in France.

M. de la Fayette and his partisans would not consent to go to the Jacobin club; and to balance its influence, they endeavored to found another society under the name of "Club of 1789," in which the friends of order and liberty were expected to meet. Mirabeau, although he had other views of his own, came to this moderate club, which, however, was soon deserted because no one was urged thither by an object of active interest. Its proposed duties were to preserve, to repress, to suspend; but these are the functions of a government, not of a club. The *monarchists*, I mean the partisans of a king and constitution, should naturally have connected themselves with this club of 1789; but Sieyès and Mirabeau, who belonged to it, would for no possible consideration have consented to lose their popularity by drawing near to Malouet or Clermont-Tonnerre, to men who were as much adverse to the impulse of the moment as they were in harmony with the spirit of the age. The moderate party were then divided into two or three different sections, while the assailants were almost always united. The prudent and courageous advocates of English institutions found themselves repulsed in all directions, because they had only truth on their side. We find, however, in the *Moniteur* of the time precious acknowledgments by the leaders of the right side of the Assembly in regard to the English constitution. The Abbé Maury said, "The English constitution which the friends of the throne and of liberty equally ought to take as a model." Cazalès said, "England, that country in which the nation is as free as the king is respected." In short, all the defenders of old abuses, seeing themselves threatened by a much greater danger than even the reform of those abuses, extolled the English government at that time as much as they had depreciated it two years before, when it was so easy for them to obtain it. The privileged classes have renewed this maneuver several times, but always without inspiring confidence: the principles of liberty cannot be a matter of tactical maneuver; for there is something which partakes of devotion in the feeling with which sincere minds are impressed for the dignity of human nature.

CHAPTER XX

Death of Mirabeau.

A man of great family from Brabant, of a sagacious and penetrating mind,[1] acted as the medium between the Court and Mirabeau: he had prevailed on him to correspond secretly with the Marquis de Bouillé, the General in whom the royal family had the most confidence. The project of Mirabeau was, it seems, to accompany the King to Compiègne in the midst of the regiments of whose obedience M. de Bouillé was certain, and to call thither the Constituent Assembly in order to disengage it from the influence of Paris and bring it under that of the Court. But Mirabeau had, at the same time, the intention of causing the English constitution to be adopted; for never will a truly superior man desire the re-establishment of arbitrary power. An ambitious character might take pleasure in such power if assured of holding it during the whole of his life; but Mirabeau was perfectly aware that if he succeeded in re-establishing an unlimited monarchy in France, the direction of such a government would not long be granted him by the Court; he desired, therefore, a representative government, in which men of talent, being always necessary, would always be of weight.

I have had in my hands a letter of Mirabeau written for the purpose of being shown to the King: in it he offered all his means of restoring to France an efficient and respected, but a limited, monarchy; he made use, among others, of this remarkable expression: "I would not want to have worked only toward a vast destruction." The whole letter did honor to the justness of his views. His death was a great misfortune at the time it happened; a transcendant superiority in the career of thought always offers great resources. "You have too much capacity," said M. Necker one day

1. Auguste de La Marck (1750–1833), a friend of Mirabeau's.

to Mirabeau, "not to acknowledge, sooner or later, that morality is in the nature of things." Mirabeau was not altogether a man of genius; but he was not far from being one by the force of talent.

I will confess, then, notwithstanding the frightful faults of Mirabeau, notwithstanding the just resentment which I felt for the attacks that he allowed himself to make on my father in public (for, in private, he never spoke of him but with admiration), that his death struck me with grief, and all Paris experienced the same sensation. During his illness an immense crowd gathered daily and hourly before his door: that crowd made not the smallest noise, from dread of disturbing him; it was frequently renewed in the course of the twenty-four hours, and persons of different classes all behaved with equal respect. A young man, having heard it said that on introducing fresh blood into the veins of a dying man a recovery might be effected, came forward and offered to save the life of Mirabeau at the expense of his own. We cannot, without emotion, see homage rendered to talent: so much does it differ from that which is lavished on power!

Mirabeau knew that his death was approaching. At that moment, far from sinking under affliction, he had a feeling of pride: the cannon were firing for a public ceremony; he called out, "I hear already the funeral of Achilles." In truth, an intrepid orator, who should defend with constancy the cause of liberty, might compare himself to a hero. "After my death," said he again, "the factious will share among themselves the shreds of the monarchy."[2] He had conceived the plan of repairing a great many evils; but it was not given to him to be the expiator of his faults. He suffered cruelly in the last days of his life; and, when no longer able to speak, wrote to Cabanis, his physician, for a dose of opium, in these words of Hamlet: "to die—to sleep." He received no consolation from religion; he was struck by death in the fullness of the interests of this world and when he thought himself near the object to which his ambition aspired. There is in the destiny of almost all men, when we take the trouble of examining it, a manifest

2. Mirabeau's physician, Dr. Cabanis, recorded the following sentence: "I carry in my heart the death of the monarchy, the corpse of which will become the prey of the factions." (quoted in Luttrell, *Mirabeau*, 270–71)

proof of a moral and religious object, of which they themselves are not always aware, and toward which they advance unconsciously.

All the parties at that time regretted Mirabeau. The Court flattered itself with having gained him; the friends of liberty reckoned on his aid. Some said that, with such distinguished talents, he could not want anarchy, as he had no need of confusion to be the first man in the state; and others were certain that he wished for free institutions, because personal value cannot find its place where these do not exist. In fine, he died in the most brilliant moment of his career,[3] and the tears of the people who followed him to the grave made the ceremony very affecting: it was the first time in France that a man indebted for celebrity to his writings and his eloquence received those honors which had heretofore been granted only to men of high birth or to distinguished commanders. The day after his death no member of the Constituent Assembly cast an unmoved eye toward the place where Mirabeau was accustomed to sit. The great oak had fallen; the rest were no longer to be distinguished.

I cannot but blame myself for expressing such regret for a character little entitled to esteem; but talent like his is so rare; and it is, unfortunately, so likely that one will see nothing equal to it in the course of one's life, that it is impossible to restrain a sigh when death closes his brazen gates on a man lately so eloquent, so animated; in short, so strongly and so firmly in possession of life.

---

3. The exact cause of Mirabeau's death is unknown. It was rumored that he was poisoned or that his death was precipitated by a sexual orgy, but it is likely that he died of natural causes, perhaps of pericarditis or gallstones. For more information, see Luttrell, *Mirabeau*, 265–73. On the occasion of Mirabeau's death, Marat wrote in *Ami du peuple:* "People, give thanks to the gods! Your greatest enemy has been cut down by the scythe of fate! . . . But what do I see? Already clever cheats are trying to work on your feelings, . . . they have represented his death as a public calamity, and you weep for him as a hero who has been sacrificed for you, as the savior of the nation." (quoted in Luttrell, *Mirabeau*, 273)

CHAPTER XXI

Departure of the King
on the 21st of June, 1791.

Louis XVI would have cordially accepted the English constitution had it been presented to him with candor and with the respect due to the head of a government; but the Assembly wounded all his affections, particularly by three decrees, which were rather hurtful than useful to the cause of the nation. They abolished the power of granting pardons,[1] that power which ought to exist in every civilized society, and which, in a monarchy, can belong only to the Crown: they required from the priests an oath of adherence to the civil constitution of the clergy, on pain of the loss of their appointments; and they wished to deprive the Queen of the power of being Regent.[2]

The greatest error, perhaps, of the Constituent Assembly, as we have already said, was to aim at creating a clerical body dependent on it, in the same way as has been done by a number of absolute sovereigns. It deviated, for this purpose, from that system of perfect equity in which it ought to have sought support. It stimulated to resistance the conscience and the honor of the clerical body. The friends of liberty wander from the true path whenever it is practicable to oppose to them generous sentiments; for true liberty can have opponents only among those who are ready to act a usurping or servile part; and the priest who refused a theo-

1. According to the Legal Code passed in October 1791.
2. According to chapter II, section 2, of the Constitution of 1791, "Women are excluded from the regency" and the "custody of the minor King shall be entrusted to his mother" (*Documentary Survey of the French Revolution*, 242, 243).

logical oath exacted by threats acted more the part of a free man than those who endeavored to make him give the lie to his opinion.

Lastly, the third decree, the one relative to the Regency, being intended to keep power out of the hands of the Queen, who was suspected by the popular party, could not fail to be personally offensive on several grounds to Louis XVI. That decree declared him the first public functionary,[3] a title wholly unsuited to a king, since every functionary must be responsible; and it is indispensable to introduce into hereditary monarchy a sentiment of respect naturally connected with the inviolability of the sovereign. This respect does not exclude the mutual compact between the King and the nation, a compact existing at all times either in a tacit or in an avowed shape; but reason and delicacy may always be made compatible when people are sincerely disposed to it.

The second article of the regency decree was to be condemned on grounds similar to those that we have already mentioned; it declared the King deprived of the throne if he went out of France.[4] This was pronouncing on what ought not to have been anticipated, the case in which a king was to be stripped of his dignity. Republican virtues and institutions elevate very greatly the people whose situation allows them to enjoy them; but in monarchical countries, the people become perverted if they are not accustomed to respect the authority which they have acknowledged. A penal code against a king is an idea without application, whether that king be strong or weak. In the latter case, the power that overturns him does not confine itself to law, in whatever manner that law may have been conceived.

It is therefore only under a prudential point of view that we are to form

3. According to chapter IV of the Constitution of 1791, "the King is the supreme head of the general administration of the kingdom" (*Documentary Survey of the French Revolution*, 251). The Constitution also stipulated (chap. II, sec. 1) that "there is no authority in France superior to that of the law; the King reigns only thereby, and only in the name of the law may he exact obedience." (*Documentary Survey of the French Revolution*, 241)

4. According to the Constitution of 1791, chapter II, section 1, 7, "If the King, having left the kingdom, does not return after invitation has been made by the legislative body, and within the period established by proclamation, which may not be less than two months, he shall be deemed to have abdicated the throne." (*Documentary Survey of the French Revolution*, 240)

an opinion of the step taken by the King in escaping from the Tuileries on the 21st of June, 1791. He had certainly met by that time with as much bad treatment as gave him a right to quit France; and he perhaps rendered a great service even to the friends of liberty by putting an end to a hypocritical situation; for their cause was injured by the vain efforts that they made to persuade the nation that the political acts of the King, from the time of his arrival at Paris, were acts of free will, when it was perfectly evident that they were not.

Mr. Fox[5] told me in England, in 1793, that at the time of the King's departure to Varennes, he should have wished that he had been allowed to quit the kingdom in peace and that the Constituent Assembly had proclaimed a republic. France would at least not have sullied herself with the crimes afterward committed against the royal family; and whether a republican form can or cannot succeed in a great country, it is always best that the trial should be made by upright men. But that which was most to be dreaded took place—the arrest of the King and his family.

A journey requiring so much management and rapidity was prepared almost as in ordinary times: etiquette is of such moment at a court that it could not be dispensed with even on this most perilous occasion; the consequence was the failure of the attempt.[6]

When the Constituent Assembly learned of the King's departure, its behavior was perfectly firm and becoming; what it had wanted till that day was a counterpoise to its unlimited power. Unfortunately, the French arrive at reason in political matters only by compulsion. A vague idea of danger hovered over the Assembly; it was possible that the King might go, as he intended, to Montmédy, and that he might receive aid from foreign

5. Charles James Fox (1749–1806), leader of the Whigs who favored the principles of the French Revolution and opposed the war with France.

6. On the King's flight to Varennes, see Mona Ozouf's entry in *A Critical Dictionary of the French Revolution*, 155–64. The escape of the royal family failed because it was poorly planned. The schedule was not meticulously prepared, and the departure was imprudently delayed; as a result, the carriage left the Tuileries Palace at two in the morning rather than at midnight. Moreover, Choiseul, who was supposed to command the first support detachment en route, defected. The implications of the Varennes episode were very important for the course of the Revolution. As Ozouf pointed out, it led to the appearance of a major schism in the country, which ultimately strengthened the power of the Jacobins.

troops; it was possible that a great party might declare for him in the interior. In short, disquietude put an end to extremes; and among the deputies of the popular party, those who had clamored on pretext of tyranny when the English constitution was proposed to them would now have willingly subscribed to it.

Never will it be possible to find grounds of consolation for the arrest of the King at Varennes: irreparable faults, crimes which must long be the cause of shame, have impaired the feeling of liberty in the minds best fitted to receive it. Had the King left the country, perhaps an equitable constitution might have arisen out of the struggle between the two parties.[7] But civil war, it will be exclaimed, was to be avoided above all things. Not above all things! There are other calamities still more to be dreaded. Generous virtues are displayed by those who fight for their opinion; and it is more natural to shed one's blood in defense of it than for one of the thousand political interests which form the habitual causes of war. Doubtless it is cruel to fight against one's fellow-citizens, but it is still more horrible to be oppressed by them; and that which of all things ought to be avoided in France is the absolute triumph of a party. For a long habit of liberty is necessary to prevent the feeling of justice from being perverted by the pride of power.

The King, on setting out, left a manifesto containing the motives for his departure; he recapitulated the treatment which he had been obliged to undergo, and declared that his authority was reduced to such a degree that he had no longer the power of governing. Amidst complaints so well founded, it was improper to insert observations of too minute a cast on the bad condition of the palace of the Tuileries. It is very difficult for hereditary sovereigns to prevent themselves from being governed by habit in the smallest as in the greatest events of life; but it is perhaps on that very account that they are better adapted than elected chiefs to a government of law and peace. The manifesto of Louis XVI closed with the memorable assurance "that on recovering his independence, he was ready to devote it to erecting the liberty of the French people on an imperishable foundation." Such was at that time the current of public feeling that no

---

7. Louis XVI intended to return to France supported by foreign troops.

one, not even the King himself, considered practicable the re-establishment of an unlimited monarchy.[8]

The Assembly, as soon as it was informed of the arrest of the royal family at Varennes, sent thither commissaries, among whom were Péthion and Barnave: Péthion, a man without information or elevation of soul, saw the misfortune of the most affecting victims without being moved by it. Barnave felt a respectful pity, particularly for the Queen; and from that time forward, he, Duport, Lameth, Regnault de St. Jean d'Angely, Chapelier, Thouret, and others united all their influence to that of M. de la Fayette to the restoration of royalty.[9]

The King and his family, on returning from Varennes, made a mournful entry into Paris; the clothes of the King and Queen were covered with dust; the two children of the royal family looked with surprise on the mass of people who came forth with an air of command into the presence of its fallen masters. Madame Elizabeth[10] appeared, in the midst of this illustrious family, like a being already sanctified and which has no longer anything in common with the world. Three of the bodyguards, placed on the outside seat of the carriage, were exposed every moment to the danger of being massacred, and deputies of the Constituent Assembly placed themselves repeatedly between them and the enraged part of the populace who wanted to kill them. It was thus that the King returned to the palace of his ancestors. Alas! what a sad presage! And how truly was it fulfilled!

8. It has been argued that, by signing this manifesto, Louis XVI proclaimed his allegiance to the older principles of his declaration of June 23, 1789, principles which were not at all compatible with those of constitutional monarchy.

9. Adrien Duport (1759–98) was a prominent French magistrate and a leading constitutional monarchist during the early stages of the French Revolution of 1789. Charles Malo François Lameth (1757–1832) was a prominent French politician and member of the Feuillants. He served in the American War of Independence and was a deputy to the Estates General in 1789. Regnault de Saint-Jean d'Angely (1761–1819) was the editor of *L'ami de patriots*, 1791–92. Thouret (1746–94) was one of the main authors of the Constitution of 1791, and Le Chapelier (1754–94) was the author of a famous law on associations (1791) that bore his name. The speeches of Duport, Thouret, and la Chapelier can be found in Furet and Halévi, *Orateurs de la Révolution française*, vol. 1.

10. Louis XVI's sister, who was executed in May 1794.

CHAPTER XXII

Revision of the Constitution.

The Assembly was constrained, by the popular ferment, to declare that the King should be kept prisoner in the palace of the Tuileries until the constitution had been presented for his acceptance. M. de la Fayette, as commander of the National Guards, had the misfortune of being doomed to carry this decree into effect. But if, on the one hand, he placed sentinels at the gates of the palace, he opposed, on the other, with conscientious energy, the party which endeavored to pronounce the King fallen from the throne.[1] He employed against those who pressed that measure the armed force in the Champ de Mars;[2] and he thus proved, at least, that it was not from views of ambition that he exposed himself to the displeasure of the King, as he drew on himself at the same time the hatred of the enemies of the throne. The only equitable manner, in my opinion, of judging the character of a man is to examine if there are no personal calculations in his conduct; if there are not, we may blame his manner of judging; but we are not the less bound to esteem him.

The republican party was the only one that came openly forward at the time of the arrest of the King. The name of the Duke of Orléans was not even mentioned; no one presumed to think of another king than Louis XVI, and he received at least the homage of having nothing but institutions opposed to him. Finally, the person of the monarch was declared inviolable; a specification was made of the cases in which a deprivation of the Crown should be incurred;[3] but if the illusion which should surround the royal person were thus destroyed, engagements propor-

1. This petition implicitly demanded the declaration of the republic.
2. The clashes between the National Guard and the people claimed more than fifty victims.
3. See articles 2, 5, and 6–8 of chapter II of the Constitution of 1791.

tionally stronger were taken to respect the law which guaranteed the inviolability of the sovereign in every possible supposition.

The Constituent Assembly always thought, but very erroneously, that its decrees possessed something of magic power, and that the people would stop in everything exactly at the line which it had traced. Its authority in this respect may be compared to that of the ribband suspended in the garden of the Tuileries to prevent the people from approaching the palace: so long as public opinion was in favor of those who had caused this ribband to be strung, it was respected by everyone; but as soon as the people would no longer have a barrier, it was not of the slightest use.

We find in some modern constitutions, as a constitutional article: "the government shall be just, and the people obedient." Were it possible to command such a result, the balance of powers would be altogether superfluous; but to succeed in putting good maxims in execution, it is necessary to combine institutions in such a way that everyone shall find his interest in maintaining them. Religious doctrines stand in no need of appealing to personal interest to acquire command over men, and it is in that, above all, that they are of a superior order; but legislators, invested with the interests of this world, fall into a kind of self-deception when they introduce patriotic sentiments as a necessary spring in the machine of society. To reckon on consequences for organizing a cause is to mistake the natural order of events. Nations become free not from their being virtuous but because fortunate circumstances, or rather a strong will, having put them in possession of liberty, they acquire the virtues which arise from it.

The laws on which civil and political liberty depend are reducible to a very small number, and it is this political decalogue alone that merits the title of constitutional articles. But the National Assembly gave that title to almost all its decrees; whether it thus aimed at keeping itself independent of the royal sanction or, like an author, acted under a degree of illusion in regard to the perfection and durability of its own work.

However, the intelligent men in the Assembly succeeded in reducing the number of constitutional articles;[4] but a discussion arose to ascertain

4. The final version of the Constitution of 1791 had 204 articles.

whether it should not be decided that every twenty years a new Constituent Assembly should be formed to revise the constitution which they had
just established, taking for granted that, in this interval, no change should
be made in it. What confidence did this show in the stability of such a
work, and how greatly has it been deceived?

At last it was decreed that no constitutional article should be modified,
except on the demand of three succeeding assemblies. This was forming an
extraordinary idea of human patience on subjects of such great importance.

The French, in general, look only at the reality of the things of this life,
and are sufficiently ready to turn principles into ridicule if they appear to
them an obstacle to the immediate success of their wishes. But the Constituent Assembly, on the other hand, acted under a domineering passion
for abstract ideas. This fashion, which was quite contrary to the spirit of
the nation, did not last long. The factious made use at first of metaphysical
arguments as motives for the most guilty actions, and they soon after overturned this structure to proclaim plainly the force of circumstances and
the contempt of general views.

The *côté droit* of the Assembly was often in the right during the course
of the session, and more often still excited the interest of the public, because it was oppressed by a stronger party and denied opportunities of
speaking. In no country is it more necessary than in France to establish
regulations in deliberative assemblies in favor of the minority; for such a
predilection exists there for the stronger party that people are apt to account it a crime in you to belong to the weaker.* After the arrest of the
King, the aristocrats, knowing that royalty had acquired defenders among
the popular party, thought it best to let the latter act, and to come less
conspicuously forward themselves. The converted deputies did what they
could to increase the authority of the executive power; but they did not,
however, venture to broach those questions, the decision of which alone

---

* An excellent work entitled *The Tactics of Deliberative Assemblies*, composed by M.
Dumont of Geneva, and containing, in part, the ideas of Mr. Bentham, an English lawyer
and profound thinker, should be perpetually consulted by the members of our legislature.
For it is by no means enough to carry a question in an assembly. It is necessary that the
weaker party should have been heard with patience; such is the advantage and the right of
a representative government.

could give solidity to the political state of France. People were afraid to speak of two chambers as of a conspiracy. The right of dissolving the legislative body, a right so necessary to the maintenance of royal authority, was not granted to it. Reasonable men were alarmed by being called aristocrats; yet the aristocrats were then no longer formidable, and it was on that very account that the name had been converted into a reproach. At that time, as well as subsequently, the stronger party in France have had the art of making the vanquished the object of public disquietude; one would say that the weak alone were to be dreaded. To over-rate the means of their adversaries is a good pretext to increase the power of the victors. We must form enemies in effigy if we wish to accustom our arm to strike a weighty blow.

The majority of the Assembly hoped to restrain the Jacobins, and yet it compromised with them, and lost ground at each victory. The constitution accordingly was drawn like a treaty between two parties, not like a work for permanency. The authors of this constitution launched into the sea an ill-constructed vessel, and thought that they found a justification for every fault by quoting the wish of such an individual or the credit of such another. But the waves of the ocean which the vessel had to traverse were not to be smoothed by such apologies.

But what course, it will be asked, could be adopted when circumstances were unfavorable to that which reason seemed to dictate? Resist, always resist, and rely for support on yourselves. The courage of an upright man is a consideration of importance, and no one can foresee what consequences it may have. Had there been ten deputies of the popular party, had there been five, three, or even one who had made the Assembly feel all the misfortunes that would necessarily result from a political work defenseless against faction; had he adjured the Assembly, in the name of the admirable principles which it had decreed and of the principles which it had overturned, not to expose to hazard so many blessings that formed the treasure of human reason; had the inspiration of thought revealed to one orator in what manner the sacred name of liberty was soon to be consigned to a disastrous association with the most cruel recollections, one man alone might perhaps have been able to arrest the destiny. But the applause, or the murmurs of the galleries, influenced questions which ought to have been discussed calmly by the most enlightened and most reflecting men. The pride which enables one to resist a multitude is of another kind than that which renders one independent of a despot, although it is the same natural impulse that enables us to struggle against oppression of every kind.

There remained only one method of repairing the errors of the laws: that method lay in the choice of men. The deputies about to succeed in the Constituent Assembly might resume imperfect labors and rectify, in the spirit of wisdom, the faults already committed. But the Assembly set out by rejecting property as a qualification, although necessary to confine the elections to the class that has an interest in the maintenance of order. Robespierre, who was about to act so great a part in the reign of blood, combated this condition as an injustice, however low the scale might be fixed; he brought forward the declaration of the rights of man in regard to equality, as if that equality, even in its most extended sense, admitted the power of acquiring everything without talent and without labor. To arrogate political rights without a title to exercise them is a usurpation as much as any other.[5] Robespierre joined obscure metaphysics to common declamation, and it was thus that he achieved a kind of eloquence. Better speeches were composed for him in his day of power; but during the Constituent Assembly no one paid attention to him, and whenever he rose to speak, those of the democrats who had any taste were very ready to turn him into ridicule, that they might obtain the credit of belonging to a moderate party.

It was decreed that to pay taxes at the annual rate of a mark of silver (about fifty-four livres) should be a necessary qualification to being a deputy. This was enough to excite complaints from the speakers in regard to all the younger brothers of families, in regard to all the men of talent, who would be excluded by their poverty from becoming representatives: yet

---

5. This was the position held by all prominent nineteenth-century liberals, from Tocqueville and Guizot to Constant and J. S. Mill. For example, Constant devoted special attention to property qualifications, which he regarded as indispensable to the proper functioning of representative government (*Principles of Politics*, 213–21). For more information, see Guéniffey, *Le nombre et la raison;* and Kahan, *The Political Culture of Limited Suffrage*, 217–44.

the rate was so small as not to confine the choice of the people to the class of men of property.

The Constituent Assembly, to remedy this inconvenience, established two stages in the elective process: it decreed that the people should name electors, who should subsequently make choice of deputies. This gradation had certainly a tendency to soften the action of the democratic element, and the revolutionary leaders were doubtless of that opinion, since they abolished it on their acquiring the ascendency. But a choice made directly by the people, and subjected to a fair qualification in point of property, is infinitely more favorable to the energy of a free government. An immediate election, such as exists in England, can alone communicate public spirit and love of country to every class. A nation becomes attached to its representatives when it has chosen them itself: but when obliged to confine itself to the electing of those who are to elect in their turn, the artificial combination casts a damp on its interest. Besides, Electoral Colleges, from the mere circumstance of their consisting of a small number of persons, are much more open to intrigue than large masses; they are open, above all, to that bourgeois intrigue that is so degrading when we see men of the middling ranks[6] apply to their lofty superiors to get places for their sons in the antechambers of the court.

In a free government the people ought to rally itself under the first class by taking representatives from among it, and the first class should endeavor to please the people by their talents and virtues. This double tie retains but little force when the act of election has to pass through two stages. The life of election is thus destroyed to avoid commotion; it is a great deal better, as in England, to balance discreetly the democratic by the aristocratic element, leaving, however, both in possession of their natural independence.[7]

M. Necker in his last work[8] proposed a new method of establishing two

6. In the original: "hommes du tiers état."

7. On this issue of direct and indirect election in England, also see Guizot, *History of the Origins of Representative Government in Europe*, 339–81. Benjamin Constant discussed the limits and benefits of direct and indirect elections in his *Principles of Politics*, 201–2, 207.

8. Necker's *Dernières vues de politique et de finance* (1802) was republished as volume XI of his *Oeuvres complètes*.

stages of election; this should consist, he thinks, in the electoral college giving a list of a certain number of candidates, out of which the primary assemblies might make a choice. The motives for this institution are ingeniously explained in M. Necker's book; but it is evident that he thought it, all along, necessary that the people should exercise fully its right and its judgment, and that distinguished men should have a permanent interest in winning its votes.

The revisers of the constitution in 1791 were incessantly accused by the Jacobins of being the advocates of despotism, even at the time that they were obliged to resort to circumlocution in speaking of the executive power, as if the name of a king could not be pronounced in a monarchical state. Yet the Constituent Deputies might still perhaps have succeeded in saving France had they been members of the following Assembly. The most enlightened deputies felt what was wanted to a constitution framed under the pressure of events, and they would have endeavored to find a remedy in the mode of interpreting it. But the party of mediocrity, which counts so many soldiers in its ranks, that party which hates talents as the friends of liberty hate despotism, succeeded in debarring, by a decree, the deputies of the Constituent Assembly from the possibility of being reelected.[9] The aristocrats and the Jacobins, having acted a very inferior part during the session, did not flatter themselves with being returned; they felt accordingly a pleasure in shutting the entrance to the next Assembly on those who were assured of the votes of their fellow-citizens. For of all agrarian laws, that which would most please the mass of mankind

---

9. The National Constituent Assembly dissolved itself on September 30, 1791, after having decreed that none of its members could be reelected in the next legislature (Robespierre had been one of the most vocal defenders of this measure). The Legislative Assembly first met on October 1, 1791, and had 745 members, most of whom belonged to the middle class. Since none had been a member of the previous Assembly, the majority of the new members lacked true political experience. Commenting on this issue, Benjamin Constant endorsed the possibility of reelection, which he regarded as an effective means of protecting political liberty. "The impossibility of reelection," he wrote, "is, in all respects, a great mistake. . . . Nothing is more opposed to liberty, and at the same time more favorable to disorder, than the forced exclusion of the representatives of the people. . . . If you set obstacles to indefinite reelection, you frustrate genius and courage of their due reward; you prepare consolation and triumph for cowardice and ineptitude." (*Principles of Politics*, p. 210)

would be a division of public votes into equal portions, talents never obtaining a greater number than mediocrity. Many individuals would flatter themselves with gaining by this plan; but the emulation which creates the wealth of mankind would be totally lost.

In vain did the first orators of the Assembly urge that successors altogether new, and elected in a time of trouble, would be ambitious of making a revolution equally striking as that which had distinguished their predecessors. The members of the extremity of the *côté gauche*, agreeing with the extremity of the *côté droit*, exclaimed that their colleagues wished to make a monopoly of power, and deputies hitherto inimical, the Jacobins and aristocrats, joyfully shook hands on thinking that they should have the good fortune of excluding men whose superiority had for two years cast them into the shade.

How great a fault under existing circumstances! But also how great an error, in point of principle, was it to forbid the people to return those who have already shown themselves worthy of its confidence! In what country do we find a sufficient number of capable persons to enable us to exclude, in an arbitrary manner, men already known, already tried, and practically acquainted with business? Nothing costs a state dearer than deputies who have to make their fortune in the way of reputation; men of acquired property of this kind also ought to be preferred to those who have still their wealth to seek.

CHAPTER XXIII

Acceptance of the Constitution, Called the Constitution of 1791.

Thus ended that famous Assembly which united so much knowledge to so many errors, which was the cause of permanent good but of great immediate evil, the remembrance of which will long serve as a pretext for attacks by the enemies of liberty.

Behold, say they, the result of the deliberations of the most enlightened men in France. But we may say to them in reply: consider what must be the situation of men who, never having exercised any political right, find themselves all at once in posession of that which is so ruinous to everyone—unlimited power: they will be long before they are aware that injustice suffered by any individual citizen, whether a friend or enemy of liberty, recoils on the head of all; they will be long before they understand the theory of liberty, which is so simple when one is born in a country where the laws and manners teach it, so difficult when one has lived under an arbitrary government in which everything is decided by circumstances, and principles always rendered subservient to them. Finally, at all times and in every country, to make a nation pass from the government of a court to the government of law is a crisis of the greatest difficulty, even when public opinion renders it unavoidable.

History should then consider the Constituent Assembly under a double point of view: the abuses which it destroyed, and the institutions which it created. Under the former it has great claims on the gratitude of mankind; under the latter it may be reproached with the most serious errors.

On the proposition of M. de la Fayette, a general amnesty was granted to all those who had participated in the King's journey or committed what could be called political offenses. He obtained likewise a decree enabling every individual to leave France, and return, without a passport. The emigration was already begun. In the next chapter I shall point out the distinction between the emigration prompted by political views and that unavoidable emigration which was of later date. But that which should fix our attention is that the Constituent Assembly rejected every measure proposed to it that would have impeded civil liberty. The minority of the nobility was actuated by that spirit of justice which is inseparable from disinterestedness. Among the deputies of the Third Estate, Dupont de Nemours,[1] who survived in spite of his courage, Thouret, Barnave, Chapelier, and so many others who fell the victims of their excellent principles certainly brought none but the purest intentions into their deliberations; but a tumultuous and ignorant majority carried their point in the decrees relative to the constitution. There was a sufficient store of knowledge in France in whatever related to the judicial branch and the details of administration; but the theory of powers required more profound information.

It was thus, then, the most painful of intellectual spectacles to see the blessings of civil liberty committed to the safeguard of a political liberty that had neither moderation nor strength.

This ill-fated constitution, so good in its foundation and so bad in its superstructure, was presented to the acceptance of the King.[2] He certainly could not refuse it, as it put an end to his captivity; but the public flattered itself that his consent was voluntary. Fêtes were held as if for a season of happiness; rejoicings were ordered that people might persuade themselves that the danger was over; the words "King," "Representative Assembly," "Constitutional Monarchy" corresponded to the real wishes of all the

---

1. Dupont de Nemours (1739–1817) was a prominent member of the Third Estate. Arrested during the Terror, he immigrated to the United States after September 4, 1797 (18 Fructidor). Madame de Staël's correspondence with him was translated into English as *De Staël–Dupont Letters. Correspondence of Madame de Staël and Pierre Samuel du Pont de Nemours and of Other Members of the Necker and du Pont Families.* For more information on Staël's views on America, see Hawkins, *Madame de Staël and the United States.*

2. From the very beginning, the relations between the monarch and the Legislative Assembly were extremely tense. Reluctant to endorse some of the Assembly's decisions, the King unwisely decided to veto them. This was the case, for example, with the Assembly's decree that the émigrés assembled on the frontiers should be liable to the penalties of death and confiscation if they remained so assembled after January 1, 1792.

French. They thought they had attained realities when they had acquired only names.

The King and Queen were entreated to go to the opera; their entrance into the house was the signal for sincere and universal plaudits. The piece was the Ballet of Psyche; at the time that the furies were dancing and shaking their flambeaus, and when the brilliancy of the flames spread all over the house, I saw the faces of the King and Queen by the pale light of this imitation of the lower regions and was seized with melancholy forebodings of the future. The Queen exerted herself to be agreeable, but a profound grief was perceptible, even in her obliging smile. The King, as usual, seemed more engaged with what he saw than with what he felt; he looked on all sides with calmness, one might almost say with indifference; he had, like most sovereigns, accustomed himself to restrain the expression of his feelings, and he had perhaps by this means lessened their intensity. After the opera, the public went out to walk in the Champs Elysées, which were superbly illuminated. The palace and garden of the Tuileries, being separated from them only by the fatal Square of the Revolution, the illumination of the palace and garden formed an admirable combination with that of the long alleys of the Champs Elysées, which were joined together by festoons of lamps.

The King and Queen drove leisurely in their carriage through the midst of the crowd, and the latter, each time that they perceived the carriage, called out: *Vive le Roi!* But they were the same people who had insulted the same King on his return from Varennes, and they were no better able to account for their applause than they had been for their insults.

I met in the course of my walk several members of the Constituent Assembly: like dethroned sovereigns, they seemed very uneasy about their successors. Certainly all would have wished like them that they had been appointed to maintain the constitution, such as it was; for enough was already known of the spirit of elections not to entertain any hope for an amelioration of affairs. But people were rendered giddy by the noise that proceeded from every quarter. The lower orders were singing, and the newspaper venders made the air re-echo with their loud calls of *La grande acceptation du Roi, la constitution monarchique,* etc. etc.

The Revolution was apparently finished, and liberty established. Yet people looked around on each other as if to acquire from their neighbors that security which they did not possess themselves.

The absence of the nobility undermined this security, for monarchy cannot exist without the participation of an aristocratic body, and, unfortunately, the prejudices of the French nobles were such that they rejected every kind of free government: it is to this great difficulty that we are to attribute the most serious defects of the constitution of 1791. For the men of rank and property offering no support to liberty, the democratic power necessarily acquired the ascendancy. The English barons, from the time of *Magna Charta,* have demanded rights for the Commons conjointly with rights for themselves. In France, the nobility opposed these rights when claimed by the Third Estate, but being too weak to struggle with the people, they quitted their country in a mass and allied themselves with foreigners. This lamentable resolution rendered a constitutional monarchy impracticable at that time, for it destroyed its preserving elements. We proceed to explain what were the necessary consequences of emigration.

PART III

CHAPTER I

On the Emigration.

It is of importance to make a distinction between the voluntary and the forced emigration. After the overthrow of the throne in 1792 and the commencement of the Reign of Terror, we all emigrated to escape the dangers with which everyone was threatened. It was not one of the least crimes of the government of that day, to have considered as culpable those who left their homes only to escape assassination at the hands of the people or of a tribunal; and to comprise in their proscriptive edicts not only men able to carry arms, but the aged, the women, and even the children. The emigration of 1791, on the other hand, being caused by no kind of danger, should be considered as an act of party; and under this point of view, we can form an opinion on it according to political principles.

At the moment the King was arrested at Varennes and brought back captive to Paris, a great number of the nobles determined on quitting their country to claim the aid of foreign powers and prevail on them to repress the revolution by force of arms. The earliest emigrants[1] obliged the nobles

---

1. Emigration occurred in several phases. The first emigrants left France immediately after July 14, 1789; others left after 1791 or shortly after the beginning of the Reign of Terror. The total number of émigrés was probably between 150,000 and 160,000 (the total population of France at that time was estimated at 26 million). For a useful overview, see M. Boffa's entry on emigration during the Revolution in *A Critical Dictionary of the French Revolution*, 324–36. For more information about the history of emigration after 1789, see Daudet, *Histoire de l'émigration pendant la Révolution française*, 3 vols.; Baldensperger, *Le mouvement des idées dans l'émigration française, 1789–1815*; and Greer, *The Incidence of the Emigration During the French Revolution*.

who had remained in France to follow them; they enjoined this sacrifice in the name of a kind of honor connected with the *esprit du corps*, and the caste of French nobles were seen covering the public roads and repairing to the camps of foreigners on the hostile frontiers. Posterity, I believe, will pronounce that the nobility on this occasion deviated from the true principles which serve as a basis to the social union. Supposing that nobles would not have done better to take part from the outset in institutions rendered necessary by the progress of information and the growth of the Third Estate, at least ten thousand more nobles around the King's person might have perhaps prevented him from being dethroned.

But without wandering into suppositions, which may always be contested, there are in politics, as in morals, certain inflexible duties; and the first of all is never to abandon our country to foreigners, even when they come forward to support with their armies the system which we consider the best. One party thinks itself the only virtuous, the only legitimate body; another the only national, the only patriotic. Who is to decide between them? Was the triumph of foreign armies a judgment of God on the French? The judgment of God, says the proverb, is the voice of the people. Had a civil war been necessary to measure the strength of the contending parties, and to manifest on which side lay the majority, the nation would by this have become greater in its own eyes, as in those of its neighbors. The Vendean leaders[2] inspire a thousand times more respect than the Frenchmen who have excited the different coalitions of Europe against their country. Victory in civil war can be obtained only by dint of courage, or justice; it is to the faculties of the soul that the success of a struggle belongs, but in order to entice foreign powers to enter a country, an intrigue, an accidental cause, or a connection with a general or minister can suffice. Emigrants have at all times betrayed the independence of their country; they would have it, as a lover wishes his mistress—dead or faithful; and the weapon which

imagine they are fighting the factious often escapes from their hands and inflicts a mortal blow on that country which they intended to save.

The nobles of France unfortunately consider themselves rather as the countrymen of the nobles of all countries than as the fellow-citizens of Frenchmen. According to their manner of judging, the race of the ancient conquerors of Europe owes itself mutual aid from one empire to another;[3] but a people, on the other hand, conscious of forming a uniform whole naturally wish to be the disposers of their own fate; and from the times of antiquity down to our days, no free, or even merely spirited, people has ever borne without horror the interference of a foreign government in its domestic quarrels.

Circumstances peculiar to the history of France have in that country separated the privileged classes and the Third Estate in a more decided manner than in any other part of Europe. Urbanity of manners concealed political divisions; but the pecuniary exemptions, the number of offices conferred exclusively on the nobles, the inequality in the application of the law, the etiquette at court, the whole inheritance of the rights of conquest transformed into arbitrary favors, created in France almost two nations out of one.[4] The consequence was that the emigrant nobles wished to treat almost the whole French people as revolted vassals; and, far from remaining in their country, either to triumph over the prevailing opinion or to unite themselves to it, they considered it a plainer course to call in the *gendarmerie* of Europe, that they might bring Paris to its senses. It was, they said, to deliver the majority from the yoke of a factious minority that they had recourse to the arms of the neighboring allies. A nation that should stand in need of foreigners to deliver it from a yoke of any kind would be so degraded that no virtue could long be displayed in it; it would have to blush at once for its oppressors and its deliverers. Henri IV ad-

3. This was one of the ideas of Boulainvilliers's *Essai sur la noblesse de France* (Amsterdam, 1732).

4. Note again the similarity between Staël's and Tocqueville's analyses of "collective individualism" under the Old Regime. In Tocqueville's view, French society was fragmented to the point that "every one of these little societies lived only for itself and was interested only in itself and in matters which directly affected it." (*The Old Regime and the Revolution*, vol. 1, 162; also see 163, 212–13)

mitted, it is true, foreign corps into his army;[5] but he had them as auxiliaries and was nowise dependent on them. He opposed English and German Protestants to the Leaguers, controlled by Spanish Catholics; but he was always surrounded by a French force of sufficient strength to make him master of his allies. In 1791 the system of emigration was false and reprehensible, for a handful of Frenchmen was lost in the midst of all the bayonets of Europe. There were, moreover, at that time, many methods of coming to a mutual understanding in France; men of great worth were at the head of government; errors in politics admitted of remedy, and judicial murders had not yet been committed.

Emigration, far from keeping up the respectability of the nobility, was the greatest blow to it. A new generation has risen up in the absence of the nobles, and as this generation has lived, prospered, and triumphed without the privileged classes, it still thinks itself capable of maintaining itself alone. The emigrants, on the other hand, living always in the same circle, are persuaded that whatever is different from their ancient habits is rebellion: they have thus acquired by degrees the same kind of inflexibility which marks the clergy. All political traditions have become in their eyes articles of faith, and abuses stand with them in the light of dogmas. Their attachment to the royal family under its misfortunes is worthy of the highest respect; but why make this attachment consist in a hatred of free institutions and in a love of absolute power? And why object to reasoning in politics as if sacred mysteries, not human affairs, were in question? In 1791 the aristocratic party separated itself from the nation in fact and by right: in one way by quitting France, in another by not acknowledging that the wish of a great people ought to have influence in the choice of its government. "What signify nations," they were accustomed to repeat. "We need armies." But do not armies form a part of nations? Does not public opinion make its way sooner or later even into the ranks of soldiers, and in what manner is it possible to stifle that which at present animates every enlightened country—the free and perfect knowledge of the interest and the rights of all?

5. It was Louis XI who in 1474 allowed Swiss soldiers to serve in the French army.

The emigrants must have convinced themselves by their own feelings, in different circumstances, that the step they had taken was reprehensible. When they found themselves in the midst of foreign uniforms, when they heard those German dialects, no sound of which recalled to them the recollections of their past life, is it possible that they could still think themselves devoid of blame? Did they not see the whole of France arrayed to defend herself on the opposite bank? Did they not experience unspeakable distress on recognizing the national music, on hearing the accents of their native province, in that camp which they were obliged to call hostile? How many of them must have returned with sorrow among the Germans, among the English, among so many other nations whom they were ordered to consider as their allies! Ah! it is impossible to transport one's household gods to a foreign hearth. The emigrants, even at the time that they were carrying on war against France, were often proud of the victories of their countrymen. As emigrants they were defeated, but as Frenchmen they triumphed: and the joy which they experienced was the noble inconsistency of generous hearts. At the battle of La Hogue,[6] James II exclaimed, on seeing the defeat of that French fleet which sustained his own cause against England, "See how my brave English fight"; and this sentiment gave him a greater right to the throne than any one of the arguments employed for his restoration. In truth, the love of country is inextinguishable, as are all the affections on which our first duties are founded. Often does a long absence or party quarrels break asunder all your connections; you no longer know an individual in that country which is yours; but at its name, or at the sight of it, your whole heart is moved; and far from its being necessary to combat such impressions as chimeras, they ought to serve as a guide to a man of virtue.

Several political writers have ascribed to emigration all the misfortunes that have happened to France. It is not fair to impute to the errors of one party the crimes committed by another; but it seems, however, clear that a democratic crisis became much more probable when all the men employed under the old monarchy, and capable, had they been willing, of

---

6. The naval battle of La Hogue, May 29–June 2, 1692, was won by the English.

contributing to recompose the new, had abandoned their country. Equality then presenting itself from all quarters, men of warm passions gave themselves up too much to the democratic torrent; and the people, seeing royalty nowhere but in the person of the King, believed that to overthrow one man sufficed to found a republic.

CHAPTER II

Prediction of M. Necker on the Fate of the Constitution of 1791.

During the last fourteen years of his life, M. Necker did not quit his estate of Coppet in Switzerland. He lived in the most complete retirement; but the repose arising from dignity does not exclude activity of mind, and he never ceased to attend, with the greatest solicitude, to every event which occurred in France. The works composed by him at different eras in the Revolution possess a prophetic character; because, in examining the defects of the different constitutions which prevailed for a time in France, he explained beforehand the consequences of these defects, and predictions of this kind could not fail to be realized.

M. Necker joined to a surprising sagacity of intellect a sensibility to the fate of mankind, and in particular of France, of which, I believe, there is no example in any writer on political topics. These topics are commonly treated in an abstract manner, and are almost always founded on calculation; but M. Necker was intent above all on considering the relations which that science bore to individual morality, to the happiness and dignity of nations. He is the Fénélon of politics, if I may venture thus to express myself, in honoring these two great men by the analogy between their virtues.

The first work published by him in 1791 is entitled *On the Administration of M. Necker, by Himself*.[1] At the close of a very profound political discussion on the various compensations that ought to have been granted to the privileged classes for the loss of their ancient rights, he says, addressing himself to the Assembly,

---

1. For a list of reviews of Necker's book, see Grange, *Les idées de Necker*, 629.

I know that I shall be blamed for my obstinate attachment to the principles of justice, and attempts will be made to debilitate it by giving it the name of aristocratic pity. I know better than you the nature of my pity. It was first for you that I felt that sentiment; but you were then without union and without strength; it was first for you that I sustained a conflict. And at the time when I complained so much of the indifference shown to you; when I spoke of the respect that was due to you; when I showed a perpetual disquietude for the fate of the people; it was then that by mere word games your enemies endeavored to ridicule my sentiments. I would willingly love others than you, now that you abandon me; I would it were in my power; but I possess not that consolation; your enemies and mine have placed between them and me a barrier which I shall never seek to burst; and they must necessarily hate me forever, since they have made me answerable for their own faults. Yet it was not I who prompted them to make an immoderate use of their former power; it was not I who rendered them inflexible when it became necessary to begin negotiating with fortune. Ah! if they were not under oppression, if they were not unhappy, how many reproaches could not I make to them! And when I defend them still in their rights and properties, they will not, I trust, believe that I think for a moment of regaining their favor. I now desire no connection with them, nor with anyone; it is with my recollections, with my thoughts, that I endeavor to live and die; when I fix my attention on the purity of the sentiments that have guided me, I find nowhere a suitable association; and when, in the want experienced by every feeling mind, I form that association, I do it in hope, with the upright men of every country, with those, so few in number, whose first passion is the love of doing good on earth.

M. Necker felt bitter regret for the loss of that popularity which he had sacrificed without hesitation to his duty. Some persons have blamed him for the importance that he set upon it. Woe to the statesmen who do not need public opinion! These are either courtiers or usurpers; they flatter themselves with obtaining, by intrigue or by terror, what generous minds wish to owe only to the esteem of their fellows.

When my father and I were walking together under those lofty trees at Coppet, which still seem to me the friendly witnesses of his noble thoughts, he asked me once whether I thought that the whole of France was infected with those popular suspicions to which he had been a victim on the road from Paris into Switzerland. "It seems to me," he said, "that in several provinces they acknowledged, down to the latest day of my administration, the purity of my intentions and my attachment to France." Hardly had he put this question to me than he dreaded being too much affected by my answer; "Let us talk no more on that subject," he said, "God reads in my heart: that is enough." I did not venture to give him a consoling answer on that day, so much of restrained emotion did I see in his whole being. Ah! how harsh and narrow-minded must be the enemies of such a man! It was to him that we ought to address the words of Ben Jonson, when speaking of his illustrious friend, the Chancellor of England. "I pray God to give you strength in your adversity; for as to greatness, you cannot want it."[2]

M. Necker, at the time when the democratic party, then in the plenitude of power, made him overtures to join them, expressed himself with the greatest energy on the disastrous situation to which the royal authority was reduced. And, although he expected, perhaps, too much from the ascendency of morality and eloquence at a time when men began to think of nothing but personal interest, he was extremely capable of availing himself of irony and reasoning when he thought them suitable. I quote the following example among many.

> I will venture to say that the political hierarchy established by the National Assembly seemed to require, more than any other social institution, the efficacious intervention of the monarch. That august mediation was perhaps alone capable of keeping up a distance between so many powers which press on each other, between so many individuals elected on similar grounds, between so many dignitaries, equal by their original profession, and still so near each other from the nature of their functions and the uncertain tenure of their places. It alone could give a certain life to the abstract and entirely constitutional gradations which ought henceforth to form the scale of subordination.

2. Ben Jonson (1572–1637), English poet and playwright, friend and rival of Shakespeare. The chancellor of England referred to here was Francis Bacon.

I can clearly perceive

Primary assemblies nominating an electoral body;

That electoral body choosing deputies to the National Assembly;

That assembly passing decrees and calling on the King to sanction and promulgate them;

The King addressing these decrees to the departments;

The departments transmitting them to the districts;

The districts issuing orders to the municipalities;

The municipalities, which for the execution of these decrees require, in case of need, the assistance of the national guards;

The national guards, whose duty it is to restrain the people;

The people who are bound to obey.

We perceive in this succession a numerical order with which there is no fault to be found; one, two, three, four, five, six, seven, eight, nine, ten; all follow with perfect regularity. But in the case of government, in the case of obedience, it is by the connection, it is by the moral relation of the different authorities that the general order is maintained. A legislator would have too easy a task if, to accomplish the grand political work of the submission of the mass to the wisdom of a few, it were enough for him to conjugate the verb to command, and to say like a schoolboy, "I will command, thou shalt command, he shall command, we shall command, &c." It is necessary, in order to establish effective subordination and to ensure the play of all the upward and downward movements, that there should be among all the conventional superiorities a proportional gradation of reputation and respect. There must be from rank to rank a distinction which has an imposing effect, and at the summit of these gradations, there must be a power which, by a mixture of reality and imagination, influences by its action the whole of the political hierarchy.

In no country are the distinctions of government more effaced than under the despotic sway of the Caliphs of the East; but nowhere are the punishments more hasty, more severe, or more multiform. The heads of the judicial order, and of the administration, have there a decoration which suffices for everything—a train of janissaries, mutes, and executioners.[3]

These latter paragraphs bear reference to the necessity of an aristocratic body, that is, of a chamber of peers, to support a monarchy.

3. For more information, see Grange, *Les idées de Necker*, 400–451.

During his last ministry, M. Necker had defended the principles of the English constitution successively against the King, the nobility, and the representatives of the people, according as each of these authorities had become the strongest. He continued the same course as a writer; and he combated in his works the Constituent Assembly, the Convention, the Directory, and Bonaparte, all four, when at the height of their prosperity; opposing to all the same principles, and apprising them that they were sowing the seeds of their own overthrow, even when succeeding in a present object; because, in political matters, that which most misleads bodies and individuals is the triumph which can be momentarily obtained over justice; a triumph which always ends by overturning those who obtain it.

M. Necker, who viewed the Constitution of 1791 with a statesman's eye, published his opinion on that subject under the first Assembly, at a time when that constitution still gave rise to a great deal of enthusiasm. His work entitled *On the Executive Power in Great Countries*,[4] is recognized by thinkers to be a classic. It contains ideas altogether new on the strength necessary to government in general; but these reflections are at first applied specifically to the order of things recently proclaimed by the Constituent Assembly; in this book, still more than in the former, one might take predictions for history, so precise and clear is the detail of the events which must necessarily arise from the defects of the institutions in question. M. Necker, on comparing the English constitution with the work of the Constituent Assembly, ends by these remarkable words: "The French will regret, when too late, their not having shown more respect to experience, and their having failed to recognize its noble origin though concealed under garments worn and rent."

He foretold in the same book the terror that was about to arise from the power of the Jacobins; and, what is still more remarkable, the terror that would be produced after them by the establishment of military despotism.

Such a political writer as M. Necker was not to be satisfied with merely exhibiting a picture of all the misfortunes that would result from the constitution of 1791: he also gave the Legislative Assembly advice on the means of escaping them. The Constituent Assembly had decreed more

---

4. For more information on Necker's book, see ibid., 434–52.

than three hundred articles which no succeeding legislature had a right to touch, except on conditions which it was almost impossible to fulfill; and yet, among these unchangeable articles was the method adopted for nominating to inferior appointments and other things of equally little importance; "so that it would be neither more easy nor less difficult to change the French monarchy into a republic, than to modify the most insignificant of all the details comprised, one knows not why, in the constitutional act."

"It seems to me," says M. Necker elsewhere,

that in a great State we cannot expect liberty and renounce at any time the following conditions.

1. Conferring exclusively the right of legislation on the national representatives under the sanction of the monarch; comprising in this right of legislation, without exception, the choice and enactment of taxes.

2. Fixing public expenditure by the same authority; with this right is evidently connected the limitation of the military force.

3. Rendering all accounts of receipt and expenditure to commissioners from among the national representatives.

4. The annual renewal of the powers necessary to levy taxes, excepting the taxes mortgaged for the payment of the interest of the public debt.

5. The proscription of every kind of arbitrary authority; and vesting in every citizen a right to bring a civil or criminal action against all public officers who should have made an abuse of their power in regard to him.

6. Prohibiting military officers to act in the interior of the kingdom otherwise than on the demand of civil officers.

7. The annual renewal by the legislature of the laws which constitute the discipline, and consequently the action and strength, of an army.

8. The liberty of the press, extended as far as is compatible with morality and public tranquillity.

9. An equal distribution of public trusts, and the legal right of all citizens to exercise public functions.

10. The responsibility of ministers and of the principal agents of government.

11. The hereditary succession to the throne, in order to prevent factions and preserve public tranquillity.

12. Conferring the executive power, fully and unreservedly, on the monarch, with all the means necessary for its exercise, that public order

may be assured and that the various powers united in the legislative body may be prevented from introducing a despotism not less oppressive than any other.

To these principles should be added the most unqualified respect for the rights of property, if that respect did not already compose one of the elements of universal morality, regardless of the form of government under which men live together.

The twelve articles which I have just pointed out offer to all enlightened men the fundamental bases of the civil and political liberty of a nation. They ought, accordingly, to have been placed separately in the constitutional act, and not have been confounded with the numerous provisions which the Assembly was willing to submit to a continual renewal of discussion.

And why was this not done? Because, in assigning to these articles a conspicuous place in the constitutional charter, a light would have been cast on two truths which it was intended to keep in the background.

The one, that the fundamental principles of the liberty of France were completely stated, either in the text or in the spirit of the declaration made by the King on the 27th of December, 1788,[5] and in his subsequent explanations.

The other, that all the orders of the state, all classes of citizens, after a certain time of wavering and agitation, would have, in all probability, concurred in giving their consent to the same principles, and would perhaps still give it were they called on to do so.

These articles, which constitute in a manner the "gospel of society," we have seen reappear, under a form nearly similar, in the declaration of the 2d of May (1814) by His Majesty Louis XVIII, dated at St. Ouen;[6]

---

5. On December 27, 1788, the King approved the doubling of the Third Estate in a document entitled *Result of the King's Council of State*. This was a major decision that concluded a three-month-long debate and acknowledged the rising influence of public opinion. For more information on the events surrounding this episode, see Doyle, *Oxford History of the French Revolution*, 92–94. For more information about the prerevolutionary phase, also see Doyle, *Origins of the French Revolution*, 131–77, and Egret, *The French Prerevolution*.

6. The declaration made by Louis XVIII (1755–1824) in May 1814 on his return to France following the defeat of Napoléon. The declaration is analyzed in detail in part V of

they reappeared also on another occasion, of which we shall speak hereafter. From the 27th of December, 1788, to the 8th of July, 1815, these
articles are what the French wished, whenever they had the power of expressing a wish.

The book *On the Executive Power in Great Countries* is the best guide
that can be followed by men called on to make or to modify a constitution
of any kind; for it may be called the political chart in which all the dangers
that are found in the track of liberty are pointed out.

In the beginning of this work M. Necker addresses himself thus to the
French nation:

> I remember the time when, on publishing the result of my long re-
> flections on the finances of France, I wrote these words: "Yes, generous
> nation, it is to you that I consecrate this work." Alas! who would have
> told me that, after the lapse of so small a number of years, there would
> come a time when I could no longer make use of the same expressions,
> and when I should have to turn my eyes toward other nations to regain
> courage to speak of justice and morality! Ah! why am I not permitted to
> say today: it is to you that I address this work, to you, nation, still more
> generous since liberty has developed your character and freed it from
> any restraint; to you, nation, still more generous since your forehead no
> longer bears the impression of a yoke; to you, nation, still more generous
> since you have made trial of your strength, and that you dictate, yourself,
> the laws that you obey! Ah! with what pleasure I should have held this
> language! my feelings still exist, but they seem to me in exile; and, in my
> sad regret, I cannot either contract new ties nor resume, even in hope,
> the favorite idea and the only passion which so long filled my soul.

I do not know, but it seems to me that never was a juster expression
given to that which we all feel: that love for France which is at present so
painful, while formerly there was not a nobler nor sweeter enjoyment.

Considerations. Louis XVIII fled to Belgium a year later, when Napoléon returned to France
during his Hundred Days.

CHAPTER III

Of the Different Parties Which Composed the Legislative Assembly.

We cannot help feeling a sentiment of profound grief on retracing the eras of a Revolution in which a free constitution might have been established in France, and on seeing not only that hope overturned, but the most distressing events taking the place of the most salutary institutions. It is not a mere recollection that we recall; it is a keen sensation of pain which revives.

The Constituent Assembly repented, toward the end of its reign, that it should have allowed itself to be carried along by popular factions. It had grown old in two years, as much as Louis XIV in forty. It was from just apprehension, in its case also, that moderation had resumed a certain sway on it. But its successors came forward with the fever of the Revolution at a time when there was nothing more to reform or destroy. The social edifice was leaning to the democratic side, and to restore it to an upright form, it was necessary to increase the power of the throne. Yet the first decree of the Legislative Assembly was to refuse the King the title of "Majesty" and to assign him an armchair only (*fauteuil*), similar in all respects to that of a president. The representatives of the people thus put on the appearance of thinking that they had a king not for the public good, but for the sake of pleasing himself, and that it was consequently well to take away as much as possible from that pleasure. The decree respecting the armchair was recalled, so many complaints did it excite among men of sense; but the blow was struck, as well on the mind of the King as on that of the people; the one felt that his position was not tenable, the other conceived the desire and the hope of a republic.[1]

---

1. The decision of the Assembly to refuse the King the title of "Majesty" and to grant

Three parties, perfectly distinct, made themselves conspicuous in the Assembly: the constitutionalists, the Jacobins, and the republicans. There were no priests, and almost no noblemen, among the constitutionalists; the cause of the privileged orders was by this time lost, but that of the throne was still under dispute, and the men of property and moderation formed a preserving party in the midst of the popular storm.

Ramond, Matthieu Dumas, Jaucourt, Beugnot, Girardin, were conspicuous among the constitutionalists:[2] they possessed courage, reason, perseverance, and could not be accused of any aristocratic prejudices. Accordingly, the struggle which they supported in favor of monarchy does infinite honor to their political conduct. The same Jacobin party which existed in the Constituent Assembly under the name of the "Mountain"[3] showed itself anew in the Legislative Assembly; but it was still less entitled to esteem than its predecessor. For in the Constituent Assembly there was reason to fear, at least during certain moments, that the cause of liberty was not the strongest, and that the partisans of the Old Regime who acted as deputies might still be formidable; but in the Legislative Assembly there was neither danger nor obstacle, and the factious were obliged to create phantoms that they might display their skill in wielding the weapons of argument.

---

him an armchair rather than a proper throne followed the declaration of Louis XVI's reservations toward the Constitution of 1791, a document that he had hesitated to sign at the outset. The symbolic connotations of the Assembly's decision were far-reaching; it amounted, among other things, to an attack on the monarch's role as an inviolable "neutral" power. As Benjamin Constant pointed out, this legal fiction (inviolability) was necessary in the interest of order and liberty itself: "Your concerns, your suspicions, must never touch him. He has no intentions, no weaknesses, no connivance with his ministers, because he is not really a man but an abstract and neutral power above the storms." (Constant, *Principles of Politics*, 237)

2. Ramond de Carbonnières (1755–1827), deputy of Paris; Mathieu Dumas (1753–1837), deputy from Seine-et-Oise. Jaucourt (1757–1852) became a member of the Tribunate in 1800 and later a peer of France during the Bourbon Restoration. Beugnot (1761–1835), deputy from Aube, was minister of the interior during the first Bourbon Restoration (1814–15) and played an important role in drafting the Charter of 1814. Stanislas de Girardin (1762–1827), after serving in the Legislative Assembly, had a long career in administration under the Empire and the Restoration.

3. See *A Critical Dictionary of the French Revolution*, 380–92, 458–73.

A singular trio, Merlin de Thionville, Bazire, and Chabot,[4] formerly a capuchin, made themselves conspicuous among the Jacobins; they were their leaders merely because, being placed in every respect in the lowest rank, they excited no envy. It was a principle with this party, which shook society to its base, to put at the head of the assailants persons possessing nothing in the edifice which they wanted to overthrow. One of the first proposals made in the Assembly by the trio of demagogues was to suppress the appellation of "honorable member," which was introduced into use, as in England: aware, doubtless, that this epithet, when addressed to any one of them, could not fail to pass for ironical.

A second party, though of merits altogether different, added strength to these ignorant men and flattered themselves, most erroneously, with being able first, to make use of the Jacobins, and afterward to keep them within bounds. The deputies from the Gironde were composed of about twenty lawyers from Bourdeaux and other parts of the South. These men, elected almost by accident, were gifted with the greatest talents, so rich is France in those men distinguished but unknown whom a representative government calls forth. The Girondists aimed at a republic, and succeeded only in overturning monarchy; they perished soon after, when endeavoring to save France and its King. This made M. de Lally say, with his accustomed eloquence, "that their life and their death were equally disastrous to the country."

To these deputies of the Gironde were joined Brissot,[5] a writer irregular in his principles as in his style, and Condorcet,[6] whose towering knowl-

---

4. Merlin de Thionville (1762–1833), deputy from Moselle and member of the extreme left. After the fall of Robespierre in July 1794, he persecuted the Jacobins and became a member of the Council of Five Hundred. Bazire (1761–94), deputy from Côte-d'Or and enemy of the Girondins, was executed on April 5, 1794. Chabot (1756–94), deputy from Lois-et-Cher, voted for the death of Louis XVI. He was arrested in November 1793 and executed the same day as Bazire.

5. Jacques-Pierre Brissot (1754–93), important journalist, deputy from Paris, and a leading member of the Girondins. He visited the United States in 1788 and later distinguished himself through his participation in the declarations of war against England and Austria and his opposition to the *Mountain* and Robespierre. He was arrested in June 1793 as he was trying to flee for Switzerland and was executed four months later.

6. Marie Jean Antoine Nicolas Caritat, Marquis de Condorcet (1743–94); prominent

edge could not be disputed, but who, in a political sense, acted a greater part by his passion than by the powers of his mind. He was irreligious in the same way as priests are bigoted, with hatred, pertinacity, and the appearance of moderation: his death too resembled martyrdom.

To give a preference to a republic over every other form of government cannot be deemed criminal if crimes are not necessary to establish it; but at the time the Legislative Assembly declared itself inimical to the remnant of royalty that still subsisted in France, the truly republican sentiments, that is, generosity toward the weak, a horror of arbitrary measures, a respect for justice, all the virtues, in short, which the friends of liberty are proud of, prompted men to take an interest in the constitutional monarchy and its head. At another period, they might have rallied under the cause of a republic, had that form been possible in France; but when Louis XVI was still alive, when the nation had received his oath, and when it, in return, had taken oaths to him in perfect freedom, when the political ascendency of the privileged orders was entirely extinguished, what confidence was it necessary to have in the future to risk, for the sake of a name, all the real advantages already possessed!

The desire of power in the republicans of 1792 was mixed with an enthusiasm for principles, and some of them offered to support royalty, if all the places in the ministry were given to their friends. In that case only, they said, shall we be sure that the opinions of the patriots will be triumphant. The choice of ministers in a constitutional monarchy is doubtless an affair of the highest importance, and the King frequently committed the fault of nominating persons that were very suspicious to the party of liberty; however, it was then but too easy to obtain their removal, and the responsibility for political events must rest, in all its weight, on the Legislative Assembly. No argument, no source of disquietude, was listened to by its leaders; to the observations of wisdom, of disinterested

---

philosopher and mathematician; deputy from Paris; cofounder (with Sieyès) of the Society of 1789; and author of, among many writings, *Esquisse d'un tableau des progrès de l'esprit humain* and *Sur le nécessité d'établir en France une Constitution nouvelle* (1793). He was arrested in March 1794 and died in prison a few months later. He defended a liberal agenda that included free public education and equal rights for women. On his political thought, see Baker, *Condorcet: From Natural Philosophy to Social Mathematics.*

wisdom, they replied by a disdainful smile indicative of that emptiness which results from vanity. Repeated efforts were made to recall to them circumstances, and to deduce general views from the past: transitions were made from theory to experience, and from experience to theory, to show them the identity of the two: yet, if they consented to reply, it was by denying the most authentic facts and contesting the most evident observations, opposing to them a few maxims that were common, although expressed in eloquent language. They looked round among themselves as if they alone had been worthy of understanding each other, and took fresh courage from the idea that all that opposed their manner of thinking was pusillanimity. These are the tokens of party spirit among Frenchmen: disdain for their adversaries forms its basis, and disdain is always adverse to the knowledge of truth. The Girondists despised the constitutionalists until they had, without intending it, made popularity descend and fix itself in the lowest ranks of society: they then saw the reproach of weakness cast on them in their turn by ferocious characters; the throne which they were attacking served them as a shelter, and it was not till after they had triumphed over it that they found themselves unprotected in front of the people. In a revolution, men have often more to dread from their successes than from their failures.

CHAPTER IV

Spirit of the Decrees
of the Legislative Assembly.

The Constituent Assembly had passed more laws in two years than the English Parliament in fifty; but these laws at least reformed abuses and were founded on general principles. The Legislative Assembly passed an equal number of decrees, although there remained nothing truly useful to be done; but the spirit of faction inspired all to which the Assembly gave the name of laws. It accused the King's brothers, confiscated the property of emigrants, and adopted against the priests a decree of proscription revolting in a still higher degree to the friends of liberty than to the sincere Catholics, so contrary was it to philosophy and equity.[1] What! will it be said, were not the emigrants and priests enemies to the Revolution? This was a very good plea for not returning such men as deputies, for not calling them to the management of public business; but what would society become if, instead of seeking support in immutable principles, men should have the power of pointing laws against their adversaries as they can point a battery? The Constituent Assembly never persecuted either individuals or classes; but the next Assembly only passed decrees suited to the moment, and we can hardly quote a resolution adopted by it which was calculated to last beyond the temporary occasion that called it forth.

Arbitrary power, against which the Revolution ought to have been directed, had acquired new strength by the Revolution itself. It was in vain that they pretended to do everything for the people; the revolutionaries were now only priests of a Moloch, called the common interest, which

1. Reference to the law of May 27, 1792, vetoed by the King, which led to the events of June 20 and August 10, 1792, and the subsequent fall of the monarchy.

required the sacrifice of the happiness of each. Persecution in politics leads to nothing but the necessity of further persecution; and to kill is not to extirpate. It has been said with the most cold-blooded intention that the dead alone return no more; but even that maxim is not true, for the children and the friends of the victims are stronger by their resentments than those who suffered were by their opinions. The object should be to extinguish hatreds, and not to compress them. Reform is accomplished in a country when its promoters have managed to make its adversaries merely bothersome, without having turned them into victims.

CHAPTER V

Of the First War Between France and Europe.

We need not be surprised that kings and princes never liked the principles of the French Revolution. "To be a royalist is my business," said Joseph II. But as the opinion of the people always makes its way into the cabinet of kings, no sovereign in Europe thought of making war on France to oppose the Revolution at its outset, when the object was only to establish a limited monarchy. The progress of knowledge was such in every part of the civilized world that, at that time, as at present, a representative government more or less similar to that of England appeared suitable and just, and that system met with no formidable opponents among either the English or Germans. Burke, from the year 1791, expressed his indignation at the crimes already committed in France, and at the false systems of policy adopted there;[1] but those of the aristocratic party on the Continent, who now quote Burke as the enemy of the Revolution, are perhaps not aware that in every page he reproaches the French with not having conformed to the principles of the English constitution.

"I recommend to the French," he says, "our constitution; all our happiness arises from it." "Absolute democracy," he adds in another place,* "is no more a legitimate government than absolute monarchy. There is but one opinion in France against absolute monarchy;† it was at its close, it was expiring without agony, and without convulsions; all the dissensions

---

* Burke's Works, vol. iii. p. 179.

† Ibid., p. 183.

1. For Burke's writings on the French Revolution after 1790, see his *Further Reflections on the Revolution in France.*

arose from the quarrel between a despotic democracy, and a government with a balance of power."

If the majority of Europe in 1789 approved the establishment of a limited monarchy in France, how then, it may be asked, does it happen that, from the year 1791, all provocations arose from foreign powers? For although France made a hasty declaration of war against Austria in 1792, the foreign powers were, in fact, the first to assume a hostile attitude toward the French, by the convention of Pilnitz and the assemblies at Coblentz.[2] The reciprocal recriminations go back to that period. Yet the public opinion of Europe and the prudence of Austria would have prevented war, had the Legislative Assembly been moderate. The greatest precision in the knowledge of dates is necessary to judge with impartiality which of the two, France or Europe, was the aggressor. A lapse of six months makes that proper in politics which was not so six months before, and people often confound ideas because they confound dates.

The foreign powers did wrong in 1791, in allowing themselves to be drawn into the imprudent measures urged by the emigrants. But after the 10th of August, 1792, when the throne was overturned, the state of things in France became wholly incompatible with social order. Yet, would not this throne have stood, had not Europe threatened France with interfering by force of arms in her domestic concerns, and revolted the pride of an independent nation by imposing laws on it? Fate alone possesses the secret of such suppositions: one thing is indisputable; it is that the convention of Pilnitz was the beginning of the long war of Europe. The Jacobins[3] were as desirous of this war as the emigrants: for both believed that a crisis of some kind or other could alone produce the chances necessary to enable them to triumph.[4]

2. The Declaration of Pilnitz (August 27, 1791) was signed by Holy Roman Emperor Leopold II and King Frederick William II of Prussia, who expressed their intention to help the king of France in case of need. The assemblies at Koblenz were organized by the émigrés.

3. A notable exception in this regard was Robespierre.

4. Austria, England, and Prussia followed closely the political developments in France and in 1791 began contemplating the possibility of intervening to support Louis XVI and restore order. The actual war began in April 1792, when France declared war on Austria; Prussia joined the Austrian side a few weeks later and invaded France in July. The battle

In the beginning of 1792, before the declaration of war, Leopold, Emperor of Germany, one of the most enlightened princes of which the eighteenth century can boast,[5] wrote to the Legislative Assembly a letter, which might be almost called familiar and confidential. Some deputies of the Constituent Assembly, as Barnave and Duport, had composed it, and the draft was sent by the Queen to Brussels, to the Count de Mercy-Argenteau, who had long been Austrian Ambassador at Paris. In this letter[6] Leopold attacked the Jacobin party by name and offered his aid to the constitutionalists. His observations were, no doubt, extremely wise; but it was not thought becoming on the part of an emperor of Germany to enter with so much detail into the affairs of France; and the minds of the deputies revolted against the advice given them by a foreign monarch. Leopold had governed Tuscany with perfect moderation, and it is but justice to add that he always showed respect to public opinion, and to the advanced knowledge of the age. He was thus a sincere believer in the good that his advice might produce. But in political discussions where the mass of a nation takes a part, it is only the voice of events that is listened to; arguments but excite the wish of answering them.

The Legislative Assembly, which foresaw a rupture ready to break out, felt also that the King could hardly take an interest in the success of Frenchmen fighting in the cause of the Revolution. The Assembly was distrustful of ministers, under the persuasion that they did not in their hearts wish to repel those enemies whose assistance they secretly invoked. The war department was entrusted in the end of 1791 to M. de Narbonne,[7]

---

of Valmy (September 20, 1792) stopped the march of the Prussian armies, which subsequently retreated from France. In November, the French occupied Belgium.

5. Leopold II (1747–92), Duke of Tuscany (1765–90), the penultimate Holy Roman Emperor (1790–92), and son of Empress Maria Theresa, personified the image of the enlightened monarch. As Grand Duke of Tuscany, Leopold endorsed a progressive constitution that, had it been ratified, would have been the first free, written liberal constitution of Europe. In the end, Emperor Joseph II opposed its ratification.

6. On December 21, 1791.

7. Louis de Narbonne-Lara (1755–1813) was nominated minister of war on December 6, 1791, and retained his position until March 9, 1792 (he emigrated soon after that). Many believed Narbonne to be the illegitimate son of Louis XV. He was one of Madame de Staël's lovers and arguably the father of her first two children. For a selection of their correspon-

who afterward lost his life at the siege of Torgau. He employed himself with unfeigned zeal in all the preparations necessary for the defense of the kingdom. Possessing rank and talents, the manners of a courtier, and the views of a philosopher, that which was predominant in his soul was military honor and French valor. To oppose the interference of foreigners under whatever circumstances always seemed to him the duty of a citizen and a gentleman. His colleagues combined against him and succeeded in obtaining his removal. They seized the moment when his popularity in the Assembly was lessened to get rid of a man who was then performing his functions of minister of war as conscientiously as he would have done under any other circumstances.

One evening, M. de Narbonne, in giving the Assembly an account of certain matters in his department, made use of this expression: "I appeal to the most distinguished members of this Assembly." At that moment the whole party of the Mountain rose up in a fury, and Merlin, Bazire, and Chabot declared that "all the deputies were equally distinguished." Aristocracy of talent was as repugnant to their feelings as aristocracy of birth.

The day after this setback, the other ministers, no longer afraid of the ascendancy of M. de Narbonne with the popular party, prevailed on the King to remove him. This ill-judged triumph was of short duration. The republicans forced the King to take ministers devoted to them, and these ministers obliged him to make use of the *initiative* given him by the constitution, by going in person to the Assembly to recommend war with Austria. I was present at the meeting in which Louis XVI was forced to a measure which was necessarily painful to him in so many ways. His features were not expressive of his thoughts, but it was not from dissimulation that he concealed them; a mixture of resignation and dignity repressed in him every outward sign of his sentiments. On entering the Assembly he looked to the right and the left, with that kind of vague curiosity which is usual to persons who are so short-sighted that their eyes seem to be of no use to them. He proposed war in the same tone of voice as he might have used in requiring the most indifferent decree possible.

---

dence, see *Madame de Staël, ses amis, ses correspondants. Choix de lettres (1778–1817)*, 71–79, 81–83, 94–100, 107–8, 113–15.

The president replied to him with the laconic arrogance adopted in this Assembly, as if the dignity of a free people consisted in insulting the King whom it had chosen for its constitutional chief.

When Louis XVI and his ministers had left the hall, the Assembly voted war by acclamation. Some members took no share in the deliberations; but the galleries applauded with transport: the deputies threw their hats in the air, and that day, the first of the bloody struggle which has torn Europe during twenty-three years, that day did not, in most minds, produce the slightest disquietude. Yet, of the deputies who voted for this war, many fell by a violent death, and those who rejoiced at it the most were unconsciously pronouncing their own death sentence.

CHAPTER VI

Of the Means Employed in 1792 to Establish the Republic.

The French are but little disposed to civil war, and have no talent whatever for conspiracies. They are little disposed to civil war because, among them, the majority almost always draws the minority after it; the party that passes for the stronger soon becomes all-powerful, for everyone joins it. They have no talent for conspiracies for the same reasons which make them extremely fitted for revolutionary movements; they stand in need of mutual excitement by a communication of their ideas; the profound silence, the solitary resolution, necessary for a conspirator does not enter into their character. They might, perhaps, be more capable of this now that Italian features are blended with their natural disposition; but we see no example of a conspiracy in the history of France; Henri III and Henri IV were each assassinated by fanatics without accomplices. The Court, it is true, under Charles IX prepared in darkness the massacre of St. Bartholomew; but it was an Italian queen[1] who communicated her artful and dissembling spirit to the instruments of which she made use. The means employed to accomplish the Revolution were not better than those generally used to form a conspiracy: in fact, to commit a crime in a public square or to contrive it in the closet is to be equally guilty, but there is the perfidy the less.

The Legislative Assembly overthrew the monarchy by means of sophistry. Its decrees perverted the good sense and depraved the morality of the nation. A kind of political hypocrisy, still more dangerous than hypocrisy in religion, was necessary to destroy the throne piecemeal while

1. Catherine de Médicis.

swearing to maintain it. Today the ministers were accused;[2] tomorrow the King's guard was disbanded;[3] on another day rewards were granted to the soldiers of the regiment of Chateauvieux, who had mutinied against their officers;[4] the massacres of Avignon found defenders in the heart of the Assembly;[5] in short, whether the establishment of a republic in France appeared desirable or not, there could be but one opinion on the choice of the means employed to attain it; and the more one felt attached to liberty, the more did the conduct of the republican party excite indignation in the bottom of the soul.

That which, in a great political crisis, ought, above all things, to be considered is whether the Revolution desired is in harmony with the spirit of the time. By endeavoring to accomplish the reinstatement of ancient institutions; that is, by endeavoring to make the human mind retrograde, all the popular passions become inflamed. But if, on the other hand, it be attempted to found a republic in a country which the day before had all the defects and all the vices to which absolute monarchies must give birth, men are obliged to exercise oppression in order to acquire freedom, and to sully themselves with crimes in proclaiming that government whose basis is virtue. A sure method of never mistaking the wish of the majority of a nation is never to follow any other than a lawful course for the attainment even of those objects which are thought most useful. So long as we allow ourselves to do nothing immoral, we are sure of never violently thwarting the course of things.

The war afterward so brilliant to the French began with defeats. The soldiers at Lisle, after being routed, killed their commander, Theobald Dillon, whose fidelity they, most unjustly, suspected. These early checks had diffused a general spirit of mistrust. Accordingly the Legislative As-

---

2. The Girondists accused the minister of foreign affairs, de Lessart, whose arrest eventually led to the fall of the Feuillants in March 1792.

3. On May 29, 1792.

4. On April 9, 1792, the Legislative Assembly honored the Swiss soldiers from the Chateauvieux regiment. They revolted at Nancy in August 1790 and were subsequently arrested.

5. The massacres occurred on October 16, 1791, when the "patriots" of Avignon, supporting annexation to France, massacred about sixty aristocrats who opposed this measure.

sembly pursued the ministers with incessant denunciations, like restive horses who cannot be spurred forward. The first duty of a government, as well as of a nation, is doubtless to ensure its independence against the invasion of foreigners. But could so false a situation continue? And was it not better to open the gates of France to the King, when desirous of quitting the country, than to act in the spirit of chicane, from morning to night, with the royal power, or rather the royal weakness; and to treat the descendant of St. Louis, when captive on the throne, like a bird fastened to the top of a tree, and against which everyone in his turn aims a dart?

The Legislative Assembly, weary even of the patience of Louis XVI, determined to present to him two decrees to which his conscience and his safety would not allow him to give his sanction. By the first, they sentenced to deportation every priest who had refused the constitutional oath, if he were denounced by twenty active citizens, that is, citizens who paid taxes; and by the second, they called to Paris a legion of Marseillois whom they knew to be determined to act the part of conspirators against the Crown. But what a decree was that of which the priests were the victims! The fate of a citizen was surrendered to a denunciation which proceeded on his presumed opinions. What is there to be feared from despotism but such a decree as this? Instead of twenty active citizens, we have only to suppose courtiers, who are active also in their manner; and we shall have the history of all the *lettres de cachet*, of all the exiles, of all the imprisonments which people wish to prevent by the establishment of a free government.

A generous impulse of the soul determined the King to expose himself to every hazard rather than accede to the proscription of the priests. He might, by considering himself as a prisoner, give his sanction to this law and protest in private against it; but he could not consent to act in religion as in politics; and if as King he dissembled, as a martyr he was true.

As soon as the veto of the King became known,[6] intelligence came from all quarters that a tumult was preparing in the suburbs of Paris. The people, having become despotic, were irritated by the slightest obstacle to

---

6. The King twice vetoed such laws, in 1791 and 1792. This was, in fact, his second veto, which occurred after France had declared war on the European powers.

their will. We saw on this occasion too the dreadful inconvenience of placing the royal authority against a single chamber. The conflict between
these two powers has, in such a case, no arbiter, and the appeal is made
to insurrection.

Twenty thousand men of the lowest rank, armed with pikes and lances,
marched to the Tuileries[7] without knowing why; they were ready to commit every crime, or could be persuaded to the noblest actions, according
to the impulse of events, and of their leaders.

These twenty thousand men made their way into the palace; their faces
bore marks of that coarseness, moral and physical, of which the disgusting
effect is not to be supported by the greatest philanthropist. Had they been
animated by any true feeling, had they come to complain against injustice,
against the dearness of corn, against the increase of taxes, against compulsory service in the army, in short, against any suffering which power
and wealth can inflict on poverty, the rags which they wore, their hands
blackened by labor, the premature old age of the women, the brutishness
of the children, would all have excited pity. But their frightful oaths mingled with cries, their threatening gestures, their deadly instruments, exhibited a frightful spectacle, and one calculated to alter forever the respect
that ought to be felt for our fellow-creatures.

All Europe knows how Madame Elizabeth, the King's sister, endeavored to prevent those around her from undeceiving the madmen who took
her for the Queen, and threatened her under that name. The Queen herself
ought to have been recognized by the ardor with which she pressed her
children to her breast. The King on this day showed all the virtues of a
saint. The time was past for saving himself like a hero; the dreadful signal
of massacre, the red cap, was placed on his devoted head; but nothing
could humiliate him, for all his life had been a continued sacrifice.

The Assembly, ashamed of its auxiliaries, sent several of the deputies
to save the royal family, and Vergniaud, perhaps the most eloquent orator
of those who have appeared at the French tribune, succeeded in dispersing
the populace in a few moments.

General la Fayette, indignant at what was passing at Paris, left his army

7. On June 20, 1792.

to appear at the bar of the Assembly and demand justice for the terrible day of 20th June, 1792.[8] Had the Girondists at that time joined him and his friends, they might perhaps still have prevented the entrance of foreign troops and restored to the King that constitutional authority which was his due. But at the instant that M. de la Fayette closed his speech by the words which so well became him, "Such are the representations submitted to the Assembly by a citizen, whose love for liberty, at least, will not be disputed"; Guadet, the colleague of Vergniaud, stepped quickly to the tribune and made a dexterous use of the distrust that every representative assembly naturally feels toward a general who interferes in domestic affairs. However, when he revived the recollection of Cromwell dictating, in the name of his army, laws to the representatives of his country, the Assembly were perfectly aware that they had neither tyrant nor soldier before them, but a virtuous citizen who, although friendly to the republican form in theory, could not tolerate crime, under whatever banner it might pretend to range itself.

8. La Fayette came to Paris on June 28, 1792, and spoke in the Legislative Assembly against the rising influence of the Jacobins. In early August, Debry asked the Legislative Assembly to condemn La Fayette's behavior. The first vote was in favor of acquittal (400 votes to 224). La Fayette was, however, indicted on August 18 and had to flee Paris on the night of August 19–20. For more information on La Fayette's role, see P. Guéniffey's entry in *A Critical Dictionary of the French Revolution*, 224–33; Gottschalk and Maddox, *La Fayette in the French Revolution*, vols. 1 and 2; and Taine, *The French Revolution*, vol. 2, 600–604.

CHAPTER VII

Anniversary of 14th July
Celebrated in 1792.

Addresses from every part of France, which at that time were sincere, because there was danger in signing them, expressed the wish of the great majority of the citizens for the support of the constitution.[1] However imperfect it might be, it was a limited monarchy, and such has, all along, been the wish of the French; the factious, or the military, have alone been able to prevent that wish from prevailing. If the leaders of the popular party have believed that the nation really wanted the republic, they would not have needed the most unjust methods to establish it. Despotic measures are never resorted to when public opinion is in favor of a plan; and what despotic measures, good heaven! were those which were then seen to proceed from the coarsest ranks of society, like vapors arising from a pestilential marsh! Marat,[2] whose name posterity will perhaps recall on purpose to connect with a man the crimes of an era, Marat made use every day of his newspaper to threaten the royal family, and its defenders, with the most dreadful punishments. Never had human speech been so much disfigured; the howlings of wild beasts might be expressed in such language.

Paris was divided into forty-eight sections, all of which used to send

1. The Legislative Assembly received many letters protesting the events of June 20, 1792. For an account of the general background of the summer of 1792, see Taine, *The French Revolution,* vol. II, 596–688.

2. Jean-Paul Marat (1743–93) was a prominent member of the Jacobins who advocated such violent measures as the September 1792 massacres of jailed "enemies of the Revolution" and was instrumental in launching the famous Reign of Terror. He was stabbed to death in his bathtub by Charlotte Corday.

deputies to the bar of the Assembly to denounce the slightest actions as crimes. Forty-four thousand municipalities contained each a club of Jacobins in correspondence with that of Paris, and that again was subservient to the orders of the suburbs.[3] Never was a city of seven hundred thousand souls so completely transformed. On all hands were heard invectives directed against the royal palace; nothing now defended it but a kind of respect which still served as a barrier around that ancient abode; but that barrier might at any moment be passed, and then all was lost.

They wrote from the departments that the most violent men were being sent to Paris to celebrate the 14th of July, and that they went there only to massacre the King and Queen. The mayor of Paris, Péthion,[4] a cold-blooded fanatic, who pushed all new ideas to an extreme because he was more capable of exaggerating than of comprehending them; Péthion, with an exterior silliness which was taken for sincerity, favored every kind of sedition. The authority of the magistracy was thus added to the cause of insurrection. The departmental administration, by virtue of an article in the constitution, suspended Péthion from his functions; the King's ministers confirmed the suspension; but the Assembly re-instated the mayor in his office, and his ascendency was increased by his momentary disgrace. A popular chief can desire nothing more than an apparent persecution, followed by a real triumph.

The Marseillois sent to the Champ de Mars to celebrate the 14th of July[5] bore, on their tattered hats, the inscription, "*Péthion or death!*" They passed before the raised seats on which the royal family were placed, calling out, *Vive Péthion!* a miserable name, which even the mischief that he did has not been able to redeem from obscurity! A few feeble voices could with difficulty be heard, when calling *Vive le Roi!* as a last adieu, a final prayer.

The expression of the Queen's countenance will never be effaced from

3. Not every municipality had a Jacobin club. According to some estimates, there were between five thousand and eight thousand Jacobin clubs in the country.

4. Pétion de Villeneuve (1756–94) was elected mayor of Paris in November 1791 and encouraged the events of August 10, 1792. Eventually he moved closer to the Girondins. He committed suicide to avoid being arrested.

5. The Marseillais arrived in Paris on July 30, 1792.

my remembrance: her eyes were swollen with tears; the splendor of her dress, the dignity of her carriage, formed a contrast with the train that surrounded her. Only a few national guards separated her from the populace; the armed men assembled in the Champ de Mars seemed collected rather for a riot than a celebration. The King repaired on foot from the pavilion, under which he sat, all the way to the altar raised at the end of the Champ de Mars. It was there that he had to take, a second time, an oath of fidelity to the constitution, of which the relics were about to crush the throne. A crowd of children followed the King with acclamations—children as yet unconscious of the crime with which their fathers were about to sully themselves.

It required the character of Louis XVI, that character of martyr which he never contradicted, to support as he did such a situation. His mode of walking, his countenance, had something remarkable in them: on other occasions one might have wished for more grandeur in his demeanor; on the present, to remain in every respect the same was enough to appear sublime. I marked at a distance his head, distinguished by its powder from the black locks of those that accompanied him; his dress, still embroidered as before, was more conspicuous when close to the coarse attire of the lower orders who pressed around him. When he mounted the steps of the altar, he seemed a sacred victim offering himself as a voluntary sacrifice. He descended again; and, crossing anew the disordered ranks, returned to take his place beside the Queen and his children. After that day the people saw him no more till they saw him on the scaffold.

CHAPTER VIII

Manifesto of the Duke of Brunswick.

It has been strongly asserted that the terms in which the manifesto of the Duke of Brunswick was expressed were one of the principal causes of the rising of the French nation against the allies in 1792.[1] I do not believe this: the first two articles of that manifesto contained what most papers of the kind since the Revolution have expressed; that is, that the foreign powers would make no conquest from France, and that they were not inclined to interfere with the interior government of the country. To these two promises, which are seldom observed, was added, it is true, the threat of treating as rebels such of the national guards as should be found with arms in their hands; as if, in any case, a nation could be culpable in defending its territory! But had the manifesto even been more moderately couched, it would not, at that time, have at all weakened the public spirit of the French. It is well known that every armed power desires victory, and has nothing more at heart than to weaken the obstacles which it must encounter to obtain it. Accordingly, the proclamations of invaders addressed to the nations whom they attack all consist in saying: "Do not resist us"; and the answer of a spirited people should be: "We will resist you."

The friends of liberty were on this occasion, as they always will be, adverse to foreign interference; but they could not, on the other hand, conceal from themselves that the King had been put in a situation that reduced him to wish for the aid of the allies. What resource could there then remain to virtuous patriots?

M. de la Fayette proposed to the royal family to come and take refuge

1. For more details, see Godechot, *La Contre-Révolution*, 75–85, 176–78. The manifesto (which had actually been drafted by the conservative Marquis of Limon at the request of the Duke of Brunswick) became publicly known in Paris on August 3, seven days before the events of August 10, 1792.

at Compiègne with his army. This was the best and safest course; but the persons who possessed the confidence of the King and Queen hated M. de la Fayette as much as if he had been an outrageous Jacobin. The aristocrats of that time preferred running every risk to obtain the re-establishment of the old government, to the acceptance of efficient aid under the condition of adopting with sincerity the principles of the Revolution, that is, a representative government. The offer of M. de la Fayette was then refused, and the King submitted to the dreadful risk of awaiting the German troops at Paris.

The royalists, who are subject to all the imprudence of hope, persuaded themselves that the defeats of the French armies would produce so much fear among the people of Paris as to render them mild and submissive whenever such intelligence reached their ears. The great error of men impassioned in politics consists in attributing all kinds of vices and meanness to their adversaries. It is incumbent on us to know how to value, in certain respects, those whom we hate, and those even whom we despise; for no man, and, still more, no mass of men, ever forfeited entirely all moral feeling. These furious Jacobins, capable at that time of every crime, were, however, possessed of energy; and it was by means of that energy that they triumphed over so many foreign armies.

CHAPTER IX

Revolution of the 10th of August, 1792—
Overthrow of the Monarchy.

Public opinion never fails to manifest itself, even in the midst of the factions which oppress it. One revolution only, that of 1789, was accomplished by the force of this opinion; but since that year, scarcely any crisis which has taken place in France has been desired by the nation.

Four days before the 10th of August, a decree of accusation was attempted to be carried in the Assembly against M. de la Fayette; he was acquitted by four hundred and twenty-four votes out of six hundred and seventy.[1] The wish of this majority was certainly against the revolution that was in the making. The forfeiture of the crown by the King was demanded; the Assembly rejected it, but the minority, who were determined to obtain it, had recourse to the people for that purpose.

The constitutional party was, nevertheless, the most numerous; and if on one hand, the nobles had not left France and on the other, the royalists who surrounded the King had cordially reconciled themselves to the friends of liberty, France and the throne might yet have been saved. It is not the first, nor will it be the last time that we shall be called upon to show in the course of this work that no real good can take place in France but by a sincere reconciliation between the royalists of the Old Regime and the constitutional royalists. But in the word "sincere," how many ideas are contained!

The constitutionalists had in vain sought leave to enter the palace of the King in order to defend him. They were prevented by the invincible

---

1. The vote took place on August 8: 400 members voted for La Fayette's acquittal and 224 against it.

prejudices of the courtiers. Incapable, however, notwithstanding the refusal they underwent, of joining the opposite party, they wandered around the palace, exposing themselves to be massacred, as a consolation for not being allowed to fight. Of this number were MM. de Lally, Narbonne, La Tour-du-Pin, Gouverner Castellane, Montmorency, and several others whose names have re-appeared on the most honorable occasions.

Before midnight on the 9th of August, the forty-eight alarm bells of the sections of Paris began to toll, and this monotonous, mournful, and rapid sound did not cease one moment during the whole night. I was at my window with some of my friends, and every quarter of an hour the voluntary patrol of the constitutionalists sent us news. We were told that the *faubourgs*[2] were advancing, headed by Santerre, the brewer, and Westermann, an officer, who afterward fought against the Vendeans.[3] No one could foresee what would happen on the morrow, and no one expected to live beyond a day. We had, nevertheless, some moments of hope during this horrible night; we flattered ourselves, I know not why, perhaps only because we had exhausted our fears.

All at once, at seven o'clock, the horrible noise of the cannon of the *faubourgs* was heard. In the first attack, the Swiss guards had the advantage. The people fled along the streets with a terror equal to their preceding fury. The King, it must be acknowledged, ought then to have put himself at the head of his troops and opposed his enemies. The Queen was of this opinion, and the courageous counsel she gave on this occasion does honor to her memory and recommends her to posterity.

Several battalions of the National Guards, and amongst others that of Les Filles St. Thomas, were full of zeal and ardor; but the King, on quitting the Tuileries, could no longer rely on that enthusiasm which constitutes the strength of armed citizens.

2. Reference to an old French term signifying the outlying parts of a city—modern-day suburbs.

3. Santerre (1752–1809) became the leader of the National Guard after the events of August 10, 1792. Westermann (1751–94) also played an important role in the events of August 10 and became later a close associate of Danton. He was arrested and executed in 1794.

Many republicans believe that if Louis XVI had triumphed on the 10th of August, the foreign troops would have arrived in Paris and have re-established the ancient despotism, rendered still more odious by the means from which it would have derived its force. It is possible that things might have come to this extremity; but what would have led them to it? In civil commotions a crime may always be rendered politically useful; but it is by preceding crimes that this infernal necessity is caused.

I was told that all my friends who formed the exterior guard of the Tuileries had been seized and massacred. I went out instantly in search of news. My coachman was stopped on the bridge by men who silently made signs to him that the killings were taking place on the other side. After two hours of fruitless attempts to pass, I heard that all those in whom I was interested were still alive, but that most of them were obliged to conceal themselves in order to avoid the proscription by which they were menaced. When I went on foot to visit them that evening, in the obscure houses where they had found an asylum, I met armed men stretched before the doors, drowsy with intoxication or half waking only to utter horrible imprecations. Several women among the populace were in the same situation, and their vociferations seemed still more odious. Whenever one of the patrols appointed to keep order advanced, respectable people fled from its approach; for what was then called keeping order was only contributing to the triumph of the assassins, and removing every obstacle in their way.

CHAPTER X

Private Anecdotes.

I cannot find courage to continue such pictures. Yet the 10th of August appeared to have in view the seizing of the reins of government, in order to direct all its efforts against the invasion of foreigners; but the massacres which took place twenty-two days after the overthrow of the throne were only wanton criminal acts. It has been said that the terror experienced in Paris, and throughout all France, decided the French to take refuge in the camps. What a singular expedient is fear for recruiting an army! But such a supposition is an offense to the nation, and I shall endeavor to show in the following chapter that it was in spite of those crimes, and not by their horrible concurrence, that the French repulsed the foreigners who came to impose the law.

To criminals succeeded criminals still more detestable. The true republicans did not remain masters one day after the 10th of August. The moment the throne they attacked was overturned, they had to defend themselves; they had shown but too much condescension toward the horrible instruments whom they had employed to establish the republic. But the Jacobins were very sure in the end to terrify them with their own idol, by dint of crimes; and it seemed as if the wretches who were most hardened in guilt endeavored to fit the head of Medusa on the different leaders of parties, in order to rid themselves of all who could not support its aspect.

The detail of these horrible massacres is revolting to the imagination and furnishes nothing for reflection. I shall, therefore, confine myself to relating what happened to me personally at this time; it is perhaps the best manner of giving an idea of it.

During the interval from the 10th of August to the 2d of September, new arrests were every day taking place. The prisons were crowded, and all the addresses of the people, which for three years past had announced, by anticipation, what the party leaders had already decided, called for the punishment of the traitors: this appellation extended to classes as well as to individuals; to talents as well as fortune; to dress as well as opinions; in short, to everything which the laws protect, and which it was the intention of these men to annihilate.

The Austrian and Prussian troops had already passed the frontier, and it was repeated on all sides that if the enemy advanced, all the honest people in Paris would be massacred. Several of my friends, Messrs. de Narbonne, Montmorency, Baumets,[1] were personally threatened, and each of them was concealed in the house of some citizen or other. But it was necessary to change their place of retreat daily, because those who gave them an asylum were alarmed. They would not at first make use of my house, being afraid that it might attract attention; but it seemed to me that being the residence of an Ambassador, and having inscribed on the door Hôtel de Suède, it would be respected, although M. de Staël was absent. It soon, however, became useless to deliberate, when there could be found no one who dared to receive the proscribed. Two of them came to my house, and I admitted into my confidence only one of my servants, of whom I was sure. I shut up my friends in the remotest chamber, and passed the night myself in the apartments looking toward the street, dreading every moment what was called the "domiciliary visits."

One morning, a servant whom I distrusted came to tell me that the denunciation and description of M. de Narbonne, who was one of the persons concealed in my house, was stuck up at the corner of my street. I thought my servant wanted, by frightening me, to penetrate my secret; but he had simply related the fact. A short time after, the formidable domiciliary visit took place in my house. M. de Narbonne, being outlawed, would have perished that very day if discovered; and notwithstanding the precautions I had taken, I knew well that if the search was rigorously made, he could not escape. It became then necessary, at whatever price, to prevent this search; I collected all my courage, and felt on this occasion

1. Briois de Baumets (1759–1800), member of the constitutionalist group; he immigrated to Germany and, later, America.

that we can always conquer our emotions, however strong, when aware that they may endanger the life of another.

Commissaries of the lowest class had been sent into all the houses of Paris to seize the proscribed; and, while they were making these visits, military posts occupied the two extremities of the street to prevent any escape. I began by alarming these men as much as I could on the violation of the rights of nations, of which they were guilty by searching the house of an ambassador; and, as their knowledge of geography was not extensive, I persuaded them that Sweden was a power which could threaten them with an immediate invasion, being situated on the frontiers of France. Twenty years after, strange to tell! my assertion became literally true; for Lubeck and Swedish Pomerania fell into the power of the French.[2]

The common people are capable of being softened instantly or not at all; there is scarcely any gradation in their sentiments, or in their ideas. I perceived that my reasonings made an impression on them, and I had the courage, with anguish in my heart, to jest with them on the injustice of their suspicions. Nothing is more agreeable to men of this class than a tone of pleasantry; for, even in the excess of their fury against the upper ranks, they feel a pleasure in being treated by them as equals. I led them back in this manner to the door, and thanked God for the extraordinary courage with which he had endowed me at that moment. Nevertheless, this situation could not last, and the slightest accident would have sufficed to betray an outlawed person, who was very well known on account of his having been recently in the ministry.

A generous and enlightened Hanoverian, Dr. Bollmann, who afterward exposed himself to deliver M. de la Fayette from the Austrian prisons, having heard of my anxieties, offered, without any other motive than the enthusiasm of goodness, to conduct M. de Narbonne to England by giving him the passport of one of his friends. Nothing was more daring than this attempt, since, if any foreigner had been arrested traveling with a proscribed person under a false name, he would have been condemned to death. The courage of Dr. Bollmann did not fail, either in the will or in

2. They were annexed to France in January 1811.

the execution, and four days after his departure, M. de Narbonne was in London.

I had obtained passports to go into Switzerland; but it would have been so distressing to find myself alone in safety, leaving so many friends in danger, that I delayed my departure from day to day, in order to learn what became of them. I was informed on the 31st of August that M. de Jaucourt, a deputy to the Legislative Assembly, and M. de Lally Tollendal had both been sent to the Abbaye; and it was already known that those only who were destined to be massacred were sent to that prison. The fine talents of M. de Lally protected him in a singular manner. He composed the defense of one of his fellow prisoners who was brought before the tribunal previous to the massacre; the prisoner was acquitted, and everyone knew that he owed his deliverance to the eloquence of Lally. M. de Condorcet admired his splendid abilities and exerted himself to save him; M. de Lally also found an efficacious protection in the sympathy of the English ambassador, who was still in Paris at this date.* M. de Jaucourt had not the same support: I procured a list of all the members of the Commune of Paris, who were then the masters of the city. I knew them only by their terrible reputation, and I sought, as chance directed, for a motive to determine my choice. I suddenly recollected that one of them, called Manuel,[3] was a dabbler in literature, having just published Letters of Mirabeau, with a preface, very badly written, it is true, but which showed at the same time an ambition to display ability. I persuaded myself that the love of applause might in some way render a man accessible to solicitation, and it was accordingly to Manuel that I wrote to ask an audience. He fixed it for the next morning at seven o'clock, at his house; this was rather a democratic hour, but I certainly did not fail to be punctual. I arrived before he had got up, and waited for him in his closet, where I saw his own portrait placed on his writing desk, which gave me hopes that at least he might be gained over a little by vanity. He came in, and I

---

* Lady Sutherland, now Marchioness of Stafford, and then English ambassadress at Paris, showed the most devoted attentions to the royal family at that frightful period.

3. Louis Pierre Manuel (1753–93), a member of the Jacobin club, took part in the events of August 10, 1792. Elected deputy to the Convention, he voted against the death penalty during the King's trial; he was arrested and executed on November 12, 1793.

must do him the justice to admit that it was through his good sentiments that I succeeded in softening him.

I represented to him the terrible vicissitudes of popularity, of which examples could be cited every day. "In six months," said I, "your power may perhaps be at an end" (in less than six months he perished on the scaffold). "Save M. de Lally and M. de Jaucourt; reserve for yourself a soothing and consoling recollection at the moment when you also may be proscribed in your turn." Manuel was a man who could feel; he was carried on by his passions, but capable of honest sentiments; for it was for having defended the King that he was condemned to death. He wrote to me on the 1st of September that M. de Condorcet had obtained the liberation of M. de Lally; and that in compliance with my entreaties, he had just set M. de Jaucourt at liberty. Overjoyed at having saved the life of so estimable a man, I determined on departing the next day; but I engaged to take up the Abbé de Montesquiou,[4] who was also proscribed, when I should have passed the barriers of Paris, and to carry him to Switzerland disguised as a servant. To make this change more easy and secure, I gave one of his attendants the passport of one of mine, and we fixed on the spot on the high road where I should find M. de Montesquiou. It was thus impossible to fail in this rendezvous, of which the hour and place were fixed, without exposing the person who was waiting for me to the suspicion of the patrols who scoured the high roads.

The news of the taking of Longwy and Verdun arrived on the morning of the 2d of September. We again heard in every quarter those frightful alarm bells, of which the sound was but too strongly engraved on my mind by the night of the 10th of August. Some wanted to prevent me from leaving, but could I risk the safety of a person who was then confiding in me?

My passports were perfectly in order, and I imagined that the best way would be to set out in a coach and six, with my servants in full livery. I thought that by seeing me in great style, people would conclude I had a

4. François-Xavier de Montesquiou-Fezensac (1755–1832) was a deputy to the Constituent Assembly. A vocal critic of the Civil Constitution of the Clergy, he eventually emigrated and later returned to France in 1795. During the Bourbon Restoration he served as minister of the interior (1814–15) and was elected to the French Academy.

right to depart, and would let me pass freely. This was very ill judged, for in such moments what of all things should be avoided is striking the imagination of the people, and the most shabby post-chaise would have conveyed me with more safety. Scarcely had my carriage advanced three steps when, at the noise of the whips of the postilions, a swarm of old women, who seemed to issue from the infernal regions, rushed on my horses, crying that I ought to be stopped; that I was running away with the gold of the nation, that I was going to join the enemy, and a thousand other invectives still more absurd. These women gathered a crowd instantly, and some of the common people, with ferocious countenances, seized my postilions and ordered them to conduct me to the assembly of the section of the quarter where I lived (the Faubourg of St. Germain). On stepping out of my carriage, I had time to whisper to the Abbé de Montesquiou's servant to go and inform his master of what had happened.

I entered this assembly, the deliberations of which bore the appearance of a permanent insurrection. The person who called himself the president declared to me that I was denounced as having the intention of carrying away proscribed persons, and that my attendants were going to be examined. He found one person missing, who was marked on my passport (it was the servant I had sent away), and, in consequence of this irregularity, he ordered me to be conducted to the Hotel de Ville by a gendarme. Nothing could be more terrifying than such an order; it was necessary to cross the half of Paris and to alight on the Place de Grêve, opposite the Hotel de Ville. On the steps leading to the staircase of that hotel, several persons had been massacred on the 10th of August. No woman had yet perished; but the next day the Princess of Lamballe[5] was murdered by the people, whose fury was already such that every eye seemed to demand blood.

It took me three hours to get from the Faubourg St. Germain to the Hotel de Ville, advancing slowly through an immense crowd, who assailed me with cries of death. Their invectives were not directed against me personally, for I was then hardly known; but a fine carriage and laced clothes

5. Marie-Thérèse de Savoie-Carignan, Princess of Lamballe (b. 1749), was killed on September 3, 1792.

were, in the eyes of the people, the marks of those who ought to be massacred. Not knowing yet how inhuman men become in revolutions, I addressed myself two or three times to the gendarmes who passed near my carriage to implore their assistance; and was answered by the most disdainful and threatening gestures. I was pregnant; but that did not disarm them; on the contrary their fury seemed to increase in proportion as they felt themselves culpable. The gendarme, however, who was placed in my coach, not being stimulated by his comrades, was moved by my situation and promised to defend me at the peril of his life. The most dangerous moment was in the Place de Grêve; but I had time to prepare myself for it, and the faces which surrounded me bore such an expression of atrocity that the aversion they inspired served to give me additional courage.

I stepped out of my carriage in the midst of an armed multitude and proceeded under an arch of pikes. In ascending the staircase, which likewise bristled with spears, a man pointed toward me the one which he held in his hand. My gendarme pushed it away with his saber: if I had fallen at this moment my life would have ended, for it is in the nature of the common people to respect what still stands erect, but the victim once struck is dispatched.

I arrived at length at the Commune, the president of which was Robespierre, and I breathed again because I had escaped from the populace: yet what a protector was Robespierre! Collot d'Herbois and Billaud Varennes[6] performed the office of secretaries, and the latter had left his beard untouched for a fortnight, that he might the better escape the slightest suspicion of aristocracy. The hall was crowded with common people; men, women, and children were exclaiming, with all their might, "*Vive la nation.*" The writing office of the Commune being a little elevated, those who were placed there could converse together. There I was seated, and while I was recovering myself, the Bailli of Virieu, Envoy of Parma, who had been arrested at the same time as myself, rose to declare that he did

---

6. Both Collot d'Herbois (1749–96) and Billaud-Varennes (1756–1819) were deputies from Paris to the Convention and members of the Committee of Public Safety (July 1793–July 1794); as such, they played a role in planning the fall of Robespierre on 9 Thermidor. They were later deported to Guyana and died overseas. For more information, see Palmer, *Twelve Who Ruled*.

not know me; that whatever my affair might be, it had not the least connection with his, and that we ought not to be confounded together. The want of chivalry of this poor man displeased me, and made me doubly eager to be useful to myself, since it appeared that the Bailli of Virieu was not disposed to spare me that trouble. I rose then and stated the right I had to depart, as being the Ambassadress of Sweden, showing the passports I had obtained in consequence of this right. At this moment Manuel arrived; he was very much astonished to find me in so painful a situation, and immediately becoming responsible for me till the Commune had decided on my fate, he conducted me out of that terrible place and locked me up with my maidservant in his closet.

We waited there for six hours, half dead with thirst, hunger, and fright: the window of Manuel's apartment looked on the Place de Grêve, and we saw the assassins returning from the prisons with their arms bare and bloody, and uttering horrible cries.

My coach with its baggage had remained in the middle of the square, and the people were proceeding to plunder it when I perceived a tall man, in the dress of a national guard, who, ascending the coach box, forbade the populace to take away anything. He passed two hours in guarding my baggage, and I could not conceive how so slight a consideration could occupy him amidst such awful circumstances. In the evening this man, with Manuel, entered the room where I was confined. He was Santerre, the brewer, afterward so notorious for his cruelty. He lived in the Faubourg St. Antoine and had several times been both witness and distributor of the supplies of corn which my father used to provide in seasons of scarcity, and for which he retained some gratitude. Unwilling also to go, as he ought to have done in his quality of commandant, to the relief of the prisoners, guarding my coach served him as a pretext; he wanted to make a boast of it to me, but I could not help reminding him what was his duty at such a moment. As soon as Manuel saw me, he exclaimed with great emotion, "Ah! how happy I am at having set your two friends at liberty yesterday!" He bitterly deplored the assassinations that were going on, but which even at this time he had no power to prevent. An abyss was opened behind the steps of every man who had acquired any authority, and if he receded he could not fail to sink into it.

Manuel conducted me home at night in his carriage; he was afraid of losing his popularity by doing it in the day. The lamps were not lighted in the streets; but we met numbers of men with torches in their hands, the glare of which was more terrifying than darkness itself. Manuel was often stopped and asked who he was, but when he answered, "*Le Procureur de la Commune,*" this revolutionary dignity was respectfully recognized.

Arrived at my house, Manuel informed me that a new passport would be given to me and that I should be allowed to depart, but with my maid-servant only. A gendarme had orders to attend me to the frontier. The following day Tallien,[7] the same who, twenty months after, delivered France from Robespierre on the 9th of Thermidor, came to my house, having been ordered by the Commune to conduct me to the barrier. We heard every instant of new massacres. Several persons much exposed were then in my room: I begged of Tallien not to name them; he promised that he would not, and he kept his word. We went together in my carriage, and left each other without having the power of communicating our thoughts to each other; the circumstances in which we were froze the words on our lips.

I still met with some difficulties near Paris which I managed to escape, and as the distance from the capital increased, the waves of the tempest seemed to subside, and in the mountains of Jura nothing reminded me of the dreadful agitation of which Paris was the theater. The French were everywhere repeating that they were determined to repulse the foreigners. I confess that I saw then no other foreigners than the bloody assassins under whose daggers I had left my friends, the royal family, and all the worthy inhabitants of France.

7. Jean-Lambert Tallien (1767–1820) was one of the most active popular leaders in the storming of the Tuileries Palace on August 10, 1792. Appointed secretary to the Commune of Paris, he eventually became a rival of Robespierre and contributed to his arrest. He was a member of the Council of Five Hundred during the Directory (1795–98), but was viewed with skepticism by both the moderates (because of his role in the Terror against the Girondins) and the extreme party (for his role in the fall of Robespierre). Later, Napoléon appointed him consul in Alicante.

CHAPTER XI

The Foreign Troops Driven from France in 1792.

The prisoners of Orléans[1] had shared the fate of those of Paris,[2] the priests had been massacred at the foot of the altars, and the royal family were captives in the temple. M. de la Fayette, faithful to the constant desire of the nation, a constitutional monarchy, had quitted his army[3] rather than take an oath contrary to that which he had so lately sworn to the King. A National Convention was formed, and the Republic was proclaimed[4] almost under the eyes of the victorious monarchs, whose armies were then only forty leagues from Paris: yet the greater part of the French officers had emigrated;[5] and what remained of the troops had never fought in a war, and the administration was in a most deplorable state. There was a grandeur in such a resolution taken in the midst of the most imminent perils; it instantly revived in every heart the interest which the French nation once inspired; and if the conquering soldiers, on their returning to their homes, had overthrown the revolutionary faction, the cause of France would have once again been gained.

1. In early September 1792, fifty-three political prisoners from Orléans were massacred at Versailles as they were being transferred to Saumur.

2. On September 2, 1792, at the Carmes Prison in Paris.

3. La Fayette went over to the Austrians on August 19, 1792. He was later arrested and imprisoned at Olmütz (1794–97).

4. On September 21, 1792, a day after the battle of Valmy, which stopped the march of foreign troops toward Paris.

5. Two-thirds of the French army officers (including those in the navy) had emigrated by September 1792.

General Dumouriez,[6] in this first campaign of 1792, displayed talents which can never be forgotten. He knew how to employ with ability the military force, which had its basis in patriotism but has since been made the tool of ambition. Amidst all the horrors which disgraced the year 1792, the public spirit which then showed itself had something in it truly admirable. The citizens, now become soldiers, devoted themselves to their country; and personal interests, the love of money and of power, had as yet no share in the efforts of the French armies. Europe consequently felt a sort of respect for the unexpected resistance which she experienced. Soon, however, the madness of crime possessed the prevailing party, and since then, every vice followed every evil deed—sad amelioration for mankind!

6. Dumouriez (1739–1823) replaced La Fayette as the leader of the Army of the North on August 17, 1792. In April 1793, he, too, defected to the enemy. He returned to France in 1803.

CHAPTER XII

Trial of Louis XVI.

What a subject! But it has been so often treated on that I shall here allow myself to make only a few particular observations.[1]

In the month of October, 1792, before the horrible trial of the King had begun, before Louis XVI had named his defenders, M. Necker stood forward to receive that noble and perilous charge. He published a memoir[2] which posterity will accept as one of the truest and most disinterested testimonies that could be given in favor of the virtuous monarch thrown into captivity.* M. de Malesherbes[3] was chosen by the King to be his advocate in the National Convention. The dreadful death of this admirable man and of his family demands the first place in our memory; but the sound reasoning and sincere eloquence of M. Necker's publication in defense of the King must render it a document for history.

It cannot be denied that Louis XVI was considered as a prisoner from the time of his departure for Varennes, and consequently he did nothing to forward the establishment of a Constitution, which the most sincere efforts would not, perhaps, have been able to maintain. But with what

---

* The property which M. Necker possessed in France was sequestered from the very day on which his *Memoire justicatif de Louis XVI* appeared.

1. On this issue, see Walzer, *Regicide and Revolution;* Jordan, *The King's Trial: Louis XVI vs. the French Revolution;* and Ozouf's entry on the trial of Louis XVI in *A Critical Dictionary of the French Revolution,* 95–106.

2. *Réflexions présentées à la nation française sur le procès de Louis XVI* (Berne and Paris, 1792).

3. Guillaume-Chrétien de Lamoignon de Malesherbes (1721–94) was a former president of the *Cour des aides* in the *Parlement of Paris* and a minister of Louis XVI's (1775–76, 1788). He served as Louis XVI's counsel for the defense and was subsequently arrested and executed in 1794. He was a relative of Tocqueville. For more information, see Wyrwa, ed., *Malesherbes, le pouvoir et les lumières.*

delicacy does not M. Necker, who always believed in the force of truth, place it before us upon this point.

Men of attentive minds—just men, will admire the patience and moderation which the King displayed when everything changed around him, and when he was continually exposed to every kind of insult; but if he had committed faults, if he had misunderstood on some points the new obligations imposed upon him, should it not be attributed to the new form of government? to that constitution in which a monarch was nothing but in appearance, in which royalty itself was out of its place; in which the head of the executive power could discern neither what he was nor what he ought to be; in which he was deceived even by words, and by the equivocal sense which might be given to them; in which he was king without any ascendency; in which he occupied the throne without enjoying any respect, in which he appeared to possess the right to command without having the means of making himself obeyed; in which he was alternately, and according to the unrestrained will of a single deliberative assembly, at one time a simple public functionary, and at another the hereditary representative of the nation? How could a monarch, suddenly placed in the trammels of a political system equally obscure and absurd, and ultimately proscribed by the deputies of the nation themselves; how could he alone be required to be consistent in the midst of the continual fluctuation of ideas? And would it not be the height of injustice to judge a monarch by all his projects, all his thoughts, in the course of a revolution so extraordinary, that it would have been necessary for him to be in perfect harmony, not only with the things which were known, but even with all those of which it would have been in vain to preconceive any just idea? [*Réflexions présentées à la nation française*, 19–20]

M. Necker goes on to retrace in his Memoir the acts of beneficence which marked the reign of Louis XVI before the Revolution; the extinction of the remains of servitude, the interdiction[4] of the torture, the suppression of the *corvée,* the establishment of the provincial administrations, the convocation of the Estates General. "Is it not Louis XVI," says he, "who, in occupying him unceasingly with the improvements of the prisons and hospitals, has given the attention of a tender father and of a compas-

4. Interdiction of torture to obtain confessions from those who were arrested.

sionate friend to the asylums of misery and the retreats of misfortune or of error? Is it not he, perhaps the only one, besides St. Louis, of all the heads of the French Empire who has given the rare example of purity of manners? Must he not besides be allowed the peculiar merit of having been religious without superstition, and scrupulous without intolerance? And is it not from him that a part of the inhabitants of France (the Protestants), persecuted during so many reigns, have received not only a legal security but a civil station which admits them to a participation in all the advantages of social order? These benefits belong to the past; but is the virtue of gratitude applicable only to other periods and other portions of life?"

The want of respect shown to Louis XVI during his trial is more striking than even his condemnation. When the President of the Convention said to him who was his King: "Louis, you may sit down!" we feel more indignation even than when he is accused of crimes which he had never committed. One must have sprung from the very dust not to respect past obligations, particularly when misfortune has rendered them sacred; and vulgarity joined to crime inspires us with as much contempt as horror. No man of real superiority has been remarked amongst those who incited the convention to condemn the King; the popular tide rose and fell at certain words and certain phrases, while the talent of so eloquent an orator as Vergniaud[5] could not influence the public mind. It is true that the greater part of the deputies who defended the King took a detestable ground. They began by declaring that he was guilty; and one among them said at the tribune that *Louis XVI was a traitor, but that the nation ought to pardon him;* and this they called the tactics of the Assembly! They pretended that it was necessary to humor the reigning opinion, that they might moderate it at a proper time. With such cautious prudence as this, how could they resist their enemies, who sprang with all their force upon the victim? In

---

5. Pierre Victurnien Vergniaud (1753–93) was a prominent lawyer and a deputy to the Legislative Assembly from the Gironde. As a leader of the Girondins, he distinguished himself as one of the greatest orators of the French Revolution. During the trial of the King, he recommended a referendum on the King's punishment and actively opposed the Montagnards and Robespierre. He fell with the other Girondins in June 1793 and was guillotined four months later.

France, they always capitulate with the majority, even when they wish to oppose it; and this miserable finesse assuredly diminishes the means instead of increasing them. The power of the minority can consist only in the energy of conviction. What are the weak in numbers if they are also weak in sentiment?

Saint-Just,[6] after having searched in vain for authentic facts against the King, finished by declaring that "no one could reign innocently"; and nothing could better prove the necessity of the inviolability of kings than this maxim; for, there is no king who might not be accused in some way or another if there were no constitutional barrier placed around him. That which surrounded the throne of Louis XVI ought to be held sacred more than any other, since it was not tacitly understood as elsewhere, but solemnly guaranteed.

The deputies from the Gironde wished to save the King; and to that end they demanded an appeal to the people. But in demanding this appeal, they continued to concur in sentiment with the Jacobins, incessantly repeating that the King deserved death. This was deserting the cause entirely. Louis XVI, says Biroteau,[7] is already condemned within my heart; but I demand an appeal to the people that he may be condemned by them. The deputies from the Gironde were right in requiring a competent tribunal, if there could exist one for such a cause: but how much more effect might they not have produced if they had required it in favor of an innocent person, instead of for one whom they pretended to be guilty. The French, it can never be too often repeated, have not yet learned in civil affairs to be moderate when they are strong, and bold when they are weak; they should transplant into politics all their military virtues, and their affairs would be improved by it.

What is most difficult to be conceived, in this terrible discussion of the national convention, is the abundance of words that everyone had ready upon such an occasion. It was natural to expect to find a concentrated fury

6. Louis Antoine Léon de Saint-Just (1767–94) was a prominent Jacobin leader and a close associate of Robespierre, with whom he served on the Committee of Public Safety. For more information, see Gross, *Saint-Just: sa politique et ses missions*.

7. Biroteau (1753–93), a lawyer from Perpignan, sided with the Girondins and voted for the death of Louis XVI. He was executed in October 1793.

in those who desired the death of the King; but to make it a subject for the display of wit, for the turning of phrases, what obstinacy of vanity in such a scene.

Thomas Paine[8] was the most violent of the American democrats: and yet, as there was neither calculation nor hypocrisy in his political exaggerations, when the sentence of Louis XVI came under discussion, he alone advised what would have done honor to France if it had been adopted, the offer to the King of an asylum in America. The Americans are grateful to him, said Paine, for having promoted their independence. Considering this resolution only in a republican point of view, it was the only one which could at that time have weakened the interest for royalty in France. Louis XVI had not those talents which are necessary to regain a crown by force; for a situation which did not excite pity would never have produced devotion. Death inflicted on the most upright man in France, but, at the same time, the least to be feared—on him who, if I may use the expression, had taken no part in his own fate, could only be a dreadful homage paid to his former greatness. There would have been more of republicanism in a revolution which had evinced less fear and more justice.

Louis XVI did not refuse, like Charles I, to acknowledge the tribunal before which he was tried; but answered to all the questions which were put to him, with unaltered gentleness. The President asked him why he had assembled the troops at the palace on the tenth of August, and he replied: "*The palace was threatened, all the Constituted Authorities saw it, and, as I myself was one of the Constituted Authorities, it was my duty to defend myself.*" How modest and unassuming was this manner of speaking of himself, and by what burst of eloquence could we be more deeply moved!

M. de Malesherbes, formerly the King's minister, stood forward to defend him. He was one of the three ministers, himself, M. Turgot, and M. Necker, who had advised the voluntary adoption of the principles of lib-

---

8. Thomas Paine (1737–1809) came to France in 1791 and received French citizenship in August 1792 before being elected a deputy to the Convention. He was excluded from the Convention in January 1793 and returned to the United States in 1802.

erty to Louis XVI. He was obliged, together with the other two, to resign his place in consequence of some opinions which the *parlements* opposed; and now, notwithstanding his advanced age, he reappeared to plead the cause of the King in the presence of the people, as he had formerly pleaded the cause of the people before the King; but the new master was implacable.

Garat,[9] then Minister of Justice, and, in times better suited to him one of the best writers of France, has told us, in his private memoirs, that when the duties of his dreadful situation compelled him to communicate to the King the sentence which condemned him to death, the King displayed, whilst listening to it, the most astonishing coolness; once only, he expressed by a gesture his contempt and his indignation; it was at the article which accused him of having wished to spill the blood of the French people. His conscience revolted at that, although he had restrained every other feeling. On the very morning of his execution, he said to one of his servants, *Go to the Queen;* but, stopping himself, he repeated, *Go to my wife.* He submitted, even at that moment, to the deprivation of his rank which had been imposed upon him by his murderers. Without doubt he believed that in everything fate executes the designs of God upon his creatures.

The King's will[10] exhibits the whole of his character. The most affecting simplicity reigns throughout: every word is a virtue, and we find in it all the intelligence which a mind just, temperate, and of infinite goodness could inspire. The condemnation of Louis XVI so affected every heart that, on account of it, the Revolution was for several years considered as accursed.

---

9. Dominique Garat (1749–1833) followed Danton as minister of justice in October 1792. In March 1793, he became minister of the interior before being imprisoned during the Terror. His *Mémoirs historiques sur le XVIIIe siècle, sur les principaux personnages de la Révolution française* were published in two volumes in 1829.

10. The King's testament was published in Soboul, *Le procès de Louis XVI*, 236–40.

CHAPTER XIII

Charles I and Louis XVI.

Many persons have attributed the disasters of France to the weakness of the character of Louis XVI; and it has been continually repeated that his stooping to recognize the principles of liberty was one of the essential causes of the Revolution. It seems to me, then, a matter of curiosity to show to those who believe that in France, at this crisis, such or such a man would have sufficed to have prevented everything; or that the adoption of such or such a resolution would have arrested the progress of events; it seems, I say, a matter of curiosity to show them that the conduct of Charles I was, in all respects, the converse of that of Louis XVI, and that, nevertheless, two opposite systems brought about the same catastrophe; so irresistible is the progress of revolutions caused by the opinion of the majority.

James I, the father of Charles, said "that men might form an opinion on the conduct of kings, since they freely allowed themselves to scrutinize the decrees of Providence; but that their power could no more be called in question than that of God." Charles I had been educated in these maxims; and he regarded as a measure equally inconsistent with duty, and with policy, every concession made by the royal authority. Louis XVI, a hundred and fifty years later, was modified by the age in which he lived; the doctrine of passive obedience, which was still received in England in the time of Charles, was no longer maintained even by the clergy of France in 1789. The English Parliament had existed from time immemorial;[1] and although it was not irrevocably decided that its consent was necessary for taxation, yet it was customary to ask its sanction. But as it granted subsidies for several years in anticipation, the King of England was not, as

1. In its current form, only since 1529.

now, under the necessity of assembling it annually; and very frequently taxes were continued without having been renewed by the votes of the national representatives. The parliament, however, on all occasions, protested against this abuse; and upon this ground commenced the quarrel between the Commons and Charles I. He was reproached with two taxes which he levied without the assent of the nation. Irritated by this reproach, he ordered, in pursuance of the constitutional right vested in him, that the parliament should be dissolved; and twelve years[2] elapsed before he called another, an interruption almost unparalleled in the history of England. The quarrel of Louis XVI began, like that of Charles I, by financial embarrassments; and it is always these embarrassments that render kings dependent upon their people; but Louis XVI assembled the Estates General, which for nearly two centuries had been almost forgotten in France.

Louis XIV had suppressed even the remonstrances of the *Parlement of Paris,* the only privilege left to that body, when he registered the bursal edicts. Henry VIII of England had caused his proclamations to be received as laws. Thus, then, both Charles and Louis might consider themselves as inheriting unlimited power; but with this difference, that the people of England always relied, and with reason, upon the past to reclaim their rights, while the French demanded something entirely new, since the convocation of the Estates General was not prescribed by any law. Louis XVI, according to the constitution, or the nonconstitution, of France, was not under any obligation to assemble the Estates General; Charles I, in omitting for twelve years to convoke the English Parliament, violated privileges which had been long recognized.

During the twelve-year suspension of the parliament under Charles, the Star Chamber,[3] an irregular tribunal which executed the will of the English monarch, exercised every imaginable species of rigor. Prynne was sentenced to lose his ears for having written, according to the tenets of the Puritans, against plays and against the hierarchy. Allison and Robins endured the same punishment because they expressed an opinion different

---

2. From 1629 to 1640.

3. The Star Chamber was the judiciary branch of the King's Council, which assumed an important role beginning with 1487 and met in a special room of Westminster Palace with a star-painted ceiling. It was abolished in 1647.

from that of the Archbishop of York; Lilburne was exposed on the pillory, inhumanly scourged, and gagged because his courageous complaints produced an effect upon the people. Williams, a bishop, underwent a similar punishment.[4] The most cruel tortures were inflicted upon those who refused to pay the taxes imposed by a mere proclamation of the King; in a host of other different cases ruinous fines were levied on individuals by the same Star Chamber; but, in general, it was against the liberty of the press that the utmost violence was displayed. Louis XVI made scarcely any use of the arbitrary measure of *lettres de cachet* for the purpose of exile or imprisonment;[5] no one act of tyranny can be laid to his charge; and, far from restraining the liberty of the press, it was the Archbishop of Sens, the King's prime minister, who, in the name of His Majesty, invited all writers to make known their opinions upon the form and the manner of assembling the Estates General.[6]

The Protestant religion was established in England; but as the Church of England recognizes the king as its head, Charles I had certainly much more influence over his church than Louis had over that of France. The English clergy, under the guidance of Laud,[7] although Protestant, was not only in all respects more independent, but more rigid than the French clergy; for the philosophic spirit had gained a footing among some of the leaders of the Gallican church; and Laud was more decidedly orthodox than the Cardinal de Rohan, the principal bishop of France. The ecclesiastical authority and the hierarchy were supported by Charles with extreme severity. The greater part of the cruel sentences which disgraced the Star Chamber had for their object the enforcing of respect for the clergy. That of France seldom defended itself, and never found defenders in others: both were equally crushed by the Revolution.

4. Prynne, Allison, Robins, Lilburne, and Williams were religious dissenters. Lilburn (1614–57) became one of the leaders of the English levelers.

5. The infamous *lettres de cachet* allowed imprisonment without any prior judgment. The King refused to abolish them in 1788.

6. On July 5, 1788.

7. Laud (1573–1645), Archbishop of London and later of Canterbury, suppressed dissent and sought to strengthen the power of the king on religious matters. He was charged by the House of Commons and executed in 1645.

The English nobility did not resort to the pernicious measure of emigration, nor to the still more pernicious measure of calling in foreigners: they encircled the throne with constancy, and combated on the side of the King during the civil war. The principles of philosophy which were in vogue in France at the commencement of the Revolution excited a great number of the nobles themselves to turn their own privileges into ridicule. The spirit of the seventeenth century did not prompt the English nobility to doubt the validity of their own rights. The Star Chamber punished with extreme severity some persons who had ventured to ridicule certain lords. Pleasantry is never interdicted to the French. The nobles of England were grave and serious, while those of France were agreeable triflers; and yet both the one and the other were alike despoiled of their privileges;[8] and, widely as they differed in all their measures of defense, they were strikingly assimilated in their ruin.

It has often been said that the great influence of Paris over the rest of France was one of the causes of the Revolution. London never obtained the same ascendant over England, because the principal English nobility lived much more in the provinces than those of France. Lastly, it has been pretended that the prime minister of Louis XVI, M. Necker, was swayed by republican principles, and that such a man as Cardinal Richelieu might have prevented the Revolution. The Earl of Strafford,[9] the favorite minister of Charles I, was of a firm, and even despotic character; he possessed one advantage over Cardinal Richelieu, that of a high military reputation, which always gives a better grace to the exercise of absolute power. M. Necker enjoyed the greatest popularity ever known in France; the Earl of Strafford was always the object of popular animosity; yet each was the victim of a revolution, and each was sacrificed by his master: the former because he was denounced by the Commons; the latter because the courtiers demanded his dismissal.

Lastly (and this is the most striking point of contrast), Louis XVI has been always blamed for not having taken the field, for not having repelled force by force, and for his insuperable dread of civil war. Charles I began

8. In reality, the English nobles did not lose all their privileges.
9. Thomas Strafford (1593–1641), a supporter of Charles I, was executed in 1641.

the civil war with motives doubtless very plausible, but still he began it. He quitted London, repaired to the country, and put himself at the head of an army which defended the royal authority to the last extremity. Charles I refused to recognize the competency of the tribunal which condemned him; Louis XVI never made a single objection to the authority of his judges. Charles was infinitely superior to Louis in capacity, in address, and in military talents—everything, in short, formed a contrast between these two monarchs, except their misfortune.

There was, however, one point of resemblance in their sentiments, which alone can account for the similarity of their destinies—Charles I was from the bottom of his heart attached to Catholicism, at that time proscribed in England by the reigning opinion; and Louis XVI was anxious to preserve the ancient political institutions of France. This similarity caused the destruction of both. It is in the art of directing public opinion, or of yielding to it at the proper moment, that the science of government consists in modern times.

CHAPTER XIV

War Between France and England.
Mr. Pitt and Mr. Fox.

During many centuries the rivalries between France and England have been the source of misery to those two countries. It used to be a contest for power; but the struggle caused by the Revolution cannot be considered under the same aspect. If there have been, in the course of twenty-three years,[1] circumstances in which England might have treated with France, it must also be allowed that during that time she has had strong reasons for making war upon her rival, and more frequently still, for defending herself against attack. The first rupture, which broke out in 1793, proceeded from motives the most just. If the Convention, while guilty of the murder of Louis XVI, had not professed and propagated principles subversive of all governments, if it had not attacked Belgium and Holland, the English might have taken no more concern in the death of Louis XVI than Louis XIV did in that of Charles I. But at the moment when the government dismissed the Ambassador of France, the English nation wished for war still more eagerly than its government.[2]

I think I have sufficiently shown, in the preceding chapters, that in 1791, during the continuance of the Constituent Assembly, and even in 1792, under the Legislative Assembly, foreign powers ought not to have acceded to the Convention of Pilnitz. If, then, English diplomacy had any share

---

1. Since 1793. This part of the book was written in 1816.

2. After the battle of Valmy (September 20, 1792), the French armies advanced beyond the borders of France. Dumouriez occupied Belgium and gained possession of Anvers's strategic location. The war between France and England began on February 1, 1793. Economic reasons played an important role, as the French occupation of Anvers threatened the commerce of the English in the North Sea.

in that great political act, it interfered too soon in the affairs of France, and Europe found itself in a bad situation because of it, since immense military forces were thus acquired by the French. But at the moment when England formally declared war against France, in 1793, the Jacobins were in complete possession of the supreme power; and not only their invasion of Holland, but their crimes and the principles which they proclaimed, made it a duty to break off all communication with them. The perseverance of England at this epoch preserved her from the troubles which threatened her internal tranquillity at the time of the mutiny of the fleet, and of the fermentation of the popular societies;[3] and likewise supported the hopes of the well-meaning, by showing them a spot upon the earth where morality and liberty were united to great power. Had the English nation been seen sending ambassadors to assassins, the true strength of that wonderful island would have abandoned her; the confidence which she inspires would have been lost.

It does not follow from these views that the Opposition, who wished for peace, and Mr. Fox,[4] who by his astonishing talents represented a party in his own person, were not actuated by the most honorable sentiments. Mr. Fox complained, and with reason, that the friends of liberty were incessantly confounded with those who polluted it; and he feared lest the reaction of so unfortunate an attempt should weaken the spirit of freedom which is the vital principle of England. In fact, if the Reformation had failed three centuries ago, what would have become of Europe? And in what state would Europe now be, if France were to be deprived of all that she has gained by her political reform?

Mr. Pitt[5] at this epoch rendered great services to England by holding with a firm hand the helm of affairs. But notwithstanding the perfect simplicity of his tastes and habits, he leaned too much to the love of power;

---

3. The mutiny of the fleet occurred from April 15 to June 30, 1797. Revolutionary societies also began to appear in England in 1789, and they were regarded with skepticism by Whigs (like Burke) and Tories alike. According to Burke, there were some forty thousand Jacobin sympathizers in England in 1793.

4. Fox was opposed to the war with France.

5. William Pitt (1759–1806), famous Tory leader and opponent of the French Revolution, served as prime minister from 1783 to 1800.

having become minister at a very early age, he never had time to live in the capacity of a private man, and by that means to experience the action of authority upon those who are subject to it. His heart had no sympathy with weakness; and the political artifices which men have agreed to call Machiavellianism were not viewed by him with all the contempt which might have been expected from a genius like his. Yet his admirable eloquence made him love the debates of a representative government; he was predisposed to liberty even by his talents, for he was ambitious of convincing, whereas men of moderate powers aspire only at command. The sarcastic tone of his speeches was singularly adapted to the circumstances in which he was placed: when all the aristocracy of sentiment and principle triumphed at the sight of popular excesses, the energetic irony of Mr. Pitt suited the Patrician who throws upon his adversaries the odious color of irreligion and immorality.

The perspicuity, the sincerity, the warmth of Mr. Fox could alone escape these sharp-edged weapons. He had no mystery in politics; for he regarded publicity as still more necessary in the affairs of nations than in any other relations of men. Even when his opinion was not followed, he was better liked than his opponent; and although force of argumentation was the distinctive characteristic of his eloquence, so much of soul was perceived beneath his reasoning that it was impossible not to be moved by it. His character, like that of his antagonist, bore the stamp of English dignity; but he had a natural candor which contact with other people could not hinder, because the benevolence of genius is unalterable.

It is not necessary to decide between these two great men, nor is there any person who would dare to think himself qualified to judge in such a cause. But the salutary reflection which ought to arise from the sublime discussions of which the English Parliament was the theater is this—that the ministerial party was always in the right when it combated Jacobinism and military despotism, but always in the wrong, and greatly in the wrong, when it made itself the enemy of liberal principles in France. The members of the Opposition, on the contrary, deviated from the noble functions which are attributed to them when they defended men whose crimes were ruining the cause of the human race; and this same Opposition has deserved well of posterity when it supported the generous few of the friends of freedom who for twenty-five years have devoted themselves to the hatred of both parties in France, and who have no strength but what they derive from one powerful alliance—the alliance of truth.

One fact may give an idea of the essential difference which exists between the Tories and the Whigs, the members of the cabinet, and the Opposition, in relation to the affairs of France. The spirit of party goes the length of stripping the most glorious actions of their true qualities so long as those who performed them live; but it is not for this the less certain that antiquity offers nothing more noble than the conduct of General la Fayette, of his wife, and of his daughters in the prisons of Olmütz.* The General was confined in these on the one hand, for having quitted France after the imprisonment of the King, and on the other, for having declined any connection with the governments which were carrying on war against his country; and the admirable Madame de la Fayette, just escaped from the dungeons of Robespierre, lost not a single day in proceeding to incarcerate herself with her husband and expose herself to all the sufferings which have abridged her life. So much firmness in a man who had been for so long a time faithful to the same cause, so much conjugal and filial love in his family, could not but interest the country of whose soil these virtues are the native growth. General Fitz-Patrick demanded, therefore, that the English ministry should intercede with their allies to obtain from them the liberty of General la Fayette.[6] Mr. Fox pleaded this cause; the English parliament heard the sublime speech, of which we shall transcribe the conclusion: and yet the representatives of a free country did not rise in a body to accede to the proposition of the orator, who on this occasion should have been only their interpreter. The ministers opposed the motion of General Fitz-Patrick by saying, as usual, that the captivity of General la Fayette concerned the powers of the Continent, and that England, in

---

* The most exact details on this affair are to be found in the excellent work of M. Emmanuel de Toulongeon, entitled *History of France from 1789*. It is of importance to strangers that they be made acquainted with the trustworthy writings of the Revolution; for never was there published on any subject so great a number of books and pamphlets in which falsehood turned itself into so many forms, that it might supply the place of talent and satisfy vanities of a thousand kinds.

6. He was released only in 1797.

meddling with it, would violate the general principle which forbids her to interfere in the internal administration of foreign countries. Mr. Fox combated admirably this wily and evasive answer. Mr. Windham,[7] Secretary of War, denied the eulogiums which Mr. Fox had pronounced on General la Fayette; and it was upon this occasion that Mr. Fox replied to him as follows:

The Secretary of War has spoken, and his principles are henceforth in open day. Those must never be pardoned who begin revolutions, and that, in the most absolute sense, without distinction of circumstances and of persons. However corrupt, however intolerant, however oppressive, however hostile to the rights and happiness of humanity a government may be; however virtuous, however moderate, however patriotic, however humane the reformer, the man who begins the justest reformation should be devoted to the most irreconcilable vengeance. If he is succeeded by men who tarnish the cause of liberty by their excesses, they may be pardoned. All our detestation of criminal revolution should be heaped upon him who begins a revolution that is virtuous. Thus, the Right Honorable Secretary of War pardons Cromwell with all his heart; for Cromwell appeared not till the second act, found things prepared, and only turned circumstances to his own profit; but our great, our illustrious ancestors, Pym, Hampden, Lord Falkland, the Earl of Bedford,[8] all these personages to whom we have been accustomed to pay honors nearly divine, for the good which they have done to the human race and to their country, for the evils from which they delivered us, for the prudent courage, the generous humanity, the noble disinterestedness with which they prosecuted their plans; these are the men who, according to the doctrine professed this day, ought to be devoted to eternal execration.

We have hitherto considered Hume[9] to be sufficiently severe when he said that Hampden died at the moment the most favorable for his glory, because, had he lived a few months longer, he would probably have dis-

7. William Windham (1750–1810) served as secretary of war 1794–1801 and 1806–7.

8. The King's attempt to arrest John Pym (1584–1643) in 1642 triggered the insurrection that eventually led to the civil war. John Hampden (1595–1643) opposed royal absolutism and supported Pym in Parliament. Lord Falkland (1610–43) was a partisan of the King. Francis Russell, Earl of Bedford, opposed royal absolutism.

9. See Hume's *History of England*, vol. V (Indianapolis: Liberty Fund, 1983).

played the latent fire of a violent ambition. But how gentle does Hume now appear when compared with the Right Honorable Secretary of War. According to the latter, men who by their crimes have blackened the glorious cause of liberty have been virtuous, in comparison of those who wished merely to deliver their country from the weight of abuses, from the scourge of corruption, and from the yoke of tyranny. Cromwell, Harrison, Bradshaw, the masked executioner by whose hand fell the head of Charles I—these are the objects of the tender commiseration and enlightened indulgence of the Right Honorable Secretary of War. Hampden, Bedford, Falkland killed in fighting for his king—such are the criminals for whom he does not find hatred enough in his heart, nor punishment enough upon earth. The Right Honorable Secretary of War has positively asserted it: in the eyes of his kings and his absolute ministers, Collot d'Herbois[10] is far from meriting so much vengeance and hatred as La Fayette.

At first I was astonished at this opinion; I now begin to comprehend it. In fact, Collot d'Herbois is a vile person and a monster; La Fayette is a great character and a man of worth. Collot d'Herbois pollutes Liberty and renders her hateful by all the crimes which he dares to clothe with her name; La Fayette honors her; he makes her an object of love, by all the virtues with which he shows her to be surrounded, by the nobleness of his principles, by the unalterable purity of his actions, by the wisdom and force of his understanding, by the gentleness, the disinterestedness, the generosity of his soul. Yes, I acknowledge it, according to the new principles, it is La Fayette who is dangerous, he is the man whom we must hate; and the *poor* Collot d'Herbois is entitled to that tender accent with which the interest of the House has been solicited for him. Yes, I do justice to the sincerity of the Right Honorable Secretary of War; he has feigned nothing, I am sure; the tone of his voice has been only the expression of his soul as often as he has implored compassion for the poor Collot d'Herbois, or summoned from every corner of the earth hatred, vengeance, and tyranny to exterminate General La Fayette, his wife and his children, his companions, and his servants.

But I, who feel otherwise, I, who am still what I have always been, I,

10. Jean-Marie Collot d'Herbois (1749–96) was a member of the Committee of Public Safety during the Reign of Terror and one of the authors of the first French republican Constitution of 1793.

who will live and die the friend of order but of liberty, the enemy of anarchy but of slavery, have thought that it was not allowed to me to remain silent after such outrages, after such blasphemies vomited forth within the precincts of an English parliament, against innocence and truth, against the rights and the happiness of the human species, against the principles of our glorious Revolution; finally, against the sacred memory of our illustrious ancestors, of those men whose wisdom, whose virtues, and whose benefits will be revered and blessed by the people of England to the latest generation.

In spite of the incomparable beauty of these words, such was the terror with which the fear of the subversion of social order then inspired the English that even the name of liberty no longer echoed in their soul. Of all the sacrifices which a man can make to his conscience as a public character, there are none greater than those to which Mr. Fox doomed himself during the French Revolution. It is nothing to support persecutions under an arbitrary government; but to find oneself abandoned by public opinion in a free country; to be deserted by one's old friends when, among them, there is such a man as Burke; to find oneself unpopular in the very cause of the people; this is a misery for which Mr. Fox deserves to be pitied as much as admired. He was seen to shed tears in the House of Commons as he pronounced the name of that illustrious Burke, who had become so violent in his new passions.[11] He inclined toward him, because he knew that his heart was broken by the death of his son; for friendship, in a character such as that of Fox, could never be altered by political feelings.

It might, however, be advantageous for England that Mr. Pitt was at the head of the state in the most dangerous crisis in which that country ever found herself: but it was not less so that a mind enlarged as was that of Mr. Fox maintained principles in spite of circumstances and knew how to preserve the household gods of the friends of freedom in the midst of

---

11. See Burke's "An Appeal from the New to the Old Whigs," in Burke, *Further Reflections on the Revolution in France*, 73–201. The break between Burke and Fox had occurred during the debates on the Quebec Bill (May 1791). Fox dismissed Burke's "A Letter to a Member of National Assembly" as "sheer madness." Madame de Staël's praise of Pitt might be read as a vicarious critique of Burke's unwillingness to distinguish between the ideas of 1789 and those of the Terror of 1793–94.

the conflagration. It is not to please the two parties that I thus praise them both, although they supported very opposite opinions. The contrary should perhaps be the case in France; the different factions are there almost always equally blamable; but, in a free country, the partisans of the ministry and the members of the opposition may all be right after their own way, and they are each frequently productive of good according to the times: the only point of importance is that the power acquired by the struggle should not be continued after the danger is past.

CHAPTER XV

Of Political Fanaticism.

The events which we have been recalling until this point have been the only kind of history for which we can find examples elsewhere. But an abyss is now about to open under our feet; we do not know what course to pursue in such a gulf, and the mind leaps in fear from disaster to disaster, till it reaches the annihilation of all hope and of all consolation. We shall pass as rapidly as we can over this frightful crisis, in which there is no individual to fix attention, no circumstance to excite interest: all is uniform, though extraordinary; all is monotonous, though horrible; and we should be in some measure ashamed of ourselves if we could contemplate these brutal atrocities sufficiently near to characterize them in detail. Let us only examine the great principle of these monstrous phenomena—political fanaticism.

Worldly passions have always played a part in religious fanaticism; and frequently, on the contrary, true faith by some abstract ideas feeds political fanaticism: the mixture is found everywhere, but its proportions are what constitutes good and evil. Social order is in itself a most peculiar structure; it is impossible, however, to imagine it as other than what it is. The concessions that we must make in order to ensure its continuing existence torment exalted souls with pity, satisfy the vanity of some, and provoke the irritation and the desires of the greater number. It is to this state of things, more or less pronounced, more or less softened by manners and knowledge, that the political fanaticism must be ascribed of which we have been witnesses in France. A sort of frenzy seized the poor in the presence of the rich; the distinctions of nobility adding to the jealousy which property inspires, the people were proud of their multitude; and all that constitutes the power and splendor of the few appeared to them mere usurpation. The germs of this sentiment have existed at all times; but we have

CHAPTER XV. *Political Fanaticism*

felt human society shaken to its foundation only during the Reign of Terror in France. We need not be surprised if this abominable scourge has left deep traces in men's minds; and the only reflection in which we can indulge, and which the remainder of this work will, I hope, confirm, is that the remedy for popular passions is to be found not in despotism, but in the rule of law.

Religious fanaticism presents an indefinite future which exalts all the hopes of the imagination; but the enjoyments of life are as unlimited in the eyes of those who have not tasted them. The Old Man of the Mountain[1] sent his subjects to death by means of allowing them delights on this earth; and we frequently see men expose themselves to death in order to live better. On the other hand, vanity takes a pride in defending the superior advantages which it possesses; it appears less guilty than the attackers, because some notion of property clings even to injustices when they have existed for a long time. Nevertheless, the two elements of religious fanaticism and political fanaticism always subsist; the will to dominate in those who are at the top of the wheel, the eagerness to make it turn in those who are on the bottom. This is the principle of all kinds of violence; the pretext changes, the cause remains, and the reciprocal fury continues the same. The quarrels of the patricians and the war of the slaves, the servile war, the war of the peasants, that which still goes on between the nobles and the bourgeois, have all equally had their origin in the difficulty of maintaining human society without disorder and without injustice. Men could not exist today, either apart or united, if respect for the law were not established in their minds: crimes of every sort would arise from that very society which ought to prevent them. The abstract power of representative governments irritates in nothing the pride of men, and it is by this institution that the torches of the furies are to be extinguished. They were lighted in a country where everything was self-love; and self-love irritated does not, with the people, resemble our fleeting nuances; it is the need to kill.

Massacres no less frightful than those of the Reign of Terror have been

---

1. The name given by the Crusaders to the chief of a Mohammedan sect called the "Assassins."

committed in the name of religion. The human race has exhausted itself for many centuries in useless efforts to constrain all men to the same belief. That end could not be attained: and the simplest idea, toleration, such as William Penn professed, has forever banished from the North of America the fanaticism of which the South has been the horrid theater. It is the same with political fanaticism; liberty alone can calm it. After a certain time, some truths will no longer be denied; and old institutions will be spoken of as ancient systems of physics, now entirely effaced by the evidence of facts.

As the different classes of society had scarcely any relations with each other in France, their mutual antipathy was of course stronger. There is no man, not even the most criminal, whom we can detest when we know him in the same way as when we imagine him. Pride places barriers everywhere, and limits nowhere. In no country have the nobles been so completely strangers to the rest of the nation: they came into contact with the second class only to offend it. Elsewhere, a simple good-heartedness, habits of life even somewhat vulgar, make people mix together, although they are separated by the law; but the elegance of the French nobility increased the envy which they inspired. To imitate their manners was as difficult as to obtain their prerogatives. The same scene was repeated from rank to rank; the irritability of a nation, lively in the extreme, inclined each one to be jealous of his neighbor, of his superior, of his master; and all, not satisfied with ruling, labored for the humiliation of each other. It is by multiplying political relations between different ranks, by giving them the means of serving each other, that we can appease in the heart the most horrible of passions—the hatred of human beings for their fellow men, the mutual aversion of creatures whose remains must all repose under the same earth and be together reborn at the last day.

CHAPTER XVI

Of the Government Called the Reign of Terror.

We know not how to approach the fourteen months which followed the proscription of the Gironde on the 31st of May, 1793. We seem as if we were descending, like Dante, from circle to circle, always lower in hell. To the animosity against the nobles and the priests succeeded a feeling of irritation against the landholders, next against talents, then even against beauty; finally, against whatever was to be found great or generous in human nature. At this epoch, facts become confused, and we are afraid of being unable to enter into such a history without leaving on the imagination indelible traces of blood. We are therefore forced to take a philosophical view of events, on which the eloquence of indignation might be exhausted without satisfying the internal sentiment which they awaken.

Doubtless, in taking away all restraints from the people, they were placed in a condition to commit every crime; but whence comes it that this people was so depraved? The government, which is spoken of as an object of regret, had time to have formed the nation which showed itself so culpable. The priests, whose instruction, example, and riches are fitted, we are told, to do so much good, had presided over the childhood of the generation which now turned against them. The class that rose into action in 1789 was of course accustomed to those privileges of feudal nobility, so particularly agreeable, we are still assured, to the persons by whom their weight must be borne. Whence comes it, then, that so many vices germinated under the ancient institutions? Let it not be pretended that the other nations of our days would have shown themselves similar if a revolution had taken place among them. French influence triggered insurrections in Holland and Switzerland, and nothing resembling Jacobinism manifested itself there. During the forty years of the history of England, which in so many points of view may be assimilated to that of France, there is no period that can be compared to the fourteen months of terror. What must we conclude from this? That for a century past no people had been so miserable as the people of France. If the negroes at St. Domingo committed a much greater number of atrocities,[1] it is because they had been still more oppressed.

It by no means follows from these reflections that the crimes deserve less detestation; but after more than twenty years, we should unite to the lively indignation of contemporaries the enlightened scrutiny which ought to serve as a guide for the future. Religious disputes provoked the English Revolution: love of equality, the subterraneous volcano of France,[2] likewise inflamed the sect of the Puritans; but the English were then really religious, and religious Protestants—a circumstance which increases at once austerity and moderation. Although England, like France, polluted herself with the murder of Charles I and the despotism of Cromwell, the reign of the Jacobins is a frightful singularity, the burden of which, in history, must be borne exclusively by France. He, however, has not thought much on the subject of civil disorders who does not know that reaction is equal to the action. The fury of revolts supplies the measure of the vices of institutions; and it is not to the government which is wished for, but to that which has long existed, that we must ascribe the moral state of a nation. At present it is said that the French have been corrupted by the Revolution. But whence come the reckless propensities which expanded themselves so violently in the first years of the Revolution, if not from a century of superstition and arbitrary power?

It seemed in 1793 that there was no more room for revolutions in France, when everything was overturned, the throne, the nobility, the clergy, and when the success of the armies gave reason to expect peace with Europe. But it is precisely when the danger is past that popular tyrannies are established: so long as there are obstacles and fears, the worst

1. Reference to the revolts in Haiti in 1791–92.
2. This idea would play a key role in Tocqueville's *The Old Régime and the Revolution*.

men observe moderation: when they have triumphed, their restrained passions show themselves without a curb.

The Girondists made several vain efforts, after the death of the King, to put some laws in activity; but they could not obtain a reception for any system of social organization; the instinct of ferocity rejected everything of the sort. Herault de Séchelles proposed a constitution scrupulously democratical;[3] the Assembly adopted it, but ordained that it should be suspended till the peace. The Jacobin party wished to exercise despotism, and this government has been mistakenly described as an anarchy. Never has a stronger authority reigned over France; but it was a strange form of power: springing out of popular fanaticism, it struck alarm into the very persons who commanded in its name; for they always feared to be proscribed in their turn by men who would go still further than they in the daring boldness of persecution. Marat alone lived without fear at this time; for his figure was so mean, his sentiments so extravagant, his opinions so sanguinary that he was sure that nobody could plunge deeper than himself in the abyss of crimes. Even Robespierre was unable to reach so infernal a security.

The last men who at this time are still worthy to occupy a place in history are the Girondists. They felt without doubt at the bottom of their hearts a keen remorse for the means which they had employed to overturn the throne; and when these very means were directed against themselves, when they recognized their own weapons in the wounds which they received, they must have reflected without doubt on that rapid justice of revolutions which concentrates in a few instants the events of several ages.

The Girondists contended every day and every hour, with an undaunted eloquence, against discourses sharpened like poignards, which carried death in every phrase. The murderous nets, with which the proscribed were enveloped on all sides, in no respect took away from them that presence of mind which alone can give effect to all the talents of the orator.

---

3. The Montagnards (the *Mountain*) presented a new constitution in June 1793, soon after the fall of the Girondins. It was drafted by, among others, Hérault de Séchelles (1759–94). Although approved by referendum, the constitution of 1793 was never applied.

M. de Condorcet, when he was put out of the protection of the law, wrote a work on the perfectibility of the human mind, which doubtless contains errors, but of which the general system is inspired by the hope of the happiness of men; this hope he nourished under the axe of the executioner at the very moment when his own destiny was ruined without resource. Twenty-two of the republican deputies were brought before the revolutionary tribunal, and their courage did not fail for a single instant.[4] When the sentence of death was pronounced upon them, one of them, Valazé, fell from the seat which he occupied; another deputy, also condemned, who was by his side and thought that his colleague was afraid, with some reproaches rudely raised him; he raised him up dead. Valazé had just plunged a poignard into his heart, with a hand so firm that he did not breathe a second after the blow was struck. Such, however, is the inflexibility of the spirit of party that these men, who defended whatever there was of respectability in France, could not flatter themselves with exciting any interest by their efforts. They struggled, they fell, they perished, while public report, the harbinger of future fame, made them no promise of any recompense. Even the constitutional royalists were so lost to common sense as to desire the triumph of the terrorists, that they themselves might thus be avenged upon the republicans. In vain were they aware that they too were proscribed by these terrorists; irritated pride prevailed over everything: in thus giving full scope to their resentments, they forgot the rule of conduct from which we should never deviate in politics: it is always to rally round the party the least bad among your adversaries, even when that party is still remote from your own views.

The scarcity of provisions, the abundance of assignats, and the enthusiasm excited by the war were the three grand springs of which the Committee of Public Safety availed itself, at once to animate and subdue the people. It terrified them, or paid them, or made them march to the frontiers, as best suited its purpose. One of the deputies to the Convention said, "We must continue the war, that the convulsions of liberty may be the stronger." It is impossible to know whether the twelve members of the Committee of Public Safety had conceived the idea of any government

4. On October 29–30, 1793.

whatsoever.[5] The direction of affairs, if we except the conduct of the war, was nothing else than a mixture of grossness and ferocity, in which no plan can be discovered, except that of making one half of the nation butcher the other. For it was so easy to be considered by the Jacobins as forming a part of the proscribed aristocracy that half the inhabitants of France incurred the suspicion, which was sufficient to lead the way to death.

The assassination of the Queen, and of Madame Elizabeth, excited perhaps still more astonishment and horror than the crime which was perpetrated against the person of the King; for no other object could be assigned for these horrible enormities than the very terror which they were fitted to inspire. The condemnation of M. de Malesherbes, of Bailly,[6] of Condorcet, of Lavoisier,[7] was the decimation of the glory of France; eighty persons were the victims of each day, as if the massacre of St. Bartholomew were to be kept in a constant state of renewal.[8] One great dif-

---

5. The Committee of Public Safety was officially established on April 6, 1793, replacing the Committee of General Defense. Robespierre, Carnot, and Saint-Just were among its twelve members. The Committee of Public Safety gave official acknowledgment to the doctrine of reason of state and ruled according to the belief that extraordinary circumstances call for extraordinary methods, as illustrated by these famous words of Marat: "It is through violence that liberty must be established, and the time has come to arrange for a temporary despotism of liberty in order to crush the despotism of kings." (quoted by D. Richet in his entry on the Committee of Public Safety, in *A Critical Dictionary of the French Revolution*, 476) The Reign of Terror was officially declared on September 5, 1793, and lasted until July 28, 1794. Madame de Staël is right to point out that the Committee of Public Safety did not rule alone but in conjunction with other rival state institutions, such as the Committee of General Security, which controlled the police, and the Commune insurectionnelle of Paris, which held military power after the fall of the monarchy on August 10, 1792. For more information, see *A Critical Dictionary of the French Revolution*, 474–78; Doyle, *The Oxford History of the French Revolution*, 247–72; and Palmer, *Twelve Who Ruled*.

6. Jean Sylvain Bailly (1736–93), a French astronomer who was elected a deputy to the Estates General, led the proceedings during the Tennis Court Oath and became mayor of Paris in July 1789. He became unpopular after he ordered the National Guard to disperse the crowd during the riotous assembly in the Champ de Mars (July 17, 1791).

7. Antoine Laurent Lavoisier (1743–94), considered the founder of modern chemistry, was arrested for his position in the Ferme générale (a tax farming company) prior to 1789. He was guillotined on May 8, 1794.

8. The Terror claimed approximately forty thousand victims (the estimates vary between sixteen and forty thousand) as a result of voluntary denunciations and quick trials

ficulty presented itself to this government, if the name of government can be given to it; it was the necessity which existed of employing all the means of civilization to carry on the war, and all the violence of the savage state to excite the passions. The populace, and even the citizens, were not struck by the misfortunes of the higher classes. The inhabitants of Paris walked about the streets, like the Turks during the plague, with this single difference, that obscure persons could easily enough preserve themselves from danger. Within view of the executions, the places of public entertainment were filled as usual; romances were published, entitled *A New Sentimental Voyage, Dangerous Friendship, Ursula and Sophia:* in short, all the insipidity and all the frivolity of life subsisted by the side of its gloomiest frenzies.

We have not attempted to dissemble what it is not in the power of men to blot out from their remembrance; but that we may breathe more at ease, we hasten to survey, in the following chapter, the virtues which did not cease to do honor to France, even at the most horrible period of her history.

---

characterized by hasty deliberations. According to Furet, the number of arrests from March 1793 to July 1794 was arguably close to a half million. The number of death sentences rose sharply after October 1793. For a good overview, see Furet's entry in *A Critical Dictionary of the French Revolution*, 137–51. A classic account can be found in Greer, *The Incidence of the Terror During the French Revolution*. For a more recent account, see Andress, *The Terror*.

CHAPTER XVII

The French Army During the Reign of Terror; the Federalists and La Vendée.

The conduct of the French army during the period of terror was truly patriotic. No generals were seen violating their oath to the state; they repulsed foreigners while they were themselves threatened with death upon the scaffold, at the slightest suspicion that might be excited against their conduct. The soldiers belonged not to any particular chief, but to France. France no longer existed but in the armies; there, however, at least, she was still beautiful: and her triumphant banners served, if we may so say, as a veil to the crimes committed in the interior. Foreigners were compelled to respect the rampart of iron which was opposed to their invasion; and, although they advanced within thirty leagues of Paris, a national feeling, still in full strength, did not permit them to arrive there. The same enthusiasm displayed itself in the navy. The crew of a man of war, *Le Vengeur*, struck by the English,[1] repeated, as with one voice, the cry of *Vive la république* while they were sinking in the ocean; and the songs of a funereal joy seemed still to re-echo from the bottom of the deep.

The French army was then unacquainted with pillage, and its chiefs sometimes marched like private soldiers at the head of their troops because they did not have money to purchase the horses which they needed. Dugommier,[2] commander in chief of the army of the Pyrénées, at the age of sixty, set out from Paris on foot to rejoin his troops on the frontiers of

1. The incident occurred not far from Brest on June 1, 1794, and was reported by Barère in the Convention.

2. Dugommier (1738–94), a French marshal who served in Guadeloupe and the Pyrénées.

Spain. The men, on whom military glory has since conferred so much renown, distinguished themselves also by their disinterestedness. They wore, without blushing, uniforms which had become threadbare in the service, a hundred times more honorable than the embroidery and decorations of every kind with which, at a later period, we have seen them bedizened.

Honest republicans, mingled with royalists, courageously resisted the Conventional Government at Toulon, at Lyons, and in some other departments. This party was known by the name of Federalists; but I do not believe that the Girondists, or their partisans, ever conceived the project of establishing a federative government in France. Nothing would be less suitable to the character of the nation, which loves splendor and bustle; for both of these require a city, which may be the focus of the talents and the riches of the empire. We may with reason complain of the corruption of a capital, and of all great assemblages of men in general; such is the condition of mankind: but in France we could scarcely bring back men's minds to virtue, but by the diffusion of knowledge and the need to obtain the votes of the public. The love of consideration or glory, in its different degrees, is the only thing that is able to raise us gradually from egoism to conscientiousness. Besides, the political and military state of the great monarchies which surround France would endanger her independence if the strength of her union were weakened. The Girondists never thought of any such plan; but, as they had many adherents in the provinces, where, by the simple effect of a national representation, political knowledge was beginning to be acquired, it was in the provinces that opposition to the factious tyrants of Paris displayed itself.

It was about this time, also, that the war of LaVendée[3] began, and nothing does more honor to the royalist party than the attempts at civil war which were then made. The people of these departments were able to resist the Convention and its successors for nearly six years, being headed by some gentlemen who drew their principal resources from their own minds.

---

3. The revolt began on March 10, 1793, as a refusal to submit to conscription and ended nine months later. On the Vendée rebellion, see Furet's entry in *A Critical Dictionary of the French Revolution*, 165–76; and Tilly, *The Vendée*.

The republicans, as well as the royalists, felt a profound respect for these warrior citizens. Lescure, La Roche Jacquelin, Charette,[4] etc., whatever their opinions might be, fulfilled a duty to which all the French at that time might have thought themselves equally bound. The country which was the theater of the Vendean war was intersected by hedges intended to enclose the different estates. These peaceful hedges served for bulwarks to the peasants become soldiers, who sustained one by one the most dangerous and most daring struggle. The inhabitants of these parts of the country had much veneration for the priests, whose influence at that time did good. But in a state where liberty has long subsisted, the public mind would not need to be excited except by public institutions. The Vendeans, it is true, demanded in their distress some succours from England; but it was only auxiliaries, not masters, whom they accepted; for their own forces were much superior to those which they borrowed from abroad. They did not therefore compromise the independence of their country. Accordingly the chiefs of la Vendée were held in consideration even by the opposite party, and they expressed themselves upon the Revolution with more moderation than the emigrants beyond the Rhine. The Vendeans having fought, so to say, man to man with the French, were not easily persuaded that their adversaries were but a handful of rebels, whom a single battalion could have brought back to their duty; and as they themselves had recourse to the power of opinions, they knew what they were, and acknowledged the necessity of compromising with them.

One problem remains still to be solved: it is, How was it possible for the government of 1793 and 1794 to triumph over so many enemies? The coalition of Austria, Prussia, Spain, and England, the civil war in the interior, the hatred with which the Convention inspired every man of consideration that remained out of prison—none of these circumstances diminished the resistance, against which foreigners saw their efforts crushed to nothing. This prodigy can be explained only by the devotion of the nation to its own cause. A million men took arms to repel the forces of the coalition; the people were animated with a frenzy, as fatal in the in-

---

4. Louis-Marie de Salgues, Marquis de Lescure (1766–93), La Rochejacquelin (1772–94), and François de Charette de la Contrie (1763–96), fought on the Vendeans' side.

terior as invincible without. Besides, the factitious but inexhaustible abundance of paper money, the low price of provisions, the degradation of the landholders, who were reduced to doom themselves eternally to misery, all tended to make the working classes believe that the yoke of inequality of fortune was at last on the point of ceasing to oppress them; this extravagant hope doubled the force which nature gave them: and social order, the secret of which consists in the endurance of the many, appeared suddenly threatened. But the military spirit, which then had no other end than the defense of the country, gave tranquillity to France by covering her with its shield. This spirit followed the same noble direction till the moment when, as we shall see later, one man turned against liberty herself the very legions that had sprung from the earth to defend her.

Of the Situation of the Friends of Liberty Out of France During the Reign of Terror.

It is difficult to relate the events of these horrible times without recalling one's own impressions in almost their original vivacity: and I know not why one should combat this natural inclination. For the best manner of representing such extraordinary circumstances is to show in what state they placed individuals in the midst of the universal tempest.

Emigration during the Reign of Terror was no longer a political measure. People escaped from France to save themselves from the scaffold, and no one could have remained there without exposing oneself to death in order to avoid ruin. The friends of liberty were more detested by the Jacobins than even the aristocrats, because they had been engaged in a closer struggle with one another, and because the Jacobins feared the constitutionalists, whom they believed to be still in possession of a very considerable influence over the mind of the nation. These friends of liberty found themselves, therefore, almost without a place of refuge upon earth. The pure royalists did not violate their principles in fighting with foreign armies against their country; but the constitutionalists could not adopt such a resolution: they were proscribed by France and viewed with an evil eye by the ancient governments of Europe, who knew little of them but from the recitals of the French aristocrats, their most furious enemies.

I concealed in my house, in the Pays de Vaud,[1] some friends of liberty respectable in every way, both for their rank and for their virtues; and as a regular permission to authorize their residence could not then be obtained from the Swiss authorities, they bore Swedish names, which M. de

1. At Coppet, in Switzerland.

Staël assigned them that he might have the pleasure of yielding them protection. Scaffolds were erected for them on the frontier of their native
country, and persecutions of every kind awaited them in foreign lands.
Thus the monks of the order of La Trappe found themselves detained in
an island in the middle of a river which separates Prussia from Russia:
each of the two countries rejected them as if tainted with a pestilence; and
yet no reproach could be alleged against them, except that they were faithful to their vows.

One particular circumstance may be of use in depicting this epoch of
1793, when perils were multiplied at every step. A young French gentleman, M. Achille du Chayla, nephew of the Count de Jaucourt, wished to
escape from France under a Swiss passport which we had sent him; for
we thought ourselves quite at liberty to deceive tyranny. At Morez, a frontier town situated at the foot of Mount Jura, suspicions were entertained
that M. du Chayla was not what his passport pretended, and he was arrested with a declaration that he must remain a prisoner till the lieutenant
of the district of Nyon should attest that he was a Swiss. M. de Jaucourt
was then staying in my house, under one of those Swedish names of which
we were the inventors. At the news of his nephew's arrest, his despair was
extreme; for the young man, at that time an object of pursuit, the bearer
of a false passport, and, besides, son to one of the chiefs of the army of
Condé, would have been instantly shot had his name been discovered.
There remained only one hope; it was to prevail upon M. Reverdil,
lieutenant-bailiff of the district of Nyon, to claim M. du Chayla as in reality
a native of the Pays de Vaud.

I went to M. Reverdil to ask this favor of him: he was an old friend of
my parents, and one of the most enlightened and most respectable men
in French Switzerland.* He at first refused, opposing to me the most
weighty motives; he was scrupulous of deviating from truth for any object
whatsoever, and besides, as a magistrate, he was fearful of compromising
his country by an act of falsehood. "If the truth is discovered," said he,

---

* M. Reverdil was chosen to preside over the education of the King of Denmark. He
wrote, during his residence in the North, very interesting memoirs of the events of which
he was a witness. These memoirs have not yet appeared.

"we shall no longer have the right of claiming our own countrymen who may be arrested in France; and thus I expose the interest of those who are entrusted to me, for the safety of a man to whom I owe nothing." This argument had a very plausible aspect: but the pious fraud which I solicited could alone save the life of a man over whose head the axe of the murderer was suspended. I remained two hours with M. Reverdil, seeking to vanquish his conscience by his humanity; he resisted long, but when I repeated to him several times, "If you say *no,* an *only* son, a man without reproach, is assassinated within twenty-four hours, and your mere word kills him," my emotion, or rather his own, triumphed over every other consideration, and the young Du Chayla was claimed. It was the first time that a circumstance presented itself to me in which two duties struggled against each other with equal force. But I still think, as I thought twenty-three years ago, that the present danger of the victim ought to prevail over the uncertain dangers of the future. There is not in the short space of existence a greater chance of happiness than to save the life of an innocent man; and I know not how it would be possible to resist this seduction, by supposing it in such a case to be one.

Alas! I was not always so fortunate in my connections with my friends. It was necessary for me a few months afterward to communicate to the man, the most susceptible of strong affection, and consequently of deep grief, M. Mathieu de Montmorency, the sentence of death pronounced upon his young brother, the Abbé de Montmorency, whose only crime was the illustrious name which he had received from his ancestors. At the same time the wife, the mother, and the mother-in-law of M. de Montmorency were alike threatened with destruction: a few days later, and all the prisoners were at this horrid epoch sent to the scaffold. One of the reflections which struck us the most forcibly in our long walks by the shores of the lake of Geneva was the contrast of the noble scenes of nature around us, and of the brilliant sun of the end of June, with the despair of man—of this prince of the earth who would have wanted to make the world carry his own mourning. Dejection had seized us: the younger we were, the less resignation we had; for in youth especially we look for happiness, we think that we have a right to it, and we revolt at the idea of not obtaining it. Yet it was in these very moments, when we were contemplating in vain the sky and the flowers, and were reproaching them with dispersing light and fragrance through the air in the presence of so many crimes, it was then that deliverance was preparing. A day of which the new name disguises, perhaps, the date from strangers, the ninth of Thermidor, carried into the hearts of Frenchmen an emotion of inexpressible joy. Poor human nature could never owe so lively a delight but to the cessation of sorrow.

CHAPTER XIX

Fall of Robespierre, and Change of System in the Government.

The men and women who were conducted to the scaffold gave proofs of a courage that nothing could shake; the prisons presented the example of the most generous acts of devotion; fathers were seen sacrificing themselves for their sons, wives for their husbands; but the party of the worthy, like the King himself, showed themselves capable only of private virtues. In general, in a country where there is no freedom, energy is found only in the factious; but in England, the support of the law and the feeling of justice render the resistance of the upper classes quite as strong as the attack of the populace could be. Had a division not taken place among the deputies of the Convention themselves, it is impossible to say how long the atrocious government of the Committee of Public Safety would have lasted.

This Committee was not composed of men of superior talent;[1] the machine of terror, the springs of which had been prepared for action by events, exercised alone unbounded power. The government resembled the hideous instrument employed on the scaffold; the axe was seen rather than the hand which put it in motion. A single question was sufficient to overturn the power of these men; it was—how many are they? But their force was measured by the atrocity of their crimes, and nobody dared attack them. These twelve members of the Committee of Public Safety distrusted one another, as the Convention distrusted them, and they distrusted it; as the army, the people, and the partisans of the revolution were all mutually filled with alarm. No name of this epoch will remain, except Robespierre.

1. For more information, see Palmer, *Twelve Who Ruled.*

Yet he was neither more able nor more eloquent than the rest; but his political fanaticism had a character of calmness and austerity which made him feared by all his colleagues.

I once conversed with him at my father's house, in 1789, when he was known merely as an advocate of the province of Artois who carried to extremes his democratical principles. His features were mean, his complexion pale, his veins of a greenish hue; he maintained the most absurd propositions with a coolness which had the air of conviction; and I could easily believe that, at the beginning of the Revolution, he had adopted sincerely certain ideas, upon the equality of fortunes as well as of ranks, which he caught in the course of his reading, and with which his envious and mischievous character was delighted to arm itself. But he became ambitious when he had triumphed over his rival in the arts of the demagogue, Danton, the Mirabeau of the mob. The latter had more spirit than Robespierre, and was more accessible to pity; but it was suspected, and with reason, that he was not proof against the seductions of money; a weakness which, in the end, always ruins demagogues; for the people cannot endure those who enrich themselves: it is a kind of austerity that no one could have convinced them to abandon.

Danton was factious, Robespierre was hypocritical: Danton was fond of pleasure, Robespierre only of power;[2] he sent to the scaffold some as counter-revolutionists, others as ultrarevolutionists. There was something mysterious in his manner which caused an unknown terror to hover about in the midst of the ostensible terror which the government proclaimed. He never adopted the means of popularity then generally in use; he was not ill dressed; on the contrary, he was the only person who wore powder in his hair; his clothes were neat, and his countenance had nothing familiar. The desire of ruling carried him, without doubt, to distinguish himself from others at the very moment when equality in everything was desired. Traces of a secret design are also perceived in the confusing discourses which he made in the Convention, and which, in some respects, recall to our recollection those of Cromwell. It is rarely, indeed, that any-

2. For modern accounts of Robespierre's life and legacy, see Scurr, *Fatal Purity;* Haydon and Doyle, *Robespierre;* and Andress, *The Terror.*

one who is not a military chief can become dictator. But the civil power had then much more influence than the military: the republican spirit led to a distrust of all the victorious generals; the soldiers themselves delivered up their leaders as soon as the least alarm with respect to their fidelity arose. Political dogmas, if the name can be applied to such wanderings of intellect, reigned at that time, and not men. Something abstract was wanted in authority, that everybody might be thought to have a share in it. Robespierre had acquired the reputation of high democratical virtue, and was believed incapable of personal views: as soon as he was suspected, his power was at an end.

The most indecent irreligion served as a lever for the subversion of the social order. There was a kind of consistency in founding crime upon impiety: it is an homage paid to the intimate union of religious opinions with morality. Robespierre conceived the idea of celebrating a festival in honor of the Supreme Being,[3] flattering himself, doubtless, with being able to rest his political ascendancy on a religion arranged according to his own notions; as those have frequently done who have wished to seize the supreme power. But in the procession of this impious festival, he decided to walk at the head of the procession in order to claim preeminence over his colleagues; and from that time he was lost. The spirit of the moment, and the personal resources of the man, were not calculated for this enterprise. Besides, it was known that he was acquainted with no other means of getting rid of competitors than by destroying them through the agency of the revolutionary tribunal, which gave murder an air of legality. The colleagues of Robespierre, not less detestable than himself, Collot d'Herbois, Billaud Varennes, attacked him to secure their own safety: the abhorrence of crime did not inspire them with this resolution; they meant to kill a man, but not to change the government.

It was not so with Tallien, the hero of the 9th of Thermidor, nor with Barras,[4] the commander of the armed force on that day, nor with several other conventionalists who then joined them. They meant, in overturning him, to break with the same blow the scepter of terror. Thus this man,

3. On June 8, 1794.
4. Barras (1755–1829) played a key role in planning Robespierre's fall in 1794.

who during more than a year had signed an unheard of number of death sentences, was seen bleeding on the very table where he was wont to affix his name to these horrible sentences. His jaw was shattered by a pistol ball; he could not even speak in his own defense: he, who had spoken so much for the proscription of others. Might it not be said that Divine justice does not disdain, in inflicting punishment, to strike the imagination of men by all the circumstances which can act upon it the most powerfully.

Of the State of Minds at the Moment When the Directorial Republic Was Established in France.

The Reign of Terror ought to be ascribed exclusively to the principles of tyranny; one finds them there completely intact. The popular forms adopted by that government were only a sort of ceremonial, which suited these savage despots; but the members of the Committee of Public Safety professed at the tribune the code of Machiavellianism, that is to say, power founded upon the degradation of men; they only took care to translate the old maxims into new terms. The liberty of the press was much more odious to them than even to the ancient feudal or theocratic states; they allowed no security to the accused, either through the means of the laws or through the means of the judges.[1] Arbitrary will, without limits, was their doctrine; it was enough for them to assign as a pretext for every violence the peculiar name of their government, *The Public Safety:* a fatal expression which implies the sacrifice of morality to what it has been agreed to call the interest of the state, that is, to the passions of those who govern.

From the fall of Robespierre to the establishment of the Republican Government under the form of a Directory, there was an interval of about fifteen months, which may be considered as the true epoch of anarchy in France.[2] Nothing is less like the period of terror than this time, though

---

1. Freedom of the press disappeared after August 10, 1792. In the revolutionary tribunals, the defendants had no legal guarantees.

2. The Directory followed the Convention and preceded the Consulate (from November 2, 1795, to November 10, 1799). Five directors shared the executive power at any time.

many crimes were still committed. The disastrous inheritance of Robespierre's laws had not been abandoned; but the liberty of the press began to revive, and truth along with it. The general wish was to establish wise and free institutions, and to get rid of the men who had governed during the reign of blood. Nothing, however, was so difficult as to satisfy this double desire; for the Convention still held the authority in its hands, and many of the friends of liberty feared that a counter-revolution might take place if those were deprived of power whose lives would be compromised by the re-establishment of the old regime. The crimes which have been committed in the name of liberty are, however, a poor security; the return of the men who had been made to suffer would, of course, be dreaded; but people are quite ready to sacrifice their principles to their security, should an opportunity present itself.

It was therefore a great misfortune for France that she was obliged to leave the republic in the hands of the members of the Convention. Some of the members were endowed with superior abilities; but those who had shared in the government of terror had necessarily contracted habits of servility and tyranny together. It was in this school that Bonaparte selected many of the men who afterward established his power; and, as they sought shelter above everything, they never felt fully assured but in despotism.

The majority of the Convention wished to punish some of the most atrocious deputies who had oppressed it; but it drew up the list of the guilty with a trembling hand, always apprehensive lest it should be itself accused of the laws which had served as a justification or pretext for every crime. The royalist party sent agents abroad, and found partisans in the interior, from the very irritation which was excited by the continuance of the Convention's power.[3] Nevertheless, the fear of losing all the advantages of the Revolution attached the people and the soldiers to the existing authority. The army always fought against foreigners with the same energy, and its exploits had already obtained an important peace for France,

---

For more information on this period, see Lefebre, *The Thermidorians and the Directory*, 239–458.

3. In the French text, "pouvoir conventionnel."

the treaty of Basel with Prussia.[4] The people also, we should add, supported unheard of evils with astonishing perseverance; famine on the one hand, and the depreciation of the paper money on the other, were reducing the lowest class of society to a state of the utmost wretchedness. If the kings of France had made their subjects undergo half these sufferings, they would have revolted on all sides. But the nation believed that they were devoting themselves for their country, and nothing equals the courage inspired by such a conviction.

Sweden having acknowledged the French Republic, M. de Staël resided at Paris as minister. I passed some months there during the year 1795, when the society of Paris was truly a very curious spectacle. Each of us was soliciting the recall of some emigrants, our friends. I obtained at this time permission for several to return; in consequence of which the deputy Legendre, a man almost from the dregs of the people, denounced me at the tribune of the Convention. The influence of women, the ascendant of good company, gilded saloons, appeared very terrible to those who were not admitted themselves, while their colleagues were seduced from them by invitations. Every tenth day (for Sunday existed no more) all the elements of the old and the new regime were seen united in the evening, though not reconciled. The elegant manners of well-educated persons penetrated through the humble costume which they still retained as in the days of terror. The men who had been converted from the Jacobin party entered for the first time into the society of the great world, and their self-love was more apt to take offense upon things which related to the tone of fashion, which they wished to imitate, than upon any other subject. The women of the old regime surrounded them, in order to obtain the return of their brothers, their sons, their husbands; and the insinuating flattery, of which they knew how to avail themselves, struck these rude ears and disposed the most bitter of the factious to what we have since seen—that is to say, to re-create a court, to bring back all its abuses, only taking great care to appropriate them to themselves.

The apologies of those who had shared in the Reign of Terror formed truly the most inconceivable school of sophistry which it was possible to

4. The treaty was signed on April 6, 1795.

witness. Some said that they had been constrained to whatever they had done, though a thousand actions of spontaneous servility or cruelty might have been cited against them. Others pretended that they had sacrificed themselves to the public good, though it was known that they had thought only on self-preservation: all threw the evil upon some individuals; and, what was a singular circumstance in a country famed for military bravery, several of the political leaders gave fear, and nothing else, as a sufficient excuse for their conduct.

A well-known member of the Convention was telling me one day, among others, that at the moment when the revolutionary tribunal was decreed, he had foreseen all the calamities which resulted from it; "and yet," added he, "the decree passed the Assembly unanimously." Now, he himself was present at that meeting, voting for what he regarded as the establishment of judicial assassination: yet it did not once occur to his mind, as he related the fact to me, that resistance from him was a thing which might have been expected. Such complete and naive lack of moral principle leaves a man in doubt almost of the very possibility of virtue.

The Jacobins who had been personally concerned in the crimes of the days of terror, such as Lebon, Carrier,[5] &c., were nearly all distinguished by the same kind of physiognomy. They might be seen in the tribune of the Convention reading their speeches, with a pale and nervous figure, going from side to side like a ferocious beast in its cage. When they were seated, they poised themselves, without rising or changing their place, in a sort of stationary agitation, which seemed to indicate merely the impossibility of repose.

In the midst of these depraved elements, there existed a party of republicans, the remnants of the Gironde, who had been persecuted with it, and were now coming forth from the prisons, or from the caverns which had served them as a refuge from death. This party was worthy of esteem

---

5. Joseph Lebon (1765–95) was a former clergyman who became a member of the Committee of General Security. He was arrested after the fall of Robespierre and condemned to death for his participation in the Terror. Jean-Baptiste Carrier (1756–94) was a deputy to the Convention who played an important role in the suppression of the Vendean revolt and, a few months later, in the fall of Robespierre. He was arrested and executed in the fall of 1794.

in many respects; but it was not cured of its democratical systems, and besides, it had a suspicious spirit which made it see everywhere favorers of the old regime. Louvet,[6] one of the Girondists who escaped the proscription, and author of a romance, *Faublas,* which foreigners often take for a picture of French manners, was a sincere republican. He trusted nobody; he brought into politics the species of faults which constituted the misery of Rousseau's life;[7] and many men of the same opinion resembled him in this respect. But the suspicions of the republicans and Jacobins in France proceeded at first from their being unable to obtain a favorable reception for their extravagant principles; and secondly, from a certain hatred against the nobles, in which some bad emotions were blended. They were right in wishing to have no nobility in France such as it had once existed; but aversion from men of noble birth is a mean sentiment which must be subdued before France can be organized in a stable manner.

In 1795, however, the plan of a republican constitution was proposed, much more reasonable and better combined than the monarchy decreed by the Constituent Assembly in 1791. Boissy d'Anglas,[8] Daunou,[9] and Lanjuinais,[10] names which always meet us whenever a ray of freedom gleams over France, were members of the Committee of the Constitution. They ventured to propose two Chambers, under the names of the Council of Ancients and the Council of Five Hundred; qualifications of property

6. Jean-Baptiste Louvet de Couvray (1760–97), deputy to the Convention and later a member of the Council of Five Hundred.

7. Reference to Jean-Jacques Rousseau.

8. François Antoine de Boissy d'Anglas (1756–1828) was an eminent French lawyer and statesman who served as a deputy (from Ardèche) to the Estates General and the Convention. He distinguished himself during the Directory through his moderate constitutionalism in the debates on the drafting of the Constitution of Year III. For more information, see Gross, "La Constitution de l'an III."

9. Pierre Claude François Daunou (1761–1840) was a Girondist deputy (from Pas-de-Calais) to the Convention and the Council of Five Hundred. He also played a key role in the creation of the Institute of France; in 1819, he was given the chair of history and ethics at the Collège de France.

10. Jean Denis, Count Lanjuinais (1753–1827), taught law at Rennes before 1789 and was elected to the Convention, where he became close to the Girondins after 1791. During the Directory, Lanjuinais was a member of the Council of Ancients, and during the Bourbon Restoration, he defended the principles of constitutional monarchy.

in order to be eligible; two steps of election, which, though not a good institution in itself, was then rendered necessary by circumstances, with a view to raise the sphere of choice; finally, a Directory composed of five persons.[11] This executive power had not yet the authority requisite for the maintenance of order; it was destitute of several indispensable prerogatives, the want of which, as we shall see later, brought on destructive convulsions.

The attempt at a republic was not without grandeur; however, that it might succeed, it would perhaps have been necessary to sacrifice Paris to France and to adopt federative forms, which, as we have stated, suit neither the character nor the habits of the nation. In a second point of view, the unity of the republican government appears impossible in a great country, and at variance with the nature of things.[12] In other respects, the attempt failed chiefly by reason of the kind of men who exclusively filled all employments; the party to which they had belonged during the period of terror rendered them odious to the nation; thus, too many serpents were thrown into the cradle of Hercules.

The Convention, instructed by the example of the Constituent Assembly, whose work had been overturned because it had abandoned it too quickly to its successors, passed the decrees of the 5th and of the 13th of Fructidor, which kept two-thirds of the existing deputies in their places: it was, however, afterward agreed that one of these thirds should be removed within eighteen months, and the other a year later. This decree produced a terrible sensation in the public opinion, and completely broke the treaty which had been tacitly signed between the Convention and people of principle. Men were willing to pardon the Convention, on condition that it renounced power; but it was natural, on the other hand, that the

---

11. For the text of the Constitution of Year III, see *Les Constitutions et les principales lois politiques de la France depuis 1789*, 73–109. An English translation can be found in *A Documentary Survey of the French Revolution*, 572–612. For an analysis of the Constitution of Year III, see Jainchill, "The Constitution of the Year III and the Persistence of Classical Republicanism," 399–435. A detailed analysis of the influence of the U.S. Constitution on the Constitution of Year III can be found in Marc Lahmer's *La Constitution américaine dans le débat français: 1795–1848*.

12. On this issue, see Benjamin Constant's posthumously published *Fragments d'un ouvrage abandonné sur la possibilité d'une constitution republicaine dans un grand pays*.

Convention should wish to retain its authority, to serve at least as a safe-guard. In these circumstances, the Parisians were somewhat too violent,[13] and were perhaps exasperated by the eager desire of occupying every place, a passion which was then beginning to ferment in men's minds. It was known, however, that persons of great acknowledged worth were marked out as the future directors; the members of the Convention wished to acquire honor by good selections; and perhaps it would have been wise to have waited for the appointed term, when the remainder of the deputies might have been legally and gradually removed. But some royalists were mingled with the party, who wished only to appropriate to themselves the places of the commonwealth; and, as has constantly happened for twenty-five years, at the moment when the cause of the Revolution seemed in the greatest danger, its defenders had on their side the people and the army, the suburbs and the soldiers. It was then that an alliance was established between the force of the people and the force of the military, which soon rendered the latter mistress of the former. The French warriors, so worthy of admiration for the resistance which they opposed to the coalesced pow-ers, made themselves, so to say, the janissaries of freedom at home. Med-dling in the internal affairs of France, they disposed of the civil authority and charged themselves with the task of effecting the different revolutions of which we have been witnesses.

The sections of Paris, on their side, were perhaps not exempt from the spirit of faction; for the cause of their tumult was of no urgent public interest, and they had only to wait eighteen months when no member of the Convention would remain in power. Impatience ruined them; they attacked the army of the Convention on the 13th of Vendemiaire, and the issue was not doubtful. The commander of this army was General Bo-naparte: his name appeared for the first time in the annals of the world on the 13th of Vendemiaire (4th of October), 1795.[14] He had already aided, but without being named, at the capture of Toulon in 1793, when that city revolted against the Convention. The party which overturned Robes-

---

13. Reference to the events of October 5, 1795, when royalists unsuccessfully tried to dissolve the Convention.

14. In fact, October 5, 1795.

pierre had left him without employment after the 9th of Thermidor; and as he had then no resource of private fortune, he asked the committees of the government for leave to go to Constantinople to train the Turks to war. In the same manner Cromwell wished to set out for America at the beginning of the English Revolution. Barras, afterward director, took an interest in Bonaparte and selected him in the committees of the Convention to be its defender. It is pretended that General Bonaparte has said that he would have taken part with the sections, if they had offered him the command of their battalions. I have my doubts of the truth of this anecdote; not that General Bonaparte was, at any period of the Revolution, attached exclusively to any opinion whatsoever; but because he always felt too strongly the instinct of force, to choose to place himself on the side which was then necessarily the weakest.

In Paris, on the day following the 13th of Vendemiaire, people feared that the Reign of Terror might be re-established. In fact, those same members of the Convention who had sought to please when they believed themselves reconciled with people of principle, could rush into every excess when they saw that their endeavors to make their past conduct forgotten were unsuccessful. But the waves of the Revolution were beginning to retire, and the lasting return of Jacobinism was already become impossible. One result, however, of the conflict of the 13th of Vendemiaire was that the Convention made a point of naming five directors who had voted for the death of the King, and as the nation in no respect approved this aristocracy of regicidal crime, it did not identify itself with its magistrates. Another result, not less unfortunate, of the 13th of Vendemiaire was a decree of the 2d of Brumaire[15] which excluded from every public employment the relatives of emigrants, and all those who in the sections had voted for *liberticidal* projects. Such was the expression of the day; for in France, at every revolution a new phrase is framed which serves all the world, that everyone may have sense or sentiment ready made to his hand, if perchance nature should have refused him the one or the other.

The decree of exclusion of the 2d of Brumaire formed a class of proscribed persons in the state, which certainly is not preferable to a privi-

15. October 24, 1795.

leged class, and is not less inconsistent with equality under the law. The Directory had the power to banish, to imprison, to transport at its pleasure, individuals who were denounced as attached to the Old Regime, nobles, and priests, to whom the benefit of the constitution was refused, and who were placed under the yoke of arbitrary will. An amnesty ordinarily accompanies the installation of every new government; but it was a sweeping proscription which distinguished that of the Directory. To what dangers was this government exposed as well by its want of constitutional prerogatives as by the revolutionary power with which it had been so prodigally invested!

Of the Twenty Months During Which the Republic Existed in France, from November 1795 to the 18th of Fructidor (4th of September) 1797.

We must do justice to the Directors, and still more to the power of free institutions, in whatever form they are introduced. The first twenty months which followed the establishment of the republic exhibit a period of administration uncommonly remarkable. Five men, Carnot,[1] Reubell,[2] Barras, La Réveillère,[3] Letourneur,[4] chosen in fury and not endowed for the most part with superior talents, arrived at power under the most unfavorable circumstances. They entered the palace of the Luxembourg, which was allotted them, without finding a table to write upon, and the state was not in better order than the palace. The paper money was reduced to almost the thousandth part of its nominal value; there were not in the public treasury a hundred thousand francs in specie; provisions were

1. Carnot (1753–1823) was elected a deputy to the Legislative Assembly and to the Convention. He was also a member of the Committee of Public Safety. After being appointed minister of war by Napoléon in 1800, Carnot voted against the nomination of Napoléon as consul for life.

2. Reubell (1747–1807), a lawyer elected to the Estates General and deputy to the Convention, participated in the repression of the Vendean revolt and sided with the Montagnards. He was a member of the Directory from 1795 to 1799.

3. La Réveillère-Lépeaux (1753–1824), lawyer, deputy to the Convention. A moderate, he left the Convention in June 1793 and fled the country to save his life. He was a member of the Directory from 1795 to 1799.

4. Letourneur (1751–1817), deputy to the Legislative Assembly and the Convention. He was a member of the Directory from 1795 to 1797.

still so scarce that the dissatisfaction of the people on this point could with difficulty be restrained; the insurrection of La Vendée was still going on; the civil disturbances had given rise to bands of robbers, known by the name of *chauffeurs,* who committed horrible excesses throughout the country; and lastly, almost all the French armies were disorganized.

In six months the Directory raised France from this deplorable situation. Money replaced the paper currency without any shock; the old landholders lived peacefully by the side of those who had recently acquired national domains; the roads, and the country, were again rendered completely safe; the armies were but too victorious; the freedom of the press re-appeared; the elections followed their legal course, and France might have been said to be free, if the two classes of nobles and priests had enjoyed the same securities as the other citizens. But the sublime perfection of liberty consists in this—that she can do nothing by halves. If you wish to persecute a single man in the state, justice will never be established for all; still more must this be the case when a hundred thousand individuals are shut out from the protecting circle of the law. Revolutionary measures therefore spoiled the constitution from the first establishment of the Directory; the latter half of the existence of this government, which lasted four years in all, was in every respect so wretched that the mischief may easily be ascribed to the institutions themselves. Impartial history, however, will place on two lines widely different the Republic before the 18th of Fructidor and the Republic after that epoch—if indeed the name of Republic can be deserved by factious authorities who overturned one another without ceasing to oppress the mass upon which they were continually falling.

During the first period of the Directory, the two extreme parties, the Jacobins and the Royalists, attacked it in the journals, each in their own mode, without meeting with any opposition from the government, which was not at all shaken by their efforts. The society of Paris was so much the more free that the class of rulers made no part of it. This separation had, and doubtless could not fail to have, in the end, many inconveniences; but, for the very reason that the government was not in fashion, people's minds were not agitated, as they have since been, by the unbridled desire of obtaining places; and there existed other objects of activity and interest.

One circumstance particularly worthy of notice under the Directory is the relation between the civil authority and the army. It has often been said that freedom, as it exists in England, is not possible in a Continental state, on account of the regular troops which must always be dependent on the head of the state. I shall reply elsewhere to these fears with respect to the continuance of liberty, which are always expressed by its enemies, by the very men who are unwilling to permit a single sincere attempt to be made in its favor. But we cannot be too much surprised at the manner in which the armies were managed by the Directory, up to the moment when, from an apprehension of the restoration of the ancient throne, it unfortunately introduced them into the internal revolutions of the state.

The best generals in Europe obeyed five directors, three of whom were only lawyers. The love of their country and of freedom was still powerful enough with the soldiers to make them yield more respect to the law than to their general, if he wished to place himself above it. However, the indefinite prolongation of the war opposed a grand obstacle to the establishment of a free government in France; for on the one hand, the ambition of conquest was beginning to take possession of the army, and on the other, the decrees for recruiting[5] which were obtained from the legislature, those decrees by means of which the Continent was afterward enslaved, were already giving fatal wounds to reverence for civil institutions. We cannot but regret that at this period the powers still at war with France, that is to say, Austria and England, did not accede to the peace. Prussia, Venice, Tuscany, Spain, and Sweden had already treated, in 1795, with a government much less regular than that of the Directory; and perhaps the spirit of invasion, which has done so much mischief to the people of the Continent, as well as to the French themselves, would not have been developed if the war had ceased before the conquests of General Bonaparte in Italy. It was still time to direct French activity to political and commercial interests. War had not till then been considered, except as a means of securing the national independence; the army thought itself destined only to maintain the Revolution; the military were not a separate order in the

5. The Law Jourdan-Delbrel (September 1798) provided for universal and mandatory conscription.

state; finally, there was still in France some disinterested enthusiasm, on which the public welfare might have been founded.

From 1793 to the beginning of 1795, England and her allies would have dishonored themselves in treating with France: what would have been said of the august ambassadors of a free nation, returning to London after having received the embrace of Marat or Robespierre? But when once the intention of establishing a regular government was manifested, no means should have been neglected to interrupt the warlike education of the French.

England, in 1797, eighteen months after the installation of the Directory, sent negotiators to Lille; but the successes of the army of Italy had inspired the chiefs of the Republic with arrogance: the Directors were already old in power, and thought themselves firmly seated in it. All governments at their commencement wish for peace: men should know how to profit by this circumstance with ability; in politics as in war, there are critical moments which we should hasten to seize. But opinion in England was heated by Burke, who, by foretelling too truly the miseries of the Revolution, had acquired a great ascendant over his countrymen. At the time of the negotiation of Lille, he wrote some letters *on a regicide peace* which revived the public indignation against France.[6] Mr. Pitt, however, had himself bestowed some praises on the constitution of 1795; and besides, if the political system adopted by France, whatever it might be, no longer endangered the security of other countries, what more could be required?

The passions of the emigrants, to which the English ministers always lent themselves too much, often led them into mistakes in their judgments upon the affairs of France. They thought to effect a powerful diversion by transporting the royalists to Quiberon:[7] they occasioned only a scene of blood, the horror of which could not be lessened by the most coura-

---

6. See Burke, *Select Works of Edmund Burke*, vol. 3: *Letters on a Regicide Peace*. Lord Malmesbury opened negotiations with France in October 1796, but they failed because England, which had territorial claims overseas (the Cap and Ceylon), was prepared only to recognize the borders of France from 1792. A second unsuccessful attempt was made in July 1797.

7. In June 1795.

geous efforts of the English squadron. The unfortunate French gentlemen, who had vainly flattered themselves with finding in Brittany a great party ready to take up arms in their cause, were abandoned in an instant. General Lemoine, the commander of the French army, has related to me with admiration the reiterated attempts of the English seamen to approach the shore and receive in their boats the emigrants enclosed on every side and endeavoring by swimming to regain the hospitable ships of England. But the English ministers, and Mr. Pitt at their head, in constantly endeavoring to promote the triumph of the pure royalists in France, paid no regard to the opinion of the country; and from this mistake arose the obstacles which they so long met with in their political combinations. The English administration, more than any other government in Europe, should have understood the history of the Revolution in France, so similar to that of England; but it would appear as if the very resemblance had been a reason for their wishing to show themselves so much the more hostile to it.

Two Singular Predictions Drawn from the History of the Revolution, by M. Necker.

M. Necker never published a political book without braving some danger, either to his fortune or to himself. The circumstances in which he published his history of the Revolution[1] might have exposed him to such a variety of fatal accidents that I made many efforts to restrain him from that proceeding. He was put upon the list of emigrants, that is to say, subjected to the penalty of death, according to the French laws; and it was already rumored on every side that the Directory intended to invade Switzerland. Nevertheless, he published, about the end of 1796, a work on the Revolution in four volumes, in which he advanced the boldest truths. No other precaution was taken in it than that of placing himself at the distance of posterity, in order to decide upon men and things. To this history full of warmth, of sarcasm, and of reasoning, he joined an analysis of the principal free constitutions of Europe; and in reading this book, where every question is sifted to the bottom, we should be discouraged from writing if we did not console ourselves with the reflection that eighteen additional years, and an individual mode of thinking, may still add some ideas to the same system.

Two very extraordinary predictions ought to be distinguished in that work; the one announces the struggle of the Directory with the Representative Body, which occurred some time afterward and was occasioned, as M. Necker had foretold, by the want of the constitutional prerogatives which were withheld from the executive power.

---

1. For more information on the reaction to Necker's *De la Révolution française*, see Grange, *Les idées de Necker*, 400–494.

"The essential arrangement in the republican constitution given to France in 1795," said he,

the arrangement of prime importance, and which may bring order or freedom into danger, is the complete and absolute separation of the two principal authorities; the one, that which enacts the laws, the other, that which directs and superintends their execution. Every kind of power has been united and confounded in the monstrous organization of the National Convention; and now by another extreme, less dangerous without doubt, not one of the connections between the two authorities, which the welfare of the state requires, has been preserved. Once again they have resorted to written maxims; and upon the faith of a small number of political theorists, a belief has been adopted that it is impossible to establish too strong a barrier between the legislative power and the executive. Let us first recollect that the lessons drawn from example give us a very different result. We know no republic in which the two powers, of which I have just spoken, were not to a certain extent blended together; and ancient times, as well as modern, present us with the same picture. Sometimes a senate, the depository of the executive authority, proposes the laws to a more numerous council, or to the mass of the citizens at large; and sometimes, likewise, this senate, exercising in an inverse direction its right of participation in the legislative power, suspends or reverses the decrees of the many. Upon the same principles is founded the free government of England, where the monarch concurs in the laws which are enacted, both by his own assent and by the presence of his ministers in the two houses of Parliament. Last of all, America has given a modified right of rejection to the President of the Congress, to that head of the state whom she has invested with executive authority; and she has at the same time admitted one of the two divisions of the legislative body to a share of this prerogative.

The republican constitution of France is the first model of a total separation between the two supreme powers, or rather the first attempt at such a separation.

The executive authority will always act alone, and without any habitual inspection on the part of the legislative authority; and in return no assent of the executive authority will be requisite to the complete enactment of laws. Finally, the two powers will have no political tie except hortatory addresses, nor any channel of communication except envoys ordinary and extraordinary.

Must not so new an organization bring inconveniences along with it? Must it not, at some future day, expose the kingdom to great danger? Let us suppose that the choice of five directors should fall, in whole or in part, upon men of a feeble or wavering character; what consideration will they be able to preserve when they appear quite separate from the legislative body, and mere obedient machines?

But if, on the contrary, the five who are chosen directors should be men of vigor, bold, enterprising, and completely united with one another, the moment might arrive when we should perhaps regret the isolation of these executive chiefs, when we should wish that the constitution had put them under the necessity of acting in presence of, or in concert with, a branch of the legislative body. The moment might perhaps arrive when we should repent of having left by the constitution itself an open field to the first suggestions of their ambition, to the first attempts of their despotism.

These bold and enterprising Directors were found; and as they were not allowed to dissolve the legislative body, they employed grenadiers,[2] instead of the legal right which the constitution should have given them. Nothing as yet presaged this crisis when M. Necker foretold it; but what is more astonishing is that he foresaw the military tyranny which was to result from the very crisis which he announced in 1796.

In another part of his work, M. Necker renders political philosophy popular by constantly mingling eloquence with reasoning. He feigns a speech of St. Louis, addressed to the French nation and truly admirable; it should be read entire, for there is a charm and a sentiment in every word. The principal object, however, of this fiction is to represent a prince, who in his illustrious life showed himself capable of a heroic devotion, declaring to the nation which had long been subjected to his ancestors that he wishes not to interfere by civil war with the efforts which they are now

2. Allusion to the coup d'état of 18 Fructidor (September 4, 1797). In 1797 Letourneur retired from the Directory and was succeeded by Barthélemy (1747–1830), a career diplomat, who allied himself with Carnot, Barras, Reubell, and La Révellière-Lépeaux and then sought help from the armies, fearing that they were losing power in the country. They called on Napoléon Bonaparte to send a general to command troops guarding the legislature at the Tuileries on 18 Fructidor, Year V. Barthélemy and Carnot were arrested and replaced by Merlin de Douai and Nicholas-Louis François de Neufchâteau. Barthélemy managed to flee to London and returned later to France after 18 Brumaire.

making to obtain liberty, even though that liberty should be republican, but that at the moment when circumstances would deceive their hopes and deliver them to despotism, he would come to aid his ancient subjects in freeing themselves from the oppression of a tyrant.

What a piercing view into futurity, and into the connection of causes and effects, must he have had, who, twenty years ago, under the Directory, formed such a conjecture!

CHAPTER XXIII

Of the Army of Italy.

The two great armies of the republic, those of the Rhine and of Italy, were almost constantly victorious, until the treaty of Campo Formio,[1] which for a short time suspended the long Continental war. The army of the Rhine, of which Moreau was General, had preserved all the republican simplicity; the army of Italy, commanded by General Bonaparte, dazzled by its conquests but was every day deviating further from the patriotic spirit which till then had animated the French armies. Personal interest was taking the place of a patriotic spirit, and attachment to one man was prevailing over a devotion to liberty. The generals of the army of Italy, likewise, sought ere long to enrich themselves, thus proportionally diminishing that enthusiasm for austere principles without which a free state cannot exist.

General Bernadotte,[2] of whom I shall have occasion to speak later, came with a division of the army of the Rhine to join the army of Italy. There was a sort of contrast between the noble poverty of the one and the irregular riches of the other: they resembled only in bravery. The army of Italy was the army of Bonaparte, that of the Rhine[3] was the army of the

---

1. The Treaty of Campo Formio was signed on October 17, 1797 (26 Vendémiaire, Year VI of the French Republic), by France and Austria. It marked the victory of Napoléon's campaigns in Italy, although France had to surrender the Venetian republic.

2. Bernadotte (1763–1844) served as minister of war in 1799 and soon after that became the brother-in-law of Napoléon, who promoted him to the rank of marshal. In 1810 Bernadotte was elected hereditary prince of Sweden; three years later, he joined the coalition against Napoléon.

3. There were, in fact, two armies of the Rhine: the army of Sambre-et-Meuse (with republican leanings) and the army of Rhin-et-Moselle (with royalist leanings). As Godechot pointed out (notes to *Considerations*, 648, n. 173), the army of Italy also had strong republican leanings.

French republic. Yet nothing was so brilliant as the rapid conquest of Italy. Doubtless, the desire which the enlightened Italians have always felt to unite themselves into one state, and thus to possess so much national strength as to have nothing either to fear or to hope from strangers, contributed much to favor the progress of General Bonaparte. It was with the cry of *Italy forever* that he passed the bridge of Lodi; and it was to the hope of independence that he owed his reception among the Italians. But the victories which subjected to France countries beyond her natural limits, far from favoring liberty, exposed it to the danger of military government.

Bonaparte was already much talked of in Paris; the superiority of his capacity in business, joined to the splendor of his talents as a General, gave to his name an importance which no individual had ever acquired from the commencement of the Revolution. But although in his proclamations he spoke incessantly of the republic, attentive men perceived that it was in his eyes a mean, and not an end. It was in this same light that he viewed all things and all men. A rumor prevailed that he meant to make himself King of Lombardy. One day I met General Augereau,[4] who had just returned from Italy, and who was cited, I believe then with reason, as a zealous republican. I asked him whether it was true that General Bonaparte was thinking of becoming a king. "No, assuredly," replied he; "he is a young man of too good principles for that." This singular answer was in exact conformity with the ideas of the moment. The sincere republicans would have regarded it as a degradation for a man, however distinguished he might be, to wish to turn the Revolution to his personal advantage. Why had not this sentiment more force and longer duration among Frenchmen!

Bonaparte was stopped in his march to Rome by signing the peace of Tolentino;[5] and it was then that he obtained the surrender[6] of the superb monuments of the arts which we have long seen collected in the Museum of Paris. The true abode of these masterpieces was, without doubt, Italy,

4. Augereau (1757–1816) was sent by Napoléon to stage the coup d'état on 18 Fructidor. He was promoted to the rank of marshal in 1804.

5. On February 19, 1797.

6. By the Holy See.

and the imagination regretted their loss; but of all her illustrious prisoners it was upon these that France justly set the highest value.

General Bonaparte wrote to the Directory that he had made the surrender of these monuments one of the conditions of the peace with the Pope. *I have particularly insisted,* said he, *on the busts of Junius and Marcus Brutus, which I wish to send to Paris before the rest.* Bonaparte, who afterward removed these busts from the hall of the legislative body, might have spared them the trouble of the journey.

CHAPTER XXIV

Of the Introduction of Military Government into France by the Occurrences of the 18th of Fructidor.

No epoch of the Revolution was more disastrous than that which substituted military rule for the well-founded hope of a representative government. I am, however, anticipating events; for the sway of a military chief was not as yet proclaimed when the Directory sent grenadiers to the two Chambers: but this tyrannical proceeding, of which the soldiers were the instruments, prepared the way for the revolution that was effected two years afterward by Bonaparte himself, when it appeared not at all strange that a military chief should have recourse to a measure in which magistrates had indulged themselves.

The Directors, however, entertained no apprehensions of the inevitable consequences of the resolution which they adopted. Their situation was dangerous; they had, as I have endeavored to show, too much arbitrary power and too little legal power. They had been invested with all the means of persecution which excite hatred, but with none of the constitutional rights which would have enabled them to defend themselves. At the moment when the second third of the Chambers was renewed by the election of 1797, the public mind became a second time impatient to remove the members of the Conventions[1] from the administration; but a second time also, instead of waiting a year, during which the majority of the Directory would have been changed and the last third of the Chambers renewed, the French vivacity urged the enemies of the government to endeavor to overturn it without delay. The opposition to the Directory

1. Former members of the Convention.

was not at first formed by pure royalists; but they gradually mingled themselves with it. Besides, in civil discord, men always end by adopting the opinions of which they are accused; and the party which attacked the Directory was thus powerfully impelled to a counter-revolution.

In every quarter a spirit of intolerable reaction appeared: at Lyons, at Marseilles, assassinations took place: the victims, it is true, were men covered with guilt; still it was assassination. The journals, in their daily proclamations of vengeance, armed themselves with calumny and announced openly a counter-revolution. In the interior, as abroad, there were two projects; one party was resolved to bring back the old regime, and General Pichegru[2] was one of their principal instruments.

The Directory, as preserver of its own political existence, had strong reasons for putting itself in a state of defense; but how could it? The defects in the constitution which M. Necker had so well pointed out rendered it very difficult for the government to make a legal resistance to the attacks of the councils. The Council of Ancients was inclined to defend the Directors, only because it occupied, though very imperfectly, the place of a chamber of peers; but as the deputies of this council were not named for life, they were afraid of rendering themselves unpopular by supporting magistrates whom the public opinion rejected. If the government had possessed the right of dissolving the Five Hundred, the mere threat of exerting this prerogative would have restrained them within bounds. In short, if the executive power had been able to oppose even a suspending *veto* to the decrees of the councils, it would have been satisfied with the means with which the law had armed it for its protection. But these very magistrates, whose authority was so limited, had great power as a revolutionary faction; and they were not scrupulous enough to confine themselves to the rules of constitutional warfare when, to get rid of their opponents, they needed only to have recourse to force. The personal interest of some individuals was seen on this occasion, as it always will be, to overturn the

---

2. General Pichegru (1761–1804) commanded the army of Rhin-et-Moselle in 1795–96 and was later elected to the Council of Five Hundred. He was arrested because of his collaboration with the royalist émigrés and the Austrians but managed to escape to London. In 1804 he returned to France and was involved in a coup against Napoléon. He was arrested and later died in prison.

barriers of the law, if these barriers are not constructed in such a way as to maintain themselves.[3]

Two directors, Barthélemy and Carnot, were on the side of the representative councils. Carnot certainly was not suspected of desiring the restoration of the old regime, but he was unwilling (and the reluctance does him honor) to adopt illegal means in order to repel the attack of the legislative power. The majority of the Directory, Reubell, Barras, and La Réveillère, hesitated some time between two auxiliaries who were equally at their disposal—the Jacobins and the army. They justly feared the former; the terrorists were still a dangerous weapon, which might overthrow him who should venture to make use of it. The Directors believed, therefore, that it was better to obtain addresses from the armies, and to request General Bonaparte, who of all the commanders in chief declared himself then most strongly against the councils, to send one of his generals of brigade to Paris to await the orders of the Directory. Bonaparte chose General Augereau, a man very decided in action and not very capable of reasoning—two qualities which rendered him an excellent instrument of despotism, provided this despotism assumed the name of revolution.

By a singular contrast, the royalists in the two councils appealed to republican principles, to the liberty of the press, to the liberty of suffrages, to every liberty, in short, and particularly to the liberty of subverting the Directory. The popular party, on the contrary, grounded itself always on circumstances and defended the revolutionary measures which served as a momentary security to the government. The republicans found themselves constrained to disavow their own principles because they were turned against themselves; and the royalists borrowed the weapons of the republicans to attack the republic. This strange combination of arms exchanged in the combat has been exhibited in other circumstances. Every minority invokes justice, and justice is liberty. A party can be judged of only by the doctrine which it professes when it is the strongest.

3. The complex political situation in 1796–97 stimulated political reflection in France. Benjamin Constant published *De la force du gouvernement actuel et de la necessité de s'y rallier* (1797), in which he called on the government's supporters to rally around the republic in order to defend it. At the same time, Madame de Staël began writing *Des Circonstances actuelles qui peuvent terminer la Révolution et des principes qui doivent fonder la république en France.*

Nevertheless, when the Directory took the fatal resolution of sending the grenadiers to seize the legislators in their seats, it had no longer need of the mischief which it resolved to do. The change of ministry, and the addresses of the armies, were sufficient to restrain the royalists; and the Directory ruined itself by pushing its triumph too far. For it was so contrary to the spirit of a republic to employ the soldiery against the representatives of the people that the state could not fail to be destroyed in the very attempt to save it by such means. On the evening of the fatal day everyone knew that a great blow was on the point of being struck; for in France men conspire in the public streets, or rather they do not conspire, but excite one another, so that he who can listen to what is said will know beforehand what is about to be done.

On the night before the entrance of General Augereau into the councils, the alarm was such that the greater number of persons of note left their houses from the fear of being arrested in them. One of my friends found an asylum for me in a small chamber which looked upon the bridge of Louis XVI. I there spent the night in beholding the preparations for the awful scene which was to take place in a few hours; none but soldiers appeared in the streets; all the citizens remained in their homes. The cannons, which were brought to surround the palace where the legislative body assembled, were rolling along the pavements; but, except their noise, all was silence. No hostile assemblage was seen anywhere, nor was it known against whom all this apparatus was directed. Liberty was the only power vanquished in that fatal struggle; it might have been said that she was seen to fly, like a wandering spirit, at the approach of the day which was to shine upon her destruction.

In the morning it was known that General Augereau had conducted his battalions into the Council of the Five Hundred, that he had arrested several of the deputies who were found there assembled in a committee, and that General Pichegru was president at the time. Astonishment was excited by the little respect which the soldiers showed for a general who had so often led them to victory; but he had been successfully characterized as a counterrevolutionary, a name which, when the public opinion is free, exercises in France a kind of magical power. Besides, Pichegru had no means of producing an effect on the imagination; he was a man of good manners, but without striking expression either in his features or in his words; the recollection of his victories did not hover around him, for there was nothing in his appearance that announced them. It has often been said that he was guided in war by the counsels of another: I know not what truth there may have been in this, but it is at least credible; for his look and conversation were so dull that they suggested no idea of his being fit for becoming the leader of any enterprise. Nevertheless, his courage and political perseverance, as well as his misfortunes, have since awakened a deserved interest in his fate.

Some members of the Council of the Ancients, with the intrepid and generous old man Dupont de Nemours and the respectable Barbé-Marbois[4] at their head, went on foot to the meeting hall and, after having ascertained that the door was shut, they returned in the same way, passing between aligned soldiers; while the people, who were looking on, seemed scarcely to be aware that it was the cause of their representatives, oppressed by an armed force, which was at stake. The fear of a counter-revolution had unfortunately disorganized the public mind: no one knew where to find the cause of liberty between those who disgraced her and those who were accused of hating her. The most honorable men, Barbé-Marbois, Tronçon-Ducoudray,[5] Camille Jordan,[6] etc., were condemned

4. François Barbé-Marbois (1745–1837), former *intendant* of Guadeloupe and Martinique, was elected to the Council of the Ancients, where he opposed the exclusion of nobles and the relatives of émigrés from public life. He was deported after 18 Fructidor, returned to France three years later, and became a senator in 1802. In 1803 he negotiated the Louisiana Purchase treaty by which Louisiana was sold to the United States. He also served as the president of the treasury until 1806. In 1814 Louis XVIII made Barbé-Marbois a peer of France.

5. Tronson Du Coudray (1750–98), a lawyer, was elected to the Council of Five Hundred and was deported to Guyana, where he died shortly thereafter.

6. Camille Jordan (1771–1821), a member of the Council of Five Hundred, was deported after 18 Fructidor and returned to France three years later. During the Bourbon Restoration, he allied himself with the French Doctrinaires and gained recognition as a gifted orator. Jordan's parliamentary discourses are difficult to find today. A collection of his speeches was published after his death, accompanied by a eulogy by Ballanche and a letter by Baron de Gérando. Jordan's analysis of the parliamentary session of 1817, "La Session de 1817, aux habitans de l'Ain et du Rhône," triggered a long response from Bonald, who criticized Jordan's assessment in a long article published in *Le Conservateur*.

to deportation beyond the sea.[7] Atrocious measures followed this first violation of all justice. The public debt was diminished by two-thirds,[8] and this operation was distinguished by the phrase *la mobiliser*, so dexterous are the French at inventing terms with a gentle sound for the harshest proceedings. The priests and the nobles were again proscribed with unrelenting barbarity. The liberty of the press was abolished as irreconcilable with the exercise of arbitrary power.[9] The invasion of Switzerland,[10] the mad project of a descent upon England, removed every hope of peace with Europe. The revolutionary spirit was conjured up, but it reappeared without the enthusiasm which once animated it; and, as the civil authority did not rest upon justice, upon magnanimity, in short, upon any of the great qualities which ought to characterize it, the ardor of patriotism turned itself toward military glory, which then at least satisfied the imagination.

7. Forty-five people were deported overseas.

8. Decree of September 10, 1797 (24 Fructidor).

9. Application of Articles 353 and 355 of the Constitution of Year III (1795), which provided for a one-year suspension of freedom of the press.

10. Beginning with January 26, 1798.

CHAPTER XXV

Private Anecdotes.

It is painful to speak of oneself, at a time especially when the most important narratives alone demand the attention of readers. Yet I cannot abstain from refuting an accusation which is injurious to me. The journals whose office it was in 1797 to insult all the friends of liberty have pretended that, from a predilection for a republic, I approved of the affair of the 18th of Fructidor. I certainly would not have counseled, had I been called upon to give advice, the establishment of a republic in France; but when it once existed, I was not of the opinion that it ought to be overturned.[1] Republican government, considered abstractedly and without reference to a great state, merits the respect which it has ever inspired; the Revolution of the 18th of Fructidor, on the contrary, must always excite horror, both by the tyrannical principles from which it proceeded and by the frightful results which were its necessary consequence. Among the individuals of whom the Directory was composed, I knew only Barras; and, far from having the slightest influence with the others, though they could not be ignorant of my fond love of liberty, they were so dissatisfied with my attachment to the proscribed that they gave orders upon the frontiers of Switzerland, at Versoix near Coppet, to arrest me and conduct me to prison at Paris; on account, said they, of my efforts to obtain the restoration of the emigrants. Barras defended me with warmth and generosity; and it was he who some time afterward obtained permission for me to return to France. The gratitude which I owed him kept up the relations of society between us.

1. Benjamin Constant held a similar view on this topic.

M. de Talleyrand[2] had returned from America a year before the 18th of Fructidor. The honest people wanted, in general, peace with Europe, which was at that time disposed to negotiate; and it was thought that M. de Talleyrand could not but be, what he has been always since found, a very able negotiator. The friends of liberty wished that the Directory should strengthen itself by constitutional measures, and that with this view they should choose ministers capable of supporting the government. M. de Talleyrand seemed then the best possible choice for the department of foreign affairs, and he much wished to accept it. I served him effectually in this respect by procuring for him an introduction to Barras, through one of my friends, and by strongly recommending him. M. de Talleyrand needed help to arrive at power; but, once there, he required not the assistance of others to maintain him in it. His appointment is the only role I had in the crisis which preceded the 18th of Fructidor, and by doing that I thought I could prevent that crisis; for there was reason to hope that M. de Talleyrand might effect a reconciliation between the two parties. Since that time I have not had the slightest connection with the various aspects of his political career.

After the 18th of Fructidor the proscription extended itself on every side; and the nation, which under the Reign of Terror had already lost the most respectable men, saw itself every day deprived of some of those who remained. Dupont de Nemours, the most chivalrous champion of liberty in France, but who could not recognize it in the dispersion of the representatives of the people by an armed force, was on the point of being proscribed. I was informed of his danger, and I immediately sent in quest of Chenier the poet,[3] who, two years before, had, at my desire, made the speech to which M. de Talleyrand was indebted for his recall. Chenier, in

2. Charles Maurice de Talleyrand-Périgord, Prince de Benevente (1754–1838), served as minister of foreign affairs under both the First Empire and the First Restoration and briefly as prime minister of France in 1815. He became one of the most versatile and influential European diplomats of his time. A close friend (and lover) of Madame de Staël, he went to America in 1794, returning to France two years later. For more information, see Waresquiel, *Talleyrand, le prince immobile;* and Cooper, *Talleyrand.*

3. Marie-Joseph Chénier (1764–1811), writer, elected to the Convention and later to the Council of Five Hundred.

spite of all that may be said against his life, was susceptible of emotion; for he had talent, and dramatic talent. He was moved by the picture of the situation of Dupont de Nemours and his family, and ran to the tribune, where he succeeded in saving him by making him pass for a man of eighty years of age, though he was scarcely sixty. This artifice was not agreeable to the pleasing Dupont de Nemours, who, so far as the mind was concerned, had always strong claims to youth.

Chenier was a man at once violent and timid; full of prejudices, though an enthusiastic admirer of philosophy; inaccessible to reasoning when it combated his passions, which he reverenced as his household gods. He walked up and down the chamber with great strides; answered without having listened; grew pale and trembled with passion when a word disagreeable to him struck his ear by itself, for want of patience to hear the remainder of the phrase. He was nevertheless a man of talent and imagination; but so much under the influence of self-love that he was astonished at what he was, instead of laboring to attain a higher perfection.

Every day increased the alarm of the good. An observation of a general, who accused me publicly of pity for the conspirators, induced me to quit Paris and withdraw to the country; for, in political conjunctures, pity is called treason. I went therefore to the house of a friend, where, by a singular chance, I met one of the most illustrious and bravest royalists of La Vendée, the Prince de la Trémouille,[4] who, though a price was set upon his head, had come with the hope of turning circumstances to the advantage of his cause. I wanted to give him asylum, which he needed more than I did. He refused my offer and proposed to leave France, since all hope of a counter-revolution was lost. We were justly surprised that the same blast should have reached us both, since our preceding situations had been very different.

I returned to Paris: every day made us tremble for some new victims who were involved in the general persecution that was carried on against emigrants and priests. The Marquis d'Ambert, who had been Bernadotte's

---

4. Prince Louis de la Trémouille was the representative of Louis XVIII in Paris. In the summer of 1797, he and other royalists were preparing a coup d'état against the Directory but their plans never came to fruition.

colonel previous to the Revolution, was taken and brought before a military commission—a terrible tribunal, the existence of which, outside of the army, is sufficient to prove the tyranny of the government. General Bernadotte sought the Directors and asked of them, as the sole reward of all his services, the pardon of his colonel; they were inflexible; they gave the name of justice to an equal distribution of misery.

Two days after the punishment of M. d'Ambert, the brother of M. de Norvins de Monbreton,[5] whom I had known in Switzerland during his emigration, entered my chamber at ten o'clock in the morning. He told me, with great agitation, that his brother was arrested and that the military commission was assembled to sentence him to death; he asked me whether I could find any means of saving him. How could I flatter myself with the hope of obtaining a favor from the Directory when the prayers of General Bernadotte had been fruitless; and yet, how could I resolve to make no attempt in behalf of a man with whom I was acquainted, and who in two hours would be shot if nobody came to his assistance? I suddenly recollected that I had seen, at the house of Barras, a General Lemoine, the same whom I have mentioned on the occasion of the Quiberon expedition, and that he had appeared to take pleasure in conversing with me. This General commanded the division of Paris and had a right to suspend the judgments of the military commission established in that city. I thanked Heaven for the idea, and instantly set out with the brother of the unfortunate Norvins: we entered together the chamber of the General, who was very much surprised to see me. He began by making apologies to me for his morning toilette and his apartment; in short, I was unable to prevent him from continually returning to the language of politeness, although I implored him not to waste an instant on it, for that instant might be irrecoverable. I hastened to tell him the reason of my visit; and, at first, he abruptly refused me. My heart throbbed at the sight of that brother who might think that I was not employing the words best fitted to obtain what I asked. I began my solicitations afresh, collecting myself, that I might assemble

---

5. Jacques Marquet, Baron of Montbreton de Norvins (1769–1854), emigrated during the Revolution and returned to France in 1797. In 1810 Napoléon appointed him director of the police in the Roman states. During the Restoration, he published a four-volume *Histoire de Napoléon* (1827–28).

all my strength; I was afraid of saying too much or too little; of losing the fatal hour, after which all would be over; or of neglecting an argument which might be successful. I looked by turns at the clock and at the General, to see which of the two powers, his soul or time, approached the term most quickly. Twice the General took the pen to sign the reprieve, and twice the fear of committing himself restrained him; at last he was unable to refuse us, and may Heaven shower blessings on him for his compliance. He delivered the redeeming paper, and M. de Monbreton ran to the tribunal, where he learned that his brother had already acknowledged everything; but the reprieve broke up the meeting, and innocence survived.

It is the duty of us women at all times to aid individuals accused of political opinions of any kind whatsoever; for what are opinions in times of faction? Can we be certain that such and such events, such and such a situation, would not have changed our own views? And, if we except a few invariable sentiments, who knows how difference of situation might have acted on us?

CHAPTER XXVI

Treaty of Campo Formio in 1797.
Arrival of General Bonaparte at Paris.

The Directory was disinclined to peace, not that it wished to extend the French dominions beyond the Rhine and the Alps, but because it thought the war useful for the propagation of the republican system. Its plan was to surround France with a belt of republics, like those of Holland, Switzerland, Piedmont,[1] Lombardy, and Genoa. Everywhere it established a directory, two councils, a constitution; in short, similar in every respect to that of France.[2] It is one of the great failings of the French, and a consequence of their social habits, that they imitate one another and wish to be imitated by everybody. They take natural varieties in each man's, or even each nation's, mode of thinking for a spirit of hostility against themselves.

General Bonaparte was assuredly less serious and less sincere than the Directory in the love of republicanism; but he had much more sagacity in appreciating circumstances. He foresaw that peace would be popular in France, because the passions were subsiding into tranquillity and the people were becoming weary of sacrifices; he therefore signed the treaty of Campo Formio with Austria. But this treaty contained the surrender of the Venetian Republic; and it is not easy to conceive how he succeeded in prevailing upon the Directory, which yet was in some respects republican, to commit the greatest possible blow according to its own principles. From the date of this proceeding, not less arbitrary than the partition of Poland, there no longer existed in the government of France the slightest

---

1. In reality, there was no republic of Piedmont.
2. See J. Godechot, *La Grande Nation*, chap. xii, 331–57.

respect for any political doctrine, and the reign of one man began when the dominion of principle ended.

Bonaparte made himself remarkable by his character and capacity as much as by his victories, and the imagination of the French was beginning to attach itself warmly to him. His proclamations to the Cisalpine and Ligurian Republics were quoted. In the one this phrase was remarked: *You were divided, and bent down by tyranny; you were not in a situation to conquer liberty.* In the other, *True conquests, the only conquests which cost no regret, are those which we make from ignorance.* In his style there reigned a spirit of moderation and dignity, which formed a contrast with the revolutionary bitterness of the civil leaders of France. The warrior then spoke like a magistrate, while magistrates expressed themselves with military violence. In his army, General Bonaparte did not enforce the laws against emigrants. He was said to be much attached to his wife, whose character was full of gentleness; it was asserted that he was feelingly alive to the beauties of Ossian; people took delight in ascribing to him all the generous qualities which place his extraordinary talents in a beautiful light. Besides, the nation was so weary of oppressors who borrowed the name of liberty, and of oppressed persons who regretted the loss of arbitrary power, that admiration did not know what to attach itself to, and Bonaparte seemed to unite all that could seduce it.

It was with this sentiment, at least, that I saw him for the first time at Paris.[3] I could not find words to reply to him when he came to me to say that he had sought my father at Coppet,[4] and that he regretted having passed into Switzerland without seeing him. But, when I was a little recovered from the confusion of admiration, a strongly marked sentiment of fear succeeded. Bonaparte, at that time, had no power; he was even

---

3. The first meeting occurred on December 6, 1797, in Talleyrand's house. On the other meetings between Madame de Staël and Napoléon, see Godechot's note to his 1983 French edition of *Considérations* (endnote 203, 650–51). Both Simone Balayé and Jacques Godechot reported rumors about earlier letters sent by Madame de Staël to Napoléon in which she allegedly courted the favor of the future emperor. Napoléon supposedly refused to answer. On this issue, also see Gautier, *Madame de Staël et Napoléon*.

4. It is unlikely that Napoléon stopped at Coppet when he passed through Switzerland in November 1797.

believed to be not a little threatened by the defiant suspicions of the Directory; so that the fear which he inspired was caused only by the singular effect of his person upon nearly all who approached him. I had seen men highly worthy of esteem; I had likewise seen monsters of ferocity: there was nothing in the effect which Bonaparte produced on me that could bring back to my recollection either the one or the other. I soon perceived, in the different opportunities which I had of meeting him during his stay at Paris, that his character could not be defined by the words which we commonly use; he was neither good, nor violent, nor gentle, nor cruel, after the manner of individuals of whom we have any knowledge. Such a being had no fellow, and therefore could neither feel nor excite sympathy: he was more or less than man. His cast of character, his spirit, his language, were stamped with the imprint of an unknown nature—an additional advantage, as we have elsewhere observed, for the subjugation of Frenchmen.

Far from recovering my confidence by seeing Bonaparte more frequently, he constantly intimidated me more and more. I had a confused feeling that no emotion of the heart could act upon him. He regards a human being as an action or a thing, not as a fellow-creature. He does not hate more than he loves; for him nothing exists but himself; all other creatures are ciphers. The force of his will consists in the impossibility of disturbing the calculations of his egoism; he is an able chess-player, and the human race is the opponent to whom he proposes to give checkmate. His successes depend as much on the qualities in which he is deficient as on the talents which he possesses. Neither pity, nor allurement, nor religion, nor attachment to any idea whatsoever could turn him aside from his principal direction. He is for his self-interest what the just man should be for virtue; if the end were good, his perseverance would be noble.

Every time that I heard him speak, I was struck with his superiority; yet it had no similitude to that of men instructed and cultivated by study or society, such as those of whom France and England can furnish examples. But his discourse indicated a fine perception of circumstances, such as the hunter has of his prey. Sometimes he related the political and military events of his life in a very interesting manner; he had even somewhat of Italian imagination in narratives which allowed of gaiety. Yet nothing could triumph over my invincible aversion for what I perceived in him. I felt in his soul a cold sharp-edged sword, which froze the wound that it inflicted; I perceived in his mind a profound irony, from which nothing great or beautiful, not even his own glory, could escape; for he despised the nation whose votes he wished, and no spark of enthusiasm was mingled with his desire of astonishing the human race.

It was in the interval between the return of Bonaparte and his departure for Egypt, that is to say, toward the end of 1797, that I saw him several times at Paris; and never could I dissipate the difficulty of breathing which I experienced in his presence. I was one day at table between him and the Abbé Sieyès—a singular situation, if I had been able to foresee what afterward happened. I examined the figure of Bonaparte with attention; but whenever he discovered that my looks were fixed upon him, he had the art of taking away all expression from his eyes, as if they had been turned into marble. His countenance was then immovable, except a vague smile which his lips assumed at random, to mislead anyone who might wish to observe the external signs of what was passing within.

The Abbé Sieyès conversed during dinner unaffectedly and fluently, as suited a mind of his strength. He expressed himself concerning my father with a sincere esteem. *He is the only man,* said he, *who has ever united the most perfect precision in the calculations of a great financier to the imagination of a poet.* This eulogium pleased me, because it characterized him. Bonaparte, who heard it, also said some obliging things concerning my father and me, but like a man who takes no interest in individuals whom he cannot make use of in the accomplishment of his own ends.

His figure, at that time thin and pale, was rather agreeable; he has since grown fat, which does not become him; for we can scarcely tolerate a character which inflicts so many sufferings on others if we do not believe it to be a torment to the person himself. As his stature is short, and his waist very long, he appeared to much more advantage on horseback than on foot. In every respect it is war, and only war, which suits him. His manners in society are constrained, without timidity; he has an air of vulgarity when he is at his ease, and of disdain when he is not: disdain suits him best, and accordingly he indulges in it without scruple.

By a natural vocation to the princely situation, he already addressed trifling questions to all who were presented to him. Are you married? was his question to one of the guests. How many children do you have? said he to another. How long is it since you arrived? When do you set out? And other interrogations of a similar kind, which establish the superiority of him who puts them over those who submit to be thus questioned. He already took delight in the art of embarrassing by saying disagreeable things—an art which he has since reduced into a system, as he has every other mode of subjugating men by degrading them. At this epoch, however, he had a desire to please, for he confined to his own thoughts the project of overturning the Directory and substituting himself in its stead; but in spite of this desire, one would have said that, unlike the prophet, he cursed involuntarily, though he intended to bless.

I saw him one day approach a French lady distinguished for her beauty, her wit, and the ardor of her opinions. He placed himself straight before her, like the stiffest of the German generals, and said to her, "*Madam, I don't like women to meddle with politics.*" "*You are right, General,*" replied she; "*but in a country where they lose their heads, it is natural for them to desire to know the reason.*" Bonaparte made no answer. He is a man who is calmed by an effective resistance; those who have borne his despotism deserve to be accused as much as he himself.

The Directory gave General Bonaparte a solemn reception,[5] which in several respects should be considered as one of the most important epochs in the history of the Revolution. The court of the palace of the Luxembourg was chosen for this ceremony. No hall would have been large enough to contain the multitude which it attracted: all the windows, and all the roofs, were crowded with spectators. The five Directors, in Roman costume, were seated on a platform at the further end of the court, and near them the deputies of the two councils, the tribunals, and the institute. Had this spectacle occurred before the subjugation of the national representation to military power on the 18th of Fructidor, it would have exhibited an air of grandeur: patriotic tunes were played by an excellent band; banners served as a canopy to the Directors, and these banners brought back the recollection of great victories.

Bonaparte arrived, dressed very simply, followed by his aides-de-camp,

5. On December 10, 1797.

all taller than himself, but nearly bent by the respect which they displayed to him. In the presence of the entire French elite, the victorious General was covered with applauses: he was the hope of everyone: republicans, royalists, all saw the present or the future in the support of his powerful hand. Alas! Of the young men who then cried *Long live Bonaparte,* how many has his insatiable ambition left alive?

M. de Talleyrand, in presenting Bonaparte to the Directory, called him *the liberator of Italy and the pacificator of the Continent.* He assured them that *General Bonaparte detested luxury and splendor, the miserable ambition of vulgar souls, and that he loved the poems of Ossian, particularly because they detach us from the earth.* The earth would have required nothing better, I think, than to let him detach himself from its concerns. Bonaparte himself then spoke with a sort of affected negligence, as if he had wished to intimate that he bore little love to the government under which he was called to serve.

He said that for twenty centuries royalty and feudality had governed the world, and that the peace which he had just concluded was the era of republican government. *When the happiness of the French,* said he, *shall be established upon better organical laws, all Europe will be free.* I know not whether by the organical laws of freedom he meant the establishment of his absolute power. However that might be, Barras, at that time his friend and president of the Directory, made a reply which supposed him to be sincere in all that he had just said, and concluded by charging him specially with the conquest of England, a mission rather difficult.[6]

On every side the hymn was sung which Chenier had composed to celebrate this day. The last stanza of it anticipates the long period of tranquil renown to which France might now look forward. It is as follows:

Contemplez nos lauriers civiques!
L'Italie a produit ces fertiles moissons;
Ceux-là croissent pour nous au milieu des glaçons;

---

6. On February 23, 1798, after inspecting the army, Napoléon submitted a report to the Directory in which he commented on the difficulty of invading England and the need to strengthen France's naval power.

Voici ceux de Fleurus, ceux des plaines belgiques.
Tous les fleuves surpris nous ont vus triomphans;
    Tous les jours nous furent prospères.
    Que le front blanchi de nos pères
Soit couvert de lauriers cueillis par leurs enfans.
Tu fus long-temps l'effroi, sois l'honneur de la terre,
    O république des François!
Que le chant des plaisirs succède aux cris de guerre,
    La victoire a conquis la paix.[7]

Alas! What is become of those days of glory and peace with which France flattered herself twenty years ago! All these blessings were in the hand of a single man: what has he done with them?

7. Admire our civic laurels!
In Italy blossomed rich harvests;
Now they grow for us amongst the fields of ice;
Here are those of Fleurus, those of the Belgian plains.
All the rivers were aghast at our triumphs;
And every day delivered our successes.
Let the noble white heads of our fathers
Be showered with honors won by their children.
O republic of the Franks,
You were once the dread of the earth,
Be now its pride!
Let songs of rejoicing follow battle cries,
Victory has won over peace. (trans. A. C.)

CHAPTER XXVII

Preparations of General Bonaparte for Proceeding to Egypt. His Opinion on the Invasion of Switzerland.

Bonaparte, at this same epoch, the close of 1797, sounded the public opinion with respect to the Directors; he saw that they were not loved, but that a republican sentiment made it impossible for a general to put himself in the place of the civil magistrates. He was one evening conversing with Barras upon his ascendancy over the Italians, who had wished to make him King of Italy and Duke of Milan. *But,* said he, *I do not think of anything of the sort in any country. You do well,* replied Barras, *not to think of it in France; for if the Directory were to send you to the Temple tomorrow, there would not be four persons who would oppose it.* Bonaparte was sitting on a couch by the side of Barras; at these words, unable to restrain his irritation, he sprang toward the fireplace: then, resuming that species of apparent tranquillity of which the most passionate among the inhabitants of the South are capable, he declared that he wished to be entrusted with a military expedition. The Directory proposed to him the invasion of England; he went to survey the coasts, and, as he soon perceived the extravagance of that project, he returned with the resolution of attempting the conquest of Egypt.

Bonaparte has always sought to lay hold of the imagination of men, and in this respect he knows well how they ought to be governed by one who is not born to a throne. An invasion of Africa, war carried into Egypt, a country almost fabulous, could not fail to make an impression on every mind. The French might easily be persuaded that they would derive great advantage from such a colony in the Mediterranean, and that it might one day furnish them with the means of attacking the English establishments in India. These schemes possessed grandeur and were fitted to augment the brilliant reputation of Bonaparte. Had he remained in France, the Directory, through all the journals which were at its nod, would have launched forth numberless calumnies and tarnished his exploits in the imagination of the idle: Bonaparte would have been reduced to dust before the thunderbolt struck him. He was therefore right in wishing to make himself a poetical personage instead of remaining exposed to the slanders of Jacobins, who, with their popular forms, are not less dextrous than courts in the propagation of scandal.

There was no money to transport an army to Egypt; and the most condemnable thing done by Bonaparte was to convince the Directory to invade Switzerland with a view to seize the treasury of Berne, which two hundred years of wisdom and economy had accumulated. The war had for its pretext the situation of the Pays de Vaud. There is no doubt but that the Pays de Vaud was entitled to claim an independent existence, which it acted right in maintaining.[1] But if the emigrants were blamed for uniting themselves to foreigners against France, should not the same principle be applied to the Swiss, who invoked the terrible assistance of the French? Besides, it was not the Pays de Vaud alone that was concerned in a war which would necessarily hazard the independence of all Switzerland. This cause appeared to me so sacred that, at that time, I still thought it not altogether impossible to induce Bonaparte to defend it. In every circumstance of my life, the errors which I have committed in politics have proceeded from the idea that men were always capable of being moved by truth, if it was presented to them with force.

I remained nearly an hour in conference with Bonaparte: he is a good and patient listener, for he wishes to know if what is said can throw any light on his own affairs: but Cicero and Demosthenes together would not draw him to the slightest sacrifice of his personal interest. Many mediocre people call that reason; it is reason of an inferior order; there is one more exalted which does not proceed by mere calculation.

Bonaparte, in conversing with me on Switzerland, alleged the situation

1. The Vaud had been dependent on the canton of Berne and became an independent canton in 1798.

of the Pays de Vaud as a motive for the entrance of the French troops. He told me that the inhabitants of that district were subject to the aristocrats of Berne, and that men could not now exist without political rights. I moderated, as well as I could, this republican ardor, by representing to him that the Vaudois were perfectly free in every civil relation, and that when liberty exists in fact, it is unnecessary, for the sake of the abstract right, to expose ourselves to the greatest of misfortunes, that of seeing foreigners in our native land. "Self-love and imagination," replied the General, "make men cling to the advantage of sharing in the government of their country, and there is injustice in excluding any portion of them from it." Nothing is more true in principle, said I, General; but it is equally true that it is by their own efforts that liberty should be obtained, and not by calling in the aid of a power which must be necessarily predominant. The word "principle" has since appeared very suspicious to Bonaparte, but it then suited him to make use of it, and he alleged it against me. I insisted anew upon the happiness and beauty of Switzerland, and the repose which she had for many centuries enjoyed. "Yes, without doubt," said Bonaparte, interrupting me, but men must have *political rights;* yes, repeated he, as if the words had been committed to memory, "*political rights.*" Then, changing the conversation, because he wished to hear no more upon the subject, he spoke to me of his love for retirement, for the country, and for the fine arts; and took the trouble of exhibiting himself to me in aspects suited to what he supposed to be the turn of my imagination.

The conversation, however, gave me some idea of the attractions which may be found in him when he assumes the air of a plain good-natured man and speaks with simplicity of himself and his projects. This art, the most formidable of all, has captivated many. At this period I still met Bonaparte occasionally in society; and he appeared to me always profoundly occupied with the relations which he wished to establish between himself and other men, keeping them at a distance or bringing them near him, according as he thought he could attach them most securely. In particular, when he was with the Directors, he was afraid of appearing like a general under the orders of his government; and in his manners with that class of superiors, he tried alternately dignity and familiarity; but he missed the true tone of both. He is a man who can be natural only when he commands.

CHAPTER XXVIII

The Invasion of Switzerland.

As Switzerland was threatened with an approaching invasion, I quitted Paris in the month of January, 1798, to rejoin my father at Coppet. He was still on the list of emigrants, and a positive law condemned to death emigrants who remained in a country occupied by the French troops. I did my utmost to induce him to quit his abode; he would not: "*At my age,*" said he, "*a man should not wander upon the earth.*" I believe that his secret motive was his reluctance to remove himself from the tomb of my mother: on this subject he had a superstition of the heart which he would have sacrificed only to the interest of his family, and never to his own. In the four years since the companion of his life had ceased to live, scarcely a day passed in which he did not go to walk near the tomb in which she reposes, and by departing he would have thought that he was abandoning her.

When the entry of the French was positively announced, my father and myself, with my young children, remained alone in the château of Coppet. On the day appointed for the violation of the Swiss territory, our inquisitive people went down to the bottom of the avenue; and my father and I, who were awaiting our fate together, placed ourselves in a balcony that had a view of the high road by which the troops were to arrive. Though it was the middle of winter, the weather was delightful; the Alps were reflected in the lake; and the noise of the drum alone disturbed the tranquillity of the scene. My heart throbbed violently from the apprehension of what might menace my father. I knew that the Directory spoke of him with respect; but I knew also the empire of revolutionary laws over those who had made them. At the moment when the French troops passed the frontier of the Helvetic confederation, I saw an officer quit his men to proceed toward our château. A mortal terror seized me; but what he said to us soon re-assured me. He was commissioned by the Directory to offer my father a safeguard. This officer, since well known under the title of Marshal Suchet,[1] conducted himself extremely well toward us; and his staff, whom he brought to my father's house the day after, followed his example.

It is impossible not to find among the French, in spite of the wrongs with which they may be justly reproached, a social spirit which makes us live at our ease with them. Nevertheless this army, which had so well defended the independence of its own country, wished to conquer the whole of Switzerland, and to penetrate even into the mountains of the small cantons, where men of simplicity retained the old-fashioned treasure of their virtues and usages. Berne and other Swiss cities possessed without doubt unjust privileges, and old prejudices were mingled with the democracy of the small cantons; but was it by force that any amelioration was to be effected in the condition of a country accustomed to acknowledge only the slow and progressive operation of time? The political institutions of Switzerland have, it is true, been improved in some respects, and up to these late times it might have been believed that even the mediation of Bonaparte[2] had removed some prejudices of the Catholic cantons. But union and patriotic energy have lost much since the revolution. The Swiss are now accustomed to have recourse to foreigners, and to share in the political passions of other nations, while the only interest of Helvetia is to be peaceful, independent, and animated by a jealous dignity of spirit.

In 1797, there was a rumor of the resistance which Berne and the small democratical cantons would make to the threatened invasion. Then, for the first time in my life, I entertained wishes against the French; for the first time in my life I experienced the painful anguish of blaming my own country enough to desire the triumph of those who fought against it. Formerly, just before the battle of Granson,[3] the Swiss prostrated themselves before God; their cruel enemies thought that they were about to surrender their arms; but they rose up and were victorious. The small cantons in 1798, in their noble ignorance of the things of this world, sent their quota

1. Napoléon appointed Suchet (1770–1826) marshal of France in 1811 and a peer of France during the Hundred Days.
2. On February 19, 1803.
3. On March 2, 1476.

to Berne; these religious soldiers kneeled before the church when they arrived in the public square. "*We do not dread,*" said they, "*the armies of France; we are four hundred, and if that is not enough, we are ready to make four hundred more of our companions march to the assistance of our country.*" Who would not be touched by this great confidence in such feeble means! But the days of the three hundred Spartans were gone by: numbers were omnipotent; and individual devotedness struggled in vain against the resources of a great state and the combination of tactics.

On the day of the first battle of the Swiss with the French, though Coppet is thirty leagues from Berne, we heard, in the silence of the evening, the discharges of cannon, which were resounding far off among the echos of the mountains. We scarcely dared to breathe, that we might the better distinguish the mournful noise; and though every probability was in favor of the French, we had still a vague hope of some miracle in behalf of justice: but time alone is her all-powerful ally. The Swiss troops were defeated in pitched battle;[4] the inhabitants, however, defended themselves long among their mountains; the women and children took up arms; priests were massacred at the foot of their altars. But there was in this small territory a national will, which the French were obliged to treat with consideration; nor did the lesser cantons ever accept the republic one and indivisible[5]—that metaphysical present which the Directory offered at the cannon's mouth. It must be allowed, however, that there was in Switzerland a party for the unity of the republic which could boast of very respectable names. The Directory never acquired any influence in the affairs of foreign nations without being supported by some portion of the natives. But these men, however decided they might be in favor of liberty, always found it difficult to maintain their popularity, because they had rallied round the overwhelming power of the French.

When Bonaparte was at the head of France, he made war to extend his empire; and that policy is easily understood. But although the Directory were desirous of obtaining possession of Switzerland as an advantageous military position, their principal aim was to extend the republican system

4. On May 3, 1798, at Morgarten.
5. The Helvetic Republic imposed by the French army lasted from 1798 until 1800.

in Europe. Now, how could they flatter themselves that they would succeed, by putting constraint on the opinion of people, especially of those who, like the Swiss, were entitled to consider themselves as the oldest friends of freedom? Violence suits despotism alone; and, accordingly, it showed itself at last under its true name—that of a military chief: to this the tyrannical measures of the Directory were a prelude.

It was likewise by a series of these combinations, half abstract and half positive, half revolutionary and half diplomatic, that the Directory wished to unite Geneva to France.[6] In this regard, they committed an act of injustice so much the more revolting that it was in opposition to all the principles which they professed. They robbed a free state of its independence, in spite of the strongly declared wish of its inhabitants; they annihilated completely the moral importance of a republic, the cradle of the Reformation, which had produced more distinguished men than the largest province of France; the democratic party, in short, did what they would have deemed a crime even in their adversaries. In fact, what would not have been said of kings and aristocrats who should have tried to deprive Geneva of its individual existence? For states, as well as men, have an individual existence. Did the French derive from their acquisition a gain equal to the loss which was occasioned to the wealth of the human mind in general? And may not the fable of the goose that laid eggs of gold be applied to small independent states which the greater are eager to occupy? Conquest destroys the very advantages of which she covets the possession.

My father, by the union of Geneva, found himself legally a Frenchman; he, who had always been so in his sentiments and in his career. To live in safety in Switzerland, at that time occupied by the armies of the Directory, it was necessary that he should obtain the erasure of his name from the list of emigrants. With this view he gave me a report to carry to Paris which was a real masterpiece of dignity and logic. The Directory, after having read it, were unanimous in the resolution to erase M. Necker's name; and, although this was an act of the most obvious justice, it gave me so much pleasure that I shall always retain a grateful remembrance of it.

6. Geneva was annexed to France on April 15, 1798.

I then negotiated with the Directory for the payment of the two million livres which my father had left deposited in the public treasury. The government acknowledged the debt, but offered payment out of the estates of the clergy, which my father refused: not that he meant thus to assume the colors of the party who consider the sale of that property illegal; but because he had never in any situation wished to make his opinions and interests coincide, that there might not be the possibility of the slightest doubt of his perfect impartiality.

CHAPTER XXIX

Of the Termination of the Directory.

After the fatal blow which, on the 18th of Fructidor, the military force inflicted on the dignity of the representatives of the people, the Directory, as we have just seen, still maintained itself for two years, without any external change in its organization. But the vital principle which had animated it existed no more, and one might have said of it, as of the giant in Ariosto,[1] that it still fought, forgetting that it was dead. The elections, the deliberations of the councils, presented nothing to excite interest; for the results were always known beforehand. The persecutions which were carried on against nobles and priests were no longer incited by popular hatred: the war had ceased to have an object since the independence of France and the limit of the Rhine were secured. But, instead of attaching Europe to France, the Directors were already beginning the fatal work which Napoleon so cruelly completed; they inspired the neighboring nations with as much aversion to the French government as princes alone had at first experienced.

The Roman republic was proclaimed from the summit of the Capitol;[2] but, in our days, the statues are the only republicans in Rome; and those must know little of the nature of enthusiasm who imagine that, by counterfeiting it, they will cause it to spring up. The free consent of the people can alone give to political institutions a certain native and spontaneous beauty, a natural harmony which guarantees their duration. The monstrous system of despotism in the means, under pretext of liberty in the end, produced nothing but governments depending upon springs, which required to be constantly repaired, and stopped the moment that they

1. Ludovico Ariosto (1474–1533), author of *Orlando furioso*.
2. On February 15, 1798.

ceased to be put in motion by external impulse. Festivals were celebrated at Paris with Grecian costumes and antique cars: but there was no fixed principle in the soul; immorality alone made rapid progress on every side; for public opinion was neither a terror nor a recompense to anyone.

A revolution had occurred in the interior of the Directory, as in the interior of a seraglio, in which the nation had taken no share. The men last chosen[3] were so little worthy of respect that France, quite weary of them, called with loud cries for a military chief; for she would neither have the Jacobins, the remembrance of whom struck her with horror, nor a counter-revolution, which the arrogance of the emigrants rendered terrible.

The lawyers who had been called in 1799 to the place of Directors, exhibited there only the ridiculous pretense of authority, without the talents and the virtues which render it respectable; the facility with which, in the course of an evening, a Director assumed the airs of a Court, was truly singular; the part must be one not very difficult to play. Gohier, Moulins—what do I know?—the most obscure of men, once appointed Directors, were already occupied the very next day with themselves; they spoke to you of their health and of their family interests, as if they had been personages dear to the whole world. They were kept in this illusion by flatterers who were people of good or bad company, but who all were fulfilling their role of courtiers, by showing to their prince the most affecting solicitude with regard to everything which could concern him, on condition of obtaining a short audience for some particular request. Among these people, those who had anything to reproach themselves with during the Reign of Terror always retained a remarkable sensibility on that subject. If you pronounced a single word which might allude to the recollection which disturbed them, they immediately related their history to you in the most minute detail, and abandoned everything to talk to you about it for hours and hours. If you returned to the affair on which you wished to converse with them, they listened to you no longer. The life of

---

3. On June 18, 1799, four directors (Reubell, La Reveillère–Lépeaux, Treilhard, and Merlin de Douai) were replaced by Sieyès, Ducos, Gohier (1746–1830), and General Moulin (1752–1819).

any individual who has committed a political crime is forever linked to that crime in order either to justify it or to live it down by the influence of power.

The nation, fatigued with this revolutionary caste, had arrived at that period in political conjunctures where men believe that it is only under the authority of a single person that repose is to be found. In this way Cromwell governed England, by offering men who had been compromised by the Revolution the shelter of his despotism. It is impossible to deny, in some respects, the truth of what Bonaparte said afterward: *I found the crown of France on the ground and picked it up;* but it was the French nation itself which required to be raised.

The Russians and Austrians had gained great victories in Italy;[4] factions were multiplying to an infinite number in the interior; and the kind of cracking which precedes the fall of a building was heard in the government. The first wish was that Joubert should put himself at the head of the state; he preferred the command of the troops and, disdaining to survive the reverses of the French armies, died nobly by the hand of the enemy. The wishes of all would have pointed out Moreau as the first magistrate of the republic—a preeminence of which his virtues certainly made him worthy; but he perhaps felt that he had not enough of political talent for such a situation, and he preferred exposing himself to military dangers rather than civil affairs.

Among the other French generals, scarcely any were known who were qualified for the civil career. One only, General Bernadotte, united, as the sequel has proved, the qualities of a statesman and of a distinguished soldier. But he was then wholly devoted to the republican party, which would no more approve the subversion of the republic than the royalists approved the subversion of the throne. Bernadotte, therefore, as we shall relate in the following chapter, limited himself to the re-establishment of the armies while he was Minister of War. No scruples whatever arrested Bonaparte's course: accordingly we shall see how he seized on the destinies of France, and in what manner he guided them.

---

4. In June 1799, the Russian and Austrian armies occupied the greatest part of Italy.

CHAPTER I

News from Egypt: Return of Bonaparte.

Nothing was more likely to produce a striking effect on the mind than the Egyptian war; and though the great naval victory gained by Nelson near Aboukir[1] had destroyed all its possible advantages, letters dated from Cairo, orders issuing from Alexandria to penetrate to Thebes, on the confines of Ethiopia, increased the reputation of a man who was not now within sight, but who at a distance seemed an extraordinary phenomenon. He put at the head of his proclamations *Bonaparte, Commander-in-chief and Member of the National Institute;* whence it was concluded that he was a friend to knowledge and a protector of letters; but the guarantee which he gave for these qualities was not any firmer than his profession of the Mahomedan faith,[2] followed by his concordat with the Pope.[3] He was already beginning to deceive Europe by a system of juggling tricks, convinced, as he was, that for everyone the science of life consists merely in the maneuvers of egoism. Bonaparte is not a man only but also a system; and if he were right, the human species would no longer be what God has made it. He ought therefore to be examined like a great problem, the solution of which is of importance to meditation throughout all ages.

Bonaparte, in reducing everything to calculation, was sufficiently acquainted with that part of the nature of man which does not obey the will

---

1. On August 1, 1798.

2. There is no evidence that Napoléon intended to convert to Islam. For more information on this topic, see Spillman, *Napoléon et l'Islam.*

3. The Concordat was signed on July 16, 1801.

to feel the necessity of acting upon the imagination; and his twofold dexterity consisted in the art of dazzling multitudes and of corrupting individuals.

His conversation with the Mufti in the pyramid of the Cheops could not fail to enchant the Parisians, for it united the two qualities by which they are most easily captivated: a certain kind of grandeur and of mockery together. The French like to be moved and to laugh at being moved: quackery is their delight, and they aid willingly in deceiving themselves, provided they be allowed, while they act as dupes, to show by some witticisms that they are not so.

Bonaparte, in the pyramid, made use of the Oriental style. "*Glory to Allah,*" said he, "*there is no true God but God, and Mahomet is his prophet. The bread stolen by the wicked turns into dust in his mouth.*" "*Thou hast spoken,*" said the Mufti, "*like the most learned of the Mullahs.*"—"*I can cause a chariot of fire to descend from Heaven,*" continued Bonaparte, "*and direct it upon the earth.*"—"*Thou art the mightiest Captain,*" replied the Mufti, "*whose hand the power of Mahomet hath armed.*"[4] Mahomet, however, did not prevent Sir Sidney Smith from arresting by his brilliant valor the successes of Bonaparte at St. Jean-d'Acre.[5]

When Napoléon, in 1805, was named King of Italy, he said to General Berthier in one of those moments when he talked of everything that he might try his ideas upon other people: "This Sidney Smith made fortune fail me at St. Jean-d'Acre; my purpose was to set out from Egypt, proceed to Constantinople, and arrive at Paris by marching back through Europe." This failure, however, made at the time a very decent appearance. Whatever his regrets might be, gigantic like the enterprises which followed them, Bonaparte found means to make his reverses in Egypt pass for successes; and although his expedition had no other result than the ruin of the fleet and the destruction of one of our finest armies, he was called the Conqueror of the East.

Bonaparte, availing himself with ability of the enthusiasm of the French for military glory, associated their self-love with his victories as well as

4. This imaginary dialogue was published in various French journals of that period.
5. In May–June 1799.

with his defeats. He gradually took possession of the place which the Revolution occupied in every head, and attached to his own name that national feeling which had aggrandized France in the eyes of foreigners.

Two of his brothers, Lucien and Joseph,[6] had seats in the Council of Five Hundred, and both in their different lines had enough of intellect and talent to be eminently useful to the General. They watched for him over the state of affairs, and when the moment was come, they advised him to return to France. The armies had been beaten in Italy and were for the most part disorganized through the misconduct of the administration. The Jacobins began to show themselves once more, the Directory was without reputation and without strength: Bonaparte received all this intelligence in Egypt, and after some hours of solitary meditation, he resolved to set out.[7] This rapid and certain perception of circumstances is precisely what distinguishes him, and opportunity has never offered itself to him in vain. It has been frequently repeated that on departing then, he deserted his army. Doubtless, there is a species of exalted disinterestedness which would not have allowed a warrior to separate himself thus from the men who had followed him, and whom he left in distress. But General Bonaparte ran such risks in traversing the sea covered with English vessels; the design which summoned him to France was so bold that it is absurd to treat his departure from Egypt as cowardice. Such a being must not be attacked with common declamations: every man who has produced a great effect on other men, to be judged, should be examined thoroughly.

A reproach of a much graver nature is the total want of humanity which Bonaparte manifested in his Egyptian campaign. Whenever he found any advantage in cruelty, he indulged in it, and yet his despotism was not sanguinary. He had no more desire to shed blood than a reasonable man has to spend money without need. But what he called necessity was in fact his ambition; and when this ambition was concerned, he did not for a moment allow himself to hesitate to sacrifice others to himself. What we call conscience was in his eyes only the poetical name of deception.

---

6. Lucien Bonaparte (1775–1840), later Prince of Canino; Joseph Bonaparte (1768–1844), later king of Naples and king of Spain (until 1814).

7. Napoléon left Egypt on August 23, 1799.

CHAPTER II

Revolution of the 18th of Brumaire.

In the time which had elapsed since Bonaparte's brothers wrote to him in Egypt to advise his return, the face of affairs had undergone a singular change. General Bernadotte had been appointed Minister of War and had in a few months restored the organization of the armies. His extreme activity repaired all the mischiefs which negligence had caused. One day, as he was reviewing the young men of Paris who were on the eve of marching to the scene of war, *My lads,* he said, *there are assuredly among you some great captains.* These simple words electrified their souls by recalling to their remembrance one of the chief advantages of free institutions, the emulation which they excite in every class.

The English had made a descent into Holland, which had been already pushed back.[1] The Prussians had been beaten at Zurich by Massena;[2] the French armies had again begun to act on the offensive in Italy. Thus, when Bonaparte returned, Switzerland, Holland, and Piedmont[3] were still under the control of France; the barrier of the Rhine, gained by the conquests of the Republic, was not disputed with her, and the force of France was on a balance with that of the other states of Europe. Who could have imagined then that of all the combinations which fortune presented to her choice, that which would lead her to be conquered and subdued was to raise the ablest of her generals to supreme power? Tyranny annihilates even the military force, to which it has sacrificed everything.

It was no longer, therefore, external reverses which, in 1799, made France desire Bonaparte; but the fear which the Jacobins excited was a

1. In October 1799.
2. In September 1799.
3. The French regained possession of Piedmont in June 1800.

powerful aid to him. They were now without means, and their appearance was nothing more than that of a specter which comes to stir the ashes: it was, however, enough to rekindle the hatred which they inspired, and the nation, flying from a phantom, precipitated itself into the arms of Bonaparte.

The President of the Directory had said on the 10th of August of the very year in which Bonaparte was made Consul; *Royalty will never raise its head again; no longer will those men be seen who pretended to be the delegates of heaven that they might oppress the earth with more security; in whose eyes France was but their patrimony, Frenchmen but their subjects, and the laws the mere expression of their good pleasure.* What was to be seen no more was, however, seen very soon; and what France wished in calling Bonaparte to the throne, peace and repose, was exactly what his character rejected as an element in which he could not live.

When Caesar overturned the Roman republic he had to combat Pompey and the most illustrious patricians of the age: Cicero and Cato contended against him; everywhere there was greatness arrayed in opposition to his. Bonaparte met with no adversaries whose names deserve to be mentioned. If the Directory had been in the fullness of its past force, it would have said, like Reubell when hints were given him that there was reason to apprehend that General Bonaparte would offer his resignation: *Very well, let us accept it, for the republic will never want a general to command its armies.* In fact, the circumstance which had rendered the armies of the French Republic formidable till then, was that they had no need of any particular man to command them. Liberty draws forth in a great nation all the talents which circumstances require.

Exactly on the 18th of Brumaire I arrived at Paris from Switzerland, and as I was changing horses some leagues from the city, I was informed that the Director Barras had just passed, on his way to his estate of Grosbois, accompanied by gendarmes. The postilions were relating the news of the day, and this popular mode of becoming acquainted with them gave them additional interest. It was the first time since the Revolution that the name of an individual was heard in every mouth. Till then it was said, the Constituent Assembly has done so and so, or the people, or the Convention; now there was no mention of any but this man, who was to be sub-

stituted for all and leave the human race anonymous; who was to mo-
nopolize fame for himself, and to exclude every existing creature from
the possibility of acquiring a share of it.

The very evening of my arrival, I learned that during the five weeks
which Bonaparte had spent at Paris since his return, he had been preparing
the public mind for the Revolution which had just taken place. Every faction had presented itself to him, and he had given hopes to all. He had
told the Jacobins that he would save them from the return of the old dynasty; he had, on the contrary, suffered the royalists to flatter themselves
that he would re-establish the Bourbons; he had insinuated to Sieyès that
he would give him an opportunity of bringing forth into light the constitution which he had been keeping in darkness for ten years; he had,
above all, captivated the public, which belongs to no faction, by general
proclamations of love of order and tranquillity. Mention was made to him
of a woman whose papers the Directory had caused to be seized; he exclaimed on the absurd atrocity of tormenting women, he who, according
to his caprice, has condemned so many of them to unlimited exile; he spoke
only of peace, he who has introduced eternal war into the world. Finally,
there was in his manner an affectation of gentleness, which formed an
odious contrast with what was known of his violence. But, after ten years
of suffering, enthusiastic attachment to ideas had given way in revolutionary characters to personal hopes and fears. After a certain time old
notions return; but the generation which has had a share in great civil
troubles is scarcely ever capable of establishing freedom: it is too soiled
for the accomplishment of so pure a work.

The French Revolution, after the 18th of Fructidor, had been nothing
but a continued succession of men who caused their own ruin by preferring their interest to their duty; thus, at least they gave an important lesson
to their successors.

Bonaparte met no obstacles in his way to power. Moreau was not enterprising in civil affairs; Bernadotte eagerly requested the Directors to
re-appoint him Minister of War. His appointment was written out, but
they had not courage to sign it. Nearly all the military men, therefore,
rallied round Bonaparte; for now that they interfered once more in the
internal revolutions, they were resolved to place one of their own body

at the head of the state, that they might thus secure to themselves the rewards which they wished to obtain.

An article of the constitution which allowed the Council of Ancients to transfer the legislative body to another city than Paris was the means employed to effect the overthrow of the Directory.

The Council of Ancients ordained on the 18th of Brumaire that the legislative body and Council of Five Hundred should, on the following day, remove to Saint Cloud, where the troops might be made to act more easily. On the evening of the 18th the whole city was agitated by the expectation of the great day that was to follow; and without doubt, apprehension of the return of the Jacobins made the majority of people of respectability wish at the time that Bonaparte might have the advantage. My own feelings, I acknowledge, were of a very mixed nature. Once the struggle began, a momentary victory of the Jacobins might occasion fresh scenes of blood; yet I experienced, at the idea of Bonaparte's triumph, a grief which might be called prophetic.

A friend of mine who was present at the meeting in St. Cloud dispatched messengers to me every hour: at one time he informed me that the Jacobins were on the point of prevailing, and I prepared to quit France anew; the instant afterward I learned that the soldiers had dispersed the national representatives and that Bonaparte had triumphed. I wept, not over liberty, for it never existed in France, but over the hope of that liberty, without which this country can only have disgrace and misery.[4] I felt within me at this instant a difficulty of breathing which, I believe, has since become the malady of all those who lived under the authority of Bonaparte.

Different accounts have been given of the manner in which the revolution of the 18th of Brumaire was accomplished. The point of chief im-

---

4. According to Jacques Godechot, the original text was most likely altered here by Madame de Staël's first editors, who are said to have cut passages in which Madame de Staël manifested a more favorable attitude to Napoléon after 18 Brumaire. A few revealing passages from Staël's correspondence with Necker from this period can be found in Guillemin, *Madame de Staël, Benjamin Constant et Napoléon*, 7; and Haussonville, *Madame de Staël et M. Necker d'après leur correspondance inédite*, 125–33.

portance is to observe on this occasion the characteristic traits of the man who has been for nearly fifteen years the master of the continent of Europe. He went to the bar of the Council of Ancients and wished to draw them into his views by addressing them with warmth and nobility; but he cannot express himself in connected discourse; it is only in conversation that his keen and decisive spirit shows itself to advantage. Besides, as he has no true enthusiasm on any subject, he is never eloquent but in abuse, and nothing was more difficult for him than to confine himself in his address to that kind of respect which is due to an assembly whom we wish to convince. He attempted to say to the Council of Ancients, "*I am the God of War and of Fortune, follow me.*" But he used these pompous words from mere embarrassment, and in their place would rather have said, "*You are all a pack of wretches, and I will have you shot if you do not obey me.*"

On the 19th of Brumaire he came to the Council of the Five Hundred, his arms crossed with a very gloomy air, and followed by two tall grenadiers who protected the shortness of his stature. The deputies, who were named Jacobins, uttered violent exclamations when they saw him enter the hall: fortunately for him his brother Lucien was president at the time; it was in vain that he rang the bell to re-establish order; cries of traitor and usurper resounded from every quarter; and one of the members, a countryman of Bonaparte, the Corsican Aréna, approached the general and shook him violently by the collar of his coat. It has been supposed, but without reason, that he had a poignard to kill him.[5] His action, however, terrified Bonaparte, who said to the grenadiers by his side, as he let his head drop over the shoulder of one of them, "*Get me out of here.*" The grenadiers carried him away from among the deputies who surrounded him, and took him from the hall into the open air. He was no sooner out than his presence of mind returned. He instantly mounted on horseback, and passing along the ranks of his grenadiers, soon determined them to what he wished should be done.

In this situation, as in many others, it has been observed that Bonaparte could be thrown into confusion when another danger than that of war was

5. Aréna (1771–1801), a military officer and deputy to the Council of Five Hundred, was arrested and executed in 1801 for participating in a conspiracy against Napoléon.

set before him; and from here some persons have ridiculously inferred that he lacked courage. Certainly, his boldness cannot be denied; but as he is nothing, not even brave, in a generous manner, it follows that he never exposes himself but when it may be advantageous. He would be much vexed at the prospect of being killed, for that would be a reverse, and he wishes to be successful in everything; he would likewise be vexed at it because death is disagreeable to the imagination; but he does not hesitate to hazard his life when, according to his views, the game, if I may be allowed the expression, is worth the risk of the stake.

After General Bonaparte left the hall of the Five Hundred, the deputies opposed to him were vehement in demanding that he should be put out of the protection of the law; and it was then that his brother Lucien, president of the Assembly, did him an eminent service by refusing, in spite of all the solicitations with which he was urged, to put that proposition to the vote. If he had consented, the decree would have passed, and no one can tell what impression it might yet have produced on the soldiers. For ten years they had uniformly abandoned those generals whom the legislative power had proscribed; and although the national representation had lost its character of legality by the 18th of Fructidor, the similarity of words often prevails over the diversity of things. General Bonaparte hastened to send an armed force to bring Lucien in safety out of the hall; as soon as he was gone, the grenadiers entered the orangery, where the deputies were assembled, and drove them away by marching from one extremity of the hall to the other, as if there had been nobody present. The deputies, driven against the wall, were forced to escape by the window into the gardens of St. Cloud with their senatorial robes. The representatives of the people had been already proscribed in France; but it was the first time since the Revolution that the civil power had been rendered ridiculous in the presence of the military; and Bonaparte, who wished to establish his dominion on the degradation of bodies as well as on that of individuals, enjoyed his success in destroying at the very outset the dignity of the deputies. From the moment that the moral force of the national representation was annihilated, a legislative body, whatever it might be, was in the eyes of the military a mere assemblage of five hundred men, much less strong and active than a battalion of the same number; and they have since been always ready at the command of their chief to correct diversities of opinion like faults in discipline.

In the Committees of the Five Hundred, Bonaparte, in the presence of the officers of his suite and some friends of the Directory, made a speech which was printed in the journals of the day. It contains a remarkable comparison, which history ought to store up. *What have they done,* said he, speaking of the Directors, *with that France which I left to them so brilliant? I left them peace, and I find war at my return: I left them victories, and I find defeats. What, in short, have they done with the hundred thousand Frenchmen, all of them my acquaintances and my companions in arms, who are now no more?* Then all at once concluding his harangue in a calm tone, he added, *This state of things cannot last; it would lead us in three years to despotism.* He took upon himself the charge of hastening the accomplishment of his prediction.

But would it not be an important lesson for the human species if these Directors, unwarlike as they were, were to rise from their ashes and were to demand of Napoléon to account for the barrier of the Rhine and the Alps conquered by the republic; for the two entries of foreign troops into Paris;[6] for the three million Frenchmen who have perished from Cádiz to Moscow;[7] and above all, for that sympathy which nations once felt with the cause of liberty in France, and which is now changed into inveterate aversion? The Directors assuredly would not be the more praiseworthy for this; but the conclusion would be that in our days an enlightened nation can do nothing worse than put itself into the hands of a single man. The public has now more sagacity than any individual; and institutions rally opinions more wisely than can be done by circumstances. If the French nation, instead of choosing that baneful foreigner,[8] who has exploited it

6. In 1814 and 1815.

7. In fact, approximately 800,000 French soldiers died in these military campaigns.

8. Corsica, where Napoléon was born in August 1769, was actually part of France at that time.

for his own advantage, and exploited it badly even in that regard—if the French nation, at that time so imposing in spite of all her faults, had formed a constitution for herself with a respectful attention to the lessons which ten years of experience had given her, she would still have been the light of the world.

CHAPTER III

Of the Establishment
of the Consular Constitution.

The most potent charm which Bonaparte employed for the establishment of his power was, as we have said, the terror which the very name of Jacobinism inspired, although every person capable of reflection was aware that this scourge could not revive in France. We willingly assume the air of fearing vanquished factions to justify general measures of rigor. All those who wish to favor the establishment of despotism are constantly endeavoring to keep the crimes of demagogues strongly in our recollection. It is an easy strategy which has little difficulty. Accordingly, Bonaparte paralyzed every kind of resistance to his will by these words: *Would you have me deliver you up to the Jacobins?* France bent before him; nor was there a man bold enough to reply, *We will combat both the Jacobins and you.* In fine, he was not loved, even at that time, but he was preferred: he has almost always presented himself simultaneously with some other source of alarm, which might cause his power to be accepted as the lesser evil of the two.

The task of discussing with Bonaparte the constitution which was to be proclaimed was entrusted to a commission of fifty members selected from the Five Hundred and from the Ancients.[1] Some of those members, who the evening before had leaped from a window to escape from the bayonets, treated seriously the abstract question of new laws, as if it had been possible to suppose that their authority was still respected. This cool-

---

1. On 19 Brumaire, deputies who were favorably disposed toward Napoléon met and created a Consular Commission that included Napoléon and two directors (Sieyès and Ducos). The deputies then divided themselves into two other committees (of twenty-five members each), which were supposed to draft a new constitution.

ness would have been noble had it been joined to energy; but abstract questions were discussed only that tyranny might be established; as in Cromwell's days, passages of the Bible were sought out to justify absolute power.

Bonaparte allowed these men, accustomed to the tribune, to dissipate in words what remained to them of character; but when their theory approached too near to practice, he cut short every difficulty by a threat of interfering no more in their affairs; that is to say, of bringing them to a conclusion by force. He took considerable pleasure in these tedious discussions, because he is himself very fond of speaking. His species of dissimulation in politics is not silence: he chooses rather to mislead by a perplexed discourse which favors alternately the most opposite opinions. In truth, deceit is often practiced more effectually by speaking than by silence. The least sign betrays those who say nothing; while, on the other hand, the impudence of active lying tends more directly to produce conviction. Bonaparte, therefore, lent himself to the subtleties of a committee which discussed the establishment of a social system like the composition of a book. There was, then, no question of ancient bodies to be treated with respect, of privileges to be preserved, or even of usages to be respected; the Revolution had so cleared away all recollections of the past from France that the plan of the new constitution was not obstructed by any remains of preceding edifices.

Fortunately for Bonaparte, in such a discussion there was no need of profound knowledge; he had only to combat reasonings, a species of weapon with which he played as he liked, and to which he opposed, when his convenience required, a logic in which nothing was intelligible except the declaration of his will. Some have believed that Bonaparte was well informed on every subject, because in this respect, as in many others, he made use of the tricks of quackery. But, as he had read little in the course of his life, his knowledge was confined to what he had picked up in conversation. By accident he may speak to you on any subject whatsoever with exactness, and even with considerable science, if he has met some person who gave him information upon it immediately before; but the next instant you discover that he does not know what every well-educated person has learned in his youth. Doubtless much of a certain kind of talent—the talent of adroitness—is necessary to enable him thus to disguise his ignorance; but none except men enlightened by sincere and regularly pursued studies can entertain just ideas on the government of nations. The old doctrine of perfidy succeeded with Bonaparte only because he added to it the prestige of victory. Without this fatal association, there would not have been two different opinions concerning such a man.

The meetings of Bonaparte with his committee were related to us every evening, and the accounts might have amused, had they not thrown us into a deep sadness as to the future lot of France. The servile spirit of courtiers began to unfold itself in the men who had shown the greatest degree of revolutionary harshness. These ferocious Jacobins were rehearsing the parts of barons and counts, which were allotted to them afterward; and everything announced that their personal interest would be the true Proteus, who would assume at will the most different appearances.

During this discussion, I met a member of the Convention whom I shall not name; for why give names where the truth of the picture does not require it? I expressed to him my worries for liberty: "Oh! Madam," replied he, "we have come to such a point that we must think of saving, not the principles of the Revolution, but only the men who made it." This wish certainly was not that of France.

It was expected that Sieyès would present already drafted that famous constitution which had been talked of for ten years as the ark of alliance which was to unite all parties; but by a singular oddity, he had written nothing on the subject. Sieyès' superiority of talent could not prevail over the misanthropy of his character: he dislikes the human race and cannot deal with it: one might say that he would rather have to do with any other beings than men, and that he renounces all business because he cannot find upon earth a species more to his taste. Bonaparte, who wasted his time neither in the contemplation of abstract ideas nor in being discouraged, perceived very quickly how the system of Sieyès might be useful to him. It was in the very artful annihilation of popular elections. Sieyès substituted for them lists of candidates,[2] out of which the Senate was to

2. Sieyès proposed three *listes de notabilités:* communal, departmental, and national. The system was extremely complex and confusing, and it amounted to abolishing popular elec-

choose the members of the legislative body and of the Tribunate; for in that constitution there were, I know not for what reason, three bodies, and even four if we reckon the Council of State, of which Bonaparte afterward availed himself so well. When the choice of deputies is not made purely and directly by the people, the government is no longer representative; hereditary institutions may accompany that of election, but it is in election that liberty consists. The important point therefore, for Bonaparte, was to paralyze popular election, because he knew it to be irreconcileable with despotism.

In this constitution, the Tribunate, composed of a hundred persons, was to speak, while the legislative body, which consisted of two hundred and fifty members, was to be silent; but it is not easy to conceive why this permission was given to the one, or this constraint imposed upon the other. The Tribunate and the legislative body were not sufficiently numerous in proportion to the population of France; and all political importance was concentrated in the conservative Senate, which united all authority but that which arises from independence of fortune. The senators had no resources except the appointments which they received from the executive power. The Senate was in effect nothing else than the mask of tyranny; it made the orders of an individual appear as if they had been discussed by many.

When Bonaparte was sure of having to deal only with men dependent on their salaries, who were divided into three bodies and named by one another, he thought himself certain of attaining his end. The glorious name of tribune denoted a pension for five years; the noble appellation of senator meant a benefice for life; and he perceived quickly enough that the one class would wish to acquire what the other would desire to preserve. Bonaparte communicated his will in different tones—sometimes by the sage voice of the Senate, sometimes by the commanded cries of the tribunes, sometimes by the quiet scrutiny of the legislative body; and this

---

tions by giving to the executive body the final power to choose the representatives from these lists. For more information, see Godechot, *Les Institutions*, 558–70; also see *Les Constitutions et les principales lois politiques de la France depuis 1789, de la France*, 109–20.

tripartite choir was reckoned the organ of the nation, though subject to the absolute control of a single master.

Sieyès' work was without doubt altered by Bonaparte. His long hawk-eyed sight made him identify and suppress whatever in the proposed institutions might, on a future day, occasion resistance: but Sieyès had ruined liberty by providing any kind of substitute for popular election.

Bonaparte himself would not perhaps have been strong enough to effect at that time so great a change in generally admitted principles; it was necessary that the philosopher should here aid the designs of the usurper. Not assuredly that Sieyès wished to establish tyranny in France; justice requires us to admit that he never took any share in it; and besides, a man of so much talent cannot love the authority of a single individual, unless that individual be himself. But he confused with his metaphysics the very simple question of elections; and it was under the shadow of the clouds thus raised that Bonaparte passed on with impunity to despotism.

CHAPTER IV

Progress of Bonaparte to Absolute Power.

The first symptoms of tyranny cannot be watched too carefully: for when once it has matured to a certain point, it can no longer be stopped. A single man enchains the will of a multitude of individuals, the greater part of whom, taken separately, would wish to be free, but who nevertheless submit because they dread one another and dare not communicate their thoughts freely. A minority not very numerous is often sufficient to resist in succession every portion of the majority which is unacquainted with its own strength.

In spite of the differences of time and place, there are points of resemblance in the history of all nations who have fallen under the yoke. It is generally after long civil troubles that tyranny is established, because it offers the hope of shelter to all the exhausted and timorous factions. Bonaparte said of himself with reason that he could play admirably upon the instrument of power. In truth, as he is attached to no principles, nor restrained by any obstacles, he presents himself in the arena of circumstances like a wrestler, no less supple than vigorous, and discovers at the first glance the points in every man or association of men which may promote his private designs. His scheme for arriving at the dominion of France rested upon three principal bases—to satisfy men's interests at the expense of their virtues, to deprave public opinion by sophisms, and to give the nation war for an object instead of liberty. We shall see him follow these different paths with uncommon ability. The French, alas! seconded him only too well; yet it is his fatal genius which should be chiefly blamed; for as an arbitrary government had at all times prevented the nation from acquiring fixed ideas upon any subject, Bonaparte set its passions in motion without having to struggle against its principles. He had it in his power to do honor to France and to establish himself firmly by respectable institutions; but his contempt of the human race had quite dried up his soul, and he believed that there was no depth but in the region of evil.

We have already seen him decree a constitution[1] in which there existed no guarantees. Besides, he took great care to leave the laws that had been published during the Revolution unrepealed, that he might at his pleasure select from this accursed arsenal the weapon which suited him. The extraordinary commissions, the transportations, the banishments, the slavery of the press, measures unfortunately introduced in the name of liberty, were extremely useful to tyranny. When he employed them, he alleged as a pretext sometimes reasons of state, sometimes the urgency of the conjuncture, sometimes the activity of his adversaries, sometimes the necessity of maintaining tranquillity. Such is the artillery of the phrases by which absolute power is defended, for circumstances never have an end; and in proportion as restraint by illegal measures is increased, the disaffected become more numerous, which serves to justify the necessity of new acts of injustice. The establishment of the sovereignty of law is always deferred till tomorrow, a vicious circle of reasoning from which it is impossible to escape; for the public spirit that is expected to produce liberty can be the outcome only of that very liberty itself.

The constitution gave Bonaparte two colleagues: he chose with singular sagacity, for his assistant consuls, two men who were of no use but to disguise the unity of his despotism: the one was Cambacérès,[2] a lawyer of great learning, who had been taught in the convention to bend methodically before terror; the other, Lebrun,[3] a man of highly cultivated mind and highly polished manners, who had been trained under the Chancellor Maupeou, under that minister who, not satisfied with the degree of arbitrary power which he found in the monarchy as it then existed, had substituted for the *parlements* of France one named by himself. Cambacérès was the interpreter of Bonaparte to the revolutionaries, Lebrun to

1. The Constitution of Year VIII. The text can be found in *Les constitutions de la France*, 109–18.

2. Carbacérès (1753–1824), a deputy to the Council of Five Hundred, was appointed minister of justice on July 20, 1799.

3. Lebrun (1739–1824), a deputy to the Estates General and the Council of Five Hundred.

the royalists: both translated the same text into two different languages. Thus two able ministers were charged with the task of adapting the old system and the new to the mixed mass of the third. The one, a great noble who had been engaged in the Revolution, told the royalists that it was their interest to recover monarchical institutions at the expense of renouncing the ancient dynasty. The other, who, though a creature of the era of disaster, was ready to promote the re-establishment of courts, preached to the republicans the necessity of abandoning their political opinions in order to preserve their places. Among these knights of circumstances, the grand master Bonaparte could create such conjunctures as he desired; while the others maneuvered according to the wind with which the genius of the storms had filled their sails.

The political army of the First Consul was composed of deserters from the two parties. The royalists sacrificed to him their fidelity to the Bourbons; the patriots, their attachment to liberty, so that no independent style of thinking could show itself under his dominion; for he was more willing to pardon a selfish calculation than a disinterested opinion. It was by the bad side of the human heart that he hoped to gain possession of it.

Bonaparte took the Tuileries for his abode: and even the choice of this residence was a political calculation. It was there that the King of France was accustomed to be seen; circumstances connected with monarchy were there presented to every eye; the very presence of the walls, if we may say so, was sufficient to re-establish everything. Toward the concluding days of the last century, I saw the First Consul enter the palace built by our kings: and though Bonaparte was still very far from the magnificence which he afterward displayed, there was visible in all around him an eagerness to vie in the courtier arts of Oriental servility, which must have persuaded him that it was a very easy matter to govern the earth. When his carriage arrived in the court of the Tuileries, his valets opened the door and put down the steps with a violence which seemed to say that even inanimate substances were insolent when they retarded his progress for a moment. He neither looked at nor thanked any person, as if he were afraid of being thought sensible to the homage which he required. As he ascended the staircase in the midst of the crowd which pressed to follow him, his eyes were not fixed on any object or any person in particular.

There was an air of vagueness and want of thought in his physiognomy, and his looks expressed only what it always becomes him to show—indifference to fortune and disdain for men.

One factor which was singularly favorable to the power of Bonaparte was that he had nothing but the mass of the nation to manage. All individual existence had been annihilated by ten years of tumult,[4] and nothing acts upon a people like military success: to resist this inclination on their part instead of profiting by it, a great strength of reason is requisite. Nobody in France could believe his situation secure; men of all classes, whether ruined or enriched, banished or recompensed, found themselves, so to speak, one by one alike in the hands of power. Thousands of Frenchmen were upon the list of emigrants, thousands more had acquired national domains; thousands were proscribed as priests or nobles; and thousands of others feared to be so for their revolutionary deeds. Bonaparte, who constantly marched between two opposite interests, took care not to terminate these inquietudes by fixed laws, which would enable every man to know his rights. To this or that man he gave back his property; from this or that other he took it away forever. A decree concerning the restitution of woods reduced one man to misery while another recovered more than he had originally possessed. Sometimes he restored the estate of the father to the son, or that of the elder brother to the younger, according as he was satisfied or dissatisfied with their attachment to his person. There was not a Frenchman who had not something to ask of the government; and that something was life: for favor then consisted not in the frivolous pleasure which one can impart, but in the hope of revisiting the land in which one was born, and of recovering a part at least of what he once possessed. The First Consul had reserved to himself, under some pretext or other, the power of disposing of the lot of all and of everyone. This unheard-of state of dependence excuses in a great measure the nation. Is universal heroism to be expected? And was there not need of heroism

---

4. Social atomization and leveling were two themes many French liberals used to account for the challenges faced by postrevolutionary France. In his *parlementary* speeches during the Restoration, Royer-Collard used a famous phrase—*la société en poussière* (atomized society)—to describe this phenomenon. A few decades later, Royer-Collard's disciple Tocqueville resorted to this same image in *The Old Régime and the Revolution* (1856).

to run the risk of the ruin and the banishment which impended over all by the application of a simple decree? A singular concurrence of circumstances placed the laws of the period of terror and the military force created by republican enthusiasm at the disposal of one man. What an inheritance for an able despot!

Those among the French who sought to resist the continually increasing power of the First Consul had to invoke liberty in order to struggle against him with success. But at this word the aristocrats and the enemies of the Revolution roared out against Jacobinism, and thus seconded the tyranny, the blame of which they have since wished to throw upon their adversaries.

To tranquillize the Jacobins, who had not yet all rallied round that court whose intentions they did not well comprehend, pamphlets were poured forth which declared that there was no reason to apprehend that Bonaparte meant to resemble Caesar, Cromwell, or Monk—obsolete parts, it was said, which were no longer suitable to the age. It is not, however, quite certain that the events of this world do not occur again and again with little variation, though such sameness is forbidden to the authors of new pieces for the stage; but the important object then was to furnish a phrase to all who wished to be decently deceived. French vanity at that time began to concern itself with diplomacy. The whole nation was informed of the secret of the comedy, and, flattered with the confidence, took pleasure in the intelligent reserve which was required of it.

The numerous journals which existed in France were soon subject to the most rigorous, but at the same time the best combined, censorship:[5] for it was wholly out of the question to impose silence upon a nation which needed to scatter its words in every direction, just as the Roman people needed to watch the games of the circus. Bonaparte then established that loquacious tyranny from which he has since derived such a great advantage. The daily papers all repeated the same thing constantly, without anyone being allowed to contradict them. The freedom of journals differs

---

5. The decree of January 17, 1800, reduced the number of journals in Paris from sixty to thirteen. Official censorship was introduced in 1804. For more information, see Hatin, *Histoire politique et littéraire de la presse en France*, vols. 7–8.

in several respects from that of books. The journals announce the news for which all classes of people are eager; and the discovery of printing, instead of being what it has been called, the safeguard of liberty, would be the most terrible weapon of despotism if the journals which constitute the sole reading of three-fourths of the nation were exclusively subject to authority. For, as regular troops are much more dangerous than a militia to the independence of nations, so hired writers introduce into public opinion much more depravity than could arise where there is no communication except by speech; in which case the judgment could be formed only upon facts. But when the curiosity for news can be satisfied with an allotted portion of lies, when no event is related unaccompanied by sophisms, when everyone's reputation depends on a calumny propagated by gazettes which are multiplied on every side, and when there is not a possibility that any person should be allowed to refute; when opinions concerning every circumstance, every work, every individual, are subject to a journalist's word of command, as the movements of soldiers to the leaders of files; then it is that the art of printing becomes what has been said of cannon—*the last reason of kings.*

Bonaparte, when he had a million armed men at his disposal, did not on that account attach less importance to the art of guiding the public mind by the newspapers: he himself often dictated articles for the journals, which might be recognized by the violent jolts of style: one can see that he would have wished to put blows instead of words in what he wrote. There is in every part of his nature a basis of vulgarity which even the gigantic height of his ambition cannot always conceal. It is not the case that he does not know how to conduct himself with perfect propriety on any given day; he is, however, at his ease only when he despises others, and as soon as he can return to that mood, he yields gladly to his inclination. Yet it was not through mere liking that he allowed himself, in his notes for the *Moniteur,* to employ the cynicism of the Revolution in the support of his power. He would permit none but himself to be a Jacobin in France. And when he inserted in his bulletins gross insults against the most respectable personages, he thought that he should thus captivate the mass of the people and soldiers by descending, in the very purple with which he was arrayed, to the level of their language and passions.

It is impossible to arrive at great power except by taking advantage of the tendency of the times: accordingly Bonaparte studied the spirit of his age with care. There had been among the men of talent of the eighteenth century, in France, a superb enthusiasm for the principles which constitute the happiness and the dignity of mankind; but under the shelter of this great oak, the venomous plants of egoism and irony flourished; and Bonaparte knew how to avail himself with ability of these baneful dispositions. He turned everything, however glorious, into ridicule, except force; *shame to the vanquished* was the declared maxim of his reign; and accordingly there is only one reproach which we would be tempted to address to the disciples of his doctrine; *yet you have not succeeded,* for they would not be affected by blame derived from feelings of morality.

It was, however, necessary to give a vital principle to this system of derision and immorality upon which the civil government was founded. These negative forces were insufficient to produce a progressive motion without the impulse of military success. Order in the administration and the finances, the embellishment of cities, the completion of canals and high roads, everything, in short, that has been praiseworthy in the management of the interior, had for its sole bases the money obtained by contributions raised upon foreigners. Nothing less was necessary than the revenues of the Continent[6] to procure these advantages for France; and, far from being founded on durable institutions, the apparent grandeur of this Colossus reposed only on feet of clay.

6. Reference to the war contributions made by the countries occupied by Napoléon.

Should England Have Made Peace with Bonaparte at His Accession to the Consulate?

When General Bonaparte was named Consul, people expected peace from him. The nation, fatigued with its long struggle, and at that time sure of confirming its independence with the barrier of the Rhine and the Alps, wished only for tranquillity; but the measures to which it had recourse were certainly ill adapted for the accomplishment of its end. The First Consul, however, took steps toward a reconciliation with England, and the ministry of the day declined his overtures. Perhaps they were in the wrong: for, two years afterward, when Bonaparte had established his power by the victory of Marengo,[1] the English government found itself obliged to sign the treaty of Amiens,[2] which was in every respect more disadvantageous than that which might have been obtained at a moment when Bonaparte was desirous of a new success, peace with England. Yet I do not join in the opinion of some persons who pretend that if the English ministry had accepted his proposals, Bonaparte would thenceforward

---

1. The Battle of Marengo (June 14, 1800) was one of the most important episodes of the Napoléonic Wars. For more information, see Hamilton, *Marengo*.

2. The treaty was signed on March 25, 1802, after French victories at Marengo and Hohenlinden, when Austria, Russia, and Naples sued for peace. The signing was made possible by William Pitt's resignation in London. Although England gained possession of two important territories (Trinidad and Tobago in the southern Caribbean and Ceylon in South Asia), the treaty terms were far from favorable to England, which agreed to give up the Cape Colony (in South Africa) and much of the West Indies to the so-called Batavian Republic (from 1795 to 1806, it designated the Netherlands as a republic modeled after the French Republic). England also agreed to withdraw from Egypt while France withdrew from the Papal States. Finally, Malta was restored to the Order of St. John of Jerusalem.

have adopted a pacific system. Nothing was more inconsistent with his nature and his interest. He cannot live but in agitation; and if anything can plead on his behalf with those who reflect on human beings, it is that he can breathe freely nowhere except in a volcanic atmosphere; his interest also recommended to him war.

Every man who becomes the chief of a great country by other means than hereditary right will scarcely be able to keep himself in his situation, unless he gives the nation either freedom or military glory, unless he becomes either Washington or a conqueror. Now, as it was difficult to have less resemblance to Washington than Bonaparte had, he could not establish and preserve absolute power except by stupefying reason and presenting to the French, every three months, a new scene, so as by the greatness and variety of events to fill up the place of that honorable but calm emulation which free states are invited to enjoy.

One anecdote will show how, from the first day of Bonaparte's accession to the Consulship, those around him were aware of the servility with which they must conduct themselves in order to please him. Among the arguments alleged by Lord Grenville[3] for not treating with Bonaparte, one was that, as the government of the First Consul depended wholly on himself, a durable peace could not be established on the life of a single individual. These words irritated the First Consul, who could not endure that the chance of his death should be discussed. In fact, he who meets with no obstacle in men becomes indignant against nature, which alone refuses to yield: it is easier for the rest of the world to die; our enemies, often even our friends, in short, our whole lot prepares us for it. The person employed to refute Lord Grenville's answer in the *Moniteur* made use of these expressions: "*As to the life and the death of Bonaparte, they, my Lord, are above your reach.*" It was thus that the people of Rome addressed their emperors by the style of "*Your Eternity.*" Strange destiny of the human species, condemned by its passions to tread the same circle, while it is constantly advancing in the career of ideas! The treaty of

3. William Wyndham Grenville (1759–1834), also known as Baron Grenville, was a prominent British Whig politician and a close ally of William Pitt the Younger. He served as foreign secretary (1791–1801) and as chancellor of Oxford (1810–34).

Amiens was concluded when Bonaparte's successes in Italy made him already master of the Continent; the terms of it were very disadvantageous for the English; and during the year that it lasted, Bonaparte indulged in such formidable encroachments that next to the fault of signing the treaty, that of not breaking it would have been the greatest. At this epoch in 1803, unfortunately for the spirit of freedom in England, and of course on the Continent, to which she serves as a beacon, the opposition, headed by Mr. Fox, followed a path altogether mistaken with respect to Bonaparte; and thenceforward their party, so honorable in other points of view, lost that influence with the nation which for many reasons it would have been desirable that it should have retained. It was already too much to have defended the French Revolution under the Reign of Terror; but it was, if possible, a still more dangerous fault to consider Bonaparte as adhering to the principles of that Revolution, of which he was the ablest destroyer. Sheridan, who by his knowledge and by his talents had the means of establishing his own fame and increasing that of his country, showed clearly to the opposition the part which she ought to play, in the eloquent speech which he delivered on the peace of Amiens.[4]

"The situation of Bonaparte and the organization of his power, are such," said Sheridan,

> that he must enter into a frightful barter with his subjects. He must promise to make them the masters of the world, that they may consent to be his slaves; and if such be his end, against what power must he turn his restless looks, if not against Great Britain. Some have pretended that he would have no other rivalship with us than that of commerce: happy were this man if he had ever entertained such views of administration; but who could believe it, he follows the old method of prohibitions and excessive taxes. He would wish, however, to arrive at our ruin by a shorter road. He conceives, perhaps, that if this country is once subjugated, he will be able to transport our commerce, our capital, and our credit to his own, as he brought the pictures and statues of Italy to Paris. But his ambitious

4. Sheridan (1751–1816) was one of the Whigs favorable to the French Revolution. The Peace of Amiens was signed on March 27, 1802. The terms were not favorable to Britain, which finally acknowledged France's hegemony in Europe.

hopes would be soon deceived: that credit would disappear under the gripe of power; that capital would sink into the earth if it were trampled at the feet of a despot; and those commercial enterprises would be devoid of vigor in the presence of an arbitrary government. If he writes in his tablets some marginal notes relative to what he means to do with the different countries which he has subdued or intends to subdue, the whole text is consecrated to the destruction of our native land. It is his first thought when he awakes; it is his prayer to whatever divinity he addresses, Jupiter or Mahomet, the God of Battles or the Goddess of Reason. An important lesson should be drawn from the arrogance of Bonaparte: he calls himself the instrument of which Providence has made choice to restore happiness to Switzerland, and splendor and importance to Italy; and we too, we should consider him as an instrument whom Providence has chosen to attach us, if possible, more firmly to our constitution, to make us feel the value of the liberty which it secures to us, to annihilate all differences of opinion in the presence of this great interest, in fine, to keep incessantly in our recollection that every man who leaves France and arrives in England thinks he has escaped from a dungeon to breathe the air and the life of independence.

Liberty would now be triumphant in the universal opinion if all who rallied round this noble hope had seen clearly at the commencement of Bonaparte's reign that the first of the counter-revolutionaries, and the only one who was then formidable, was the man who clothed himself with the national colors that he might re-establish with impunity all that had vanished before them.

The dangers with which the ambition of the First Consul threatened England are marked out with as much truth as force in the speech which we have just quoted. The English ministry is therefore amply justified in having begun the war anew; but, although in the sequel they may have lent more or less countenance to the personal enemies of Bonaparte, they have never gone the length of authorizing an attempt against his life; such an idea did not occur to the leaders of a Christian people. Bonaparte was in great danger from the infernal machine, a mode of assassination the most blamable of all because it threatened the life of a great number of persons at the same time with that of the Consul. But the English ministers had no share in this conspiracy; there is reason to believe that the Chouans, that is to say, the Jacobins of the aristocratic party, were alone guilty. On this occasion,[5] however, a hundred and thirty revolutionaries were transported, though they had no concern in the infernal machine. But it seemed natural to take advantage of the alarm which this event caused to get rid of all whom it was desirable to proscribe. A singular mode, we must acknowledge, of treating the human species! The men, it will be said, who were treated thus were odious characters. That may be true; but what though it be? Will France never learn that there is no respect of persons in the eye of the law? The agents of Bonaparte adopted the extravagant principle of striking both parties when one of them was in the wrong; and this they called impartiality. About the same time, a man to whom we may spare the disgrace of being named proposed that all who should be convicted of an attempt against the life of the First Consul should be burned alive. The proposal of cruel punishments seems to belong to another age than ours; but flattery is not always satisfied with platitudes, and meanness very easily becomes ferocity.

5. On December 24, 1800, the First Consul narrowly escaped the explosion of a bomb in the rue Saint-Nicaise. He subsequently used this attempt on his life as a pretext for eliminating his Jacobin opponents.

CHAPTER VI

Of the Solemn Celebration of the Concordat at Nôtre-Dame.

At the epoch of the accession of Bonaparte the sincerest partisans of the Catholic faith, after having long been victims of a political inquisition, aspired to nothing more than perfect religious liberty. The general wish of the nation was limited to this: that all persecution of priests should cease for the future; that no kind of oath should be required of them any longer; that the state, in short, should in no respect interfere with anyone's religious opinions. The Consular government, therefore, would have satisfied opinion by maintaining in France a complete toleration, like what exists in America, among a people whose constant piety and severe mores, which are its proof, cannot be called in question. But the First Consul was occupied with no such holy thoughts; he knew that if the clergy resumed a political consistence, their influence would promote the interests of despotism; and his intention was to prepare the way for his arrival at the throne.

He needed a clergy, as he needed chamberlains, titles, decorations, in short, all the ancient caryatides of power; and he alone was in a situation to restore them. Complaints have been made of the return of old institutions; and it must never be forgotten that it was Bonaparte who brought them back. It was he who reorganized the clergy to render them subservient to his designs. The revolutionaries, who, fourteen years ago, were still formidable, would never have allowed a political existence to be thus restored to the priests if a man whom they considered in some respects as one of their party had not assured them, when he presented a concordat with the Pope, that the measure was the result of profound combinations and would be useful in maintaining the new institutions. The revolutionaries, with a few exceptions, are more violent than shrewd, and for that very reason are flattered by being treated as able men.

Bonaparte assuredly is not religious; and the species of superstition of which some traces have been discovered in his character relates solely to the worship of himself. He has faith in his own fortune and has manifested the sentiment in different ways. But from Mahometanism to the religion of the fathers of the desert, from the agrarian law to the ceremonial of the court of Louis XIV, his understanding is ready to conceive, and his character to execute, what circumstances may require. As his natural inclination, however, was toward despotism, he liked what favored it; and he would have preferred the old regime of France more than any person if he could have persuaded the world that he was lineally descended from St. Louis.

He has often expressed his regret that he did not reign in a country where the monarch was also head of the church, as in England and Russia; but as he found the French clergy still devoted to the court of Rome, he chose to negotiate with it. One day he assured the prelates that, in his opinion, there was no religion but the Catholic, which was truly founded on ancient traditions; and on this subject he usually displayed to them some erudition acquired the day before. Then, when he was with the philosophers, he said to Cabanis,[1] *Do you know what this concordat is which I have just signed? It is the vaccination of religion, and in fifty years there will be none in France.* It was neither religion nor philosophy which he cared for in the existence of a clergy entirely submissive to his will; but as he had heard mention made of the alliance between the altar and the throne, he began by raising up the altar. The celebration of the concordat was, therefore, if we may use the expression, a full-dressed rehearsal of his coronation.

In the month of April, 1802, he ordered a grand ceremony at Nôtre-Dame. He was present with regal pomp and named for orator at this inauguration, whom? the Archbishop of Aix, the same who had delivered

---

1. Pierre Jean Georges Cabanis (1757–1808) was a close friend of Mirabeau's and a prominent member of the French Ideologues. He was elected deputy to the Council of Five Hundred and was later an opponent of Napoléon.

the coronation sermon in the cathedral of Rheims on the day when Louis XVI was crowned. Two motives determined him to this choice: the ingenious hope that the more he imitated the monarchy, the more he suggested the idea of himself being invested with it; and the perfidious design of so degrading the Archbishop of Aix as to render him wholly dependent and give the world the measure of his own ascendancy. He has always wished, when the thing was possible, that a man of note, in adhering to him, should do some action blamable enough to ruin him in the esteem of every other party. To burn one's ships was to make a sacrifice of reputation to him: he wished to convert men into a sort of coin which derives its value only from the impress of the master; subsequent events have proved that this coin could return into circulation with a fresh image.

On the day of the concordat, Bonaparte went to the church of Nôtre-Dame, in the old royal carriages, with the same coachmen, the same footmen walking by the side of the door; he had the whole etiquette of the court most minutely detailed to him; and though first consul of a republic, applied to himself all this pomp of royalty. Nothing, I allow, ever excited in me so strong a feeling of resentment. I had shut myself up in my house that I might not behold the odious spectacle; but I heard the discharges of cannon which were celebrating the servitude of the French people. For was there not something peculiarly disgraceful in having overturned the ancient regal institutions, surrounded at least with noble recollections, to take back the same institutions in the forms of upstarts and with the chains of despotism? On that day we might have addressed to the French the beautiful words of Milton to his countrymen: *We shall become the shame of free nations, and the plaything of those which are not free; is this, strangers will say, the edifice of liberty which the English boasted of building? They have done nothing but precisely what was requisite to render them forever ridiculous in the eyes of all Europe.*[2] The English at least have not fulfilled this prediction.

---

2. In his political writings John Milton (1608–76) put forward a strong defense of freedom of the press and endorsed the principles of classical republicanism, which he regarded as compatible with Christianity. For more information see John Milton, *Areopagitica and Other Political Writings of John Milton* (Indianapolis, Ind.: Liberty Fund, 1999), 2–51, 415–45.

In returning from Nôtre-Dame, the First Consul said in the midst of his generals, *Is it not true that today everything appeared restored to the ancient order?* "Yes," was the noble reply of one of them,[3] "except two million Frenchmen, who have died for liberty and who cannot be brought to life." Millions more have perished since, but for despotism.

The French are bitterly accused of irreligion. One of the principal causes of this unhappy result is that the various factions for twenty-five years have always wished to direct religion to a political end, and nothing is less favorable to piety than to employ it for any other end than itself. The nobler its sentiments are in their own nature, the more repugnance they inspire when hypocrisy and ambition take advantage of them. After Bonaparte was Emperor, he appointed the same Archbishop of Aix of whom we have been speaking to the Archbishopric of Tours: the Archbishop, in turn, in one of his pastoral charges, exhorted the nation to acknowledge Napoléon as legitimate sovereign of France. The minister who had the superintendence of religious affairs, while he was walking with a friend of mine, showed him this charge and said: "See, he calls the Emperor great, generous, illustrious: all that is very well; but *legitimate* is the important word in the mouth of a priest." During twelve years from the date of the concordat, the ecclesiastics of every rank have never let an opportunity pass of praising Bonaparte in their way; that is, by calling him the envoy of God, the instrument of his decrees, the representative of Providence upon earth. The same priests have since doubtless preached another doctrine; but how can it be supposed that a clergy, always at the orders of the existing authority, whatever that may be, should add to the ascendency of religion over the soul?

The catechism which was received in every church during the reign of Bonaparte threatened with eternal punishment whoever should not love and defend the dynasty of Napoléon. If you do not love Napoléon and his family, said the catechism (which, with this exception, was the catechism of Bossuet), what will happen to you? Answer: Then we shall incur

---

3. Probably General Delmas (1766–1813).

everlasting damnation.* Was it to be believed, however, that Bonaparte would dispose of hell in the next world because he gave the idea of it in the present? The truth is that nations have no sincere piety, except in countries where the doctrine of the church is unconnected with political dogmas, in countries where the priests exercise no power over the state, in countries, in short, where a man may love God and Christianity with all his soul without losing, and still more without obtaining, any worldly advantage by the manifestation of this sentiment.

---

* P. 55. Q. What are the duties of Christians toward the princes who govern them, and what are our duties in particular toward Napoléon I, our Emperor?

A. Christians owe to the princes who govern them, and we owe in particular to Napoléon I, our Emperor, love, respect, obedience, fidelity, military service, the taxes which are imposed for the preservation and defense of the empire and his throne. . . . To honor and serve the Emperor is therefore to honor and serve God himself.

Q. Are there not particular motives which ought to attach us more strongly to Napoléon I, our Emperor?

A. Yes; for it is he whom God hath raised up in difficult times to re-establish the public worship of the holy religion of our ancestors, and to be its protector. He has restored and preserved public order by his profound and active wisdom: he defends the state by his powerful arm; he has become the anointed of the Lord by the consecration which he hath received from the sovereign Pontiff, the head of the Catholic church.

Q. What ought we to think of those who should fail in their duty toward our Emperor?

A. According to the Apostle Paul, they would resist the established order of God himself, and would render themselves worthy of everlasting damnation.

CHAPTER VII

M. Necker's Last Work
Under the Consulship of Bonaparte.

M. Necker had a conversation with Bonaparte as he passed into Italy by Mount St. Bernard a little time before the battle of Marengo; during this conversation, which lasted two hours, the First Consul made a rather agreeable impression on my father by the confidential way in which he spoke to him of his future plans. No personal resentment therefore animated M. Necker against Bonaparte when he published his book entitled *Last Political and Financial Views.*[1] The death of the Duc d'Enghien had not yet occurred; many people hoped for much benefit from the government of Bonaparte; and M. Necker was in two respects dependent upon him: both because he was desirous that I should not be banished from Paris, where I loved to live, and because his deposit of two million was still in the hands of the government, in other words, of the First Consul. But M. Necker, in his retirement, had imposed the propagation of truth as an official duty upon himself, the obligations of which no motive could induce him to neglect. He wished order and freedom, monarchy and a representative government to be given to France; and as often as any deviation from this line occurred, he thought it his duty to employ his talent as a writer, and his knowledge as a statesman, to endeavor to bring back men's minds toward this goal. At that time, however, regarding Bonaparte as the defender of order and the preserver of France from anarchy, he called him *the necessary man,*[2] and in several passages of his books

---

1. The book was published in 1802.

2. The phrase "necessary man" is from Necker's *Dernières vues de politique et de finance,* 7. After calling Napoléon "a necessary man," however, Necker went on (in sec. VIII) to

praised his abilities again and again with the highest expressions of esteem. But this praise did not pacify the First Consul. M. Necker had touched upon the point which his ambition felt most acutely by discussing the project he had formed of establishing a monarchy in France of which he was to be the head, and of surrounding himself with a nobility of his own creation. Bonaparte did not wish that his design should be announced before it was accomplished; still less was he disposed to allow its faults to be pointed out. Accordingly, as soon as this work appeared, the journalists received orders to attack it with the greatest fury. Bonaparte distinguished M. Necker as the principal author of the Revolution: for if he loved this Revolution because it had set him on the throne, he hated it by his instinct of despotism: he would have wished to have the effect without the cause. Besides, his genius in hatred sagaciously suggested to him that M. Necker, who suffered more than anyone from the misfortunes which had struck so many respectable people in France, would be deeply wounded by being designated, though in the most unjust manner, as the man who had prepared them.

No claim for the restoration of my father's deposit was admitted after the publication of his book in 1802; and the First Consul declared, in the circle of his court, that he would not permit me to return to Paris anymore because, he said, I had given my father such false information on the state of France. Assuredly my father had no need of me for anything in this world, except, I hope, for my affection; and when I arrived at Coppet, his manuscript was already in the press.[3] It is curious to observe what it was in this book that could excite so keenly the resentment of the First Consul.

In the first part of his work,[4] M. Necker analyzed the consular constitution as it then existed, and examined also the hypothesis of the royalty established by Bonaparte as it might then be foreseen. He laid it down as

---

draw attention to the highly complex and difficult task faced by the First Consul. For more information, see ibid., 272.

3. In *Ten Years of Exile*, Madame de Staël acknowledged that she encouraged her father to write and publish the book. For more information, see *Ten Years of Exile*, pt. I, chap. viii, 38. Also see Haussonville, *Madame de Staël et M. Necker d'après leur correspondance inédite*, 71–142.

4. Entitled *Sur la constitution française du 22 frimaire an VIII*.

a maxim that there is no representative system without direct election by the people, and that nothing authorizes a deviation from this principle.[5] Then proceeding to examine the aristocratical institution which was to serve as a barrier between the national representation and the executive power, M. Necker judged beforehand the Conservative Senate to be what it has since shown itself, a body to whom everything would be referred and which could do nothing, a body which received on the first of every month salaries from the very government it was supposed to control. The senators were necessarily mere commentators on the will of the Consul.[6] A numerous assembly became conjointly responsible for the acts of an individual; and everyone felt more at liberty to degrade himself under the shadow of the majority.

M. Necker then foretold the suppression of the Tribunate as it took place under the Consulate. "The tribunes," he said,

> will think twice of it before they render themselves troublesome or run the risk of displeasing a senate which every year must fix their political lot and perpetuate them or not in their places. The constitution, in giving the Conservative Senate the right of renewing annually the legislative body and the Tribunate by fifths, does not explain in what manner the operation is to be executed: it does not say whether the fifth which is to give way to another shall be determined by lot or by the arbitrary selection of the Senate. It cannot be doubted that when a right of seniority shall be established, the fifth which ranks first in point of time should be selected to go out at the end of five years, and each of the other fifths in a succession arranged on the same principle. But the question is still very important when applied merely to the members of the Tribunate and of the legislative body, who are chosen together at the outset of the constitution; and if the Senate, without having recourse to lot, should assume the right of naming at pleasure the fifth which is to go out annually during five years (this is what it did), freedom of opinion will be henceforth restrained in a very powerful manner.

There is truly a singular disproportion in the power given to the Conservative Senate: it can remove from the Tribunate whomsoever it shall

---

5. Necker, *Dernières vues de politique et de finance*, 15–17, 20–21.
6. Ibid., 36–37.

think fit, as far as one-fifth of the whole; yet it is not itself authorized to act in the preservation or defense of the constitution, unless by the advice and direction of the Tribunate. What a superiority in one sense, what an inferiority in the other! No part of the structure seems to have been built with symmetry.*[7]

On this point I would venture to dissent from my father's opinion; there was a kind of unity in this incoherent organization; it aimed constantly and craftily at resembling liberty while it was introducing slavery. Ill-contrived constitutions are well calculated to effect such a result; but that always proceeds from the evil intention of the framer; for every sincere mind knows today in what the natural and spontaneous springs of liberty consist.

Then passing to the examination of the mute legislative body, of which we have already spoken, M. Necker says, with respect to the power of introducing laws,

> The government, by an exclusive appropriation, is alone to propose laws. The English would deem themselves ruined as a free people if the exercise of such a right were taken away from their parliament, if the most important and most civic prerogative were ever to escape from their hands. The monarch himself shares in it only indirectly and through the medium of those members of the House of Lords and the House of Commons, who are at the same time his ministers.
>
> The representatives of the nation, who come from all parts of a kingdom or republic to assemble annually in the capital, and who again return to their homes in the intervals between their sessions, necessarily collect valuable notions on the improvements of which the administration of the state is susceptible. Besides, the power of proposing laws is a political faculty, fruitful in social ideas and of universal utility. In order to exercise it, it requires an investigating spirit and patriotic soul, whilst, to accept or refuse a law, judgment alone is necessary. Such was the limited office of the ancient *parlements* of France. Reduced to this function, and unable to judge of objects except one by one, they never acquired general ideas.†[8]

---

* Last Views on Politics and Finance, p. 41.
† Last Views on Politics and Finance, p. 53.
7. Ibid., 38–40.
8. Ibid., 47–48.

The Tribunate[9] was instituted to denounce all kinds of arbitrary proceedings: imprisonments, banishments, blows aimed at the liberty of the press. M. Necker shows that as its election depended on the Senate, and not on the people, it was not strong enough for such a function. However, as the First Consul meant to give it many occasions of complaint, he preferred the suppression of it, whatever might be its tameness. The name alone was too republican for the ears of Bonaparte.

It is thus that M. Necker afterward expresses himself on the responsibility of the agents of power:

> Let us in the meantime point out an arrangement of more real consequence, though in a way quite opposite to all ideas of responsibility, and meant to declare the agents of government independent. The consular constitution says that all agents of the government, besides ministers, cannot be prosecuted for acts relative to their functions, but in virtue of a decision of the Council of State; and then the prosecution is carried on before the ordinary tribunals. Let us observe in the first place that in virtue of a decision of the Council of State, and in virtue of a decision of the First Consul, are two things that amount to the same; for the Council does not of its own accord deliberate upon any subject; the Consul, who names and dismisses the members at his will, takes their opinions, either assembled in a body or, more frequently, distributed into sections, according to the nature of the business; and in the last resort, his own decision is the rule. But this is of little importance; the principal object of the arrangement which I have stated is to exempt the agents of the government from every species of inspection and prosecution on the part of the tribunals without the consent of the government itself. Thus, however audaciously, however scandalously a receiver or assessor of taxes may prevaricate, the First Consul must determine, before anything can be

9. The Tribunate had one hundred members appointed for five years by the Senate; one-fifth of the tribunes were renewable every year. As Madame de Staël argued, in spite of its flaws, this institution could have prevented tyranny in the long run had it been allowed to function smoothly. Napoléon came into conflict with the Tribunate in 1802, after the majority of the senators had nominated Daunou, whom the First Consul profoundly disliked, as a candidate for the Tribunate. Napoléon used this pretext to expel the twenty most-independent-minded tribunes (among them Chénier, Bailleul, Daunou, and Constant) and replaced them with obedient individuals who were unlikely to challenge his authority. For more information, see *Ten Years of Exile*, pt. I, chap. ii, 6–7; and pt. I, chap. ix, 42–43.

done, whether there is ground of accusation. In like manner he will be the sole judge if other agents of his authority deserve to be called to account for any abuse of power; it is of no importance whether the abuse relates to contributions, to requisitions of personal labor, to supplies of any kind, to the quartering of soldiers, and to forced enlistments, designated by the name of conscription. Never has a moderate government been able to exist on such terms. I shall not here adduce the example of England, where such political laws would be considered as a total dissolution of freedom; but I will say that under the ancient French monarchy, neither a parliament nor an inferior court of justice would have asked the consent of the prince to punish the acknowledged misconduct of a public agent or a manifest abuse of power; a particular tribunal, under the name of The Court of Aids, had the ordinary jurisdiction over claims and offenses concerning the revenue, and had no need of a special permission to discharge this duty in all its extent.

In fine, Agent of Government is too vague an expression; authority in its immense circumference may have ordinary and extraordinary agents; a letter of a minister, of a prefect, of a lieutenant of police, is sufficient to constitute an agent; and if in the exercise of their functions they are all out of the reach of justice, without a special permission from the prince, the government will have in its hands men whom such an exemption will render very bold, and who will likewise be sheltered from shame by their direct dependence on the supreme authority. What chosen instruments for tyranny![10]

Might we not say that M. Necker, when he wrote these words in 1802, foresaw what the Emperor has since done with his Council of State? We have seen the functions of the judicial order pass gradually into the hands of that administrative authority, which was without responsibility as it was without bounds; we have even seen it usurp the prerogatives of legislation; and this divan had only its master to dread.

M. Necker, after having proved that there was no Republic in France under the Consular government, easily concluded that it was Bonaparte's intention to arrive at royalty; and he then developed in a very forcible

---

10. Necker, *Dernières vues de politique et de finance*, 72–75.

manner the difficulty of establishing a moderate monarchy,[11] without having recourse to great nobles previously existing, who are usually inseparable from a prince of ancient lineage. Military glory may certainly supply the place of ancestors; it acts upon the imagination even more powerfully than recollections; but as a king must surround himself with superior ranks, it is impossible to find a sufficient number of citizens illustrious by their exploits to constitute an aristocracy altogether new which may serve as a barrier to the authority which had created it. Nations are not Pygmalions who adore their own work; and the Senate, composed of new men chosen from among a crowd of equals, had no consciousness of energy and inspired no respect.

Let us hear on this topic M. Necker's own words. They apply to the Chamber of Peers, such as it was hastily constituted by Bonaparte in 1815;[12] but they apply especially to the military government of Napoléon, which, however, in 1802, was very far from being established as we have since seen it.

> If then, either by a political revolution or by a revolution in opinion, you have lost the elements which produce great nobles, consider yourselves as having lost the elements which produce moderate hereditary monarchy and turn your views, whatever difficulties you may encounter, to another social system.
>
> I do not believe that Bonaparte, with all his talent, all his genius, and all his power, could succeed in establishing at the present day in France a moderate hereditary monarchy. The opinion is important: I shall allege my reasons; let others judge.
>
> I wish at the outset to observe that this opinion is contrary to what we have heard repeated since the election of Bonaparte. France, it was often said, is about to have recourse to the government of one man; that is a point gained for monarchy. But what do such words mean? nothing at all. For we do not wish to speak indifferently of monarchy elective or hereditary, despotic or moderate, but solely of moderate hereditary monarchy; and without doubt the government of any Asiatic prince that you

11. Ibid., 196–221.
12. By the Additional Act during the Hundred Days.

may choose to name is more distinct from the monarchy of England, than the American Republic.[13]

There is an instrument, unconnected with republican ideas, unconnected with the principles of moderate monarchy, which may be used for the establishment and support of a hereditary government. It is the same which placed and perpetuated the imperial sway in the hands of the great families of Rome, the Julii, the Claudii, the Flavii, and which was afterward employed to subvert their authority: I mean military force—the praetorian guards, the armies of the East and West. May heaven save France from a similar destiny![14]

What a prophecy! If I have insisted several times on the singular merit which M. Necker has had in his political works of predicting events, it is to show how a man deeply versed in the science of constitutions may know their result beforehand. It has been often said in France that constitutions are nothing and circumstances everything. Such language becomes the worshippers of arbitrary power, but the assertion is as false as it is slavish.

The resentment of Bonaparte at the publication of this work was extremely keen, because it drew an early attention to his dearest projects, and those which were the most exposed to the attacks of ridicule. A sphinx of a new species, he turned his wrath against the man who solved his riddles. The importance which arises from military glory may, it is true, supply everything: but an empire founded on the chances of battles was not enough for the ambition of Bonaparte; he wished to establish his dynasty, although he could in his lifetime support only his own greatness.

The Consul Le Brun wrote to M. Necker a letter, dictated by Bonaparte, in which all the arrogance of ancient prejudices was combined with the rude harshness of the new despotism. In it M. Necker was likewise accused of having been the man who caused a double number of deputies to be allowed to the Third Estate, of having constantly the same scheme of constitution, etc. The enemies of freedom hold all the same language, however different the situation from which they proceed. M. Necker was then advised to meddle no more with politics, and to leave them to the

13. Necker, *Dernières vues de politique et de finance*, 249–50.
14. Ibid., 253–54.

First Consul, who only was capable of governing France with wisdom; thus despots always consider thinking men to be superfluous in affairs. The Consul finished with declaring that I, the daughter of M. Necker, should be exiled from Paris merely on account of the *Last Views on Politics and Finances* published by my father.[15]

I have since, I hope, merited this exile by my own conduct; but Bonaparte, who took the trouble of inquiring that he might wound more effectually, wished to disturb the privacy of our domestic life by holding up my father to me as the author of my exile. This reflection occurred to my father, who gave ready admission to every scruple; but, thanks to Heaven, he was able to satisfy himself that it never for an instant haunted me.

A very remarkable thing in the last and perhaps the best political work of M. Necker is that, after having in preceding books combated with much force the republican system in France, he examines for the first time what would be the best form that could be given to that kind of government.[16] On the one hand, the sentiments of opposition to the despotism of Bonaparte, which animated M. Necker, inclined him to employ the only weapons that could still reach such an adversary; on the other, at a moment when there was no reason to dread the danger of exciting the public mind too keenly, a political philosopher amused himself with examining a most important question to the full extent of the truth.

The most remarkable idea in this examination is that, when once we decide in favor of a republic, instead of wishing to bring it as near to a monarchy as possible, we should, on the contrary, place all its strength in popular elements. As the dignity of such an institution reposes only on the assent of the nation, the power which, in this case, is to fill the place of every other should be made to appear in a variety of forms. This profound maxim is the basis of that scheme of a republic of which M. Necker details all the parts—though with the often repeated caution that he would not advise a great country to adopt it.

15. See *Ten Years of Exile*, pt. I, chaps. x–xi, 50–64. In 1803, Madame de Staël left France after having asked Joseph Bonaparte to plead with Napoléon to change his mind (63). She was invited to Joseph's estate at Mortfontaine, where she spent three days (accompanied by her elder son, Auguste de Staël).

16. Necker, *Dernières vues de politique et de finance*, 237–71.

He concludes his last work with some general considerations on finances.[17] They contain two essential truths: First, the consular government was in a much better situation in this respect than the king of France had ever been, because on the one hand, the increase of territory increased the receipts, while on the other, the reduction of the debt diminished the expenses; and, besides, the taxes were more productive, though the people were less burdened, by reason of the suppression of tithes and feudal rights. In the second place, M. Necker affirmed, in 1802, that credit could never exist without a free constitution: not, assuredly, that the lenders of the present day have an enthusiastic love of liberty, but because the calculation of their interest teaches them that confidence can be put only in durable institutions, and not in ministers of finance, whom caprice has chosen, whom caprice may remove, and who, in the retirement of their closet, decide upon what is just and unjust without ever being illuminated by the broad daylight of public opinion.

Bonaparte, in truth, maintained his finances by the produce of foreign contributions and by the revenue of his conquests; but he could not have borrowed freely the most inconsiderable portion of the sums which he collected by force. It would be good advice to sovereigns in general who wish to know the truth with respect to their government, that they should judge rather from the manner in which their loans are filled up than from the testimony of their flatterers.

Though Bonaparte could find in M. Necker's work no words concerning himself which were not flattering, he let loose against him with unheard-of bitterness the journals which were all at his command; and from that time this system of calumny has never ceased. The same writers, under different colors, have never varied in their hatred against a man who was the advocate of the most rigid economy in the finances and of such institutions in government as compel rulers to be just.

17. Ibid., 275–341.

CHAPTER VIII

Of Exile.

Among all the prerogatives of authority, one of the most favorable to tyranny is the power of banishing without trial. The *lettres de cachet* of the Old Regime had been justly held forth as one of the most urgent motives for effecting a revolution in France: yet it was Bonaparte, the chosen man of the people, who, trampling underfoot all the principles the support of which had caused the popular insurrection, assumed the power of banishing whoever displeased him even a little, and of imprisoning without any interference on the part of the tribunals whoever displeased him more. I can understand, I admit, how the greater part of the old courtiers rallied round the political system of Bonaparte; they had only one concession to make to him, that of changing their master. But how could the republicans submit to his tyranny—the republicans, whom every word, every act, every decree of his government must have shocked?

A very considerable number of men and women of different opinions have suffered by these decrees of exile, which give the sovereign of the state a more absolute authority than even that which can result from illegal imprisonments. For it is more difficult to carry into effect a violent measure than to exert a species of power which, though terrible in reality, has something benign in its form. The imagination clings to an insurmountable obstacle; great men—Themistocles, Cicero, Bolingbroke, were extremely wretched in exile; Bolingbroke,[1] in particular, declares in his writings that death seemed to him less terrible.

To remove a man or a woman from Paris, to send them, as it was then called, to breathe the air of the country, was designating a severe punishment by such gentle expressions that the flatterers of power turned it easily

---

1. Bolingbroke (1678–1751) spent eight years in exile in France, from 1715 to 1723.

into derision. Yet the fear of such an exile was sufficient to make all the inhabitants of the principal city of the empire incline toward servitude. The scaffolds may at last rouse resistance; but domestic vexations of every kind which are the result of banishment weaken resistance and cause you to dread only the displeasure of the sovereign who can impose upon you so wretched an existence. You may pass your life voluntarily out of your own country: but when you are constrained to do so, you are incessantly imagining that the objects of your affection may be sick, while you are not permitted to be near them and will perhaps never see them again. The affections of your choice, often family affections too, your habits of society, the interests of your fortune, are all compromised; and what is still more cruel, every tie is relaxed and you finally become a stranger in your native land.

I have often thought, during the twelve years of exile to which Bonaparte condemned me, that he could not feel the misfortune of being deprived of France. He had no French recollections in his heart. The rocks of Corsica alone retraced to him the days of his infancy; but the daughter of M. Necker was more French than he. I reserve for another work,[2] of which several passages are already written, all the circumstances of my exile, and of the journeys, even to the confines of Asia, which were the consequences of it. But as I have almost forbidden myself to draw portraits of living characters, I could not give to the history of an individual the kind of interest which it ought to have. In the meantime, I must limit myself to retracing what may enter with propriety into the general plan of this work.

I discovered sooner than others (and I am proud of it) the tyrannical character and designs of Bonaparte. The true friends of liberty are guided in such subjects by an instinct which does not deceive them. To render my situation at the beginning of the consulship still more painful, people of fashion in France thought that they saw in Bonaparte the man who saved them from anarchy or Jacobinism; and they therefore blamed strongly the spirit of opposition which I exhibited against him. Whoever in politics foresees tomorrow excites the resentment of those who think

2. *Ten Years of Exile.*

only of today. More courage, I will venture to say, was requisite to support the persecution of society than to encounter that of power.

I have always retained the recollection of one of these drawing-room punishments, if I may so express myself, which the French aristocrats know so well how to inflict on those who do not participate in their opinions. A great part of the ancient nobility had rallied round Bonaparte; some, as has since appeared, to resume the habits of courtiers; others in the hope that the First Consul would restore the old dynasty. It was known that I had declared myself decidedly against the system of government which Napoléon was following and was preparing; and the partisans of arbitrary power gave, as usual, the name of antisocial to opinions which tend to exalt the dignity of nations. If some of the emigrants who returned under the reign of Bonaparte were to call to mind the fury with which they then blamed the friends of liberty who continued always attached to the same system, perhaps they would learn indulgence by recollecting their errors.

I was the first woman whom Bonaparte exiled; but a great number, adherents of opposite opinions, soon shared my fate. Among others, a very interesting personage, the Duchess de Chevreuse,[3] died of grief occasioned by her exile. She could not, when at the point of death, obtain permission from Napoléon to return once more to Paris to consult her physician and enjoy a last sight of her friends. Whence proceeded this luxury in mischief, if not from a sort of hatred against all independent beings? And as women, on the one hand, could in no respect promote his political designs, while on the other hand they were less accessible than men to the hopes and fears of which power is the dispenser, they gave him a dislike for rebels, and he took pleasure in addressing to them vulgar and injurious words. He hated the spirit of chivalry as much as he sought after etiquette—a bad selection undoubtedly from the manners of ancient days. He likewise retained from his early habits during the Revolution a Jacobinical antipathy to the brilliant society of Paris, over which the women exercised a great ascendancy; he dreaded in them the art of pleasantry

3. Hermesinde de Narbonne-Pelet, Duchess of Cheuvreuse, was exiled to her castle at Luynes. She died in Lyon in 1813.

which, it must be allowed, belongs particularly to French women. Had Bonaparte been satisfied with acting the proud part of a great general and first magistrate of the republic, he would have soared in all the height of his genius far above the small but pointed shafts of drawing-room wit. But when he entertained the design of becoming an upstart king, a citizen gentleman upon the throne, he exposed himself as a fine aim to the mockery of fashion; and to restrain it, as he has done, he was obliged to have recourse to terror and the employment of spies.

Bonaparte wished me to praise him in my writings, not assuredly that any additional praise would have been remarked in the fumes of the incense which surrounded him; but he was vexed that I should be the only writer of reputation in France who had published books during his reign without making any mention of his gigantic existence, and at last with inconceivable rage he suppressed my work on Germany.[4] Till then my disgrace had consisted merely in my removal from Paris; but from that time I was forbidden to travel and was threatened with imprisonment for the remainder of my days. The contagion of exile, the noble invention of the Roman emperors, was the most cruel aggravation of this punishment. They who came to see the banished exposed themselves to banishment in their turn; the greater part of the Frenchmen with whom I was acquainted avoided me, as if I had been tainted with a pestilence. This appeared to me like a comedy when the pain it gave was not extreme; and as travelers under quarantine mischievously throw their handkerchiefs to the passersby, to compel them to share in the wearisome sameness of their confinement, so when I happened to meet a man of Bonaparte's court in the streets of Geneva I was tempted to terrify him by my polite attentions.

My generous friend, M. Matthieu de Montmorenci, had come to see me at Coppet and received, four days after his arrival, a *lettre de cachet*, by which he was banished as a punishment for having given the consolation of his presence to a woman who had been his friend for twenty-five years. I know not what I would not have done at this moment to avoid such a pain. At the same time Madame Recamier, who took no concern

4. For more information, see *Ten Years of Exile*, pt. II, chap. i, 101–10. Madame de Staël's two sons unsuccessfully attempted to meet with Napoléon at Fontainebleau.

in politics beyond a courageous interest for the proscribed of all opinions, came also to see me at Coppet, where we had met several times already. And would it be believed? The most beautiful woman in France, who on this ground alone should have found defenders everywhere, was exiled because she had come to the country seat of an unfortunate friend a hundred and fifty leagues from Paris. This coalition of two women settled on the shore of the lake of Geneva appeared too formidable to the master of the world, and he incurred the ridicule of persecuting them. But he had once said, *Power is never ridiculous,* and assuredly he put this maxim thoroughly to the proof.

How many families have we not seen divided by the fear which was caused by the slightest connections with the exiled? At the commencement of the tyranny, there were some distinguished examples of courage, but vexation gradually alters our sentiments; we are exhausted by constant opposition, and we begin to think that the disgraces of our friends are occasioned by their own faults. The sages of the family assemble to say that there must not be too much communication kept up with Mr. or Mrs. such a one; their excellent sentiments, it is declared, cannot be doubted, but their imagination is so lively! In truth they would willingly proclaim all these poor proscribed sufferers to be great poets on condition that their imprudence be admitted as a reason for neither seeing them nor writing to them. Thus friendship, and even love, are frozen in every heart; private qualities fall with the public virtues; men no longer care for one another, after having ceased to care for their country; and they learn only to employ a hypocritical language which contains a softened condemnation of those who are out of favor, a skillful apology for the powerful and the concealed doctrine of egoism.

Bonaparte had above every other man the secret of producing that cold isolation which presented men to him individually and never collectively. He was unwilling that a single person of his time should exist by his own means, that a marriage should be celebrated, a fortune acquired, a residence chosen, a talent exercised, or any resolution taken without his leave; and, what is remarkable, he entered into the minutest details of the relations of each individual, so as to unite the empire of the conqueror to the inquisition of the gossip, and to hold in his hands the finest threads as well as the strongest chains.

The metaphysical question of the free will of man became altogether useless under the reign of Bonaparte; for no person could any longer follow his own will, either in the most important circumstances or in the most trifling.

CHAPTER IX

Of the Last Days of M. Necker.

I would not speak of the feeling which the death of my father produced in me were it not an additional means of making him known. When the political opinions of a statesman are still in many respects the subject of debate in the world, we should not neglect to give to his principles the sanction of his character. Now what better proof can be given than the impression which it produced upon the people, who were most qualified to judge him? It is now twelve years since death separated me from my father, and every day my admiration of him has increased; the recollection which I have retained of his talents and virtues serves me as a point of comparison to appreciate the worth of other men; and though I have traversed all Europe, a genius of the same style, a moral principle of the same vigor, has never come within my way. M. Necker might be feeble from goodness and wavering from reflection; but when he believed that duty was concerned in a resolution, he thought that he heard the voice of God; and whatever attempts might be made to shake him, he listened only to it. I have even now more confidence in the least of his words than I should have in any individual alive, however superior that individual might be. Everything that M. Necker has said is firm in me as a rock; what I have gained myself may disappear; the identity of my being consists in the attachment which I bear to his memory. I have loved those whom I love no more; I have esteemed those whom I esteem no more; the waves of life have carried all away, except this mighty shade whom I see upon the summit of the mountain, pointing out to me with its finger the life to come.

I owe no real gratitude on earth but to God and my father; the remainder of my days has passed in contention; he alone poured his blessing over them. But how much has he not suffered! The most brilliant prosperity distinguished one-half of his life; he was rich; he had been named prime minister of France; the unbounded attachment of Frenchmen had recompensed him for his devotedness to their cause. During the seven years of his first retirement, his works had been placed in the first class of those of statesmen, and perhaps he was the only individual who had shown himself profoundly skilled in the art of governing a great country without ever deviating from the most scrupulous morality or even the most refined delicacy. As a religious writer,[1] he had never ceased to be a philosopher; as a philosopher, he had never ceased to be religious; eloquence had not hurried him away beyond the limits of reason, nor had reason ever deprived him of a single emotion of true eloquence. To these great advantages he had joined the most flattering success in society: Madame du Deffant,[2] who was acknowledged to have more lively smartness of conversation than any other woman in France, declared in her letters that she had met with no man more pleasing than M. Necker. He too possessed the same charm of conversation, but he employed it only among his friends. In fine, the universal opinion of France in 1789 was that no minister had ever carried further every kind of talent and virtue. There is not a city, not a town, not a corporation in France from which we have not addresses expressing this sentiment. I transcribe here from among a thousand others that which was written to the republic of Geneva by the city of Valence.

Gentlemen Syndics,

Amid the enthusiasm of liberty which inflames the whole French nation, and which penetrates us with a deep sense of the goodness of our august monarch, we have thought that we owe you a tribute of gratitude. It was in the bosom of your republic that M. Necker first saw the light; it was in the abode of your public virtues that his heart was trained to the practice of all those of which he has given us an affecting spectacle; it was in the school of your good principles that he imbibed that gentle

---

1. Necker had published *De l'importance des opinions religieuses* in 1788. For more information about his religious and philosophical views, see Grange, *Les idées de Necker,* 517–614.

2. Marie de Vichy-Chambrond, Marquise of Deffand (1697–1780), was famous for her Parisian salon, which attracted such well-known writers as Montesquieu, D'Alembert, and Condorcet.

and consoling morality which strengthens confidence, inspires respect, and prescribes obedience to legitimate authority. It was likewise among you, gentlemen, that his soul acquired that firm and vigorous temper which the statesman needs when he devotes himself with intrepidity to the painful duty of laboring for the public good.

Penetrated with veneration for so many different qualities, the union of which in M. Necker exalts our admiration, we think that we owe to the citizens of Geneva a public testimony of our gratitude for having formed in its bosom a minister so perfect in every respect.

We desire that our letter may be recorded in the registers of your republic, that it may be a lasting monument of our veneration for your respectable fellow-citizen.

Alas! could it have been foreseen that so much admiration would be followed by so much injustice; that he who cherished France with a pre-dilection almost too great would be reproached with entertaining the sentiments of a stranger; that one party would call him the author of the Revolution because he respected the rights of the nation, and that the leaders of that nation would accuse him of having wished to sacrifice it to the defense of the monarchy? So in former times, as I am fond of re-peating, the Chancellor de l'Hôpital was alternately threatened by the Catholics and the Protestants; so Sully[3] would have sunk under party hatred if the firmness of his master had not supported him. But neither of these statesmen had that lively imagination of the heart which renders us accessible to every kind of pain. M. Necker was calm before God, calm at the approach of death, because at that instant conscience alone spoke. But while he was yet occupied with the interests of this world, there was not a reproach which did not hurt him, not an enemy whose ill-will did not wound him, not a day in which he did not subject himself to twenty different examinations, sometimes to accuse himself of evils which he could not have prevented, sometimes to place himself in the rear of events and weigh anew the different resolutions which he might have taken. The purest enjoyments of life were poisoned to him by the unprecedented per-

3. Maximilien de Béthune, Baron of Rosny and Duke of Sully (1560–1641), minister of Henri IV.

secutions of party spirit. This party spirit showed itself even in the manner in which the emigrants, in the time of their distress, applied to him for aid. Several, when they wrote to him on this subject, apologized for not being able to visit him because the chief man among them had forbidden them to do so. They judged well at least of M. Necker's generosity when they believed that this submission to the impertinence of their leaders would not prevent him from doing them service.

The slavery of the press, among other inconveniencies, placed literary decisions in the hands of the government. The consequence was that by means of the journalists, the police disposed, for the time at least, of the literary success of a writer in the same way as it granted licenses for gambling. Accordingly the writings of M. Necker during the concluding period of his life were not judged impartially in France; and this was an additional evil which he had to bear in his retirement. The last but one of his works, entitled *A Course of Religious Morality*, is, I venture to affirm, one of the best-written devotional books, one of the strongest in thought and eloquence, of which the Protestants can boast; and I have often found it in the hands of persons whose hearts have been stricken with sorrow. Yet the journals under Bonaparte made scarcely any mention of it; and the little that they said gave no correct idea of it. There have been in like manner in other countries some examples of masterpieces in literature which were not rightly estimated till long after the death of their author. It is painful to reflect that one who was so dear to us was deprived even of the pleasure which his talents as a writer indisputedly deserved.

He beheld not the day of justice shine forth for his memory, and his life ended in the very year[4] in which Bonaparte was about to declare himself Emperor, that is, at an epoch when no kind of virtue was held in honor in France. Such was the delicacy of his soul that the reflection which tormented him during his last illness was the fear of having been the cause of my exile; and I was not near to restore him to confidence. He wrote to Bonaparte with a feeble hand, requesting him to recall me when he should

4. Necker's health declined in late March 1804; he passed away during the night of April 9–10. Madame de Staël was in Berlin when she learned of her father's illness. She returned to Coppet on May 19, 1804. For more information, see *Ten Years of Exile*, pt. I, chap. xvi, 81–83.

be no more. I sent this sacred request to the Emperor; he returned no answer: magnanimity always appeared to him affectation, and he spoke of it pretty freely as a virtue only of the drama; had he known its powerful influence, he would have been at once a better and an abler man. After so many sorrows and the exercise of so many virtues, the capacity for affection appeared to have increased in my father at the age when it diminishes in other men; and everything about him announced that when he ceased to live he returned to Heaven.

CHAPTER X

Abstract of M. Necker's Principles on Government.

It has been often said that religion is necessary for the people; and I think it easy to prove that men of an exalted rank have still more need of it. The same is true of morality in its connections with politics. Men have never been weary of repeating that it suits individuals, and not nations; the truth, on the contrary, is that it is to the government of states that fixed principles are especially applicable. As the existence of this or that individual is fleeting and transitory, it sometimes happens that a bad action is useful to him for the moment in a conjuncture where his personal interest is compromised; but as nations are durable, they cannot disregard the general and permanent laws of intellectual order without proceeding to their ruin. The injustice which may be advantageous to one man by way of exception is always injurious to successions of men, whose lot must necessarily fall under the general rule. But the circumstance which has given some currency to the infernal maxim which places politics above morality is that the leaders of the state have been confounded with the state itself. These chiefs have often experienced that it was more convenient and advantageous for them to extricate themselves at any price from a present difficulty; and they have drawn out into principles the measures to which their selfishness or their incapacity induced them to have recourse. A man embarrassed in his affairs would willingly establish the theory that borrowing at interest is the best financial system which can be adopted. Now immorality of every kind is also borrowing at interest; it saves for the moment and ruins later.

M. Necker, during his first ministry, was not in a situation to think of the establishment of a representative government. In proposing courts of provincial administration, he wished to set a limit to the power of ministers and to give influence to enlightened men and rich proprietors in all parts of France. M. Necker's first maxim in government was to avoid arbitrary power and to limit the action of the ministry in everything that was not necessary to the maintenance of order. A minister who wishes to do everything, to order everything, and who is jealous of power as a personal enjoyment, is fit for courts but not for nations. A man of genius, when such a man finds himself by chance at the head of public affairs, should try to render himself useless. Good institutions embody and establish those lofty ideas which no individual, whoever he may be, can put in action for more than a short time.

To hatred of arbitrary power M. Necker joined great respect for opinion and a deep interest for that abstract, yet real being called the people, which has not ceased to be the object of pity, though it has shown itself to be formidable. He believed it was necessary to secure to the people knowledge and comfort, two inseparable blessings. He did not wish to sacrifice the nation to privileged casts; but he was at the same time of the opinion that ancient customs should be dealt with gently on account of new circumstances. He believed in the necessity of distinctions in society, that the rudeness of power might be diminished by the voluntary ascendancy of consideration; but aristocracy, according to his conception, was an institution intended to excite the emulation of all men of merit.

M. Necker hated wars of ambition, estimated very highly the resources of France, and believed that such a country, governed by the wisdom of a true national representation and not by the intrigues of courtiers, had nothing to desire or fear in the middle of Europe.

However beautiful, it will be said, the doctrine of M. Necker might be, it has not succeeded, and therefore was not adapted to men as they are. An individual may not obtain from heaven the favor of aiding the triumph of the truths which he proclaims; but are they the less truths on that account? Though Galileo was thrown into prison, have not the laws of nature discovered by him been since universally acknowledged? Morality and freedom are as certainly the only bases of the happiness and dignity of the human race as the system of Galileo is the true theory of the celestial motions.

Consider the power of England: whence does it proceed? from her virtues and her constitution. Suppose for a moment that this island, now so prosperous, were all at once deprived of her laws, of her public spirit, of the freedom of the press, of her parliament, which derives its strength from the people and gives them back its own in return, how her fields would be dried up! How her harbors would be forsaken! The very agents of arbitrary power, unable any longer to obtain their subsidies from a country without credit and without patriotism, would regret the liberty which for so long a time had at least supplied them with treasures.

The misfortunes of the Revolution resulted from the unreflecting resistance of the privileged ranks to what reason and force demanded; this question is still debated after twenty-seven years. The dangers of the struggle are lessened because the parties are weaker, but its issue will be the same.[1] M. Necker disdained Machiavellianism in politics, quackery in finances, and arbitrary power in government. He thought that the highest talent consisted in bringing society into harmony with the immutable though silent laws to which the Divinity has subjected human nature. On this ground he may be attacked: for it is the ground on which, if he were alive, he would still place himself.

He did not plume himself on that kind of talent which is requisite to constitute the leader of a faction or a despot; he had too much order in his understanding, and too much peace in his soul, to be fit for those great irregularities of nature which swallow up the age and the country in which they appear. But if he had been born an Englishman, I say with pride that

---

1. The political context of the first years of the Bourbon Restoration (1814–16) was marked by heated controversies in the (in)famous *Chambre introuvable*, dominated by the ultraconservatives. The newly elected chamber provided an open arena for vigorous political debates among partisans of the Old Regime, supporters of constitutional monarchy and representative government, and those who wanted to continue the Revolution. The legacy of the French Revolution made the entire situation extremely complex, for the country had witnessed not only the "noble" moment of 1789 that marked the fall of absolute monarchy of divine right, but also the dark moment of the Terror of 1793–94. Hence, in reopening the debate over the legitimacy of the principles of 1789, the Restoration had to come to terms with the violent episodes of the French Revolution. For more information, see Craiutu, *Liberalism Under Siege*, chaps. 2–3, 7–9; and Berthier de Sauvigny, *The Bourbon Restoration*, pt. I, chaps. 1–5; part II, chaps. 2–6; pt. III, chaps. 3, 5.

no minister would ever have surpassed him; for he was a firmer friend to liberty than Mr. Pitt, more austere than Mr. Fox, and not less eloquent, not less energetic, nor less penetrated with the dignity of the state than Lord Chatham. Ah! why was he not permitted, like that nobleman, to utter his last words in the senate of his country, in the midst of a nation which can judge, which can be grateful, and whose enthusiasm, far from being the presage of slavery, is the recompense of virtue!

In the meantime, let us return to the examination of that political personage who forms the most complete contrast to the principles which we have just sketched; and let us see whether Bonaparte himself does not help to prove the truth of those principles, which alone could have maintained him in power and preserved the glory of the French name.

Bonaparte Emperor.
The Counter-revolution Effected by him.

When Bonaparte, at the close of the last century, put himself at the head of the French people, the whole nation desired a free and constitutional government. The nobles, long exiled from France, aspired only to return in peace to their homes; the Catholic clergy invoked toleration; as the republican warriors had effaced by their exploits the splendor of the distinctions of nobility, the feudal race of ancient conquerors respected the new victors, and a revolution had taken place in the public mind. Europe was willing to resign to France the barrier of the Rhine and the Alps; and the only thing that remained was to secure these advantages by repairing the evils which the acquisition of them had brought along with it. But Bonaparte conceived the idea of effecting a counter-revolution to his own advantage by retaining in the state nothing new except himself. He re-established the throne, the clergy, and the nobility; a monarchy, as Mr. Pitt said, without legitimacy and without imitation; a clergy who were only the preachers of despotism; a nobility composed of old and new families who exercised no magistracy in the state and served only as a gaudy decoration of arbitrary power.[1]

---

1. On this issue, see Furet, *Revolutionary France*, 219–25, 248–51; and Bergeron, *France Under Napoléon*, 3–22. Madame de Staël's words must be taken with a grain of salt and might be more appropriate to a later phase of Napoléon's rule (after 1808). As many historians have pointed out, the great conquests of 1789 did not disappear in 1804, when Napoléon became emperor. Moreover, the new privileges sanctioned by Napoléon were not hereditary; on the contrary, as Furet argued, "the dialectic of equality and status wove Napoleonic society together more closely than ever" (250). Yet, it is revealing that toward the end of his reign, in 1813, Napoléon predicted: "After me, the Revolution—or, rather,

Bonaparte opened the door to ancient prejudices, flattering himself that he could arrest them precisely at the point which suited his omnipotence. It has been often said that he would have kept his place if he had been moderate. But what is meant by moderate? If he had established with sincerity and dignity the English constitution in France, he would doubtless still have been emperor. His victories made him a prince; it was his love of etiquette, his thirst for flattery, titles, decorations, chamberlains, that made re-appear in him the character of an upstart. But however rash his system of conquest might be, from the moment that his soul became so miserable as to see no grandeur except in despotism, it was perhaps impossible for him to do without continual wars; for what would a despot be without military glory in a country like France? Could the nation be oppressed in the interior without giving it the fatal compensation of ruling elsewhere in its turn? Absolute power is the scourge of the human race; and all the French governments which have succeeded the Constituent Assembly have perished by yielding to this seduction under some pretext or other.

At the moment when Bonaparte wished to be named emperor, he believed it was necessary to give new confidence, on the one hand, to the revolutionaries with respect to the possibility of the return of the Bourbons, and on the other, to prove to the royalists that in attaching themselves to him, they separated themselves irremediably from the cause of the ancient dynasty. It was to accomplish this double end that he perpetrated the murder of a prince of the blood, the Duke d'Enghien.[2] He passed the Rubicon of crime, and from that day his downfall was written in the book of destiny.

One of the Machiavellian politicians of the court of Bonaparte said on this occasion *that the assassination of D'Enghien was much worse than a crime, for it was a fault.* I have, I acknowledge, a profound contempt for

---

the ideas which formed it—will resume their course. It will be like a book from which the marker is removed, and one starts to read again at the page where one left off" (Furet, *Revolutionary France*, 265–66). His words vindicated to some extent Madame de Staël's opinion.

2. The Duke d'Enghien, the son of the last Condé, lived in the town of Baden, a few kilometers away from the French border. At the recommendation of Fouché, Bonaparte sent his men to arrest the duke, who was considered a potential conspirator capable of sowing discord and turmoil in France. He was brought to Vincennes, where he was executed on March 21, 1804.

all those politicians whose talent consists in showing themselves superior to virtue. Let them for once show themselves superior to egoism; that will be more uncommon, and even more ingenious.

Nevertheless, those who blamed the murder of the Duke d'Enghien as a bad speculation were right even in this view of the matter. The revolutionaries and the royalists, in spite of the terrible cement of innocent blood, did not deem themselves irrevocably united to the lot of their master. He had made interest the deity of his partisans; and the partisans of his doctrine practiced it against himself when misfortune struck him.

In the spring of 1804, after the death of the Duke d'Enghien and the abominable prosecution of Moreau and Pichegru, when every mind was filled with a terror which might in an instant be changed into revolt, Bonaparte sent for some senators with whom he conversed with affected negligence on the proposition which had been made to him of declaring himself emperor, treating it as a matter on which he had not yet come to a fixed resolution. He reviewed the different lines of conduct which might be adopted for France—a republic, the recall of the ancient dynasty, lastly, the creation of a new monarchy; like a person conversing on the affairs of another and examining them with perfect impartiality. Those who talked with him resisted with the most vehement energy every time he exhibited arguments in favor of any other power than his own. At last, Bonaparte allowed himself to be convinced: *Very well*, said he, *since you believe that my nomination to the title of Emperor is necessary to the happiness of France, take at least precautions against my tyranny—Yes, I repeat it, against my tyranny. Who knows if, in the situation in which I am about to be placed, I shall not be tempted to abuse my power?*

The senators went away moved by this amiable candor, the consequences of which were the suppression of the Tribunate, all-complaisant as it was; the establishment of the exclusive power of the Council of State as an instrument in the hand of Bonaparte; the government of the police, a permanent body of spies; and, in the sequel, seven state prisons where those who were confined could be judged by no tribunal, as their lot depended merely on the decision of the ministers.[3]

---

3. In early May 1804, the Tribunate asked that Napoléon be given the title "Hereditary

To maintain such a tyranny, it was necessary to satisfy the ambition of all who would engage in its support. The contributions of the whole of Europe afforded scarcely a sufficient supply of money; and accordingly Bonaparte sought other treasures in vanity.

The principal moving power of the French Revolution was the love of equality. Equality in the eye of the law partakes of justice, and consequently of liberty: but the desire of annihilating every superior rank is one of the pettinesses of self-love. Bonaparte well knew the influence of this failing in France, and this is the mode in which he availed himself of it. The men who had participated in the Revolution were not willing that there should be classes above them. Bonaparte rallied them round his standard by promising them the titles and dignities of which they had stripped the nobles. "Do you wish for equality?" said he to them. "I will do better still, I will give you inequality in your own favor: MM. de la Trémouille, de Montmorency, &c. will be, according to law, private citizens of the state, while the titles of the old regime and the offices at court will be possessed, if it so pleases the Emperor, by the most vulgar names." What a strange idea! Would not one have thought that a nation so prompt at laying hold of improprieties would have delivered itself up to the inextinguishable laugh of the gods of Homer at seeing all those republicans disguised as dukes, counts, and barons, and making their attempts in the study of the manners of great lords, like men repeating a part in a play? A few songs indeed were composed on these upstarts of every kind, kings and footmen; but the splendor of victories and the force of despotism made everything succeed, for some years, at least. Those republicans who had been seen disdaining the rewards given by our monarchs had no longer room enough upon their coats for the broad badges, German, Italian, and Russian, that bedecked them. A military order, the iron crown,[4] or the Legion of Honor might be accepted by warriors, in whom such distinctions recalled their wounds and their exploits; but did the ribbons and keys

---

Emperor of the French." A plebiscite followed in which fewer than ten thousand voters failed to vote. The coronation ceremony took place at Nôtre Dame on December 2, 1804.

4. The Order of the Iron Crown was created by Napoléon (as King of Italy) in 1805 to reward outstanding civil and military exploits.

of a chamberlain, with all the other apparatus of courts, suit men who had stirred heaven and earth to abolish such vain pomp? An English caricature represents Bonaparte as cutting up the red cap of liberty into shreds to make a grand *cordon* of the Legion of Honor. How exact an image of the nobility invented by Bonaparte, who could boast of nothing but the favor of their master! The French troops can no longer be regarded but as the soldiers of an individual, after having once been the defenders of the nation. Ah! how great were they then!

Bonaparte had read history in a confused way; little accustomed to study, he made much less use of what he had learned from books than of what he had picked up by his observation of men. There remained, however, in his head a certain respect for Attila and Charlemagne, for feudal laws and Oriental despotism, which he applied indiscriminately, never making a mistake as to what would instantaneously promote his power, but on other points quoting, blaming, praising, reasoning, as chance conducted him. He would speak in this way for hours together, with so much the more advantage that nobody interrupted him, except by the involuntary applauses which always burst forth on such occasions. It is a singular circumstance that, in conversation, several of Bonaparte's officers have borrowed from their leader this heroical gabble, which in truth has no meaning but at the head of eight hundred thousand men.

Bonaparte, therefore, to make at once a Carolingian and an Oriental empire, bethought himself of creating fiefs in the countries conquered by him, and of investing with them his generals or principal ministers. He fixed the rights of primogeniture, he issued decrees concerning substitutions, he did one the service of concealing his former situation under the unknown title of Duke of Rovigo;[5] while, on the contrary, by taking away from Macdonald,[6] from Bernadotte, from Massena,[7] the names which they had rendered illustrious by so many noble exploits, he as it were defrauded

5. General Savary (1774–1833), one of Napoléon's most faithful collaborators, became Duke of Rovigo in May 1808.

6. Etienne-Jacques-Joseph-Alexandre MacDonald, Duke of Taranto (1765–1840), commander of the French army at Naples in 1799, was promoted to the rank of marshal in 1809.

7. André Masséna (1758–1817) was a military officer who became Duke of Rivoli (in 1808) and Prince of Essling (in 1809).

renown of its rights and remained alone, as he desired, in possession of the military glory of France.

It was not enough to have degraded the republican party by entirely changing its nature; Bonaparte wished also to deprive the royalists of that dignity which they owed to their perseverance and their misfortunes. He gave the greater part of the offices of his household to nobles of the Old Regime. He thus flattered the new race by mingling them with the old, and as he himself united the vanity of an upstart to the gigantic talents of a conqueror, he loved the flattery of the courtiers of the former reign because they were more skillful in that art than the new men, whatever might be the eagerness of the latter to distinguish themselves in the same career. As often as a gentleman of the old court called back to recollection the etiquette of the days that were gone and proposed an additional bow, a certain mode of knocking at the door of an antechamber, a more ceremonious manner of presenting a dispatch, of folding a letter, or concluding it with such or such a form, he was received as if he had made a contribution to the happiness of the human race. The code of imperial etiquette is the most remarkable document of the meanness to which the human race may be reduced. The followers of Machiavellian principles will say that it is in this way that men must be deceived; but is it true that men are deceived in our days? Bonaparte was obeyed (let us not cease to repeat it) because he gave military glory to France. Whether that was a benefit or the contrary, it was at least a clear and unsophisticated fact. But all the Chinese farces which were played off before his car of triumph were agreeable only to his servants, whom, had it been convenient for him, he might have led in a hundred other ways. Bonaparte frequently took his court for his empire; he liked better to be treated as a prince than as a hero; perhaps, at the bottom of his soul, he was conscious that he had more right to the first of these titles than to the second.

The partisans of the Stuarts, when the crown was offered to Cromwell, took their ground upon the principles of the friends of liberty to oppose him, and it was not till the epoch of the Restoration that they resumed the doctrine of absolute power; but at least they remained faithful to the ancient dynasty. A great part of the French nobility hastened to the courts

CHAPTER XI. *Bonaparte Emperor*

of Bonaparte and his family. When a man of very high birth was re-proached for having become chamberlain to one of the princesses, *But what would you have me to do?* he said. *I must serve someone.* What a reply! Does it not contain the full condemnation of governments founded upon the spirit of a court?

The English nobles preserved much more dignity in their civil distur-bances; for they did not commit two enormous faults from which the French nobles cannot easily exculpate themselves: the one, that of having joined foreigners against their own country; the other, that of having ac-cepted places in the palace of a man who, according to their maxims, had no right to the throne; for the election of the people, supposing that Bona-parte could have alleged it in his favor, was not in their eyes a legitimate title. Assuredly they have no right to be intolerant after such proofs of compliance; and less injury is done, in my opinion, to the illustrious House of Bourbon by wishing for constitutional limits to the authority of the throne than by having held places under a new sovereign tainted by the assassination of a youthful warrior of the ancient race.

Could the French nobles who served Bonaparte in the employments of the palace pretend that they were constrained to do so? Far more petitions were refused than places given; and those who did not choose to submit to the desires of Bonaparte in this respect were not obliged to make part of his court. Adrian and Mathieu de Montmorency, whose names and char-acters drew attention, Elzear de Sabran, the Duke and Duchess of Duras, several others also, though not in great numbers, would have no concern with employments offered by Bonaparte; and although courage is req-uisite to resist that torrent which in France carries everything in the di-rection of power, these courageous persons preserved their virtuous pride without being obliged to renounce their country. In general, to do nothing is almost always possible, and it is proper it should be so, since there is no excuse for acting contrary to one's principles.

There were certainly none of the French nobles who fought in the ar-mies like the courtiers who were personally connected with the dynasty of Bonaparte. Warriors, whoever they are, may allege a thousand excuses, and better than excuses, according to the motives which influenced them and the conduct which they followed. For at every epoch of the Revolution France has existed; and surely the first duties of a citizen are to his country.

Never had a man the art of multiplying the ties of dependence more ably than Bonaparte. He surpassed everybody in his knowledge of the great and the little means of despotism; he concerned himself perseveringly with the dress of the women, that their husbands, ruined by their expenses, might be obliged to have recourse to him more frequently. He wished likewise to strike the imaginations of the French by the pomp of his court. The old soldier who smoked at the door of Frederick II was sufficient to make him respected by all Europe. Bonaparte without doubt had enough of military talents to obtain the same result by the same means; but to be master was not all that he desired: he wished also to be a tyrant; to oppress Europe and France, one had to resort to all the means of degrading the human species; and accordingly the wretch has succeeded but too well!

In life, the balance of human motives to good or evil is usually in equilibrium, and it is conscience which decides. But, when under Bonaparte, more than forty million sterling of revenue and eight hundred thousand armed men threw their weight into the scale of bad actions, when the sword of Brennus was on the same side with the gold to make the balance incline; how powerful was the seduction! Yet the calculations of ambition and avarice would not have been sufficient to render France submissive to Bonaparte; something great is required to excite masses of people, and it was military glory which intoxicated the nation while the nets of despotism were spread out by some men whose meanness and corruption cannot be sufficiently emphasized. They treated constitutional principles as a chimera, like the courtiers of the old governments of Europe, whose places they aspired to occupy. But their master, as we shall soon see, coveted more than the crown of France, and did not limit himself to that bourgeois despotism with which his civil agents would have wished him to be satisfied at home, that is to say, among us.

CHAPTER XII

Of the Conduct of Napoléon
Toward the Continent of Europe.

Two very different plans of conduct presented themselves to Bonaparte when he was crowned Emperor of France. He might confine himself to the barrier of the Rhine and the Alps, which Europe did not dispute with him after the battle of Marengo, and render France, thus enlarged, the most powerful empire in the world. The example of constitutional liberty in France would have acted gradually, but with certainty, on the rest of Europe. It would no longer have been said that freedom is suitable only for England because it is an island; or for Holland because it is a plain; or for Switzerland because it is a mountainous country; and a Continental monarchy would have been seen flourishing under the shadow of the law, than which there is nothing more holy upon earth except the religion from which it emanates.

Many men of genius have exerted all their efforts to do a little good and to leave some traces of their institutions behind them. Destiny, in its prodigality toward Bonaparte, put into his hands a nation at that time containing forty million men, a nation whose amiable manners gave it a powerful influence on the opinions and taste of Europe. An able ruler at the opening of the present century might have rendered France happy and free without any effort, merely by a few virtues. Napoléon is guilty no less for the good which he has not done than for the evils of which he is accused.

In short, if his devouring activity felt itself restrained in the finest monarchy in the world, if to be merely Emperor of France was too pitiful a lot for a Corsican who, in 1790, was a second lieutenant, he should at least have stirred up Europe by the pretext of some great advantages to herself.

The re-establishment of Poland, the independence of Italy, and the deliverance of Greece were schemes that had an air of grandeur; peoples might have felt an interest in the revival of other peoples. But was the earth to be inundated with blood that Prince Jerome might fill the place of the Elector of Hesse;[1] and that the Germans might be governed by French rulers who took to themselves fiefs of which they could scarcely pronounce the titles, though they bore them, but on the revenues of which they easily laid hold in every language? Why should Germany have submitted to French influence? This influence communicated no new knowledge and established no liberal institutions within her limits, except contributions and conscriptions still heavier than all that had been imposed by her ancient masters. There were, without doubt, many reasonable changes to be made in the constitutions of Germany; all enlightened men knew it; and for a long time accordingly they had shown themselves favorable to the cause of France, because they hoped to derive from her an improvement of their own condition. But without speaking of the just indignation which every people must feel at the sight of foreign soldiers in their territory, Bonaparte did nothing in Germany but with the view of establishing there his own power and that of his family: was such a nation made to serve as a footstool to his vanity? Spain too could not but reject with horror the perfidious means which Bonaparte employed to enslave her. What, then, did he offer to the empires which he wished to subjugate? Was it liberty? Was it strength? Was it riches? No; it was himself, always himself, with whom the world was to be regaled in exchange for every earthly blessing.

The Italians, in the confused hope of being finally united in one state; the unfortunate Poles, who implore Hell as well as Heaven that they may again become a people, were the only nations who served the Emperor voluntarily. But he had such a horror for the love of liberty that, though he needed the Poles as auxiliaries, he hated in them the noble enthusiasm

1. In 1807 Jérôme Bonaparte (1784–1860), the youngest brother of Napoléon, became king of Westphalia (which included Hesse); his reign ended in 1813. When his nephew, Prince Louis Napoléon, became president of the French Republic in 1848, Jérôme was made governor of Les Invalides, in Paris, and was later appointed marshal of France and president of the Senate.

which condemned them to obey him. This man, so able in the arts of dissimulation, could not avail himself even hypocritically of the patriotic sentiments from which he might have drawn so many resources; he could not handle such a weapon, and he was always afraid lest it be shattered in his hand. At Posen, the Polish deputies came to offer him their fortunes and their lives for the re-establishment of Poland. Napoléon answered them with that gloomy voice and that hurried declamation which have been remarked in him when under constraint, consisting of a few words about liberty, well or ill put together, which cost him such an effort that it was the only lie which he could not pronounce with apparent ease. Even when the applauses of the people were in his favor, the people were still disagreeable to him. This instinct of despotism made him raise a throne without foundation and forced him to fail in what was his vocation here below, the establishment of political reform.

The means of the Emperor to enslave Europe were audacity in war and shrewdness in peace. He signed treaties when his enemies were half beaten, that he might not drive them to despair, but yet weaken them so much that the axe which remained in the trunk of the tree might cause it at length to perish. He gained some friends among the old sovereigns by showing himself in everything the enemy of freedom. Accordingly, it was the nations who finally rose up against him; for he had offended them more even than kings. Yet it is surprising still to find partisans of Bonaparte elsewhere than among the French, to whom he at least gave victory as a compensation for despotism. His partisans, especially in Italy, were in general friends of liberty who had erroneously flattered themselves with obtaining it from him, and who would still prefer any great event to the dejection into which they are now fallen. Without wishing to enter upon the interests of foreigners, of which we have determined not to speak, we may venture to affirm that the particular benefits conferred by Bonaparte, the high roads necessary to his projects, the monuments consecrated to his glory, some remains of the liberal institutions of the Constituent Assembly, of which he occasionally permitted the application outside France, such as the improvement of jurisprudence and public education, or the encouragements given to the sciences: all these benefits, desirable as they might be, could not compensate for the degrading yoke that placed a burden on the character of the people. What superior genius has been developed during his reign, or will be developed for a long time to come, in the countries where he ruled? If he had desired the triumph of a wise and dignified liberty, energy would have been displayed on every side, and a new impulse would have animated the civilized world. But Bonaparte has not procured for France the friendship of a single nation. He has made up marriages, rounded and united provinces, remodeled geographical maps, and counted souls, in the manner since received, to complete the dominions of princes; but where has he implanted those political principles which are the ramparts, the treasures, and the glory of England? those institutions which are invincible after a duration of even ten years; for they have by that time produced so much happiness that they rally all the citizens of a country in their defense?

CHAPTER XIII

Of the Means Employed by Bonaparte to Attack England.

If there is any glimpse of a plan in the truly incoherent proceedings of Bonaparte toward foreign nations, it was that of establishing a universal monarchy, of which he was to be declared the head, giving kingdoms and duchies as fiefs, and re-instituting the feudal system as it was formerly established by conquest. It does not even appear that he meant to limit himself to the boundaries of Europe, and his views certainly reached as far as Asia. In short, his inclination was to march constantly forward, as long as he met with no obstacles; but he had not calculated that, in so vast an enterprise, an obstacle might not only arrest his progress but entirely destroy the edifice of an unnatural prosperity, which would be annihilated the moment that it ceased to ascend.

To make the French nation support war, which, like all nations, desired peace—to oblige foreign troops to follow the banners of France, a motive was necessary which might in appearance, at least, connect itself with the public good. We have endeavored to show in the preceding chapter that, if Napoléon had taken the liberty of nations for his standard, he would have aroused Europe without employing the means of terror; but his imperial power would have gained nothing, and he certainly was not a man to conduct himself by disinterested sentiments. He wanted a rallying word which might make people believe that he had the advantage and independence of Europe in view, and he chose the freedom of the seas. The perseverance and financial resources of the English were without doubt obstacles to his projects, and he had besides a natural aversion to their free institutions and the haughtiness of their character. But what was particularly convenient for him was to replace the doctrine of representative government, founded on the respect due to nations, with mercantile and commercial interests, on which men may speak without end, reason without limits, and never attain the object. The motto of the unfortunate periods of the French revolution, *Liberty and Equality,* gave the people an impulse which could not be agreeable to Bonaparte; but the motto of his banner—*The Liberty of the Seas*—conducted him wherever he wished, and made the voyage to the Indies as necessary as the most reasonable peace, if such a peace should be suddenly for his advantage. Lastly, he had in these rallying words the singular advantage of animating the mind without directing it against power. M. de Gentz[1] and M. A. W. de Schlegel,[2] in their writings upon the Continental system, have treated completely of the advantages and disadvantages of the maritime ascendancy of England when Europe is in its ordinary situation. But it is at least certain that this ascendancy, a few years ago, was the only balance to the dominion of Bonaparte, and that there would not have remained perhaps a single corner of the earth in which a sufferer could have escaped from his tyranny if the English ocean had not encircled the Continent with its protecting arms.

But, it will be said, though we admire the English, yet France must always be the rival of their power; and at all times her leaders have endeavored to combat them. There is only one way of being the equal of England, and that is by imitating her. If Bonaparte, instead of planning that ridiculous farce of an invasion, which has only served as a subject for English caricatures, and that Continental blockade, a measure more serious, but likewise more fatal; if Bonaparte had wished only to become superior to England in her constitution and her industry, France would now be in possession of a commerce founded upon credit, and of a credit founded upon a national representation and upon the stability which such a representation gives. But the English ministry is unfortunately too well aware that a constitutional monarchy is the sole means of securing durable prosperity to France. When Louis XIV struggled successfully at sea

1. Friedrich von Gentz (1764–1832), prominent conservative German political thinker, translator of Burke's *Reflections on the Revolution in France,* and adviser to Metternich.

2. August Wilhelm von Schlegel (1767–1845) was a prominent German Romantic writer and friend of Madame de Staël.

against the English fleets, the financial riches of the two countries were then nearly the same; but since liberty has been consolidated in England for eighty or a hundred years, France cannot bring herself into equilibrium with her rival except by legal securities of the same nature. Instead of taking this truth for his compass, what did Bonaparte do?

The gigantic idea of the Continental blockade was like a species of European crusade against England, of which Napoléon's scepter was the rallying sign. But if, in the interior, the exclusion of English merchandise gave some encouragement to manufacturers, the ports were deserted and commerce annihilated. Nothing rendered Napoléon more unpopular than that increase in the price of sugar and coffee which affected the daily habits of all classes. By burning in the cities which were subject to him, from Hamburg to Naples, the productions of English industry, he disgusted every witness of these *autos-da-fé* in honor of despotism. In the public square at Geneva, I saw some poor women throw themselves on their knees before the pile on which the merchandise was burning, with supplications that they might be allowed to snatch in time from the flames some pieces of cotton or woollen stuff to clothe their infants in misery. Such scenes must have occurred everywhere; and though statesmen, in an ironical style, then said that they were of no consequence, they were the living picture of a tyrannical absurdity—the Continental system. What has been the result of the terrible anathema of Bonaparte? The power of England has increased in the four quarters of the globe, her influence over foreign governments has been unlimited; and it ought to be so, considering the magnitude of the evil from which she preserved Europe. Bonaparte, whom the world persists in calling able, has, however, found the awkward art of multiplying everywhere the resources of his adversaries, and in particular of so augmenting those of England that he has not been able to succeed in doing her more perhaps than one single injury (though that one perhaps is the greatest of all)—the injury of increasing her military forces to such a degree that apprehensions might be entertained for her freedom were it not that confidence may be placed in her public spirit.

It cannot be denied that it is very natural for France to envy the prosperity of England; and this sentiment has caused her to allow herself to be deceived with respect to Bonaparte's attempts to raise her industry to a level with that of England. But is it by armed prohibitions that riches are created? The will of sovereigns can no longer direct the system of commerce and industry among nations: they must be left to their natural development, and their interests must be supported according to their own wishes.[3] As a woman does not procure more homage to herself by being angry at that which is offered to her rival, so a nation can succeed in commerce and industry only by finding means of attracting voluntary tributes, and not by proscribing competition.

The official gazette writers were ordered to insult the English nation and government. In the daily papers, absurd appellations, such as *perfidious islanders, avaricious merchants,* were incessantly repeated, with occasional variations which never deviated too far from the text. In some writings the authors went back as far as William the Conqueror to characterize the battle of Hastings[4] as a revolt, and ignorance rendered it easy for baseness to propagate the most pitiful calumnies. Bonaparte's journalists, to whom no one could reply, disfigured the history, the institutions, and the character of the English nation. This too is one of the scourges arising from the slavery of the press: France has undergone them all.

As Bonaparte had more respect for himself than for those who were under him, he sometimes in conversation allowed himself to say much good of England, either because he wished to prepare men's minds for a situation in which it would be convenient for him to treat with England, or rather because he wished to escape for a moment from the false language which he imposed upon his servants. It was as much as to say, *Let us make our people lie.*

---

3. Economic liberalism has always had an uncertain existence in France. During the last decade of his life, Benjamin Constant, Madame de Staël's close friend, published a number of important articles in which he touched on the relationship between economic freedom and political liberty. See Constant, *De la liberté chez les modernes,* 543–70, 596–602; and Constant, *Commentaire sur l'ouvrage de Filangeri,* pt. II, 105–224.

4. On October 14, 1066.

CHAPTER XIV

On the Spirit of the French Army.

It must not be forgotten that the French army was admirable during the first ten years of the war of the Revolution. The qualities which were wanting in the men employed in the civil career were found in the military: perseverance, devotedness, boldness, and even goodness when their natural disposition was not altered by the impetuosity of attack. The soldiers and officers were often beloved in foreign countries, even where their arms had done mischief; not only did they meet death with that inconceivable energy which will at all times be found in their blood and their heart, but they supported the most horrid privations with unprecedented serenity. The fickleness of which the French are justly accused in political affairs becomes respectable when it is transformed into indifference to danger, and even indifference to pain. The French soldiers smiled in the midst of the most cruel situations and encouraged one another in the agonies of suffering, either by a sentiment of enthusiasm for their country or by a witticism which rekindled the cheerful gaiety to which the very lowest classes of society in France are always alive.

The Revolution had brought the fatal art of recruiting[1] to singular perfection; but the good which it had done by rendering every rank accessible to merit excited in the French army an unbounded emulation. It was to these principles of freedom that Bonaparte was indebted for the resources which he employed against liberty herself. Ere long the army under Napoléon retained little of its popular virtues, except its admirable valor and a noble sentiment of national pride; but how much was it fallen, fighting for a single man, while its predecessors, while its own veterans, ten years

---

1. Reference to the Law Jourdan-Delbrel of September 5, 1798, which introduced mandatory military service.

before, had devoted themselves only for their country! Soon too the troops of almost every Continental nation were forced to combat under the banners of France. What patriotic sentiment could animate the Germans, the Dutch, the Italians, when they had no security for the independence of their native land, or rather when its subjugation bore heavily upon them? They had no common tie except one and the same leader; and on that account nothing was less solid than their association, because enthusiasm for a man, whoever he may be, is necessarily fluctuating; the love only of our country and of freedom cannot change, because it is disinterested in its principle. That which constituted the particular prestige of Napoléon was the idea which was entertained of his fortune; attachment to him was attachment to oneself. A fond belief prevailed with respect to the various kinds of advantages to be obtained under his banners; and as he was both an admirable judge of military merit and knew how to recompense it, any private soldier in the army might nourish the hope of becoming a marshal of France. Titles, births, the services of courtiers had little influence on promotion in the army. There a spirit of equality prevailed in spite of the despotism of the government, because Bonaparte had need of force, which cannot exist without a certain degree of independence. Accordingly, under the Emperor, that which was of most value was assuredly the army. The commissaries who afflicted the conquered countries with contributions, imprisonments, and exile; those clouds of civil agents who came like vultures after the victory to pounce upon the field of battle, did much more to make the French detested than the poor gallant conscripts who passed from childhood to death in the belief that they were defending their country. It belongs to men skilled in the military art to pronounce upon Bonaparte's talents as a captain. But to judge of him in this respect merely by such observations as are within the reach of everybody, it appears to me that his ardent selfishness perhaps contributed to his early triumphs as it did to his final reverses. In the career of arms, as well as in every other, he was destitute of that respect for men, and of that sentiment of duty, without which nothing great is durable.

Bonaparte, as a general, never spared the blood of his troops; he gained his astonishing victories by a prodigal waste of the soldiers which the Revolution had supplied. By marching without extra ammunition he rendered his movements uncommonly rapid, but he thus doubled the evils of war to the countries which were the theater of action. In short, even the style of his military maneuvers has some connection with the rest of his character: he always risks the whole for the whole, counting on the faults of his enemies, whom he despises, and ready to sacrifice his partisans, for whom he cares little if he does not by their means obtain the victory.

In the Austrian war, in 1809, he quitted the island of Lobau when he judged the battle to be lost, and crossed the Danube in the company only of Marshal Berthier and M. de Czernitchef,[2] one of the intrepid aides-de-camp of the Emperor of Russia. Bonaparte said to them, with undisturbed tranquillity, that *after having gained forty battles, it was not extraordinary to lose one*. When he reached the other side of the river, he went to bed and slept till the morning of the following day, without inquiring after the fate of the French army, which his generals saved while he slept. What a singular trait of character! And yet in the greater part of important occasions there is no man more active or more bold. But it would appear that he cannot sail except with a favorable wind, and that misfortune freezes him completely, as if he had made a magical compact with fate and was unable to proceed without her.

Posterity, and already many of our contemporaries, will object to the adversaries of Bonaparte the enthusiasm with which he inspired his army. We will treat this subject as impartially as possible when we shall have arrived at the fatal return from Elba. Who could deny that Bonaparte was in many respects a man of transcendent genius? He saw as far as the knowledge of evil can extend; but there is something beyond that—the region of good. Military talents are not always a proof of superior intellect; in this career, many accidents may contribute to success; besides, that kind of quick survey of circumstances which is necessary for conducting men in the field of battle has no resemblance to the close and accurate observation which the art of government requires. One of the greatest misfortunes of the human race is the impression which the success of force pro-

2. Alexandre I. Czernitchef (1779–1857), prominent Russian general and diplomat. In 1809 Russia supported France in the war against Austria.

duces upon the mind. And nonetheless, there will be neither liberty nor morality in the world if we do not bring ourselves to consider a battle like any other transaction in the world, merely according to the goodness of the cause and the utility of the result.

One of the greatest evils done by Napoléon to France was to have given a taste for luxury to those warriors who were so well satisfied with glory in the days when the nation still existed. An intrepid marshal, covered with wounds and impatient for more, demanded for his hotel a bed so covered with gilding and embroidery that there was not to be found in Paris one that came up to his wishes. *Very well,* said he in his peevishness, *give me a truss of straw, I shall sleep well enough upon it.* In fact, there is no medium for these men between the pomp of the One Thousand and One Nights and the rigid life to which they were accustomed.

Bonaparte must likewise be accused of having altered the French character by forming it to the habits of dissimulation, of which he gave the example. Many military leaders became diplomats in the school of Napoléon, capable of concealing their true opinions, of studying circumstances, and of bending to them. Their courage remained the same, but everything else was changed. The officers who were most closely attached to the person of the Emperor, far from having preserved the lively courtesy of the French, became cold in their manners, circumspect, disdainful; they gave a slight salutation with the head, spoke little, and seemed to share their master's contempt for the human species. Soldiers have always generous and natural emotions; but the doctrine of passive obedience which parties, opposite in their interests though in agreement with their maxims, have introduced among their chiefs, has necessarily altered all that was great and patriotic in the troops of France.

An armed force, it is said, ought to be essentially obedient. That is true on the field of battle, in the presence of the enemy, and in relation to military discipline. But could the French be ignorant, or ought they to have been ignorant, that they were sacrificing a nation in Spain? Was it possible or was it right for them not to know that at Moscow they were not defending their homes, and that Europe was in arms only because Bonaparte had successively availed himself of every country in it to enslave the whole? Some people wanted to make the army a kind of corporation, separate from the nation and incapable of union with it. In this case the unfortunate people would always have two enemies, their own troops and those of foreigners, since all the virtues of citizens are forbidden to warriors.

The army of England is as submissive to discipline as that of the most absolute state of Europe; but the officers do not therefore make less use of their reason, both as citizens, by taking part when they return home in the public concerns of their country; and as soldiers, by knowing and respecting the empire of the law in what regards them. An English officer would never arrest an individual, nor fire upon the people in commotion, till the forms ordained by the constitution had been observed. There is an intention of despotism whenever there is a wish to forbid men to use the reason which God has given them. Obedience to their oath, it will be said, is sufficient; but what is there which requires the employment of reason more than the knowledge of the duties attached to this very oath? Is it to be believed that the oath taken to Bonaparte could oblige any officer to carry off the Duc d'Enghien from the foreign land which ought to have been an asylum to him? Whenever maxims opposed to liberal sentiments are established, it is for the purpose of using them as a battery against our adversaries, but on condition that these adversaries do not employ them in return against us. It is only knowledge and justice which gives no ground of apprehension to any party. What, then, is the result of this emphatical maxim: *The army should not judge but obey?* The result is that in civil troubles the army always determines the lot of empires, but determines ill, because it is excluded from the use of reason. It was in consequence of this blind obedience to its leaders, which the French army had been taught to esteem a duty, that it supported the government of Bonaparte; yet how much has it been blamed for not overturning his power! Civil bodies, to justify their servility to the Emperor, laid the blame upon the army; and it is easy to make the partisans of absolute power, who usually are not very strict logicians, say in the same breath, first that military men should never have an opinion upon any political subject, and next that they are very blamable for having lent themselves as instruments to the unjust wars of Bonaparte. Surely those who shed their blood for the state have some right to know whether it is for the state that they really fight. Not that the army should be the government; Heaven defend us from such an evil! But if the army ought to keep itself apart from all public affairs in all that concerns their habitual direction, the freedom of the country is not the less under its protection; and when despotism endeavors to obtain the mastery, it should refuse to support it. What! it will be said, would you have the army deliberate? If you give the name of deliberation to a knowledge of its duty and to the employment of its faculties in fulfilling its obligations, I shall reply that if you forbid it today to reason against your orders, you will be dissatisfied tomorrow that it did not reason against the orders of another. All the parties which require, in politics as in faith, the renunciation of the exercise of thought, mean only that, whatever happens, we should think as they do. Yet, when soldiers are transformed into machines, we have no right to complain if these machines yield to force. In governing men, it is impossible to succeed without the influence of opinion. The army, like every other association, ought to know that it constitutes a part of a free state, and that it ought to defend the constitution established by law for and against all. Must not the French army bitterly repent at this day of that blind obedience to its chief which has ruined France? If the soldiers had not ceased to be citizens, they would still have been the support of their country.

It must be allowed, however, and with sincerity, that regular troops are an unhappy invention; and if they could be suppressed at once throughout the whole of Europe, mankind would have made a great step toward the perfection of social order. Had Bonaparte stopped in his career after some of his victories, his name and the reputation of the French armies produced at that time such an effect that he might have been satisfied with the National Guard for the defense of the Rhine and the Alps. Every advantage in human affairs was at his disposal; but the lesson which he was destined to give to the world was of another nature.

At the time of the last invasion of France, a general of the Allies declared that every French private citizen would be shot who should be found with arms in his hand; some of the French generals had occasionally been guilty of the same injustice in Germany; and yet the soldiers in regular armies have much less interest in the fate of defensive war than the inhabitants of the country. Were it true, as this general said, that citizens are not permitted to defend themselves against regular troops, all the Spaniards would be guilty and Europe would be still subject to Bonaparte; for it must not be forgotten that the private inhabitants of Spain were the first who commenced the struggle; they were the first who thought that the probability of success was nothing when it was a duty to resist. None of these Spaniards, and, at a subsequent period, none of the Russian peasants, formed part of the regular troops; yet this circumstance only rendered them more worthy of our admiration for the firmness with which they fought for the independence of their country.

CHAPTER XV

Of the Legislation and Administration Under Bonaparte.

The unlimited despotism and the shameless corruption of the civil government under Bonaparte has not yet been sufficiently delineated. It might be supposed that after the torrent of abuse which is always poured forth in France against the vanquished, there would remain no ill to be spoken against a fallen power which the flatterers of the subsequent regime have not exhausted. But as they who attacked Bonaparte wished still to spare the doctrine of despotism; as many of those who load him with reproach today had praised him yesterday, they were obliged, in order to introduce some consistency into conduct in which nothing is systematic except baseness, to carry their outrages even beyond what the man deserves, and yet in many respects to observe a prudent silence on a system from which they still wanted to benefit. The greatest crime of Napoléon, however, that for which every man of reflection, every writer qualified to be the dispenser of glory among posterity, will never cease to accuse him before mankind, was the mode in which he established and organized despotism. He founded it on immorality; for so much knowledge was diffused through France that absolute power, which elsewhere rests on ignorance, could there be maintained only by corruption.

Is it possible to speak of legislation in a country where the will of a single man decided everything—where this man, uncertain and fluctuating as the waves of the sea during a tempest, was unable to endure the barriers of his own will if the regulation of the evening was opposed to the next day's desire of change? A counselor of state once thought proper to represent to him that the resolution which he was about to take was inconsistent with the Code Napoléon. *Very well*, said he, *the Code Napoléon was made for the welfare of the people; and if that welfare requires other mea-sures, we must adopt them.* What a pretext for unlimited power is the public welfare! Robespierre did well in giving that name to his government. Shortly after the death of the Duke d'Enghien, while Bonaparte was still troubled at the bottom of his soul by the horror which that assassination had inspired, he said in a conversation upon literature with an artist very capable of forming a judgment upon the subject: "Reason of state, do you observe, has with the moderns supplied the place of the fatalism of the ancients. Corneille is the only French tragic writer who has felt this truth. Had he lived in my time, I would have made him my prime minister."

There were two kinds of instruments of imperial power, laws and de-crees. The laws received the sanction of the semblance of a legislative body; but the real exercise of authority was to be found in the decrees which emanated directly from the Emperor and were discussed in his council. Napoléon left the fine speakers of the Council of State, and the mute deputies of the legislative body, to deliberate and decide on some abstract questions in jurisprudence, with the view of giving his govern-ment a false air of philosophical wisdom. But when laws relative to the exercise of power were concerned, all the exceptions, as well as all the rules, were under the jurisdiction of the Emperor. In the Code Napoléon, and even in the criminal code, some good principles remain, derived from the Constituent Assembly: the institution of juries, for instance, the anchor of French Hope—and several improvements in the mode of procedure which have brought that branch of jurisprudence out of the darkness in which it lay before the Revolution, and in which it still lies in several states of Europe. But of what value were legal institutions when extraordinary tribunals named by the Emperor, special courts, and military commissions judged all political offenses—that is to say the very offenses in which the unchangeable aegis of the law is most required? In the succeeding volume we shall show how the English have multiplied precautions in political prosecutions to protect justice more efficaciously from the encroachments of power. What examples has not Bonaparte's reign exhibited of those extraordinary tribunals, which became habitual! For when one arbitrary act is permitted, the poison spreads itself through all the affairs of the state. Have not rapid and dark executions polluted the soil of France? The military code in all countries except England interferes too much with the civil. But under Bonaparte it was enough to be accused of interfering with the recruitment of soldiers in order to bring the accused before a military commission. It was thus that the Duke d'Enghien was tried. Bonaparte never once left a political offense to the decision of a jury. General Moreau and those who were accused along with him were deprived of that right; but they were fortunately brought before judges who respected their conscience. These judges, however, were not able to prevent the perpetration of iniquities in that horrible trial, and the torture was introduced anew in the nineteenth century by a national chief whose power ought to have emanated from opinion.

Under the reign of Bonaparte, it was difficult to distinguish legislative measures from measures of administration, because both were equally dependent on the supreme authority. On this subject, however, we shall make one main observation. Whenever the improvements of which the different branches of the government were susceptible in no respect struck at the power of Bonaparte, but on the contrary promoted his plans and his glory, he made, in order to effect them, an able use of the immense resources which the dominion of nearly all Europe gave him. And as he possessed a great talent for discovering, among a number of men, those who could be useful instruments of service to him, he generally employed persons very well qualified for the affairs with the care of which they were entrusted. We owe to the imperial government the museums of the arts and the embellishments of Paris, high roads, canals which facilitate the mutual communications of the departments; in short, all that could strike the imagination by showing, as in the Simplon and Mont Cenis, that nature obeyed Bonaparte with almost as much docility as men. These various prodigies were accomplished because he could cause to bear on any particular point the taxes and the labor of eighty million men; but the kings of Egypt and the Roman emperors had, in this respect, equally great titles to glory. In what country did Bonaparte take any concern about the moral development of the people? What means, on the contrary, did he not employ in France to stifle the public spirit which had grown up in spite of the bad governments to which faction had given birth?

All the local authorities in the provinces were gradually suppressed or annulled; there remains in France only one focus of movement—Paris; and the instruction which arises from emulation faded away to nothing in the provinces, while the carelessness with which the schools were kept up completed the consolidation of that ignorance which agrees so well with slavery. Yet as those who are endowed with intellect feel the necessity of exerting it, all who had any talent went immediately to the capital to endeavor to obtain places. Hence proceeds that rage for being employed and pensioned by the state which degrades and devours France. If men had anything to do at home; if they could take a share in the administration of their city or department; if they had an opportunity of making themselves useful there, of gaining consideration, and of cheering themselves with the hope of being one day elected a deputy; we should not see everyone hastening to Paris who can flatter himself with prevailing over his rivals by an intrigue or a flattery the more.[1]

No employment was left to the free choice of the citizens. Bonaparte took delight in issuing decrees concerning the nomination of doorkeepers and sergeants dated from the first capitals in Europe. He wished to exhibit himself as present everywhere, as sufficient for everything; in fine, as the sole governing being upon earth. It was, however, only by the tricks of a mountebank that a man could succeed in multiplying himself to such a degree; for the substance of power always falls into the hands of the subaltern agents who exercise the details of despotism. In a country where there is neither any intermediate independent body nor freedom of the press, there is one thing which a despot, whatever be the superiority of his genius, can never know; and that is the truth which could be disagreeable to him.

Commerce, credit, all that demands spontaneous activity in the nation and a sure defense against the caprices of government, were ill adapted to the system of Bonaparte. The contributions of foreign countries were its only basis. By treating the public debt with respect, an appearance of good faith was given to the government without actually hindering it very

---

1. This strongly centralized structure continued during the first years of the Bourbon Restoration. For more information, see Craiutu, *Liberalism Under Siege*, chaps. 3 and 6.

much, given that the sum was so small. But the other creditors of the public treasury knew that their payment or nonpayment was to be considered as a chance, on the determination of which their right was the circumstance which had the least influence. Accordingly nobody thought of lending to the state, however powerful its chief might be; and for the very reason that he was too powerful. The revolutionary decrees accumulated during fifteen years of disorder were taken or let alone according to the exigency of the moment. On every affair there was generally one law on this side and another on that, which the ministers applied according to their convenience. Sophisms, which were a mere article of superfluity, since authority was all-powerful, justified by turns the most opposite measures.

What a shameful establishment was that of the police! This political inquisition has in modern times taken the place of religious inquisition. Was the chief beloved who needed to weigh down the nation with such a bondage? He made use of some to accuse others, and boasted of practicing the old maxim of dividing in order to command which, thanks to the progress of human reason, is now an artifice very easily discovered. The revenue of this police was worthy of its employment. The gaming houses of Paris supplied the funds for its support: and thus it hired vice with the money of the vice which paid it. It escaped public attention by the mystery which enveloped it; but when chance brought into open day a prosecution in which the agents of the police were in some way concerned, is it possible to conceive anything more disgusting, more perfidious, or more mean than the disputes which arose between these wretches? Sometimes they declared that they had professed one opinion to make use secretly of the opposite; sometimes they boasted of the snares which they had prepared to induce malcontents to conspire, with the view of betraying them as soon as a conspiracy was formed; and yet the depositions of such men were received by the tribunals! The unfortunate invention of this police has since been directed against the partisans of Bonaparte in their turn; had they not reason to think that it was the bull of Phalaris,[2] of which, after having conceived the fatal idea of it, they were themselves undergoing the punishment?

---

2. The tyrant of Agrigento (570–554 B.C.), who is said to have had his enemies burned inside an iron bull.

CHAPTER XVI

Of Literature Under Bonaparte.

This very police for which we have not terms contemptuous enough, terms which put a sufficient distance between an honest man and the creature who could enter into such a den, was entrusted by Bonaparte with the charge of directing the public mind in France. In fact, when there is no freedom of the press, and when the power of the police does not confine itself to matters of censorship, but dictates to a whole people the opinions which they are to entertain on politics, on religion, on morals, on books, and on individuals, into what a state must a nation fall which has no other nourishment for its reflections than that which despotic authority permits or prepares? We have therefore no reason to be surprised at the degradation of literature and literary criticism in France. There is certainly nowhere more talent or more quickness in attaining proficiency than among the French. We may see what astonishing progress they are constantly making in the sciences and in erudition, because those two paths have no connection with politics; whilst literature can now produce nothing great without liberty.[1] The masterpieces of the age of Louis XIV will be adduced in opposition to us; but the slavery of the press was much less severe under that sovereign than under Bonaparte. Toward the end of the reign of Louis XIV, Fénélon and other reflecting men were already engaged in the discussion of questions essential to the interests of society. Poetical genius in every country exhausts itself periodically and revives only at certain intervals. But the art of prose composition, which is inseparable from thought, embraces necessarily the whole philosophical sphere of ideas; and when men of letters are doomed to wheel about in madrigals and idylls, the dizziness of flattery soon seizes them; and they can produce

---

1. On the connection between literature and politics, also see Madame de Staël, *Politics, Literature, and National Character,* 139–265.

nothing that will pass beyond the suburbs of the capital and the boundaries of the present time.

The task imposed on writers under Bonaparte was singularly difficult. They were to combat with fury the liberal principles of the Revolution, but were to respect all the interests which depended on it; so that liberty was annihilated while the titles, estates, and offices of the revolutionaries were sacred. Bonaparte one day said, speaking of J. J. Rousseau, *He was the cause of the Revolution. For my part, I have no reason to complain of him; for it was in the Revolution that I caught the throne.* Such was the language which was to serve as a text for writers to sap incessantly constitutional laws and the everlasting rights on which they are founded, and yet exalt the despotic conqueror who had been produced by the storms of the Revolution, and had afterward calmed them. When religion was concerned, Bonaparte seriously declared in his proclamations that France should distrust the English because they were heretics; but when he wished to justify the persecutions which had been endured by the most venerable and the most moderate of the heads of the church, Pope Pius VII,[2] he accused him of fanaticism. The watchword was to denounce as a partisan of anarchy whoever published any kind of philosophical opinion; but if a noble seemed to insinuate that the ancient princes were more skillful than the new in the dignity of courts, he was without fail marked out as a conspirator. In fine, it was necessary to reject all that was valuable in every system of opinions to make up the worst of human plagues, tyranny in a civilized country.

Some writers have endeavored to frame an abstract theory of despotism in order, if I may say so, to whitewash it anew, and so give it an air of philosophical novelty. Others, on behalf of the upstart men, have plunged into Machiavellianism, as if depth were to be found there; and have held up the power of the creatures of the Revolution in the light of a sufficient security against the return of the old governments, as if there were only interests in the world, and the career of the human species had no connection with virtue. All that remains of this trickery is a certain combi-

---

2. Pope Pius VII was arrested by Napoléon's men in July 1809 after refusing to sign a new Concordat. He was able to return to the Vatican only in 1814.

nation of phrases unsupported by any true idea, and yet duly constructed according to the rules of grammar, with verbs, nominatives, and accusatives. The paper suffers everything, said a man of wit. Doubtless it is the only sufferer, since men retain no remembrance of sophisms; and fortunately for the dignity of literature, no monument of this noble art can be raised on false bases. The accents of truth are essential to eloquence, just principles to reasoning, courage of soul to the impetuous excursions of genius; and nothing of this is to be found in writers who follow the direction of force, from whatever point of the compass it may blow.

The journals were filled with addresses to the Emperor, with the strolls of the Emperor, with those of the princes and princesses, with ceremonies and presentations at court. These journals, faithful to the spirit of servitude, found the means to be insipid at the very moment of the subversion of the world; and had it not been for the official bulletins,[3] which came from time to time to inform us that the half of Europe was conquered, we might have believed that we were living under arbors of flowers and that we had nothing better to do than to count the steps of their Imperial Majesties and Highnesses, and to repeat the gracious words which they had condescended to let fall upon the head of their prostrate subjects. Was it thus that men of letters and magistrates capable of thought should have conducted themselves in the presence of posterity?

Some persons, however, tried to print books under the censorship of the police; what was the consequence? a persecution like that which forced me to fly by Moscow to seek an asylum in England.[4] The bookseller Palm was shot in Germany for having refused to name the author of a pamphlet which he had printed.[5] And, if more numerous examples of proscriptions cannot be quoted, the reason is that despotism was exerted so strongly that at last all submitted to it, as to those terrible laws of nature, disease

---

3. Bulletins of the Grand Army.

4. The printed copies of *On Germany* were destroyed by the police in October 1810; the original manuscript survived and was sent to Vienna. The book finally appeared in London in 1813. For more information, see *Ten Years of Exile,* 101–10; also see *Madame de Staël, ses amis, ses correspondants. Choix de lettres (1778–1817),* 395–425.

5. The reason was that the editor had distributed an anti-French tract entitled *L'Allemagne dans sa profond humiliation.*

and death. It was not merely the endless rigors to which you were exposed under so persevering a tyranny; but you could enjoy no literary glory in your own country when journals, as numerous as under a free government, and yet all following abjectly the same language, teased you with the witticisms which were prescribed to them. For my part I have furnished continual refrains to the French journalists for fifteen years—the melancholy of the North, the perfectibility of the human species, the muses of romance, the muses of Germany. The yoke of authority and the spirit of imitation were imposed upon literature as the official journal dictated the articles of faith in politics. The sagacious instinct of despotism made the agents of the literary police feel that originality in the manner of writing may conduct to independence of character; and that great care must be taken not to suffer English and German books to be introduced into Paris, if it is meant to check the French writers, while they observe the rules of taste, from keeping pace with the progress of the human mind in countries where civil troubles have not retarded its advancement.

Finally, of all the pains which the slavery of the press can inflict, the bitterest is to see what you most love or most respect insulted in the public papers without the possibility of procuring the insertion of a reply in the same gazettes, which are necessarily more popular than books. What cowardice to attack the grave when the friends of the deceased cannot take up their defense! What cowardice in these mediocre and unscrupulous writers, when backed by authority, to attack the living too, and to serve as a vanguard to all the proscriptions of which absolute power, when the least suspicion is suggested to it, is so prodigal! What a style is that which bears the seal of the police! When we read, by the side of this arrogance and meanness, the discourses of Englishmen or Americans, of public men, in short, who, in addressing other men, seek only to impress upon them their sincere conviction, we felt ourselves moved as if the voice of a friend had all at once reached the ear of a forsaken being who knew not where to find a fellow creature.

CHAPTER XVII

A Saying of Bonaparte
Printed in the Moniteur.

It was not enough that every act of Bonaparte should bear the stamp of a despotism becoming always more audacious; it was further necessary that he himself reveal the secret of his own government, disdainful enough of mankind that he should reveal it openly. In the *Moniteur* of the month of July, 1810, he caused these words to be inserted, addressed to his brother Louis Bonaparte's second son,[1] who was then destined to be Grand Duke of Berg. *Never forget,* says he, *in whatever situation my politics and the interest of my empire may place you, that your first duties are to me, your second to France; and that all your other duties, even your duties toward the people whom I may have entrusted to your care, come only afterward.* This is no libel, it is not the opinion of a faction: it is the man himself, it is Bonaparte in person, who brings against himself a severer accusation than posterity would ever have dared to do. Louis XIV was accused of having said in private, *I am the state;* and enlightened historians have with justice grounded themselves upon this language in condemning his character. But if, when that monarch placed his grandson on the throne of Spain, he had publicly taught him the same doctrine that Bonaparte taught his nephew, perhaps even Bossuet would not have dared to prefer the interests of kings to those of nations. He who chose thus to substitute his gigantic *self* in the place of the human species was a man chosen by the people—a man whom the friends of freedom for an instant mistook as the representative of their cause! Many have said, he is the child of the Revolution; yes, without doubt; but a parricidal child: should they then have acknowledged him?

1. The future Emperor Napoléon III.

CHAPTER XVIII

On the Political Doctrine of Bonaparte.

One day M. Suard, who more than any other lettered Frenchman united the tact of literature with a knowledge of the great world, was speaking boldly before Bonaparte of the picture of the Roman emperors in Tacitus: "Very well," said Napoléon; "but he ought to have told us why the Roman people suffered, and even liked those bad emperors. It is that which it was of importance to explain to posterity." Let it be our endeavor not to incur, with respect to the Emperor of France himself, the censure which he passed on the Roman historian.

The two principal causes of Napoléon's power in France were, above all, his military glory and the art with which he re-established order without attacking those selfish passions to which the Revolution had given birth. But not everything was included in these two problems.

It is pretended that, in discussions in the Council of State, Napoléon displayed a universal sagacity. I have some doubts of the ability ascribed to a man who is all-powerful; it is much more difficult for us, the common people, to earn our celebrity. One is not, however, master of Europe during fifteen years without having a piercing view of men and things. But there was in the mind of Bonaparte an incoherence which is a marked feature of those who do not range their thoughts under the law of duty. The power of commanding had been given by nature to Bonaparte; but it was rather because other men did not act upon him, than because he acted upon them, that he became their master. The qualities which he lacked served his purpose as well as the talents he possessed; and he made himself obeyed only by degrading those whom he subjected. His successes are astonishing; his reverses more astonishing still. What he performed, aided by the energy of the nation, is admirable; the state of torpor in which he left it can scarcely be conceived. The multitude of men of talent whom he employed is extraordinary; but the characters whom he debased have done more harm to the cause of liberty than the service that could be rendered to it by all the powers of intelligence. To him, above all, may be applied the fine image of despotism, in the "Spirit of Laws";[1] "he cut up the tree by its roots to obtain its fruit," and perhaps he has even dried up the soil.

In a word, Bonaparte, the absolute master of eighty million men, and meeting nowhere with opposition, knew neither how to found a single institution in the state nor durable power for himself.[2] What, then, was the destructive principle which haunted his triumphal steps? What was it? the contempt of mankind, and consequently of all the laws, all the studies, all the establishments, and all the elections of which the basis is respect for the human race. Bonaparte was intoxicated with the vile draught of Machiavellism; he resembled in many respects the Italian tyrants of the fourteenth and fifteenth centuries; and as he had read but little, the natural tendency of his character was not counteracted by the effect of information. The Middle Ages being the most brilliant era in the history of the Italians, many of them have but too much respect for the maxims of government at that period, and those maxims were all collected by Machiavelli.

Reading lately in Italy his famous treatise of *The Prince*, which still finds believers among power-holders, a new fact and a new conjecture appeared to me worthy of notice. In the first place, letters of Machiavelli found in the manuscripts of the Barberini library and published in 1813 prove clearly that he published his *Prince* in order to reconcile himself with the Medicis. They had put him to the rack on account of his efforts in favor of liberty; he was ruined, in bad health, and without resources;

---

1. Montesquieu, *The Spirit of the Laws*, book 5, chap. 13, 59.

2. This statement must be taken with a grain of salt. Napoléon's legacy includes, among other things, the famous Napoleonic Code (enacted in 1804) and the introduction of the modern professional conscript army. For an overview of Napoléon's institutional legacy (the administration, the fiscal and judicial systems, education, the army, and the relations between the state and the church), see Bergeron, *France Under Napoléon*, 23–84; and Alexander, *Bonapartism and Revolutionary Tradition in France*. A detailed study of legislation under Napoléon can be found in Beck, *French Legislators, 1800–1834.*

he gave up his principles, but it was after having been put to the torture—in our days, people yield to slighter things.

This treatise of *The Prince,* where we find unhappily that superiority of mind which Machiavelli had displayed in a better cause, was not composed, as has been believed, to render despotism odious by showing the frightful resources which despots must employ to maintain their authority. This supposition is too refined to be admitted.[3] I am inclined to think that Machiavelli, detesting above everything the yoke of foreigners in Italy, tolerated, and even encouraged, the means, whatever they were, which the princes of the country could employ in order to be masters, hoping that they would one day be powerful enough to repulse the German and French troops. Machiavelli analyzes the art of war in his writings like a military man; he reverts continually to the necessity of a military organization entirely national; and if he sullied his reputation by his indulgence for the crimes of the Borgias, it was perhaps because he felt too strongly the desire of attempting every means of recovering the independence of his country. Bonaparte did not certainly examine the *Prince* of Machiavelli in this point of view; but he sought there what still passes for profound wisdom with vulgar minds, the art of deceiving mankind. This policy must fall in proportion to the extension of knowledge, as the belief in witchcraft has fallen since the true laws of natural philosophy have been discovered.

A general principle, whatever it might be, was displeasing to Bonaparte, as a thing foolish or hostile. He listened only to the considerations of the moment, and examined things merely with a view to their immediate utility; for he would have wished to stake the whole world in an annuity on his own life. He was not sanguinary but indifferent respecting the lives of men, considering them but as a means of attaining his end or as an obstacle to be removed out of his way. He was even less irascible than he often seemed to be: he wished to terrify by his words, in order to spare himself the act by the threat. Everything with him was means or end; nothing involuntary was to be found either in good or evil. It is pre-

---

3. This interpretation of Machiavelli as the founder of "Machiavellianism" has recently been challenged and nuanced by scholars (such as Quentin Skinner and Maurizio Viroli) who emphasized his republicanism. The classical biography of Machiavelli remains Ridolfi, *The Life of Niccolò Machiavelli.*

tended that he said, "I have so many conscripts to expend by the year"; and it is probable that he held that language, for Bonaparte had contempt enough for his hearers to delight in a kind of sincerity which is nothing less than impudence.

He never believed in exalted sentiments, either in individuals or in nations; he considered the expression of these sentiments as hypocrisy. He believed that he held the key of human nature by fear and by hope, skillfully presented to the selfish and the ambitious. It must be allowed that his perseverance and activity were never slackened on behalf of the slightest interests of despotism; but it was that very despotism which was destined one day to fall upon his head. An anecdote, in which I happened to have some share, may give an additional idea of the system of Bonaparte relative to the art of governing.

The Duke of Melzi,[4] who was for some time vice president of the Cisalpine Republic, was one of the most distinguished characters which Italy, so fertile in every production, has brought forth. Born of a Spanish mother and an Italian father, he blended the dignity of one nation with the vivacity of the other; and I am not sure whether even in France a man could be cited more remarkable for his powers of conversation, and for the more important and essential talent of knowing and appreciating all those who acted a political part in Europe. The First Consul was obliged to employ him, because he had the greatest influence over his fellow-citizens, and because his attachment to his country was unquestioned. Bonaparte did not like to make use of men who were disinterested and whose principles, whatever they might be, were not to be shaken; he was therefore continually circumventing Melzi, in order to corrupt him.

Having caused himself to be crowned King of Italy in 1805, Bonaparte went to the legislative body of Lombardy and informed the Assembly that he had the intention of giving a considerable estate to the Duke of Melzi as a testimony of public gratitude toward him: this, he hoped, would render him unpopular. Being then at Milan, I saw that same evening M. de

---

4. Francesco Melzi d'Eril (1753–1816) became vice president of the Cisalpine Republic in 1801. Four years later, he was appointed grand chancellor of the Kingdom of Italy and was ennobled in 1807.

Melzi, who was quite in despair at the perfidious trick that Napoléon had played him, without having given him the slightest warning. As Bonaparte would have been irritated by a refusal, I advised M. de Melzi to appropriate instantly to a public establishment the revenues with which Napoléon wanted to overwhelm him. He followed my advice, and the next day, walking with the Emperor, he told him that such was his intention. Bonaparte, seizing him by the arm, exclaimed, "This, I would wager, is an idea of Madame de Staël; but take my advice, and do not give in to the romantic philanthropy of the eighteenth century; there is only one thing to do in this world: that is to get continually more money and more power; all the rest is chimerical." Many people will say that he was right; I think, on the contrary, that history will show that by establishing this doctrine, by setting men loose from the ties of honor everywhere but on the field of battle, he prepared his partisans to abandon him, according to his own precepts, when he should cease to be the strongest; and indeed he may well boast of having met with more disciples faithful to his system than adherents devoted to his misfortunes. He consecrated his policy by fatalism, the only religion suitable to this devotedness to fortune; and his prosperity constantly increasing, he ended by making himself the high priest and idol of his own adoration, believing in himself as if his desires were presages and his designs oracles.

The duration of the power of Bonaparte was a perpetual lesson of immorality. If he had always succeeded, what should we have been able to say to our children? There would have been left, it is true, the solace of religious resignation; but the mass of the inhabitants of the world would have sought in vain to discover the intentions of Providence in human affairs.

Nevertheless, in 1811, the Germans still called Bonaparte the man of fate, and the imagination even of some Englishmen was dazzled by his extraordinary talents. Poland and Italy still hoped for independence from him, and the daughter of the Caesars had become his consort.[5] This badge of honor caused him a transport of joy foreign to his nature; and for some

5. After divorcing Joséphine de Beauharnais, Napoléon married Marie Louise, Archduchess of Austria, in 1810.

time it might be believed that his illustrious partner would change the character of the man with whom destiny had connected her. Even at this time Bonaparte lacked but one good sentiment to have become the greatest monarch upon earth; either that of paternal affection, which induces men to take care of the inheritance of their children; or pity for the French who rushed to death for him whenever he gave the signal; or equity toward foreign nations who gazed at him with wonder; or, finally, that kind of prudence natural to every man toward the middle of life, when he sees the approach of the vast shadows by which he must soon be enveloped: one virtue, one single virtue would have sufficed to have fixed all human prosperity on the head of Bonaparte. But the divine spark did not exist.

The triumph of Bonaparte in Europe, as well as in France, was founded on a great equivocation which endures with a number of people. The nations persisted in considering him the defender of their rights at the very moment when he was their greatest enemy. The strength of the French Revolution, of which he had been the inheritor, was immense, because it was composed of the will of the French and of the secret desires of other nations. Napoléon made use of this power against the old governments during several years, before the people discovered that their interest was not his object. The same names still subsisted: it was still France, lately the center of popular principles; and although Bonaparte destroyed republics and stimulated kings and princes to acts of tyranny, in opposition even to their own natural moderation, it was yet believed that all this would end in liberty; and he often himself talked of a constitution, at least when speaking of the reign of his son. Nonetheless, the first step that Bonaparte made toward his ruin was the enterprise on Spain;[6] for he there met with a national resistance, the only one from which no corruption or diplomatic art could set him free. He had not suspected the danger which awaited his army in a war of villages and mountains; he did not believe in the power of the soul; he counted bayonets, and there being scarcely any in Spain before the arrival of the English troops, he had not learned

---

6. From 1807 to 1813. The French army's occupation of the north of Spain provoked the revolt of May 1808. The war began after Napoléon installed his brother Joseph Bonaparte as the king of Spain. The war ended in 1813, when Ferdinand VII (of the Bourbon dynasty) became the king of Spain.

to dread the only invincible power—the enthusiasm of a whole nation. *The French*, said Bonaparte, *are nervous machines*, by which he meant to explain that mixture of obedience and mobility which constitutes their character. This reproach is perhaps well founded; but amidst these defects they have displayed an invincible perseverance during nearly thirty years; and it was because Bonaparte flattered their ruling passion that he reigned. The French long believed that the imperial government would preserve them from the institutions of the Old Regime, which to them are peculiarly odious. They also long confounded the cause of the Revolution with that of a new master; many people with good intentions suffered themselves to be deluded by this motive; others held the same language, though they had no longer the same opinion; and it was long before the nation lost its interest in Bonaparte. But from that moment forward an abyss was hollowed under his steps.

CHAPTER XIX

Intoxication of Power;
Reverses and Abdication of Bonaparte.

"I am tired of this old Europe," said Napoléon before his departure for Russia. He met indeed nowhere any obstacle to his will, and the restlessness of his character required a new aliment. Perhaps also the strength and clearness of his judgment were impaired when he saw men and things bending before him in such a manner that it became no longer necessary for him to exercise his thoughts upon any of the difficulties of life. There is in unlimited power a kind of giddiness which seizes on genius as on stupidity, and overthrows them both alike.

The Oriental etiquette which Bonaparte had established in his court intercepted that kind of knowledge which is acquired amidst the easy communications of society. When there were four hundred people in his saloon, a blind man might have thought himself alone, so deep was the silence that prevailed. The marshals of France, amidst the fatigues of war, at the moment of the crisis of a battle, used to enter the tent of the Emperor to ask his orders without being allowed to sit down. His family did not suffer less than strangers from his despotism and his pride. Lucien preferred living a prisoner in England to reigning under the orders of his brother.[1] Louis Bonaparte, whose character is generally esteemed, was constrained by his probity to renounce the throne of Holland;[2] and can it be believed that when conversing with his brother during two hours by themselves, and that brother obliged by indisposition to lean painfully against the wall, Napoléon never offered him a chair: he used to continue

1. From 1810 until 1814.
2. Louis Bonaparte was the king of Holland from 1806 to 1810.

standing himself, from the fear that anyone should think of using the familiarity with him of sitting in his presence.

The dread which he inspired in later times was such that nobody dared to address him first upon any subject. Sometimes he conversed with the greatest simplicity, surrounded by his court and in his Council of State. He suffered, and even encouraged, contradiction upon administrative or judicial affairs which had no connection with his power. It was curious to remark how sensibly those persons were affected whom he had suffered for a moment to breathe freely; but when the master re-appeared, it was in vain to ask the ministers to present a report to the Emperor against an unjust measure. If the question was about the victim of some error, some individual caught by accident in that great net thrown over the human race—the agents of power would invoke the difficulty of addressing Napoléon, as if he had been the Great Lama. Such a stupor caused by power would have raised a smile if the situation of men without refuge under this despotism had not inspired the deepest pity.

The compliments, the hymns, the adorations without number and without measure which filled his journals, might have tired a man of such transcendent mind; but the despotism of his character was stronger than his reason. He liked true praise less than base flattery, because the one only showed his merit while the other attested his authority. In general he preferred power to glory; for the exertion of power pleased him too much to make him think of posterity, on whom it cannot act. But one of the results of absolute power which contributed the most to precipitate Bonaparte from his throne was that by degrees no one dared to state to him the truth on any subject. He ended by not knowing that it was cold at Moscow in November, because there could be found no one among his courtiers who had enough of the Roman to inform him of a thing so simple.[3]

In 1811, Napoléon had inserted, and disavowed at the same time, in the *Moniteur* a sacred note, printed in the English papers as having been ad-

---

3. Napoléon decided to leave Moscow on October 19, 1812, when the temperatures were still mild. In early November they dropped significantly, hindering the orderly retreat of the French army.

dressed by his Minister of Foreign Affairs to the Ambassador of Russia. It was there said that Europe could enjoy no peace so long as England and its constitution subsisted. Whether this note was authentic or not, it bore at least the stamp of the school of Napoléon, and certainly expressed his ideas. An instinct which he could not account for taught him that so long as a center of justice and liberty existed in the world, the tribunal which was to pass sentence upon him held its permanent meetings.

Bonaparte connected perhaps with the wild idea of the war of Russia that of the conquest of Turkey, of a return into Egypt, and of some attempts on the English establishments in India. Such were the gigantic plans with which he marched for the first time to Dresden,[4] dragging after him the armies of all the continent of Europe, whom he obliged to march against the powerful nation situated on the limit of Asia. Pretexts were of small importance to a man who had attained such a degree of power; still it was necessary to adopt a phrase on the expedition to Russia which the courtiers might use as the word of command. This phrase was that *France was obliged to make war on Russia, because that power did not maintain the Continental blockade against England.* Now, at this very time, Bonaparte himself was continually granting licenses at Paris for exchanges with the merchants of London; and the Emperor of Russia might with more propriety have declared war against him for violating the treaty by which they had mutually engaged to hold no commercial intercourse with England. But who would now take the trouble of justifying such a war? No one; not even Bonaparte; for his respect for success is such that he must condemn himself for having incurred such great reverses.

Nevertheless, the feeling of admiration and terror which Bonaparte inspired was so great that little doubt was entertained of his triumph. While he was at Dresden in 1812, surrounded by all the sovereigns of Germany, at the head of an army of five hundred thousand men composed of almost all the nations of Europe, it seemed impossible, according to human calculation, that his expedition should fail. In his fall, indeed, the

4. Napoléon arrived in Dresden on May 9, 1812, where he hoped to meet the Emperor of Austria and the German princes in order to convince them to endorse his Russian campaign.

intervention of Providence has been more manifested to the world than in any other event; and the elements were first employed to strike the ruler of men. At present we can hardly imagine that if Bonaparte had succeeded in his expedition against Russia, there would not have been a single corner of Continental ground where one could have escaped from his power. All the ports were shut, and the Continent was, like the tower of Ugolino, walled up on all sides.

Threatened with imprisonment by a prefect,[5] extremely docile to power, if I showed the least intention of withdrawing for a day from my dwelling, I escaped when Bonaparte was just entering into Russia, fearing I should find no outlet in Europe if I deferred my project any longer.[6] I had already but two ways of going to England, by Constantinople or by St. Petersburg. The war between Russia and Turkey rendered the road by the latter almost impracticable; I did not know what would become of me, when the Emperor Alexander had the goodness to send me a passport to Vienna. On entering his empire, acknowledged as absolute, I felt myself free for the first time since the reign of Bonaparte; not only on account of the personal virtues of the Emperor Alexander, but because Russia was the only country which Napoléon had not compelled to feel his influence. None of the old governments can be compared to a tyranny which is engrafted upon a revolution, a tyranny which had employed even the extension of knowledge to chain even further every form of liberty.

It is my intention at a future day to write what I observed of Russia; I shall here only remark, without turning from my subject, that it is a country little known, because almost all we have seen of that nation is a small number of courtiers, whose defects are always greater in proportion as the power of a monarch is less limited. They are distinguished, for the most part, only by that intrepid bravery common to all classes; but the Russian peasantry, that numerous class of the nation whose knowledge

5. Capelle was the prefect of the department of Lyon.

6. Madame de Staël left Coppet on May 23, 1812. She headed for Berne, Innsbruck, and Vienna and arrived in Moscow on August 1, 1812. She then left for Saint Petersburg, Stockholm, and London, where she arrived on June 18, 1813. For more information, see Staël, *Ten Years of Exile*, pt. II, chaps. v–xx, 131–229; and *Madame de Staël, ses amis, ses correspondants. Choix de lettres (1778–1817)*, 427–79.

does not extend beyond the earth they cultivate and the heavens they contemplate, have qualities that are really admirable. The mildness of these people, their hospitality, their natural elegance, are extraordinary; no danger exists in their eyes; they think nothing impossible when their master commands. The word "master," of which courtiers make an object of flattery and policy, does not produce the same effect on a people almost Asiatic. The monarch, being at the head of public worship, constitutes a part of their religion, and the peasants prostrate themselves before the Emperor as they salute the church by which they pass; no servile feeling mingles itself with these demonstrations of their sentiments.

Thanks to the enlightened wisdom of the present sovereign, every possible amelioration will take place gradually in Russia.[7] But nothing is more absurd than the observations commonly repeated by those who dread the enlightened ideas of Alexander. "Why," they exclaim, "does that Emperor, for whom the friends of liberty are such enthusiasts; why does he not establish at home the constitutional government which he recommends to other nations?" It is one of the thousand artifices of the enemies of human reason to endeavor to prevent what is possible and desirable for one nation by demanding things that are impossible for another. There is as yet no Third Estate in Russia: how, then, could a representative government be established there? The intermediary class between the boyards and the people is almost entirely missing. It would be possible to augment the power of the great nobles, and by so doing, destroy the work of Peter I; but that would be going back instead of forward; for the power of the Emperor, however absolute, is an amelioration in the state of society, compared to what the Russian aristocracy formerly was. Russia, in regard to civilization, has only attained that period of history in which, for the good of nations, it becomes necessary to limit the power of the privileged class by that of the crown. Thirty-six religions, including those that are pagan,

---

7. See the letter sent by Madame de Staël to Tsar Alexander I in 1814, in *Madame de Staël, ses amis, ses correspondants. Choix de lettres (1778–1817)*, 476. The tsar did not live up to Madame de Staël's hopes, as he refused to endorse the friends of constitutional liberty in France. It would be worth comparing these optimistic words of Madame de Staël with the account of Astolphe de Custine, who visited Russia two decades later (translated into English as *Empire of the Czar*).

and thirty-six different nations are not collected, but scattered over an immense territory. On one hand, the Greek creed accords with perfect toleration, and on the other, the vast space occupied by the population leaves every man the freedom of living according to his mores. There is not yet to be found, in this order of things, knowledge that could be concentrated or individuals who could make institutions work. The only tie which unites nations who are almost in a pastoral state, and whose dwellings appear like wooden tents erected in the plain, is respect for the monarch and national pride. Other ties will be successively brought forth by time.

I was at Moscow exactly a month before Napoléon's army entered its walls; and I did not dare to remain but a very short time, fearing its immediate approach. When walking on the top of the Kremlin, the palace of the ancient tzars, which commands the vast capital of Russia and its eighteen hundred churches, I thought it was the lot of Bonaparte to see empires at his feet, as Satan offered them to our Savior. But it was when there remained nothing more for him to conquer in Europe that Fate seized upon him, and made him fall with as much rapidity as he had risen. Perhaps he has since learned that whatever may be the events in the earlier scenes, there is a potency in virtue which always reappears at the fifth act of the tragedy; as, among the ancients, the knot was severed by a god when the action was worthy of his intervention.

The admirable perseverance of the Emperor Alexander in refusing the peace which Bonaparte offered him, according to his practice when victorious; the energy of the Russians, who set fire to Moscow that the martyrdom of one holy city might redeem the Christian world; all this certainly contributed greatly to the misfortunes of Bonaparte's troops in the retreat from Russia. But it was that cold, that "cold of Hell," such as is pictured by Dante, that alone could annihilate the army of Xerxes.

We who have French hearts had accustomed ourselves, during the fifteen years of the tyranny of Napoléon, to consider his armies beyond the Rhine as no more belonging to France. They no longer defended the interests of the nation, they only served the ambition of one man; there was nothing in that which could awaken the love of their country; and far from wishing for the triumph of those troops, a great part of whom were foreigners, their defeat might be considered as a blessing even for France. Besides, the more we are attached to liberty in our own country, the more we feel that it is impossible to rejoice in victories the result of which must be the oppression of other nations. But who can hear a description of the evils which overwhelmed the French in the war of Russia without heart-rending sorrow?

Incredible man!—he had witnessed sufferings from which thought re-coils,[8] he knew that the French grenadiers, whom Europe never names but with respect, became the toy of a few Jews and of some old women at Wilna, so much was their physical strength weakened, long before they could die; he received proofs of respect and of attachment from that army when they were perishing for him one by one; and he refused, six months after, at Dresden, a peace which would leave him master of France as far as the Rhine and of the whole of Italy.[9] He had come rapidly to Paris after the retreat from Russia to collect new forces, having, with firmness more theatrical than natural, crossed Germany, where he was detested but still feared. In his last bulletin[10] he had given an account of the disasters of his army, which he had rather exaggerated than concealed. He is a man who delights so much in calling forth strong emotions that when he cannot conceal his losses, he exaggerates them in order to do always more than another. During his absence, some attempted against him the most gen-erous conspiracy (that of Mallet) of which the history of the French Rev-olution presents an example;[11] and which, therefore, terrified him more than the coalition itself. Alas! why did not this patriotic conspiracy suc-ceed? France would have had the glory of freeing herself, and it would not have been under the ruins of the country that her oppressor would have been crushed.

General Mallet was a friend to liberty, and attacked Bonaparte on that

8. During the retreat of the French army from Russia.

9. On June 4, 1813, a truce was signed at Pleiswitz; it lasted until August 10, 1813. On June 27, England, Prussia, Austria, and Russia signed a treaty that sought to open nego-tiations with France. Napoléon, who wanted to preserve the borders of 1812, rejected Met-ternich's proposals, and the war began again in August 1813.

10. The 29th Bulletin of the Grand Army.

11. On October 23, 1812, General Mallet attempted a coup d'état that failed.

ground. Bonaparte was well aware that none was more dangerous for him; and when he returned to Paris, he talked of nothing but *ideologie*.[12] He had conceived a horror for this very innocent word because it meant the theory of thought. It was singular enough to dread nothing but what he called the ideologues at a moment when all Europe was armed against him. It would have been noble if, in consequence of this fear, he had sought, in preference to everything, the esteem of philosophers; but he detested every man capable of an independent opinion. Even from a political point of view, he leaned too much to the belief that men were to be governed only by their interest; this old maxim, however common it may be, is often false. The greater number of those on whom Bonaparte had heaped places and wealth deserted his cause; but his soldiers, attached to him by his victories, did not abandon him. He laughed at enthusiasm; and yet it was by enthusiasm, or at least military fanaticism, that he was supported. The frenzy of battles, which has something of greatness even in its excess, constituted the only strength of Bonaparte. Nations can never be in the wrong; a vicious principle never acts long on the mass: men are perverse only individually.

Bonaparte performed, or rather the nation performed for him, a miracle: notwithstanding his immense losses in Russia, a new army was created in less than three months, which was able to march into Germany and to gain new battles. It was then that the demon of pride and folly took possession of Bonaparte in such a manner that reasoning founded on his own interest can no longer explain the motives of his conduct: it was at Dresden that he mistook the last apparition of his tutelary genius.

The Germans, long indignant, rose at length against the French who occupied their territory; national pride, the great strength of human nature, again displayed itself among the sons of Germany. Bonaparte was then taught what becomes of allies who have been constrained by force; and that whatever is not voluntary is destroyed at the first reverse of fortune. The sovereigns of Germany fought with the intrepidity of soldiers; and it seemed as if the Prussians and their warlike king were animated by

12. The concept "ideology" was coined by Destutt de Tracy. For more information, see Freeden, *Ideology: A Very Short Introduction;* and Welch, *Liberty and Utility.*

the remembrance of the personal insult offered some years before by Bonaparte to their beautiful and virtuous queen.[13]

The liberation of Germany had long been the object of the wishes of the Emperor of Russia. When the French were repulsed from his country, he devoted himself to this cause, not only as a sovereign but as a general; and he several times exposed his life, not in the character of a monarch guarded by his courtiers, but in that of an intrepid soldier. Holland welcomed her deliverers and recalled that house of Orange whose princes are now, as heretofore, the defenders of independence and the magistrates of liberty.[14] Whatever was the influence at this period of the English victories in Spain, we shall speak elsewhere of Lord Wellington, for we must pause at that name; we cannot take an incidental notice of it.[15]

Bonaparte returned to Paris; and even at this moment France might have been saved. Five members of the Legislative Assembly, Gallois, Raynouard, Flaugergues, Maine de Biran, and Lainé, asked for peace at the peril of their lives.[16] Each of those persons might be designated by his particular merit; and the last I have named, Lainé,[17] perpetuates every day by his conduct and talents the remembrance of an action which alone would suffice to honor the character of any person. If the Senate had joined with the five members of the legislative body, and the generals had supported the Senate, France would have been the disposer of her own fate; and whatever course she had taken, she would have remained France. But fifteen years of tyranny subverts all ideas and changes all sentiments; the very men who would expose so nobly their lives in war are not aware that

13. Louise de Mecklembourg-Strelitz (1776–1810), Queen of Prussia, opposed Napoléon in 1806.

14. In November 1813, Holland rebelled against Napoléon. The Prince of Orange was recalled and became king of the Netherlands (Holland and Belgium) in 1815.

15. Arthur Wellesley, first Duke of Wellington (1769–1852). Wellington defeated Napoléon at Waterloo on June 18, 1815, and subsequently served as prime minister (1828–30).

16. After the battle of Leipzig in October 1813, Napoléon rejected the peace offer made by Metternich. While the Senate agreed with the Emperor, some members of the legislative body, including Raynouard, Lainé, Gallois, and Maine de Biran, expressed their concern with the Emperor's policy in December 1813.

17. Joseph Lainé (1767–1835) served as president of the Chamber of Deputies during the First Bourbon Restoration (1814–15) and minister of the interior (1816–18). He was elected to the French Academy in 1816.

the same courage and the same honor command resistance in the civil career to the enemy of all the despotism.

Bonaparte answered the delegation of the legislative body with a kind of concentrated fury; he expressed himself ill, but his pride was seen to pierce through his confused language. He said "that France wanted him more than he wanted France," forgetting that it was himself who had reduced her to that state. He added "that a throne was but a piece of wood upon which a carpet was spread, and that all depended on the person by whom it was occupied." Finally, he continued to appear intoxicated with himself. A singular anecdote, however, might lead us to believe that he was already struck with that stupor which seems to have taken possession of his character during the last crisis of his political life. A person worthy of credit told me that, conversing with him alone, the day before his departure for the army in the month of January, 1814, when the allies had already entered France, Bonaparte confessed in this private interview that he did not possess the means of resisting; they discussed the question, and Bonaparte showed him, without reserve, the worst side of things; and, what will scarcely be believed, he fell asleep while talking on such a subject, without any preceding fatigue that could explain so singular an apathy. This did not prevent his displaying an extreme activity in his campaign of 1814; he suffered himself, no doubt, to be misled by a presumptuous confidence; and on the other hand, physical existence, through enjoyments and facilities of all kinds, had gained possession of this man, formerly so intellectual. His soul seemed in some sort to have become gross along with his body. His genius now pierced only at intervals through that covering of egoism which a long habit of being considered everything had made him acquire. He sunk under the weight of prosperity before he was overthrown by misfortune.

It is pretended that he would not consent to relinquish the conquests which had been made by the Republic, and that he could not bring himself to allow that France should be weakened under his reign. If this consideration determined him to refuse the peace that was offered to him at Châtillon[18] in March, 1814, it is the first time that the idea of a duty acted

18. The Congress of Châtillon-sur-Seine convened on February 3, 1814, after Napo-

on his mind; and his perseverance on this occasion, however imprudent, would deserve some esteem. But it rather appears that he relied too much on his talents after having had some success in Champagne, and that he concealed from himself, as might have been done by one of his flatterers, the difficulties he had to surmount. They were so much accustomed to fear him that none of them dared to tell him the facts that interested him the most. If he happened to assert that in such a place there was a body of twenty thousand French, no one had the courage to inform him that there were only ten thousand; if he observed that the Allies were only in such a number, no one ventured to prove that this number was double. His despotism was such that he had reduced men to be but the echo of himself; and his own voice returning to him from all sides, he was alone amidst the crowd that encircled him.

In short, he did not perceive that enthusiasm had passed from the left bank of the Rhine to the right; that he had no longer to do with undecided governments, but with irritated nations; and that on his side, on the contrary, there was only an army and no longer a nation; for in this great contest France remained neutral, without seeming to think that what regarded him regarded herself. The most warlike of nations saw, almost with indifference, the success of those very foreigners with whom they had often fought so gloriously; and the inhabitants of the towns and villages gave but little aid to the French soldiers, not being able to persuade themselves that after twenty-five years of victory, so strange an event as the entry of the Allies into Paris could ever happen. It did, however, happen! this terrible justice of destiny. The Allies were generous; Alexander, as we shall see hereafter, displayed a constant magnanimity. He was the first to enter the conquered city as a powerful protector and as an enlightened philanthropist; but even in admiring him, who could be a Frenchman and not be overwhelmed with sorrow?

From the moment that the Allies crossed the Rhine and penetrated into France, it seemed to me that the wishes of the friends of France ought to have been completely changed. I was then in London, and one of the

---

léon's defeat at La Rothière. Napoléon refused again the terms proposed by the representatives of Austria, Russia, England, and Prussia.

English ministers asked me what were my wishes? I had the boldness to answer him that I wished that Bonaparte should be *victorious, and killed*. I found in Englishmen sufficient greatness of mind to have no need of concealing this French sentiment in their presence. I was, however, forced to hear, amidst the transports of joy with which the city of the conquerors resounded, that Paris had fallen into the power of the Allies. It seemed to me at that moment that there was no longer a France: I thought the pre-diction of Burke accomplished, and that there where France existed we should henceforth see but an abyss. The Emperor Alexander, the Allies, and the constitutional principles adopted by the wisdom of Louis XVIII dissipated this sad foreboding.[19]

Bonaparte then heard on all sides the truth which had been so long kept in captivity. It was then that ungrateful courtiers deserved the contempt entertained by their master for the human race. If the friends of liberty respect public opinion, desire publicity, and seek everywhere for the sin-cere and free support of the national voice, it is because they know that only the vilest of souls appear in the secrets and intrigues of arbitrary power.

There was, however, something of grandeur in the farewell of Na-poléon to his soldiers and to their eagles, so long victorious; his last cam-paign had been long and skillful; in short, the fatal illusion which con-nected him with the military glory of France was not yet destroyed. The Congress at Paris has accordingly to reproach itself with having put him in a situation that admitted of his return.[20] The representatives of Europe ought frankly to confess this fault; and it is unjust to make the French nation bear the blame. It was certainly without any sinister intention that the ministers of the foreign powers allowed to hover over the throne of Louis XVIII a danger which threatened, at the same time, the whole of Europe. But why do not those who suspended this sword plead guilty to the mischief which it caused?

Many people like to claim that Bonaparte, had he not attempted the

19. The Charter of 1814 was "granted" by Louis XVIII in June 1814 upon his return to France.

20. Reference to the Treaty of Paris, signed on May 30, 1814.

war of Spain or that of Russia, would still be Emperor; and this opinion is flattering to the partisans of despotic power, who think that so fine a government cannot be overturned by the nature of things, but only by accidental causes. I have already said what an attentive consideration of France will confirm, that Bonaparte stood in need of war to establish and preserve absolute power. A great nation would not have borne the monotonous and degrading pressure of despotism if military glory had not incessantly animated or exalted the public mind. The continual promotion to various ranks, in which every class of the nation had the means of participating, rendered the conscription less painful to the peasantry. The interest perpetually excited by victory supplied the place of interest in other things; ambition was the active principle of government in its smallest ramifications; titles, money, power, all were given by Bonaparte to the French in place of their liberty. But, to be enabled to deal around these disastrous indemnities, he required nothing less than Europe to devour. If Napoléon had been what one may term a rational tyrant, he would not have been able to struggle against the activity of the French, which required an object. He was a man condemned by his destiny either to the virtues of Washington or to the conquests of Attila; but it was easier to reach the confines of the civilized world than to stop the progress of human reason; and public opinion in France would soon have accomplished what was brought about by the arms of the Allies.

From this time forward it is not he alone who will occupy the history of which we aim at sketching a picture, and our ill-fated France is about to appear again after fifteen years during which nothing was spoken of but the Emperor and his army. What reverses we have to describe! what evils we have to dread! We shall be obliged to require of Bonaparte once more an account of France, since that country, too confiding and too warlike, trusted her fate a second time in his hands.

In the different observations which I have made about Bonaparte, I have abstained from his private life, with which I am unacquainted, and which does not concern the interests of France. I have not advanced a single doubtful point in regard to his history; for the calumnies thrown out against him seem to me still more vile than the adulations of which he was the object. I flatter myself with having estimated him as all public men ought to be estimated: with reference to the effects of their conduct on the prosperity, information, and morality of nations. The persecutions which Bonaparte made me undergo have not, I can faithfully declare, at all biased my opinion. On the contrary, I have rather felt a necessity for resisting that kind of fascination produced on the imagination by an extraordinary genius and a formidable destiny. I should even gladly have allowed myself to be led away by the satisfaction which lofty minds find in defending an unfortunate man, and by the pleasure of thus putting themselves more in opposition to the writers and speakers who, so lately prostrate before him, are now incessantly pouring abuse on him, keeping, however, I imagine, a watchful eye on the height of the rocks which imprison him.[21] But one cannot be silent in regard to Bonaparte even in the day of his misfortune, because his political doctrine still reigns in the minds both of his enemies and of his partisans. For of the whole inheritance of his dreadful power, there remains nothing to mankind but the baneful knowledge of a few secrets the more in the art of tyranny.

21. At Sainte-Helena.

✤ ✤ ✤ ✤ ✤ ✤   PART V*   ✤ ✤ ✤ ✤ ✤ ✤

CHAPTER I

Of What Constitutes Legitimate Royalty.

In considering royalty, as all institutions ought to be judged with reference to the happiness and dignity of nations, I shall say generally, but with due respect to exceptions, that princes of old established families are much more likely to promote the welfare of a country than those princes who have raised themselves to a throne.[1] Their talents are commonly less remarkable, but their disposition is more pacific; they have more prejudices but less ambition; they are less dazzled by power because they are told from their infancy that they were destined to it; and they do not fear so much to lose it, which renders them less uneasy and less suspicious. Their mode of living and acting is more simple, as they are under no necessity of recurring to artificial means to strike the public, and have nothing new to gain in point of respect: the habits and traditions serve as their guides. Add to this that outward splendor, a necessary attribute of royalty, seems perfectly in place in the case of princes whose forefathers have stood for centuries at the same elevation of rank. When a man is suddenly raised,

* We think it incumbent on us to mention again that a part of the third volume of this work was not revised by Madame de Staël. Some of the subsequent chapters will perhaps appear unfinished; but we felt it a duty to publish the MS. in the state in which we found it, without taking on us to make any addition whatever to the production of the author.

It is proper also to remark that this portion of the work was written in the early part of the year 1816, and that it is consequently of importance to refer to that period the opinions, whether favorable or unfavorable, pronounced by the author. (*Note by the Editors.*)

1. For an overview of the historical context of 1814–15, see Furet, *Revolutionary France*, 269–84.

the first in his family, to the highest dignity, he requires the illusion of glory to cast into the shade the contrast between royal pomp and his former situation of a private individual. But the glory calculated to inspire the respect which men willingly bestow on ancient pre-eminence can be acquired only by military exploits; and the world well knows how the great captains and conquerors almost always conduct themselves in civil affairs.

Besides, hereditary succession in a monarchy is indispensable to the tranquillity, I will even say to the morality and progress, of the human mind. Elective royalty offers a vast field to ambition; the factions resulting from it have infallibly the effect of corrupting the heart and of diverting the thoughts from every occupation which does not point to the interest of tomorrow. But the prerogatives granted to birth, whether for founding a class of nobility or for fixing the succession to the throne in a single family, stand in need of being confirmed by time; they differ in that respect from natural rights, which are independent of every conventional sanction. Now, the principle of hereditary succession is best established in old dynasties. But in order that this principle may not become contrary to reason, and to that general good for the sake of which it has been adopted, it must be indissolubly connected with the reign of law. For were it necessary that millions should be governed by one man according to his will or caprice, it would be better, in such a case, that he were a man of genius; and genius is more likely to be found when we have recourse to election than when we are regulated by the chance of birth.

In no country is hereditary succession more solidly established than in England, although that country has rejected the legitimacy founded on divine right, to substitute for it the hereditary succession sanctioned by a representative government. All sensible people are perfectly able to understand how, by virtue of laws passed by the delegates of a people and accepted by the king, it is the interest of nations, who also are hereditary and even legitimate, to acknowledge a dynasty called to the throne by right of primogeniture. If, on the other hand, royal power was founded on the doctrine that all power proceeds from God, nothing could be more favorable to usurpation; for it is not, in general, power that is wanting to usurpers; for the same men who proffered incense to Bonaparte are at this day the advocates for divine right. All their theory consists in asserting that force is force, and that they are its high priests; we require a different worship with different ministers, and it is then only that we believe monarchy shall be durable.

A change of dynasty, even when legally pronounced, has never taken place except in countries where the overturned government was arbitrary; for the personal character of the sovereign, being then decisive of the fate of the people, it became necessary, as we have often seen in history, to dispossess those who were unfit to govern; while, in our own day, the respectable sovereign of England was accounted the ruler for a considerable time after his faculties were gone,[2] because the responsibility of ministers admitted of postponing the act for a regency. Thus, on the one hand, a representative government inspires greater respect for the sovereign in those who are unwilling to transform the affairs of this world into dogmas lest the name of God should be taken in vain; while on the other hand, conscientious sovereigns do not have to fear that the welfare of the country should be wholly dependent on their individual lives.

Legitimacy, such as it has been recently proclaimed, is then altogether inseparable from constitutional limitations. Whether the limitations that formerly existed in France were insufficient to oppose an effectual barrier to the encroachments of power, or whether they were gradually infringed and obliterated, is a point of little importance: they ought to commence from this time forward, even if the antiquity of their origin could not be proved.[3]

One is ashamed to go back to the evidence of history to prove that a thing equally absurd and unjust ought neither to be adopted nor maintained. It has not been argued in favor of slavery that it has lasted four thousand years; nor did the state of servitude which succeeded it appear more equitable for having subsisted above ten centuries; the slave trade has never been defended as an ancient institution of our fathers. The inquisition and torture, which are of older date, have, I confess, been reestablished in one country in Europe;[4] but this did not, I imagine, take

2. The reference is to King George III (1738–1820) of England. Because of severe mental illness, he was incapacitated during the last ten years of his reign.

3. For more information on this topic, see bk. I, chap. xi, of Staël, *Considerations.*

4. In 1814, by King Ferdinand VII of Spain.

place with the approbation even of the defenders of all ancient usages. It would be curious to know to which generation among our fathers the gift of infallibility was granted. Which is that past age which ought to serve as a model to the present, and from which one cannot make the slightest departure without falling into pernicious innovations? If every change, whatever be its influence on the general good and progress of mankind, be censurable merely because it is a change, it will not be difficult to oppose to the ancient order of things invoked by you, another order of things still more ancient to which it has succeeded. At that rate, the fathers of those of your ancestors whom you wish to take as guides, and the fathers of those fathers, would be entitled to complain of their sons and grandsons, as of a turbulent youth impatient to overthrow their wise institutions. What human being gifted with good sense can pretend that a change in manners and opinion ought not to produce corresponding change in our institutions? Must government, then, be always three hundred years behind? Or shall a new Joshua command the sun to stand still in his course? "No," it will be said; "there are things that ought to be changed, but the government ought to be immutable." There could not be a more effectual way of rendering revolutions inevitable; for if the government of a country refused to participate in any degree in the progressive advance of men and things, it will necessarily be overthrown by them. Can men coolly discuss whether the form of the governments of the present time ought to be in correspondence with the needs of the existing generation, or of those which are no more? Whether it is in the dark and disputed antiquity of history that a statesman ought to look for his rule of conduct; or whether that statesman should possess the talents and firmness of Mr. Pitt, should know where power resides, whither opinion tends, and where he is to fix his point of support to act on the national feeling? For without the nation, nothing is to be done—with it, everything except that which would tend to degrade it: bayonets are the only instruments for that sad purpose. In recurring to the history of the past, as to the law and the prophets, the same thing that happened to the latter happens to history: it becomes the subject of a war of endless controversy. Shall we at present aim at ascertaining from the documents of the age whether a perverse king, Philip the Fair, or a mad king, Charles VI, had ministers who, in their name, allowed the nation to be of some account? Besides, the facts in French history, far from supporting the doctrine which we combat, confirm the existence of a primitive compact between the nation and the king, as fully as human reason demonstrates its necessity. I have, I believe, proved that in Europe, as in France, it is liberty that is ancient and despotism that is modern; also that those defenders of the rights of nations who are stigmatized as innovators have always appealed to the past. Even were this truth not evident, the result would be only a more pressing demand on us as a duty to introduce the reign of that justice which may not as yet have commenced. But the principles of liberty are so deeply engraven on the heart of man that, if the history of every government presents a picture of the efforts of power to encroach, it exhibits likewise a picture of popular struggles against these efforts.

CHAPTER II

Of the Political Doctrine of Some French Emigrants and Their Adherents.

The opponents of the French Revolution of 1789, whether nobility, clergy, or lawyers, repeated incessantly that no change was necessary in regard to government, because the intermediary bodies which then existed were sufficient to prevent despotic measures; and they now proclaim despotic forms as a re-establishment of the old regime. This inconsistency in point of principle is consistency in point of interest. So long as the privileged classes served as a limit to the royal authority, they were averse to arbitrary power in the Crown; but since the time that the people has found means to take the place of the privileged classes, the latter have rallied under the royal prerogative and would give the character of rebellion to all constitutional opposition and to all political liberty.

These persons found the power of kings on divine right to be an absurd doctrine, which caused the overthrow of the Stuarts, and which, even at that time, was denied by their most enlightened adherents, from a dread that it would forever bar their return to England. Lord Erskine,[1] in his admirable pleading in favor of the Dean of St. Asaph, on a question relative to the liberty of the press, begins by quoting Locke's treatise on the points of divine right and passive obedience, in which that celebrated philosopher positively declares that every agent of royal authority who goes beyond the latitude allowed by law should be considered an instrument of tyranny, and that on this account it is lawful to shut one's door and repel him by force, as if we were attacked by a robber or a pirate. Locke

---

1. Lord Thomas Erskine (1750–1823) defended Thomas Paine in 1792. He served as chancellor in 1806–7.

admits the objection so often repeated, that a doctrine of this kind dis-
seminated among the people might encourage insurrections. "There exists
no truth," he says, "which may not lead to error, no remedy which may
not become a poison. There is not one of the gifts which we hold from
the bounty of God of which we could make use, if the possible abuse of
them were a reason for depriving us of their use. On this view, the Gospels
ought not to have been published; for although they are the foundation
of all the moral obligations which unite men in society, yet an imperfect
knowledge and an injudicious study of the Holy Word has led many men
to madness. Weapons necessary for defense may serve for vengeance and
murder. The fire that warms us exposes us to conflagration; the medicines
which cure us may cause our death. Finally, one could not instruct men
on any point of government, one could not profit by any of the lessons
of history, if the excesses to which false reasoning may be carried were
always to be brought forward as an argument to prevent freedom of
thought."[2]

The sentiments of Mr. Locke, said Lord Erskine, were published three
years after the accession of King William to the throne of England, and
at a time when that monarch had raised the author to a high rank in the
state. But Bolingbroke, no less famous than Locke in the republic of letters
and in the theater of the world, expresses himself on this question in the
same manner. He who had armed himself to restore James II to the throne
laid the greatest stress on exculpating the Jacobites from what he considered a dangerous calumny—the charge of attempting to found the claims
of James II on divine right, and not on the English constitution. And it
was from the Continent, to which he had been banished by the House of
Hanover, that he wrote what follows: "The duty of a people," says Bolingbroke, "is now so clearly established that no man can be unacquainted
with the circumstances in which he ought to obey, or those in which he
ought to resist. Conscience has no longer to contend with reason. We
know that we ought to defend the crown at the cost of our fortune and

---

2. Staël does not indicate the exact source of this quote. In *Two Treatises of Government*
(1689) Locke criticized the doctrine of the divine right of kings and advocated the principle
of constitutionalism (separation of powers, rule of law).

our life, if the crown protects us and does not depart from the limits assigned by law; but we know likewise that if it exceed these limits, it is our duty to resist it."[3]

I shall observe incidentally that this divine right, refuted so long ago in England, is kept up in France by an equivocation. Its advocates urge the established phrase: "by the grace of God, king of France and Navarre." The words so often repeated, that our kings hold their crown from God and their sword, were intended to free them from the extraordinary pretension advanced by the popes to crown and to remove sovereigns. The emperors of Germany, who undoubtedly were elective, assumed, in like manner, the title of "Emperor by the grace of God." The kings of France, who in virtue of the feudal system rendered homage for this or that province, were not less in the habit of using this form; while princes and archbishops, down to the humblest members of the feudal body, took the title of lords and prelates by the grace of God. At this day the king of England employs the same form, which in fact is nothing but an expression of Christian humility; yet a positive law in England declares guilty of high treason whoever should support divine right. These pretended privileges of despotism, which never can have any other support than that of force, are like the passage in St. Paul: "Let every soul be subject unto the higher powers; for there is no power but of God." Bonaparte insisted greatly on the authority of this apostle; he obliged all the clergy of France and the Low Countries to preach on this text; and in fact one could not well refuse to Bonaparte the title of "a higher power on earth." But what could be the meaning of St. Paul, except that the Christians ought not to interfere with the political factions of his time? Will it be alleged that St. Paul meant to justify tyranny? Did he not himself resist the orders issued by Nero when he preached the Christian faith? And were the martyrs obedient to the prohibition of professing their worship enjoined to them by the emperors? St. Peter calls government very properly a *human order*. There is

3. Staël does not indicate the exact source of this quote. Henry St. John Bolingbroke (1678–1751) was a prominent British politician and writer. He was educated at Oxford, entered Parliament in 1701, and soon after became a member of the Tory party. His works, which include *A Dissertation on Parties* (1736) and *The Patriot King* (1769), were widely read in eighteenth-century America and influenced Burke.

not a single question, either in morals or politics, in which we are under the necessity of admitting what is called authority. The conscience of men is to them a perpetual revelation, their reason an unalterable fact. That which constitutes the essence of the Christian religion is the harmony of our private feelings with the words of Jesus Christ. That which constitutes society is the principles of justice applied in different ways, but always recognized as the basis of power and of law.

The nobility, as we have shown in the course of this work, had passed, under Richelieu, from the condition of independent vassals to that of courtiers. One would almost say that a change of dress was indicative of a change of character. Under Henri IV, the French dress had in it something chivalrous; but the large perukes and that sedentary and affected dress that was worn at the court of Louis XIV did not begin till under Louis XIII. During the youth of Louis XIV, the impulse given by the faction called the *fronde* still called forth some energy; but in his latter years, in the regency, and during the reign of Louis XV, can we quote a single public man who deserves a name in history? What court intrigues occupied the great nobles! And in what a state of ignorance and frivolity did not the Revolution find the greatest part of them!

I have spoken of emigration, its motives, and its consequences. Of the nobles who took that step, some remained constantly out of France and followed the Royal Family with a commendable fidelity. The majority returned to France under the reign of Bonaparte, and many of them became confirmed in his school in the doctrine of passive obedience, of which they made the most scrupulous trial in submission to him whom they were bound to consider a usurper. That the emigrants are justly irritated by the sale of their property I can well conceive; such a confiscation is infinitely less justifiable than the highly legal disposal of the property of the church. But must a resentment, in other respects very natural, be directed against all the good sense of which mankind is in possession in this world? One would say that the progress of the age, the example of England, and even a knowledge of the actual state of France, are so foreign to their minds that they would, I believe, be tempted to strike out the word "nation" from their language as a revolutionary term. Would it not be better, even as a matter of calculation, to become frankly reconciled to all the principles which accord with the dignity of man? What proselytes can they make with this doctrine *ab irato*,[4] without any other foundation than personal interest? They want an absolute king, an exclusive religion, an intolerant priesthood, a court nobility founded on genealogy, a Third Estate acquiring from time to time distinction by *lettres de noblesse*, a population immersed in ignorance and without rights, an army acting as a mere machine, ministers without responsibility, no liberty of the press, no juries, no civil liberty; but they would have police spies and hired newspapers to extol this work of darkness. They want a king of unbounded authority that he may be able to restore to them all the privileges that they have lost, and which the deputies of the nation, be they who they may, would never consent to restore. They desire that the Catholic religion alone should be tolerated: some because they flatter themselves that thus they should recover the property of the church; others because they hope to find zealous auxiliaries of despotism in some of the religious orders. The clergy of France contended formerly against the Crown, in support of the authority of Rome; but at present all persons of the privileged classes are leagued together. It is the people only which has no other support than itself. These men desire a Third Estate incapable of occupying any elevated station, that all such offices may be reserved for the nobles. They would have the people receive no education, that they may be a flock more easily guided. They would have an army with officers accustomed to arrest, denounce, and put to death; in short, more the enemies of their fellow-citizens than of foreigners. For to re-establish the old state of things in France, without the glory that existed on the one part and the portion of liberty that existed on the other; without the habits of the past which are broken; and all this in opposition to the invincible attachment to the new order of things—a foreign force would be necessary to keep the nation in a state of perpetual compression. These men are averse to juries because they wish for the re-establishment of the old *parlements* of the kingdom. But besides that these *parlements* were formerly unable, notwithstanding their honorable efforts, to prevent either arbitrary condemnation, *lettres de cachet*, or taxes imposed in spite of their remonstrances,

4. Latin phrase used in civil law signifying "in anger."

they would be in the situation of other privileged persons; they would no longer be animated by their former spirit of resistance to the encroachments of ministers. Re-instated against the wish of the nation, and merely by the will of the sovereign, how could they act in opposition to kings, who might say to them, "If we do not continue to support you, the nation, which is no longer disposed to bear with you, will overthrow you"? Finally, to maintain a system in contradiction to the public wish, it is necessary to have the power of arresting anyone, as well as to give ministers the means of imprisoning without trial, and of preventing the accused from printing a single line in their defense. Society in such a state would be the prey of a few and the bane of the many. Henri IV would be as much disgusted by such a state of things as Franklin; and there is, in the history of France, no period so remote as to offer anything similar to such barbarism. At a time when all Europe seems to advance toward gradual improvement, ought one to pretend to make use of the just horror inspired by a few years of revolution to establish oppression and degradation in a nation once invincible?

Such are the principles of government disclosed in a number of writings by emigrants and their adherents; or rather such are the consequences of this party egoism; for we cannot give the name of principles to that theory which interdicts refutation and does not bear the light. The situation of the emigrants dictates to them the opinions which they advance, and hence the reason that France has always dreaded that power should be lodged in their hands. It is not the former dynasty that inspires any aversion to the country; it is the party which wishes to reign in its name. When the emigrants were recalled by Bonaparte, he was able to restrain them; and the public did not perceive that they had influence. But as they call themselves exclusively the defenders of the Bourbons, there has existed an apprehension that the gratitude of that family toward them might lead to entrusting the military and civil authority to those against whom the nation had contended during twenty-five years, and whom it had always seen in the ranks of the hostile armies. Nor is it the individuals composing the emigrant party who displease those of the French who never quitted their country; they have been intermingled in the camps, and even in the court of Bonaparte. But as the political doctrine of the emigrants is contrary to the national welfare, to the rights for which two million men have perished on the field of battle, to the rights for which (and this is still more grievous) crimes committed in the name of liberty have recoiled on France, the nation will never willingly bend under the yoke of emigrant opinions; and it is the dread of seeing itself constrained to this which has prevented it from taking part in the recall of its ancient princes. The constitutional charter, by giving a guarantee to the good principles of the Revolution, is the palladium of the throne and of the country.[5]

5. For more information about the political doctrine of the ultraconservative right under the Restoration, see Oechslin, *Le mouvement ultra-royaliste sous la Restauration;* Rials, *Révolution et Contre-Révolution au XIXème siècle;* and Rémond, *The Right Wing in France.*

Of the Circumstances That Render the Representative Government at This Time More Necessary in France Than in Any Other Country.

The resentment of those who have suffered greatly by the Revolution and who cannot flatter themselves with recovering their privileges but by intolerance of religion and despotism of the Crown, is, as has just been said, the greatest danger to which France can be exposed. Her happiness and her glory consist in a treaty between the two parties, taking the constitutional charter as the basis. For besides that the prosperity of France depends on the advantages acquired by the mass of the nation in 1789, I do not know anything that could be more humiliating to the French than to be sent back to servitude like children subjected to chastisement.

Two great historical facts may be, in some respects, compared to the restoration of the Bourbons: the return of the Stuarts in England and the accession of Henri IV. Let us first examine the more recent of the two: we shall afterward return to the former, which concerns France more directly.

Charles II was recalled to England after the crimes of the revolutionaries and the despotism of Cromwell;[1] the reaction always produced on the minds of the ordinary people by crimes committed under the pretext of a noble cause repressed the zeal of the English people toward liberty. It was almost the entire nation which, represented by its parliament, de-

---

1. In 1660.

manded the return of Charles II; it was the English army[2] that proclaimed him; no foreign troops interfered in this restoration, and in this respect, Charles II was in a much better situation than that of the French princes. But as a parliament was already established in England, the son of Charles I was not called on either to accept or to grant a new charter. The difference between him and the party who had caused the Revolution related to quarrels of religion: the English nation desired the Reformation and considered the Catholic religion as irreconcilable with liberty. Charles II was then obliged to call himself a Protestant; but as, in the bottom of his heart, he professed another faith, he cunningly deceived public opinion during his whole reign; and when his brother,[3] who had more violence of temper, permitted all the atrocities which the name of Jefferies[4] recalls, the nation felt the necessity of having at its head a prince who should be king by means of liberty, instead of being king in despite of liberty. Some time after, an act was passed excluding from the succession every prince who should be a Catholic or who should have espoused a princess of that religion. The principle of this act was to maintain hereditary succession by not entrusting to chance for a sovereign, but by formally excluding whoever should not adopt the political and religious faith of the majority of England. The oath pronounced by William III, and subsequently by all his successors, proves the contract between the nation and the king; and a law of England, as I have already mentioned, declares guilty of high treason whoever shall support the divine right, that is, the doctrine by which a king possesses a nation as a landholder possesses a farm, the people and the cattle being placed on the same footing, and the one having as little as the other a right to alter their situation. When the English welcomed back the old family with delight, they were hopeful that it would adopt a new doctrine; but the direct inheritors of power refusing this, the friends of liberty rallied under the standard of him who submitted to the condition without which there is no legitimacy. The Revolution of France, down to the fall of Bonaparte, is greatly similar to

2. General Monk played a key role in this regard.

3. The future King James II (1633–1701), who reigned from 1685 to 1688.

4. English magistrate famous for his ruthlessness. George Jeffreys was arrested and imprisoned during the Revolution of 1688.

that of England. Its resemblance with the war of the League and the accession of Henry IV is less striking; but in return, we say it with pleasure, the spirit and character of Louis XVIII recalls to our minds Henri IV much more than Charles II.

The abjuration of Henri IV,[5] considered only in regard to its political influence, was an act by which he adopted the opinion of the majority of the French. The Edict of Nantes may also be compared to the declaration of the 2d of May, 1814, by Louis XVIII;[6] that wise treaty between the two parties appeased them during the life of Henri IV. By citing these two eras, so different in themselves, and on which one might long dispute, for rights alone are incontestible, while facts frequently give rise to different interpretations, my aim has been only to show what history and reason confirm: that is, that after great commotions in a state, a sovereign can resume the reins of government only in as far as he sincerely adopts the prevailing opinion of his country, seeking, however, at the same time to render the sacrifices of the minority as little painful as possible. A king ought, like Henri IV, to renounce, in some measure, even those who have adhered to him in times of adversity; for, if Louis XIV was to blame in pronouncing the well-known words *"L'état, c'est moi,"* a benevolent sovereign should, on the other hand, say *"Moi, c'est l'état."*

The mass of the people has, ever since the Revolution, dreaded the ascendancy of the old privileged orders; besides, as the princes had been absent for twenty-three years, they had become unknown to the nation; and the foreign troops, in 1814, traversed a great part of France without

---

5. In July 1593.

6. In the Declaration of Saint-Ouen, Louis XVIII acknowledged the newly gained civil liberties and promised to give France a new liberal constitution. This was the famous Charter of 1814 that was "granted" by the new king a month later. The Charter sought to bring social peace in a country divided among rival factions and groups that were fiercely opposed to each other. This goal was clearly conveyed by the language of reconciliation as illustrated by the symbolic references to the "great family" of French citizens and the emphasis on the need to live as "brothers" in love, peace, and reconciliation. The Charter provided for the creation of a two-chamber *parlement,* the Chamber of Deputies being elected by electoral colleges according to a narrow franchise. To be qualified to vote, individuals had to be at least thirty years of age and pay a direct tax of three hundred francs (Article 40). For more information, see Rosanvallon, *La monarchie impossible;* Furet, *Revolutionary France,* 269–75; and Craiutu, *Liberalism Under Siege,* 70–75.

hearing either regret expressed for Bonaparte or a decided wish for any form of government. It was then a political combination, not a popular movement, that reinstated the ancient dynasty in France; and if the Stuarts, recalled by the nation without any foreign aid and supported by a nobility that had never emigrated, lost their crown by seeking to enforce their divine right, how much more necessary was it for the House of Bourbon to make again a compact[7] with France, that they might soften the grief necessarily caused to a proud people by the influence of foreigners on its interior government! Hence the necessity of an appeal to the nation to sanction what force had established. Such, as we shall presently see, was the opinion of a man, the Emperor Alexander, who, although a sovereign with unlimited powers, possesses sufficient superiority of mind and soul to excite jealousy and envy like persons in private life. Louis XVIII, by his constitutional charter and, above all, by the wisdom of his declaration of the 2d of May, by his surprising extent of information and his imposing grace of manner, supplied in many respects what was wanting in point of popular inauguration on his return. But we are still of the opinion, and we shall presently state our reasons, that Bonaparte would not within a year[8] have been welcomed by a considerable party if the King's ministers had truly established a representative government along with the principles of the Charter in France, and if an interest for constitutional liberty had replaced that for military renown.

7. The Charter of 1814 was not, properly speaking, a contract between the King and the nation, since it was Louis XVIII who "granted" and "conceded" the constitution to his subjects.

8. During the Hundred Days in the spring of 1815.

Of the Entry of the Allies into Paris, and the Different Parties Which Then Existed in France.

The four great powers, England, Austria, Russia, and Prussia, who formed a coalition in 1813 to repel the aggressions of Bonaparte, had never before acted in union, and no Continental state was able to resist such a mass of force. The French nation might perhaps have still been capable of defending itself before despotism had compressed all its energy; but as the struggle on the part of France was to be sustained only by soldiers, army against army, the balance of numbers was entirely, and beyond all proportion, in favor of the foreigners. The sovereigns who led on these troops, amounting, as well regulars as militia, to nearly eight hundred thousand men, displayed a bravery that gives them an inextinguishable right to the affection of their people; but amidst these great personages we must specially mention the Emperor of Russia, who contributed most eminently to the success of the coalition of 1813.

Far from thinking that the merit of the Emperor Alexander is exaggerated by flattery, I would almost say that sufficient justice is not done him, because, like all the friends of liberty, he labors under the preconception existing against the way of thinking in what is called the good company of Europe. People are always attributing his political views to personal calculations, as if in our days disinterested sentiments could no longer enter the human heart. Doubtless, it is of high importance to Russia that France should not be crushed, and France can be restored only by the aid of a constitutional government supported by the assent of the nation. But was the Emperor Alexander actuated by selfish thoughts when he conferred on the part of Poland ceded to him by the last treaties those rights which human reason at present calls for in all directions? Some wish to reproach him with the admiration which he testified during a time for Bonaparte; but was it not natural that great military talents should dazzle a young sovereign of a warlike spirit? Was it possible that he, distant as he was from France, should penetrate, like us, through the artifices of which Bonaparte made a frequent use, in preference even to all the other means at his command? When the Emperor Alexander acquired a thorough knowledge of the enemy with whom he had to contend, what resistance did he not oppose to him? One of his capitals was taken: still he refused that peace which Napoléon offered him with extreme eagerness. After the troops of Bonaparte were driven from Russia, Alexander carried all his force into Germany to aid in the deliverance of that country; and when the remembrance of the French power still caused hesitation in regard to the plan of campaign proper to be followed, he decided that it was indispensable to march to Paris;[1] and all the successes of Europe are connected with the boldness of that resolution. It would be painful to me, I confess, to render homage to this determination, had not the Emperor Alexander in 1814 acted a generous part toward France; and had not he, in the advice that he gave, constantly respected the honor and liberty of the nation. The liberal side is that which he has supported on every occasion;[2] and if he has not made it triumph so much as might have been wished, ought we not at least to be surprised that such an instinct for what is noble, such a love of what is just, should have been born in his heart, like a flower of heaven, in the midst of so many obstacles?

I have had the honor of conversing several times with the Emperor Alexander at St. Petersburg and at Paris, at the time of his reverses as at the time of his triumph.[3] Equally unaffected, equally calm in either situation, his mind, penetrating, judicious, and wise, has ever been consistent. His conversation is wholly unlike what is commonly called an official con-

1. On March 24, 1814.
2. In reality, Tsar Alexander I endorsed a number of illiberal policies after 1812 and did not introduce representative institutions in Russia, as Madame de Staël had hoped he would.
3. Madame de Staël met the tsar for the first time on August 17, 1812. She recounted her conversations and impressions in *Ten Years of Exile*, pt. II, chap. xvii, 201–5. For more information about her sojourn in Russia, see Fairweather, *Madame de Staël*, 391–415.

versation; no insignificant question, no mutual embarrassment condemns those who approach him to those Chinese phrases, if we may so express ourselves, which are more like bows than words. The love of humanity inspires the Emperor Alexander with the desire of knowing the true sentiments of others, and of treating, with those whom he thinks worthy of the discussion, on the great views which may be conducive to the progress of social order. On his first entrance into Paris, he discoursed with Frenchmen of different opinions like a man who can venture to enter the lists of conversation without reserve.

In war his conduct is equally courageous and humane; and of all lives it is only his own that he exposes without reflection. We are justified in expecting from him that he will be eager to do his country all the good which the state of its knowledge admits. Although he keeps on foot a great armed force, we should do wrong to consider him in Europe as an ambitious monarch. His opinions have more sway with him than his passions; and it is not, so far as I can judge, at conquest that he aims; a representative government, religious toleration, the improvement of mankind by liberty and the Christian religion are no chimeras in his eyes. If he accomplishes his designs, posterity will award him all the honors of genius; but if the circumstances by which he is surrounded, if the difficulty of finding instruments to second him, do not permit of his realizing his wishes, those who shall have known him will at least be apprised that he had conceived the most elevated views.

It was at the time of the invasion of Russia by the French that the Emperor Alexander saw the Prince Royal of Sweden, formerly General Bernadotte, in the town of Abo, on the borders of the Baltic.[4] Bonaparte had made every effort to prevail on that prince to join him in his attack against Russia: he had made him the tempting offer of Finland, so lately taken from Sweden, and so bitterly regretted by the Swedes. Bernadotte, from respect to Alexander and from hatred to the tyranny which Bonaparte exercised over France and Europe, joined the coalition and refused the proposals of Napoléon, which consisted principally in a permission

---

4. August 27–30, 1812.

granted to Sweden to take or re-take all that might suit her, either among her neighbors or her allies.

The Emperor of Russia, in his conference with the Prince Royal of Sweden, asked his advice as to the means that ought to be employed against the invasion of the French. Bernadotte explained them like an able general who had formerly defended France against foreigners, and his confidence in the final result of the war had considerable weight. Another circumstance does great honor to the sagacity of the Crown Prince of Sweden. When news was brought to him that the French had entered Moscow, the envoys of the different powers who were then in his palace at Stockholm were thunderstruck; he alone declared firmly that from the date of that event, the campaign was lost to the conquerors; and addressing himself to the Austrian envoy at a time when the troops of that power still formed a part of the army of Napoléon: "You may," he said, "write to your Emperor that Napoléon is lost, although the capture of Moscow seems the greatest exploit in his military career." I was near him when he expressed himself in this way, and did not, I confess, put entire faith in his predictions. But his profound knowledge of the art of war disclosed to him an event at that time least expected by others. In the vicissitudes of the ensuing year, Bernadotte rendered eminent services to the coalition, as well by participating, with activity and intelligence, in the war at moments of the greatest difficulty, as in keeping up the hopes of the Allies when, after the battles gained in Germany by the new army raised, as if from the earth, by the voice of Bonaparte they began once more to consider the French as invincible.

Yet Bernadotte has enemies in Europe, because he did not enter France with his troops at the time that the Allies, after their triumph at Leipzig, passed the Rhine and marched on Paris. It is, I believe, very easy to justify his conduct on this occasion. Had the interest of Sweden required the invasion of France, it would have been incumbent on him, in making the attack, to forget that he was a Frenchman, as he had accepted the honor of being the head of another state; but Sweden was interested only in the deliverance of Germany; to bring France into a state of subjugation is incompatible with the security of the northern powers. It was therefore allowable to General Bernadotte to stop short on reaching the frontiers of his native land; to decline bearing arms against that country to which he was indebted for his existence and his fame. It has been pretended that he was ambitious to succeed Bonaparte;[5] no one knows what an ardent man may imagine in respect to fame; but it is at least certain that by not rejoining the Allies with his troops, he deprived himself of every chance of success through their means. Bernadotte therefore showed on this occasion only an honorable feeling, without being able to flatter himself with deriving from it any personal advantage.

A singular anecdote relative to the Prince Royal of Sweden deserves to be put on record. Bonaparte, far from wishing him to be chosen by the Swedish nation, was very dissatisfied at it, and Bernadotte had reason to fear that he would not allow him to quit France. In the field Bernadotte has considerable boldness, but in all that relates to politics he is prudent; and knowing perfectly how to feel his ground, he marches with force only toward that point of which fortune opens to him the path. For several years back he had dexterously kept himself in a middle state between the good and bad graces of the Emperor of France; but having too much talent to be ranked among the officers formed for blind obedience, he was always more or less suspected by Napoléon, who did not like to find a saber and an independent mind in the same man. Bernadotte, on relating to Napoléon in what manner his election had just taken place in Sweden, looked at him with those dark and piercing eyes which give something very singular to the expression of his features. Bonaparte walked beside him and stated objections which Bernadotte refuted as tranquilly as possible, endeavoring to conceal the keenness of his wishes; finally, after an hour's conversation, Napoléon said suddenly to him: "Well, let fate be fulfilled!" Bernadotte soon caught the words, but to be the more assured of his good fortune, he repeated them as if he had not understood their meaning: "Let fate be fulfilled," said Napoléon once more, and Bernadotte departed to reign over Sweden. There are some examples of points being gained in conversation with Bonaparte, in contradiction to his interest; but it is one of those chances, connected with his temper, on which no one can count.

5. Bernadotte stopped his advance at Liège in late February 1814. His ambition was to succeed Napoléon with the aid of Tsar Alexander I.

Bonaparte's campaign against the allies in the winter of 1814 is generally admitted to have been very able; and even those Frenchmen whom he had proscribed forever could not themselves avoid wishing that he should succeed in saving the independence of their country. What a fatal combination, and how unprecedented in history! A despot was then defending the cause of liberty by endeavoring to repulse the foreigners whom his ambition had brought on the French territory! He did not deserve of Providence the honor of repairing the mischief that he had done. The French nation remained neutral in the great struggle about to decide its fate; that nation formerly so animated, so vehement, was ground to dust by fifteen years of tyranny. Those who knew the country were well aware that life remained at the bottom of those paralyzed souls, and union in the midst of the apparent diversity produced by discontent. But one would have said that, during his reign, Bonaparte had covered the eyes of France like those of a falcon who is kept hood-winked until let loose on his prey. People did not know where the country was; they would no longer hear of Bonaparte, nor of any of the governments whose names were mentioned. The moderate conduct of the European powers prevented them from being considered as enemies, without its being possible, however, to welcome them as allies. France, in this condition, underwent the yoke of foreigners because she had not redeemed herself from that of Bonaparte; from what evils would she have escaped if, as in the early days of the Revolution, she had preserved in her heart a sacred horror of despotism!

Alexander entered Paris almost alone, without guards, without any precautions; the people were pleased at this generous confidence, the crowd pressed around his horse, and the French, so long victorious, did not yet feel themselves humiliated in the first moments of their defeat. Every party hoped for a deliverer in the Emperor of Russia, and certainly he carried that wish in his breast. He stopped at the house of M. de Talleyrand, who having, throughout all the stages of the Revolution, preserved the reputation of a man of much talent, was capable of giving him correct information on every point. But, as we have already mentioned, M. de Talleyrand considers politics as a maneuver to be regulated by the prevailing winds, and stability of opinion is by no means his characteristic. This is called cleverness, and something of this cleverness is perhaps necessary to veer on thus to the end of a mortal life; but the fate of a country should be guided by men whose principles are invariable; and in times of trouble, above all, that flexibility which seems the height of political art plunges public affairs into insurmountable difficulties. Be this as it may, M. de Talleyrand is, when he aims at pleasing, the most agreeable man whom the old government produced; it was chance that placed him amidst popular dissensions; he brought to them the manners of a court; and those graces which ought to be suspected by the spirit of democracy have often seduced men of coarse dispositions, who felt themselves captivated without knowing how. Nations which aim at liberty should beware of choosing such defenders; those poor nations without armies, and without treasure, inspire attachment only to conscientious minds.

A government proclaimed in Paris by the victorious armies of Europe was an event of high interest to the world; whatever that government might be, it could not be concealed that the circumstances which led to its establishment rendered its position very difficult; no people possessed of a spirit of pride can bear the intervention of foreigners in its interior affairs. In vain will these foreigners do whatever is reasonable and wise; their influence is sufficient to pervert even happiness itself. The Emperor of Russia, impressed with the importance of public opinion, did all that was in his power to leave to that opinion as much liberty as circumstances allowed. The army was desirous of a regency, in the hope that, under the minority of the son of Napoléon, the same government and the same military employments would be kept up. The nation wished that which it will always wish—the maintenance of constitutional principles. Some individuals believed that the Duke of Orléans,[6] a man of talent, a sincere friend of liberty, and a soldier in the cause of France at Jemmappes, would serve as a mediator between the different interests; but at that time he had hardly lived in France, and his name was indicative rather of a treaty than of a party. The impulse of the allied sovereigns was naturally in favor of the old dynasty; it was called for by the clergy, the nobles, and the adherents whom they were collecting in some departments of the south and west.

6. The future King Louis-Philippe I (r. 1830–48).

But at the same time, the army contained scarcely any officers or soldiers reared in obedience to princes absent for so many years. The interests accumulated by the Revolution, the suppression of tithes and feudal rights, the sale of national lands, the extinction of the privileges of the nobility and clergy; all that constitutes the wealth and greatness of the mass of the people rendered it necessarily inimical to the partisans of the old government, who came forward as the exclusive defenders of the royal family; and until the constitutional charter had given proof of the moderation and enlightened wisdom of Louis XVIII, it was natural that the return of the Bourbons should excite an apprehension of all the inconveniences attendant on the restoration of the Stuarts in England.

The Emperor Alexander estimated all those circumstances, as would have been done by an enlightened Frenchman, and was of the opinion that a compact ought to be concluded, or rather renewed, between the nation and the king. For if in former ages the barons assigned limits to the throne and required of the monarch the maintenance of their privileges, it was fair that France, which now formed only one people, should, by its representatives, possess those rights which the nobles enjoyed formerly, and enjoy still in several countries of Europe. Besides, Louis XVIII having returned to France only by the support of foreigners, it was of importance to draw a veil over that sad circumstance by voluntary and mutual securities between Frenchmen and their king. Policy as well as equity recommended this system; and if Henri IV, after a long civil war, submitted to the necessity of adopting the creed of the majority of the French, a man of so much judgment as Louis XVIII might well conquer such a kingdom as France by accepting a situation similar to that of the king of England: in truth it is not so much to be disdained.

Of the Circumstances Which Accompanied the First Return of the House of Bourbon in 1814.

When the return of the Bourbons was decided on by the European powers, M. de Talleyrand brought forward the principle of legitimacy to serve as a rallying point to the new spirit of party that was about to prevail in France. Doubtless, we cannot too often repeat that hereditary succession to the throne is an excellent pledge for tranquillity and comfort; but as the Turks also enjoy this advantage, we may well conclude that certain other conditions are necessary to ensure the welfare of a state. Moreover, nothing is more distressing at a critical conjuncture than those slogans which prevent most men from exercising their reasoning powers. Had the revolutionaries proclaimed not mere equality, but equality under the law, this qualification would have been sufficient to excite some reflection in the public mind. The case would be the same with legitimacy, if we add to it the necessity of limiting the royal power. But either of these words, "equality" or "liberty," when without qualification, are only such as would justify sentinels who should fire on him that did not instantly give the watch-word on the demand "who comes here."

The senate was pointed out by M. de Talleyrand to discharge the functions of representatives of the French nation on this solemn occasion.[1] Had the senate the power of assuming this right? And that power, which it legally had not, was it entitled to by its past conduct? As there was not

---

1. In early April 1814, the Senate entrusted a committee of five distinguished individuals (including Barbé-Marbois and Destutt de Tracy) with the task of drafting a new constitution that was approved on April 6. Nonetheless, Louis XVIII, taking note of the opposition of the royalists to the Senate's project, decided to endorse a different constitutional text.

time to convene deputies from the departments, was it not at least necessary to call together the legislative body? That assembly had given proofs of decision in the latter period of the reign of Bonaparte, and the nomination of its members belonged somewhat more to France herself. However, the senate pronounced[2] the forfeiture of the crown by that same Napoléon to whom it was indebted for its existence. The forfeiture was grounded on principles of liberty; why were not these recognized before the entrance of the allies into France? The senators, it will be said, were then without strength; all power was in the hands of the army. There are, we must admit, circumstances in which the most courageous men have no means of being active; but there are none that oblige men to do anything contrary to conscience. The noble minority of the senate, Cabanis, Tracy, Lanjuinais, Boissy d'Anglas, Volney,[3] Collaud,[4] Chollet,[5] &c., had fully proved during several years that a passive resistance was possible.

Senators, among whom there were several members of the National Convention, called for the return of the old dynasty, and M. de Talleyrand boasted that on this occasion he obtained the call of *Vive le Roi* from those who had voted the death of Louis XVI. But what good was to be expected from this kind of address, and would there not have been more dignity in excluding these men from such a deliberation? Is it necessary to deceive even the guilty? And if they are so bent to servitude as to bow the head to proscription, what purpose is gained by making use of them? Finally, it was this senate which prepared the constitution to be presented to the acceptance of Louis XVIII; and in those articles so essential to the liberty of France, M. de Talleyrand, at that time all-powerful, admitted the in-

2. On April 2, 1814.

3. Constantin François Chasseboeuf Volney (1757–1820), eminent French philosopher and historian, deputy to the Estates General in 1789. He was the author of *Les Ruins, ou meditations sur les révolutions des empires* (1791). Thomas Jefferson translated the first twenty chapters of this influential book for an American edition. In 1792, Volney purchased land in Corsica and established an agrarian community (later dissolved) based on his ideals. He was arrested during the Reign of Terror. Volney subsequently traveled to the United States, where he lived until 1798. He edited *Tableau du climat et du sol des États-Unis* in 1803.

4. General Collaud (1754–1819) was elected to the Senate in 1801.

5. Chollet (1747–1826), deputy to the Council of Five Hundred from 1795 to 1799 and member of the Senate after 18 Brumaire.

troduction of a most ridiculous condition, a condition calculated to invalidate all the others: the senators declared themselves, and along with them their pensions, hereditary. That men hated and ruined should make awkward efforts to preserve their situation is perfectly natural, but ought M. de Talleyrand to permit it? And ought we not to conclude, from this apparent negligence, that a man of his sagacity was already wanting to please the nonconstitutional royalists by allowing the public to lose the respect otherwise due to the principles advanced in the declaration of the senate? This was facilitating to the King the means of disdaining that declaration and of returning without any kind of previous engagement.

Did M. de Talleyrand at that time flatter himself that by this excess of complaisance, he should escape the implacable resentment of party spirit? Had he had during life enough of constancy in point of gratitude to imagine that others would not fail toward him in that respect? Did he hope that he alone should escape the shipwreck of his party, when all history informs us that there are political hatreds which never admit of reconciliation? Prejudiced men, whatever be the reform in question, never forgive those who have in any degree participated in new ideas; no penitence, no quarantine, can give them confidence in this respect; they make use of the individuals who have abjured; but if these pretended converts would retain a remnant of their past principles, even in small points, their fury is forthwith rekindled against them. The partisans of the old regime consider those of a representative government as in a state of revolt against legitimate and absolute power. What mean, then, in the eyes of these nonconstitutional royalists, the services which the old friends of the Revolution may render their cause? They are considered a beginning of expiation and nothing more. How did M. de Talleyrand not feel that, for the interest of the King as for that of France, it was necessary that a constitutional compact should tranquilize the public mind, consolidate the throne, and present the French nation to the eyes of all Europe not as rebels who ask forgiveness, but as citizens who become connected with their sovereign by mutual duties?

Louis XVIII returned without having recognized the necessity of such a compact; but being personally a man of a very enlightened mind, and whose ideas extended far beyond the circle of courts, he supplied it, in some measure, by his declaration of 2nd May, dated from St. Ouen. He thus granted what the nation wished him to accept; but this declaration, superior to the constitutional charter in regard to the interests of liberty, was so well conceived that it satisfied the public at the time. It justified the hope of a happy union of legitimacy in the sovereign and legality in the institutions. The same king might be a Charles II in hereditary right and a William III by his enlightened views. Peace seemed concluded between the opposing parties; the situation of courtier was left to those who were fit for it; the Chamber of Peers was composed of the men whose families were rendered illustrious by history and of the men of merit in the present age; in short, the nation hoped to repair her misfortunes by redirecting that intense activity, which had previously consumed herself as well as Europe, toward the securing of constitutional liberty.

There were only two kinds of danger that could extinguish these hopes: one, if the constitutional system was not followed by an administration with energy and sincerity; the other, if the congress of Vienna should leave Bonaparte at the island of Elba in the presence of the French army. This was a sword suspended over the throne of the Bourbons. Napoléon, by contending against foreigners to the last moment, had regained somewhat in the opinion of the French, and had perhaps more partisans at that time than during his lawless prosperity. It was thus necessary, for the support of the Restoration, that the Bourbons, on the one hand, should triumph over the recollection of victory by pledges given to liberty and, on the other, that Bonaparte should not be settled within thirty leagues of his old soldiers. No greater error could ever have been committed with regard to France.

CHAPTER VI

Of the Aspect of France and of Paris During Its First Occupation by the Allies.

It would be altogether wrong to feel surprise at the grief experienced by the French on seeing their celebrated capital occupied in 1814 by foreign armies. The sovereigns who became masters of it behaved at that time with the greatest equity; but it is a cruel misfortune for a nation to have to express even gratitude to foreigners, as it is a proof that its fate depends on them. French armies had, it is true, entered more than once almost all the capitals of Europe, but none of these cities were of so great importance relative to their respective countries as Paris relative to France. The monuments of the fine arts, the recollections of men of genius, the splendor of society, all contributed to render Paris the central point of Continental civilization. For the first time since Paris occupied such a rank in the world did the flag of foreigners wave on its ramparts. The dome of the Hotel of the Invalids had been lately decorated with standards, the trophies of forty battles, and now the banners of France could be displayed only under the orders of her conquerors. I have not, I believe, extenuated in this work the picture of the faults which reduced the French to this deplorable condition, but the more they suffered from them, the more they were entitled to esteem.

The best way of judging of the sentiments that actuate large masses is to consult one's own impressions. We are sure of discovering the feelings of the multitude by a reference to our own; and it is thus that men of ardent imaginations are able to foresee the popular movements with which a nation is threatened.

After ten years of exile[1] I landed at Calais, and I anticipated great plea-

---

1. In reality, Madame de Staël returned to France after twelve years of exile. She left London on May 8, 1814, and arrived in Paris on May 12.

sure on revisiting that beautiful France which I had so much regretted; my sensations were quite different from what I expected.[2] The first men whom I perceived along the shore wore the Prussian uniform; they were the masters of the town and had acquired that right by conquest. But I felt as if I were witnessing the re-establishment of the feudal system, such as it is described by old historians, when the inhabitants of the country served only to cultivate the ground of which the warriors of Germany were about to reap the fruits. Oh France, France! None but a foreign tyrant would have reduced you to such a state; a French sovereign, be he who he might, would have loved you too much ever to expose you to it.

I continued my journey, my heart always afflicted by the same thoughts; on approaching Paris, Germans, Russians, Cossacks, and Baskirs presented themselves to my sight in every direction; they were encamped around the church of St. Denis, where repose the ashes of the kings of France. The discipline enjoined by their leaders prevented the soldiers from doing injury to anyone, at least any other injury than that oppression of soul which it was impossible to remove. At last, I entered that city in which had been spent the most happy and most brilliant days of my life; I entered it as if I were passing through a painful dream. Was I in Germany or in Russia? Had they imitated the streets and squares of the capital of France to revive the remembrance of them after it had ceased to exist? In short, all was trouble in my mind; for in spite of the bitterness of my pain, I esteemed the foreigners for having shaken off the yoke. I felt unqualified admiration for them at this time; but to see Paris occupied by them, the Tuileries, the Louvre guarded by troops who had come from the frontiers of Asia, to whom our language, our history, our great men were all less known than the meanest Khan of Tartary—this was insupportable grief. If such was the impression on me, who could not have returned to France under Bonaparte's sway, what must have been the feelings of those warriors, covered with wounds and so much the prouder of their military fame, as it had for a long time constituted the only fame of France?

A few days after my arrival I wished to go to the opera; I had repeatedly

2. For more information, see Solovieff, *Madame de Staël, ses amis, ses correspondants. Choix de lettres (1778–1817)*, 481–84. Staël's letters to the Count of Harrowby (May 19, 1814) and Bernadotte (June 4, 1814) offer a good overview of the political context of that time. Also see Fairweather, *Madame de Staël*, 433–64.

in my exile figured to my recollection this daily amusement of Paris as far more graceful and brilliant than all the extraordinary entertainments of other countries. The performance was the ballet of Psyche, which for twenty years back had invariably been represented, but under very different circumstances. The staircase of the opera was lined with Russian sentinels; entering the house I looked around on all sides to discover a face which I might recognize, but I perceived only foreign uniforms; hardly did a few Parisians of the middling class show themselves in the pit, that they might not lose their ancient habits; in other respects the spectators were entirely changed; the performance alone remained the same. The decorations, the music, the dancing had lost none of their charms, and I felt myself humiliated by seeing French elegance so lavishly displayed before those sabers and mustachios, as if it had been the duty of the vanquished again to contribute to the amusement of the victors.

At the Theâtre François the tragedies of Racine and Voltaire were represented before foreigners more jealous of our literary fame than eager to confess it. The elevation of sentiment expressed in the tragedies of Corneille could no longer find a pedestal in France; it was no easy matter to avoid a blush on hearing them pronounced. Our comedies, in which the art of gaiety is carried so far, were amusing to our conquerors when it was no longer in our power to enjoy them, and we were almost ashamed even of the talents of our poets when they seemed chained like us to the chariot of the victors. No officer of the French army, to their honor be it said, appeared at the theater during the occupation of the capital by the Allies; they walked about sorrowfully and without uniforms, being unable to bear their military decorations since they had been unable to defend the sacred territory of which the charge had been entrusted to them. The irritation which they felt did not allow them to understand that it was their ambitious, selfish, and rash leader who had brought them to the state they were in: reflection could not accord with the passions by which they were agitated.

The situation of the King returning with foreigners amidst that army which necessarily hated them presented difficulties without number.[3] In-

---

3. This general feeling of uncertainty and powerlessness was nicely conveyed by Charles de Rémusat, who recalled the following conversation of his parents: "Here we are, after

dividually, he did all that intelligence and goodness can inspire to a sovereign who wanted to please, but he had to do with feelings of too strong a cast to be satisfied by the means employed under the old government. It was the support of the nation that was needed to regain the army; let us examine whether the system adopted by the ministers of Louis XVIII could accomplish that object.[4]

eighteen years, still on the same point, neither able to see clearly into the future nor capable of entrusting ourselves entirely to the present. Everything is still less completed than on the day when our son was born." (Rémusat, *Mémoires de ma vie*, vol. 1, 202–3) (trans. A. C.)

4. For a general view on the First and Second Bourbon Restorations, see Vaulabelle, *Histoire des deux Restaurations jusqu'à l'avénement de Louis-Philippe*, vols. 4 and 5; Gorce, *La Restauration: Louis XVIII;* and Sauvigny, *The Bourbon Restoration*. For a detailed analysis of the Charter of 1814, see Rosanvallon, *La monarchie impossible*.

CHAPTER VII

Of the Constitutional Charter Granted by the King in 1814.

I have a pride in here reminding the reader that the declaration signed by Louis XVIII at St. Ouen in 1814 contained almost all the articles in support of liberty proposed by M. Necker to Louis XVI in 1789, before the Revolution of the 14th of July burst forth.

That declaration did not bear the date of a reign of nineteen years,[1] in which lies the question of a divine right or a constitutional compact. The silence observed in that respect was extremely prudent, since it is clear that a representative government is irreconcilable with the doctrine of divine right. All the disputes between the English and their kings have arisen from that inconsistency. In fact, if kings are absolute masters of the people, they ought to exact taxes instead of asking for them; but if they have anything to ask from their subjects, it necessarily follows that they have also something to promise them. Moreover, the King of France, having in 1814 reascended the throne by the aid of a foreign force, his ministers ought to have suggested the idea of a contract with the nation, of the consent of its deputies; in short, the idea of anything that could convey a guarantee and bear evidence of the wish of Frenchmen, even if these principles had not been generally recognized in France. It was much to be apprehended that the army which had taken an oath to Bonaparte and had fought nearly twenty years under him should regard as null the oaths required by European powers. It was thus of importance to connect and blend the French

---

1. By using the phrase "*De notre règne le dix-neuvième*" ("in the nineteenth year of our reign") to date the Charter on his return to France in 1814, Louis XVIII implicitly claimed that his reign had started nineteen years earlier. This apparently minor detail implied that all previous regimes, including the empire, had been illegitimate.

military with the French people by all possible forms of voluntary acquiescence.

What, it will be said, would you plunge us again in the anarchy of primary assemblies? By no means; that which public opinion called for was an abjuration of the system on which absolute power is founded, but the public would have aimed at no chicanery with the ministry of Louis XVIII in regard to the mode of accepting the constitutional charter. It would have been sufficient only to consider it as a contract, not as an edict of the King;[2] for the Edict of Nantes of Henri IV was abolished by Louis XIV; and every act which does not rest on mutual engagements can be revoked by the authority from which it emanates.

Instead of at least inviting the two chambers to choose the commissioners who were to examine the act of constitution, the ministers caused these commissioners to be named by the King. The chambers would very probably have elected the same men; but it is one of the errors of the ministers of the old government to want to introduce the royal authority everywhere, while one ought to make a sparing use of this authority wherever it is not indispensably needed. All that we can allow a nation to do, without its leading to disorder, tends to extend information, to fortify public spirit, and increase the harmony between the government and the people.

On the 4th of June, 1814, the King came to the two chambers to make a declaration of the constitutional charter. His speech was full of dignity, talent, and propriety; but his Chancellor[3] began by calling the constitutional charter a decree of reform. What a fault! Did not this imply that what was granted by the King might be withdrawn by his successors? Nor was this all; in the preamble to the charter, it was said that power in all its plenitude was vested in the person of the King, but that its exercise had often been modified by the monarchs who preceded Louis XVIII, such as Louis VI, Philippe the Fair, Louis XI, Henri II, Charles IX, and

2. The use of the word "*octroi*" (concession) carried strong symbolic connotations that affirmed both the royal sovereignty and the continuity with the French monarchical tradition. As such, it eliminated any possibility of conceiving of the Charter as a social contract (or social pact) between the monarch and his subjects.

3. Dambray.

Louis XIV. The examples were certainly ill-chosen; for without dwelling on Louis XI and Charles IX, the ordonnance of Louis VI, in 1127, relieved the Third Estate of the towns from a state of servitude, and it is rather long since the French nation have forgotten this favor. As to Louis XIV, his is not the name to be introduced when we speak of liberty.

No sooner had I heard these words than I became apprehensive of the greatest future evils; for such indiscreet pretensions were still more calculated to expose the throne than to threaten the rights of the nation. The latter was at that time so powerful in its interior that nothing was to be dreaded for her; but it was exactly because public opinion was all-powerful that people could not avoid being irritated at ministers who thus put to hazard the protecting authority of the King without having any real strength to support it. The charter was preceded by the old form used in ordonnances, "We accord, we make concession and grant." But the mere name of charter, consecrated by the history of England, recalls the engagements which the Barons obliged King John to sign in favor of the nation and themselves.[4] Now, in what manner could the concessions of the Crown become a fundamental law of the state if they were nothing more than a favor from the King? Scarcely was the constitutional charter read when the Chancellor hastened to ask the members of the two chambers to swear fidelity to it. What would then have been said of a reclamation by a deaf person who should have got up to excuse himself from taking an oath to a constitution of which he had not heard a single article? Well! this deaf party was the French people; and it was because its representatives had acquired the habit of being dumb under Bonaparte that they desisted from any objection on the occasion. The consequence was that many of those who, on the 4th of June, swore to obey in all respects a code of laws which they had not even had time to understand, disengaged themselves but too easily ten months after from a promise so lightly given.

It was curious to see assembled in the presence of the King the two assemblies, the Senate and the legislative body, who had so long served Bonaparte. The senators and the deputies still wore the uniform given them by Napoléon; they made their bows turning to the rising instead of

4. Magna Carta (1215).

the setting sun; but their salute was as lowly as before. The Court of the House of Bourbon was in the galleries, holding up white handkerchiefs and calling *Vive le Roi* with all their might. The former adherents of the imperial government, the senators, marshals, and deputies, found themselves surrounded by these transports, and they had the practice of submission to such a degree that all the habitual smiles of their features served, as usual, for the admiration of power. But ought anyone who knew the human heart to put trust in such demonstrations? And would it not have been better to bring together representatives freely elected by France than men who at that time could be actuated only by interests, and not by opinions?

Although the charter was in several respects calculated to satisfy the public wish, it still left many things to be desired. It was a new experiment, while the English constitution had stood the test of time; and when the charter of the one country is compared with the constitution of the other, everything is in favor of England, whether we look to the people, to the grandees, or even to the King, who in a free country does not have the power of separating himself from the general interest.

The unconstitutional part of the royalists, whose words we are obliged incessantly to take note of, because it is above all by words that they act, have all along repeated that if the King had acted like Ferdinand VII,[5] if he had re-established, purely and simply, the old form of government, he would have had nothing to dread from his enemies. But the King of Spain had the army at his disposal, while that of Louis XVIII was not attached to him. The priesthood also forms an auxiliary army to the King of Spain; in France the ascendancy of the priesthood is at an end; in short, everything forms a contrast in the political and moral situation of the two countries; and he who endeavors to compare them merely indulges his fancy without at all considering the elements of which power and public opinion are composed.

But Bonaparte, it will still be said, knew how to beguile or to control the spirit of opposition! Nothing would be more fatal for any government

---

5. Upon his return to Spain in December 1813, Ferdinand VII rejected the liberal Cádiz constitution (passed in 1812) and reestablished political absolutism and the Inquisition.

in France than to imitate Bonaparte. His war-like exploits were of a nature that produced a fatal illusion in regard to his despotism; still Napoléon was found unable to resist the effect of his own system, and certainly no other hand was capable of wielding that club which recoiled even on his head.

In 1814, the French appeared less difficult to govern than at any other period of the Revolution; for they were rendered passive by despotism, and they were weary of the agitation to which the restless character of their master had doomed them. But, far from putting trust in this deceitful torpor, it would have been better to encourage them, if we may say so, to want to be free, that the nation might serve as a support to the royal authority against the army. It was important to replace military enthusiasm with political interests in order to nourish that public spirit which in France always stands in need of it. But of all yokes it was most impracticable to re-establish the ancient one; and the greatest precautions should have been taken to guard against whatever recalled it. There are yet but few Frenchmen who know thoroughly what liberty is; and Bonaparte certainly did not render them nice judges of it; but all institutions tending to hurt equality produce in France the same ferment which the reintroduction of Popery caused formerly in England.

The dignity of the peerage differs as much from nobility by genealogy as a constitutional monarchy from a monarchy founded on divine right; but it was a great error in the charter to keep up all titles of nobility, whether ancient or recent. After the restoration, we met in all directions with counts and barons created by Bonaparte, by the court, and sometimes even by themselves; while the peers alone ought to be considered the dignitaries of the country, in order to destroy the feudal nobility and replace it with a hereditary magistracy which, extending only to the eldest son, would not establish distinctions of blood and family in the country.[6]

Does it follow from these observations that the people in France were unhappy under the First Restoration? Was not justice and even the greatest kindness displayed toward everyone? Doubtless; and the French will

---

6. The hereditary peerage was introduced during the Second Restoration in August 1815 and was abolished during the July Monarchy in December 1831.

long repent that they were not then sufficiently aware of it. But if there are faults which justly irritate you against those who commit them, there are others which cause you disquietude for the fate of a government that you esteem; and of this description were those committed by the agents of the royal authority. The friends of liberty, the most sincerely attached to the King, wished a guarantee for the future; and their desire in that respect was just and reasonable.

CHAPTER VIII

Of the Conduct of the Ministry During the First Year of the Restoration.

Several English writers on politics advance that history shows the impossibility of getting a constitutional monarchy adopted with sincerity by a race of princes who have enjoyed unlimited authority during several centuries. The French ministry in 1814 had only one method of refuting this opinion: this was by manifesting in everything the superior mind of the King, to a degree that might convince the public that he yielded voluntarily to the improved knowledge of his age; because, if he lost as a sovereign, he gained as an enlightened man. The King on his return personally produced this salutary impression on those who had contact with him; but several of his ministers seemed to make a point of destroying this great advantage produced by the wisdom of the monarch.

A man since raised to an eminent station said, in an address to the King in the name of the department of the Lower Seine, that the Revolution had been nothing else than a twenty-five-year rebellion. By pronouncing these words, he disqualified himself from being useful in public affairs; for if this revolution be nothing else than a revolt, why consent to its operating a change in all our political institutions, a change consecrated by the constitutional charter? Consistency required that this objection should be answered by saying that the charter was a necessary evil to which people ought to submit so long as the misfortunes of the times required. How could such a mode of thinking be calculated to inspire confidence? How could it confer any stability or any strength on an order of things nominally established? A certain party considered the constitution as a wooden dwelling, the inconveniences of which were to be borne with during the interval necessary to reconstruct the true mansion, the old government.[1]

In public the ministers spoke of the charter with the greatest respect, particularly when they proposed measures which were destroying it piece by piece; but, in private, they smiled at the name of this charter, as if the rights of a nation were an admirable topic for pleasantry. What frivolity, good heavens! and this on the brink of an abyss! Is there, then, in the habits of courts something which perpetuates levity of mind even to advanced age? Gracefulness is often the result of this levity, but it costs dearly in the serious periods of history.

The first proposition submitted to the legislative body was the suspension of the liberty of the press. The ministry cavilled about the words of the charter, which were as clear as possible; and the newspapers were subjected to censorship.[2] If it was thought that the newspapers could not yet be left to themselves, it was at least incumbent on the ministry, after becoming responsible for their contents, to commit the direction of these papers (now official by the mere circumstance of the censorship) to wise men who would in no case permit the least insult to the French nation. How strange that a party evidently the weaker, weak to a high degree, as

---

1. On the one hand, the *ultras* accused the authors of the Charter of trying to import and artificially copy the English (unwritten) constitution without paying due attention to the old traditions and mores of France. Their motto was *"Restons Français et ne soyons pas Anglais!"* ("Let us remain French and not be English!") On the other hand, the *ultras* sought to downplay the novelty of the Charter by arguing that the latter was grounded on the same principles that had previously underpinned the institutions of the Old Regime. This thesis appears, for example, in Vitrolles' writings (as well as in Montlosier's *De la monarchie française*, 1814).

2. The Law of October 21, 1814, seemed to contradict Article 8 of the Charter of 1814 recognizing freedom of the press as a fundamental principle of the new political order: "Frenchmen have the right to publish and to have printed their opinions, while conforming to the laws which are necessary to restrain abuses of that liberty." Nonetheless, the Charter left open the possibility of temporary (preventive) forms of censorship in order to prevent and/or punish certain abuses of freedom of the press committed by those who sought to use the press to subvert the foundations of the new political order. This was the motivation behind the Law of October 21, 1814. A liberal justification of the law was given by François Guizot in his memoirs (*Memoirs to Illustrate the History of My Time*, vol. 1, 394–95). Benjamin Constant took an opposite view in this debate. For more information, see Craiutu, *Liberalism Under Siege*, 256–62.

the fatal return of Bonaparte showed but too clearly! How strange that this party should assume, toward so many million men, the tone of a preacher on a fast-day! How strange to declare to all that they are criminal in various ways, at various times, and that they ought, by relinquishing every claim to liberty, to expiate the evils which they caused in their efforts to obtain it! The writers of this party would, I believe, have permitted only for one short day a representative government, had it consisted in a few deputies robed in white and coming, with halters round their necks, to ask pardon for France. Others, with a milder tone, said, as in the time of Bonaparte, that it was proper to preserve the interests of the Revolution, provided its principles were annihilated. This was saying nothing less than that they still feared the interests, and that they hoped to weaken them by separating them from the principles.

Is this a proper manner of treating a nation of twenty-five million, lately the conquerors of Europe? Foreigners in spite, and perhaps even on account, of their triumph showed much more respect to the French nation than those newspaper writers who, in every successive government, had been the purveyors of sophistic arguments for the stronger party. These newspapers, whose tone, however, was thought to be dictated by ministry, attacked all individuals, dead or alive, who had been the first to proclaim even the principles of the constitutional charter. We were obliged to hear the venerable names which have an altar in our hearts, constantly insulted by party writers without having the power of replying, without being able even once to say how far these illustrious tombs were placed above their unworthy attacks, and what champions we have in Europe, and in posterity, for the support of our cause. But what can be done when all the discussions are ordered beforehand, and when no accent of the soul can pierce through writings devoted to the cause of meanness? At one time they insinuated the advantages of exile or discussed the objections to personal liberty. I have heard it proposed that government should consent to the liberty of the press, on condition of being invested with the power of arbitrary imprisonment; as if it were possible for one to write when laboring under a threat of being punished, without trial, for having written!

When the partisans of despotism have recourse to the bayonet, they act consistently; but when they employ the forms of reasoning to establish their doctrine, it is in vain that they flatter themselves with success in their deception. It is in vain to try to deprive a nation of knowledge and publicity; it becomes the more distrustful; and all the depths of Machiavellian policy are but wretched child's play when compared to the strength, at once natural and supernatural, of complete sincerity. There are no secrets between a government and a people: they understand, they know each other.[3] One can seek support in this or that party; but to believe that one can introduce by stealth the institutions against which public opinion is on the watch, implies a total ignorance of what the public has become in our day.

A series of resolutions tended to re-establish all things on the old footing; the constitutional charter was hemmed round in such a way as to render it eventually so different from the original whole as to make it fall, in a manner, of itself, stifled under the pressure of etiquette and ordinances. At one time it was proposed to reform the Institute which has been the glory of enlightened France, and to impose anew on the French Academy the old eulogies on Cardinal de Richelieu and Louis XIV exacted for more than a century; at another time decrees were passed for oaths to be taken in the ancient form and without reference to the charter; and when this triggered complaints, the example of England was brought forward; but it was introduced in France to sanction anything against liberty but never in favor of it. Yet it was very easy on this, as on every other occasion, to refute the explanation given to the example of England. The King of England, swearing himself to maintain the constitutional laws of the kingdom, the public functionaries take the oaths to him only. But is it worthwhile to begin an argument when the sole purpose of the adversaries is to find words to hide their intentions?

The institution of nobility as created by Bonaparte answered in truth no other purpose than to show the absurdity of that multitude of titles without reality to which only puerile vanity can attach importance. In the peerage, the eldest son inherits the titles and rights of his father; but the rest of the family returns into the class of citizens; and, as we have fre-

---

3. On publicity and public opinion during the Restoration, see Craiutu, *Liberalism Under Siege*, 246–56.

quently repeated, they form not a race of nobles but a hereditary magistracy, on whom certain honors are conferred on account of the public utility of the peerage, and not in consequence of inheritance by conquest, an inheritance which constitutes feudal nobility. The titles of nobility sent in all directions by the Chancellor of France in 1814 were necessarily injurious to the principles of political liberty. For what is meant by ennobling, except declaring that the Third Estate, in other words the nation, is made up of plebeians; that it is not honorable to be merely a citizen, and that certain worthy individuals must be raised above this state of humility? Now these individuals were, in general, persons who were known to be ready to sacrifice the rights of the nation to the privileges of the nobility. A taste for privileges in those who possess them by right of birth has at least a certain grandeur; but what can be more servile than those members of the Third Estate who offer to serve as a footstool to those who wish to mount over their heads?

Letters of nobility take date in France from the reign of Philip the Bold; their principal object was to confer an exemption from the taxes paid exclusively by the Third Estate. But the old nobles of France never considered as their equals those who were not noble by birth; and in this they were right; for nobility loses all its empire on the imagination whenever it does not go back to the shades of antiquity. Thus, letters of nobility are equally to be rejected on the ground of aristocracy as on that of liberty. Let us attend to what is said of them by the Abbé de Velly, a very judicious historian,[4] and acknowledged as such, not only by public opinion but by the royal censors of his time.* "The most remarkable thing in letters of nobility is that they require at the same time a financial supply for the king, who must be indemnified for the portion of taxation of which the descendants of the new noble are relieved, and an alms for the people, who undergo a surcharge in consequence of this exemption. It belongs to the Chamber of Accounts to decide on both. The king may remit both; but he seldom remits the alms, as that regards the poor. This is the place for quoting the remark of a celebrated jurist. *This abolition of plebeianship*

---

* Velly, vol. iii, p. 424.
4. Abbé de Velly (1709–59) was the author of *Histoire générale de la France* (1755).

is, if the truth may be spoken, nothing more than an erasure of which the mark remains; it seems indeed rather a fiction than a truth, the prince possessing no power to reduce an entity to a non-entity. This is what makes us in France so anxious to conceal the origin of our titles of nobility, in the hope of making them appear to belong to that earliest class of gentility, or immemorial rank, which alone constituted nobility in former ages."

On reading what has been published on these topics in Europe since the discovery of printing, or that only which is quoted from ancient chronicles, we are surprised to see how ancient in every country are the principles of the friends of liberty; and in what manner just views penetrate through the superstitions of certain periods in the minds of those who have in any way published their independent reflections. We have certainly on our side the reason of every age, and this cannot be denied to form a kind of legitimacy like any other.

Religion being one of the grand springs of every government, the conduct to be held in that respect necessarily occupied the serious attention of ministers; and the principle in the charter which it was incumbent on them to maintain with the greatest scruple was universal toleration. Although there still exists in the south of France some traces of that fanaticism which so long caused blood to be shed in these provinces, although the ignorance of some of the inhabitants of that country is equal to their warmth of temper, was it necessary to allow the Protestants to be insulted in the streets by sanguinary songs announcing the assassinations which were subsequently committed?[5] Was it not time for the purchasers of church lands to tremble when they saw the Protestants of the south marked out for massacre? Did not the peasantry, who pay neither tithe nor feudal dues, see their cause also in that of the Protestants; in short, in that of the principles of the Revolution, acknowledged by the King himself, but constantly evaded by the ministers? There are complaints, and but too just complaints in France, of a want of religion in the people; but if the intention be to make use of the clergy to reinstate the old form of government, we may be assured that the irritation thus caused will increase incredulity.

5. The so-called White Terror in the region of Nîmes in 1814–15.

What, for instance, could have been contemplated by substituting for the *fête* of Bonaparte on the 15th of August a procession to celebrate the vow of Louis XIII which consecrates France to the Holy Virgin? The French nation has, it must be admitted, a tremendous share of warlike asperity to be made to go through so meek a ceremony. Courtiers follow this procession with due devotion for the sake of places, as married women perform pilgrimages that they may have children; but what good is done to France by solemnly attempting to re-introduce ancient usages which have lost their influence on the people? This is accustoming them to make a mockery of religion instead of reviving their former habits of veneration for it. To attempt restoring power to fallen superstition is to imitate Don Pedro of Portugal, who, when he had attained the throne, brought from the tomb the remains of Inès de Castro to have them crowned. She was no more a queen for that.

Yet these remarks are far from being applicable to the funeral ceremony in memory of Louis XVI celebrated at St. Denis on the 21st of January. No one was able to witness that spectacle without emotion. The whole heart shares in the sufferings of that princess[6] who returned to the palace not to enjoy its splendor, but to honor the dead and to seek out their bleeding remains. This ceremony was, in the opinion of some, impolitic; but it excited so much sympathy that no blame could attach to it.

A free admission to all public employments is one of the principles on which the French lay the greatest stress. But, although this principle was declared sacred by the charter, the nominations made by ministers, particularly in the diplomatic department, were altogether confined to the aristocratic class. The army saw introduced into it too many general officers who had never made war but in a drawing room, and even there not always with success. In short, there was clearly no disposition but to bestow offices on the courtiers of former days, and nothing was so painful to those of the Third Estate who were conscious of possessing talent or wanted to excite emulation in their sons.

The finances, that department which is felt more immediately by the people, were in some respects managed with ability; but the promise given

6. Marie-Thérèse (1778–1851), daughter of Louis XVI.

to suppress the long list of excise duties comprised under the name of *droits reunis*[7] was not performed, and the popularity of the restoration suffered greatly by it.

Finally, the duty of the ministry, above all things, was to obtain that the princes should exercise no interference in public business unless in responsible employments. What would the English nation say if the King's sons or brothers had seats in the cabinet, voted for war or peace, in short, took a share in public business, without being subjected to the first principle of that government, responsibility, from which the King alone is exempted? The proper place for princes is the House of Peers; it is there that they ought to take the oath to observe the constitutional charter, an oath which they took only when Bonaparte was marching on Paris. Was not this an acknowledgment that they had till then neglected one great means of gaining the confidence of the people? Constitutional liberty is, for the princes of the House of Bourbon, the magic word which alone can open to them the gates of the palace of their ancestors. The art which they might employ to evade the pronunciation of it would be very easily observed; and this word, like the images of Brutus and Cassius, would excite greater attention in proportion as greater pains had been taken to avoid it.

There existed no common concert among ministers; no plan recognized by the whole; the ministry of police, an institution detestable in itself, was apprised of nothing and was employed about nothing; for if there be laws, however few, what can be done by a minister of police? Without having recourse to the employment of spies, to arrests, in short, to the whole abominable edifice of despotism founded by Bonaparte, statesmen must know the direction of public opinion and the true way to act in conformity to it. You must either command an army that will obey you like a machine or derive your strength from the sentiments of the nation; the science of politics stands in need of an Archimedes to supply it with a point of support.

M. de Talleyrand, whose thorough acquaintance with the parties that have agitated France cannot be contested, being at the congress of Vienna,

---

7. The new minister of finance, Baron Louis (1755–1837), refused to eliminate the *droits réunis,* indirect taxes on alcohol, tobacco, and salt.

could not influence the conduct of government in domestic affairs. M. de Blacas,[8] who had shown the most chivalrous attachment to the King in his exile, inspired the courtiers with the old jealousies of the *oeil de boeuf,* which do not leave a moment of repose to those who are thought to be in favor with the monarch; and yet M. de Blacas was, perhaps, of all those who returned with Louis XVIII, the most capable of forming an estimate of the situation of France, however new it might be to him. But what could be done by a ministry constitutional in appearance and counter-revolutionary in reality; a ministry composed, in general, of men who were upright, each in his own way, but who were governed by opposite principles, although the first wish of each was to please at court? Everyone said, *this cannot last,* although at that time the situation of everyone was easy; but the want of strength, that is of a durable foundation, created a general restlessness. It was not arbitrary strength that was desired, for that is only a convulsion from which, sooner or later, there always results a disastrous reaction, while a government established on the true nature of things goes on in a course of progressive consolidation.

As people saw the danger without forming a clear idea of the remedy, some persons adopted the unfortunate notion of proposing for the ministry of war Marshal Soult,[9] who had lately commanded with distinction the armies of Bonaparte. He had found means to gain the heart of certain royalists by professing the doctrine of absolute power which he had long practiced. The adversaries of all constitutional principles feel in themselves much more analogy to the Bonapartists than to the friends of liberty, because the change of the master's name is all that is wanted to make the two parties agreed. But the royalists did not perceive that this name was everything, for despotism could not then be established with Louis XVIII, either on account of his personal qualities or because the army were not disposed to lend itself to such a purpose. The true party of the King should

8. Pierre de Blacas d'Aups (1771–1839) had been Louis XVIII's main adviser in exile. He later served as ambassador in Naples.

9. Marshal Soult (1769–1851) led the battle of Toulouse against Wellington in April 1814. He subsequently rallied to Louis XVIII but defected to Napoléon during the Hundred Days in 1815. He returned to France in 1819 and served later as prime minister (1839–40, 1845–47).

have been the immense majority of the nation, which desires a representative constitution. All connection with the Bonapartists was then to be avoided, because they could not but subvert the monarchy of the Bourbons, whether they served them with integrity or aimed at deceiving them. The friends of liberty, on the other hand, were the natural allies among whom the King's party should have sought support; for, from the moment that the King granted a constitutional charter, he could employ with advantage those only who professed its principles.

Marshal Soult asked the erection of a monument for the emigrants who fell at Quiberon; he who, during twenty years, had fought for the cause adverse to theirs: it was a disavowal of all his past life, and still this abjuration was gratifying to a number of royalists. But in what consists the strength of a general from the moment that he loses the attachment of his fellow soldiers? When a man of a popular party is obliged to sacrifice his popularity, he is no longer of use to the new party that he embraces. The pertinacious royalists will always inspire more esteem than the converted Bonapartists.

The royalists thought to gain the army by appointing Marshal Soult minister of war; they were deceived: the great error of persons educated under the old government consists in attaching too much importance to leaders of every description. In our day the masses are everything, the individuals comparatively nothing. If the marshals lose the confidence of the army, generals of equal ability with their superiors soon come forward; if these generals are overset in their turn, soldiers will be found capable of replacing them. The same may be said in regard to civil administration; it is not men but systems which shake or guarantee power. Napoléon, I confess, forms an exception to this truth; but besides that his talents are extraordinary, he has farther studied, in the different circumstances in which he has been placed, to lay hold of the opinions of the moment, to seduce the passions of the people at the time he wished to enslave them.

Marshal Soult did not perceive that the army of Louis XVIII ought to be led by principles altogether different from that of Napoléon; the plan should have been to detach it gradually from that eagerness for war, from that frenzy of conquest by means of which so much military success had been obtained and such cruel evils inflicted on the world. But a respect for law, a sentiment of liberty, could alone operate this change. Marshal Soult, on the contrary, believed that despotism was the secret of everything. Too many people persuade themselves that they will be obeyed like Bonaparte by exiling some, by removing others from office, by stamping with the foot, by knitting the eyebrows, by replying haughtily to those who address them with respect; in short, by practicing all those arts of impertinence which men in office acquire in twenty-four hours, but which they often repent during the whole of life.

The intentions of the Marshal failed from the numberless obstacles of which he had not the slightest idea. I am persuaded that the suspicion of his acting a treacherous part is groundless. Treason among the French is, in general, nothing but the result of the momentary seduction of power; they are scarcely ever capable of combining it beforehand. But a Coblentz emigrant would not have committed so many faults in regard to the French army if he had been in the same situation; for he would at least have observed his adversaries, whereas Marshal Soult struck at his former subordinates, without suspecting that since the fall of Bonaparte there was such a thing as opinion, legislation, or, in short, the possibility of resistance. The courtiers were persuaded that Marshal Soult was a superior man because he said that one should govern with a scepter of iron. But where is this scepter to be forged, when you have on your side neither army nor people? In vain do you dwell on the necessity of bringing back to obedience, of subjecting, punishing, &c.; none of these maxims act of themselves, and you may pronounce them in the most energetic tone without being any the stronger for it. Marshal Soult had shown great ability in the method of administering a conquered country; but France was not one after the foreign troops were withdrawn.

CHAPTER IX

Of the Obstacles Which Government Encountered During the First Year of the Restoration.

We proceed to state the obstacles which the ministry of the Restoration had to surmount in 1814, and we shall have no fear in expressing our opinion on the system that ought to have been followed to triumph over them; the picture of this era is certainly not yet foreign to the present time.

All France had been cruelly disorganized by the reign of Bonaparte. What forms the strongest charge against that reign is the evident degradation of knowledge and virtue during the fifteen years that it lasted. After Jacobinism was past, there remained a nation that had not participated in its crimes, and the revolutionary tyranny might be considered a calamity of nature, under which the people had succumbed without being debased. The army could then boast of having fought only for the country, without aspiring to wealth, to titles, or to power. During the four years of the rule of the Directory, a trial had been made of a form of government which was connected with grand ideas; and if the extent of France and its habits rendered that form of government irreconcilable with general tranquillity, at least the public mind was electrified by the individual efforts which a republic always excites. But after military despotism and the civil tyranny founded on personal interest, of what virtues could we find any trace in the political parties with which the imperial government had surrounded itself? The masses in all orders of society, the military, peasants, nobles, men in trade, still possessed great and admirable qualities; but those who came forward on the scene of public business presented, with a few exceptions, the most miserable spectacle. The day after the fall of Bonaparte there was no activity in France but at Paris, and at Paris only among a few thousand persons running after the money and offices of government, whatever that government might be.

The military were and still are the most energetic body in a country where, for a long time, distinction has been awarded only to one kind of virtue—bravery. But ought those warriors who were indebted for their fame to liberty, to carry slavery among foreign nations? Ought those warriors who had so long supported the principles of equality on which the Revolution is founded, to exhibit themselves, if I may so speak, tattooed with orders, ribbons, and titles, which the Princes of Europe had given them that they might escape the tribute required from them? The majority of French generals, eager after distinctions of nobility, bartered their fame, like savages, for bits of glass.

It was in vain that, after the Restoration, government, while it was far too negligent of officers of the second rank, heaped favors on those of the higher class. From the time that Bonaparte's warriors wished to become courtiers, it was impossible to satisfy their vanity in that respect; for nothing can make new men belong to an ancient family, whatever be the title that is given to them. A well-powdered general of the old government excites the ridicule of those veteran mustachios which have conquered the whole of Europe. But a chamberlain from the family of a farmer or trades-man is hardly less ridiculous in his way. It was therefore impossible, as we have just said, to form a sincere alliance between the old and the new court; the old court indeed necessarily bore an appearance of bad faith in endeavoring to remove, in this respect, the quick-sighted apprehensions of the great lords created by Bonaparte.

It was equally impossible to give Europe a second time to be parcelled out among the military, whom Europe had at last conquered; and yet they were persuaded that the restoration of the old dynasty was the only cause of the treaty of peace which made them lose the barrier of the Rhine and the ascendency in Italy.

The secondhand royalists, to borrow an English phrase, that is, those who, after having served Bonaparte, offered to be instrumental in intro-ducing the same despotic principles under the Restoration; these men, calculated only to inspire contempt, were fit for nothing but intrigue. They were to be dreaded, it was said, if they were left unemployed; but nothing should be more guarded against in politics than to employ those whom we dread: for it is perfectly certain that they, discovering this feeling, will act as we act toward them merely by the tie of self-interest, which is broken, and rightly so, by adverse fortune.

The emigrants expected indemnities from the old dynasty for the property which they had lost by remaining faithful to it, and their complaints in this respect were certainly very natural. But they should have been helped without invalidating, in any manner, the sale of the national property, and made to comprehend what the Protestants had learned under Henri IV—that although they had been the friends and defenders of their King, they ought for the good of the state to consent that the King should attach himself to the interest that was predominant in the country over which he wished to reign. But the emigrants never conceive that there are Frenchmen in France, and that these Frenchmen are to be reckoned for something, nay for a great deal.

The clergy reclaimed their former possessions, as if it were possible to dispossess five million proprietors in a country, even if their titles were not by this time consecrated by all laws ecclesiastical and civil. Certainly France under Bonaparte has lost almost as much in point of religion as in point of information. But is it necessary that the clergy should form a political body in the state and possess territorial wealth in order that the French people may be brought back to more religious sentiments? Moreover, when the Catholic clergy exercised great power in France, it procured in the seventeenth century the repeal of the Edict of Nantes; and this same clergy in the eighteenth century opposed, down to the time of the Revolution, the proposition of M. de Malesherbes to restore the Protestants to the rights of citizens.[1] How, then, could the Catholic priesthood, if re-constituted as an order of the state, admit the article of the charter which proclaims religious toleration? In short, the general disposition of the nation is such that a foreign force alone could make it endure the re-establishment of the church in its previous form. Such an object would require the bayonets of Europe to remain permanently on the soil of

1. In 1787–88.

France, and a measure of this nature would certainly not reanimate the attachment of the French to the clergy.

Under the reign of Bonaparte nothing was properly carried on but war; everything else was willfully and voluntarily abandoned. People seldom read anymore in the provinces, and at Paris the public hardly know books but through the newspapers; which, such as they are, exercise a control over thought, since it is by them only that opinions are formed. We should blush to compare England and Germany with France in regard to general instruction. Some distinguished men still conceal our poverty from the eyes of Europe; but the instruction of the people is neglected to a degree that threatens every sort of government. Does it follow that public education ought to be exclusively entrusted to the clergy? England, the most religious country in Europe, has never admitted such an idea. Nor is it thought of either in the Catholic or Protestant part of Germany. Public education is a duty of government to the people, on which the former cannot levy the tax of this or that religious opinion.

That which the clergy of France wishes, that which it has always wished, is power; in general, the demands which we hear urged in the name of the public interest may be resolved into the ambition of groups or of individuals. If a book is published on politics, if you have difficulty in understanding it, if it appears ambiguous, contradictory, confused, translate it by these words, "I wish to become a minister," and all its obscurity will be explained to you. In fact, the predominant party in France is that which calls for places; the others are but accidental shades at the side of this uniform color; the nation, however, neither is nor can be of any account in this party.

In England when a ministry is changed, all who occupy places given by ministers do not imagine that they can receive places from their successors; and yet there exists but a very slight difference between the different parties in England. Tories and Whigs both desire monarchy and liberty, although they differ in the degree of their attachment to each. But in France, people thought themselves entitled to receive appointments from Louis XVIII because they had held places under Bonaparte; and a number of persons who call themselves patriots thought it strange that the King should not compose his counsel of those who had sentenced his brother to death. Incredible madness of the love of power! The first article of the rights of man in France is that it is necessary that every Frenchman should hold a public employment.

The caste of place-hunters have no idea of living but at the public expense; neither industry nor commerce, nor anything which proceeds from ourselves, appears to them a suitable source of income. Bonaparte had accustomed certain men who called themselves the nation to be pensioned by government; and the disorder which he had introduced into the affairs of everyone, as much by his gifts as by his acts of injustice, was such that at his abdication an incalculable number of persons, without any independent resource, offered themselves for places of any kind, no matter whether in the navy, the magistracy, the civil or military departments. Dignity of character, consistency of opinion, inflexibility of principle, all the qualities of a citizen, of a man of high spirit, of a friend of liberty, no longer exist in the active candidates formed by Bonaparte. They are intelligent, bold, decisive, dextrous dogs in the chase, ardent birds in the pursuit of prey; but that inward conscience which renders one incapable of deceiving, of being ungrateful, of showing servility toward power or harshness toward misfortune; all these virtues which exist in our nature as well as in reflection were treated as chimerical or as romantic exaggeration, even by the young men of that school. Alas! the misfortunes of France will give her back enthusiasm; but at the time of the Restoration there was scarcely any such thing as a decided wish on any point; and the nation was with difficulty awakened from the despotism which had given to men a movement so mechanical that even the vivacity of their action was no exercise of the will.

This, then, the royalists will still repeat, was an admirable opportunity for reigning by force. But, we say it once more, the nation consented to be subservient to Bonaparte only to obtain through him the splendor of victory; the dynasty of the Bourbons could not and ought not to make war on those who had re-established them. Were there any means of introducing slavish obedience at home when the army was by no means attached to the throne and when the population, being almost wholly renewed since the princes of the house of Bourbon had quitted

France, princes who were known only to persons of the age of forty and upward?

Such were the principal elements of the Restoration. We shall examine particularly the spirit of society at this date, and we shall finish by a sketch of the methods which, in our opinion, could alone triumph over these various obstacles.

CHAPTER X

Of the Influence of Society on Political Affairs in France.

Amidst the difficulties which the government had to overcome in 1814, we must place in the first rank the influence which the conversation of the saloons exercised on the fate of France. Bonaparte had resuscitated the old habits of a court and had joined to them, besides, all the faults of the less refined classes. The result was that a thirst of power and the vanity that it inspires had assumed characteristics still more strong and violent among the Bonapartists than among the emigrants. So long as there is no liberty in a country, everyone aims at getting favor, because the hope of obtaining a place is the only vivifying principle which animates society. The continual variations in the mode of expressing oneself, the confused style of political writings, whose mental restrictions and flexible explanations lend themselves to any interpretation; bows made and bows refused; sallies of passion and effusions of condescension, have no other object than to obtain favor, further favor, and still additional favor. It follows that people suffer quite enough by not getting it, because it is only by means of it that they obtain the tokens of kindness in the human countenance. One must possess great loftiness of soul and steadiness of opinion to dispense with it; for even your friends make you feel the value of exclusive power by the eagerness of their attention to those who possess it.

In England the adherents of the Opposition are often better received in society than those of the court; in France, before inviting a person to dinner, you ask if he be in the good graces of ministers; and in a time of famine, it might be even well to refuse bread to those who happen to be out of favor at court.

The Bonapartists had enjoyed the homage of society during their reign in the same way as the royalist party that succeeded them, and nothing hurt them so much as to occupy only the second place in the very saloons where they were so lately pre-eminent. The men of the old government had, besides, that advantage over them which is conferred by grace and the habit of good manners of former days. There consequently subsisted a perpetual jealousy between the old and the new men of title; and, among the latter, stronger passions were awakened by every little circumstance to which the various pretensions gave birth.

The King had not, however, re-established the conditions required under the old government to be admitted at court; he received, with a politeness perfectly well measured, all those who were presented to him; but though places were too often given to those who had served Bonaparte, nothing was more difficult than to appease those vanities that had become easily alarmed. Even in society it was wished that the two parties should mingle together, and each, apparently at least, complied. The most moderate in their party were still the royalists who had returned with the King, and who had not quitted him during his entire exile: the Count of Blacas, the Duke of Grammont, the Duke of Castries, the Count of Vaudreuil, etc. Since their conscience bore witness that they had acted in the most honorable and disinterested manner, according to their opinion, their minds were calm and benevolent. But those whose virtuous indignation against the party of the usurper was the most difficult to repress were the nobles or their adherents who had solicited places to the same usurper during his power, and who separated themselves from him very abruptly on the day of his fall. The enthusiasm for legitimacy of such a chamberlain of *Madame Mère* or of such a lady-in-waiting of *Madame Sœur* knew no bounds; and we whom Bonaparte had proscribed during the whole course of his reign, we examined ourselves to know whether we had not been his favorites at times when a certain delicacy of mind obliged us to defend him against the invectives of those whom he had loaded with favors.

We very often perceive a kind of tempered arrogance in the aristocrats, but the Bonapartists had certainly still more of it during the days of their power; and at least the aristocrats then adhered to their ordinary weapons: a constrained air, ceremonious politeness, conversations in a low tone of voice; in short, all that the perceptive eyes can observe but that proud characters disdain. It was easy to guess that the ultraroyalists forced themselves to treat the opposing party decently; but it cost them still more to show them to the friends of liberty than to the generals of Bonaparte; and the latter obtained from them attentions which obedient subjects always owe, in conformity with their system, to the agents of royal authority, whoever they may be.

The defenders of liberal ideas, equally adverse to the partisans of the old and new despotism, might have complained of seeing the flatterers of Bonaparte preferred to them; those men who offered no other guarantee to their new master but the sudden desertion of the old. But of what importance to them were the miserable disputes of society? It is possible, however, that such motives may have excited the resentment of a certain class of persons, at least as strongly as the most essential interests. But was this a reason for replunging the world in misery by the recall of Bonaparte and, at the same time, setting at stake the independence and liberty of the country?

In the first years of the Revolution, much may have been suffered from the terrorism of society, if it can be so called; and the aristocracy made a dextrous use of its established respectability to declare such or such an opinion out of the pale of good company. This first-rate company exerted, in former days, an extensive jurisdiction; some were afraid of being banished from it; others wished to be received into it; and the great lords and the great ladies of the old regime were beset with the most active pretensions for their favor. But nothing similar existed under the Restoration; Bonaparte, by imitating courts in a coarse manner, had dissipated their illusions; fifteen years of military despotism change everything in the customs of a country. The young nobles partook of the spirit of the army; they still retained the good manners which their parents had inculcated; but they possessed no real instruction. Women feel nowhere a necessity for being superior to men; and only a few gave themselves that trouble. There remained in Paris a very small number of amiable people of the old regime; for old persons had, for the most part, sunk under long misfortunes or were soured by inveterate resentments. The conversation of new men was necessarily more interesting: they had performed an active part; they took the lead of events while their adversaries could scarcely be dragged on in their train. Foreigners sought more eagerly those who had made themselves known during the Revolution; and in this respect, at least, the self-love of the latter must have been satisfied. Moreover, the old empire of good company in France consisted in the difficult conditions which were required to form a part of it, and in the liberty of conversation amidst a very select society: these two great advantages could no longer be found.

The mixture of ranks and parties had led to the adoption of the English fashion of large companies, which prevents any choice among the persons invited and consequently diminishes much the value of the invitation. The fear inspired by the imperial government had destroyed every habit of independence in conversation; the French under that government had almost all acquired a diplomatic reserve, so that social intercourse was confined to insignificant phrases which in no way reminded us of the daring spirit of France. There was certainly nothing to fear in 1814, under Louis XVIII; but the habit of reserve was acquired; and besides, the courtiers chose that it should be the fashion not to talk of politics nor treat of any serious subject: they hoped by this conduct to lead the nation back to frivolity, and consequently to submission; but the only result they obtained was that of rendering conversation insipid and depriving themselves of every means of knowing the real opinion of individuals.

Yet this society, little attractive as it was, proved a singular object of jealousy to a great number of Bonaparte's courtiers; and with their vigorous hands they would willingly, like Samson, have overthrown the edifice in order to make a ruin of the hall where they were not admitted to the banquet. Generals rendered illustrious by conquest wished to be made chamberlains, and their wives ladies in waiting: a singular ambition for a warrior who calls himself the defender of liberty! What, then, is this liberty? Is it only the national property, military rank, and civil employments? Does it consist in the wealth and power of a few men rather than of others? Or are we charged with the noble mission of introducing into France a sentiment of justice, a sentiment of dignity in all classes, fixed principles, and respect for knowledge and personal merit?

It would, notwithstanding, have been better policy to have given these generals places as chamberlains, since such was their wish; but the conquerors of Europe would really have found the life of a courtier embarrassing; and they might well have allowed the King to live within his palace with those to whom he had been habituated during his long years of exile. In England, who cares whether such or such a man is in the King's household? Those who follow this pursuit do not in general mix in public business; and we have never heard that Fox or Pitt wanted to pass their time in such a manner. It was Napoléon alone who could put into the heads of the soldiers of the republic all these fancies of citizen-gentlemen which made them necessarily dependent on the favor of courts. What would Dugommier, Hoche, Goubert, Dampierre, and so many others who fell for the independence of their country have said if, in recompense of their victories, they had been offered a place in the household of a prince, whoever he might be? But the men formed by Bonaparte have all the passions of the Revolution and all the vanities of the old regime. There was but one means of obtaining the sacrifice of these petty things—that of substituting in their stead great national interests.

Finally, the etiquette of courts in all its rigor can hardly be reestablished in a country where those habits are lost. If Bonaparte had not mingled with all these things the life of camps, he would have been insupportable. Henri IV lived familiarly with all the distinguished persons of his time; and Louis XI himself used to sup with the citizens and to invite them to his table. The Emperor of Russia, the Archdukes of Austria, the princes of the house of Prussia, those of England, in short, all the sovereigns of Europe live, in some respects, like private individuals. In France, on the contrary, the princes of the Royal Family scarcely ever go out of the circle of the court. Etiquette, as it existed formerly, is completely in contradiction to the manners and opinion of the age; it has the double inconveniency of giving occasion to ridicule, and yet of exciting envy.[1] No person wants to be excluded from anything in France, not even from those distinctions which are laughed at; and since there is as yet no open and public road to the service of the state, disputes are agitated on every question to which the civil code of court introductions can give rise. They hate each other for opinions on which life may depend; but they hate each other still more

1. A similar point was made by Tocqueville in *Democracy in America*.

on account of all those combinations of self-love which two reigns and two orders of nobility have called forth and multiplied. The French have become so difficult to satisfy, from the infinite increase in the pretensions of all classes, that a representative constitution is as necessary to deliver government from the numberless claims of individuals as it is to preserve individuals from what is arbitrary in government.

CHAPTER XI

Of the System Which Ought to Have Been Followed in 1814, to Maintain the House of Bourbon on the Throne of France.

Many people think that if Napoléon had not returned, the Bourbons had nothing to fear. I am not of this opinion; for such a man, it must at least be allowed, was an alarming pretender; and if the House of Hanover could fear Prince Edward,[1] it was madness to leave Bonaparte in a position which invited him as it were to form audacious projects.

M. de Talleyrand, in re-assuming in the Congress of Vienna almost as much ascendancy in the affairs of Europe as French diplomacy had exercised under Bonaparte, certainly gave great proofs of his personal skill. But should the French government, after changing its nature, have interfered with the affairs of Germany? Were not all the just resentments of the German nation yet too recent to be effaced? It was then the first duty of the King's ministers to have asked of the Congress of Vienna the removal of Bonaparte to a greater distance. Like Cato in the Roman senate when he repeated incessantly, "Carthage must be destroyed," the ministers of France ought to have laid aside all other interests till Napoléon was no longer within view of France and Italy.

It was on the coast of Provence that men attached to the royal cause might have been useful to their country by preserving it from Bonaparte. The plain good sense of the Swiss peasants, I remember, induced them to foretell, in the first year of the Restoration, that Bonaparte would return. Every day attempts were made in society to convince of this the persons

---

1. Charles Edward Stuart (1720–88), grandson of James II, who (unsuccessfully) attempted to return to Scotland in 1745.

who could make themselves heard at court. But since the etiquette which prevails only in France did not allow the monarch to be approached, and because ministerial gravity, another inconsistency in the present times, removed to a distance from the first servants of the state those who could have told them what was going on, an unprecedented lack of foresight proved the ruin of the country. But even if Bonaparte had not landed at Cannes, the system followed by the ministers, as we have endeavored to prove, had already endangered the Restoration, and left the King without any real strength in the midst of France. Let us first examine the conduct which government ought to have adopted in respect to each party, and conclude by recalling those principles which ought to guide the direction of affairs and the choice of men.[2]

The army, it has been said, was difficult to bring round. No doubt, if the intention was to maintain an army in order to conquer Europe and establish despotism in the interior, that army must have preferred Bonaparte as a military chief to the princes of the Bourbon family; nothing could change such a disposition. But if, while paying regularly the appointments and pensions of the military who had shed so much glory on the French name, the court had convinced the army that it was neither feared nor wanted, since it had been determined to take a liberal and peaceful policy as a guide; if, far from insinuating, in a whisper, to the officers that they would gain favor by supporting the encroachments of authority they had been told that the constitutional government, having the people on its side, would tend to diminish the number of the troops of the line, transforming the military into citizens and converting a warlike spirit into civil emulation, the officers would perhaps have regretted for some time longer their former importance. But the nation, of whom they constitute a part more than in any other army, since they are taken from all its classes, this nation, satisfied with its constitution and relieved from the apprehension of what of all things it fears most, the return of the privileges of the nobles and the clergy, would have calmed the military instead of irritating them by its disquietudes. It was useless to try to imitate Bonaparte in order

---

2. For more on the historical and political context of the first period of the Bourbon Restoration, see Alexander, *Rewriting the French Revolutionary Tradition*, 1–80.

to please the army; so fruitless an attempt could bring only ridicule on those who made it; but, by adopting a system altogether different, even directly contrary, they could have obtained that respect which arises from justice and obedience to the law; that path at least had not been trodden by Bonaparte.

In regard to the emigrants whose property was confiscated, what had been already done in 1814 might have been repeated; an extraordinary supply might have been asked of the legislative body to acquit the personal debts of the King. And since there would have been no tribute to pay to foreigners had not Bonaparte returned, the deputies would have acceded to the wish of the monarch, and would have respected the manner in which he employed an occasional supplement to his civil list.* Let it be asked with sincerity if, when the royalist cause seemed desperate, the emigrants had been told in England, "Louis XVIII shall ascend the throne of France, but with the condition of being limited to the powers possessed by the King of England; and you, who will return with him, shall obtain all the indemnities and favors which a monarch, according to your own wishes, can grant; but if property be restored to you, it shall be by his gift, not by your own rights; if you acquire any power it shall be by your personal talents, not by the privileges of your class," would not they all have consented to this treaty? Why then suffer themselves to be intoxicated by a moment of prosperity? And if, I take a pleasure in repeating it, Henri IV, who had been a Protestant, and Sully, who remained one, knew how to restrain the pretensions of their fellow soldiers, why did the ministers of Louis XVIII lack the art of governing the dangerous friends whom Louis XVI himself designated in his will as having greatly injured him by a mistaken zeal?

---

* In 1815 the King gave orders that out of this supplement the two million deposited by my father in the Royal Treasury should be restored to his family, and the order was about to be executed at the time of the landing of Bonaparte. The justice of our demand could not be contested; but I do not less admire the conduct of the King, who, though regulating with the utmost economy many of his personal expenses, would not retrench those which equity required. Since the return of His Majesty, the capital of two million has been paid to us by an inscription on the Great Book of 100,000 francs a year.

The existing clergy, or rather that which it was wished to re-establish, was another difficulty which presented itself from the first year of the Restoration. The conduct of government toward the clergy ought to be the same as toward all other classes: toleration and liberty, taking things as they are. If the nation desires a rich and powerful clergy in France, it will know how to re-establish it; but if no one wishes for it, then it will only alienate more and more the French from piety to present religion to them as a tax and the priests as men who seek to enrich themselves at the expense of the people. The persecutions which the priests suffered during the Revolution are continually cited: it was then a duty to serve them by every possible means; but the re-establishment of the political influence of the clergy has no connection with the just compassion which the sufferings of the priests inspired. It is the same with the nobility; their privileges ought not to be renewed as a compensation for the injustice they have suffered. Again it does not follow, because the remembrance of Louis XVI and his family awaken a deep and painful interest, that absolute power should be the necessary consolation to be offered to his descendants. This would be imitating Achilles when he caused the sacrifice of slaves on the tomb of Patroclus.

The nation always exists; it cannot die; and it must on no account be deprived of the institutions which belong to it. When the horrors which have been committed in France are described merely with the indignation which they naturally awaken, every mind is in sympathy; but when they are made the means of exciting hatred against liberty, the tears which spontaneous regret would have caused to flow are dried up.

The great problem which ministers had to solve in 1814 could have been studied in the history of England. They ought to have taken as a model the conduct of the House of Hanover, not that of the House of Stuart.

But it will be said, what marvellous effects would the English constitution have produced in France, since the Charter which resembles it so nearly has not saved us? First, greater confidence would have been placed in the duration of the Charter if it had been founded on a compact with the nation, and if the princes of the royal family had not been surrounded by persons professing, for the most part, unconstitutional principles. No one has dared to build on such unstable ground, and factions have remained on the alert, waiting for the fall of the edifice.

It was of importance to establish local authorities in the towns and villages, to create political interests in the provinces in order to diminish the ascendancy of Paris, where people aim at getting everything by favor.[3] It would have been possible to revive a desire for public esteem in those individuals who had terribly dispensed with it by making the suffrages of their fellow-citizens necessary to their being chosen deputies. A numerous election for the Chamber of Representatives (six hundred deputies at least; the English House of Commons has more) would have given a greater respectability to the legislative body, and consequently many distinguished persons would have engaged in that career. It has been acknowledged that the qualification of age, fixed at forty years,[4] was a damp to every kind of emulation. But the ministers dreaded deliberative assemblies above everything; and, influenced by their old experience of the early events of the Revolution, they directed all their efforts against the freedom of speech in the Assembly. They did not perceive that, in a country intoxicated with military ardor, the freedom of debate is a protection instead of a danger, since it adds to the strength of the civil power.

To increase as much as possible the influence of the Chamber of Peers, there should have been no obligation to preserve all the former senators, unless they had a right to that honor by their personal merit. The peerage ought to have been hereditary and composed wisely of the ancient families of France, which would have given it dignity; and of men who had acquired an honorable name in the civil and military career. In this manner the new nobility would have derived luster from the old, and the old from

3. In a letter to Louis de Kergolay of June 29, 1831, Tocqueville commented on the limitations of the Charter of 1814, which, in his view, was destined to be a short-lived constitution. The Bourbons, argued Tocqueville, should have paid more attention to channeling the emerging democratic elements and principles rather than attempting to preserve or reform old and inefficient institutions. Furthermore, they should have furthered administrative decentralization and promoted self-government that would have strengthened the communal and departmental system in France. For more information, see Tocqueville, *Selected Letters on Politics and Society*, 55–56.

4. Cf. Article 38 of the Charter of 1814.

the new; they would thus have advanced toward that constitutional blending of classes without which there is nothing but arrogance on one side and servility on the other.

It would also have been well not to have condemned the Chamber of Peers to deliberate in secret. This was depriving it of the surest means of acquiring an ascendancy over the public mind. The Chamber of Deputies, although they had no real title to popularity, since they were not elected directly, exercised more power on public opinion than the Chamber of Peers solely because the speakers were known and heard.

Finally, the French desire the fame and the happiness attached to the English constitution, and the experiment is well worth a trial; but the system once adopted, it is essential that the language, the institutions, and the customs should be brought to conformity with it. For it is with liberty as with religion; hypocrisy in a noble cause is more revolting than its complete abjuration. No address ought to be received, no proclamation issued, that did not formally remind us of the respect due to the Constitution, as well as to the throne. The superstition of royalty, like all other superstitions, alienates those whom the simplicity of truth would have attracted.

A public education not under the management of religious orders, to which we cannot return, but a liberal education, the establishment of schools in all the departments for mutual instruction;[5] the universities, the polytechnic school, everything which could restore the splendor of learning to France, ought to have been encouraged under the government of so enlightened a prince as Louis XVIII. In this manner it would have been practicable to divert the public mind from military enthusiasm and compensate to the nation for the absence of that fatal glory which produces so much evil, whether it is gained or lost.

No arbitrary act, and we are happy in insisting on that fact, no arbitrary act was committed during the first year of the Restoration. But the existence of the police,[6] forming a ministry as under Bonaparte, was discor-

---

5. The "mutual" form of education (in which the instructor was helped by the best students) developed in England and Germany; it was linked to Protestantism.

6. The ministry of police was abolished in 1814 and reestablished a year later.

dant with the justice and mildness of the royal government. The principal employment of the police was, as we have already stated, the inspection of the newspapers, and the spirit of the latter was detestable. Even admitting that this inspection was necessary, the censor should at least have been chosen among the deputies and peers; but it was violating all the principles of representative government to put into the hands of ministers themselves the direction of that opinion by which they are to be tried and enlightened. If the liberty of the press had existed in France,[7] I will venture to affirm that Bonaparte would never have returned; the danger of his return would have been pointed out in such a manner as would have dispelled the illusions of obstinacy; and truth would have served as a guide instead of producing a fatal explosion.

Finally, the choice of ministers, that is, of the party from which they should have been chosen, was the most important condition for the safety of the Restoration. In times when men are occupied with political debates, as they were formerly with religious quarrels, free nations can be governed only by the aid of those whose opinions are in correspondence with the opinions of the majority. I shall begin, then, by describing those who ought to have been excluded before pointing out the men who ought to have been chosen.

None of the men who committed any crime in the Revolution, that is, who shed innocent blood, can be in any way useful to France. They are reprobated by the public and their own disquietude leads them into deviations of every kind. Give them repose and security; for who can say what he would have done amidst such great agitations? He who has not been able to keep his conscience and his honor clear in any struggle whatever may still be dextrous enough to serve himself, but can never serve his country.

Among those who took an active part in the government of Napoléon, a great number of military men have virtues which do honor to France, and some administrators possess rare abilities from which advantages may be derived; but the principal chiefs, the favorites of power, those who

7. For more on freedom of the press under the Bourbon Restoration, see Hatin, *Histoire politique et littéraire de la presse en France*, vol. 8.

enriched themselves by servile acquiescence, those who delivered up France to that man who perhaps would have respected the nation if he had met with any obstacle to his ambition, any greatness of soul in those by whom he was surrounded—there could be no choice more contrary than that of such men to the dignity as well as safety of the Crown. If it is the system of the Bonapartists to be always the slaves of power, if they bring their science of despotism to the foot of every throne, ought ancient virtues to be brought in alliance with their corruption? If it were intended to reject all liberty, better in that case would it have been to have gone over to the ultra-royalists, who were at least sincere in their opinion and considered absolute power as an article of faith. But is it possible to rely on the promises of men who have set aside all political scruples? They have abilities, it is said; ah! accursed be those abilities which can dispense with even one true feeling, with one just and firm act of morality! And of what utility can be the talents of those who overwhelm you when you are sinking? Let a dark speck appear on the horizon, their features lose by degrees their gracious look; they begin to reason on the faults that have been committed; they bitterly accuse their colleagues and make gentle lamentations for their master; until, by a gradual metamorphosis, they are transformed into enemies; they who had so lately misled princes by their Oriental adulation!

After having pronounced these exclusions, there remains, and a great blessing it is, there remains, I say, no choice but that of the friends of liberty; either they who have preserved that opinion unsullied since 1789 or they who, less advanced in years, follow it now and adopt those principles in the midst of the efforts made to stifle them; a new generation, which has arisen in these later times and on whom our future hopes depend.

Such men are called upon to terminate the Revolution by liberty,[8] and

8. This was the main task of postrevolutionary French liberals: "closing" the Revolution by coming to terms with the legacy of the Terror of 1793–94. To this effect, they championed the main principles of 1789 and the civil liberties enshrined in the Declaration of the Rights of Man and of Citizen—the rights of man, political liberty, freedom of association, and the like—while also vigorously condemning the ideas that, in their view, had made the Terror possible. This attitude was nicely illustrated by Guizot: "As a destructive [phenomenon],

it is the only possible close to that sanguinary tragedy. Every effort to sail against the torrent will but overset the boat; but let this torrent enter into channels, and all the country which it laid waste will be fertilized.[9]

A friend of liberty in the situation of minister to the king would respect the supreme chief of the nation and be faithful to the constitutional monarch, in life and death; but he would renounce those officious flatteries which weaken belief in what is true instead of increasing attachment. Many sovereigns in Europe are very well obeyed without requiring to be deified. Why, then, in France are writers on every occasion so prodigal of this incense? A friend of liberty would never suffer France to be insulted by any man who depended, in any degree, on government. Do we not hear some emigrants saying that the king alone is the country, that no confidence can be placed in Frenchmen, &c.? What is the consequence of this insensate language? What is it? That France must be governed by foreign armies. What an outrage! What blasphemy! Undoubtedly those armies are now stronger than we are; but they would never have the voluntary assent of a French heart; and to whatever state Bonaparte may have reduced France, there is in a minister who is a friend of liberty such a dignity of character, such a love for his country, such a noble respect for the monarch and the laws, as would check all the arrogance of a military force, whoever might be its leaders. Such ministers, never committing an arbitrary act themselves, would not be in the dependence of the military; for it was much more to establish despotism than to defend the country that the different parties courted the troops of the line. Bonaparte pretended, as in the times of barbarism, that the whole secret of social order consisted

---

the Revolution is done and there is no question of returning to it; as founding moment, it only commences now" (François Guizot, Review of Montlosier's *De la monarchie française*. *Archives, Philosophiques, Politiques et Littéraires*, vol. III, 397). For more information, see Manent, *An Intellectual History of Liberalism*, 80–83.

9. During the first years of the Restoration, reconciling democracy as a new type of society with representative government seemed a daunting task. By democracy as social condition, French liberals referred to the advent of a new type of society which brought forth a new configuration of mores, sentiments, laws, and institutions. The image of democracy as an irresistible torrent ("in full spate") that needed strong dikes to contain and purify it appeared in the *parlementary* speeches during the first years of the Bourbon Restoration. For more information, see Craiutu, *Liberalism Under Siege*, 104–12.

in bayonets. How, without them, will it be said, could the Protestants and Catholics, Republicans and Vendeans, be made to go on together? All these elements of discord existed in England in 1688 under different names; but the invincible ascendancy of a constitution set afloat by skillful and upright pilots brought everything under submission to the law.

An assembly of deputies really elected by the nation exercises a majestic power, and the ministers of the monarch, if their souls were filled with the love of country and of liberty, would find everywhere Frenchmen ready to aid them, even without their knowledge; because, in that case, opinion and not interest would form the tie between the governors and the governed. But if you employ, and this we shall not cease to repeat, if you employ individuals who hate free institutions to carry them on, however upright they may be, however well resolved to adhere to their promise, a discordance will always be felt between their natural inclinations and their imperious duty.

The artists of the seventeenth century painted Louis XIV as a Hercules with a large peruke on his head; very old doctrines, reproduced in a popular assembly, present an equally great disparity. All that edifice of old prejudices which some seek to re-establish in France is nothing but a castle of cards which the first breath of wind will overset. We can calculate only on two kinds of force in this country: public opinion, which calls for liberty, and the foreign troops who obey their sovereigns; all the rest is mere trifling.

Thus, whenever a minister pretends that his countrymen are not made for freedom, accept this act of humility in his quality of Frenchman as a resignation of his place; for that minister who can deny the almost universal desire of France knows his country too ill to be capable of directing its affairs.

CHAPTER XII

What Should Have Been the Conduct
of the Friends of Liberty in 1814?

The friends of liberty, we have already said, could alone have contributed in an efficacious manner to the establishment of constitutional monarchy in 1814; but how ought they to have acted at that period? This question, no less important than the former, deserves also to be treated. We shall discuss it frankly, since we, for our own part, are persuaded that it was the duty of all good Frenchmen to defend the Restoration and the constitutional charter.

Charles Fox, in his history of the two last kings of the House of Stuart, says that "a restoration is commonly the most dangerous, and the worst, of all revolutions." He was right in applying this maxim to the two reigns of Charles II and James II, whose history he was writing; he saw, on the one side, a new dynasty which owed its crown to liberty, whilst the old dynasty thought itself despoiled of its natural right by the limitation of absolute power, and consequently avenged itself on all those who had entertained such intentions. The principle of hereditary succession, so indispensable in general to the repose of nations, was necessarily averse to it on this occasion. The English then did very wisely in calling to the throne the Protestant branch, and without this change their constitution would never have been established. But when the chance of hereditary succession has given you for a monarch such a man as Louis XVIII, whose serious studies and quietude of mind are in harmony with constitutional liberty; and when, on the other hand, the chief of a new dynasty showed himself, during fifteen years, to be the most violent despot of modern times, how can such a combination in any way remind us of the wise William III and the sanguinary and superstitious James II?

William III, although he owed his crown to election, often found that the manners of liberty were not very gracious and would, if he had been able, have made himself a despot like his father-in-law. Sovereigns of ancient date think themselves, it is true, independent of the choice of the people; the popes, in like manner, think themselves infallible; the nobles are proud of their genealogy; every man and every class have their disputed pretensions. But what was there to fear at this time from those pretensions in France? Liberty had nothing to dread at the time of the First Restoration but the very calamity which befell it: a military commotion bringing back a despotic chief, whose return and whose defeat served as a pretext and a motive for the establishment of foreign armies in France.

Louis XVIII possessed the essence of a magistrate in his mind and his disposition. In as much as it would be absurd to consider time past as the despot of the present, no less would it be desirable to add, when it can be done, the support of the one to the improvement of the other. The upper chamber had the advantage of inspiring some great lords with a taste for new institutions. In England the most decided enemies of arbitrary power are found among the patricians of the first rank; and it would be a great happiness for France if the nobility would at length acquire a knowledge of, and an attachment for, free institutions. There are qualities connected with illustrious birth of which it would be fortunate that the state could avail itself. A people made only of the bourgeois could with difficulty establish itself in the midst of Europe unless it had recourse to military aristocracy, the most fatal of all to liberty.

Civil wars must end by mutual concessions, and already the great lords were observed yielding to liberty in order to please the King; the nation would have gained ground every day; the trackers of power, who scent where it lies and throw themselves on its path, did not then cling to the extreme royalists. The army began to assume a liberal tone; this was, in truth, because it regretted the loss of its former influence in the state; but at all events the cause of reason derived advantage from its ill-humor. We heard Bonaparte's generals endeavoring to speak of the liberty of the press, of the liberty of the person; to pronounce those phrases which they had received as a watch-word, but which they would at last have comprehended by dint of frequent repetition.

The most respectable military men lamented the defeats of the army, but they recognized the necessity of putting a stop to continual reprisals, which would, in the course of time, destroy civilization. For if the Russians were to avenge Moscow at Paris, and the French Paris at St. Petersburg, these bloody marches of soldiers across Europe would annihilate all knowledge and all the enjoyments of social life. Besides, did the first entry of foreign troops into Paris efface the numerous triumphs of the French? Were these not still present to the recollection of all Europe? Did Europe ever speak of French valor but with respect? And was it not just, however painful, that the French should feel in their turn the dangers attached to their unjust wars? Finally, was that irritation which excited some individuals to desire the overthrow of a government proposed by foreigners a patriotic feeling? Certainly the European nations had not taken up arms to replace the Bourbons on the throne; and therefore the coalition ought not to have been attributed to the old dynasty: it was impossible to deny that the descendants of Henri IV were French; and Louis XVIII had conducted himself in the negotiation for peace as such, when, after all the concessions made before his arrival, he had been able to preserve untouched the old territory of France. It was not then conformable to truth to say that national pride demanded new wars; France had still a great share of glory, and if the nation had known how to reject Bonaparte and to become free like England, never would she have seen the British flag wave a second time on her ramparts.

No confiscation, no exile, no illegal arrest took place during ten months;[1] what a progress was this on emerging from fifteen years of tyranny! England hardly attained this noble result thirty years after the death of Cromwell. In short, there was no doubt that in the succeeding session, the liberty of the press would have been decreed. Now to this law, the first of a free state, may be applied the words of Scripture, "Let there be light, and there was light."

The chief error in the charter, which lay in the mode of election and in the condition of eligibility, was already acknowledged by all enlightened men, and changes in this respect would have been the natural con-

1. From April 1814 to February 1815.

sequence of the liberty of the press, because that liberty always places great truths in a conspicuous light. Genius, a talent for writing, the exercise of thought, all that the reign of bayonets had stifled was reviving by degrees; and if a constitutional language was held to Bonaparte, it was because people had respired for ten months under Louis XVIII.[2]

Some vain people complained; a few imaginations were alarmed; a few venal writers, by talking every day to the nation of its happiness, made it doubtful of it; but when the champions of thought had entered the lists, the French would have recognized the voice of their friends; they would have learned by what dangers national independence was threatened; what motives they had to remain at peace abroad as at home, and to regain the esteem of Europe by the exercise of civil virtues. The monotonous stories of war become confounded in the memory or lost in oblivion; the political history of the free nations of antiquity is still present to every mind and has served as a study to the world for two thousand years.

2. This complex social and political context created a unique environment that triggered an exceptional revival of arts and sciences. Many writings and memoirs of that period conveyed the feeling of living in a time of great change after decades of spiritual desolation. For more information, see Craiutu, *Liberalism Under Siege*, 19–26.

CHAPTER XIII

Return of Bonaparte.

No, never shall I forget the moment when I learned from one of my friends, on the morning of the 6th of March, 1815,[1] that Bonaparte had disembarked on the coast of France; I had the misfortune to foresee instantly the consequences of that event, such as they have since taken place, and I thought that the earth was about to open under my feet. For several days after the triumph of this man the aid of prayer failed me entirely, and in my trouble it seemed to me that the Deity had withdrawn from the earth and would no longer communicate with the beings whom he had placed there.

I suffered in the bottom of my heart from personal circumstances; but the situation of France absorbed every other thought.[2] I said to M. de Lavalette,[3] whom I met almost at the hour when this news was resounding around us: "There is an end of liberty if Bonaparte triumphs, and of national independence if he is defeated." The event has, I think, but too much justified this sad prediction.

It was impossible to avoid an inexpressible irritation before the return and during the progress of Bonaparte. During the previous month, all

1. In fact, Napoléon landed on March 1, 1815, at Golfe-Jean. See Furet, *Revolutionary France*, 275–80.

2. On March 10, 1815, Madame de Staël and her family (with the exception of Auguste) left Paris for Switzerland; Napoléon arrived in Paris ten days later. On behalf of the Emperor, Joseph Fouché, Duke of Otrante (1759–1820), sent Madame de Staël a courteous note on March 24, followed by a similar letter signed by Joseph Bonaparte on April 5, in which Joseph Bonaparte quoted Napoléon as endorsing Madame de Staël's ideas. See Solovieff, ed., *Madame de Staël, ses amis, ses correspondants. Choix de lettres (1778–1817)*, 494. To Joseph Bonaparte she commented somewhat favorably on Napoléon's return (ibid., 493).

3. Antoine Chamans, Count of La Valette (1769–1830), former close associate of Napoléon.

those who had any acquaintance with revolutions had felt the air charged with storms; repeated notice of this was given to persons connected with government; but many among them regarded the disquieted friends of liberty as relapsing, and as still believing in the influence of the people, in the power of revolutions. The most moderate among the aristocrats thought that public affairs regarded government only, and that it was indiscreet to interfere with them. They could not be made to understand that to be acquainted with what is passing in a country where the spirit of liberty ferments, men in office should neglect no opinion, be indifferent to no circumstance, and multiply their numbers by activity instead of wrapping themselves up in a mysterious silence. The partisans of Bonaparte were a thousand times better informed on everything than the servants of the King; for the Bonapartists, as well as their master, were aware of what importance every individual can be in a time of trouble. Formerly everything depended on men in office; at present those who are out of office act more on public opinion than government itself, and consequently forecast better the future.

A continual dread had taken possession of my soul several weeks before the disembarkation of Bonaparte. In the evening, when the beautiful buildings of the town were illuminated by the rays of the moon, it seemed to me that I saw my happiness and that of France, like a sick friend whose smile is the more amiable because he is on the eve of leaving us. When told that this terrible man was at Cannes, I shrunk before the certainty as before a poignard; but when it was no longer possible to escape that certainty, I was but too well assured that he would be at Paris in a fortnight. The royalists made a mockery of this terror; it was strange to hear them say that this event was the most fortunate thing possible, because we should then be relieved from Bonaparte, because the two chambers would feel the necessity of giving the King absolute power, as if absolute power was a thing to be given! Despotism, like liberty, is assumed and is never granted. I am not sure that among the enemies of every constitution there may not have been some who rejoiced at the convulsion which might recall foreigners and induce them to impose an absolute government on France.

Three days were passed in the inconsiderate hopes of the royalist party. At last, on the 9th of March, we were told that nothing was known of the

Lyon telegraph because a cloud had prevented reading the communication. I was at no loss to understand what this cloud was. I went in the evening to the Tuileries to attend the King's levee; on seeing him, it seemed to me that, with a great deal of courage, he had an expression of sadness, and nothing was more touching than his noble resignation at such a moment. On going out, I perceived on the walls of the apartment the eagles of Napoléon which had not yet been removed, and they seemed to me to have re-assumed their threatening look.

In the evening, at a party, one of those young ladies who, with so many others, had contributed to the spirit of frivolity which it was attempted to oppose to the spirit of faction, as if the one could contend against the other; one of these young ladies, I say, came up to me, and began jesting on that anxiety which I could not conceal: "*What, Madam,*" said she to me, "*can you fear that the French will not fight for their legitimate King against a usurper?*" How, without discrediting oneself, could one answer a phrase so adroitly turned? But after twenty-five years of revolution, ought one to flatter oneself that legitimacy, an idea respectable but abstract, would have more ascendancy over the soldiers than all the recollections of their long wars? In fact, none of them contended against the supernatural ascendancy of the genius of the African isles; they called for the tyrant in the name of liberty: they rejected in its name the constitutional monarch; they brought six hundred thousand foreigners into the bosom of France to efface the humiliation of having seen them there during a few weeks; and this frightful day of the 1st of March, the day when Bonaparte again set foot on the soil of France, was more fertile in disasters than any epoch of history.

I will not launch out, as has been but too much done, into declamations of every kind against Napoléon. He did what it was natural to do in trying to regain the throne he had lost, and his progress from Cannes to Paris is one of the greatest conceptions of audacity that can be cited in history. But what shall we say of the enlightened men who did not see the misfortunes of France and of the world in the possibility of his return? A great general, it will be said, was wanted to avenge the reverses experienced by the French army. In that case, Bonaparte ought not to have proclaimed the treaty of Paris; for if he was unable to reconquer the barrier of the Rhine sacrificed by that treaty, what purpose did it answer to expose that which France possessed in peace? But, it will be answered, the secret intention of Bonaparte was to restore to France her natural barriers. But was it not clear that Europe would guess that intention, that she would form a coalition to resist it, and that, particularly at the time in question, France was unable to resist united Europe? The Congress[4] was still assembled; and although a great deal of discontent was produced by several of its resolutions, was it possible that the nations would make choice of Bonaparte for their defender? Was it he who had oppressed them whom they could oppose to the faults of their princes? The nations were more violent than the sovereigns in the war against Bonaparte; and France, on taking him back for her ruler, necessarily brought on herself the hatred both of governments and of nations. Will anyone dare to pretend that it was for the interest of liberty that they recalled the man who had during fifteen years shown himself most dextrous in the art of being master, a man equally violent and deceitful? People spoke of his conversion, and there were not wanting believers in this miracle; less faith certainly was required for the miracles of Mahomet. The friends of liberty have been able to see in Bonaparte only the counterrevolution of despotism and the revival of an old regime more recent, but on that account more formidable; for the nation was still completely fashioned to tyranny, and neither principles nor public virtue had had time to take root. Personal interests only, and not opinions, conspired for the return of Bonaparte, and they were mad interests which were blinded in regard to their own danger and accounted the fate of France as nothing.

Foreign ministers have called the French army a perjured army; but this epithet cannot be justified. The army that abandoned James II for William III was then also perjured; and besides, the English rallied under the son-in-law and the daughter to dethrone the father, a circumstance still more cruel. Well, it will be said, be it so; each army betrayed its duty. I do not admit even the comparison; the French soldiers, in general under the age of forty, did not know the Bourbons, and they had fought for twenty years under the orders of Bonaparte; could they fire on their Gen-

4. The Congress of Vienna (1814–15).

eral? And from the moment that they refused to fire on him, would they not be prevailed on to follow him? The men really to blame are those who, after having become close to Louis XVIII, after obtaining favors from him and making him promises, were capable of joining Bonaparte. The word, the dreadful word "treachery," is applicable to them; but it is cruelly unjust to address it to the French army. The governments that placed Bonaparte in a situation to return ought to take the blame of his return. For to what natural feeling could an appeal be made to persuade soldiers that they ought to kill the General who had led them twenty times to victory? The General whom foreigners had overturned, who had fought against foreigners at the head of Frenchmen less than a year before? All the reflections which made us hate that man and love the King were adapted neither to the soldiers nor to the subaltern officers. They had been fifteen years faithful to the Emperor; that Emperor advanced toward them without defense; he called them by their names; he spoke to them of the battles which they had gained with him; how was it possible to resist? In a few years the name of the King, the blessings of liberty, would have captivated every mind, and the soldiers would have learned from their parents to respect the public welfare. But scarcely ten months had passed since the removal of Bonaparte, and his departure dated from an event which must necessarily put warriors in despair, the entry of foreigners into the capital of France.

But the accusers of our country will say, if the army are excusable, what shall we think of the peasantry, of the inhabitants of the towns who welcomed Bonaparte? I will make in the nation the same distinction as in the army. Enlightened men could see nothing but a despot in Bonaparte; but, by a concourse of very distressing circumstances, this despot was presented to the people as the defender of its rights. All the benefits acquired by the Revolution, benefits which France will never voluntarily renounce, were threatened by the continuous imprudent actions of the party which aims at making a conquest of Frenchmen, as if they still were Gauls; and the part of the nation which most dreaded the return of the old government thought they saw in Bonaparte the means of preserving themselves from it. The most fatal combination that could overwhelm the friends of liberty was that a despot should put himself in their ranks, be placed, as it were, at their head, and that the enemies of all liberal ideas should have a pretext for confounding popular violence with the evils of despotism, thus making tyranny pass as if it were on the account of liberty herself.

The result of this fatal combination has been that the French have incurred the hatred of sovereigns for desiring to be free, and of nations for not knowing how to be so. Doubtless, great faults must have been committed to produce such a result; but the reproaches provoked by these faults would plunge all ideas into confusion if we did not endeavor to show that the French, like every other people, were victims of those circumstances which produce great convulsions in the order of society.

If blame is at all events to be imputed, would there then be nothing to say against those royalists who allowed the King to be taken from them without drawing a single trigger in his defense? They ought certainly to rally under the new institutions, since it is evident that there remains to the aristocracy nothing of its former energy. It was assuredly not because the nobles were not, like all Frenchmen, of the most brilliant courage; but because they are ruined by their confidence as soon as they become the stronger party, and by discouragement as soon as they become the weaker. Their blind confidence arises from their having made a dogma of politics; and from their trusting, like Turks, to the triumph of their faith. The cause of their discouragement is that three-quarters of the French nation being at present in favor of the representative government, the adversaries of this system, so soon as they cease to have six hundred thousand foreign bayonets in their service, are in such a minority that they lose all hopes of defending themselves. Were they willing to make a treaty with reason, they would again become what they ought to be, the support alternately of the people and of the throne.

CHAPTER XIV

Of the Conduct of Bonaparte on His Return.

If it was a crime to recall Bonaparte, it was silliness to wish to disguise such a man as a constitutional sovereign. From the moment that he was taken back, a military dictatorship should have been conferred on him, the conscription re-established, the nation made to rise in mass so as not to be embarrassed about liberty when independence was compromised. Bonaparte was necessarily lowered in public opinion when made to hold a language quite contrary to that which had been his during fifteen years. It was clear that he could not proclaim principles so different from those that he had followed when all-powerful but because he was forced to it by circumstances; now, what is such a man when he allows himself to be forced? The terror he inspired, the power resulting from that terror, no longer existed; he was a muzzled bear which, though still heard to murmur, is nevertheless obliged by his guides to dance as they think proper. Instead of imposing the necessity of holding constitutional language for whole hours together on a man who had a horror of abstract ideas and legal restraints, he ought to have been in the field four days after his arrival at Paris, before the preparations of the allies were completed and, above all, while the astonishment caused by his return still shook the imagination. His object should have been to excite the passions of the Italians and Poles; to promise the Spaniards to expiate his faults by restoring to them their Cortes; in short, to take liberty as a weapon, not as an incumbrance.

> *Quiconque est loup, agisse en loup,*
> *C'est le plus certain de beaucoup.*[1]

1. Whoever is wolf acts as wolf:
   It is most certain of much.

From "Le Loup devenu berger" ("The Wolf Become Shepherd"), by Jean de La Fontaine (*Fables*, bk. 3).

Some friends of liberty,[2] endeavoring to pass an illusion on themselves, attempted to justify their renewed connection with Bonaparte by making him sign a free constitution; but there was no excuse for serving Bonaparte elsewhere than on the field of battle. Foreigners, once at the gates of France, should have been prevented from entering it; in that way only was the esteem of Europe herself to be regained. But it was degrading the principles of liberty to clothe in them a former despot; it was giving hypocrisy a place among the most sincere of human truths. In fact, how would Bonaparte have supported the constitution which he was made to proclaim? When responsible ministers should have refused compliance with his will, what would he have done with them? And if these same ministers had been severely accused by the deputies for having obeyed him, how would he have restrained an involuntary motion of his hand as a signal to his grenadiers to go a second time and drive out, at the point of the bayonet, the representatives of another power than his own?

What! this man would have read every morning in the newspapers insinuations on his faults, on his errors! Sarcasms would have approached his imperial paw, and he have withheld a blow! He was accordingly often seen ready to reassume his true character; and since that character was such, he could find strength only in showing it. Military Jacobinism, one of the greatest scourges of the world, was, if still practicable, the only resource of Bonaparte. On his pronouncing the words "law" and "liberty," Europe became tranquil; she felt that it was no longer her old and terrible adversary.[3]

---

2. Among them was Madame de Staël's close friend Benjamin Constant, the author of the new constitution entitled *Additional Act* (April 1815). A part of their correspondence during this period is found in Solovieff, ed., *Madame de Staël, ses amis, ses correspondants. Choix de lettres (1778–1817)*, 494–506.

3. Napoléon realized that he had to make a series of liberal concessions to those who advocated the principles of representative government and constitutional monarchy. In a private conversation, he acknowledged: "The taste of constitutions, debates, and speeches has revived. Authority is questioned." (quoted in Lucas-Dubreton, *The Restoration and the July Monarchy*, 13) Napoléon abolished censorship of the press and signed an "Additional Act to the Constitutions of the Empire," drafted by his former opponent Benjamin Constant. The preamble of the act clearly indicates the new spirit that ruled over the country: "The emperor wishes to give to the representative system its full extension, while combining

Another great fault that Bonaparte was made to commit was the establishment of a House of Peers. The imitation of the English constitution, so often recommended, had at last taken hold of the minds of the French and, as always happens, they carried the idea to an extreme; for a peerage can no more be created in a day than a dynasty; hereditary rank for the future stands in need of hereditary rank in the past. You can, doubtless, I repeat it, associate new with old names; but the color of the past must blend with that of the present. Now what signified that antechamber of peers in which all the courtiers of Bonaparte took their places? There were among them some very estimable men; but others could be mentioned whose sons would have desired to be spared their father's name instead of receiving an assurance of its continuance. What elements for forming the aristocracy of a free country, such as should merit the respect of the monarch as well as of the people! A king, entitled to voluntary respect, finds his security in national liberty; but a dreaded chief, rejected by half the nation, and called in by the other half only as an instrument of military success, why should he aim at a kind of esteem which he could never obtain? Bonaparte, in the midst of all the shackles imposed on him, was unable to display the genius which he still possessed: he let things proceed and commanded no longer. His discourse showed signs of a fatal presentiment, whether it was that he thoroughly knew the strength of his enemies or that he was impatient of being no longer the absolute master of France. That habit of dissimulation which ever formed a part of his character ruined him on this occasion; he has played a part the more with his accustomed facility; but the circumstances were too serious to allow him to get through it by cunning; and the undisguised action of his despotism and impetuosity could alone give him even a momentary chance of success.

---

in the highest degree political liberty with the power necessary to secure respect abroad for the independence of the French people and the dignity of the throne." Also see Hatin, *Histoire politique et littéraire de la presse en France*, vol. VIII, 132.

CHAPTER XV

Of the Fall of Bonaparte.

I have not yet spoken of that warrior who caused the fortune of Bonaparte to fade; of him who pursued him from Lisbon to Waterloo, like that adversary of Macbeth who was to be endowed with supernatural gifts in order to be his conqueror. Those supernatural gifts were the most noble disinterestedness, inflexible justice, talents whose source was in the soul, and an army of free men. If anything can console France for having seen the English in the heart of her capital, it is that she will at least have learned what liberty has made them.

The military genius of Lord Wellington could not have been the work of the constitution of his country; but his moderation, the magnanimity of his conduct, the energy which he derived from his virtues—these come from the moral atmosphere of England; and what crowns the grandeur of that country and its General is that while on the convulsed soil of France the exploits of Bonaparte sufficed to make him an uncontrolled despot, he by whom he was conquered, he who has not yet committed one fault or lost one opportunity of triumph, Wellington will be in his own country only an unparalleled citizen, but as subject to the law as the most obscure individual.

I will venture to affirm, however, that our France would not, perhaps, have fallen had any other than Bonaparte been its chief. He was extremely dextrous in the art of commanding an army; but he knew not how to rally a nation. The revolutionary government itself understood better how to awaken enthusiasm than a man who could be admired only as an individual, never as the defender of a sentiment or an idea. The soldiers fought extremely well for Bonaparte; but France did little for him on his return. In the first place, there was a numerous party against Bonaparte, a numerous party for the King, who did not consider it their duty to oppose foreign armies. But even if every Frenchman could have been convinced that in any situation whatever the duty of a citizen is to defend the independence of his country, no one fights with all the energy of which he is capable when the object is only to repel an evil, not to obtain a good. The day after the triumph over the foreign troops we were certain of being enslaved in the interior. The double power which would at once have repulsed the invader and overthrown the despot existed no longer in a nation that had preserved only military vigor, which is by no means similar to public spirit.

Besides, Bonaparte reaped even among his adherents the bitter fruits of the doctrine which he had sown. The only thing he had extolled was success; the only thing he praised was opportunity; whenever there was any question of opinion, of devotedness, of patriotism, the dread he had of the spirit of liberty excited him to turn every sentiment which could lead to it into ridicule. But those were the only sentiments which could induce the perseverance which attaches itself to misfortune; those sentiments alone possess an electric power and form an association from one extremity of a country to the other, without its being necessary even to communicate in order to be unanimous. If we examine the various interests of the partisans of Bonaparte and of his adversaries, we shall explain forthwith the motives of their differences of opinion. In the South, as in the North, the manufacturing towns were for him and the seaports against him, because the Continental blockade had favored manufactures and destroyed commerce. All the different classes of the defenders of the Revolution might, in some respects, prefer a chief whose want of legitimacy was itself a guarantee, since it placed him in opposition to the old political doctrines; but the character of Bonaparte is so adverse to free institutions that those among the partisans of the latter who thought proper to connect themselves with him did not second him with all their might, because they did not belong to him with all their heart: they had an afterthought and an after hope. If, as is extremely doubtful, there still remained any means of saving France after she had provoked Europe, it could only be in a military dictatorship or in the republican form. But nothing was more absurd than to found a desperate resistance on a falsehood: with this you can never have the whole man.

The same system of egoism which always governed Bonaparte induced him to aim, at whatever cost, at a great victory instead of trying a defensive system which would have better suited France, especially if he had been supported by the public mind. But he arrived in Belgium having, it is said, in his carriage a scepter, a robe, in short, all the baubles of imperial sway; for the only thing he understood well was that kind of pomp mixed with a sort of quackery. When Napoléon returned to Paris after his lost battle,[1] he had surely no idea of abdicating, and his intention was to demand from the two chambers supplies of men and money, in order to try another struggle. The legislature ought, in these circumstances, to have granted everything rather than yield to the foreign powers.[2] But if the chambers were perhaps wrong in abandoning Bonaparte in this extremity, what shall we say of the manner in which he abandoned himself?

What! This man, who had just convulsed Europe by his return, sends in his resignation like a mere general and does not once attempt to resist! There is a French army under the walls of Paris that desired to fight the invaders, and he is not in the midst of it, as a chief or as a soldier! This army falls back behind the Loire, and he crosses the Loire to embark where his person may be in safety, while it was his own torch that had set France in flames![3]

We cannot permit ourselves to accuse Bonaparte of wanting courage in these circumstances any more than in those of the preceding year. He did not command the French army during twenty years without having shown himself worthy of his station. But there is a firmness of soul that conscience alone can give; and Bonaparte, instead of this decisive will, which is independent of events, had a kind of superstitious faith in fortune which did not allow him to proceed without her auspices. From the day

---

1. The Battle of Waterloo (June 1815).

2. After the battle of Waterloo, the deputies, worried by Napoléon's intention to assume dictatorial power, voted (at the initiative of La Fayette) in favor of a motion declaring that any attempt to dissolve the Chamber would be considered high treason. The Chamber of Peers passed a similar resolution.

3. Initially, Napoléon wanted to leave for the United States. To this effect, he went to Rochefort but found the port blocked by the English navy. He surrendered himself to the English on July 15.

he felt that misfortune had taken hold of him, he resisted no longer; from the day his own destiny was overthrown, he thought no more of the destiny of France. Bonaparte had confronted death with intrepidity in the field, but he did not choose to inflict it on himself; and this resolution is not without some dignity. This man has lived to give the world a moral lesson, the most striking, the most sublime, that nations have ever witnessed; it seems as if Providence has been pleased, like a severe tragic poet, to make the punishment of this great culprit arise out of the very crimes of his life.

Bonaparte, who during ten years had stirred up the world against the most free and religious country which social order in Europe has yet produced, against England, delivers himself up into her hands; he who during ten years had every day insulted that nation, makes an appeal to her generosity; in short, he who never spoke of laws but with contempt, who so lightly ordered arbitrary imprisonments, invokes the liberty of England and would use it as a shield. Ah! why did he not give that liberty to France? Neither he nor the French would then have been exposed to the mercy of conquerors.

Whether Napoléon live or die, whether he reappear or not on the continent of Europe,[4] one single motive still leads me to speak of him; it is the ardent desire that the friends of liberty should separate entirely their cause from his, and that they should be careful not to confound the principles of the Revolution with those of the imperial government. There is not, and I believe I have proved it, a counterrevolution more fatal to liberty than that which he accomplished. If he had been of an old dynasty, he would have pursued equality with extreme animosity under whatever form it might have presented itself; he paid his court to priests, to nobles, and to kings, in the hope of being himself accepted as a legitimate monarch. It is true that he sometimes made them the object of abuse and that he did them harm when he saw that he could not enter into the confederation of past times; but his inclinations were aristocratic even to pettiness. If the principles of liberty are destroyed in Europe, it is only because he eradicated them from the mind of nations. He seconded despotism everywhere by giving it support in the hatred of the nations against France.

4. Napoléon was still alive when Madame de Staël wrote these lines.

He perverted human intellect by imposing, during fifteen years, on his pamphleteers an obligation to write and display every system which could mislead reason and stifle knowledge. To establish liberty requires superior men in every department; Bonaparte would have men of talents only in the military line; and never, under his reign, could a reputation be founded on the management of civil business.

At the beginning of the Revolution, a crowd of illustrious names did honor to France; and it is one of the principal characters of an enlightened age to possess many distinguished men, but hardly one superior to all the rest. Bonaparte subjugated the age in that respect, not because he was superior in information but, on the contrary, because he had something of the barbarism of the middle ages. He brought from Corsica a different age, different expedients, a different character, from anything that we had in France; and this novelty favored his ascendancy over the minds of men. Bonaparte is single where he reigns, and no other distinction can be compatible with his own.

Different opinions may be entertained of his genius and of his qualities; there is about this man something enigmatic which prolongs curiosity. Everyone represents him under different colors, and each may be right, according to the point of view which he chooses; those who would concentrate his portrait in a few words would give only a false idea of him. To attain some general result, we must pursue different ways: it is a labyrinth, but a labyrinth that has a clue—egoism. Those who knew him personally may have found him in domestic life possessing a kind of goodness which the world certainly never perceived. The devoted attachment of some truly generous friends is what speaks the most in his favor. Time will bring to light the principal traits of his character; and those who are willing to admire every extraordinary man have a right to think him such. But he never could, and never can, bring anything but desolation on France.

God preserve us, then, from him, and forever! But let us beware of calling those men Bonapartists who support the principles of liberty in France; for with much more reason might that name be given to the partisans of despotic power, to those who proclaim the political maxims of the man they proscribe: their hatred of him is only a dispute about interests; a real love of generous sentiments forms no part of it.

CHAPTER XVI

Of the Declaration of Rights
Proclaimed by the Chamber of
Representatives, 5th of July, 1815.

Bonaparte signed his second abdication on the 22d of June, 1815; and on the 8th of the following month the foreign troops entered the capital. During this very short interval, the partisans of Napoléon lost a great deal of precious time in trying to secure, against the will of the nation, the crown to his son.[1] Besides, the Chamber of Representatives contained a number of men who would certainly not have been elected without the influence of party-spirit; and yet it sufficed that, for the first time during fifteen years, six hundred Frenchmen elected in any manner by the people should be assembled together and deliberate in public, in order that the spirit of liberty and the talent of speaking might reappear. Men entirely new in the career of politics spoke with distinguished ability: others, who had not been heard of during the reign of Bonaparte, recovered their old vigor, and yet, I repeat it, there were deputies in that Chamber whom the nation, if left to itself, would never have accepted. But such is the strength of public opinion when men feel themselves in its presence, such is the enthusiasm inspired by a forum where you are heard by all the enlightened men of Europe, that those sacred principles, obscured by long years of despotism, reappeared in less than a fortnight; and in what circumstances did they appear! When factions of all kinds were kindled in the assembly itself, and when three hundred thousand foreign soldiers were near the walls of Paris.

1. Napoléon II.

A *bill* of rights, for I have a pleasure on this occasion[2] in making use of the English expression, which recalls only happy and august recollections; a bill of rights was proposed and carried in the midst of these disasters; and in the few words we are about to read, there exists an immortal power—truth.*

I stop at this last act, which preceded by a few days the complete invasion of France by foreign armies: it is there that I finish my historical reflections. In fact, there is no more a France so long as foreign armies occupy our territory. Let us cast our eyes, before ending, toward those general ideas which have guided us throughout the course of the work; and let us, if possible, present a picture of that England which we have so often held up as a model to the legislators of France, by accusing them every time that they departed from it.[3]

* The author intended to have inserted here the Declaration of the Chamber of Representatives, eliminating whatever was not in harmony with the principles professed in this work. This task is of too delicate a nature for the editors to take on themselves to complete it.

This chapter is evidently nothing but an outline. Notes in the margin of the manuscript pointed out the principal facts of which Madame de Staël purposed treating, and the distinguished names she meant to cite. (Note by the original editors)

2. On July 4, 1815. This declaration, titled *Déclaration des Droits des Français et des principes fondamentaux de leur constitution*, drew inspiration from the English Bill of Rights of 1689 rather than the Declaration of the Rights of Man and of Citizen of 1789. The new declaration, drafted by Garat, former deputy to the Estates General and former minister of justice, stipulated, among other things, popular sovereignty, division of powers, the inviolability of the monarch, freedom of the press, and freedom of religion. After the entry of foreign armies in Paris (July 5) and the return of Louis XVIII (July 8), the Chamber was officially dissolved on July 13 and Garat's declaration was abandoned.

3. There are significant differences between the published and the original version of this chapter. For more information, see the account given by Chinatsu Takeda, "Présentation des documents," in *Revue française d'histoire des idées politiques* (Paris: Picard, 2003), no. 18, 2e., 355–61. Madame de Staël's original version of this chapter is reproduced on pp. 365–68.

PART VI

CHAPTER I

Are Frenchmen Made to Be Free?

Frenchmen are not made to be free, says a certain party composed of Frenchmen who want to do the honors of the nation in such a way as to represent it as the most miserable of all human associations. What indeed is more miserable than to be incapable either of respect for justice, or of love for our country, or of energy of soul; virtues of which the whole, of which any one singly, is sufficient to render a nation worthy of liberty? Foreigners do not fail to lay hold of these expressions, and to glorify themselves as if they were of a nobler race than the French. This ridiculous assertion, however, means only one thing, that it suits certain privileged persons to be acknowledged as alone fitted to govern France with wisdom, and that the rest of the nation should be regarded as factious.

We shall examine, under a more philosophic and impartial point of view, what is meant by a "people made to be free." I would simply answer: it is a people who wish to be free; for I do not believe that history affords one example of the will of a whole nation not being accomplished. The institutions of a country, whenever they are below the degree of knowledge diffused throughout it, tend necessarily to raise themselves to the same level. Now, since the latter years of Louis XIV down to the French Revolution, spirit and energy have belonged to individuals, while government has been on the decline. But it will be said that the French, during the Revolution, incessantly wandered between follies and crimes. If it was so, this must be attributed, I cannot too often repeat, to their former political institutions; for it was they that had formed the nation; and if they were of a nature to enlighten only one class of men and deprave the mass, they were certainly good for nothing. But the sophistry of the enemies of human reason lies in their requiring that a people should possess the virtues of liberty before they obtain liberty; while it cannot acquire these virtues till after having enjoyed liberty, since the effect cannot precede the cause. The first quality of a nation that begins to be weary of exclusive and arbitrary governments is energy. Other virtues can be only the gradual result of institutions which have lasted long enough to form a public spirit.

There have been countries, like ancient Egypt, in which religion, being identified with policy, left a passive and stationary character on the manners and habits of men. But, in general, nations are seen to improve or to retrograde according to the nature of their government. Rome has not changed her climate, and yet, from the Romans to the Italians of our days, we can run through the whole scale of the modifications which men undergo by diversity of government. Doubtless, that which constitutes the dignity of a people is to know how to give itself a suitable government; but this work may encounter great obstacles, and one of the greatest certainly is the coalition of the old states of Europe to prevent the progress of new ideas. We must then make an impartial estimate of its difficulties and its efforts before deciding that a nation is not made to be free, which at bottom is a phrase devoid of meaning; for, can there exist men to whom security, emulation, the peaceable application of their industry, and the untroubled enjoyment of the fruits of their labor are not suitable? And if a nation was condemned by a curse of Heaven never to practice either justice or public morality, why should one part of this nation account itself exempt from the curse pronounced on the race? If all are equally incapable of virtue, what part shall oblige the other to possess it?

During twenty-five years, it will still be said, there has been no government founded by the Revolution which has not shown itself mad or wicked. Be it so; but the nation has been incessantly agitated by civil troubles, and all nations in that situation resemble each other. There exist in mankind dispositions which always reappear when the same circumstances call them forth. But if there is not an era of the Revolution in which crime has not borne its part, neither is there one in which great virtues have not been displayed. The love of country, the desire of securing independence at whatever cost, have been constantly manifested by the patriotic party; and if Bonaparte had not enervated public spirit by introducing a thirst for money and for honors, we would have seen miracles performed by the intrepid and persevering character of some of the men of the Revolution. Even the enemies of new institutions, the Vendeans, have exhibited the character which makes men free. They will rally under liberty when liberty shall be offered them in its true features. A keen resolution and an ardent spirit exist, and will always exist, in France. There are powerful souls among those who desire liberty; there are such among the young men who are coming forward, some exempt from the prejudices of their fathers, others innocent of their crimes. When all is seen, when all is known of the history of a revolution; when the most active interests excite the most violent passions, it seems to contemporaries that nothing equal to this has stained the face of the earth. But when we recall the wars of religion in France and the troubles of England, we perceive, in a different form, the same party spirit and the same crimes produced by the same passions.

It seems to me impossible to separate the necessity of the improvement of society from the desire of improving oneself; and, to make use of the title of Bossuet's work,[1] in a different sense from that which he gives to it, policy is sacred because it contains all the motives which actuate men in a mass and bring them closer or further from virtue.

We cannot, however, conceal that people have as yet acquired in France only few ideas of justice. They do not imagine that an enemy can have a right to the protection of the laws when he is conquered. But in a country where favor and want of favor have so long disposed of everything, how should people know what principles are? The reign of courts has permitted the French to display only military virtues; a very limited class were occupied in the management of civil affairs; and the mass of the nation having nothing to do, learned nothing and did not at all exercise itself in political virtues. One of the wonders of English liberty is the number of men who occupy themselves with the interests of each town, of

---

1. The full title of Bossuet's book is *Politics Drawn from Holy Scripture.*

each province, and whose mind and character are formed by the occupations and the duties of citizens. In France, intrigue was the only field for exercising oneself, and a long time is necessary to enable us to forget that unhappy science.

The love of money, of titles, in short of all the enjoyments and all the vanities of society, re-appeared under the reign of Bonaparte: these form the train of despotism. In the frenzy of democracy, corruption at least was of no avail; and, even under Bonaparte, several warriors have remained worthy, by their disinterestedness, of the respect which foreigners have for their courage.

Without resuming here the unhappy history of our disasters, let us say it boldly, there are, in the French nation, energy, patience under misfortune, audacity in enterprise, in one word strength; and its aberrations will always be to be dreaded until free institutions convert a part of this strength into virtue. Certain commonplace ideas put in circulation are often what most mislead the good sense of the public, because the majority of men receive them for truths. There is so little merit in finding them that one is induced to think that reason alone can make them be adopted by so many persons. But in party times the same interests inspire the same discourses, without their acquiring more truth when a hundred times repeated.

The French, it is said, are frivolous, the English serious; the French are quick, the English grave; the former, therefore, must be governed despotically, and the latter enjoy liberty. It is certain that if the English were still contending for this liberty, people would find in them a thousand defects that would stand in its way; but the fact among them refutes the argument. In our France troubles are apparent, while the motives of these troubles can be comprehended only by reflecting minds. The French are frivolous because they have been doomed to a kind of government which could be supported only by encouraging frivolity; and as to quickness, the French possess it much more in the spirit than in the character. There exists among the English an impetuosity of a much more violent nature, and their history exemplifies it in a multitude of cases. Who could have believed, two centuries ago, that a regular government could ever have been established among these factious islanders? The uniform opinion at that time on the Continent was that they were incapable of it. They have deposed, killed, overturned more kings, more princes, and more governments than the rest of Europe together; and yet they have at last obtained the most noble, the most brilliant, and most religious order of society that exists in the Old World. Every country, every people, every man are fit for liberty by their different qualities; all attain or will attain it in their own way.

But before endeavoring to describe the admirable monument of the moral greatness of man presented to us by England, let us cast a glance on some periods of her history similar in all respects to that of the French Revolution. People may perhaps become reconciled with the French on seeing in them the English of yesterday.

CHAPTER II

Cursory View of the History of England.

It is painful to me to represent the English character in a disadvantageous light, even in past times. But this generous nation will listen without pain to all that reminds it that it is to its actual political institutions, to those institutions which it is in the power of other nations to imitate, that it owes its virtues and its splendor. The puerile vanity of believing themselves a separate race is certainly not worth, in the eyes of the English, the honor of encouraging mankind by their example. No people in Europe can be put on a parallel with the English since 1688; there are a hundred and twenty years of social improvement between them and the Continent. True liberty, established for more than a century among a great people, has produced the results which we witness; but in the preceding history of this people, there is more violence, more illegality, and, in some respects, a still greater spirit of servitude than among the French.

The English always quote *Magna Charta* as the most honorable title of their ancient genealogy as free men; and in truth, such a contract between a nation and its king is an admirable thing. So early as the year 1215, personal liberty and the trial by jury are declared there in terms which might be used in our days. At this same period of the middle age there was, as we have mentioned in the Introduction, a movement of liberty throughout Europe. But knowledge and the institutions created by knowledge, not being yet diffused, there resulted nothing stable from this movement in England until 1688, that is, almost five centuries after *Magna Charta*. During all this period the charter was subject to incessant infractions. The successor of him who had signed it (Henry III, the son of John) made war on his barons to release himself from the promises of his father.[1]

---

1. This war ended in 1266 when Henry III Plantagenet reaffirmed the promises made in *Magna Charta*.

The barons had on this occasion favored the Third Estate, that they might find support in the people against the authority of the king. Edward I, the successor of Henry III, swore eleven times to maintain the great charter, which proves that he violated it even more often than that. Neither kings nor nations observe political oaths, except when the nature of things is such as to command sovereigns and satisfy the people. William the Conqueror had dethroned Harold; the House of Lancaster, in its turn, overset Richard II, and the act of election which called Henry IV to the throne was sufficiently liberal to be afterward imitated by Lord Somers in 1688. On the accession of Henry IV, in 1399, attempts were made to renew the great charter, and the King at last promised to respect the franchises and liberty of the nation. But the nation did not then know how to make herself respected. The war with France,[2] the intestine wars between the Houses of York and Lancaster[3] gave rise to the bloodiest scenes, and no history exhibits so many violations of individual liberty, so many executions, so many conspiracies of every kind. The result was that in the time of the famous Warwick,[4] the "king-maker," a law was passed enjoining obedience to the actual sovereign, whether rightfully so or not, in order to avoid the arbitrary judicial condemnations to which changes in government necessarily gave rise.

Next came the House of Tudor, which, in the person of Henry VII, united the rights of York and Lancaster.[5] The nation was weary of civil war: the spirit of servitude succeeded, for a time, the spirit of faction. Henry VII, like Louis XI and Cardinal Richelieu, subjected the nobility and found means to establish the most complete despotism. Parliament, which has since been the sanctuary of liberty, served at that time only to sanction the most arbitrary acts by a false appearance of national consent; for there is not a better instrument of tyranny than an assembly when it is degraded. Flattery conceals itself under the appearance of general opinion, and fear, felt in common, almost resembles courage; so much do men

2. The Hundred Years' War (1337–1475).
3. The War of the Two Roses (1455–85).
4. Richard Neville, Earl of Warwick (1428–71).
5. Henry VII Tudor, King of England, reigned from 1485 to 1509.

animate each other in an enthusiasm for power. Henry VIII[6] was still more despotic than his father, and more lawless in his desires. The Reformation, as far as he adopted it, served him surprisingly to persecute both orthodox Catholics and sincere Protestants. He made the English Parliament commit the most humiliating acts of servitude. It was the Parliament which took charge of the processes brought against the innocent wives of Henry VIII. It was it which solicited the honor of condemning Catherine Howard,[7] declaring there was no need of the royal sanction to bring a bill of impeachment against her, that they might save the King (her husband), as they said, the pain of trying her. Thomas More,[8] one of the most noble victims of the tyranny of Henry VIII, was accused by Parliament, as well as all those whose death the King desired. The two houses pronounced it a crime of high treason not to regard the King's marriage with Anne of Clèves as legally dissolved; and Parliament, stripping itself of power, decreed that the King's proclamations should have the force of law, and that they should be considered as having even the authority of revelation in matters of faith; for Henry VIII had made himself the head of the church in England, even while preserving the Catholic doctrine. It was then necessary to shake off the supremacy of Rome without exposing himself to the charge of dogmatic heresy. It was at this time that the bloody law of the Six Articles[9] was passed, a law which established the points of doctrine to which it was necessary to conform: the real presence; the communion in one element; the inviolability of monastic vows (notwithstanding the abolition of convents); the utility of private mass; the celibacy of the clergy; and the necessity of auricular confession. Whoever did not admit the first point was burned as a heretic; and he who rejected the five others was put to death as a felon. Parliament thanked the King for the divine

6. Henry VIII Tudor was King of England from 1509 to 1547. He managed to sever the Church of England from the Roman Catholic Church and establish himself as the supreme head of the church in England after being excommunicated by the pope in 1533.

7. Catherine Howard, who married Henry VIII in 1540, was accused of adultery, found guilty, and executed in 1542. She was the fifth of Henry VIII's six wives.

8. Thomas More (1480–1535), grand chancellor under Henry VIII, opposed the reform of the church. He was imprisoned in the Tower of London and executed.

9. Drafted by Henry VIII in 1539.

study, for the labor and the pains which His Majesty had bestowed on the composition of this law.

Yet Henry VIII opened the path to the religious reformation. It was introduced into England by his guilty amours, as *Magna Charta* had owed its existence to the crimes of John Lackland. It is thus that ages advance, proceeding unconsciously toward the object of human destiny.

Parliament, under Henry VIII, did violence to the conscience as well as to the person. It ordered, under pain of death, that the King should be considered the head of the church; and all who refused to acknowledge this perished martyrs to their courage. Parliaments changed the religion of England four times. They consecrated the schism of Henry VIII and the Protestantism of Edward VI; and when Queen Mary[10] caused old men, women, and children to be cast into the flames, hoping thus to please her fanatic husband, even these atrocities were sanctioned by a Parliament lately Protestant.

The Reformation reappeared with Elizabeth,[11] but the spirit of the people and of Parliament was not the less servile. That queen had all the grandeur which despotism conducted with moderation can confer. The reign of Elizabeth in England may be compared to that of Louis XIV in France.

Elizabeth had more capacity than Louis XIV, and finding herself at the head of Protestantism, the principle of which is toleration, she could not, like the French monarch, join fanaticism to absolute power. Parliament, which had compared Henry VIII to Samson for strength, to Solomon for prudence, and to Absalom for beauty, sent its speaker to declare, on his knees, to Queen Elizabeth that she was a divinity. But not confining itself to these insipid servilities, it stained itself with a sanguinary flattery in seconding the criminal hatred of Elizabeth against Mary Stuart,[12] calling for the condemnation of her enemy and wishing thus to remove from the

---

10. Mary I (Mary Tudor), daughter of Henry VIII, was Queen of England from 1553 to 1558, when she unsuccessfully tried to restore Catholicism in England by persecuting Protestants (hence her nickname, "Bloody Mary"). She married Philip II of Spain in 1554.

11. Elizabeth I, Queen of England, reigned from 1558 to 1603.

12. Mary Stuart was Queen of Scotland from 1542 to 1567. She was arrested in 1586 and condemned to death for conspiring against Elizabeth I.

Queen the shame of a measure which she desired; but it only dishonored itself in her train.

The first king of the House of Stuart,[13] equally weak but more regular in his morals than the successor of Louis XIV, professed constantly the doctrine of absolute power, without having in his character the means of supporting it. Information was spreading in all directions. The impulse given to the human mind at the beginning of the sixteenth century was diffusing itself more and more; religious reform fermented in every mind. At last burst out the revolution under Charles I.[14]

The principal points of analogy between the revolutions of England and France[15] are: a king brought to the scaffold by the spirit of democracy, a military chief getting possession of power, and the restoration of the old dynasty. Although religious and political reform have many things in common, yet when the principle that puts men in movement is somehow connected with what they deem their duty, they preserve more morality than when their impulse has no other motive than a desire of recovering their rights. The passion for equality was, however, so great in England that the King's daughter, the Princess of Gloucester, was put apprentice to a mantua-maker. Several traits of this kind equally strange might be quoted, although the management of public affairs during the revolution of England did not descend into such coarse hands as in France. The commoners, having earlier acquired importance by trade, were more enlightened. The nobility who had at all times joined these commoners against the usurpations of the throne did not form a separate caste as among the French.[16] The blending of occupations, which does not prevent the dis-

13. James I reigned from 1603 to 1625.

14. Charles I was King of England from 1625 to 1649. His conflict with Parliament triggered the civil war that led to the Revolution of 1648–49. He was tried and executed for high treason in January 1649.

15. On this issue, also see Guizot, *Histoire de la Révolution d'Angleterre depuis Charles I à Charles II.*

16. A few decades later Tocqueville, in *The Old Régime and the Revolution*, developed further this famous comparison between France and England by drawing on the different patterns of alliance between the monarch, the middle class, and the nobles in the two countries. For more information about the image of England in French political thought, see

tinction of ranks, had existed for a length of time. In England the nobility of the second class was joined to the commoners.* The families of peers alone were apart, while in France one knew not where to find the nation, and everyone was impatient to get out of the mass that he might enter into the privileged class. Without entering on religious discussions, it cannot be denied that the opinions of the Protestants, being founded on inquiry, are more favorable to knowledge and to the spirit of liberty than the Catholic religion, which decides everything by authority and considers kings equally infallible with popes, unless popes happen to be at war with kings. Lastly, and it is here that we must admit the advantages of an insular position, Cromwell conceived no projects of conquest on the Continent; he excited no anger on the part of kings who did not consider themselves threatened by the political experiments of a country that had no immediate communication with Continental ground. Still less did the nations take part in the quarrel; and the English had the remarkable good fortune of neither provoking foreigners nor calling in their aid.

The English rightly say that in their last civil troubles they had nothing that bore a resemblance to the eighteen months of the Reign of Terror in France. But in viewing the whole of their history, we shall find three kings deposed and put to death, Edward II, Richard II, and Henry VI; one king assassinated, Edward V; Mary of Scotland and Charles I perishing on the

---

Jennings, "Conceptions of England and Its Constitution in Nineteenth-Century French Political Thought."

* I quote here the text of an address of the Commons under James I, which is an evident demonstration of this truth.

Declaration of the House of Commons in regard to its privileges, drawn up by a committee chosen to present that address to James I.

The Commons of this realm contain not only the citizens, burgesses, and yeomanry, but also the whole inferior nobility of the kingdom, knights, squires, and gentlemen, many of which are come immediately out of the most noble families; and some others of their worth advanced to the high honor of your Majesty's privy council, and otherwise have been employed in very honorable service; in sum, the sole persons of the higher nobility excepted, they contain the whole power and flower of your kingdom; first, with their bodies your wars; secondly, with their purses your treasures are upheld and supplied; thirdly, their hearts are the strength and stability of your royal seat. All these, amounting to many millions of people, are representatively present in us of the House of Commons.

scaffold; princes of the blood royal dying a violent death; judicial assassinations in greater number than in all the rest of Europe together; along with I know not what of harsh and factious, which hardly indicated the public and private virtues of which England has afforded an example for the past century. Doubtless, it would be impossible to keep an open account of the vices and virtues of both nations; but in studying the history of England, we do not begin to see the English character, such as it rises progressively to our eyes since the foundation of liberty, except in a few men at the time of the Revolution and under the Restoration. The era of the return of the Stuarts, and the changes accomplished on their expulsion, again offer new proofs of the all-powerful influence of political institutions on the character of nations. Charles II and James II reigned, the one in an arbitrary, the other in a tyrannical manner;[17] and the same acts of injustice which had sullied the history of England in earlier ages were renewed at a period when knowledge had made however a very great progress. But despotism produces in every country, and in every time, nearly the same results; it brings back darkness in the midst of day. The most noble friends of liberty, Russell and Sidney,[18] perished under the reign of Charles II; and a number of other persons of less celebrity were in like manner unjustly condemned to death. Russell refused to redeem his life on condition of acknowledging that resistance to the sovereign, however despotic he may be, is contrary to the Christian religion. Algernon Sidney said, on mounting the scaffold, "I come here to die for the good old cause, which I have cherished since my infancy." The day after his death there were found writers who attempted to ridicule these beautiful and simple words. Flattery of the basest kind, that which surrenders the rights of nations to the good pleasure of sovereigns, was exhibited in all quarters. The University of Oxford condemned all the principles of liberty and showed itself a thousand times less enlightened in the seventeenth century than the barons in the beginning of the thirteenth. It proclaimed that there existed no mutual contract, either express or implied, between nations and

17. Charles II reigned from 1660 to 1685; James II, from 1685 to 1688. The Glorious Revolution of 1688 brought William III of Orange to the throne of England.

18. Lord William Russell (1639–83), an opponent of Charles II, was executed for participating in a conspiracy against the King (in which Algernon Sidney was also involved).

their kings. It was a town destined to be a center of learning that sent forth this declaration, which placed a man above all laws, divine and human, without imposing on him either duties or restraints. Locke, then a young man, was expelled from the university for having refused his adherence to this servile doctrine; so true it is that men of reflection, whatever be the object of their occupation, are always agreed in regard to the dignity of human nature.

Parliament, although very obsequious, was still an object of dread; and Louis XIV feeling, with remarkable sagacity, that a free constitution would give great strength to England, bribed not only the ministry but the King himself to prevent the establishment of such a constitution. It was not, however, from the dread of example that he wished to see no liberty in England. France was at that time too remote from any spirit of resistance to give him the least disquietude; it was solely, and the diplomatic documents prove it, because he considered a representative government as a source of wealth and power to the English. He caused 200,000 livres to be offered to Charles II if he would become a convert to the Catholic faith and convoke no more parliaments. Charles II, and after him James II, accepted these subsidies without venturing to adhere to all the conditions. The prime ministers, the wives of these prime ministers, received presents from the ambassador of France on promising to render England submissive to the influence of Louis XIV. Charles II would have desired, it is said in the negotiations published by Dalrymple,[19] to bring over French troops into England that they might be employed against the friends of liberty. We cannot easily persuade ourselves of the truth of these facts when we know the England of the eighteenth and nineteenth centuries. There were still remains of a spirit of independence among some members of Parliament; but as the liberty of the press did not support them in the public opinion, they could not oppose the strength of that opinion to the strength of government. The law of *Habeas Corpus*,[20]

19. James Dalrymple (1619–1695), a Scottish statesman who opposed the Stuarts, was the author of *The Institutions of the Law of Scotland* (1681).

20. *Habeas corpus* is a basic individual right against arbitrary arrest and imprisonment, dating back to the thirteenth century. It was properly formalized only in 1679, when the

on which individual liberty is founded, was passed under Charles II, and yet there never were more violations of that liberty than under his reign, for laws without security are of no avail. Charles II made the towns surrender to him all their privileges, all their particular charters; nothing is so easy to a central authority as to overthrow each separate part in succession. The judges, to please the King, gave to the crime of high treason a greater extension than what had been fixed three centuries before, under the reign of Edward III. To this serious tyranny was joined as much corruption, as much frivolity, as Frenchmen can be reproached with at any period. The English writers, the English poets, who are now animated by the truest sentiments and the purest virtues, were under Charles II coxcombs, sometimes sad, but always immoral. Rochester, Wycherley, above all, Congreve[21] drew pictures of human life which appear parodies of hell. In some of these pictures the sons jest on the old age of their fathers; in others, the younger brothers long for the death of their eldest brother; marriage is there treated according to the maxims of Beaumarchais; but there is no gaiety in these saturnalia of vice; the most corrupt men cannot laugh at the sight of a world in which even the wicked could not make their way. Fashion, which is still the weakness of the English in small matters, trifled at that time with whatever was most important in life. Charles II had over his court, and his court had over his people, the influence which the regent had over France.[22] And when we see in English galleries the portraits of the mistresses of this King, arranged methodically together, we cannot persuade ourselves that little more than a century has yet passed since so depraved a frivolity seconded the most absolute power among Englishmen. Finally, James II, who made an open declaration of the opinions which Charles II introduced by underhand practices, reigned

English Parliament voted the law of habeas corpus. The original Latin meaning, "you have the body," refers to a civil proceeding used to review the legality of a prisoner's confinement in criminal cases. In other words, it is a court petition that orders that a person being detained be produced before a judge for a hearing to decide whether the detention is lawful.

21. John Wilot, second Count of Rochester (1647–80), was the author of poems and of a rich correspondence with his wife (published in 1686). William Wycherley (1640–1716), a playwright, wrote *The Country Wife* (1673). William Congreve (1670–1729), a playwright, wrote *The Old Bachelor* (1690).

22. The Duke of Orléans.

during three years with a tyranny happily without moderation, since it was to his very excesses that the nation was indebted for the peaceful and wise revolution on which its liberty was founded. Hume, the historian, a Scotsman, a partisan of the Stuarts, and a defender of royal prerogative in the way in which an enlightened man can be so, has rather softened than exaggerated the crimes committed by the agents of James II. I insert here only a few of the traits of this reign in the way they are related by Hume.[23]

Such arbitrary principles had the court instilled into all its servants that Feversham, immediately after the victory,[24] hanged above twenty prisoners; and was proceeding in his executions when the Bishop of Bath and Wells warned him that these unhappy men were now by law entitled to a trial, and that their execution would be deemed a real murder. This remonstrance, however, did not stop the savage nature of Colonel Kirke, a soldier of fortune who had long served at Tangiers and had contracted, from his intercourse with the Moors, an inhumanity less known in European and in free countries. At his first entry into Bridgewater, he hanged nineteen prisoners without the least inquiry into the merits of their cause. As if to make sport with death, he ordered a certain number to be executed while he and his company should drink the King's health, or the Queen's, or that of Chief Justice Jefferies.[25] Observing their feet to quiver in the agonies of death, he cried that he would give them music to their dancing, and he immediately commanded the drums to beat and the trumpets to sound. By way of experiment, he ordered one man to be hung up three times, questioning him at each interval whether he repented of his crime: but the man obstinately asserting that, notwithstanding the past, he still would willingly engage in the same cause, Kirke ordered him to be hung in chains. One story commonly told of him is memorable for the treachery, as well as barbarity, which attended it. A young maid pleaded for the life of her brother and flung herself at Kirke's feet, armed with all the charms which beauty and innocence, bathed in tears, could bestow upon her. The tyrant was inflamed with desire, not softened into love or clemency. He promised to grant her request, pro-

23. See Hume's *History of England*, vol. 6, chap. LXX, 462–66.
24. Hume refers to the victory of James II against the Duke of Monmouth in 1685.
25. George Jeffreys (1648–89), chief justice of England, was imprisoned after the Revolution of 1688.

vided that she, in her turn, would be equally compliant to him. The maid yielded to the conditions: but after she had passed the night with him, the wanton savage the next morning showed her, from the window, her brother, the darling object for whom she had sacrificed her virtue, hanging on a gibbet, which he had secretly ordered to be there erected for the execution. Rage and despair and indignation took possession of her mind and deprived her forever of her senses. All the inhabitants of that country, innocent as well as guilty, were exposed to the ravages of this barbarian. The soldiery were let loose to live at free quarters; and his own regiment, instructed by his example and encouraged by his exhortations, distinguished themselves in a particular manner by their outrages. By way of pleasantry he used to call them *his lambs;* an appellation which was long remembered with horror in the west of England.

The violent Jefferies succeeded after some interval; and showed the people that the rigors of law might equal, if not exceed, the ravages of military tyranny. This man, who wantoned in cruelty, had already given a specimen of his character in many trials where he presided; and he now set out with a savage joy, as to a full harvest of death and destruction. He began at Dorchester; and thirty rebels being arraigned, he exhorted them, but in vain, to save him, by their free confession, the trouble of trying them. And when twenty-nine were found guilty, he ordered them, as an additional punishment of their disobedience, to be led to immediate execution. Most of the other prisoners, terrified with this example, pleaded guilty; and no less than two hundred and ninety-two received sentence at Dorchester. Of these, eighty were executed. Exeter was the next stage of his cruelty; two hundred and forty-three were there tried, of whom a great number were condemned and executed. He also opened his commission at Taunton and Wells; and everywhere carried consternation along with him. The juries were so struck with his menaces that they gave their verdict with precipitation; and many innocent persons, it is said, were involved with the guilty. And on the whole, besides those who were butchered by the military commanders, two hundred and fifty-one are computed to have fallen by the hand of justice. The whole country was strewed with the heads and limbs of traitors. Every village, almost, beheld the dead carcass of a wretched inhabitant. And all the rigors of justice, unabated by any appearance of clemency, were fully displayed to the people by the inhuman Jefferies.

Of all the executions during this dismal period, the most remarkable were those of Mrs. Gaunt and Lady Lisle, who had been accused of harboring traitors. Mrs. Gaunt was an anabaptist noted for her beneficence, which she extended to persons of all professions and persuasions. One of the rebels, knowing her humane disposition, had recourse to her in his distress and was concealed by her. Hearing of the proclamation which offered an indemnity and rewards to such as discovered criminals, he betrayed his benefactress and bore evidence against her. He received a pardon as a recompense for his treachery; she was burned alive for her charity.

Lady Lisle was widow of one of the regicides who had enjoyed great favor and authority under Cromwell, and who having fled after the Restoration to Lauzanne in Swisserland, was there assassinated by three Irish ruffians, who hoped to make their fortune by this piece of service. His widow was now prosecuted for harboring two rebels the day after the battle of Sedgemoor; and Jefferies pushed on the trial with an unrelenting violence. In vain did the aged prisoner plead that these criminals had been put into no proclamation; had been convicted by no verdict; nor could any man be denominated a traitor till the sentence of some legal court was passed upon him; that it appeared not by any proof that she was so much as acquainted with the guilt of the persons, or had heard of their joining the rebellion of Monmouth; that though she might be obnoxious on account of her family, it was well known that her heart was ever loyal, and that no person in England had shed more tears for that tragical event in which her husband had unfortunately borne too great a share; and that the same principles which she herself had ever embraced she had carefully instilled into her son, and had, at that very time, sent him to fight against those rebels whom she was now accused of harboring. Though these arguments did not move Jefferies, they had influence on the jury. Twice they seemed inclined to bring in a favorable verdict; they were as often sent back with menaces and reproaches; and at last were constrained to give sentence against the prisoner. Notwithstanding all applications for pardon, the cruel sentence was executed. The King said that he had given Jefferies a promise not to pardon her.

Even those multitudes who received pardon were obliged to atone for their guilt by fines, which reduced them to beggary; or, where their former poverty made them incapable of paying, they were condemned to cruel whippings or severe imprisonments. . . . The people might have been willing on this occasion to distinguish between the King and his ministers; but care was taken to prove that the latter had done nothing but what was agreeable to their master. Jefferies, on his return, was immediately, for those eminent services, created a peer; and was soon after vested with the dignity of chancellor.[26]

Such were the sufferings which a king could impose on Englishmen, and such was the treatment which they supported. It was in 1686 that England exhibited to Europe such examples of barbarity and servility; and two years after, when James II was deposed and the constitution established, began that period of one hundred and twenty-eight years down to our days, in which a single session of Parliament has not passed without adding some improvement to the state of society.

James II was highly culpable; yet we cannot deny that there was treason in the manner in which he was abandoned. His daughters deprived him of the crown.[27] The persons who had professed for him the greatest attachment, and who owed him the greatest gratitude, left him. The officers broke their oath; but success having, according to an English epigram, excused this treason, it no longer bore the name.*

William III was a firm and wise statesman, accustomed, by his situation of Stadtholder in Holland, to respect liberty whether he naturally liked it or not. Queen Anne,[28] who succeeded him, was a woman without talents and with no strong attachments but to prejudices. Although in possession of a throne which, according to the principles of legitimacy, she ought to have relinquished to her brother, she preserved a predilection for the doctrine of divine right; and although the party of the friends of liberty had made her queen, she always felt an involuntary disinclination to them. Yet political institutions were by this time acquiring so much strength that,

---

* Treason does never prosper: what's the reason?
  Why, when it prospers, none dare call it treason.

26. For Hume's account of this period, see *The History of England*, vol. 6, chap. lxx, 449–95.

27. Mary II and Anne Stuart. Mary married William III of Orange, who succeeded James II on the throne of England.

28. Queen Anne reigned from 1702 to 1714.

abroad as at home, this reign was one of the most glorious in the annals of England. The House of Hanover completed the securities of religious and political reform; yet, till after the battle of Culloden, in 1746, the spirit of faction often got the better of the spirit of justice.[29] A price of 30,000 livres was put on the head of Prince Edward, and much as people feared for liberty, they had difficulty in resolving on the only manner of establishing it, that is, on respecting principles, whatever be the circumstances of the moment.

But if we read with care the reign of the three Georges,[30] we shall see that, during that period, morality and liberty have been in a course of uninterrupted advancement. What a beautiful spectacle is this constitution, unsteady on leaving its harbor, like a vessel launched into the sea, and at last spreading wide its sails and giving a spring to all that is great and generous in the human mind! I know that the English will assert that they have at all times had a stronger spirit of liberty than the French; that from the time of Caesar they repelled the Roman yoke; and that the code of these Romans, composed under the emperors, was never introduced into the English laws; it is equally true that by adopting the Reformation, the English founded at once morality and liberty on a firmer basis. The clergy, having always sat in Parliament along with the lay lords, had no distinct power in the state, and the English nobility showed themselves more factious, but less of courtiers, than the nobility of France. These differences are, it cannot be denied, to the advantage of England. In France, the beauty of the climate, the relish for society, all that embellishes life operated in favor of arbitrary power, as in the countries of the South, in which the pleasures of existence are sufficient for man. But as soon as the call for liberty takes possession of the mind, even the defects with which the French are reproached, their vivacity, their self-love, attach them more to what they have determined to conquer. They are the third people, reckoning the Americans, who are making the trial of a represen-

29. On April 16, 1746, at Culloden (Scotland), the army led by the Duke of Cumberland defeated the army of Charles Edward Stuart.

30. George I of Hanover (r. 1714–27), George II (r. 1727–60), and George III (r. 1760–1820).

tative government, and the example of their predecessors begins at last to guide them. In whatever way we consider each nation, we find in it always that which will render a representative government not only possible but necessary. Let us then examine the influence of that government in the country which had first the glory of establishing it.

CHAPTER III

Of the Prosperity of England, and the Causes by Which It Has Been Hitherto Promoted.

In the year 1813, the English had been twenty-one years at war with France, and for some time the whole Continent had been in arms against them. Even America, from political circumstances foreign to the interests of Europe, made a part of this universal coalition.[1] During several years the respectable monarch of Great Britain was no longer in possession of his intellectual faculties.[2] The great men in the civil career, Pitt and Fox, were now no more, and no one had yet succeeded to their reputation. No historical name could be cited at the head of affairs, and Wellington alone attracted the attention of Europe. Some ministers, several members of the opposition, lawyers, men of science and literature enjoyed a great share of the public esteem; and if on the one hand, France, in bending beneath the yoke of one man, had seen the reputation of individuals disappear; on the other, there was so much ability, information, and merit among the English that it had become very difficult to take the first rank amidst this illustrious crowd.

On my arrival in England, no particular person was present to my thoughts: I knew scarcely anyone in that country; but I went there with confidence.[3] I was persecuted by an enemy of liberty, and therefore be-

1. The war between the United States and England lasted from June 1812 to December 1814. The Americans were never allied with Napoléon against the English.
2. See note 2, p. 539.
3. Madame de Staël arrived in London on June 17, 1813. A few days later, she was presented to the Queen and the Prince Regent. For more information, see Fairweather, *Madame de Staël*, 417–46.

lieved myself sure of an honorable sympathy in a country where every institution was in harmony with my political sentiments. I counted also greatly on my father's memory as a protection, and I was not deceived. The waves of the North Sea, which I crossed in going from Sweden, still filled me with dread when I perceived at a distance the verdant isle that had alone resisted the subjugation of Europe. Yet it contained only a population of twelve million; for the five or six additional million which compose the population of Ireland had often, during the course of the last war, been a prey to intestine divisions.[4] Those who will not acknowledge the ascendency of liberty in the power of England are perpetually repeating that the English would have been vanquished by Bonaparte, like every Continental nation, if they had not been protected by the sea. This opinion cannot be refuted by experience; but I have no doubt that if, by a stroke of the Leviathan, Great Britain had been joined to the European continent, she would indeed have suffered more; her wealth would, no doubt, have been diminished; but the public spirit of a free nation is such that it would never have submitted to the yoke of foreigners.

When I landed in England, in the month of June 1813, intelligence had just arrived of the armistice concluded between the Allied Powers and Napoléon. He was at Dresden, and it was still in his power to reduce himself to the miserable lot of being Emperor of France as far as the Rhine, and King of Italy. It was probable that England would not subscribe to this treaty;[5] her position was therefore far from being favorable. A long war menaced her anew; her finances appeared exhausted; at least if we were to judge of her resources according to those of every other country of the world. The bank note, serving instead of coin, had fallen one-fourth on the Continent; and if this paper had not been supported by the patriotic spirit of the nation, it would have involved the ruin of public and private affairs. The French newspapers, comparing the state of the finances of the two countries, always represented England as overwhelmed with debt, and France as mistress of considerable treasure. The comparison was true;

---

4. Allusion to Irish opposition to England. In 1798, two years before the Union Act, which linked the two countries, the English defeated a revolt in Ireland.

5. The Treaty of Pleiswitz (May 29, 1813).

but it was necessary to add that England had the disposal of unbounded resources by her credit, while the French Government possessed only the gold which it held in its hands. France could levy millions in contributions on oppressed Europe; but her despotic sovereign could not have succeeded in a voluntary loan.

From Harwich to London you travel by a high road of nearly seventy miles, which is bordered, almost without interruption, by country houses on both sides; it is a succession of habitations with gardens, interrupted by towns; almost all the people are well clad; scarcely a cottage is in decay, and even the animals have something peaceful and comfortable about them, as if there were rights for them also in this great edifice of social order. The price of everything is necessarily very high; but these prices are for the most part fixed: there is such an aversion in that country to what is arbitrary that when there is no positive law, there is first a rule, and next a custom, to secure, as far as possible, something positive and fixed even in the smallest details. The dearness of provisions, occasioned by enormous taxes, is, no doubt, a great evil; but if the war was indispensable, what other than this nation, that is, this constitution, could have sufficed for its expenses? Montesquieu is right in remarking that free countries pay far more taxes than those who are governed despotically; but we have not yet ascertained, though the example of England might have taught us, the extent of the riches of a people who consent to what they give and consider public affairs as their own. Thus the English nation, far from having lost by twenty years of war, gained in every respect, even in the midst of the Continental blockade. Industry, become more active and ingenious, made up in an astonishing manner for the want of those productions which could no longer be drawn from the Continent. Capitals, excluded from commerce, were employed in the cultivation of waste lands and in agricultural improvements in various counties. The number of houses increased everywhere, and the extension of London, within a few years, is scarcely credible.[6] If one branch of commerce fell, another arose soon. Men whose property was increased by the rise of land appropriated a large portion of their revenue to establishments of public charity. When

6. The population of London rose from 745,000 inhabitants in 1801 to 1,250,000 in 1815.

the Emperor Alexander arrived in England,[7] surrounded by the multitude, who felt so natural an eagerness to see him, he inquired where the lower orders were, because he found himself surrounded only by men dressed like the better class in other countries. The extent of what is done in England by private subscription is enormous: hospitals, houses of education, missions, Christian societies were not only supported but multiplied during the war; and the foreign who felt its disasters, the Swiss, the Germans, and the Dutch, were perpetually receiving from England private aid, the produce of voluntary gifts. When the town of Leyden was almost half destroyed by the explosion of a vessel laden with gunpowder,[8] the English flag was soon after seen to appear on the coast of Holland; and as the Continental blockade existed at that time in all its rigor, the people on the coast thought themselves obliged to fire on this perfidious vessel; she then hoisted a flag of truce and made known that she brought a considerable sum for the people of Leyden, ruined by their recent misfortune.

But to what are we to attribute all these wonders of a generous prosperity? To liberty, that is to the confidence of the nation in a government which makes the first principle of its finances consist in publicity; in a government enlightened by discussion and by the liberty of the press. The nation, which cannot be deceived under such a state of things, knows the use of the taxes which it pays, and public credit supports the amazing weight of the English debt. If, without departing from proportions, anything similar were tried in the governments of the European continent that are not representative, not a second step could be made in such an enterprise. Five hundred thousand proprietors of public stock form a great guarantee for the payment of the debt in a country where the opinion and interest of every man possess influence. Justice, which in matters of credit is synonymous with ability, is carried so far in England that the dividends due to French proprietors were not confiscated there, even when all English property was seized in France. The foreign stockholder was not even made to pay an income tax on his dividends, though that tax was paid by the English themselves. This complete good faith, the perfection of policy,

7. In June 1814.
8. On January 12, 1807.

is the basis of the finances of England; and the confidence in the duration of this good faith is connected with political institutions. A change in the ministry, whatever it may be, occasions no prejudice to credit, since the national representation and publicity render all dissimulation impossible. Capitalists who lend their money are of all people in the world the most difficult to deceive.

There still exist old laws in England which cause some obstacles to different enterprises of industry in the interior; but some are progressively abolished, and others are fallen into disuse. Thus everyone creates resources for himself, and no man endowed with any activity can be in England without finding the means of acquiring property by doing that which contributes to the good of the state. The government never interferes in what can be equally well done by individuals: respect for personal liberty extends to the exercise of the faculties of every man; and the nation is so jealous of managing its own affairs, whenever possible, that in several respects London lacks a police necessary to the comfort of the town, because the ministers cannot encroach on the local authorities.

Political security, without which there can be neither credit nor accumulated capital, is not, however, sufficient to bring forth all the resources of a nation; men must be excited to labor by emulation, while the law secures to them the fruits of labor. Commerce and industry must be honored, not by recompenses bestowed on such or such an individual, which supposes two classes in a country, one of which believes it has the right to pay the other; but by an order of things which allows each man to reach the highest rank, if he is worthy. Hume says "that commerce stands still more in need of dignity than of liberty";[9] and indeed, the absurd prejudice which forbade the French nobles to engage in business was more prejudicial than all the other abuses of the Old Regime to the progress of wealth in France. Peerages have been recently given in England to merchants of the first class; when once made peers, they do not remain in business, because it is understood that they should serve their country in another manner. But it is their functions as magistrates, and not the prejudices of a caste, which removes them from the occupations of trade, into which

---

9. See Hume's essay "Of Commerce" in *Essays*, 253–67.

the younger sons of the greatest families, when called on by circumstances, enter without hesitation. The same family is often connected with peers on one side and, on the other, with the plainest merchants of a provincial town. This political order stimulates all the faculties of the individual, because there are no bounds to the advantages which riches and talent may attain; and because no exclusion withholds either alliances, or employment, or society, or titles from the last of English citizens, if he is worthy of being the first.

But it will be said that in France, even under the old government, individuals without high birth were named to the greatest places. Yes; they were sometimes employed where they were useful to the state; but a bourgeois citizen could in no case be made the equal of a man of noble family. How was it possible to give decorations of the first order to a man of talent, without high birth, when genealogical titles were requisite to have the right of wearing them? Have we ever seen the title of duke and peer conferred on one who could have been called an upstart? And was not this word *parvenu* in itself an offense? Even the members of the French parliament could never, as we have already stated, cause themselves to be considered the equals of the nobility of sword. In England, rank and equality are combined in the manner most favorable to the prosperity of the state, and the happiness of the nation is the object of all social distinctions. There, as everywhere else, historical names inspire that respect of which a grateful imagination cannot refuse the tribute; but the titles remaining the same, though passing from one family to another, there results from this a salutary ignorance in the minds of the people, which leads them to pay the same respect to the same titles, whatever may be the family name to which they are attached. The great Marlborough[10] was called Churchill, and was certainly not of so noble an origin as the ancient house of Spencer, to which the present Duke of Marlborough belongs; but without speaking of the memory of a great man, which would have sufficed to honor his descendants, the people of the better classes only know that the Duke of Marlborough of our days is of more illustrious descent than the famous General, and the respect in which he is held by the mass of the nation

10. John Churchill, first Duke of Marlborough (1650–1722).

neither gains nor loses from that circumstance. The Duke of Northumberland,[11] on the contrary, descends, by the female branch only, from the famous Percy Hotspur;[12] and, nevertheless, he is considered by everybody as the true heir of that house. People exclaim against the regularity of ceremonials in England; the seniority of a single day, in point of nomination to the peerage, gives one peer precedence of another named some hours later. The wife and daughter share the advantages of the husband or father; but it is precisely this regularity of ranks which prevents qualms of vanity; for it may happen that the last created peer is of a nobler birth than he by whom he is preceded; he may at least think so; and everyone takes his share of self-love without injuring the public.

The nobility of France, on the contrary, could be classed only by the genealogist of the court. His decisions, founded on parchments, were without appeal; and thus, whilst the English aristocracy is the hope of all, since every person can attain it, French aristocracy was necessarily the despair of all, since it was impossible for an individual to obtain, by the efforts of his whole life, that which chance had refused him. It is not the *inglorious order* of birth, said an English poet to William III, which has raised you to the throne, but genius and virtue.

In England they have made respect for ancestry serve to form a class which gives the power of flattering men of talents by associating them with it. In fact, we cannot too often ask, what folly can be greater than that of arranging political associations in such a way as may lead a celebrated man to regret that he is not his own grandson; for, once ennobled, his descendants of the third generation obtained by his merit privileges that could not be granted to himself. Thus in France all persons were eager to quit trade, and even the law, whenever they had money enough to purchase a title. Hence it happened that no career, except that of arms, was ever carried as far as it might have been; and it has thus been impossible to judge how far the prosperity of France would extend if it enjoyed in peace the advantages of a free constitution.

---

11. Hugh Smithson Percy, first Duke of Northumberland (1715–86).

12. Percy Hotspur (1364–1403), second Count of Northumberland, played an important role in the War of the Roses.

All classes of respectable individuals are accustomed to meet in England in different committees when engaged in any public undertaking, in any act of charity supported by voluntary subscriptions. Publicity in business is a principle so generally admitted that though the English are by nature the most reserved of men, and the most averse to speak in society, there are always seats for spectators in the halls where the committees meet and an elevation from which the speakers address the assembly.

I was present at one of these discussions, in which motives calculated to excite the generosity of the hearers were urged with much energy. The question was sending of relief to the inhabitants of Leipzig after the battle fought under the walls of that town.[13] The first who spoke was the Duke of York, the King's second son and the first person in the kingdom after the Prince Regent, a man of ability and much esteemed in the direction of his department; but who has neither the habit of, nor a taste for, speaking in public. He, however, conquered his natural timidity because he was thus hopeful of giving useful encouragement. Courtiers in an absolute monarchy would not have failed to insinuate to a king's son, first, that he ought not to do anything which cost him trouble; and, secondly, that he was wrong to commit himself by haranguing the public in the midst of merchants, his colleagues in speaking. This idea never entered the Duke of York's mind, nor that of any Englishman, whatever might be his opinion. After the Duke of York, the Duke of Sussex, the King's fifth son, who expresses himself with great ease and elegance, spoke in his turn; and the man the most respected and esteemed in all England, Mr. Wilberforce,[14] could scarcely make himself heard, so much was his voice drowned in acclamations. Obscure citizens, holding no other rank in society than their fortune or their zeal for humanity, followed these illustrious names; every one, according to his powers, insisted on the honorable necessity in which England was placed of helping those of her allies who had suffered more than herself in the common contest. The auditors subscribed before their

13. In October 1813.

14. William Wilberforce (1759–1833), a member of Parliament, fought for the abolition of slavery. The Slavery Abolition Act was passed shortly after his death, in 1833. Madame de Staël and her son, Auguste, became strong supporters of Wilberforce after meeting him at a dinner in London. For more information, see Fairweather, *Madame de Staël*, 428–29.

departure, and considerable sums were the result of this meeting. It is thus that are formed the ties which strengthen the unity of the nation; and it is thus that social order is founded on reason and humanity.

These respectable assemblies do not merely aim at encouraging acts of humanity; some of them serve particularly to consolidate the union between the great nobility and the commercial class, between the nation and the government; and these are the most solemn.

London has always had a Lord Mayor, who presides during a year in the council of the city, and whose administrative powers are very extensive. They are very careful in England not to concentrate everything in ministerial authority; they choose that in every county, in every town, local interests should be placed in the hands of men chosen by the people to manage them. The Lord Mayor is usually a merchant in the city, and not always a great merchant; but often a trader in whom a great many individuals may see their equal. The Lady Mayoress, for it is thus the Mayor's wife is called, enjoys, during a year, all the honors attached to the most distinguished ranks of the state. The election of the people and the power of a great city are honored in the man by whom they are represented. The Lord Mayor gives two grand official dinners, to which he invites English of all classes and foreigners. I have seen at his table sons of the King, several of the ministers, ambassadors of foreign powers, the Marquis of Lansdowne, the Duke of Devonshire, as well as gentlemen of the highest respectability on various accounts: some sons of peers; others members of the House of Commons; merchants, lawyers, literary men, all English citizens, all equally attached to their noble country. Two of the King's ministers rose from table to address the company; for while on the Continent a minister confines himself, even in the midst of select society, to the most insignificant phrases, the heads of government in England always consider themselves as representatives of the people and endeavor to win its approbation with as much solicitude as the members of the opposition; for the dignity of the English nation soars above every office and every title. Various toasts, of which the objects were political interests, were given according to custom: sovereigns and nations, glory and independence were celebrated, and there at least the English showed themselves the friends of the liberty of the world. In fact, a free nation may have an exclusive spirit in regard to the advantages of trade or power; but it ought to associate itself in every country with the rights of mankind.

This meeting took place in an ancient edifice in the city, whose gothic vaults have witnessed the bloodiest struggles: tranquillity has reigned in England only in conjunction with liberty. The official dress of all the members of the Common Council is the same as it was several centuries ago. Some customs of that period are likewise preserved, and the imagination is affected by them; but this is because the recollections of former ages do not recall odious prejudices. Whatever is Gothic in the habits, and even in some of the institutions of England, seems a ceremony of the worship of the age; but neither the progress of knowledge nor the improvement of the laws suffers from it in any respect.

We cannot believe that Providence has placed this fine monument of social order so near to France merely to give us the pain of never being able to equal it; and we shall examine with attention that which we should wish to imitate with energy.

CHAPTER IV

Of Liberty and Public Spirit
Among the English.

The first basis of all liberty is individual security; and nothing is finer than English legislation in this respect. A criminal suit is in every country a horrible spectacle. In England the excellence of the procedure, the humanity of the judges, the precautions of every kind taken to secure the life of the innocent man, and means of defense to the guilty mingle a sentiment of admiration with the anguish of such a discussion. *How will you be tried?* says the officer of the court to the accused. *By God and my country,* replies the latter. *God grant you good deliverance,* rejoins the officer of the court. From the opening of the proceedings, if the prisoner be confused, if he commit himself by his answers, the judge sets him in the proper path and takes no account of inconsiderate words which might escape him. In the progress of the trial he never addresses himself to the accused, fearing that the emotion naturally experienced by the latter might expose him to injure himself. Indirect witnesses, that is, witnesses who depose on hearsay, are never admitted, as in France. In short, all the precautions have the interest of the accused for their object. Religion and liberty preside over the imposing act which permits man to condemn his fellow creature to death. The admirable institution of juries, which in England goes back to a very remote period, introduces equity into the administration of justice. Those who are momentarily invested with the right of sending a guilty person to death have a natural sympathy with the habits of his life, as they are in general chosen in a class nearly similar to his own; and when juries are obliged to find a criminal guilty, he himself is at least certain that society has done everything to procure his acquittal, if he had deserved it; and this conviction cannot but produce some tranquillity in his heart.

For the past century, there is perhaps no example in England of a capital conviction in which the innocence of the individual was discovered too late. The citizens of a free state have so large a share of good sense and conscientiousness that, with these two directing lights, they never err.

We know what a noise was produced in France by the sentence pronounced against Calas,[1] by that against Lally;[2] and shortly before the Revolution, president Dupaty published a most energetic pleading in favor of three accused persons who had been condemned to die on the wheel, and whose innocence was proved after their death. Such misfortunes could not occur under the laws and criminal procedure of England; and public opinion, that court of appeal, would, with the liberty of the press, make known the slightest error in that respect, were it possible that it could be committed.

Moreover, offenses which have no connection whatever with politics are not those in which we have to dread the application of arbitrary power. In general, it is of little consequence to the great personages of this world in what way robbers and assassins are tried; and no person has an interest in wishing that the laws should not be respected in such trials. But when political crimes are in question, those crimes with which opposite parties reproach each other with so much hatred and bitterness, then it is that we have seen in France all kinds of extraordinary tribunals, created by existing circumstances, applied to such an individual and justified, it was said, by the greatness of the offense; while it is exactly when this offense is of a nature to excite the passions strongly that we are under the greatest necessity of recurring for its trial to the dispassionate firmness of justice.

The English had been vexed like the French, like every people of Europe, where the empire of law is not established, by the Star Chamber,[3] by extraordinary commissions, by the extension of the crime of high treason to all that was displeasing to the possessors of power. But since liberty has been consolidated in England, not only has no individual accused of

1. Calas was a prominent Protestant condemned to death in 1762 for allegedly having murdered his son in Toulouse. The Royal Council found him not guilty in 1765.

2. Wrongly condemned to death (for having surrendered Pondichéry to the English) and executed in 1766.

3. See note 3, p. 342, above.

an offense against the state ever had to dread a removal from his natural judges—who could admit such a thought?—but the law gives to him more means of defense than to any other, because he has more enemies. A recent circumstance will show, in all its beauty, this respect of the English for justice, one of the most admirable traits of their admirable government.

Three attempts have been made, during the present reign, on the life of the King of England, and certainly it was very dear to his subjects. The veneration which he inspires under his present malady has something affecting and delicate, of which one would never have thought an entire nation capable; and yet none of the assassins who endeavored to kill the King have been condemned to death. Having been found to show symptoms of mental derangement, this was made the object of an inquiry the more scrupulous in proportion to the violence of public indignation against them. Louis XV was wounded by Damien toward the middle of the last century,[4] and it is asserted that this wretch also was deranged; but supposing even that he possessed his reason to a degree that merited a capital punishment, can a civilized nation tolerate the tortures to which he was condemned? And it is said that those tortures had inquisitive and voluntary witnesses: what a contrast between such barbarity and the proceedings in England! But let us beware of deducing from this any consequence unfavorable to the French character; it is arbitrary government that depraves a nation, and not a decree of Heaven awarding every virtue to one and every vice to another.

Hatfield is the name of the third of the madmen who attempted to assassinate the King of England. He chose the day when the King reappeared at the theater after a long illness, accompanied by the Queen and the royal family. At the moment the King entered the house was heard the report of a pistol fired in the direction of his box; and as he stepped back a few paces, the public were, for a moment, doubtful whether the murder had not been committed; but when the courageous monarch again advanced to relieve the crowd of spectators, whose disquietude was extreme, nothing can express the transport they felt. The musicians, by a

4. In January 1757.

spontaneous impulse, struck up the sacred tune, "God Save the King," and this prayer produced, in the midst of the public anxiety, an emotion of which the recollection still lives in the bottom of the heart. After such a scene, many persons unacquainted with the virtues of liberty would have loudly demanded a cruel death for the assassin, and the courtiers would have been seen acting the part of the populace in their frenzy, as if the excess of their affection no longer left them masters of themselves: nothing of this kind could take place in a free country. The King, in the capacity of magistrate, was protector of his assassin from a feeling of justice, and no Englishman imagined it was possible to please his sovereign by the sacrifice of the immutable law which represents the will of God on earth.

Not only was the course of justice not hastened a single hour, but we shall see, by the preamble to the pleading of Mr. Erskine, now Lord Erskine,[5] what precautions are adopted in favor of a state criminal. Let us add that in trials for high treason, the defender of the accused has a right to plead in his defense. In ordinary cases of felony, he can only examine witnesses and call the attention of the jury to their answers. And what a defender was he who was given to Hatfield? Erskine, the most eloquent lawyer in England, the most ingenious in the art of pleading. It was thus that his speech began:*

> Gentlemen of the Jury. The scene which we are engaged in, and the duty which I am not merely privileged but appointed by the authority of the court to perform, exhibits to the whole civilized world a perpetual monument of our national justice.
>
> The transaction, indeed, in every part of it, as it stands recorded in the evidence already before us, places our country, and its government,

---

* I cannot too strongly recommend to French readers the collection of the speeches of Erskine, who was raised to the rank of chancellor after a long and distinguished career at the bar. Descended from one of the oldest families in Scotland, he set out in life as an officer; and afterward, being without fortune, entered on the profession of the law. The particular circumstances to which the pleadings of Lord Erskine relate are all opportunities for displaying, with unrivaled strength and sagacity, the principles of criminal jurisprudence which ought to serve as a model to every people.

5. Thomas Erskine (1750–1823), a prominent lawyer and Whig politician, served as chancellor in 1806–7 and was an acquaintance of Madame de Staël.

its inhabitants, and its laws upon the highest pinnacle of moral elevation that social order can attain. It appears that, on the 15th day of May last, His Majesty, after a reign of forty years, not merely in sovereign power but spontaneously in the very hearts of his people, was openly shot at (or to all appearance shot at), in a public theater in the center of his capital, and amidst the loyal plaudits of his subjects; yet not a hair of the head of the supposed assassin was touched. In this unparalleled scene of calm forbearance, the King himself, though he stood first in personal interest and feeling, as well as in command, gave an example of calmness and moderation equally singular and fortunate.

Gentlemen, I agree with the Attorney General (indeed there can be no possible doubt) that if the same pistol had been maliciously fired by the prisoner in the same theater at the meanest man within its walls, he would have been brought to immediate trial and, if guilty, to immediate execution. He would have heard the charge against him for the first time when the indictment was read upon his arraignment. He would have been a stranger to the names and even to the existence of those who were to sit in judgment upon him, and of those who were to be witnesses against him; but upon the charge of even this murderous attack upon the King himself, he is entirely covered with the armor of the law. He has been provided with counsel by the King's own judges, and not of their choice but of his own. He has had a copy of the indictment ten days before his trial. He has had the names, descriptions, and abodes of all the jurors returned to the court; he has enjoyed the important privilege of peremptorily rejecting them without assigning the motive of his refusal. He has had the same description of every witness who could be received to accuse him; and there must at this hour be twice the testimony against him that would be legally competent to establish his guilt on a similar prosecution by the meanest and most helpless of mankind.

Gentlemen, when this unfortunate catastrophe happened, I remember to have said to some now present that it was, at first view, difficult to go back to the principle of those indulgent exceptions to the general rules of procedure, and to explain why our ancestors extended to conspiracies against the king's person the precautions which concern treasons against government. In fact, in cases of political treason, passions and interests of great bodies of powerful men being engaged and agitated, a counterpoise became necessary to give composure and impartiality to criminal tribunals; but a mere murderous attack upon the king's person, not at all connected with his political character, seemed a case to be ranged and dealt with like a similar attack upon any private man.

But the wisdom of the law is greater than any man's wisdom; how much more, therefore, than mine! An attack upon the king is considered to be parricide against the state; and the jury and the witnesses, and even the judges, are its children. It is fit, on that account, that there should be a solemn pause before we rush to judgment; and what can be a more sublime spectacle of justice than that of a whole nation declared disqualified from judging during a limited period? Was not a fifteen days' quarantine necessary to preserve the mind from the contagion of so natural a partiality?

What a country is that in which such words are only the plain and accurate exposition of the existing state of things!

The civil jurisprudence of England is much less entitled to praise; the suits in it are too tedious and too expensive. It will certainly be ameliorated in course of time, as it has already been in several respects; for what, above all things, characterizes the English government is the possibility of improving itself without convulsion. There remain in England old forms, originating in the feudal ages, which surcharge the civil administration of law with a number of useless delays; but the constitution was established by engrafting the new on the old, and if the result has been the keeping up of certain abuses, it can, on the other hand, be said that liberty has in this way received the advantage of claiming an ancient origin. The condescension for old usages does not extend in England to anything that concerns individual security and liberty. In that respect, the ascendancy of reason is complete, and it is on the basis of reason that all reposes.

Before we proceed to the consideration of political powers, without which civil rights would possess no guarantee, we must speak of the only infraction of individual liberty with which England can be reproached— the impressment of seamen.[6] I will not urge the motives founded on the great interest which a country whose power is maritime has to maintain

---

6. A random and arbitrary means of recruitment used by the Royal Navy until the middle of the nineteenth century.

itself in this respect in strength; nor will I say that this kind of violence is confined to those who have already served either in the mercantile or in the Royal Navy, and who consequently know, as soldiers do on land, the kind of obligation to which they are subjected. I shall prefer to admit frankly that it is a great abuse, but an abuse which will doubtless be reformed in some way; for in a country in which the thoughts of all are turned toward the improvement of the state of society, and where the liberty of the press is favorable to the extension of public spirit, it is impossible that truths of every kind should not, in the long run, attain effectual circulation. We may predict that at a period more or less remote, we shall see important changes in the mode of recruiting the navy of England.

"Well!" exclaim the enemies of all public virtue, "supposing the good that is said of England to be well founded, the only result is that it is a country ably and wisely governed, as every other country might be; but it is by no means free in the way that philosophers understand freedom, for ministers are masters of everything in that as in other countries. They purchase votes in Parliament in such a way as to obtain constantly a majority; and the whole of this English constitution, which we hear spoken of with so much admiration, is nothing but the art of bringing political venality into play." Mankind would be much to be pitied were the world thus stripped of all its moral beauties, and it would then be difficult to comprehend the views of the Divinity in the creation of man; but happily these assertions are combated by facts as much as by theory. It is inconceivable how ill England is known on the Continent, in spite of the little distance that separates the two. Party spirit rejects the light which it would receive from this immortal beacon; and people refuse to look at anything in England but her diplomatic influence, which is not, as I shall explain in the sequel, the fair side of that country.

Can people in good faith persuade themselves that the English ministers give money to the members of the House of Commons or to members of the House of Peers to vote on the side of government? How could the English ministers, who render so exact an account of the public money, find sums of sufficient magnitude to bribe men of such large fortune, to say nothing whatever of their character? Mr. Pitt, several years ago, threw himself on the indulgence of the House in consequence of having lent 40,000 livres to support some commercial establishments during the last war; and what is called secret service money is of too small amount to command the least political influence in the interior of the country. Moreover, would not the liberty of the press, the torch which sheds light on the smallest details of the life of public men, would it not expose those presents of corruption which would forever ruin those who had received them as well as the ministers who had bestowed them?

There did, I confess, exist under Mr. Pitt's predecessors some examples of bargains concluded for government in such a way as to give an indirect advantage to members of Parliament; but Mr. Pitt abstained altogether from expedients so unworthy of him; he established a free competition for loans and contracts; and yet no man exercised a greater sway over both houses. "Yes," it will be said, "peers and members of the commons are not gained by money, but their object is places for themselves and their friends; and corruption in this way is as effectual as in the other." Doubtless, the favors at the disposal of the Crown form a part of the prerogative of the king, and consequently of the constitution. This influence is one of the weights in the balance so wisely combined; and moreover, it is as yet very limited. Never would ministry have either the power or the idea of making any change in what regards the constitutional liberties of England. Public opinion presents in that respect an invincible barrier. Public delicacy consecrates certain truths as above attack; and the opposition would no more think of criticizing the institution of the peerage than the ministerial party would presume to blame the liberty of the press. It is only in the circle of momentary circumstances that certain personal or family considerations can influence the direction of some minds; but never to a degree to cause the infraction of constitutional laws. Even if the King wanted to exempt himself from these laws, the responsibility of ministers would not permit them to support him in it: and those who compose the majority in the two houses would be still less disposed to renounce their real rights as lords, representatives, and citizens to acquire the favor of a court.

Fidelity to a party is one of the virtues founded on respect for public spirit, from which the greatest advantages result to English liberty. If tomorrow the ministers go out of office, those who voted with them and to whom they have given places quit those places along with them. A man would be dishonored in England were he to separate himself from his political friends for his own particular interest. Public opinion in this respect is so strong that a man of a very respectable name and character was known, not very long ago, to commit suicide because he reproached himself to have accepted a place independent from his party. Never do you hear the same mouth give utterance to two opposite opinions; and yet, in the existing state of things in England, the differences lie in shades, not colors. Tories, it has been said, approve of liberty and love monarchy, while Whigs approve of monarchy and love liberty; but between these two parties, no question could arise about a republican or a regal form of government, about the old or the new dynasty, liberty or servitude; in short, about any of those extremes and contrasts which we have seen professed by the same men in France, as if we ought to say of power as of love that the object is of no consequence provided one be always faithful to the sentiment, that is, to devotedness to power.

Dispositions of a very opposite character are the objects of admiration in England. For nearly half a century the members of the opposition have been in place only three or four years; yet party fidelity has not been shaken among them; and even recently, at the time I was in England, I saw lawyers refuse places of 7 or 8000 livres a year, which were not immediately connected with politics, only because they had engagements of opinion with the friends of Fox. Were a man in France to refuse a place of 8000 livres a year, truly his relations would think it high time to take out against him a statute of lunacy.

The existence of a ministerial and opposition party, although it cannot be prescribed by law, is an essential support of liberty founded on the nature of things. In every country where you see an assembly of men constantly in accord, be assured that despotism exists, or that despotism, if not the cause, will be the result of unanimity. Now, as power and the favors at the disposal of power possess attraction for men, liberty could not exist but with this fidelity to party, which introduces, if we may use the phrase, a discipline of honor into the ranks of members enrolled under different banners.

But if opinions are formed beforehand, how can truth and eloquence operate on the assembly? How can the majority change when circumstances require it, and of what avail is discussion if no one can vote according to his conviction? The case is not so: what is called fidelity to your party consists in not separating your personal interests from those of your political friends, and in your not treating separately with men in power. But it often happens that circumstances or arguments influence the mass of the assembly, and that the neutral party, whose number is considerable, that is, the men who do not take an active part in politics, produce a change in the majority. It is in the nature of the English government that ministers cannot remain in office without having this majority in their favor; yet Mr. Pitt, although he lost it for an interval during the first illness of the King, was enabled to keep his place because public opinion, which was in his favor, enabled him to dissolve Parliament and have recourse to a new election.[7] In short, public opinion bears the sway in England, and it is public opinion that constitutes the liberty of a country.

The jealous friends of this liberty desire a reform in Parliament and maintain that there is no truth in the existence of a representative government so long as the elections shall be so managed as to put the choice of a great number of deputies at the disposal of the ministry. The ministry, it is true, can influence a number of elections, such as those of the Cornish boroughs and some others of the same nature, in which the right of electing has been preserved although the electors have, in a great measure, disappeared; while towns of which the population is greatly increased have not so many deputies as their population would require, or have even none at all.[8] We may reckon, in the number of the prerogatives of the Crown, the right of introducing by its influence sixty or eighty members into the House of Commons out of six hundred and fifty-eight who compose it;

7. Pitt was in power during the periods 1783–1801 and 1804–6.

8. The so-called rotten boroughs. At the beginning of the nineteenth century, the English electoral system did not adequately reflect the country's new social, political, and economic conditions. Three major industrial cities—Manchester, Birmingham, and Leeds—with a total population of approximately half a million did not send a single representative to the House of Commons. In addition to many "rotten" boroughs in which there were hardly any voters left, there were many pocket boroughs in which elections were tightly controlled by a single individual or family. For more information, see Brock, *The Great Reform Act*.

but this abuse, for it is one, has not, down to the latest times, altered the strength and independence of the English Parliament.

The bishops and archbishops, who have seats in the House of Peers, vote likewise almost always with the ministry, except in points relative to religion. It is not from corrupt motives but from a sense of propriety that prelates appointed by the king do not in general attack ministers; but all these different elements that enter into the composition of the national representation do not prevent it from proceeding under the eye of public opinion; nor prevent men of importance in England, whether for talent, fortune, or personal respectability, from being in general members of the House. There are great proprietors and peers who dispose of certain seats in the House of Commons in the same way as ministers; and when these peers are in the opposition, the members whom they have caused to be elected vote in like manner on their side. All these accidental circumstances make no change in the nature of the representative government. What, above all, is of importance is the publicity of debate and the admirable forms of deliberation which protect the minority. Deputies elected by lot would, with the liberty of the press, represent the national opinion in a country more faithfully than the most regularly elected deputies, if they were not guided and enlightened by that liberty.

It would, however, be desirable to make a gradual suppression of elections that have become illusory, and that, on the other hand, a fairer representation be given to population and property in order to re-animate a little the spirit of Parliament which the reaction against the French Revolution has rendered in some respects too docile toward the executive power.[9] But there exists a dread of the strength of the popular element composing the third branch of the legislature, although modified by the discretion and dignity of the members of the House of Commons. There are, however, some men in that assembly whose opinions are very decided in favor of democracy. Not only must that be the case wherever opinion is free, but it is even desirable that the existence of such opinions should remind the grandees of the country that they cannot preserve the advantages of their rank otherwise than by consulting the rights and welfare of the nation. Yet it

9. This was the goal of the famous Reform Act of 1831–32.

would be a great error to imagine on the Continent that the opposition party is democratic. What strange democrats would be the Duke of Devonshire, the Duke of Bedford, the Marquis of Stafford! On the contrary, it is the high aristocracy of England which serves as a barrier to royal authority. Opposition are, it is true, more liberal than ministers in their principles: to combat power is sufficient to give a new temper to the mind and heart. But how could one fear a revolutionary commotion on the part of individuals possessed of every kind of property which order causes to be respected; of fortune, rank, and, above all, of knowledge? For knowledge, when real and profound, gives men a consistency equal to that of wealth.

In the House of Commons in England, no attempts are made at that kind of eloquence which excites the multitude; discussion predominates in that assembly, the spirit of business presides there, and there prevails perhaps too great a strictness in regard to oratorical display. Even Burke, whose political writings are now so much admired, was not listened to with attention when speaking in the Lower House, because he introduced into his speeches ornaments foreign to his subject and belonging properly to literature. Ministers are often required to give, in the House of Commons, particular explanations which do not at all enter into the debates. The deputies from the different towns or counties apprise the members of government of the abuses which may occur in local administration, of the reforms and improvement of which it is susceptible; and these habitual communications between the representatives of the people and the heads of the executive power produce the happiest results.

"If the majority of Parliament is not bribed by ministers," say those who think they are pleading their own cause by demonstrating the degradation of mankind, "at least you will admit that candidates expend enormous sums on their elections." It cannot be denied that in certain elections there exists venality, notwithstanding the severity of the law. The greatest part of the cost consists in traveling expenses, that is, in bringing to the place of election voters who live at a great distance. The consequence is that none except very opulent persons can venture to run the risk of coming forward as candidates for such places, and that the expense of elections is sometimes carried to a foolish extreme in England, like expense of every kind in other monarchies. Yet in what country can popular elections exist without endeavors to win the favor of the people? This is precisely the grand advantage of the institution. It happens then for once that the rich stand in need of the class which in general is dependent on them. Lord Erskine told me that in his career of counselor and member of the House of Commons, there was perhaps not one inhabitant of Westminster to whom he had not occasion to speak; so great are the political relations between the citizens and men of the highest rank. Nominations by a court are almost always influenced by the most narrow motives; the broad day of popular election cannot be borne but by individuals remarkable for some quality or other. Merit will always triumph at last in countries where the public is called on to point it out.

That which is particularly characteristic of England is a mixture of chivalrous spirit with an enthusiasm for liberty, the two most noble sentiments of which the human heart is susceptible. Circumstances have brought about this fortunate result, and we ought to admit that new institutions would not suffice to produce it: the recollection of the past is necessary to consecrate aristocratic ranks; for if they were all of the creation of power, they would be subject, in part, to the inconveniences experienced in France under Bonaparte. But what can be done in a country where the nobility should be inimical to liberty of every kind? The Third Estate could not form a union with them; and as it would be the stronger of the two, it would incessantly threaten the nobility until the latter had submitted to the progress of reason.

The English aristocracy is of a more mixed kind in the eyes of a genealogist than that of France; but the English nation seems, if we may say so, one entire body of gentlemen. You see in every English citizen what he may one day become, since no rank lies beyond the reach of talent, and since high ranks have always kept up their ancient splendor. It is true that that which, above all, constitutes nobility, in the view of an enlightened mind, is being free. An English nobleman or gentleman (taking the word "gentleman" in the sense of a man of independent property) exercises, in his part of the country, some useful employment to which no salary is attached: as a justice of the peace, sheriff, or lord lieutenant in the county where his property is situated; he influences elections in a manner that is suitable, and that increases his credit with the people; as a peer or member of the House of Commons, he discharges a political function and possesses a real importance. This is not the idle aristocracy of a French nobleman, who was of no consideration in the state whenever the king refused him his favor; it is a distinction founded on all the interests of the nation. And we cannot avoid being surprised that French nobles should have preferred the life of a courtier, moving on the road from Versailles to Paris, to the majestic stability of an English peer on his estate, surrounded by men to whom he can do a thousand acts of kindness, but over whom he can exercise no arbitrary power. The authority of law is in England predominant over all the powers of the state, as Fate in ancient mythology was superior to the authority of the gods themselves.

To the political miracle of a respect for the rights of everyone founded on a sentiment of justice, we must add the equally skillful and fortunate union of equality under the law to the advantages arising from the separation of ranks. Everyone in that country stands in need of others for his comfort, yet everyone is there independent of all by his rights. This Third Estate, which has become so prodigiously aggrandized in France and in the rest of Europe, this Third Estate, the increase of which necessitates successive changes in all old institutions, is united in England to the nobility, because the nobility itself is identified with the nation. A great number of peers owe the origin of their dignity to the law, some to commerce, others to a military career, others to political eloquence; there is not one virtue nor one kind of talent which has not its place, or which may not flatter itself with attaining it; and everything in the social edifice conduces to the glory of that constitution which is as dear to the Duke of Norfolk as to the meanest porter in England, because it protects both with the same equity.

> *Thee I account still happy, and the chief*
> *Among the nations, seeing thou art free,*
> *My native nook of earth! Thy clime is rude,*
> *Replete with vapours, and disposes much*
> *All hearts to sorrow, and none more than mine:*
> . . . .
> *Yet, being free, I love thee. . . .* *

* Cowper.

These verses are by a poet of admirable talents, but whose happiness was destroyed by his extreme sensibility.[10] He was laboring under a mortal disease of melancholy; and when love, friendship, philosophy, everything added to his sufferings, a free country yet awakened in his soul an enthusiasm which nothing could extinguish.

All men are more or less attached to their country; the recollections of infancy, the habits of youth form that inexpressible love of the native soil which we must acknowledge as a virtue, for all true feeling constitutes its source. But in a great state, liberty and the happiness arising from that liberty can alone inspire true patriotism: nothing accordingly is comparable to public spirit in England. The English are accused of selfishness, and it is true that their mode of life is so well regulated that they generally confine themselves within the circle of their habits and domestic affections; but what sacrifice is too great for them when the interest of their country is at stake? And among what people in the world are services rendered, felt, and rewarded with more enthusiasm? When we enter Westminster Abbey, all those tombs, sacred to the men who have been illustrious for centuries past, seem to reproduce the spectacle of the greatness of England among the dead. Kings and philosophers repose under the same roof: it is there that quarrels are appeased, as has been well observed by the celebrated Walter Scott.* You behold the tombs of Pitt and Fox beside each other, and the same tears bedew both; for they both deserve the profound regret which generous minds ought to bestow on that noble elite of our species who serve to support our confidence in the immortality of the soul.

Let us recollect the funeral of Nelson,[11] when nearly a million persons scattered throughout London and the neighborhood contemplated in silence the passage of his coffin. The multitude were silent, the multitude

---

* Genius, and taste, and talent gone,
  For ever tomb'd beneath the stone,
  Where, taming thought to human pride!
  The mighty chiefs sleep side by side.
  Drop upon Fox's grave the tear,
  'Twill trickle to his rival's bier.

10. William Cowper (1731–1800) was an English poet and hymnodist. His works include *Olney Hymns* (1779) and translations of Homer's *Iliad* and *Odyssey*.

11. Horatio Nelson (1758–1805) was a famous English admiral who died in the battle of Trafalgar on October 21, 1805.

evinced as much respect in the expression of its grief as might have been expected from the most polished society. Nelson had given as a signal, on the day of Trafalgar, "England expects every man to do his duty"; he had accomplished that duty, and when expiring on board his vessel, the honorable obsequies which his country would grant him presented themselves to his thoughts as the beginning of a new life.

Nor yet let us be silent on Lord Wellington, although in France we cannot but suffer by the recollection of his glory. With what transport was he not received by the representatives of the nation, by the Peers and by the Commons! No ceremony was required to convey this homage rendered to a living man; but the transports of the English people burst forth on all sides. The acclamations of the crowd resounded in the lobby before he entered the House; when he appeared, all the members rose with a spontaneous motion, unrequired by any formality. The homage which is dictated elsewhere was here inspired by emotion. Yet nothing could be more simple than the reception of Lord Wellington: there were no guards, no military pomp to do honor to the greatest general of the age in which Bonaparte lived; but the day was celebrated by the voice of the people, and nothing like it could be seen in any other country upon earth.

Ah! what a fascinating enjoyment is that of popularity! I know all that can be said on the inconstancy, and even the caprice of popular favor; but those reproaches are more applicable to ancient republics, where the democratic forms of government led to the most rapid vicissitudes. In a country governed like England, and, moreover, enlightened by that torch without which all is darkness, the liberty of the press, men and things are judged with great equity. Truth is submitted to the observation of everyone, while the various constraints that are employed elsewhere produce necessarily great uncertainty in judgments. A libel that glides across the compulsory silence to which the press is condemned may change public opinion in regard to any man, for the praise or the censure ordered by government is always suspicious. Nothing can be clearly and solidly settled in the minds of men but by free discussion.

"Do you pretend," it may be said, "that there is no mutability in the judgment of the English people, and that they will not offer incense today to him whom they would perhaps tear in pieces tomorrow?" Doubtless, those who are at the head of government should be subject to lose the favor of the people if they are not successful in the management of public affairs. The depositaries of authority ought to be fortunate; that is one of the conditions of the advantages that are granted to them. Besides, power having always a tendency to deprave those who possess it, it is always to be wished, in a free country, that the same men should not remain too long in office; and it is right to change ministers, were it only for the sake of changing. But reputation, once acquired, is very durable in England, and public opinion may be considered as the conscience of the state.

If anything can seduce the English nation from equity, it is misfortune. An individual, persecuted by any power whatever, might inspire an undeserved, and consequently a fleeting interest. But this noble error belongs, on the one hand, to the generosity of the English character, and on the other, to that sentiment of liberty which makes all feel the desire of defending themselves mutually against oppression; for it is in that respect especially that, in politics, we should treat our neighbor as ourselves.

The state of information and the energy of public spirit are more than a sufficient answer to the arguments of those men who pretend that the army would overpower the liberty of England if England were a Continental state. It is, without doubt, an advantage to England that her strength consists rather in her marine than in her land forces. It requires more knowledge to be a captain of a ship than a colonel; and none of the habits acquired at sea lead one to desire to interfere in the interior affairs of the country. But were nature, in a lavish mood, to create ten Lord Wellingtons, and were the world again to witness ten battles of Waterloo, it would never enter the heads of those who so readily give their lives for their country to turn their force against it; or, if so, they would encounter an invincible obstacle among men as brave as themselves, and more enlightened, who detest the military spirit although they know how to admire and practice warlike virtues.

That sort of prejudice which persuaded the French nobility that they could serve their country only in the career of arms does not exist at all in England. Many sons of lords are counselors; the bar participates in the respect that is felt for the law; and in every career civil occupations are held in esteem. In such a country there is nothing as yet to be feared from military power: only ignorant nations have a blind admiration for the sword. Bravery is a superb quality when we expose a life dear to our family, and when, with a mind filled with virtue and knowledge, a citizen becomes a soldier to maintain his rights as a citizen. But when men fight only because they will not take the trouble to employ their minds and their time in some steady pursuit, they cannot be long admired by a nation where industry and reflection hold the first rank. The satellites of Cromwell overthrew a civil power which had neither strength nor dignity; but since the existence of the constitution, and of public spirit which is its soul, princes or generals would only excite in the whole nation a feeling of contempt for their folly were they at any time to dream of enslaving their country.

CHAPTER V

Of Knowledge, Religion, and Morals Among the English.

What constitutes the knowledge of a nation are sound political ideas spread among all classes and a general instruction in sciences and literature. In the first respect, the English have no rivals in Europe; in the second, I know nothing that can be compared to them, except the Germans of the North. Still the English would have an advantage which can belong only to their institutions, which is that the first class of society devotes itself as much to study as the second. Mr. Fox wrote learned dissertations on Greek during his hours of leisure from parliamentary debates; Mr. Windham has left several interesting treatises on mathematics and literature. The English have at all times honored learning: Henry VIII, who trampled everything underfoot, yet respected men of letters when they did not come in opposition to his disorderly passions. The great Elizabeth was well versed in the ancient languages and even spoke Latin with facility. That foppery of ignorance with which we had reason to reproach the French nobility was never introduced among the princes or nobility of England. One would think that the former were persuaded that the divine right by which they hold their privileges entirely exempted them from the study of human science. Such a manner of thinking could not exist in England and would only appear ridiculous. Nothing factitious can succeed in a country where everything is subjected to publicity. The great English nobility would be as much ashamed of not having had a distinguished classical education as men of the second rank in France were, heretofore, of not going to court; and these differences are not connected, as some pretend, with French frivolity. The most persevering scholars, the deepest thinkers, have belonged to that nation, which is capable of everything when it chooses; but its political institutions were so defective that they perverted its natural good qualities.

In England, on the contrary, the institutions favor every kind of intellectual progress. The juries, the administrations of counties and towns, the elections, the newspapers give the whole nation a great share of interest in public affairs. The consequence is that it is better informed; and that, at a venture, it would be better to converse with an English farmer on political questions than with the greater number of men on the Continent, even the most enlightened. That admirable good sense which is founded on justice and security exists nowhere but in England or in the country that resembles it, America. Reflection must remain a stranger to men who have no rights; since as soon as they perceive the truth, they must be first unhappy, and soon after filled with the spirit of revolt. It must be admitted also that in a country where the armed force has almost always been naval, and commerce the principal occupation, there must necessarily be more knowledge than where the national defense is confided to the troops of the line; and where industry is almost entirely directed to the cultivation of the ground. Commerce, placing men in relation with the interests of the world, extends the ideas, exercises the judgment, and, from the multiplicity and diversity of transactions, makes the necessity of justice continually to be felt. In countries where the only pursuit is agriculture, the mass of the population may be composed of serfs attached to the soil and devoid of all information. But what could be done with tradesmen who are enslaved and ignorant? A maritime and commercial country is, therefore, necessarily more enlightened than any other; yet there remains much to be done to give the English people a sufficient education. A considerable portion of the lowest class can as yet neither read nor write; and it is doubtless to remedy this evil that the new methods of Bell and Lancaster[1] are so warmly encouraged, because they are calculated to bring education within the reach of the indigent. The lower orders are perhaps better informed in Switzerland, in Sweden, and in some parts of the north of Germany; but in none of these countries is found that vigor of liberty which

---

1. Andrew Bell (1753–97) and Joseph Lancaster (1778–1838) founded the mutual education system involving the best students in the teaching process.

will preserve England, it is to be hoped, from the reaction occasioned by the French Revolution. In a country where there is an immense capital, great riches concentrated in a small number of hands, a court, all that can tend to the corruption of the people, time is needed for knowledge to extend itself and to oppose successfully the inconveniences attached to the disproportion of fortunes.

The peasantry of Scotland is better informed than that of England, because there is less wealth in the hands of a few and more prosperity among the people. The Presbyterian religion established in Scotland excludes the episcopal hierarchy maintained by the English church. Consequently, the choice of the simple ministers of public worship is better there; and as they live retired in the mountains, they devote their time to the instruction of the peasants. It is also a great advantage for Scotland not to be subject, like England, to a very oppressive and very ill-planned poor's tax, which keeps up mendicity and creates a class of people who dare not quit the parish where relief is guaranteed to them.[2] The city of Edinburgh is not so much absorbed as London by public affairs, and does not contain such a mixture of wealth and luxury; philosophical and literary interests play there a greater role. But, on the other hand, the remains of the feudal system are more felt in Scotland than in England. Juries in civil affairs have been but recently introduced, and there are not nearly so many popular elections in proportion as among the English. Commerce has there less influence, and the spirit of liberty is, with some exceptions, displayed with less energy.

In Ireland, the ignorance of the people is frightful; but that must be attributed, in part, to superstitious prejudices and, in part, to the almost total privation of the benefits of a constitution. Ireland has been united to England only for a few years;[3] she has felt till now all the evils of arbitrary power, and has often avenged herself of it in a most violent manner. The nation being divided into two religions, forming also two political parties, the English government since Charles I has granted every advantage to

2. The Poor Laws had existed since the reign of Elizabeth I; they confined the poor to workhouses in which work was mandatory. The 1601 law remained in effect until 1832.

3. Since 1800.

the Protestants in order to enable them to keep in submission the Catholic majority. Swift, an Irishman and as fine a genius as any in the three king-doms,* wrote, in 1740, on the miserable state of Ireland. The attention of enlightened men was strongly excited by the writings of Swift, and the improvements which took place in that country may be dated from that time. When America declared herself independent, and England was obliged to acknowledge her as such, the necessity of paying attention to Ireland was felt every day more strongly by reflecting minds. The illus-trious talents of Mr. Grattan,[4] which thirty years later have again aston-ished England, were remarked so early as 1782 in the parliament of Ire-land; and by degrees that country was at length brought to a union with Great Britain. Superstitious prejudices are still, however, the source of a thousand evils there; for to reach the same point of prosperity as England, the knowledge connected with a reform in religion is as necessary as the free spirit of a representative government. The political exclusion to which the Irish Catholics are condemned is contrary to the true principles of justice; but it seems difficult to put in possession of the benefits of the constitution men who are irritated by ancient resentment.

Hitherto then we can admire in the Irish nation only a great character of independence and a great deal of natural quickness; but in that country people do not yet enjoy either the security or the instruction which are the result of religious and political liberty. Scotland is, in many respects, the opposite of Ireland, and England retains something of both.

---

* It is related that Swift felt a foreboding that his faculties would abandon him, and that, walking one day with a friend, he saw an oak, the head of which was withered, though the trunk and roots were yet in full vigor. "It is thus I shall be," said Swift; and his sad prediction was accomplished. When he had fallen into such a state of stupor that for a whole year he had not uttered a word, he suddenly heard the bells of St. Patrick's, of which he was the Dean, ringing in full peal, and asked what it meant. His friends, in raptures that he had recovered his speech, hastened to inform him that it was in honor of his birthday that these signs of joy were taking place. "Ah!" he exclaimed, "all that is unavailing now"; and he returned to that silence which death soon after confirmed. But the good he had done sur-vived him, and it is for this that men of genius appear on the earth.

4. Henry Grattan (1746–1820), Irish Protestant and member of the parliament in Dublin, fought for Irish independence.

Since it is impossible in England to be minister without sitting in one of the houses of Parliament, and without discussing the affairs of state with the representatives of the nation, it unavoidably follows that such ministers bear, in general, no resemblance to the class of governors in an absolute monarchy. The esteem of the public is, in England, the first aim of men in power; they scarcely ever make a fortune in the ministry. Mr. Pitt died leaving nothing but debts, which the Parliament paid. The under-secretaries of state, the clerks, all persons connected with the administration, enlightened by public opinion and their own pride, possess the most perfect integrity. Ministers cannot favor their partisans unless the latter are sufficiently distinguished not to provoke the discontent of Parliament. It is not enough to have the favor of the master to remain in place; it is necessary also to have the esteem of the representatives of the nation; and this can only be obtained by real ability. Ministers appointed by court intrigue, as we have seen continually in France, would not support themselves twenty-four hours in the House of Commons. Their mediocrity would be ascertained in an instant; they would not appear there bepowdered and in the full costume of the ministers of the old government and of the court of Bonaparte. They would not be surrounded with courtiers acting the same part with them which they themselves act with the King, and bursting into raptures at the justness of their commonplace ideas and the depth of their false conceptions. An English minister enters either house alone, without any particular dress, without a distinctive mark; no sort of quackery comes to his aid; everybody questions and judges him; but, on the other hand, he is respected by all, if he deserves it, because being able to pass only for what he is, the esteem he enjoys is due to his personal worth.

"They do not pay their court to princes in England as in France," it will be said, "but they seek popularity, which does not less impair the truth of character." In a well-organized country like England, to desire popularity is to wish for the just recompense of all that is noble and good in itself. There have existed, in all times, men who were virtuous, notwithstanding the inconveniences and the perils to which they were exposed in consequence; but when social institutions are combined in such a manner that private interests and public virtues accord, it does not hence follow that these virtues have no other basis than personal interest. They are only more general, because they are advantageous as well as honorable.

The science of liberty (if we may use that expression) at the point at which it is cultivated in England supposes in itself a very high degree of education and knowledge. Nothing can be more simple than that doctrine, once the principles on which it reposes have been adopted; but it is nevertheless certain that, on the Continent, we seldom meet with any person who, in heart and mind, understands England. It would seem as if there were moral truths amidst which we must be born, and which the beating of the heart inculcates better than all the discussions of theory. Nevertheless, to enjoy and practice that liberty which unites all the advantages of republican virtues, of philosophical knowledge, of religious sentiments, and monarchical dignity, a great share of understanding is requisite in the people, and a high degree of study and virtue in men of the first class. English ministers must unite with the qualities of a statesman the art of expressing themselves with eloquence. It thence follows that literature and philosophy are much more appreciated, because they contribute efficaciously to the success of the highest ambition. We hear incessantly of the empire of rank and of wealth among the English; but we must also acknowledge the admiration which is granted to real talents. It is possible that, among the lowest class of society, a peerage and a fortune produce more effect than the name of a great writer; this must be so; but if the question regards the enjoyments of good company and consequently of public opinion, I know no country in the world where it is more advantageous to be a man of superiority. Not only every employment, every rank may be the recompense of talent; but public esteem is expressed in so flattering a manner as to confer enjoyments more keenly felt than any other.

The emulation which such a prospect must excite is one of the principal causes of the incredible extent of information and knowledge diffused in England. Were it possible to make a statistical report of knowledge, in no country should we find so great a proportion of persons conversant in the study of ancient languages, a study, unfortunately, too much neglected in France. Private libraries without number, collections of every kind, subscriptions in abundance for all literary undertakings, establishments for public education exist in all directions, in every county, at the extremity as in the center of the kingdom; in short, we find at each step altars erected to thought, and these altars serve as a support to those of religion and virtue.

Thanks to toleration, to political institutions, and the liberty of the press, there is a greater respect for religion and for morals in England than in any other country in Europe. In France people take a pleasure in saying that it is precisely for the sake of religion and morals that censors have been at all times employed; but let them compare the spirit of literature in England since the liberty of the press is established there with the different writings which appeared under the arbitrary reign of Charles II, and under the regent or Louis XV in France. The licentiousness of published works was carried among the French in the last century to a degree that excites horror. The case is the same in Italy, where, however, the press has at all times been subjected to the most cumbersome restrictions. Ignorance in the mass of the people and the most lawless independence in men of superior parts is always the result of constraint.

English literature is certainly of all others that in which there are the greatest number of philosophic works. Scotland contains, at this day, very powerful writers in that department, with Dugald Stewart[5] at their head, who in retirement pursues with ardor the search of truth. Literary criticism is carried to the highest pitch in the reviews, particularly in that of Edinburgh;[6] in which writers, formed to render themselves illustrious, Jeffrey, Playfair, Mackintosh,[7] do not disdain to enlighten authors by the opinions they pass on their works. The most learned writers on questions of juris-

---

5. Dugald Stewart (1753–1828), a prominent Scottish philosopher and disciple of Thomas Reid, was a member of the Scottish School of Common Sense, which flourished in Scotland in the late eighteenth and early nineteenth centuries.

6. The famous *Edinburgh Review,* one of the most influential magazines of the nineteenth century, was founded in 1802 by Francis Jeffrey, Sydney Smith, and Henry Brougham. For more information, see Fontana, *Rethinking the Politics of Commercial Society.*

7. Francis Jeffrey (1773–1850) was a founder of the *Edinburgh Review* and member of the House of Commons (from 1834). John Playfair (1748–1819) was an eminent mathematician and geologist. James Mackintosh (1765–1832) was the author of *Vindiciae Gallicae* (1791).

prudence and political economy, such as Bentham, Malthus, Brougham,[8] are more numerous in England than anywhere else because they have a well-founded hope that their ideas will be translated into practice. Voyages to every part of the world bring to England the tributes of science, which are not less welcome than those of commerce; but in the midst of so many intellectual treasures of every kind, we cannot cite any of those irreligious or licentious works with which France has been inundated: public opinion has reprobated them from the moment that it had cause to dread them; and it acquits itself of this with greater willingness because it is the only sentinel for this purpose. Publicity is always favorable to truth; and as morality and religion are truth in its highest character, the more you permit men to discuss these subjects, the more they become enlightened and dignified. The courts of justice would very properly punish in England any publication offensive to character and morals; but no work bears that mark of official inspection (*censure*) which casts a previous doubt on the assertions it may contain.

English poetry, which is fostered neither by irreligion, nor the spirit of faction, nor licentiousness of manners, is still rich and animated, experiencing nothing of that decline which threatens successively the literature of most other countries in Europe. Sensibility and imagination preserve the immortal youth of soul. A second age of poetry has arisen in England because enthusiasm is not there extinct, and because nature, love, and country always exercise great power there. Cowper lately, and now Rogers, Moore, Thomas Campbell, Walter Scott, Lord Byron, in different departments and degrees, are preparing a new age of glory for English poetry; and while everything on the Continent is in a state of degradation, the eternal fountain of beauty still flows from the land of freedom.

In what empire is Christianity more respected than in England? Where are greater pains taken to propagate it? Whence do missionaries proceed in so great number to every part of the world? The Society[9] which has taken on itself to transmit copies of the Bible into countries where the light

8. Henry Brougham (1778–1868) was a prominent Whig politician. As lord chancellor from 1830 to 1834, he was responsible for the passage of the Reform Act of 1831–32 and the Slavery Abolition Act of 1833.

9. The British and Foreign Bible Society, founded in London in 1804.

of Christianity is obscured, or not yet displayed, transmitted quantities of them into France during the war, and this care was not superfluous. But I should at present deviate from my subject were I to enter here on what would constitute an apology for France in that respect.

The Reformation placed the cultivation of knowledge among the English in harmony with the feelings of religion. This has been of great advantage to that country; and the high degree of piety of which individuals there are capable leads always to austerity in morals, and scarcely ever to superstition. The particular sects of England, the most numerous of which is that of the Methodists, have no other view than the maintenance of the severe purity of Christianity in the conduct of life. Their renunciation of pleasures of every kind, their persevering zeal in well-doing announce to mankind that there are in the Gospel the germs of sentiments and of virtues still more fruitful than all those that we have seen displayed even to the present day, and the sacred flowers of which are perhaps destined for future generations.

In a religious country good morals also necessarily exist, and yet the passions of the English are very strong; for it is a great error to believe them of a calm disposition because they have habitually cold manners. No men are more impetuous in great things; but they resemble the dogs sent by Porus[10] to Alexander, who disdained to fight against any other adversary than the lion. The English abandon their apparent tranquillity and give themselves up to extremes of all kinds. They go in quest of danger; they wish to attempt extraordinary things; they desire strong emotions. Activity of imagination and the restraint of their habits render such emotions necessary to them; but these habits themselves are founded on a great respect for morality.

The freedom of the newspapers, which some persons would represent to us as contrary to delicacy of mores, is one of the most efficacious causes of that delicacy: everything in England is so well known, and so discussed, that truth in all matters is unavoidable; and one might submit to the judgment of the English public as to that of a friend, who should enter into the details of your life, into the shades of your character, to weigh every

---

10. Indian prince (ca. 327 B.C.) who fought against Alexander the Great.

action, in the spirit of equity, agreeably to the situation of each individual. The greater the weight of public opinion in England, the greater boldness is necessary to act in violation of it; accordingly the women who brave it go to a daring length. But how rare are these violations of it, even in the highest class, the only one in which such examples can at times be cited! In the second rank, among the inhabitants of the country, we find nothing but good marriages and private virtues, a domestic life entirely consecrated to the education of a numerous family, who, brought up in a complete conviction of the sacred nature of marriage, would not permit a light thought on this subject to enter the mind. As there are no convents in England, the daughters are commonly educated at the house of their parents; and one can see by their information and their virtues which of the two is better for a female, education on this plan or on that which is practiced in Italy.

"At least," it will be said, "those trials for divorce in which the most indecent discussions are admitted are a source of scandal." They shouldn't, however, be so, since the result is such as I have just mentioned. These trials are an old usage, and from this point of view, certain people ought to defend them; but be this as it may, the dread of the scandal is a great restraint. And besides, people in England are not disposed as in France to make such subjects a topic of pleasantry. A degree of austerity corresponding to the spirit of the early Puritans is displayed in these trials. The judges, as well as the spectators, come to them with a serious disposition, and the consequences are highly important since the maintenance of the domestic virtues depends on them, and there is no liberty without these virtues. Now, as the spirit of the age was not favorable to them, the useful ascendancy of these trials for divorce is a fortunate chance; for chance there almost always is in the good or evil that can be produced by adhering to old usages, as occasionally they are suitable to the present time, and at other periods no longer applicable to it. Happy the country in which the misconduct of women can be punished with so much wisdom, without frivolity, and without vengeance! They are permitted to have recourse to the protection of the man for whom they have sacrificed everything; but they are, in general, deprived of all the brilliant advantages of society. I do not know whether legislation could invent anything at once stronger and milder.

An indignant feeling will perhaps be excited by the practice of requiring a sum of money from the seducer of a woman. As everything in England is stamped with a noble feeling, I will not lightly pass sentence on a custom of this nature, since it is preserved. It is necessary to punish in some way the trespasses of men against morals, since public opinion is in general too lax in regard to them, and no one will pretend that a heavy pecuniary loss is not a punishment. Moreover, the public sensation produced by these distressing trials renders it almost always a duty on the man to espouse the woman whom he has seduced; and this obligation is a pledge that neither levity nor falsehood is mingled with the sentiments which men allow themselves to express. When in love there is nothing but love, its irregularities are both more rare and more excusable. It is, however, difficult to me to understand why the fine payable by the seducer should go to the husband: often, indeed, the husband does not accept it, but appropriates it to the poor. However, there is reason to think that two motives have given rise to this custom: one to furnish to a husband, when of a class without property, the means of educating his children when the mother, whose duty it was, is lost to him; the other, and this is a more essential point, to bring forward the husband in a case involving the misconduct of his wife, in order to examine if he be not culpable in a similar way in regard to her. In Scotland, infidelity on the part of the husband dissolves a marriage like infidelity on the part of the wife, and a sentiment of duty in a free country always puts the strong and the weak on a level.

In England all is constituted in such a way that the interest of each class, of each sex, of each individual lies in conforming themselves to morality. Political liberty is the supreme instrument of this admirable combination. "Yes," it will still be said, "if you look at words and not at things; the truth is, that the English are always governed by interest." As if there were any resemblance between the interest that leads to virtue and that which causes a deviation to vice! Doubtless, England is not a planet distinct from ours, in which personal advantage is not, as elsewhere, the spring of human action. Men cannot be governed by reckoning always on devotedness and sacrifices; but when the whole of the institutions of a country are such that there is an advantage in being upright, there results from it a certain habit of integrity which becomes engraven on every heart: it is transmitted by remembrance, the air we breathe is impregnated with it, and we are no longer under the necessity of reflecting on the inconveniences of every kind that would ensue from certain improprieties; the force of example is enough to preserve them.

CHAPTER VI

Of Society in England, and of Its Connection with Social Order.

It is not probable that we shall ever see in any country, not even in France, such a society as we there enjoyed during the first two years of the Revolution and the period that preceded it. Foreigners who flatter themselves with finding anything of the kind in England are much disappointed, for they often get bored there. Although that country contains the most enlightened men and the most interesting women, the enjoyments which society can procure are but rarely met with. When a foreigner understands English well and is admitted to small circles composed of the superior men of the country, he tastes, if he be worthy of them, the most noble enjoyments which the communication of reflecting beings can afford; but it is not in these intellectual feasts that the society of England consists. People in London are invited every day to vast assemblies where they elbow each other as in the pit of a theater. The women form there the majority and the crowd is, in general, so great that even their beauty does not have enough room for display; still less can any pleasure of the mind be thought of. Considerable physical force is required to cross the salons without being stifled and to get back to one's carriage without accident; but I do not well see that any other superiority is necessary in such a crowd. Accordingly, serious men soon renounce the tax which in England is called fashionable company; and it is, it must be confessed, the most tiresome combination which can be formed out of such distinguished elements.

These reunions arise from the necessity of admitting a very great number of persons into the circle of one's acquaintance. The list of visitors which an English lady receives is sometimes of twelve hundred persons.

French society is infinitely more exclusive: the aristocratic spirit which regulated the formation of its circles was favorable to elegance and amusement, but nowise in correspondence with the nature of a free state. Thus, in frankly admitting that the pleasures of society are found very rarely, and with great difficulty, in London, I shall examine if these pleasures are compatible with the social order of England. If they are not, the choice cannot be a matter of doubt.

Men of large property in England generally discharge some public duty in their respective counties; and, from a wish to be returned to Parliament or to influence the election of their relations and friends, they pass eight or nine months in the country. The consequence is that social habits are entirely suspended during two-thirds of the year, and it is only by meeting every day that people form familiar and easy connections. In the part of London where the higher circles reside, there are whole months in summer and autumn during which the town has the appearance of being visited by a contagion, such is the solitude that prevails. The meeting of Parliament seldom takes place until January, and people do not come to London till that time. The men living much on their estates pass half the day in riding or sporting; they come home fatigued and think only of taking rest, or sometimes even of drinking, although the reports made of English manners in this respect are grossly exaggerated, particularly if referred to the present time. However, such a mode of life does not fit people for the pleasures of society. The French being called neither by their business nor by their taste to live in the country, one might find at Paris during the whole year houses in which to enjoy very agreeable conversation; but the consequence also is that Paris alone enjoyed existence in France, while in England political life is felt in every county. When the interests of the country come under the jurisdiction of everyone, the most attractive conversation is that of which public business is the object. Now, in considering this subject, we do not so much regard the lightheartedness of spirit as the real importance of the things discussed. Often does a man, in other respects far from agreeable, captivate his hearers by the power of his reasoning and information. In France, the art of being agreeable lay in never exhausting a subject and in never dwelling too long on those which were not interesting to women. In England, women never come conspicuously forward in discourse; the men have not accustomed them to take a share in general conversation: when they leave the room after dinner, conversation of this kind becomes more keen and animated. The mistress of a house does not, as among the French, think herself obliged to lead the conversation, and particularly to take care that it does not languish. People are quite resigned to this evil in English society; and it seems much easier to bear than the necessity of taking a conspicuous part for the sake of re-animating the discourse. English women are extremely timid in this respect; for in a free country, men preserving their natural dignity, females feel themselves subordinate.[1]

The case is not the same in an unlimited monarchy such as existed in France. As nothing there was impracticable or determinate, the conquests made by elegance and grace were unbounded, and women necessarily triumphed in contests of this kind. But in England what ascendancy could a woman, even the most amiable, exercise in the midst of popular elections, of the eloquence of Parliament, and the inflexibility of the law? Ministers have no idea that a woman could send them a request on any subject whatever unless she had neither brother, son, nor husband to undertake it. In the country of the greatest publicity, state secrets are better kept than anywhere else. There are here no intermediates, if we may use the expression, between the newspapers and the ministerial cabinet; and this cabinet is the most discreet in Europe. There is no example of a woman having known, or at least having told, what ought to have been kept secret. In a country where domestic manners are so regular, married men have no mistresses; and it is only mistresses who dive into secrets and particularly who reveal them.

Amongst the means of rendering society more animated we must reckon coquetry: now, this hardly exists in England, except among young men and women who may perhaps subsequently intermarry; conversation gains nothing by it, but the reverse. Indeed, so low in general is their tone of voice that these persons can scarcely hear each other; but the consequence is that people are not married without being acquainted; while in

---

1. For a splendid account of the role of women in French society, see Ozouf, *Women's Words*.

France, to save the tediousness of these timid amours, young girls were never introduced into company until their marriage had been concluded on by their parents. If there are in England women who deviate from their duty, it is with so much mystery or with so much publicity that the desire of pleasing in company, of exhibiting their fascinations, of shining by grace and sprightliness of mind has no connection whatever with their conduct. In France the power of conversation led to everything; in England talents of this kind are appreciated, but they are nowise useful to the ambition of those who possess them; public men and the people make a choice, among the candidates for power, of very different marks of superior faculties. The consequence is that people neglect what is not useful, in this as in everything else. The national character, moreover, being strongly turned toward reserve and timidity, a powerful motive is necessary to triumph over these habits, and this motive is found only in the importance of public discussions.

It is difficult to give a thorough explanation of what in England is called shyness, that is, the embarrassment which confines to the bottom of the heart the expressions of natural benevolence; for one often meets the coldest manners in persons who would show themselves most generous toward you if you stood in need of their aid. The English are as far from being at ease among each other as with foreigners; they do not speak till after having been introduced to each other; familiarity becomes established only after long acquaintance. In England one scarcely ever sees the younger branches live after their marriage in the same house with their parents; home is the prevailing taste of the English, and this inclination has perhaps contributed to make them detest the political system which, in other countries, permits exile or arbitrary arrest. Each family has its separate dwelling; and London consists of a vast number of houses of small size, shut as close as boxes, and into which it is not much easier to penetrate. There are not even many brothers or sisters who go to dine at each other's houses without invitation. This formality does not render life very amusing; and in the taste of the English for traveling, the motive is partly a desire to withdraw from the constraint of their customs, as well as the necessity of escaping from the fogs of their country.

In every country the pleasures of society concern only the first class, that is, the unoccupied class; who, having a great deal of leisure for amusement, attach much importance to it. But in England, where everyone has his career and his employment, it is natural for men of rank, as for men of business in other countries, to prefer physical relaxation, walks, the country, in short, pleasure of any kind in which the mind is at rest rather than conversation, in which one must think and speak with almost as much care as in the most serious business. Besides, the happiness of the English being founded on domestic life, it would not suit them that their wives should, as in France, make a kind of family selection of a certain number of persons constantly brought together.

We must not, however, deny that with all these honorable motives are mixed certain defects, the natural results of all large associations of men. In the first place, although in England there is much more pride than vanity, a good deal of stress is laid on marking by manners the ranks which most of the institutions tend to bring closer together. There prevails a certain degree of egoism in the habits, and sometimes in the character. Wealth and the tastes created by wealth are the cause of it: people are not disposed to submit to inconvenience in anything, so great is their power of being comfortable in everything. Family ties, so intimate as regards marriage, are far from intimate in other relations, because the substitutions[2] render the eldest sons too independent of their parents, and separate also the interest of the younger brothers from those of the inheritor of the fortune. The entails[3] necessary to the support of the peerage ought not, perhaps, to be extended to other classes of proprietors; it is a remnant of the feudal system, of which one ought, if possible, to lessen the vexatious consequences. From this it happens likewise that most of the women are without marriage portions, and that in a country where the institution of convents cannot exist, there are a number of young ladies whom their mothers have a great desire to get married, and who may, with reason, be

2. The substitutions were legal procedures by which one could bequeath to someone all or a part of one's assets with the mandate of transmitting them to a third person designated in advance. The substitutions were outlawed by the Convention in October 1792.

3. In French, *majorats*, a form of substitution required to support a title of nobility. The *majorats* were abolished in France in June 1790, reestablished by Napoléon in 1806, and outlawed in 1835.

uneasy as to their prospects. This inconvenience produced by the unequal partition of fortunes is sensibly felt in society; for the unmarried men take up too much of the attention of the women, and wealth in general, far from conducing to the pleasure of social intercourse, is necessarily hurtful to it. A very considerable fortune is required to receive one's friends in the country, which is, however, the most agreeable mode of living in England: fortune is necessary for all the relations of society; not that people would take pride in a sumptuous mode of life; but the importance attached by everybody to the kind of enjoyment called *comfortable* would prevent any person from venturing, as was formerly the case in the most agreeable societies in Paris, to make up for a bad dinner by amusing anecdotes.

In all countries the pretensions of young persons of fashion are engrafted on national defects; they exhibit a caricature of these defects, but a caricature has always some traits of an original. In France the pretenders to elegance endeavored to strike and tried to dazzle by all possible means, good or bad. In England this same class of persons wish to be distinguished as disdainful, indifferent, and completely satiated of everything. This is disagreeable enough; but in what country of the world is not self-conceit a resource of vanity to conceal natural mediocrity? Among a people where everything bears a salient aspect, as in England, contrasts are the more striking. Fashion has remarkable influence on the habits of life, and yet there is no nation in which one finds so many examples of what is called *eccentricity*, that is, a mode of life altogether original, and which makes no account of the opinion of others. The difference between the men who live under the control of others and those who live to themselves is recognized everywhere; but this opposition of character is rendered more conspicuous by the singular mixture of timidity and independence remarkable among the English. They do nothing by halves, and they pass all at once from a slavish adherence to the most minute usages to the most complete indifference as to what the world may say of them. Yet the dread of ridicule is one of the principal causes of the coldness that prevails in English society: people are never accused of insipidity for keeping silence; and as nobody requires of you to animate the conversation, one is more impressed by the risks to which one exposes oneself by speaking than by the inconvenience of silence. In the country where people have the greatest attachment to the liberty of the press, and where they care the least for the attacks of the newspapers, the sarcasms of society are very much dreaded. Newspapers are considered the volunteers of political parties, and in this as in other respects, the English are very fond of keeping up a conflict; but slander and irony, when they take place in society, irritate highly the delicacy of the women and the pride of the men. This is the reason that people come as little forward as possible in the presence of others. Animation and grace necessarily lose greatly by this. In no country of the world have reserve and taciturnity ever, I believe, been carried so far as in certain societies in England; and if one falls into such companies, it is easy to conceive how a disrelish of life may take possession of those who find themselves confined to them. But out of these frozen circles, what satisfaction of mind and heart may not be found in English society when one is happily placed there? The favor or dislike of ministers and the court are absolutely of no account in the relations of life; and you would make an Englishman blush were you to appear to think of the office which he holds or of the influence he may possess. A sentiment of pride always makes him think that these circumstances neither add to nor deduct in the slightest degree from his personal merit. Political disappointments cannot have any influence on the pleasures enjoyed in high society; the party of opposition is as brilliant as the party in power: fortune, rank, intellect, talents, virtues are shared among them; and never do either of the two think of drawing near to or keeping at a distance from a person by those calculations of ambition which have always prevailed in France. To quit one's friends because they are out of power and to draw near to them because they possess it is a kind of tactics almost unknown in England; and if the applause of society does not lead to public employment, at least the liberty of society is not impaired by combinations foreign to the pleasures which may be tasted there. One finds there almost invariably the security and the truth which form the bases of all enjoyment, because they form their security. You have not to dread those perpetual broils which in other countries fill life with disquietude. What you possess in point of connection and friendship you can lose only by your own fault, and you never have reason to doubt the expressions of benevolence addressed to you, for they will be surpassed by the actual performance and consecrated by time. Truth, above all, is one of the most distinguished qualities of the English character. The publicity that prevails in business, the discussions by which people arrive at the bottom of everything have doubtless contributed to this habit of absolute truth which cannot exist but in a country where dissimulation leads to nothing but the mortification of being exposed.

It has been much repeated on the Continent that the English are not polite, and a certain habit of independence, a great aversion to restraint may have given rise to this opinion. But I know no politeness, no protection, so delicate as that of the English toward women in every circumstance of life. Is there question of danger, of trouble, of a service to be rendered, there is nothing that they neglect to aid the weaker sex. From the seamen who, amidst the storm, support your tottering steps to English gentlemen of the highest rank, never does a woman find herself exposed to any difficulty whatever without being supported; and everywhere do we find that happy mixture which is characteristic of England, a republican austerity in domestic life and a chivalrous spirit in the relations of society.

A quality not less amiable in the English is their disposition to enthusiasm.[4] This people can see nothing remarkable without encouraging it by the most flattering praises. One acts then very rightly in going to England, in whatever state of misfortune one is placed, if conscious of possessing in oneself anything that is truly distinguished. But if one arrives there like most of the rich idlers of Europe, who travel to pass a carnival in Italy and a spring in London, there is no country that more disappoints expectation; and we shall certainly quit it without suspecting that we have seen the finest model of social order, and the only one which for a long time supported our hopes in human nature.

I shall never forget the society of Lord Grey, Lord Lansdowne, and Lord Harrowby. I cite their names because they all three belong to different parties,[5] or to shades of different parties, which comprise almost all

4. On the issue of enthusiasm, also see the last three chapters of Madame de Staël's *On Germany* (bk. II, pt. IV, chaps. x–xii).

5. Lord Grey (1764–1845) and Lord Lansdowne (1780–1863) were Whigs; Lord Harrowby (1762–1847) was a Tory.

the political opinions of England. There are other names which I should, in like manner, have had much pleasure in mentioning.

Lord Grey is one of the most ardent friends of liberty in the House of Peers: the nobleness of his birth, of his figure, and of his manners preserves him most decidedly from that kind of vulgar popularity which some are eager to attribute to the partisans of the rights of nations; and I would defy anyone not to feel for him every kind of respect. His eloquence in Parliament is generally admired. To eloquence of language he joins a force of interior conviction which makes his audience participate in his feelings. Political questions produce emotion in him because a generous enthusiasm is the source of his opinions. As in company he always expresses himself with calmness and simplicity on topics that interest him the most, it is by the paleness of his look that we sometimes become aware of the keenness of his feelings; but it is without desiring either to conceal or display the affections of his soul that he speaks on subjects for which he would give up his life. It is well known that he has twice refused to be prime minister because he could not agree in certain points with the prince who was ready to appoint him. Whatever diversity of opinion there may be on the motives of that resolution, nothing appears more natural in England than to decline being minister. I would not then notice the refusal of Lord Grey had his acceptance implied the slightest renunciation of his political principles; but the scruples by which he was determined were carried too far to be approved by everybody. And yet the men of his party, while they censured him in this respect, did not think it possible to accept without him any of the offices that were offered to them.

The house of Lord Grey offers an example of those domestic virtues so rare elsewhere in the highest class. His wife, who lives only for him, is worthy, by her sentiments, of the honor that Heaven has allotted her in uniting her with such a man. Thirteen children, still young, are educated by their parents and live with them, during eight months of the year, at their country seat in the extremity of England, where they have hardly ever any other variety than their family circle and their habitual reading. I happened to be one evening in London in this sanctuary of the most noble and affecting virtues; Lady Grey had the politeness to ask her daughters to play music; and four of these young persons, of angelic candor and grace, played duets on the harp and piano with a harmony that was admirable and that showed a great habit of practicing together; their father listened to them with affecting sensibility. The virtues which he displays in his family afford a pledge of the purity of the vows that he makes for his country.

Lord Lansdowne is also a member of the opposition; but, less decided in his political opinions, it is by a profound study of administration and finance that he has already served and will still serve his country. Affluent and high in rank, young and singularly fortunate in the choice of his domestic partner, none of these advantages dispose him to indolence; and it is by his superior merit that he stands in the foremost rank in a country where nothing can exempt a man from owing distinction to personal exertion. At his seat at Bowood, I have met the most delightful assemblage of enlightened men that England, and consequently the world, can offer. Sir James Mackintosh, pointed out by public opinion to continue Hume and to surpass him by writing the history of the constitutional liberty of England, a man of such universal information and such brilliancy of conversation that the English quote him with pride to foreigners to prove that in this respect also they are capable of taking a lead; Sir Samuel Romilly,[6] the luminary and honor of that English jurisprudence which in itself is the object of the respect of all mankind; poets, literary men not less distinguished in their career than statesmen in politics; all contributed to the pure splendor of such a society, and of the illustrious master of the house. For in England the culture of intellect and the practice of morality are almost always combined; in fact, at a certain level they do not admit of separation.

Lord Harrowby, president of the Privy Council, is naturally a member of the ministerial, or Tory, party; but in the same way that Lord Grey has all the dignity of aristocracy in his character, Lord Harrowby partakes, by his mind, of all the knowledge of the liberal party. He knows foreign literature, and that of France in particular, somewhat better than ourselves.

6. Samuel Romilly (1757–1818) was a prominent Whig legal reformer, close friend of Mirabeau, and author of, among others, *Thoughts on the Probable Influence of the Late Revolution in France upon Great Britain* (1790).

I had the honor of seeing him sometimes amidst the most critical moments of the war before last;[7] and while in other quarters one is obliged to behave and speak in a certain way before a minister when public affairs are discussed, Lord Harrowby would have felt himself offended had people considered him otherwise than personally when conversing on questions of general interest. We see neither at his table nor at that of the other English ministers any of those subordinate flatterers who surround powerful people in an absolute monarchy. There is in England no class in which such men could be found, nor any men in office who would listen to them. As a speaker, Lord Harrowby is distinguished for the purity of his language and the brilliant irony of which he knows how to make an appropriate use. Accordingly he justly attaches much more importance to his personal reputation than to his temporary office. Lord Harrowby, seconded by his intelligent partner, exhibits in his house the most complete example of what a conversation may be when literary and political by turns, and when both subjects are treated with equal ease.

In France we have a number of women who have acquired reputation merely by the power of conversation or by writing letters which resembled conversation.[8] Madame de Sévigné is the first of all in this department; but subsequently Madame de Tencin, Madame du Deffant, Madlle. de l'Espinasse, and several others have acquired celebrity by the quality of their mind. I have already said that the state of society in England hardly admitted of distinction in this way, and that examples of it could not be cited. There are, however, several women remarkable as writers: Miss Edgeworth, Madame D'Arblay, formerly Miss Burney, Mrs. Hannah Moore, Mrs. Inchbald, Mrs. Opie, Miss Baillie are admired in England and read with avidity in French; but they live in general in complete retirement, and their influence is confined to their books. Were we to cite a woman uniting in the highest degree that which constitutes the strength and moral beauty of the English character, it would be necessary to seek her in history.

Lady Russell, the wife of the illustrious Lord Russell, who was be-

7. Allusion to the war against Napoléon (1813–14).
8. For more information on this issue, see Ozouf, *Women's Words*.

headed under Charles II for opposing the encroachments of royal power, seems to me the true model of an Englishwoman in all her perfection. The court that tried Lord Russell asked him what person he desired to serve him as secretary during his trial; he made choice of Lady Russell *because,* he said, *she unites the information of a man to the tender affection of a wife.* Lady Russell, who adored her husband, sustained, nevertheless, the presence of his iniquitous judges and the barbarous sophistry of their questions with all the presence of mind with which the hope of being useful inspired her; but it was in vain. When the sentence of death was pronounced, Lady Russell threw herself at the feet of Charles II, imploring him in the name of Lord Southampton, whose daughter she was, and who had devoted himself for the cause of Charles I. But the remembrance of services rendered to the father had no effect on the son, whose frivolity did not prevent his being cruel. Lord Russell, in parting from his wife to go to the scaffold, pronounced these memorable words: "Now the bitterness of death is past." There are indeed affections of which the whole of our existence may be composed.[9]

Letters written by Lady Russell after the death of her husband have been published and bear the stamp of the deepest affliction, moderated by religious resignation. She lived to bring up her children; she lived because she did not think it lawful to give herself a voluntary death. By weeping continually she became blind, and the remembrance of him she had so loved was ever alive in her heart. She had one moment of joy when liberty was established in 1688, when the sentence pronounced against Lord Russell was repealed, and his opinions triumphed. The partisans of William III, and Queen Anne herself, often consulted Lady Russell on public affairs as having preserved some sparks of the light of Lord Russell. It was by that title she answered their call, and, amidst the deep mourning

9. Lady Russell (1636–1723) was the second daughter of Thomas Wriothesley, the fourth Earl of Southampton. Her second husband, Lord William Russell, was charged with complicity in the Rye House Plot in 1683 and was convicted of high treason and executed. In *L'amour dans le mariage,* Guizot eulogized Lady Russell; Guizot's book appeared in English in New York in 1864 under the title *Love in Marriage* and in London in 1883 as *The Devoted Life of Rachel Lady Russell.* For more information, see Schwoerer, "William, Lord Russell: The Making of a Martyr, 1683–1983."

of her soul, interested herself in the noble cause for which the blood of her husband had been shed. She appeared always the widow of Lord Russell, and it is by the constancy of that feeling that she claims admiration. Such again would a true Englishwoman be if a scene so tragical, a trial so terrible, could be renewed in our days, and if, thanks to liberty, such calamities were not removed forever. The duration of the sorrows caused by the loss of those we love often absorbs, in England, the life of persons by whom they are felt. If women there have not personally active habits, they live so much more strongly in the objects of their attachment. The dead are not forgotten in that country, where the human soul possesses all its beauty; and that honorable constancy which struggles with the instability of this world exalts the feelings of the heart to the rank of things eternal.

CHAPTER VII

Of the Conduct of the English
Government Outside of England.

In expressing, as much as I could, my admiration for the English nation, I have never ceased to attribute its superiority over the rest of Europe to its political institutions. It remains for us to offer a sad proof of this assertion: it is that, in things where the constitution does not command, the English government justly incurs the same reproaches which absolute power has ever deserved on earth. If, by some circumstances which are not met with in history, a nation had possessed, a hundred years before the rest of Europe, the art of printing, the compass, and, what is more valuable, a religion which is only a sanction of the purest morality, that nation would certainly be far superior to those who had not obtained similar advantages. The same may be said of the benefits of a free constitution; but these benefits are necessarily limited to the country which that constitution governs. When Englishmen exercise military or diplomatic employments on the Continent, it is still probable that men brought up in the atmosphere of all the virtues participate in them individually. But it is possible that power, which corrupts almost all men when they go beyond the circle of the dominion of law, may have misled many Englishmen when they had to render an account of their conduct abroad to ministers only, and not to the nation. In truth, that nation, so enlightened in other things, is ill-informed of what passes on the Continent: it lives in the interior of its own country, if we may use the expression, like every man in his own house; and it is only after a length of time that it learns the history of Europe, in which her ministers often act too great a part, by means of its blood and treasures. The conclusion is that every country, at every time, should defend itself from the influence of foreigners, be they who they may; for the nations who are the most free at home may have rulers very jealous of the prosperity of other states, and may become the oppressors of their neighbors if they find a favorable opportunity.

Let us, however, examine how far there is truth in what is alleged of the conduct of the English out of their country. When, unfortunately for themselves, they were obliged to send troops to the Continent, those troops observed the most perfect discipline. The disinterestedness of the English army and of its commanders cannot be disputed; we have seen them paying in an enemy's country more regularly than the enemy paid their own countrymen, and never do they neglect to blend the cares of humanity with the calamities of war. Sir Sidney Smith,[1] in Egypt, protected the envoys of the French army in his own tent; and often declared to his allies, the Turks, that he would perish sooner than suffer the rights of nations to be violated toward his enemies. During the retreat of General Moore[2] in Spain, English officers threw themselves into a river where some Frenchmen were on the point of drowning in order to save them from a danger to which they were exposed by accident, and not by arms. Finally, there is no occasion in which the army of the Duke of Wellington, directed by the magnanimity and the conscientious severity of its illustrious chief, has not sought to relieve the inhabitants of the countries through which it passed. The splendor of English bravery, we must acknowledge, has never been sullied by cruelty or by pillage.

The military force transported to the colonies, and particularly to India, ought not to be made responsible for the acts of authority of which there may be reason to complain. The regular troops obey passively in countries considered as subjected, and which are not protected at all by the constitution. But in the colonies, as elsewhere, the English officers cannot be accused of depredation; it is the persons holding civil employments who are reproached with enriching themselves by unlawful means. In fact, the conduct of these persons during the first years of the conquest of India deserves the highest blame and furnishes another proof of what we cannot too often repeat, that every man charged with the command of others, if

1. Sidney Smith (1764–1840) was an admiral in the English navy.
2. Sir John Moore (1761–1809) was a prominent officer in the English army.

he is not himself subject to the law, obeys nothing but his passions. But since the trial of Mr. Hastings, the attention of the English nation being directed toward the frightful abuses which till then had been tolerated in India, the public spirit has obliged government to attend to them.[3] Lord Cornwallis carried his virtues, and Lord Wellesley his knowledge, to a country necessarily unhappy because subjected to a foreign dominion.[4] But the good performed by these two governors is felt every day more and more. There existed no courts of justice in India to which an appeal could be made from the injustice of men in office; the proportion of taxes was not at all fixed. Courts are now established according to the English form; some natives even occupy places of the second rank; the taxes are fixed by a regular scale and cannot be augmented. If persons in office enrich themselves now, it is because their appointments are very considerable. Three-fourths of the revenue of the country are consumed in the country itself; commerce is free in the interior; the corn trade in particular, which had given rise to so cruel a monopoly, is now on a footing more favorable to the Indians than to government.

England has adopted the principle of governing the inhabitants of the country according to their own laws. But the very toleration by which the English distinguish themselves so honorably from their predecessors in the government of India, whether Mahometans or Christians, obliges them to employ no other arms than those of persuasion in order to destroy prejudices which have taken root for thousands of years. The difference of castes is still humiliating to human nature, and the power of fanaticism is such that the English have not hitherto been able to prevent women from burning themselves alive after the death of their husbands. The only triumph which they have obtained over superstition has been that of pre-

3. Warren Hastings (1732–1818) was the first governor-general of British India, from 1773 to 1785. He was impeached in 1787 for corruption (Burke was one of his most vocal critics) and acquitted in 1795.

4. Lord Cornwallis and Lord Wellesley were governors of India. During his tenure (1786–93), Lord Cornwallis introduced several judicial reforms and set up the criminal courts. Lord Wellesley, who served as governor-general between 1798 and 1805, extended the dominions of the British in India by introducing the Subsidiary Alliance system, which brought the Indian states within the purview of the British power of jurisdiction.

venting mothers from throwing their children into the Ganges in order to send them to paradise. Attempts are being made to establish respect for an oath among them, and hopes are still entertained of being able to diffuse Christianity among them at some future time. Public education is very carefully attended to by the English in authority, and it was at Madras that Dr. Bell established his first school. In short, it may be hoped that the example of the English will form those nations sufficiently to enable them to give themselves one day an independent political existence. Every enlightened man in England would applaud the loss of India if it took place in consequence of the benefits conferred on it by government. It is one of the prejudices of the Continent to believe the power of the English connected with the possession of India; that oriental empire is almost an affair of luxury and contributes more to splendor than to real strength. England lost her American provinces and her commerce has been increased by it. Were the colonies that remain to her to declare themselves independent, she would still possess her naval and commercial superiority because she has in herself a principle of action, of progress, and of duration which places her always above exterior circumstances.

It has been said on the Continent that the slave trade was suppressed in England from political calculation in order to ruin the colonies of other countries by that abolition. Nothing is more false in every point of view. The English Parliament, pressed by Mr. Wilberforce, debated this question during twenty years, in which humanity struggled with what apparently was interest.[5] The merchants of Liverpool and of various parts of England demanded vehemently the continuance of the trade. The colonists talked of that abolition as certain persons in France express themselves at present on the liberty of the press and political rights. If you would believe the colonists, that person must be a Jacobin who could wish to put an end to the buying and selling of men. Maledictions against philosophy in the name of that superior wisdom which pretends to rise above it by maintaining things as they are, even when they are abominable; sarcasms without number on philanthropy toward the Africans or fraternity with negroes; finally, the whole arsenal of personal interest was poured

5. On Wilberforce, see note 14, p. 656, above.

forth in England, as elsewhere, by the colonists, by that species of privileged persons who, fearing a diminution of their income, defended it in
the name of the public good. Nevertheless, when England pronounced the
abolition of the slave trade, in 1806, almost all the colonies of Europe were
in her hands, and if ever it could be injurious to be just, it was on this
occasion. There has since happened what always will happen—a resolution commanded by religion and philosophy has not produced the least
political inconvenience. In a short space of time, good treatment, by increasing the number of the slaves, has made up for the wretched cargoes
imported every year, and justice has found her place, because the true
nature of things always fits in with her.

The English ministry, then of the Whig party, had proposed a bill for
the abolition of the slave trade: they gave in their resignation to the King
because they had not obtained from him the emancipation of the Catholics. But Lord Holland, the nephew of Mr. Fox and heir of the principles,
of the knowledge, and of the friends of his uncle, reserved to himself the
noble satisfaction of still carrying to the House of Peers the King's sanction to the act for the abolition of the slave trade. Mr. Clarkson,[6] one of
the virtuous men who labored during twenty years with Mr. Wilberforce
at the accomplishment of this eminently Christian work, in giving an account of this meeting says that at the moment when the bill received the
royal assent, a ray of sunshine, as if to celebrate this affecting triumph,
darted from the clouds which that day covered the sky. Certainly, if it
were tedious to hear so much spoken of the fine weather which was said
to consecrate the military parades of Bonaparte, pious minds may surely
be permitted to hope for a benevolent token from their Creator while they
are burning on his altar that incense which is most pleasing to him, the
doing of good to mankind. Such was on this occasion the sole policy of
England, and when the Parliament, after public debates, adopts any decision whatever, its principal aim is almost always the good of humanity.
But can it be denied, it will be said, that England is encroaching and domineering abroad? I now come to her faults, or rather to those of her min-

---

6. Thomas Clarkson (1760–1846), a prominent English abolitionist educated at Cambridge, played a key role in the abolition of the slave trade in 1833.

istry; for the party, and a very numerous one it is, that disapproves the conduct of government in this respect cannot be accused of it.

There is a people who will one day be very great: these are the Americans. One stain only obscures the perfect splendor of reason that vivifies that country; slavery still subsists in the Southern provinces; but when the Congress shall have found a remedy for that evil, how shall we be able to refuse the most profound respect to the institutions of the United States? Whence comes it then that many English allow themselves to speak with disdain of such a people? "They are shopkeepers," they repeat. And how did the courtiers of Louis XIV talk of the English themselves? The people of Bonaparte's court also, what did they say? Do not the nobility that are unemployed, or that are employed only in the service of a prince, disdain that hereditary magistracy of the English which is founded solely on its utility to the whole nation? The Americans, it is true, declared war against England at a very ill-chosen time[7] with respect to Europe; for England then resisted alone the power of Bonaparte. But America on this occasion looked only to what concerned her own interest; and she can certainly not be suspected of having wished to favor the imperial system. Nations have not yet attained that noble feeling of humanity which should extend itself from one part of the world to the other. As neighbors they feel a mutual hatred; while those at a distance are unknown to each other. But could that ignorance of the affairs of Europe which impelled the Americans to declare war unseasonably against England justify the burning of Washington? It was not warlike establishments that were destroyed, but peaceful edifices sacred to national representation, to public instruction, to the transplantation of arts and sciences into a country once covered by forests and conquered only by the labor of men on savage nature. What is there more honorable for mankind than this new world, which has established itself without the prejudices of the old; this new world where religion is in all its fervor without needing the support of the state to maintain it; where the law commands by the respect which it inspires, without being enforced by any military power? It is possible, alas! that Europe may be destined, like Asia, to exhibit one day the spectacle of a stationary civi-

---

7. In June 1812, during the Napoléonic Wars.

lization,[8] which, not having been able to advance, has become degraded. But does it thence follow that England, old and free, should refuse the tribute of admiration inspired by the progress of America because former resentments and some features of resemblance excite a family hatred between the two countries?

Finally, what will posterity say of the recent conduct of the English ministry toward France?[9] I shall confess I cannot approach this subject without being seized with an inward tremor, and yet, were it necessary, I would not hesitate to declare that if one of the two nations, France or England, must be annihilated, it would be better that that country which can reckon a hundred years of liberty, a hundred years of knowledge, a hundred years of virtue should preserve the trust which Providence has placed in its hands. But does this cruel alternative exist? And why has not a rivalship of so many ages led the English government to think that it is a duty of chivalry, as well as of justice, not to oppress that France which in her contests with England, during the whole course of their common history, animated her efforts by a generous jealousy? The opposition party has been at all times more liberal and better informed respecting the affairs of the Continent than the party in power; it ought, of course, to have been entrusted with the conclusion of peace. Moreover, it was the rule in England that peace ought not to be signed by the same ministers who had conducted the war. It is felt that the irritation against the enemy which serves to carry on war with vigor leads to the abuse of victory; and this manner of reasoning is no less just than favorable to real peace, which must not merely be signed, but must be established in the minds and hearts. Unfortunately, the party of opposition had committed the error of supporting Bonaparte. It would have been more natural to have seen his despotic system defended by the friends of power and opposed by the friends of liberty. But the question became very complex in England, as everywhere else; the partisans of the principles of the Revolution thought it their duty to support a tyranny for life to prevent, in various places, the

8. This was the conventional image of Asia (i.e., India and China) in nineteenth-century Europe.

9. An allusion to the two treaties of Paris (1814 and 1815), which brought France back to the borders of 1792 and imposed heavy reparations on the French.

return of more lasting forms of despotism. But they did not see that one kind of absolute power opens the way for all others; and that by again giving to the French the habits of servitude, Bonaparte had destroyed the energy of public spirit. One peculiarity of the English constitution, which we have already noticed, is the necessity in which the opposition believe themselves placed of opposing the government on all possible grounds. This habit, applicable only to ordinary circumstances, ought to have been relinquished at a crisis when the contest was so national that even the existence of the country depended on its issue. The opposition ought to have frankly joined government against Bonaparte; for the government, by opposing him with perseverance, nobly fulfilled its duty. The opposition made its stand on the desire of peace, which is in general very welcome to the people; but on this occasion, the good sense and energy of the English impelled them to war. They felt that it was impossible to treat with Bonaparte; and all that the government and Lord Wellington did to overthrow him contributed powerfully to the repose and greatness of England. But at this period when the nation had reached the summit of prosperity, at this period when the English government deserved a vote of thanks for the part it could claim in the triumph of its heroes, the fatality which seizes all men who have reached the height of power marked the treaty of Paris with the seal of reprobation.

The English ministry had already had the misfortune to be represented at the Congress of Vienna by a man whose private virtues are highly worthy of esteem, but who has done more harm to the cause of nations than any diplomatist of the Continent.[10] An Englishman who reviles liberty is a false brother more dangerous than strangers, since he seems to speak of what he knows and to do the honors of what he possesses. The speeches of Lord Castlereagh in Parliament are stamped with a kind of cold irony singularly pernicious when applied to all that is dignified in this world. For most of those who defend generous sentiments are easily discouraged when a minister in power treats their wishes as chimerical, when he makes

10. Robert Stewart, second Marquess of Londonderry and Viscount Castlereagh (1769–1822), was a prominent English diplomat who represented England at the Congress of Vienna. In 1804 Pitt appointed Castlereagh secretary of state for war and the colonies. He also served as foreign secretary from 1812 to 1822.

a mockery of liberty, as of perfect love, and puts on the appearance of an indulgent air toward those who cherish it by imputing to them nothing but an innocent folly.

The deputies of several countries of Europe, at present weak but formerly independent, came to solicit some rights, some securities from the representative of the power which they adored as free. They returned with an anguished heart, not knowing whether Bonaparte or the most respectable nation in the world had done them most lasting mischief. One day, their conferences will be published and history can hardly present a more remarkable document. "What!" they said to the English minister, "does not the prosperity, the glory of your country arise from this constitution, some principles of which we demand, when you are pleased to dispose of us for this pretended balance of which we form one of the make-weights in your scales?" "Yes," they were answered, with a sarcastic smile, "liberty is a usage of England; but it is not suitable to other countries." The only one[11] among kings, or among men, that ever put to the torture not his enemies but his friends has distributed, according to his good pleasure, the scaffold, the galleys, and the prison among citizens who, having fought in defense of their country under the standard of England, claimed her support as having, by the generous avowal of Lord Wellington, powerfully aided his efforts. Did England protect them? The North Americans would willingly support the Americans of Mexico and Peru, whose love for independence must have increased when they have seen the torture and the inquisition restored at Madrid. Well, what fears the Congress of the North in succoring its brethren of the South?[12] The alliance of England with Spain. In all directions the influence of the English government is dreaded, precisely in a contrary sense to the support which the oppressed have a right to hope from it.

But let us return, with all our soul and all our strength, to that France which alone we know. "During twenty-five years," it is said, "she has incessantly tormented Europe by her democratic excesses and her military

11. King Ferdinand VII of Spain.

12. In 1815 Spain was counting on the support of England to suppress the independence movements in Central and Latin America.

despotism. England has suffered cruelly by her continual attacks, and the English have made immense sacrifices to defend Europe. It is perfectly just that in her turn France should expiate the evil of which she has been the cause." Everything in these accusations is true except the conclusion that is drawn from them. Of what use is the law of retaliation in general, and above all, the law of retaliation exercised against a nation? Is a people today what it was yesterday? Does not a new and innocent generation come to replace that which has been found guilty? Will you comprise in the same proscription women, children, old men, even the victims of the tyranny that has been overthrown? The unhappy conscripts, concealed in woods to escape the wars of Bonaparte, but who, when forced to carry arms, conducted themselves like intrepid warriors; the fathers of families ruined already by the sacrifices they have made to purchase the exemption of their sons; and what, finally! do so many classes of men, on whom public misfortune presses equally although they have certainly not borne an equal share in the fault—do they deserve to suffer on account of a few? If it be hardly practicable in a question of political opinion to try one man with equity, how then can a nation be tried? The conduct of Bonaparte toward Prussia was taken as a model in the second treaty of Paris; in pursuance of which fortresses and provinces are occupied by one hundred and fifty thousand foreign soldiers.[13] Can the French be in this manner persuaded that Bonaparte was unjust and that they ought to hate him? They would have been better convinced of it if his doctrine had in no respect been followed. And what did the proclamation of the Allies promise? Peace to France so soon as Bonaparte should cease to be her chief. Ought not the promise of powers whose decisions were free to be as sacred as the oaths of the French army pronounced in the presence of foreigners? And because the ministers of Europe commit the error of placing in the island of Elba a General, the sight of whom cannot but excite the emotions of his soldiers, must enormous contributions exhaust the poor during five years? And what is still more grievous, must foreigners humiliate the French as the French humiliated other nations; that is, provoke, in the soul of Frenchmen, the same feelings which raised up Europe against them?

13. Napoléon imposed extremely harsh conditions on Prussia in 1806 at Tilsit.

Is it supposed that the abuse of a nation formerly so strong is likely to be as effectual as the punishment inflicted on students at school? Certainly, if France allows herself to be instructed in this manner; if she learns humility toward foreigners when they are the stronger party, after having made an abuse of victory when she had triumphed over them, she will have deserved her fate.

But some persons will still say, what then was to be done to restrain a nation always prone to conquest, and which had taken back its former chief only in the hope of again enslaving Europe? I have mentioned in the preceding chapters what I consider to be incontestable, that is, that the French nation will never be sincerely tranquil until she shall have secured the object of her efforts, a constitutional monarchy. But in putting aside for a moment this view of the case, was not the dissolution of the army, the carrying off the artillery, the levying contributions a sufficient assurance that France, thus weakened, would neither be desirous nor able to go beyond her limits? Is it not clear to every observer that the hundred and fifty thousand men who occupy France have but two objects, either to partition her territory or to prescribe laws for her interior government? Partition her territory! Alas! Since policy committed the human sacrifice of Poland, the mangled remains of that unhappy country still agitate Europe; its wrecks are incessantly rekindled to serve it as firebrands. Is it to strengthen the present government that a hundred and fifty thousand soldiers occupy our territory? Government has more effectual means of maintaining itself; for as it is destined to be one day supported by Frenchmen only, the foreign troops who remain in France, the exorbitant contributions which they exact excite daily a vague discontent which is not always justly directed to the proper objects.

I willingly admit, however, that England as well as Europe had a right to desire the return of the former dynasty of France; and that, in particular, the high degree of wisdom evinced by the King in the first year of his restoration rendered it a duty to make him a reparation for the cruel return of Bonaparte. But ought not the English ministers, who know better than any ministry whatever, by the history of their country, the effects of a long revolution on the public mind, ought they not to maintain constitutional securities with as much care as they maintain the ancient dynasty? Since they brought back the royal family, ought they not to be watchful that the rights of the nation should be as well respected as those of legitimacy? Is there but one family in France, although that family be royal? And ought the engagements taken by that family toward twenty-five million persons to be broken for the sake of pleasing a few ultraroyalists?* Shall the name of the charter be still pronounced at a time when there is not a shadow of the liberty of the press; when the English newspapers cannot penetrate into France; when thousands of individuals are imprisoned without examination; when most of the military men brought to trial are condemned to death by extraordinary tribunals, by prevotal courts, by courts-martial composed of the very men against whom the accused have fought during twenty-five years; when most of the forms are violated in these trials, counsel interrupted or reprimanded; finally, when arbitrary rule prevails everywhere and the charter[14] nowhere, though it ought to be defended as zealously as the throne, since it was the safeguard of the nation? Could it be pretended that the election of the deputies who suspended that charter was regular? Do we not know that twenty persons named by the prefects were sent into each electoral college to make choice there of the enemies of every free institution as pretended representatives of a nation which, since 1789, has been invariable only on one single point, the hatred that it has shown for their power? A hundred and eighty Protestants were massacred in the department of the Gard[15] without a single man having suffered death in punishment of these crimes, without the terror caused by these assassinations having permitted the courts to condemn them. It was very readily asserted that those who perished were Bonapartists, as if it were not also necessary to prevent Bonapartists from being massacred. But this imputation was likewise as false as all those which are commonly cast upon victims. The man who has not been tried is innocent; still more

---

* All this was written during the session of 1815, and it is known that no one was more eager than Madame de Staël to do homage to the beneficial effects of the *ordonnance* of the 5th of September of that year.—(*Note of the Editors.*)

14. The Charter of 1814. For more information about the political context and the parliamentary debates during the first years of the Restoration, see Craiutu, *Liberalism Under Siege*, 19–85, 192–97.

15. The so-called White Terror of 1815.

the man who is assassinated; still more the women who have perished in these bloody scenes. The murderers, in their atrocious songs, pointed out for the poignard those who profess the same religion as the English and the most enlightened half of Europe. This English government, which has re-established the papal throne, sees the Protestants threatened in France; and far from coming to their aid, adopts against them those political pretexts which the parties have employed against each other from the beginning of the Revolution. An end should be put to the argument of force which might be applied in turn to the opposite factions by merely changing proper names. Would the English government now have the same antipathy for Protestantism as for republics? Bonaparte also was in many respects of this way of thinking. The inheritance of his principles is fallen to certain diplomatists like the conquests of Alexander to his generals; but conquests, however much to be condemned, are better than a doctrine founded on the degradation of mankind. Will the English ministry still be permitted to say that it considers it a duty not to interfere in the interior affairs of France? Must it not be interdicted from such an excuse? I ask it in the name of the English people; in the name of that nation whose first virtue is sincerity, and which is unconsciously led astray into political perfidy. Can we repress the laugh of bitterness when we hear men who have twice disposed of the fate of France urge this hypocritical pretext only to avoid doing her a service, to avoid restoring to the Protestants the security that is due to them, to avoid demanding the sincere execution of the constitutional charter? For the friends of liberty are also the brethren of the English people in religion. What, Lord Wellington is officially charged by the powers of Europe with superintending France since he is charged to answer for her tranquillity; the note that invests him with that power is published; in that same note the Allied Powers have declared, and the declaration is honorable to them, that they considered the principles of the constitutional charter to be those that ought to govern France; a hundred and fifty thousand men are under the orders of him to whom such a dictatorship is granted; and the English government will still come forward and say that it cannot interfere in our affairs? Lord Castlereagh, who, in his capacity of Foreign Secretary, had declared in the House of Commons several weeks before the battle of Waterloo* that England did not in any manner pretend to impose a government upon France, the same man, in the same place, declares the following year† that if, at the expiration of the five years, France should be represented by another government, the English ministry would not be so absurd as to consider itself bound by the conditions of the treaty. But in the same speech in which this incredible declaration is made, the scruples of the noble Lord, in regard to the influence of the English government in France, revive as soon as he is asked to prevent the massacres of the Protestants and to guarantee to the French people some of the rights which it cannot lose without lacerating its bosom by civil war or without biting the dust like slaves. And let it not be pretended that the English people desires to make its enemies bear its yoke! It is proud, it has a right to be so, of twenty-five years and a day. The battle of Waterloo has filled it with a just pride. Ah! nations that have a country partake the laurels of victory with the army! Citizens are warriors, warriors are citizens; and of all the joys which God permits to man on earth, the most lively is perhaps that of the triumph of one's country. But this noble emotion, far from stifling generosity, re-animates it; and if the voice of Mr. Fox, so long admired, could be once more heard; if he should ask why English soldiers acted as jailers to France; why the army of a free people treats another people like a prisoner of war who has to pay his ransom to his conquerors: the English nation would learn that an injustice is committed in its name; and from that instant there would arise from all quarters, in its bosom, advocates of the cause of France. Could it not be asked, in the midst of the English Parliament, what England would now be if the troops of Louis XIV had taken possession of her territory at the time of the restoration of Charles II; if they had seen encamped in Westminster the French army that had triumphed on the Rhine; or, what would have been still more disastrous, the army which subsequently fought against the Protestants of the Cevennes? These armies would have re-established the Catholic worship and suppressed Par-

* Debate of 25th May 1815.
† Debate of 19th February 1816.

liament; for we see from the dispatches of the French ambassadors that Louis XIV offered them to Charles II with that intention. What would England then have become? Europe would have heard of nothing but the murder of Charles I, of the excesses of the Puritans in favor of equality, of the despotism of Cromwell, who made himself be felt abroad as at home, since Louis XIV put on mourning for him. Writers would have been found to maintain that this turbulent and sanguinary people ought to be brought back to its duty, and ought to resume the institutions that were those of their fathers at the time when their fathers had lost the liberty of their ancestors. But should we have seen that fine country at the height of power and glory which the universe admires today? An unsuccessful attempt to obtain liberty would have received the name of rebellion, crime, in short, every epithet lavished on nations when they desire to have rights and do not know how to obtain possession of them. The countries which were jealous of the maritime power of England under Cromwell would have taken delight in her humiliation. The ministers of Louis XIV would have said that the English were not made to be free, and Europe would not have been able to contemplate the beacon which has guided her in the tempest and ought to direct her course in the calm.

There are in France, it is said, none but extreme royalists or Bonapartists; and the two parties are equally, it must be confessed, favorers of despotism. The friends of liberty are, it is asserted, in small number and without strength to compete against these two inveterate factions. The friends of liberty, being virtuous and disinterested, cannot, I admit, contend actively against the eager passions of those whose only objects are money and place. But the nation is with them; all who are not paid, or do not aim at being paid, are on their side. The progress of the human mind is favorable to them from the very nature of things. They will succeed gradually, but surely, in founding in France a constitution similar to that of England, if England herself, who is the guide of the Continent, forbid her ministers to show themselves everywhere the enemies of the principles which she so well knows how to maintain at home.

CHAPTER VIII

Will Not the English Hereafter Lose Their Liberty?

Many enlightened persons who know to what a height the prosperity of the French nation would rise, were the political institutions of England established among them, are persuaded that the English are actuated by a previous jealousy and throw every obstacle in the way of their rivals obtaining the enjoyment of that liberty of which they know the advantages. In truth, I do not believe in such a feeling, at least on the part of the nation. It has pride enough to be convinced, and with reason, that for a long time still it will take the lead of all others; and were France to overtake and even surpass her in some respects, England would still preserve exclusive sources of power peculiar to her situation. As to the government, he who directs it, the Foreign Secretary, seems to have, as I have said, and as he himself has proved, such a contempt for liberty that I truly believe he would dispose of it at a cheap rate even to France; and yet the prohibition of export from England has been almost entirely confined to the principles of liberty, while we, on the other hand, would have wished that in this respect also the English had been pleased to impart to us the products of their industry.

The English government desires, at whatever sacrifice, to avoid a return of war; but it forgets that the most absolute kings of France never ceased to form hostile projects against England, and that a free constitution is a far better pledge for the stability of peace than the personal gratitude of princes. But what ought above all, in my opinion, to be represented to the English, even to those who are exclusively occupied with the interests of their country, is that if, for the sake of preventing the French from being factious or free, term it as you will, an English army must be kept up in the territory of France, the liberty of England becomes exposed by this convention so unworthy of her. A people does not accustom itself to violate national independence among its neighbors without losing some degrees of energy, some shades in the purity of doctrine when the point is to profess at home what is disavowed abroad. England partitioning Poland, England occupying Prussia in the style of Bonaparte would have less strength to resist the encroachments of its own government in the interior. An army on the Continent may involve her in new wars, and the state of her finances should make these wars an object of dread. To these considerations, which have already had a strong impact in Parliament at the time of the discussion of the property tax, we must add the most important of all, the imminent danger of the military spirit. The English, in doing injury to France, in carrying thither the poisoned arrows of Hercules, may, like Philoctetes, inflict a wound on themselves. They humiliate their rival, they trample her underfoot, but let them beware. The contagion threatens them; and if in compressing their enemies they should stifle the sacred fire of their own public spirit, the vengeance or the policy to which they abandon themselves would burst, like bad firearms, in their hands.

The enemies of the English constitution on the Continent are incessantly repeating that it will perish by the corruption of Parliament, and that ministerial influence will increase to such a point as to annihilate liberty: nothing of the kind is to be dreaded. The English Parliament always obeys national opinion, and that opinion cannot be corrupted in the sense attached to that expression, that is, be bribed. But that which is seductive for a whole nation is military glory; the pleasure which the youth find in a camp life, the ardent enjoyments procured to them by success in war are much more conformable to the taste of their age than the lasting benefits of liberty. A man must possess a degree of talent to rise in a civil career; but every vigorous arm can handle a saber, and the difficulty of distinguishing oneself in the military profession is by no means in proportion to the trouble necessary to think and become educated. The employments which in that career become numerous give government the means of holding in its dependence a very great number of families. The newly invented decorations offer to vanity recompenses which do not flow from the source of all fame, public opinion; finally, to keep up a considerable standing army is to sap the edifice of liberty in its foundation.

In a country where law reigns and where bravery founded on patriotic feelings is superior to all praise, in a country where the militia are worth as much as the regular troops, where, in a moment, the threat of a descent created not only an infantry but a cavalry equally fine and intrepid, why forge the instrument of despotism? All those political reasonings on the balance of Europe, those old systems which serve as a pretext to new usurpations, were they not known by the proud friends of English liberty when they would not permit the existence of a standing army, at least in such numbers as to make it a support to government? The spirit of subordination and of command together, that spirit necessary in an army, renders men incapable of knowing and respecting what is national in political powers. Already do we hear some English officers murmuring despotic phrases, although their accent and their language seem to yield with difficulty to the wilted words of servitude.

Lord Castlereagh said in the House of Commons that England could not rest contented with blue coats while all Europe was in arms. It is, however, the blue coats which have rendered the Continent tributary to England. It is because commerce and finances had liberty for their basis, that is, because the representatives of the nation lent their strength to government, that the lever which has poised the world could find its supporting point in an island less considerable than any of the countries to which she lent her aid. Make of this country a camp, and soon after a court, and you will see its misery and humiliation. But could the danger, which history points out in every page, not be foreseen, not be repelled by the first thinkers in Europe, whom the nature of the English government calls to take a part in public affairs? Military glory doubtless is the only seduction to be dreaded by energetic men; but as there is an energy far superior to that of the profession of arms, the love of liberty, and as this liberty inspires at once the highest degree of valor when our country is exposed and the greatest disdain for the military spirit when subordinate to a perfidious diplomacy; we ought to hope that the good sense of the English people and the intelligence of its representatives will save liberty from the only enemy against which it has to guard—continual war and that military spirit which war brings in its train.

What a contempt for knowledge, what impatience of the restraints of law, what a desire of power do we not see in all those that have long led the life of camps! Such men find as much difficulty in submitting to liberty as the nation in submitting to arbitrary rule; and in a free country, it is necessary that as far as possible every man should be a soldier, but that no one should be so exclusively. English liberty having nothing to dread but a military spirit, Parliament, it seems to me, should on that account take into its serious consideration the situation of France; it ought to do so likewise from that universal feeling of justice which is to be expected from the most enlightened assembly in Europe. Its own interest commands it, it is necessary to restore the spirit of liberty, naturally weakened by the reaction caused by the French Revolution; it is necessary to prevent the pretensions of vanity in the Continental style which have found their way into certain families. The English nation in all its extent is the aristocracy of the rest of the world by its knowledge and virtues. What would a few puerile disputes on genealogy be beside this intellectual pre-eminence? Finally, it is necessary to put an end to that contempt for nations on which the policy of the day is founded. That contempt, artfully spread abroad, might, like religious incredulity, attack the foundation of the finest of creeds in the very country where its temple has been consecrated.

Parliamentary reform, the emancipation of the Catholics, the situation of Ireland, all the different questions which can still be debated in the English Parliament will be resolved in conformity to the national interest and do not threaten the state with any danger. Parliamentary reform may be accomplished gradually by giving annually some additional members to towns that have lately become populous, and by suppressing, with indemnities, the rights of certain boroughs which have now scarcely any voters.[1] But property has such a sway in England that the partisans of disorder would never be chosen representatives of the people, were a par-

---

1. The famous Reform Bill of 1831–32 brought much-needed change to an electoral system that did not accurately reflect England's new political, social, and economic conditions.

liamentary reform in all its extent to be accomplished in a single day. Men of talent without fortune might perhaps thus lose the possibility of being returned, as the great proprietors of either party would no longer have seats to give to those who do not have the property necessary to get elected in counties and towns. The emancipation of the Irish Catholics is demanded by the spirit of universal toleration which ought to govern the world; yet those who oppose it do not reject this or that worship; but they dread the influence of a foreign sovereign, the Pope, in a country where the rights of citizens should take priority of everything. It is a question which the interest of the country will decide,[2] because the liberty of the press and of public debate allows no ignorance to prevail in England in what concerns the interior of the country. Not a fault would be committed were foreign affairs equally well understood in that assembly. It is of serious importance to England that the condition of Ireland should be different from what it has hitherto been; a greater share of happiness and consequently of knowledge ought to be diffused there. The union with England ought to procure to the Irish people the blessings of the constitution; and so long as the English government insists on the necessity of arbitrary acts for suspending the law it has by no means accomplished its task, and Ireland cannot be sincerely identified with a country which does not impart to it all its rights. Finally, the administration of Ireland is a bad example for the English, a bad school for their statesmen; and were England to subsist long between Ireland and France in the present state of things, she would find it difficult to avoid suffering from the perverse influence which her government exercises habitually on the one and at the present moment on the other.

A people can confer happiness on the man who serves them only by the satisfaction of his conscience; they cannot inspire attachment to any but the friends of justice, to hearts disposed to sacrifice their interest to their duty. Many and many a heart is there of this nature in England; there are, in these reserved characters, hidden treasures to be discerned only by

2. The Catholic Relief Act was passed a decade later, in 1829. The act reduced or removed many of the restrictions on Roman Catholics that had been previously introduced and allowed Catholics to hold many high-ranking governmental, administrative, and judicial offices as well as to serve in Parliament.

sympathy, but which show themselves with force as soon as the occasion calls them forth: it is on these that the maintenance of liberty reposes. All the aberrations of France have not thrown the English into opposite extremes; and although, at this moment, the diplomatic conduct of their government be highly reprehensible, Parliament lets no session pass without improving some old law, framing new ones, discussing questions of jurisprudence, agriculture, or political economy, with an intelligence always on the increase; in short, making daily improvements, while people in other countries would gladly turn into ridicule that progress without which society would have no object that could be rationally explained.

But will English liberty escape that operation of time which has devoured everything on earth? Human foresight is not capable of penetrating into the remote future; yet we see, in history, republics overturned by conquering empires or destroying themselves by their own conquests; we see the nations of the North taking possession of countries in the South because these countries fell into decay, and also because the necessity of civilization carried a part of the inhabitants of Europe with violence toward her Southern regions. Everywhere we have seen nations perish from want of public spirit, from want of knowledge, and, above all, in consequence of the prejudices which, by subjecting the most numerous part of a people to a state of slavery, servitude, or any other injustice, rendered it foreign to the country which it alone could defend. But in the actual state of social order in England, after the duration, for a century, of institutions which have formed the most religious, most moral, and most enlightened nation of which Europe can boast, I should be unable to conceive in what way the prosperity of a country, that is, its liberty, could ever be threatened. At the very moment when the English government leans toward the doctrine of despotism, although it was a despot with whom it contended; at the very moment when legitimacy, violated in a formal manner by the Revolution of 1688, is held up by the English government as the only principle necessary to social order; in this moment of temporary deviation, one already perceives that by degrees the vessel of the state will regain its balance: for of all storms, that which prejudice can excite is the most easily calmed in the country of so many great men, in the center of so much knowledge.

Can a Limited Monarchy Have Other Foundations Than That of the English Constitution?

We find in Swift's Works a small tract entitled *Polite Conversation*,[1] which comprises all the commonplace ideas that enter into the discourse of the fashionable world. A witty man had a plan of making a similar essay on the political conversations of the present day. "The English constitution is suitable only to Englishmen; the French are not worthy of receiving good laws: people should be on their guard against theory and adhere to practice." What signifies it, some will say, that these phrases are tedious if they convey a true meaning? But it is their very falsehood that makes them tedious. Truth on certain topics never becomes common, however often repeated; for every man who pronounces it feels and expresses it in his own way; but the watchwords of party spirit are the undoubted signs of mediocrity. We may almost take for granted that a conversation beginning by these official sentences promises only a combination of tedium and sophistry. Laying aside, then, that frivolous language which aims at profundity, it seems to me that thinking men have not even yet discovered other principles of monarchical and constitutional liberty than those which are admitted in England.

Democrats will say that there ought to be a king without a patrician body, or that there ought to be neither; but experience has demonstrated the impracticability of such a system. Of the three powers, aristocrats dis-

---

1. The full title of Swift's book is *A Complete Collection of Genteel and Ingenious Conversation According to the Most Polite Mode and Method Now Used at Court and in the Best Companies of England* (1738).

pute only that of the people: thus, when they pretend that the English constitution cannot be adapted to France, they merely say that there must be no representatives of the people; for it is certainly not a nobility or hereditary royalty which they dispute. It is thus evident that we cannot deviate from the English constitution without establishing a republic by eliminating hereditary succession; or a despotism by suppressing the commons: for of the three powers, it is impossible to take any one away without producing one or other of these two extremes.

After such a revolution as that of France, constitutional monarchy is the only peace, the only treaty of Westphalia, if we may use the expression, which can be concluded between actual knowledge of society and hereditary interests; between almost the whole nation and the privileged classes supported by the powers of Europe.

The King of England enjoys a power more than sufficient for a man who wishes to do good; and I can hardly conceive how it is that religion does not inspire princes with scruples on the use of unbounded authority: pride in this case gets the ascendancy over virtue. As to the commonplace argument of the impossibility of being free in a Continental country where a numerous standing army must be kept up, the same persons who are incessantly repeating it are ready to quote England for a contrary purpose, and to say that in that country a standing army is not at present dangerous to liberty. The diversity of arguments of those who renounce every principle goes to an unheard-of length: they avail themselves of circumstances when theory is against them; of theory, when circumstances demonstrate their errors: finally, they wheel round with a suppleness which cannot escape the broad light of discussion, but which may mislead the mind when it is not permitted either to silence or to answer sophists. If a standing army give greater power to the King of France than to the King of England, the ultra-royalists, according to their way of thinking, will enjoy that excess of strength, and the friends of liberty do not dread it if the representative government and its securities are established in France with sincerity and without exception. The existence of a Chamber of Peers necessarily reduces, it is true, the number of noble families: but will public interest suffer by this change? Would the families known in history complain of seeing associated in the peerage new men whom the sovereign and public opinion might think worthy of that honor? Should the nobility, which has most to do to reconcile itself with the nation, be the most obstinately attached to inadmissible pretensions? We, the French people, have the advantage of being more ingenious, but at the same time more stupid than any other people of Europe; I am not aware that we ought to boast of it.

Arguments deserving a more serious examination, because they are not inspired by mere frivolous pretensions, were renewed against the Chamber of Peers at the time of Bonaparte's constitution. Human reason had, it was said, made too great progress in France to bear with any hereditary distinctions. M. Necker had treated that question fifteen years before, like a writer undaunted either by the vanity of prejudices or the self-conceit of theories; and it appears to me admitted by every reflecting mind that the respect with which a conservative element surrounds a government is to the advantage of liberty as well as order, by rendering a recurrence to force less necessary. What obstacle would there then be in France more than in England to the existence of a numerous, imposing, and enlightened House of Peers? The elements of it exist, and we already see how easy it would be to give them a happy combination.

What, it will still be said, for all political sayings are worth the trouble of being combated on account of the multitude of common minds who respect them; you then wish that France should be nothing but a copy, and a bad copy, of the English government? Truly, I do not see why the French or any other nation should reject the use of the compass because they were Italians[2] who discovered it. There are in the administration of a country, in its finances, in its commerce, in its armies a number of things connected with localities, and necessarily varying according to them; but the fundamental parts of a constitution are the same throughout. The republican or monarchical form is prescribed by the size and situation of a country; but there are always three elements given by nature: deliberation, execution, and preservation; and these three elements are necessary to secure to the citizens their liberty, their fortune, the peaceful development of their faculties, and the rewards due to their labor. What people is there

---

2. In fact, the compass was invented by the Chinese.

to whom such rights are not necessary, and by what other principles than those of England can we obtain their lasting enjoyment? Can even all the defects which people are so ready to attribute to the French serve as a pretext to refuse them such rights? In truth, were the French rebellious children, as their great parents in Europe pretend, I would the rather advise giving them a constitution, which should be in their eyes a pledge of equity in those who govern them; for rebellious children, when in such numbers, can be more easily corrected by reason than restrained by force.

A lapse of time will be necessary in France before it will be practicable to create a patriotic aristocracy; for the Revolution having been directed still more against the privileges of the nobles than against the royal authority, the nobility now second despotism as their safeguard.[3] It might be said with some truth that this state of things is an argument against the creation of a Chamber of Peers, as too favorable to the power of the Crown. But first, it is in the nature of an upper house in general to lean toward the throne; and the opposition of the peers in England is almost always a minority. Besides, there can be introduced into a Chamber of Peers a number of noblemen friendly to liberty; and those who may not be so today will become so from the mere circumstance that the discharge of the duties of a high magistracy alienates a person from a court life and attaches him to the interest of the country. I shall not fear to profess a sentiment which a number of persons will term aristocratic, but with which all the circumstances of the French Revolution have impressed me: it is that the noblemen who have adopted the cause of a representative government, and consequently of equality before the law, are, in general, the most virtuous and most enlightened Frenchmen of whom we can yet boast. They combine, like the English, the spirit of chivalry with the spirit of liberty;[4] they have, besides, the generous advantage of founding their opinions on their sacrifices, while the Third Estate must necessarily find its own in the general interest. Finally, they have to support, almost daily, the ill-will of their class, sometimes even of their family. They are

3. See Furet, *Revolutionary France*, 284–98.
4. Burke put forward a similar claim in *Reflections on the Revolution in France*.

told that they are traitors to their order because they are faithful to the country; while men of the opposite extreme, democrats without the restraint of reason or morality, have persecuted them as enemies of liberty, looking to nothing but their privileges and refusing, very unfairly, to believe in the sincerity of their renunciation. These illustrious citizens, who have voluntarily exposed themselves to so many trials, are the best guardians of liberty on which a country can rely; and a Chamber of Peers ought to be created for them, even if the necessity of such an institution in a constitutional monarchy were not acknowledged even to demonstration.

"No kind of deliberative assembly, whether democratic or hereditary, can succeed in France. The French are too desirous of making a display, and the necessity of producing effect carries them always from one extreme to another." "It is sufficient then," certain men say, who constitute themselves the guardians of the nation, that they may declare it in a perpetual minority; "it is sufficient then that France have provincial states instead of a representative assembly." Certainly I ought to respect provincial assemblies more highly than anyone, since my father was the first and the only minister who established them, and who lost his place for having supported them against the *parlements*. It is doubtless very wise, in a country as large as France, to give the local authorities more power and more importance than in England; but when M. Necker proposed to assimilate, by provincial assemblies, the provinces called elective (*pays d'élection*) to the *pays d'état;*[5] that is, to give to the old provinces the privileges possessed only by those whose union to France had been more recent, there was in Paris a *parlement* which could refuse to register money edicts or any other law emanating directly from the throne. This right of *parlement* was a very bad outline of a representative government, but at least it was one; and now that all the former limits of the throne are overturned, what would be thirty-three provincial assemblies, dependent on ministerial despotism and possessing no means of opposing it? It is good

---

5. Before 1789 the term *pays d'élection* was applied to provinces that did not have estates to assist in local government and in the assessment and collection of taxes. Its opposite was *pays d'état*.

that local assemblies should discuss the repartition of taxes and verify the public expenses; but popular forms in the provinces, subordinate to an unlimited central power, is a great political monstrosity.

Let us frankly say that no constitutional government can be established if, in the outset, we introduce into all places, whether of deputies or of the agents of the executive power, the enemies of the constitution itself. The first condition to enable a representative government to proceed is that the elections should be free; for they will then produce in men of integrity a wish for the success of the institution of which they will form a part. A deputy is alleged to have said in company, "People accuse me of not being for the constitutional charter; they are very wrong, I am always mounted on this charter; but it is indeed to ride it to death." Yet after this charming effusion, this deputy would probably take it very much amiss to be suspected of wanting good faith in politics; but it is too much to desire to unite the pleasure of revealing one's secrets to the advantage of keeping them. Do people think that, with these concealed, or rather with these too well-known intentions, a fair experiment of representative government is made in France? A minister declared lately in the Chamber of Deputies that, of all powers, the one over which royal authority should exercise the greatest influence was the power of elections; which is saying in other terms that the representatives of the people ought to be named by the King. At that rate the officers of the Household ought to be named by the people.

Let the French nation elect the men she shall think worthy of her confidence, let not representatives be imposed on her, and, least of all, representatives chosen among the constant enemies of every representative government: then, and then only, will the political problem be solved in France.[6] We may, I believe, consider it a certain maxim that when free institutions have subsisted twenty years in a country, it is on them the blame must be cast if we do not perceive a daily improvement in the morality, the intelligence, and the happiness of the nation that possesses them.

---

6. It will be recalled that on September 5, 1816, Louis XVIII dissolved the (in)famous *Chambre introuvable* and called for new elections.

It is for these institutions, when arrived at a certain age, to answer, if we may say so, for men; but at the commencement of a new political establishment, it is for men to answer for the institutions:[7] for we can in no degree estimate the strength of a citadel if the commanding officers open the gates or attempt to undermine the foundations.

7. Montesquieu made a similar argument in *The Spirit of the Laws.*

CHAPTER X

Of the Influence of Arbitrary Power
on the Spirit and Character of a Nation.

Frederic II, Maria Theresa, and Catherine II inspired so just an admiration by their talents for governing that it is very natural, in the countries where their memory still lives and their system is strictly followed, that the public should feel, less than in France, the necessity of a representative government. On the other hand, the regent and Louis XV gave in the last century the saddest example of all the misfortunes, of all the degradations attached to arbitrary power. We repeat then that we have here only France in view; and she must not suffer herself, after twenty-seven years of revolution, to be deprived of the advantages she has reaped and be made to bear the double dishonor of being conquered at home and abroad.

The partisans of arbitrary power quote the reigns of Augustus in ancient history, of Elizabeth and of Louis XIV in modern times, as a proof that absolute monarchy can at least be favorable to the progress of literature. Literature in the time of Augustus was little more than a liberal art, foreign to political interests. Under Elizabeth, religious reform stimulated the mind to every kind of development; and the government was the more favorable to it as its strength lay in the very establishment of that reform. The literary progress of France under Louis XIV was caused, as we have already mentioned in the beginning of this work, by the display of intellect called forth by the civil wars. That progress led to the literature of the eighteenth century; and so far is it from being right to attribute to the government of Louis XIV the masterpieces of human intellect that appeared in that age, we must rather consider them almost all as attacks on that government. Despotism, then, if it well understands its interest, will not encourage literature, for literature leads men to think, and thought passes sentence on despotism. Bonaparte directed the public mind toward military success; he was perfectly right according to his object: there are but two kinds of auxiliaries for absolute power, the priests and the soldiers. But are there not, it is said, enlightened despotisms, moderate despotisms? None of these epithets, by which people flatter themselves they will produce an illusion in regard to the word to which they are appended, can mislead men of good sense. In a country like France, you must destroy knowledge if you wish the principles of liberty not to revive. During the reign of Bonaparte and subsequently, a third method has been adopted: it was to make the press instrumental to the oppression of liberty by permitting the use of it only to certain writers enjoined to comment on every error with the more assurance that it was forbidden to reply to them. This is consecrating the art of writing to the destruction of thought, and publicity itself to darkness; but deception of this kind cannot long continue. When government wishes to command without law, its support must be sought in force, not in arguments; for though it be forbidden to refute them, the palpable falsehood of these arguments suggests a wish to combat them; and to silence men effectually, the best plan is not to speak to them.

It would certainly be unjust not to acknowledge that various sovereigns in possession of arbitrary power have known how to use it with discretion; but is it on a chance that the lot of nations should be staked? I shall here quote an expression of the Emperor Alexander which seems to me worthy of being consecrated. I had the honor of seeing him at Petersburg at the most remarkable moment of his life, when the French were advancing on Moscow, and when, by refusing the peace which Bonaparte offered as soon as he thought himself the victor, Alexander triumphed over his enemy more dextrously than his generals did afterward. "You are not ignorant," said the Emperor of Russia to me, "that the Russian peasants are slaves. I do what I can to improve their situation gradually in my dominions; but I meet elsewhere with obstacles which the tranquillity of the empire enjoins me to treat with caution." "Sire," I answered, "I know that Russia is at present happy, although she has no other constitution than the personal character of your Majesty." "Even if the compliment you pay me were true," replied the Emperor, "*I should be nothing more than a fortunate accident.*" Finer expressions could not, I think, have been pronounced by a monarch whose situation could blind him in regard to the condition of men. Not only does arbitrary power deliver nations to the chances of hereditary succession; but the most enlightened kings, if they are absolute, could not, if they would, encourage in their nation strength and dignity of character. God and the law alone can command man in the tone of a master without degrading him.

Do people figure to themselves how ministers such as Lord Chatham, Mr. Pitt, Mr. Fox would have been supported by the princes who appointed Cardinal Dubois or Cardinal Fleury?[1] The great men in French history, the Guises, Coligny, Henri IV, were formed in times of trouble because those troubles, in other respects disastrous, prevented the stifling action of despotism and gave a great importance to certain individuals. But in England only is political life so regularly constituted that genius and greatness of soul can arise and show themselves without agitating the state.

From Louis XIV to Louis XVI half a century elapsed: a true model of what is called arbitrary government when people wish to represent it in its mildest colors. There was not tyranny, because the means to establish it were wanting; but it was only through the disorder of injustice that any liberty could be secretly acquired. He who wished to become of any account or to succeed in any business was obliged to study the intrigue of courts, the most miserable science that ever degraded mankind. There is there no question either of talents or virtues; for never would a superior man have the kind of patience necessary to please a monarch educated in the habits of absolute power. Princes thus formed are so persuaded that it is always personal interest which suggests what is told to them, that it must be without their consciousness that one can have influence over them. Now, for this kind of success, to be always on the spot is better than the possession of every possible talent. Princes stand in the same relation to courtiers as we to our servants: we should be offended if they gave us advice, if they spoke to us in an urgent tone, even on our own interests; but we are displeased to see them put on a discontented look, and a few words addressed to us at an appropriate moment, a few flatteries which

---

1. Cardinal Dubois (1656–1723) and Cardinal Fleury (1653–1743) were prominent French statesmen during the reigns of Louis XIV and Louis XV.

would appear to fall accidentally from them, would completely govern us if our equals, whom we meet on leaving our house, did not teach us what we are. Princes, having to do only with servants of good taste, who insinuate themselves more easily into their favor than our attendants into ours, live and die without ever having an idea of the real state of things. But courtiers, though they study the character of their master with a good deal of sagacity, do not acquire any real information even as to the knowledge of the human heart, at least that knowledge that is necessary to direct nations. A king should make it a rule to take as prime minister a man displeasing to him as a courtier; for never can a superior mind bend itself to the exact point necessary to captivate those to whom incense is offered. A certain tact, half common, half refined, serves to make one's way at court: eloquence, reasoning, all the transcendent faculties of the mind and soul would offend like rebellion or would be overpowered with ridicule. "What unsuitable discourse; what ambitious projects!" would say the one; "What does he wish; what does he mean!" would say the other; and the prince would participate in the astonishment of his court. The atmosphere of etiquette operates eventually on everybody to such a degree that I know no one sufficiently bold to articulate a significant word in the circle of princes who have remained shut up in their courts. The conversations must be unavoidably confined to the fine weather, to the chase, to what they drank yesterday, to what they will eat tomorrow; finally, to all sorts of things that have neither meaning nor interest for anybody. What a school is this for the mind, and for the character! What a sad spectacle is an old courtier who has passed many years in the habits of stifling all his feelings, dissembling his opinions, waiting the breath of a prince that he may respire, and his signal that he may move! Such men, at last, destroy the finest of all sentiments, respect for old age, when they are seen, bent by the habit of bowing, wrinkled by false smiles, pale more from boredom than from years, and standing for hours together on their trembling legs in those antechambers where to sit down at the age of eighty would seem almost a revolt.

One prefers, in this career, the young men, giddy and foppish, who can boldly display flattery toward their masters, arrogance toward their inferiors, and who despise the part of mankind which is above as well as that which is below them. They proceed thus, trusting only to their own merit until some loss of favor awaken them from the fascination of folly and of wit together; for a mixture of the two is necessary to succeed in the intrigues of courts. Now, in France, from rank to rank, there have always been courts, that is, houses, in which was distributed a certain quantity of favor for the use of those who aimed at money and place. The flatterers of power, from the clerks to the chamberlains, have adopted that flexibility of language, that facility of saying everything, as of concealing everything, that cutting tone in the style of decision, that condescension for the fashion of the day as for a great authority which has given rise to the levity of which the French are accused; and yet this levity is found only in the swarm of men who buzz around power. This levity they must have to change their party readily; they must have it not to enter thoroughly into any study, for otherwise it would cost them too much to say the contrary of what they would have seriously learned; by ignoring many things, one affirms everything more easily. In short, they must have this levity to lavish, from democracy down to legitimacy, from the republic down to military despotism, all the phrases most opposite in point of meaning, but which still bear a resemblance to each other, like persons of the same family, equally superficial, disdainful, and calculated never to present but one side of a question in opposition to that which circumstances have rendered common. The artifices of intrigue at this time intermeddling with literature as with everything else, there is no possibility for a poor Frenchman who reads to learn anything else than that which it is expedient to say, not that which really is. In the eighteenth century, on the contrary, men in power had no apprehension of the influence of writings on public opinion, and they left literature almost as undisturbed as the physical sciences still are at this day. The great writers have all combated, with more or less reserve, the different institutions founded on prejudices. But what was the result of this conflict? That the institutions were vanquished. One might apply to the reign of Louis XV, and to the kind of happiness found under it, the saying of the man who was falling from the third story of a house: "This is very pleasant, if it would but last."

Representative governments, it will still be objected to me, have not existed in Germany, and yet learning has made immense progress there. Nothing has less resemblance than Germany and France.[2] There is a methodical spirit in the German governments which much diminishes the irregular ascendancy of courts. No coteries, no mistresses, no favorites, nor even ministers who can change the order of things are to be found there. Literature proceeds without flattering anyone; the rectitude of character and the abstract nature of studies are such that even in the time of civil troubles, it would be impossible to compel a German writer to play those strange tricks which have justly led to the remark that, in France, paper suffers everything, so much is required of it. You acknowledge then, I shall be told, that the French character has invincible defects which are hostile to the knowledge, as well as to the virtues, without which liberty cannot exist? By no means; I say that an arbitrary, fluctuating, capricious, and unstable government, full of prejudice and superstition in some respects, and of frivolity and immorality in others, that this government, such as it existed once in France, had left knowledge, intellect, and energy only to its adversaries. And, if it be impossible that such an order of things should be in accordance with the progress of knowledge, it is still more certain that it is irreconcilable with purity of morals and dignity of character. We already perceive that, notwithstanding the misfortunes of France, marriage is far more respected since the Revolution than it was under the old system. Now, marriage is the support of morals and of liberty. How should women have confined themselves to domestic life under an arbitrary government and not have employed all their seductive means to influence power? They were certainly not animated by an enthusiasm for general ideas, but by the desire of obtaining places for their friends; and nothing was more natural in a country where men in favor could do everything, where they disposed of the revenues of the state, where they were stopped by nothing but the will of the King, necessarily modified by the intrigues of those by whom he was surrounded. How should any scruple have been felt to employ the credit of women who were in favor to obtain from a minister any exception whatever to a rule that did not exist? Can it be believed that Madame de Montespan

2. This point is developed in Madame de Staël's *On Germany*.

under Louis XIV, or Madame du Barry under Louis XV, ever received a refusal from ministers?[3] And without approaching so near the throne, where was the circle upon which favor did not act as at court, and where everyone did not employ all possible means to achieve one's purpose? In a nation, on the contrary, regulated by law, what woman would have the useless effrontery to solicit what was unfair or rely more on her entreaties than on the real claims of those whom she recommended? Corruption of morals is not the only result of those continual solicitations, of that activity of intrigue of which French women, particularly those of the first class, have but too frequently set the example; the passions of which they are susceptible, and which the delicacy of their organs renders more lively, disfigure in them all that is amiable in their sex.

It is in free countries only that the true character of a woman and the true character of a man can be known and admired. Domestic life inspires all the virtues in women; and the political career, far from habituating men to despise morality as an old tale of the nursery, stimulates those who hold public functions to the sacrifice of their personal interests, to the dignity of honor, and to all that greatness of soul which the habitual presence of public opinion never fails to call forth. Finally, in a country where women are at the bottom of every intrigue, because favor governs everything, the morals of the first class have nothing in common with those of the nation, and no sympathy can exist between the persons who fill the salons and the bulk of the people. A woman of the lowest order in England feels that she has some kind of analogy with the Queen, who has also taken care of her husband and brought up her children in the way that religion and morality enjoin to every wife and mother. But the morals to which arbitrary government leads transform women into a sort of third factitious sex, the sad production of a depraved social order. Women, however, may be excusable for taking political matters as they are and for finding pleasure in those lively interests from which they seem separated by their natural destiny. But what are men who are brought up under arbitrary government? We have seen some of them amidst the Jacobins, under Bo-

3. The Marquise de Montespan (1640–1707) and the Countess du Barry (1743–93) were the mistresses of Louis XIV and Louis XV, respectively.

naparte, and in foreign camps—everywhere except in the incorruptible band of the friends of liberty. They take their stand on the excesses of the Revolution to proclaim despotism; and twenty-five years are opposed to the history of the world, which displays nothing but the horrors committed by superstition and tyranny. To believe in the good faith of these partisans of arbitrary power, we must suppose that they have never read what preceded the era of the French Revolution; and we know some who may well found their justification on their ignorance.

Our Revolution, as we have already stated, almost followed the different phases of that of England, with the same regularity which the crises of a similar malady present. But the question which now agitates the civilized world consists in the application of all the fundamental truths upon which social order rests. The greed of power has led men to commit all the crimes which sully history; fanaticism has seconded tyranny; hypocrisy, violence, fraud, and the sword have enchained, deceived, and devastated the human race. Two periods alone have illumined the globe: the history of some centuries of Greece and Rome. Slavery, by limiting the number of citizens, allowed the republican government to be established even in extensive countries, and thence resulted the greatest virtues. Christianity, by liberating slaves and by civilizing the rest of Europe, has since conferred on individual existence a good which is the source of all others. But despotism, that disorder within order, has all along maintained itself in several countries; and all the pages of our history have been stained, either by religious massacres or judiciary murders. Suddenly Providence permitted England to solve the problem of constitutional monarchies; and America, a century later, that of federal republics. Since this period, not one drop of blood has been shed unjustly by tribunals in either of these countries. For sixty years past religious quarrels have ceased in England, and they never existed in America. The venom of power, which has corrupted so many men during so many ages, has undergone at last, by representative governments, a salutary innoculation, which has destroyed all its malignity. Since the battle of Culloden, in 1746, which may be considered the close of the civil troubles that commenced a hundred years before, not one abuse of power can be cited in England. There exists not one worthy citizen who has not said, *"Our happy constitution,"* because there exists no one who has not felt its protection. This chimera, for such whatever is sublime has always been called, stands there realized before our eyes. What feeling, what prejudice, what hardness of mind or heart can prompt us, in recalling what we have read in our history, not to prefer the sixty years of which England has given us an example? Our kings, like those of England, have been alternately good and bad; but their reign presents at no time sixty years of internal peace and liberty together. Nothing equal to it has even been thought possible in any other epoch. Power is the protector of order; but it is also its enemy by the passions which it excites: regulate its exercise by public liberty, and you will have banished that contempt for mankind which exempts all vices from restraint and justifies the art of profiting by them.

CHAPTER XI

Of the Mixture of Religion with Politics.

It is very often said that France has become irreligious since the Revolution. No doubt at the period of all crimes, the men who committed them must have thrown off the most sacred of restraints. But the general disposition of men at present is not connected with fatal causes, which happily are very remote from us. Religion in France, as it was preached by priests, has always mixed itself with politics; and from the time when the popes absolved subjects from their oath of fidelity to their kings, until the last catechism sanctioned by the great majority of the French clergy, a catechism in which, as we have seen, those who did not love and serve the Emperor Napoléon were threatened with eternal damnation; there is not a period in which the ministers of religion have not employed it to establish political dogmas, all differing according to circumstances. In the midst of these changes, the only invariable thing has been intolerance toward whatever was not conformable to the prevailing doctrine. Never has religion been presented merely as the most inward worship of the heart, without any connection with the interests of this world.

We are subject to the reproach of irreligion when we do not accord in opinion with the ecclesiastical authorities in the affairs of government; but a man may be irritated against those who seek to impose upon him their manner of thinking in politics and, nevertheless, be a very good Christian. It does not follow that because France desires liberty and equality in the eye of the law, that the country is not Christian; quite the contrary. Christianity accords eminently with this opinion. Thus, when man shall cease to join what God has separated, religion and politics, the clergy will have less power and less influence, but the nation will be sincerely religious. All the art of the privileged persons of both classes consists in establishing that he who wishes for a constitution is partisan and biased; and he who dreads the influence of the priests in the affairs of this world, an unbeliever. These tactics are well known, for, like all the rest, they have only been renewed.

Sermons in France, as in England, in times of party have often treated of political questions, and, I believe, they have but little edified persons of a contrary opinion by whom they were heard. We do not much attend to a sermon which we hear in the morning from a preacher with whom we have been disputing the day before; and religion suffers from the hatred which political questions inspire against the priests who interfere in those discussions.

It would be unjust to pretend that France is irreligious because the nation does not apply, according to the wish of some members of the clergy, the famous text that all power comes from God; a text, the honest interpretation of which is easy, but which has been wonderfully useful in treaties made by the clergy with all governments supporting themselves on the divine right of force. I will cite on this occasion some passages of the Pastoral Instruction of the Bishop of Troyes,[1] who, when he was almoner to Bonaparte, delivered a discourse at the christening of the King of Rome at least as edifying as that with which we are going to be engaged. It is unnecessary to add that this Instruction is of 1816. The date of a publication in France can always be recognized by the opinion which it contains.

The Bishop of Troyes says, "France wishes for her King, but her legitimate King, because legitimacy is the first treasure of a nation, and a benefit so much the more invaluable as it compensates for all others and can by no other be supplied." Let us pause one moment to pity the man who thinks thus for having served Napoléon so long and so well. What an effort! What constraint! But, after all, the Bishop of Troyes does no more in this respect than many others who still hold places; and we must render him at least the justice that he does not call for the proscription of his fellow-flatterers of Napoléon: this is no small matter.

I will pass over the flattering language of the pastoral letter; a language

1. Anne-Antoine (1747–1825), Count of Boulogne and Bishop of Troyes (from 1809) and Peer of France (from 1822 to his death).

which a man ought to permit himself the less to use toward power, the more he respects power. Let us proceed to less benign things:

France wishes for her King; but, in wishing for him, she does not pretend that she can choose another; and, happily, she does not have this fatal right. Far from us be the thought that kings hold their authority from the people, and that the option which the people may have had of choosing them includes the right of recalling them. . . . No, it is not true that the people is sovereign, nor that kings are its trustees. . . . This is the cry of sedition, the dream of independence; it is the foul chimera of turbulent democracy; it is the most cruel falsehood that our vile tyrants ever invented to deceive the multitude. We do not mean to refute seriously this disastrous sovereignty. . . . But it is our duty, in the name of religion, to protest against this anarchical and antisocial doctrine, vomited amongst us with the revolutionary lava; and to guard the faithful committed to our care against this double heresy, political and religious, equally rejected by the greatest doctors and the greatest legislators, not less contrary to natural than to divine right, nor less destructive of the authority of kings than of the authority of God.

The Bishop of Troyes, in fact, does not seriously treat that question, which had, however, appeared worthy of the attention of some thinkers; but it is easier to convert a principle into heresy than to investigate it by discussion. There are, however, some Christians in England, in America, and in Holland; and since social order has been founded, honest persons have been known to believe that all power emanated from the nation, without whom no power could exist. It is in this manner that by employing religion to direct politics the French are liable to continual reproaches of impiety; which simply means that there are in France a great many friends of liberty who are of the opinion that a compact should exist between nations and sovereigns. It seems to me that we can believe in God and yet think in this manner.

By a singular contradiction this same Bishop, so orthodox in politics, cites the famous passage which served him, no doubt, as a justification in his own eyes when he was the almoner of the Usurper: "*All power comes from God; and he who resists power, resists God himself.*" "Behold, beloved brethren, the public right of religion, without which no one has the right to command, nor the obligation to obey. Behold that first sovereignty from which all others are derived, and without which all others would have neither basis nor sanction; it is the only constitution adapted to all places as well as to all times; the only one which can enable us to do without others, and without which no other can maintain itself. This is the only one which can never be subject to revision; the only one which cannot be shaken by any faction, and against which no rebellion can prevail; against which, in short, nations and kings, masters and subjects can do nothing: all power comes from God; and he who resists power resists God himself." Is it possible in a few words to collect a greater number of fatal errors and servile calculations? Thus Nero and Robespierre, Louis XI and Charles IX, the most sanguinary of men, ought to be obeyed, if he who resists power resists God himself! Nations or their representatives are the only power which should have been excepted in this implicit respect for authority. When two parties in the state are contending together, how shall we seize the moment when one of them becomes sacred, that is to say, the stronger? Those French then were wrong who did not quit the King during twenty-five years of exile! For certainly during that time it was Bonaparte to whom we could not refuse the right which the Bishop of Troyes proclaims, that of power. Into what absurdities writers fall, who wish to reduce into theories, into dogmas, into maxims the interests of the moment! The sword, in truth, is less degrading than speech when it is thus used. It has been a hundred times repeated that the phrase in the Gospel "All power comes from God," and the other, "Render to Caesar the things that are Caesar's," had solely for their object to remove all political discussion. Jesus Christ desired that the religion he preached should be considered by the Romans as entirely unconnected with public affairs; "My reign is not of this world," said he. All that is required of the ministers of religion is to fulfill in this respect, as in all others, the intentions of Christ.

"Appoint, O Lord!" says the Prophet, "a legislator over them, that the nations may know that they are men." It would not be amiss that kings should also learn that they are men, and certainly they must be ignorant of it unless they contract engagements toward the nation whom they govern. When the Prophet prays to God to establish a king, it is, as all religious men pray to God, to preside over every event of this life; but how is a dynasty specially established by Providence? Is it prescription that is the sign of a divine mission? The popes have excommunicated and deposed princes from the remotest times. They excluded Henri IV on account of his religion; and powerful motives recently impelled a pope to concur in the coronation of Bonaparte. It will then belong to the clergy to declare, when necessary, that such a dynasty, and not such another, is chosen by the will of God. But let us follow the pastoral instruction, "Appoint a legislator," that is to say, "a king who is the legislator above all, and without whom there can be no law; a supreme legislator who will speak and make laws in your name; one legislator, and not several; for the more there are, the worse will the laws be made; a legislator with unrivaled authority, that he may do good without hindrance; a legislator who, obedient himself to his own laws, cannot bind anyone to submit to his passions and caprices; finally, a legislator who, making only just laws, would thus lead his people to real liberty." A man who will make laws for himself alone will *have neither passions nor caprices;* a man surrounded by all the snares of royalty will be the only legislator of a people and *will make none but just laws!* There is, obviously, no example of the contrary; we have never seen kings abuse their power; no priests such as the Cardinals of Lorraine, Richelieu, Mazarin, Dubois who excited them to it! And how is that doctrine compatible with the constitutional charter which the King himself has sworn? This King whom France desires; for the Bishop of Troyes allows himself to say this, although, according to him, France has no right to form a wish on the subject; this King, who is established by the Lord, has promised on oath that there should be various legislators, and not one only, although the Bishop of Troyes pretends that *the more there are, the more imperfect will be the laws.* Thus the information acquired by administration; thus the wishes collected in the provinces by those who live there; thus the sympathy arising from the same wants and the same sufferings, all this is not equivalent to the information of a single king who *represents himself,* to make use of a somewhat singular expression of the Bishop of Troyes. One would think that one had already attained what, in this kind of composition, cannot be surpassed, if the following passage did not claim a preference.

"Thus, beloved brethren, have we seen this senate of kings under the name of Congress[2] consecrate the legitimacy of all dynasties as a principle, as the aegis of their throne and the surest pledge of the happiness of nations and of the tranquillity of states. We are kings, they said, because we are kings: for so require the order and stability of the social world: so requires our own security; and they have said it without much concerning themselves whether they were not thus in opposition to the *ideas* called *liberal,* and still less whether the partition which they made of the countries which they found to suit them were not the most solemn denial given to sovereign peoples." Would not one think that we had quoted the most ironical satire against the Congress of Vienna, did we not know that such could not have been the intention of the author? But when a writer goes to such a degree of absurdity, he is not aware of the ridicule incurred, for methodical folly is very serious. *We are kings because we are kings,* the sovereigns of Europe are made to say; "*I am, that I am,*" are the words of Jehovah in the Bible; and the ecclesiastical writer takes on himself to attribute to monarchs what can be suitable only to the Deity. *The kings,* he said, *did not much concern themselves whether the partitioning of the countries which they found to suit them was in harmony with the ideas called liberal.* So much the worse, in truth, if they have managed this partitioning like a banker's account, paying balances in a certain number of souls, or of fractions of souls, to make up a round sum of subjects! So much the worse if they have consulted nothing but their convenience, without thinking of the interests and wishes of the people! But the kings, be assured, reject the unworthy eulogy that is thus addressed to them; they, doubtless, reject also the blame which the Bishop of Troyes ventures to cast on them, although that blame contains an odious flattery under the form of a reproach.

"It is true that several of them have been seen to favor, at the hazard of being in contradiction with themselves, those popular forms and other new theories which their ancestors did not know, and to which, until our days, their own countries had been strangers, without being the worse for their ignorance; but, we do not fear to say it, it is the malady of Europe, and the most alarming symptom of its decline; it is in that way that Prov-

2. The Congress of Vienna (September 1814–June 1815).

idence seems to attack it to accelerate its dissolution. Let us add to this mania of re-casting governments and supporting them by books that tendency of innovating minds to make a blending of all modes of worship as they wish to make of all parties, and to believe that the authority of princes acquires for itself all the strength and authority of which they strip religion; and we shall have the two greatest political dissolvents which can undermine empires, and with which Europe, sooner or later, must fall into shreds and rottenness." Such then is the object of all these homilies in favor of absolute power; it is religious toleration that must make Europe fall, sooner or later, into shreds and rottenness. Public opinion is favorable to this toleration; it is then necessary to prescribe whatever can serve as an organ to public opinion: then the clergy of the only admitted religion will be rich and powerful; for, on the one hand, they will call themselves the interpreters of that divine right by which kings reign, and, on the other, the peoples being allowed to profess nothing but the prevailing religion, the ecclesiastics solely must be charged, as they demand, with public education and with the direction of conscience, which supports itself on the Inquisition, as arbitrary power on the police.

The fraternity of all Christian communities, such as the Holy Alliance[3] proposed by the Emperor Alexander has made humanity expect, is already condemned by the censure passed on the *blending of the forms of worship*. What social order is proposed to us by these partisans of despotism and of intolerance, these enemies of knowledge, these adversaries of humanity, when it bears the name of people and nation! Whither could one fly were they to have command? A few words more on this pastoral instruction of which the title is so mild and the words so bitter.

"Alas!" says the Archbishop of Troyes, addressing himself to the King, "seditious men, the better to enslave us, already begin to speak to us of our rights, that they may make us forget yours. Sire, we have doubtless rights, and they are as ancient as the monarchy: the right of belonging to you as the head of the great family, and of calling ourselves your subjects,

---

3. The Holy Alliance was a powerful coalition among Russia, Austria, and Prussia created in 1815 at the initiative of Tsar Alexander I of Russia. It was signed by the three powers in Vienna on September 26, 1815.

because that word signifies your children." One cannot avoid thinking that the writer, a man of intelligence, himself smiled when he proposed, as the only right of the French people, that of calling themselves the subjects of a monarch who should dispose, according to his good pleasure, of their property and their lives. The slaves of Algiers can boast of rights of the same kind.

Lastly, see on what rests all the scaffolding of sophistry prescribed as an article of faith because reasoning could not support it. What a use of the name of God! And how can one expect that a nation to whom one says this is religion should not become unbelievers, for the misfortune of itself and for that of the world!

"Beloved brethren, we shall not cease to repeat to you what Moses said to his people: *Ask your forefathers and the God of your fathers, and go back to the source.* Consider that the less we deviate from beaten paths the greater is our security. Consider, in short, that to despise the authority of ages is to despise the authority of God, since it is God himself who makes antiquity; and that to desire to renounce it is, in any event, the greatest of crimes, even were it not the greatest of misfortunes." *It is God that makes antiquity.* Doubtless; but God is likewise the author of the present, on which the future is about to depend. How silly would this assertion be did it not contain a dextrous artifice! It is as follows: all upright people are affected when reminded of their ancestors; the idea of their fathers seems always to join itself to the idea of the past. But does this noble and pure feeling lead to the re-establishment of the torture, of the wheel, of the Inquisition, because in remote ages abominations of that kind were the work of barbarous manners? Can we support what is absurd and criminal because absurdity and criminality once existed? Were not our fathers culpable toward their fathers when they adopted Christianity and abolished slavery? *Reflect that the less we deviate from the beaten paths the greater is our security,* says the Bishop of Troyes; but to enable this path to have become beaten, it must have been necessary to pass from antiquity to later times; and we now wish to profit by the information of our days, that posterity may also have an antiquity proceeding from us, but which she may change, in her turn, if Providence continue to protect, as it has done, the progress of the human mind in all directions.

I should not have dwelt so long on the composition of the Bishop of Troyes did it not contain the quintessence of all that is daily published in France. Will good sense escape from it unimpaired? And what is still worse, will the sentiment of religion, without which men have no refuge in themselves, be able to resist this mixture of policy and religion, which bears the obvious character of hypocrisy and egoism?

CHAPTER XII

Of the Love of Liberty.

The necessity of free governments, that is to say, of limited monarchies in great states and independent republics in those which are small, is so evident that we are tempted to believe no one can refuse sincerely to admit this truth; and yet, when we meet with men of good faith who combat it, we would wish, for our own satisfaction, to account for their motives. Liberty has three classes of opponents in France: the nobles who consider honor as consisting in passive obedience and the nobles who possess more reflection but less candor, and believe that the interests of their own aristocracy are identified with the interests of absolute power; the men whom the French Revolution has disgusted with the ideas which it profaned; finally, the Bonapartists, the Jacobins, all those devoid of political consciousness. The nobles who connect honor with passive obedience altogether confound the spirit of ancient chivalry with that of the courtiers of the last centuries. The ancient knights doubtless were ready to die for their king, and so would every warrior for his leader; but as we have already said, they were by no means the partisans of absolute power: they sought to encompass that power with barriers, and placed their glory in defending a liberty which, though aristocratical, was still liberty. As to the nobles who are convinced that the privileges of the aristocracy must now rest upon the despotism which they once were instrumental in limiting, we may say to them, as in the romance of *Waverly:* "What concerns you is not so much whether James Stuart shall be King, as whether Fergus Mac Ivor shall be Earl."[1] The institution of a peerage accessible to merit is to nobility what the English constitution is to monarchy. It is the only mode of preserving either the one or the other: for we live in an age in

1. *Waverly* (1814) is a famous novel by Sir Walter Scott.

which the world does not readily imagine that the minority, and a very small minority, can have a right which is not for the advantage of the majority. A few years ago, the Sultan of Persia had an account given to him of the English constitution by the ambassador of England at his court. After having listened to it and, as we shall see, understood it tolerably well: "I can conceive," he said, "that the order of things which you describe to me is better framed than the government of Persia for the duration and happiness of your empire; but it seems to me much less conducive to the enjoyment of the monarch." This was an accurate statement of the question; only that it is better even for the monarch to be guided in the administration of affairs by public opinion than incessantly to run the risk of being in opposition to it. Justice is the aegis of all and of everyone: but in its quality of justice, it is the great number which has the preferable claim to protection.

We have next to speak of those whom the misfortunes and the crimes of the French Revolution have terrified, and who fly from one extreme to the other, as if the arbitrary power of an individual were the only sure protection against demagogy. It was thus that they exalted the tyranny of Bonaparte, and it is thus that they would render Louis XVIII a despot if his superior wisdom did not protect him from it. Tyranny is an upstart, and despotism a grandee; but both are equally offensive to human reason. After having witnessed the servility with which Bonaparte was obeyed, it is difficult to conceive that the republican spirit is that which is to be dreaded in France. The diffusion of knowledge and the nature of things will bring liberty to France; but the nation assuredly will not spontaneously show itself either factious or turbulent.

Since for so many ages every generous soul has loved liberty; since the noblest actions have been inspired by her; since antiquity and the history of modern times exhibit to us so many prodigies effected by public spirit; since we have seen so lately what nations can do; since every reflecting writer has proclaimed; since not one political work of lasting reputation can be cited which is not animated by this sentiment; since the fine arts, poetry, the masterpieces of the theater, which are intended to excite emotion in the human heart, all exalt public liberty; what are we to say of those little men, great only in folly, who, with an accent insipid and affected as

their whole being, declare to you that it is very bad taste to trouble yourselves with politics; that after the horrors which we have witnessed nobody
cares for liberty; that popular elections are an institution altogether vulgar;
that the people always make a bad choice; and that genteel persons are
not suited to go, as in England, and mingle with the populace? *It is bad
taste to trouble ourselves with politics.* Good heavens! Of what then, good
heaven, are those young people to think who were educated under the
government of Bonaparte merely to go and fight, without any instruction,
without any interest in literature or the fine arts? Since they can have
neither a new idea nor a sound judgment on such subjects, they would,
at least, be men if they were to occupy themselves with their country, if
they were to deem themselves citizens, if their life were to be in any way
useful. But what would they substitute for the politics which they affect
to proscribe? Some hours passed in the antechamber of ministers to obtain
places which they are not qualified to fill; some trivial parlor conversations, beneath the understanding of even the silliest of the women to whom
they address them. When they were encountering death they might escape
without blame, because there is always greatness in courage: but in a country which, thanks to Heaven! will be at peace, to have no attainments
beyond the level of a chamberlain, and to be unable to impart other knowledge or dignity to their native land—this is bad taste indeed. The time is
gone by when young Frenchmen could set the fashion in everything. They
have still, it is true, the frivolity of former days; but they have no longer
the graces on account of which that frivolity might be pardoned.

After the horrors which we have witnessed, it is said, *nobody now wishes to
hear the name of liberty.* If sensible characters give themselves up to an
involuntary and distempered hatred (for so must it be named, since it
depends on certain recollections, certain associations of terror, which it is
impossible to vanquish), we would say to them with a poet of the present
day, that liberty must not be compelled to stab herself like Lucretia because
she has been violated. We would bid them remember that the massacre
of St. Bartholomew has not caused the proscription of the Catholic faith.
We would tell them, in short, that the fate of truth is not dependent on
the men who put this or that motto on their banners, and that good sense
has been given to every individual to judge of things as they are in them-

selves, and not according to accidental circumstances. The guilty of all times have tried to avail themselves of a generous pretext in order to excuse bad actions: there are few crimes in the world which their authors have not ascribed to honor, to religion, or to liberty. It does not follow, I think, that it is on that account necessary to proscribe whatever is beautiful upon earth. In politics especially, as there is room for fanaticism as well as for bad faith, for devotedness as well as for personal interest, we are subject to fatal errors when we do not have a certain force of understanding and of soul. If on the day after the death of Charles I, an Englishman, cursing with reason that crime, had implored Heaven that there might never again be freedom in England, we might certainly have felt an interest in that emotion of a good heart which in its agitation confounded all the pretexts of a great crime with the crime itself; and would have proscribed, had it been able, even the sun, which had risen on that day as usual. But if so unthinking a prayer had been heard, England would not at this day serve as an example to the world; the universal monarchy of Bonaparte would be weighing Europe to the ground; for, without the aid of this free nation, Europe would not have been in a situation to work out her own deliverance. Such arguments and many others might be addressed to persons whose very prejudices merit respect because they spring from the affections of the heart. But what are we to say of those who treat the friends of liberty as Jacobins, while they themselves have been ready instruments in the hands of the imperial power? We were forced, they say, to be so. Ah! I know some who could likewise speak of constraint, and who yet escaped it. But since you have allowed yourselves to be compelled, at least allow us to endeavor to give you a free constitution, in which the empire of the law will prevent anything wrong from being required of you: for, as appears to me, you are in danger of giving way too readily to circumstances. They whom nature has endued with a disposition to resist, have no reason to fear despotism; but you, who have crouched under it so well, should wish that at no time, under no prince, in no shape may it ever again touch you.

The epicureans of our days would wish that knowledge might improve our physical existence without exciting intellectual development; they would have the Third Estate labor to render social life more agreeable and comfortable without desiring to benefit from the advantages which it has gained for all. In former days the general style of life had little delicacy or refinement, and the relations in society were likewise much more simple and stable. But now that commerce has multiplied everything, if you do not give motives of emulation to talent, the love of money will fill the vacancy. You will not raise up the castles of feudal chieftains from their ruins; you will not recall to life the princesses who with their own hands spun the vests of the warriors; you will not even restore the reign of Louis XIV. The present times do not admit of that sort of gravity and respect which then gave so much ascendancy to that court. But you will have corruption, and corruption without refinement of mind; the lowest degradation to which the human species can fall. It is not then between knowledge and the ancient system of feudal manners that we are to choose, but between the desire of distinction and the eagerness to become rich.

Examine the adversaries of freedom in every country, you will find among them a few deserters from the camp of men of talent, but in general, you will see that the enemies of freedom are the enemies of knowledge and intelligence. They are proud of their deficiency in this respect; and one must agree that such a negative triumph can be easily achieved.

The secret has been found of presenting the friends of liberty as the enemies of religion: there are two pretexts for the singular injustice which would forbid to the noblest of sentiment of this earth, the alliance with Heaven. The first is the Revolution; as it was effected in the name of philosophy, an inference has thence been drawn that to love liberty it is necessary to be an atheist. Certainly, it is because the French did not unite religion to liberty that their revolution deviated so soon from its primitive direction. There might be certain dogmas of the Catholic Church which were not in agreement with the principles of freedom; passive obedience to the Pope was as difficult to be defended as passive obedience to the King. But Christianity has in truth brought liberty upon earth; justice toward the oppressed, respect for the unfortunate; finally, equality before God, of which equality under the law is only an imperfect image. It is by confusion of thought, voluntary in some, blind in others, that endeavors have been made to represent the privileges of the nobility and the absolute

power of the throne as doctrines of religion. The forms of social organization can have no concern with religion except by their influence on
the maintenance of justice toward all, and of the morals of each individual.
The rest belongs to the science of this world.

It is time that twenty-five years, of which fifteen belong to military
despotism, should no longer place themselves as a phantom between history and us, and should no longer deprive us of all the lessons and of all
the examples which it offers us. Is Aristides to be forgotten, and Phocion,
and Epaminondas in Greece; Regulus, Cato, and Brutus at Rome; Tell in
Switzerland; Egmont and Nassau in Holland; Sidney and Russell in England;[2] because a country that had long been governed by arbitrary power
was delivered, during a revolution, to men whom arbitrary power had
corrupted? What is there so extraordinary in such an event as to change
the course of the stars, that is, to give a retrograde motion to truth, which
was before advancing with history to enlighten the human race? By what
public sentiment shall we be moved henceforth if we are to reject the love
of liberty? Old prejudices have now no influence upon men except from
calculation; they are defended only by those who have a personal interest
in defending them. What man in France desires absolute power from pure
love or for its own sake? Inform yourself of the personal situation of its
partisans, and you will soon know the motives of their doctrine. On what
then would the fraternal tie of human associations be founded if no enthusiasm were to be developed in the heart? Who would be proud of being
a Frenchman after having seen liberty destroyed by tyranny, tyranny broken to pieces by foreigners, unless the laurels of war were at least rendered
honorable by the conquest of liberty? We should have to contemplate a
mere struggle between the selfishness of those who were privileged by
birth and the selfishness of those who are privileged by events. But where
would then be France? Who could boast of having served her, since nothing would remain in the heart, either of past times or of the new reform?

Liberty! Let us repeat her name with so much the more energy that the
men who should pronounce it, at least as an apology, keep it at a distance

---

2. What all these characters shared was military virtue and courage in the fight for
liberty.

through flattery: let us repeat it without fear of wounding any power that deserves respect; for all that we love, all that we honor is included in it. Nothing but liberty can arouse the soul to the interests of social order. The assemblies of men would be nothing but associations for commerce or agriculture if the life of patriotism did not excite individuals to sacrifice themselves for their fellows. Chivalry was a warlike brotherhood which satisfied that thirst for self-devotion which is felt by every generous heart. The nobles were companions in arms, bound together by duty and honor; but since the progress of the human mind has created nations, in other words, since all men share in some degree in the same advantages, what would become of the human species were it not for the sentiment of liberty? Why should the patriotism of a Frenchman begin at this frontier and cease at that, if there were not within this compass hopes, enjoyments, an emulation, a security which make him love his native land as much through the genuine feelings of the soul as through habit? Why should the name of France awaken so invincible an emotion if there were no other ties among the inhabitants of this fine country than the privileges of some and the subjection of the rest?

Wherever you meet with respect for human nature, affection for fellow-creatures, and that energy of independence which can resist everything upon earth and prostrate itself only before God; there you behold man the image of his Creator, there you feel at the bottom of the soul an emotion which so penetrates its very substance that it cannot deceive you with respect to truth. And you, noble Frenchmen, for whom honor was freedom, you who by a long series of exploits and greatness ought to consider yourselves as the elite of the human race, permit the nation to raise itself to a level with you; she, too, has rights of conquest; every Frenchman may now call himself a gentleman if every gentleman is not willing to be called a citizen.

It is indeed a remarkable circumstance that throughout the world, wherever a certain depth of thought exists, there is not to be found an enemy of freedom. As the celebrated Humboldt[3] has traced upon the

3. Alexander von Humboldt (1769–1859) was a famous Prussian scientist and explorer whose scientific achievements were admired by all the leading names of his epoch, from

mountains of the New World the different degrees of height which permit the development of this or that plant, so might we predict what extent, what elevation of spirit is requisite to enable a man to conceive the great interests of mankind in their full connection and in all their truth. The evidence of these opinions is such that they who have once admitted them can never renounce them, and that from one end of the world to the other, the friends of freedom maintain communication by knowledge, as religious men by sentiments; or rather knowledge and sentiment unite in the love of freedom as in that of the Supreme Being. Is the question the abolition of the slave trade, or the liberty of the press, or religious toleration? Jefferson thinks as La Fayette; La Fayette, as Wilberforce; and even they who are now no more are reckoned in the holy league. Is it then from the calculations of interest, is it from bad motives that men so superior, in situations and countries so different, should be in such harmony in their political opinions? Without doubt knowledge is requisite to enable us to soar above prejudices: but it is in the soul also that the principles of liberty are founded; they make the heart palpitate like love and friendship, they come from nature, they ennoble the character. One connected series of virtues and ideas seems to form that golden chain described by Homer, which in binding man to Heaven delivers him from all the fetters of tyranny.

Goethe and Napoléon to Jefferson and Darwin. Simón Bolívar once claimed that "Alexander von Humboldt has done more for America than all its conquerors; he is the true discoverer of America." Von Humboldt also had a genuine interest in politics. During the July Monarchy, he was frequently employed in diplomatic missions to the court of the king of France, with whom he maintained cordial personal relations. His brother, Wilhelm von Humboldt (1767–1835), was a well-known political thinker and founder of Humboldt University in Berlin. Wilhelm von Humboldt's ideas had a strong influence on J. S. Mill's *On Liberty*.

Select Bibliography on Madame de Staël

PRIMARY SOURCES

Complete Works

Madame de Staël. *Oeuvres complètes de Mme la baronne de Staël publiées par son fils.* Paris: Treuttel et Würtz, 1821.

Major Publications of Madame de Staël (*in French*)

Considérations sur la Révolution française. Edited by J. Godechot. Paris: Tallandier, 1983.

Corinne ou l'Italie. Edited by S. Balayé. Paris: Gallimard, 1807, 1985.

De la littérature. Edited by G. Gengembre and J. Goldzink. Paris: Flammarion, 1991.

De l'Allemagne. Critical edition by S. Balayé. 5 vols. Paris: Hachette, 1958–1960.

Delphine. Edited by B. Didier. 2 vols. Paris: Flammarion, 2000.

Des Circonstances actuelles qui peuvent terminer la Révolution et des principes qui doivent fonder la république en France. Critical edition edited by L. Omacini. Paris and Geneva: Droz, 1979.

Dix années d'exil. Critical edition edited by S. Balayé and M. Bonifacio. Paris: Fayard, 1996. English edition: *Ten Years of Exile.* Translated by Avriel H. Goldberger. DeKalb: Northern Illinois University Press, 2000. A previous English translation by Doris Beik was published under the same title by *Saturday Review* in 1972.

For a representative selection from Madame de Staël's rich correspondence, see Georges Solovieff, ed., *Madame de Staël, ses amis, ses correspondants. Choix de lettres (1778–1817).* Paris: Klincksieck, 1970. Madame de Staël's correspondence with Dupont de Nemours was edited and translated into English by James F. Marshall as *De Staël–Dupont Letters. Correspondence of Madame de Staël and Pierre Samuel du Pont de Nemours and of Other Members of the Necker and du Pont Families.* Madison: University of Wisconsin Press, 1968.

Sources of Information on Madame de Staël

Cahiers Staëliens. Vols. 1–54. Published by the *Société des études staëliennes* (founded in 1929 at Coppet; http://www.stael.org/) and Éditions Honoré Champion, this series is an essential source of information on Staël's life and works. Over the years the society has sponsored many colloquia whose proceedings have been published as separate volumes of *Cahiers Staëliens.* The society's Web site contains many valuable bibliographical references (more than 6,000 entries) that are essential to any student of Staël's works and life.

For an overview of the Coppet group, see *Coppet, creuset de l'esprit libéral: les idées politiques et constitutionnelles du group de Madame de Staël,* Coppet colloquium, May 15–16, 1998, edited by Lucien Jaume (Aix-en-Provence and Paris: Presses Universitaires d'Aix-Marseille et Economica, 2000).

Useful Web Sites on the French Revolution and Napoléon

http://userweb.port.ac.uk/~andressd/frlinks.htm
http://chnm.gmu.edu/revolution/
http://www.napoleon.org/en/home.asp

MAJOR SECONDARY WORKS
AND BIBLIOGRAPHIES

Bailleul, Jacques-Charles. *Examen critique de l'ouvrage posthume de Mme. la Bnne. de Staël, ayant pour titre: Considérations sur les principaux événemens de la Révolution française.* 2 vols. Paris: Ant. Bailleul, 1818.

Balayé, Simone. *Les Carnets de voyage de Madame de Staël.* Geneva: Droz, 1971.

———. *Madame de Staël: Lumières et Liberté.* Paris: Klincksieck, 1979.

Berger, Morroe, trans. and ed. *Politics, Literature, and National Character, by Germaine de Staël.* New Brunswick, N.J.: Transaction, 2000.

Bonald, Louis de. *Observations sur l'ouvrage de Madame la baronne de Staël: considérations sur les principaux événemens de la révolution française.* Paris: A. Le Clere, 1818. A new French edition was published under the title *La vraie Révolution: réponse à Madame de Staël,* edited by Michel Toda. Etampes: Clovis, 1997.

Bredin, Jean-Denis. *Une singulière famille: Jacques Necker, Suzanne Necker et Germaine de Staël*. Paris: Fayard, 1999.

Diesbach, Ghislain de. *Madame de Staël*. Paris: Perrin, 1983.

————. *Necker ou la faillite de la vertu*. Paris: Perrin, 1978.

Fairweather, Maria. *Madame de Staël*. London: Constable, 2005.

Folkenflick, Vivian, ed. and trans. *An Extraordinary Woman: Selected Writings of Germaine de Staël*. New York: Columbia University Press, 1987.

Guillemin, H. *Madame de Staël, Benjamin Constant et Napoléon*. Paris: Plon, 1959.

Gutwirth, Madelyn, Avriel Goldberger, and Karyna Szmurlo, eds. *Germaine de Staël: Crossing the Borders*. New Brunswick, N.J.: Rutgers University Press, 1991.

Gwynne, Griffith E. *Madame de Staël et la Révolution française*. 2nd ed. Paris: Nizet, 2005.

Haussonville, Comte de. *Madame de Staël et Necker d'après leur correspondance inédite*. Paris: Calmann-Lévy, 1925.

Hawkins, Richmond Laurin. *Madame de Staël and the United States*. Cambridge, Mass.: Harvard University Press, 1930.

Herrold, Christopher. *Mistress to an Age: A Life of Madame de Staël*. London: Hamish Hamilton, 1958.

Fundamental Texts

Baker, Keith M., ed. *The Old Regime and the French Revolution*. Vol. 7 of University of Chicago Readings in Western Civilization. Chicago: University of Chicago Press, 1987.

Duguit, L., H. Monnier, and R. Bonnard, eds. *Les Constitutions et les principales lois politiques de la France depuis 1789*. Paris: Librairie Générale de Droit et de Jurisprudence, 1952.

Hampsher-Monk, Iain, ed. *The Impact of the French Revolution: Texts from Britain in the 1790s*. Cambridge: Cambridge University Press, 2005.

Stewart, John Hall, ed. *A Documentary Survey of the French Revolution*. New York: Macmillan, 1951.

General Background

Acton (Lord). [John Emerich Edward Dalberg-Acton.] *Lectures on the French Revolution*. Indianapolis: Liberty Fund, 2000.

Alexander, Robert. *Bonapartism and Revolutionary Tradition in France*. Cambridge: Cambridge University Press, 1991.

Alexander, Robert. *Rewriting the French Revolutionary Tradition*. Cambridge: Cambridge University Press, 2004.

Andress, David. *The Terror: The Merciless War for Freedom in Revolutionary France*. New York: Farrar, Straus and Giroux, 2006.

Avenel, Henri. *Histoire de la presse française depuis 1789 jusqu'à à nos jours*. Paris: Flammarion, 1900.

Baker, Keith. *Condorcet: From Natural Philosophy to Social Mathematics*. Chicago: University of Chicago Press, 1982.

————. *Inventing the French Revolution*. Cambridge: Cambridge University Press, 1990.

Baker, Keith, ed. *The French Revolution and the Creation of Modern Political Culture*. Vol. 1: *The Political Culture of the Old Regime*. Oxford: Pergamon Press, 1987.

Baldensperger, Fernand. *Le mouvement des idées dans l'émigration française, 1789–1815*. Paris, 1924.

Barnave, Antoine. *Power, Property, and History: Barnave's Introduction to the French Revolution and Other Writings*. Translated and edited by Emanuel Chill. New York: Harper, 1971.

Beck, Thomas D. *French Legislators, 1800–1834: A Study in Quantitative History*. Berkeley: University of California Press, 1974.

Beik, Paul H., ed. *The French Revolution*. New York: Harper and Row, 1970.

Belanger, Claude, et al. *Histoire générale de la presse française*. Vol. 1. Paris: PUF, 1967.

Bénétruy, J. *L'atelier de Mirabeau: Quatre proscrits Genevois dans la tourmente révolutionnaire*. Geneva: Société d'Histoire et d'Archéologie, 1962.

Bergeron, Louis. *France Under Napoleon*. Princeton: Princeton University Press, 1981.

Bertier de Sauvigny, Guillaume de. *The Bourbon Restoration*. Philadelphia: University of Pennsylvania Press, 1966.

Blythe, James M. *Ideal Government and the Mixed Constitution in the Middle Ages*. Princeton: Princeton University Press, 1992.

Brewer, John. *The Pleasures of the Imagination: English Culture in the Eighteenth Century*. Chicago: University of Chicago Press, 1997.

Brix, Michel. "*Les Considérations sur la Révolution française* et la philosophie de l'histoire." In *Annales Benjamin Constant*. *31–32*. *Le groupe de Coppet et l'histoire. Actes du VIIIe colloque de Coppet* (Chateau de Coppet, 5–8 juillet 2006). Lausanne & Genève: Institut Benjamin Constant & Éditions Slatkine, 2007, 203–14.

Brock, Michael. *The Great Reform Act.* London: Hutchinson University Library, 1973.

Burke, Edmund. *Further Reflections on the Revolution in France.* Edited by Daniel E. Ritchie. Indianapolis: Liberty Fund, 1992.

———. *Select Works of Edmund Burke.* Vol. 2: *Reflections on the Revolution in France.* Indianapolis: Liberty Fund, 1999.

———. *Select Works of Edmund Burke.* Vol. 3: *Letters on a Regicide Peace.* Indianapolis: Liberty Fund, 1999.

Carré de Malberg, Raymond. *Contribution à la théorie générale de l'État.* 2 vols. Paris: Éditions du CNRS, 1962.

Chaussinand-Nogaret, Guy, ed. *Mirabeau entre le roi et la Révolution: Notes à la cour suivies de Discours.* Paris: Hachette, 1986.

Chinard, Gilbert. "La correspondance de Madame de Staël avec Jefferson." *Revue de littérature comparée* 2 (1922).

Constant, Benjamin. *Commentaire sur l'ouvrage de Filangeri.* Paris: Les Belles Lettres, 2004.

———. *De la liberté chez les modernes.* Edited by Marcel Gauchet. Paris: Hachette, 1980.

———. "De Madame de Staël et de ses ouvrages." In *Oeuvres.* Edited by Alfred Roulin. Paris: Gallimard, Bibliothèque de la Pléiade, 1957, 825–52.

———. *Fragments d'un ouvrage abandonné sur la possibilité d'une constitution republicaine dans un grand pays.* Edited by H. Grange. Paris: Aubier, 1991.

———. *Political Writings.* Edited and translated by Biancamaria Fontana. Cambridge: Cambridge University Press, 1988.

Cooper, Duff. *Talleyrand.* New York: Harpers, 1932.

Craiutu, Aurelian. *Liberalism Under Siege: The Political Thought of the French Doctrinaires.* Lanham, Md.: Lexington Books, Rowman and Littlefield, 2003.

Craveri, Benedetta. *The Age of Conversation.* New York: New York Review Books, 2006.

Daudet, Ernest. *Histoire de l'émigration pendant la Révolution française.* 3 vols. Paris, 1904–7.

Doyle, William. *Origins of the French Revolution.* 3rd ed. Oxford: Oxford University Press, 1999.

————. *The Oxford History of the French Revolution.* Oxford: Oxford University Press, 1989.

Echeverria, Durand. "The Pre-revolutionary Influence of Rousseau's *Contrat Social.*" *Journal of the History of Ideas* (1972): 551–52.

Egret, Jean. *The French Prerevolution, 1787–1788.* Chicago: University of Chicago Press, 1977.

————. *Necker, ministre de Louis XVI.* Paris: Champion, 1975.

Ellis, Harold A. *Boulainvilliers and the French Monarchy: Aristocratic Politics in Early Eighteenth-Century France.* Ithaca: Cornell University Press, 1988.

Fontana, Biancamaria. *Rethinking the Politics of Commercial Society: The Edinburgh Review, 1802–1832.* Cambridge: Cambridge University Press, 1985.

Forsyth, Murray. *Reason and Revolution: The Political Thought of the Abbé Sieyès.* Leicester: Leicester University Press, 1987.

Freeden, Michael. *Ideology: A Very Short Introduction.* Oxford: Oxford University Press, 2003.

Furet, François. *Interpreting the French Revolution.* Cambridge: Cambridge University Press, 1981.

————. *Revolutionary France: 1770–1880.* Oxford: Blackwell, 1995.

Furet, François, and Mona Ozouf, eds. *A Critical Dictionary of the French Revolution.* Cambridge, Mass.: Harvard University Press, 1989.

Furet, François, and Ran Halévi, eds. *Orateurs de la Révolution française.* Vol. 1: *Les Constituants.* Paris: Gallimard, Bibliothèque de la Pléiade, 1989.

Gauchet, Marcel. *La Révolution des droits de l'homme.* Paris: Gallimard, 1989.

————. "Staël." In *A Critical Dictionary of the French Revolution*, edited by François Furet and Mona Ozouf. Cambridge, Mass.: Harvard University Press, 1989.

Gautier, Paul. *Madame de Staël et Napoléon.* Paris: Plon, 1902.

Gengembre, Gérard, and Jean Goldzinck. "Causalités historiques et écriture de l'histoire dans *Considérations sur la Révolution française.*" In *Annales Benjamin Constant. 31–32. Le groupe de Coppet et l'histoire. Actes du VIIIe colloque de Coppet* (Chateau de Coppet, 5–8 juillet 2006). Lausanne & Genève: Institut Benjamin Constant & Éditions Slatkine, 2007, 215–26.

Godechot, Jacques. *La contre-révolution.* Paris: PUF, 1961.

————. *La grande nation: l'expansion révolutionnaire de la France dans le monde de 1789 à 1799.* Paris: Aubier Montaigne, 1983.

————. *Les institutions de la France sous la Révolution et l'empire.* 2nd ed. Paris: PUF, 1968.

Gorce, Pierre de la. *La Restauration: Louis XVIII*. Paris: Plon, 1926.

Gottschalk, Louis R., and Margaret Maddox. *La Fayette in the French Revolution*. Vol. 1: *Through the October Days*. Chicago: University of Chicago Press, 1969. Vol. 2: *From the October Days Through the Federation*. Chicago: University of Chicago Press, 1973.

Grange, Henri. *Les idées de Necker*. Paris: Klincksieck, 1974.

Greer, Donald. *The Incidence of the Emigration During the French Revolution*. Cambridge, Mass.: Harvard University Press, 1951.

————. *The Incidence of the Terror During the French Revolution: A Statistical Interpretation*. Cambridge, Mass.: Harvard University Press, 1935.

Griffith, Robert. *Le Centre perdu: Malouet et les "monarchiens" dans la Révolution française*. Grenoble: Presses Universitaires de Grenoble, 1988.

Gross, Jean-Pierre. "La Constitution de l'an III: Boissy d'Anglas et la naissance du libéralisme constitutionnel." *Annales historiques de la Révolution française*, no. 323. http://ahrf.revues.org/document1028.html.

————. *Saint-Just: sa politique et ses missions*. Paris: Bibliothèque nationale, 1976.

Guéniffey, Patrice. *Le nombre et la raison. La Révolution française et les élections*. Paris: Éditions de l'École des Hautes Études en Sciences Sociales, 1993.

Guizot, François. *L'amour dans le mariage. Étude historique*. Paris: Hachette, 1855.

————. *Histoire de la civilisation en Europe suivie de Philosophie politique: de la souveraineté*. Edited by Pierre Rosanvallon. Paris: Hachette, 1985.

————. *Histoire de la civilisation en France depuis la chute de l'Empire Romain*. Paris: Didier, 1859.

————. *Histoire de la Révolution d'Angleterre depuis Charles I à Charles II*. 2 vols., 1826–27. English translation, 2 vols., Oxford, 1838.

————. *The History of Civilisation in Europe*. Edited by Larry Siedentop and translated by William Hazlitt. London: Penguin, 1997.

————. *History of the Origins of Representative Government in Europe*. Edited by Aurelian Craiutu. Indianapolis: Liberty Fund, 2002.

————. *Memoirs to Illustrate the History of My Time*. Vol. I. Translated by J. W. Cole. London: R. Bentley, 1858.

Hamilton, Jill. *Marengo: The Myth of Napoleon's Horse*. London: Fourth Estate, 2000.

Hatin, Eugène. *Histoire politique et littéraire de la presse en France*. Paris: Poulet-Malassis et de Broise, 1861.

Haydon, Colin, and William Doyle, eds. *Robespierre*. Cambridge: Cambridge University Press, 2006.

Hesse, Carla. *The Other Enlightenment*. Princeton: Princeton University Press, 2001.

Hoffman, Ronald, and Peter J. Albert, eds. *The Bill of Rights: Government Proscribed*. Charlottesville: University Press of Virginia, 1997.

Hume, David. *The History of England*. 6 vols. Indianapolis: Liberty Fund, 1983.

Hurt, John J. *Louis XIV and the Parlements: The Assertion of Royal Authority*. Manchester: Manchester University Press, 2002.

Jainchill, Andrew. "The Constitution of the Year III and the Persistence of Classical Republicanism." *French Historical Studies* 26, no. 3 (2003): 399–435.

Jaume, Lucien. "Coppet, creuset du libéralisme comme 'culture morale.'" In *Coppet, creuset de l'esprit libéral*. Paris: Presses Universitaires d'Aux-Marseille, 2000, 225–39.

Jennings, Jeremy. "Conceptions of England and Its Constitution in Nineteenth-Century French Political Thought." *Historical Journal* 29, no. 1 (1986): 65–85.

Jordan, David. *The King's Trial: Louis XVI vs. the French Revolution*. 2nd ed. Berkeley: University of California Press, 2004.

Kahan, Alan. *The Political Culture of Limited Suffrage*. London: Palgrave, 2003.

Kennedy, Michael L. *The Jacobin Clubs in the French Revolution: The First Years*. Princeton: Princeton University Press, 1982.

Kenyon, J. P., ed. *Halifax, Complete Works*. London: Penguin, 1969.

Lahmer, Marc. *La constitution américaine dans le débat français: 1795–1848*. Paris: L'Harmattan, 2001.

Lefebre, George. *The Thermidorians and the Directory: Two Phases of the French Revolution*. Translated by Robert Baldick. New York: Random House, 1964.

Livois, René de. *Histoire de la presse française*. Vol. 1: *Des origines à 1881*. Paris: Les Temps de la Presse, 1965.

Lucas-Dubreton, J. *The Restoration and the July Monarchy*. New York: Putnam's, 1929.

Luttrell, Barbara. *Mirabeau*. Carbondale: Southern Illinois University Press, 1990.

Maistre, Joseph de. *Considerations on France*. Edited and translated by Richard Lebrun. Cambridge: Cambridge University Press, 1994.

Malouet, Victor. *Mémoires*. 2 vols. Paris: Didier, 1868.

Manent, Pierre. *An Intellectual History of Liberalism*. Princeton: Princeton University Press, 1994.

Margerison, Kenneth. "History, Representative Institutions, and Political Rights in the French Pre-revolution (1787–1789)." *French Historical Studies* 15:1 (1987): 68–97.

Montesquieu, *The Spirit of the Laws*. Translated by Anne Cohler, Basia Miller, and Harold Stone. Cambridge: Cambridge University Press, 1989.

Mounier, J.-J. *Considérations sur les gouvernements*. Paris, 1789.

Mousnier, Roland. *Les institutions de la France sous la monarchie absolue, 1598–1789*. 2 vols. Paris: PUF, 1974–78.

Necker, Jacques. *Compte rendu*. Paris, 1781.

———. *De la Révolution française*. Part I. Republished in *Oeuvres complètes de M. Necker*, vol. 9. Edited by Auguste de Staël. Paris: Treuttel et Würtz, 1821.

———. *Dernières vues de politique et de finance* (1802). Republished in *Oeuvres complètes de M. Necker*, vol. 11. Edited by Auguste de Staël. Paris: Treuttel et Würtz, 1821.

———. *Réflexions présentées à la nation française: sure le proces intente a Louis XVI*. Paris: Volland, 1792.

Oechslin, J.-J. *Le mouvement ultra-royaliste sous la Restauration*. Paris: Librairie Générale de Droit et de Jurisprudence, 1960.

Ozouf, Mona. "L'opinion publique." In *The French Revolution and the Creation of Modern Political Culture*. Vol. 1: *The Political Culture of the Old Regime*, Edited by K. Baker. Oxford: Pergamon Press, 1987.

———. *Women's Words: Essay on French Singularity*. Chicago: University of Chicago Press, 1997.

Palmer, R. R. *Twelve Who Ruled*. Princeton: Princeton University Press, 1941. New ed. 1970.

Pochmann, Henry A. *German Culture in America*. Madison: University of Wisconsin Press, 1957.

Rémond, René. *The Right Wing in France: From 1815 to De Gaulle*. Philadelphia: University of Pennsylvania Press, 1968.

Rémusat, Charles. *Mémoires de ma vie*. Vol. 1. Ed. Charles-H. Pouthas. Paris: Plon, 1958.

Rials, Stéphane. *Révolution et contre-révolution au XIXème siècle*. Paris: Albatros, 1987.

Ridolfi, R. *The Life of Niccolò Machiavelli*. London: Routledge and K. Paul, 1963.

Rosanvallon, Pierre. *La monarchie impossible. Les Chartes de 1814 et de 1830*. Paris: Fayard, 1994.

Schwoerer, Lois G. "William, Lord Russell: The Making of a Martyr, 1683–1983." *Journal of British Studies* 24, no. 1 (January 1985): 41–71.

Scurr, Ruth. *Fatal Purity: Robespierre and the French Revolution*. New York: Henry Holt, 2006.

Sieyès, Emmanuel Joseph. *Political Writings*. Edited and translated by Michael Sonenscher. Indianapolis: Hackett, 2003.

Soboul, Albert. *Le procès de Louis XVI*. Paris: Julliard, 1966.

Solovieff, Georges, ed. *Madame de Staël, ses amis, ses correspondants. Choix de lettres (1778–1817)*. Paris: Klincksieck, 1970.

Spillman, George. *Napoléon et l'Islam*. Paris: Academique Perrin, 1969.

Taine, Hippolyte. *The French Revolution*. Translated by John Durand. Indianapolis: Liberty Fund, 2002.

Takeda, Chinatsu. "Deux origines du courant libéral en France." In *Revue française d'histoire des idées politiques* (2003): 18, no. 2, 233–57.

Ticknor, George. *Life, Letters, and Journals of George Ticknor*. 2 vols. Boston and New York: Houghton Mifflin, 1909.

Tilly, Charles. *The Vendée*. Cambridge, Mass.: Harvard University Press, 1964.

Tocqueville, Alexis de. *The Old Régime and the Revolution*. Vol. 1. Translated by Alan S. Kahan. Edited by F. Furet and F. Mélonio. Chicago: University of Chicago Press, 1998.

———. *Selected Letters on Politics and Society*. Edited by Roger Boesche and translated by Roger Boesche and James Toupin. Berkeley: University of California Press, 1985.

Tribouillard, Stéphanie. *"Les Considérations sur la Révolution française* et l'historiographie libérale de la Révolution du premier XIXe siécle." In *Annales Benjamin Constant. 31–32. Le groupe de Coppet et l'histoire. Actes du VIIIe colloque de Coppet* (Chateau de Coppet, 5–8 juillet 2006). Lausanne & Genève: Institut Benjamin Constant & Éditions Slatkine, 2007, 227–48.

Valensise, Marina. "The French Constitution in Pre-revolutionary Debate." *Journal of Modern History* 60 (suppl.) (1988): 22–57.

Van Kley, Dale. "New Wine in Old Wineskins: Continuity and Rupture in the Pamphlet Debate of the French Prerevolution, 1787–1789." *French Historical Studies* 17, no. 2 (1991): 447–65.

Vaulabelle, Achille de. *Histoire des deux Restaurations jusqu'à l'avénement de Louis-Philippe*. Vols. 4 and 5. Paris: Perrotin, 1855 and 1856.

Vile, M. J. C. *Constitutionalism and the Separation of Powers*. 2nd ed. Indianapolis: Liberty Fund, 1998.

Walzer, Michael, ed. *Regicide and Revolution: Speeches at the Trial of Louis XVI*. New York: Columbia University Press, 1993.

Waresquiel, Emmanuel de. *Talleyrand, le prince immobile*. Paris: Fayard, 2003.

Welch, Cheryl. *Liberty and Utility: The French Ideologues and the Transformation of Liberalism*. New York: Columbia University Press, 1984.

Wyrwa, Marek, ed. *Malesherbes, le pouvoir et les Lumières*. Paris: Éditions France-Empire, 1989.

Index

Persons whose names begin with prefixes such as *d'*, *de*, *du*, *l'*, and *van* will be found under the main element of the name (e.g., Barante, Prosper de) unless that element is considered by common usage or spelling an integral part of the name (e.g., Dupont de Nemours; La Fayette).

This book is set in Fournier, a font based on types cut by Pierre Simon Fournier circa 1742 in his *Manuel Typographique*. These types were some of the most influential designs of the eighteenth century, being among the earliest of the transitional style of type-face, and were a stepping stone to the more severe modern style made popular by Bodoni later in the century. They had more ver-tical stress than the old-style types, greater contrast between thick and thin strokes, and little or no bracketing on the serifs.

Printed on paper that is acid-free and meets the requirements of the American National Standard for Permanence of Paper for Printed Library Materials, z39.48-1992. ♾

Book design by Louise OFarrell
Gainesville, Florida
Typography by Apex CoVantage
Madison, Wisconsin
Printed and bound by Worzalla Publishing Company
Stevens Point, Wisconsin